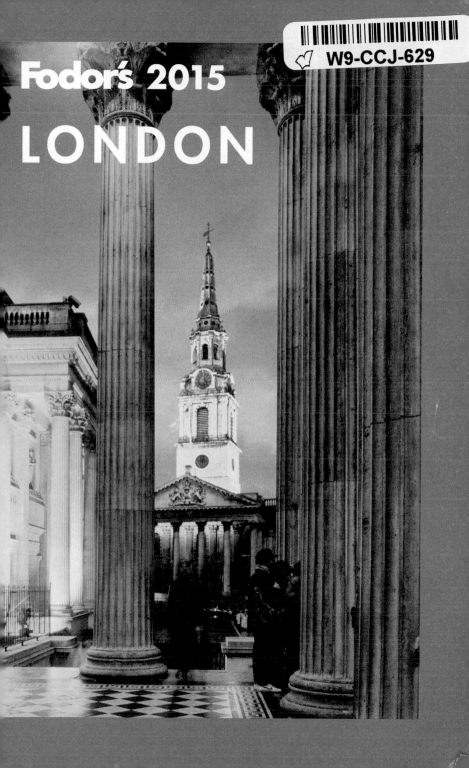

Fodor's 2015
LONDON

W9-CCJ-629

WELCOME TO LONDON

History and tradition greet you at every turn in London; it's also one of the coolest, most modern cities in the world. If London contained only landmarks such as Westminster Abbey and Buckingham Palace, it would still rank as one of the world's great destinations, but Britain's capital is much more. People come to glimpse the royals and stop by hot galleries; to take in theater and trendy shops; to sample tea and scones or cutting-edge cuisine. When you need a break from the action, pop into a pub, relax in a park—or take a walk and make London your own.

TOP REASONS TO GO

★ **Architectural Icons:** The Tower of London and Big Ben are quintessential London.

★ **Art Museums:** From the National Gallery to the Tate Modern, a visual feast awaits.

★ **Top Theater:** Whether it's Shakespeare or avant-garde drama, the play's the thing.

★ **City of Villages:** Unique neighborhoods from Mayfair to the East End invite discovery.

★ **Shopping:** Fun markets, famous flagship department stores, chic boutiques.

★ **Parks and Squares:** Distinctive green spaces large and small are civilized retreats.

Fodor's LONDON 2015

Publisher: Amanda D'Acierno, *Senior Vice President*

Editorial: Arabella Bowen, *Editor in Chief*; Linda Cabasin, *Editorial Director*

Design: Fabrizio La Rocca, *Vice President, Creative Director*; Tina Malaney, *Associate Art Director*; Chie Ushio, *Senior Designer*; Ann McBride, *Production Designer*

Photography: Melanie Marin, *Associate Director of Photography*; Jessica Parkhill and Jennifer Romains, *Researchers*

Maps: Rebecca Baer, *Senior Map Editor*; David Lindroth, Mark Stroud (Moon Street Cartography) *Cartographers*

Production: Linda Schmidt, *Managing Editor*; Evangelos Vasilakis, *Associate Managing Editor*; Angela L. McLean, *Senior Production Manager*

Sales: Jacqueline Lebow, *Sales Director*

Marketing & Publicity: Heather Dalton, *Marketing Director*; Katherine Punia, *Senior Publicist*

Business & Operations: Susan Livingston, *Vice President, Strategic Business Planning*; Sue Daulton, *Vice President, Operations*

Fodors.com: Megan Bell, *Executive Director, Revenue & Business Development*; Yasmin Marinaro, *Senior Director, Marketing & Partnerships*

Writers: Jo Caird, Kate Hughes, Jack Jewers, James O'Neill, Ellin Stein, Alex Wijeratna

Editors: Kristan Schiller (lead editor), Bethany Beckerlegge, Amanda Sadlowski

Production Editor: Elyse Rozelle

ISBN 978-0-8041-4258-8

ISSN 0149-631X

SPECIAL SALES

This book is available at special discounts for bulk purchases for sales promotions or premiums. For more information, e-mail specialmarkets@randomhouse.com

PRINTED IN THE UNITED STATES OF AMERICA

10 9 8 7 6 5 4 3 2 1

CONTENTS

Fodor's Features

CONTENTS

ABOUT
THIS GUIDE

Fodor's Ratings

Everything in this guide is worth doing—we don't cover what isn't—but exceptional sights, hotels, and restaurants are recognized with additional accolades. **Fodor's**Choice★ indicates our top recommendations, and **Best Bets** call attention to notable hotels and restaurants in various categories. Care to nominate a new place? Visit Fodors.com/contact-us.

Trip Costs

We list prices wherever possible to help you budget well. Hotel and restaurant price categories from $ to $$$$ are noted alongside each recommendation. For hotels, we include the lowest cost of a standard double room in high season. For restaurants, we cite the average price of a main course at dinner or, if dinner isn't served, at lunch. For attractions, we always list adult admission fees; discounts are usually available for children, students, and senior citizens.

Hotels

Our local writers vet every hotel to recommend the best overnights in each price category, from budget to expensive. Unless otherwise specified, you can expect private bath, phone, and TV in your room. For expanded hotel reviews, facilities, and deals visit Fodors.com.

Restaurants

Unless we state otherwise, restaurants are open for lunch and dinner daily. We mention dress code only when there's a specific requirement and reservations only when they're essential or not accepted. To make restaurant reservations, visit Fodors.com.

Credit Cards

The hotels and restaurants in this guide typically accept credit cards. If not, we'll say so.

Top Picks		Hotels &
★ **Fodor's**Choice		**Restaurants**
		⊞ Hotel
Listings		↪ Number of
⊠ Address		rooms
⊠ Branch address		⦿ Meal plans
☎ Telephone		✕ Restaurant
🖷 Fax		⬠ Reservations
⊕ Website		🏛 Dress code
✉ E-mail		⊟ No credit cards
🔖 Admission fee		⑤ Price
⊘ Open/closed		**Other**
times		⇨ See also
Ⓜ Subway		☞ Take note
✛ Directions or		🏌 Golf facilities
Map coordinates		

EXPERIENCE
LONDON

LONDON TODAY

Welcome to London! Variously described by poets and statesmen as "modern Babylon," "Unreal City," "enormous Babel," and ". . . the City of the free." Indeed majestic London's always been a city in flux and these days it's hard to turn a corner without stumbling into some work-in-progress crater so vast you can only imagine what was there before. This latest wave of development was turbo-charged as the city became a safe haven during the global economic crisis. New neighborhoods continually rise up and burst to the fore—a visit to the eastern edge of the City should provide you with your quotient of London hipness. The creative fervor that swirls through London like fog shows up in DIY galleries, mini boutiques, and ace hotels.

While many images are seared on your consciousness before you arrive—the guards at Buckingham Palace, the red double-decker buses, and the River Thames—time does not stand still in this ancient and yet gloriously modern city. Instead, "London, the buskin'd stage . . . The heart, the centre of the living world!" is in revolution, and evolves, organically, historically through time.

Ask any time-pressed but savvy local and they'll tell you that . . .

Today's London . . .
. . . is heading skyward.

London's loosened its collar and showcases some spectacular new architecture, with the pyramid-shaped Shard providing an iconic beacon for the city. With the exceptions of Canary Wharf, the Swiss Re HQ ("the Gherkin"), the Lloyd's of London building, and the London Eye, London's skyline has traditionally been low-key, with little of the swagger of, say, Shanghai or Manhattan. But a spectacular crop of soaring new office towers with wonderful monikers—the Quill, the Shard, the Pinnacle, the Cheese Grater, and the Walkie Talkie—is revitalizing the city skyline. Not everyone loves Renzo Piano's pointy Shard and its 87-floor cloud-piercing "vertical city" at London Bridge, which has a stunning viewing gallery on the 72nd floor. However, once you visit it, your understanding of the true greatness of the city will explode.

WHAT'S NEW

We really shouldn't begrudge it, but some of London's top cultural attractions seem to be in a Cold War upgrade arms race and are investing heavily in new galleries, exhibits, refurbs, expansions, and assorted shiny new bells and whistles. Look, then, for the new £45-million rehang at Tate Britain that allows you to walk through 500 years of British art organized in strict chronological order, including new galleries on visionary painter William Blake and sculptor Henry Moore. Similarly, Shakespeare's Globe has recreated an atmospheric oak-paneled entirely candlelit 350-seat Jacobean *indoor* theater—the Sam Wanamaker Playhouse—where you'll catch intimate bawdy Jacobean

. . . is more global.

The nationalities *keep* coming, and London now swipes the crown as one of *the* most cosmopolitan cities on Earth. White Britons are in the minority for the first time (according to the latest census), representing 45% of London's population of 8.2 million, while Asians make up 18%, black Londoners 13%, European "White Others" 13%, and mixed-race residents at 5%. But London's always been a city of immigrants—from the 10th century, the city had Cymric Brythons, Belgae and Gauls, East Saxons, and Mercians, Danes, Swedes, and Norwegians, plus Jutes, Franks, and Angles. Today, Londoners simply shrug and are "Begone with their business."

. . . is more happening.

Have you picked up one of those free daily London *Evening Standard* newspapers lately? They're stuffed with a smorgasbord of world-class shows, plays, performances, readings, concerts, fashion follies, cabaret, talks, auctions and blockbuster art exhibitions. Whether it's contemporary art and old masters paintings at the Frieze London art fair or a one-off guest chef's eight-course surprise meal, London is one of the most happening places on the planet.

. . . is better connected.

Finally, you'll notice that the public transport's gotten more frequent and more reliable. While London's traffic often seems more chaotic than New York City's, the Congestion Charge, the £10-per-day fee imposed on vehicles entering central London, has reduced both traffic and pollution. While the Underground now runs 24 hours a day on weekends, massive tunneling continues apace on London's flagship, high-speed, Cross Rail underground railway line, which includes new interchanges at Paddington, Tottenham Court Road, and Farringdon stations, slated to open in 2018. Meanwhile, don't miss London's distinctive sky-blue hire bikes, Barclay's Cycle Hire, known locally as "Boris Bikes," after London Mayor Boris Johnson. With 8,733 bikes available at 612 docking stations, you'll find (after laying down £7 for a weekly pass) that the first half hour's free, an hour's a quid, and two hours is only £6.

plays, historical music and vocalists, and groundbreaking collaborations with groups like the Royal Opera House. And watch out for a radical £120-million renovation at the Southbank Centre, where the Queen Elizabeth Hall, Purcell Room, and Hayward Gallery will soon encompass a slick "floating" glass pavilion linking up the venues and a new national literature center and poetry library.

WHAT'S WHERE

The following numbers refer to chapters.

2 **Westminster, St. James's, and Royal London.** This is the place to embrace the "Gran turismo" label. Snap pictures of the mounted Horse Guards, watch kids clambering onto the lions in Trafalgar Square, and visit stacks of art in the fantastic national galleries. Do brave the crowds to peruse historic Westminster Abbey and its ancient narrative in stone.

3 **Mayfair and Marylebone.** You might not have the wallet for London's most prestigious shops, but remember window-shopping in Mayfair is free. Meanwhile, boutique shops in Marylebone are a refreshing change from gaudy Oxford Street a few blocks south.

4 **Soho and Covent Garden.** More sophisticated than seedy these days, the heart of London puts Theatreland, strip joints, Chinatown, burger boîtes, and the trendiest of film studios side by side. Nearby Charing Cross Road is an old bibliophile's bookfest. And hold tight among the hectic hordes in Leicester Square, London's crowd-packed answer to Times Square. Covent Garden's historic piazza is one of the busiest, most raffishly enjoyable parts of the city.

5 **Bloomsbury, Holborn, and Islington.** Once the bluestocking and intellectual center of London, elegant Bloomsbury is now also a mixed business district—albeit with the mother lode of museums at its heart. The British Museum has enough amazing artifacts to keep you busy for a month of Sundays; otherwise, offerings are limited, though the Law Courts, University of London, and quaint Lamb's Conduit Street are worth a gander.

6 **The City.** London's Wall Street might be the oldest part of the capital, but thanks to futuristic skyscrapers and a sleek blade-of-light Millennium Bridge, it looks like the newest. History fans won't be short-changed, however: head for the baroque dome of St. Paul's Cathedral; the Victorian iconography of Tower Bridge; and the grisly medieval terrors of the Tower of London.

7 **East London.** Once famed for the noxious 19th-century slums immortalized by Charles Dickens and Jack the Ripper, today the area's become a fulcrum of London's contemporary art scene and a trendy youth-quake party zone. For spit-and-sawdust sensations of market London on the weekend, dive headfirst into the eclectic wares

WHAT'S WHERE

at Spitalfields, Brick Lane (popular for curry houses and 24-hour bagel bakeries), and Columbia Road's much-loved flower market.

8 South of the Thames. Die-hard culture vultures could spend a lifetime here. The Southbank Centre—including the National Theatre and Royal Festival Hall, the Haywood Gallery, Shakespeare's Globe, and Tate Modern—showcases the capital's crowning artistic glories. Or put it all in aerial perspective from the 72nd floor of the mesmerizing pyramid-shaped Shard.

9 Kensington, Chelsea, Knightsbridge, and Belgravia. Although the many boutiques of King's Road have lost much of their heady '60s swagger, the free museums are as awe-inspiring as ever. Kensington High Street (or "Ken High Street" to locals) is slightly more affordable than King's Road; otherwise, flash your cash at London's snazziest department stores, Harrods and Harvey Nichols.

10 Notting Hill and Bayswater. For that effortlessly hip west London demeanor, hang out in its coolest residential postal code: Notting Hill, north of Kensington. Around Portobello Road, Notting Hill Gate is a trendsetting

square mile of multiethnic finds, galleries, bijou shops, and see-and-be-seen-in restaurants. Nearby, Bayswater mixes eclectic ethnic fashions, fresh-food shops, and Chinese restaurants.

11 Regent's Park and Hampstead. Surrounded by the supremely elegant "terraces"—in truth, mansions as big as palaces—designed by 19th-century architect John Nash, Regent's Park is a Regency extravaganza. The nearby hilltop villages of Hampstead and Primrose Hill attract residents like Kate Moss, Gwyneth Paltrow, and Jude Law.

12 Greenwich. The Royal Observatory, Sir Christopher Wren architecture, the Old Royal Naval College, *Cutty Sark*, and Greenwich Meridian Line all add up to one of the best Thames-side excursions beyond the cut-and-thrust of central London.

13 The Thames Upstream. As an idyllic retreat from the city, stroll around London's historic gardens and enjoy the stately homes of Kew, Richmond, and Putney. Better yet, take a river cruise and end up at the famous Maze of Hampton Court Palace.

LONDON PLANNER

When to Go

The heaviest tourist season runs mid-April through mid-September, with another peak around Christmas—though the tide never really ebbs. Late spring is the time to see the surrounding countryside and the Royal parks and gardens at their freshest; fall brings autumnal beauty and fewer people. Summer gives the best chance of good weather, although the crowds are most intense. Winter can be dismal—the sun sets at 4 and it's dark by 5—but all the theaters, concerts, and exhibitions go full-speed ahead, and Christmas lights bring a touch of festive magic to the busy streets. For a schedule of festivals, check ⊕ *www.visitlondon.com.*

When Not to Go

The October "half-term," when schools in the capital take a break for a week, results in most attractions being overrun by children. The start of August can be a very busy time, and hot weather makes Tube travel a sweaty nightmare. Air-conditioning is far from the norm in London, even in hotels; so although it rarely tops 90°F, it can feel much hotter. And shopping in central London just before Christmas borders on the insane.

Addresses

Central London and its surrounding districts are divided into 32 boroughs—33, counting The City of London. More useful for navigating, however, are the subdivisions of London into postal districts. Throughout the guide we've given the abbreviated postal code for most listings. The first one or two letters give the location: N means north, NW means northwest, and so on. Don't expect the numbering to be logical, however. (You won't, for example, find W2 next to W3.) The general rule is that the lower numbers, such as W1 or SW1, are closest to the city center.

Getting Around

London is, above all, a walker's city, and will repay every moment you spend exploring on foot. But if you're in a rush, there are other options. By far the easiest and most practical way to get around is on the Underground, or "Tube." Trains run daily from early morning to beyond midnight during the week and 24 hours on weekends on five key lines. Frequent buses crisscross London and often have their own lanes, which only buses and black taxis can use. They are a great way to see London, but routes are more complicated than the Tube's; scan the route posted at the bus stop and check the number and destination on the front of the bus. Ask the bus conductor if in doubt.

Put a deposit on an Oyster card for £5, which will allow you to use London's transport—including bus, Tube, tram, DLR, London Overground, and most National Rail services in London—at a lower cost than using paper tickets. The plastic card can be topped up as often as you want, and your £5 deposit will be reimbursed when you hand the card back.

Alternatively, buy a Travelcard pass (from £8.80 per day in the central Zones 1 and 2), which offers unlimited use of the Tube, buses, and the commuter rail. Check ⊕ *www.tfl. gov.uk* for details on ongoing Tube renovations.

⇨ *For further details on transport around London, see the Travel Smart section at the end of this book.*

London Hours

The usual shop hours are Monday–Saturday 9–6 and Sunday 11–5. Around Oxford Street, High Street Kensington, and Knightsbridge, hours are 9:30–6, with late-night hours (until 7:30 or 8) on Wednesday or Thursday.

Many businesses are closed on Sunday and national ("bank") holidays, except in the center, where most open 10–4. Banks are open weekdays 9:30–4:30; offices are generally open 9–6.

The major national museums and galleries are open daily, mainly 10–6, and often they're open late one night a week.

Deal or No Deal?

There's no getting around it: London can be as expensive as—or even *more* expensive than—New York, Paris, or any other large global city. So it's much better to accept this fact in advance and factor it into your vacation planning, tailoring outings and trips that will reflect your interests—and your budget.

Often, booking in advance, harnessing cut-price and low-season deals, and taking advantage of Internet specials for flights and hotel rooms can cut down on costs. London is also great at offering things for free (particularly the museums), and the quality of the culture, entertainment, parks, relaxation, and general fun to be had in the city means that if you target your spending wisely, you'll go home penny-pinched but deeply satisfied.

How's the Weather?

It's a long-standing joke that Londoners—and the English in general—chat obsessively about the weather. The London drizzle generates a fatalism that kicks off any conversation with a long-suffering nod to the heavens. Winter is usually dreary, cold, and wet (with occasional snow), spring is colorful and fair, June to August can be anything from a total washout to a long, hot summer and anything in between, while autumn can be "Indian-summer" warm, cool, or mild—or all three. Come prepared for anything—layers and a brolly are your best friends. One thing is sure: it's virtually impossible to forecast London weather, but you can be fairly certain that it will *not* be what you expect.

The following are the average daily maximum and minimum temperatures for London.

WHAT IT COSTS		
	In London	**In New York**
Pair of theater tickets	£40–£95	$70–$240
Museum admission	Usually free; sometimes £4–£16	Usually $5–$25; rarely free
Fast-food value meal	£6	$7
Tall latte	£3.90	$4
Pint of beer in a pub	£3.90 and up	$6 and up
1-mile taxi ride before tip	£7	$6
Subway ride within city center	Up to £5.50 without Oyster or Travelcard	$2.50

AVERAGE LONDON TEMPERATURES

LONDON
TOP ATTRACTIONS

Westminster Abbey

(A) The pillars of this early–English Gothic edifice stand around the stone tombs of the great men and women who built Britain. The Abbey also continues to play a preeminent role in the spiritual life of the nation, from the coronation of 38 sovereigns to royal weddings and state funerals.

Buckingham Palace

(B) Not the largest or prettiest royal residence, the palace at the heart of London is nonetheless a must-see for the glimpse it affords into the life of the Royal Family. The opulence of the 19 State Rooms open to the public are jaw-dropping, and don't forget the collection of old masters and gilded state carriages at the Queen's Gallery and Royal Mews stables next door.

Tower of London

(C) The Tower is London at its historic, gory best. Every brick tells a grisly story, and the ax-blows and fortunes that have risen and fallen within this 20-towered mini-city provide an inexhaustible supply of intrigue.

St. Paul's Cathedral

(D) Sir Christopher Wren's masterpiece never fails to take the breath away. Climb the enormous dome, one of the world's largest, to experience the acoustics of the Whispering Gallery, and higher still to the Golden Gallery for far-reaching views across London.

British Museum

(E) "Mankind's Attic" has been wowing visitors to London since 1753. Its unrivalled 8-million-strong collection spans all recorded history, including the Elgin Marbles, the Rosetta Stone, Egyptian mummies, and the warrior treasures of Sutton Hoo.

Shakespeare's Globe

(F) You can catch a Shakespeare play almost every evening in London. But standing in the open-air "pit" or yard with the "groundlings" on a floor of sawdust in a scrupulously re-created oak version of the original thatched Tudor theater for which Shakespeare wrote is a genuine thrill.

Tate Modern

(G) The world's most visited modern art gallery, Tate Modern is a hip and hugely successful feature of London's artistic landscape. Passing judgment on the latest controversial exhibit inside the giant sloping Turbine Hall has become almost a civic duty among art-loving Londoners.

London's Central Parks

(H) A whopping 25% of London is parkland, so it is mighty hard to choose between St. James's Park (those fairy tale views), Kensington Gardens (the beloved

Peter Pan statue), Hyde Park (pedelos on the Serpentine Lido), and Regent's Park's rose gardens.

Hampton Court Palace

(I) Henry VIII's palace has a Tudor-turreted charm, augmented by Wren's touch, and a picturesque Thames-side location, all of which make for a great day out. Not even dour Oliver Cromwell, who moved here in 1653, could resist its charms.

National Gallery

(J) There are enough amazing world-class paintings at this collection of 2,300 masterpieces to have the most casual art enthusiast drooling with admiration. Note the raised front entrance and its great photo op: Big Ben and Nelson's Column framed by a pedestrianized Trafalgar Square.

LONDON ROYAL LEGACY

Don't know your House of Tudor from your House of Hanover? Here's the lowdown on the most famous kings and queens who have influenced London, and where you can still see their mark.

Queen Mary I
(A) "Bloody Mary" (r. 1553–58, House of Tudor), the Roman Catholic daughter of Henry VIII and his first wife, Catherine of Aragon, persecuted Protestants in an attempt to reverse the Reformation and return England to Roman Catholicism. She imprisoned her half sister, Elizabeth—daughter of Anne Boleyn—in the Tower, suspecting her of a plot against her, but there was no evidence and Elizabeth came to the throne after her death.

Edward the Confessor
(B) Edward (r. 1042–66, House of Wessex) came to the throne in 1042 and ordered the construction of the original Westminster Abbey, which was consecrated in 1065, just a week before he died.

William the Conqueror
(C) The Battle of 1066 was won by William (r. 1066–87, House of Normandy) when he shot the then-king Harold through the eye with an arrow at the battle of Hastings. He is credited with starting the building of the White Tower in the Tower of London, though it wasn't completed until after his death.

Queen Elizabeth I
(D) The "Virgin Queen" (r. 1558–1603, House of Tudor) never married—perhaps because she thought that any man might try to wrest control from her (though she did move Robert Dudley, Earl of Leicester, into rooms close to her own at Hampton Court Palace). She oversaw a golden age of playwriting and poetry and famously inspired her troops as they prepared to battle the Spanish Armada.

1

Henry VIII

(E) A true Renaissance man, Henry (r. 1509–47, House of Tudor) was keen to bring new ideas to the Royal Court. All of Henry's six wives, who were famously "divorced, beheaded, died, divorced, beheaded, survived," lived at Hampton Court Palace. Henry was desperate for a male heir—the main reason for having two of his wives executed: Anne Boleyn and Catherine Howard.

George III

(F) His frequent bouts of irrational behavior led to the nickname "The Mad One" but George (r. 1760–1820, House of Hanover) is now thought to have suffered from an inherited metabolic illness and often secluded himself at Kew Palace. With the Declaration of Independence in 1776, he lost the American colonies. One of the most cultured monarchs, George donated 65,000 of his books to the British Museum.

Duke and Duchess of Cambridge

(G) It's exciting to catch a glimpse of the Windsors and heir Prince William on a royal walkabout—so go to ⊕ www.royal. gov.uk and search for "Future engagements" under the Latest News and Diary section to catch the Duke and Duchess of Cambridge at a public event.

Charles I

(H) "The Martyr" (r. 1625–49, House of Stuart) is famous for losing the English Civil War, and was beheaded at Banqueting House—a twist of fate, as Charles had commissioned the palace to be decorated with paintings showing a monarch being received into heaven.

Queen Victoria

(I) Famous for the longest reign so far in British history, 63 years, Victoria (r. 1837–1901, House of Hanover) was born in, and spent her childhood at, Kensington Palace, where she learned she would become queen at age 18.

GIVE THE SPORTS SCENE A GO

Sport in the capital is best watched, rather than participated in. If you're lucky enough to score a ticket for a Premier League football match, you'll experience a seething mass of mockery and chanting. Rugby Union, Championship tennis, horse racing, and Test cricket impinge on Londoners' horizons at crucial times of the year, too, but you're unlikely to see grown men crying at the outcome of the Wimbledon Men's Final, or beating each other up about the Ashes.

Boating

The Boat Race. Join over a quarter of a million zealous devotees along the crammed banks of the River Thames for a glimpse of the annual Oxford and Cambridge University "Boat Race," held on the last Saturday of March or first Saturday of April. Sink a few pints and soak up the Barbour-clad "Oxbridge-y" Thames-side atmosphere as these crack heavyweight eight-man University crews clash oars, occasionally sink, and generally tussle head-to-head for supremacy. First raced in 1829, the 4-mile route is a historic stretch between Putney and Chiswick bridges. ⊠ *Putney Bridge, Putney* ⊕ *www. theboatrace.org.*

Cricket

At its best, Test cricket can be a slow-build of smoldering tension and unexpected excitement. At its worst, it can be too slow for the casual observer, as five-day games crawl toward a draw, or as rain stops play. But try to visit Lord's—the home of cricket—for just one day of a Test match to see the English upper classes on full display.

Lord's. Lord's—the home of Marylebone Cricket Club (MCC)—has been hallowed cricketing turf since 1814 and MCC rules codified the game. Tickets for major Test matches are hard to come by: obtain an application form and enter the lottery to purchase them. Forms are sent out in early December or apply online. Test Match tickets cost between £28 and £95. Cheaper county matches can be seen by standing in line on match day. ⊠ *Marylebone Cricket Club, Lord's Cricket Ground, St. John's Wood Rd., St. John's Wood* ☎ *020/7432–1000* ⊕ *www.lords. org* Ⓜ *St. John's Wood.*

Football

London's top teams—Tottenham Hotspur, Arsenal, and Chelsea—are world-class and often progress in the Champions League. It's unlikely you'll get tickets for anything except the least popular Premier League games during the August–May season, despite the high ticket prices—£41 for a walk-up match day seat at Chelsea, and £126 for the most expensive tickets at Arsenal.

Tennis

Wimbledon Lawn Tennis Championships. The Wimbledon Lawn Tennis Championships are famous for Centre Court, rain, strawberries and cream, and an insistence on players wearing white. Thankfully, rain's been banished on Centre Court by the retractable roof but whether you can get tickets for Centre Court all comes down to the luck of the draw—there's a ballot system for advance purchase. See the website for details. You can also buy entry to roam on the outside courts, where even top-seeded players compete early on. Get to Wimbledon Tube station as early as possible and join the queue; 500 show court tickets are sold daily, too. ⊠ *The All England Lawn Tennis Club, Church Rd.* ☎ *020/8944–1066* ⊕ *www.wimbledon.com.*

FREE (AND ALMOST FREE) THINGS TO DO

1

The exchange rate may vary a bit, but there is one conversion that will never change: £0 = $0. Here are our picks for the top free things to do in London.

CONCERTS

St. Martin-in-the-Fields, St. Stephen Walbrook, St. Olaves, and St. James's Church have free lunchtime concerts, as does St. Giles-in-the-Fields on Friday and St. George, Bloomsbury on Sunday. There are also regular organ recitals at Westminster Abbey.

Of the music colleges, the Royal Academy of Music, the Royal College of Music, the Guildhall, Trinity College, and the Royal Opera House have free recitals. For contemporary ears, the area outside the National Theatre at the Southbank Centre has an eclectic range of music weekdays at 5:45 pm, Saturday at 1 pm and 5:45 pm, and Sunday at 1 pm. There's free jazz and classical Thursday to Saturday (plus two Sundays per month) at the Dysart Arms (☎ 0208/940–8005) in Richmond and live jazz at the Lamb & Flag (✉ 33 Rose St. ☎ 0207/497–9504) in Covent Garden, from 8 pm one Sunday a month. For free blues before 8:30 pm, head to the Ain't Nothin But . . . blues bar in Soho (✉ 20 Kingly St. ☎ 020/7287–0514).

FILM, THEATER, AND OPERA

If all seats have been sold, the National Theatre sells £5 standing tickets on the day of performances at their Olivier and Lyttleton theaters. Standing-only tickets are between £4 and £15 at the Royal Opera House, and 67 tickets are available from the box office from 10 am on the day of most performances. Under 30?

Becoming an "Access all Arias" member of the English National Opera is free, and allows you to buy £10 tickets. Standing-only tickets for £5 are a historically appropriate way to experience Shakespeare's Globe. At Sloane Square, the Royal Court Theatre has four standing-only tickets for 10 pence each at the Jerwood Theatre Downstairs, available an hour before performances; otherwise *all* tickets are £10 on Monday.

OFFBEAT EXPERIENCES

Join a blood-curdling, two-hour Jack the Ripper evening walking tour of Spitalfields to retrace the innocuous spots and alleyways where five young prostitutes were slashed to death and disemboweled by the Ripper over a 12-week period in 1888.

SIGHTSEEING ON THE CHEAP

Prop yourself on the top deck of a double-decker bus for a ride through the most scenic parts of the city. Routes 9 and 15 also operate Heritage routes on the traditional Routemaster buses. You can use your Oyster card or buy tickets from machines at the bus stops for the following routes:

Bus 11: King's Road, Sloane Square, Victoria station, Westminster Abbey, Houses of Parliament and Big Ben, Whitehall, Trafalgar Square, the Strand, the Royal Courts of Justice, Fleet Street, and St. Paul's Cathedral.

Bus 19: Sloane Square, Knightsbridge, Hyde Park Corner, Green Park, Piccadilly Circus, Shaftsbury Avenue, Oxford Street, Bloomsbury, and Angel Islington.

Bus 88: Oxford Circus, Conduit Street, Piccadilly Circus, Haymarket, Trafalgar Square, Whitehall, Horse Guards Parade, Westminster station, Westminster Abbey, Horseferry Road, and Tate Britain.

VISIT WORLD-FAMOUS MUSEUMS

London's museums are one of the capital's crown jewels, and many have free entry. *This list includes museums listed elsewhere in our content (check index for full listings), plus extras.*

Major Galleries

Giddy art lovers will target the big four—the **National Gallery**, the **National Portrait Gallery**, **Tate Britain**, and **Tate Modern**. The National Gallery has 2,300 masterpieces from 1250 to 1900 while the world's largest collection of portraits is next door at the National Portrait Gallery. Tate Britain takes you on a chronological walk through 500 years of British art and Tate Modern showcases contemporary art and installations.

Academies and Galleries

Must-visits include the 1768 **Royal Academy of Arts** for its sell-out exhibitions on artists like Monet and the diminutive **Courtauld Gallery** at Somerset House, which has a classy capsule collection from the early medieval period to the Post Impressionists. The **Queen's Gallery** at Buckingham Palace showcases the Royal Collection and hosts blockbusters on greats like Leonardo da Vinci. The **Dulwich Picture Gallery** exhibits exquisite European old masters from 1600 to the 1700s and the **Guildhall Art Gallery** has awesome Pre-Raphaelites.

House Museums

London's historic house museums are treats within treats: the art and the house itself. One of the finest is the private **Wallace Collection** at the majestic damask-filled 1788 Hertford House on Manchester Square, which hosts European old masters and French decorative arts from the 15th to 19th century. Other stand-alone historic humdingers with old masters and antiques-strewn interiors include **Apsley House**, **Kenwood House**, and **Leighton House** in Holland Park.

Contemporary Art

With London now a global art hub, you'll find excellent contemporary art galleries splattered around. The **Serpentine Gallery** in Hyde Park may be small but packs a mean modern art punch. The **Hayward Gallery** at the Southbank Centre concentrates on bleeding-edge exhibitions while the **Whitechapel Gallery** kindles the East London art scene. Private galleries like the **Saatchi Gallery** and **Maureen Paley** push up-and-comers and unknowns, while **White Cube** features bankable Brits and esoteric premiers.

Major Museums

The **British Museum** was the world's first national public museum in 1753 and still captivates with its vast collection of artifacts from the Rosetta Stone to Ramesses the Great. A 105-foot Diplodocus greets you at the **Natural History Museum** with its Victorian treasure trove of 70 million artifacts spanning 4.5 billion years while the **Science Museum** has a collection of 300,000 items showcased in 12 galleries. The **Victoria & Albert Museum** is stuffed with amazing jewelry and design exhibits. At St. Pancras, the permanent exhibition at the **British Library** has manuscripts like Magna Carta, the Gutenberg Bible, and Shakespeare's First Folio.

British History

The **Museum of London** explores London since before Roman times while the **Museum of London Docklands** tells the 2,000-year story of the port of London. The **Royal Observatory, Greenwich**, tells of Britain's role in the story of navigation and astronomy, and is the home of the Prime Meridian while the **National Maritime Museum** charts British naval ascendancy. The **National Army Museum, IWM London**, and **Household Cavalry Museum** venerate Britain's military history, while the **RAF Museum** houses Spitfires and a Lancaster bomber. You'll find all the clocks have stopped at just before 5 pm at the **Churchill War Rooms**, which preserves the World War II Cabinet War Rooms, and you can operate a "dead man's handle" on a 1930s Underground train at the **London Transport Museum** in Covent Garden. Shakespeare's **Globe** theater is an enthralling replica of the original.

Royal Palaces

London's a royal wonderland, with royal palaces doubling down as de facto royal museums. You can get into **Buckingham Palace** from July to October and tour 19 impossibly grand State Rooms, including the Queen's Throne Room. **Kensington Palace** is home to Prince William and Kate and you can glide through former King William III and Queen Mary II's closet. The turrets, tapestries, and kitchens fascinate all-comers at **Hampton Court Palace**, as do the Crown Jewels at Royal Palace and Fortress at the **Tower of London**. **Kew Palace** and **Eltham Palace** are two other prize royal retreats.

Best for Kids

Kids adore the gory Black Death scenes and gruesome Jack the Ripper rides at the **London Dungeon** and are intrigued by the waxwork models of celebs like J-Lo at **Madame Tussauds**. The eclectic **Horniman Museum** has 350,000 quirky objects amassed by a Victorian tea trader and there are scientific, medical, and surgical specimens galore at the **Wellcome Collection, Royal Institution**, and **Hunterian Museum**. The **London Fire Brigade Museum**, tiny **Pollock's Toy Museum**, and **The Guards Museum Toy Soldier Centre** on Birdcage Walk all cater brilliantly to the whims of kids of all ages.

One-Man Shows

London is fab at preserving the homes of native sons and daughters, with the best including the Charles Dickens Museum, Florence Nightingale Museum, Freud Museum, Handel House Museum, plus artist William Hogarth's House and essayist Thomas Carlyle's House on Cheyne Row. Candlelit tours at Dennis Severs' House in Spitalfields chart the tale of a 17th-century French Huguenot silk merchants' family, and the Sir John Soane Museum is crammed with antiquities from the namesake neoclassical architect and collector.

Etc

Some museums aren't classifiable. The Geffrye Museum is dedicated to 11 urban middle-class living rooms from 1630 to the present, while the Old Operating Theatre Museum and Herb Garret attached to St Thomas's Church, Southwark, displays the earliest wooden operating theater from 1822. The Petrie Museum of Egyptian Archaeology at University College, London, is worth seeing for its 80,000-strong collection of archaeology from ancient Egypt and Sudan.

A LONDON HISTORIC PUB CRAWL

A brilliant, beery, and *traditional* way to see London and its medieval backstreets is on a "pub crawl." This walk takes you through some of the city's most historically textured neighborhoods. Settle back with a pint and drink in all the history.

The South Bank

Like Chaucer's *Canterbury Tales* pilgrims, we start in Southwark near London Bridge. Head down Borough High Street to the **George Inn,** a long black-and-white affair with wonky galleries, warped beams, open fires, and smoothed oak wooden stairs. First chronicled in 1542, the pub's mentioned in Charles Dickens's *Little Dorrit.* Cross Borough High Street and take the Bedale Street entrance to **Borough Market;** walk along until it turns into Cathedral Street, with the striking **Southwark Cathedral** on your right. At the fork head left to Sir Francis Drake's **Golden Hind** replica galleon and walk past Pickfords Wharf to reach the **Anchor Bankside.** This old tavern was originally built in 1615 and was frequented by William Shakespeare and other players and actors from the nearby Globe, Swan, and Rose theaters. Head up to the roof terrace for sweeping views of the River Thames and **St. Paul's Cathedral.**

Across the Thames

Cross Southwark Bridge to The City. On the corner of Bow Lane, **Ye Olde Watling** was originally built before the Great Fire, and promptly torched. Rebuilt around 1668, again in 1901, and again after the Blitz, it's named after Watling Street, the Roman road on which it sits.

Head west along Watling Street to St. Paul's Cathedral and take a left down Creed Lane from Ludgate Hill. Wind your way down to Queen Victoria Street and turn right to **The Blackfriar** at No 174. The Grade II–listed spectacular interior is all marble and brass bas-reliefs of Dominican friars interspersed with aphorisms and quotes. Head north up New Bridge Street and turn left onto Fleet Street to the 1667 **Ye Olde Cheshire Cheese** at No. 145. Dr. Samuel Johnson, author of the first dictionary, used to drink here, as did Charles Dickens, Voltaire, Mark Twain, Oscar Wilde, and Teddy Roosevelt.

Bloomsbury

Wander west along Fleet Street, then walk north up Fetter Lane to the hidden-away **Ye Olde Mitre** at 1 Ely Court, which has served brews since 1546. Look for the old maypole cherry tree trunk (in the front bar) that Elizabeth I supposedly once danced around. For the final stretch, walk north up Gray's Inn Road, then left onto Theobald's Road before turning right onto quaint Lamb's Conduit Street, to find **The Lamb,** notable for its 1720s wooden horseshoe bar with etched-glass "snob screens" to shield the well-to-do from women of dubious distinction. Head west along Great Ormond Street to the far side of Queen Square to find **The Queens Larder,** where Queen Charlotte reputedly rented out a cellar to store special food for her sickly husband, George III. Just north is Russell Square Tube station, or you can continue southwest to the British Museum, which faces the **Museum Tavern,** where Karl Marx would take time off from researching *Das Kapital.*

Where to Start:	On the South Bank at the London Bridge Tube/rail station.
Length:	4 miles (about 1½ hours without stopping). Just part of this walk will give you a taste of the oldest bits of London.
Where to Stop:	Russell Square Tube station or Tottenham Court Road.
Best Time to Go:	Weekday afternoons (most pubs open late in the morning).
Worst Time to Go:	Busy summer weekends may be too crowded.
Eating and Drinking:	All the pubs will serve food at lunchtime. Stop when you're hungry or pick up some tasty grub in Borough Market and stop in either Gray's Inn Fields or Lincoln's Inn Fields for a picnic.
Diversions:	From the Anchor, consider continuing along the riverside to Tate Modern, before crossing over the River Thames to ferret out Ye Olde Watling or The Blackfriar.
Pub Highlights:	The Anchor, The Blackfriar, George Inn, The Lamb, Ye Olde Cheshire Cheese, Ye Olde Watling, Ye Olde Mitre.

IN PURSUIT OF THE EAST END ART SCENE

From the atmospheric period streets of Whitechapel and Spitalfields to the warehouses-turned-galleries of Hackney, a tour of the East End's art spaces presents the area in all its rich variety.

Whitechapel and Bethnal Green

To start your tour, Tube it to Aldgate East Station, then walk east along Whitechapel High Street to the **Whitechapel Gallery**, a center for exciting exhibitions since its founding in 1901. Head back towards the Tube, then turn left into Commercial Street, go north past Spitafields Market, then right, at the Ten Bells pub into Fournier Street, with its handsome, 18th-century, former Huguenot silk weavers' workshops. Turn left into Brick Lane, then right into Cheshire Street, known for quirky shops like the Duke of Uke (for all your ukulele needs). The shops give way to a railway line as Cheshire Street turns into Dunbridge Street, and then Three Colts Lane, as you walk directly east, until you come to industrial Herald Street, where you'll turn left. At No. 21 is the **Maureen Paley** gallery, founded by an American expat who's now a doyenne of the East End art scene.

Hackney

Turn right onto Witan Street and then left onto Cambridge Heath Road. The **V&A Museum of Childhood** is just past Bethnal Green Tube station. Continue heading north (take Bus 106 or 254 if you're flagging) to just past Hackney Road. A few yards on the right is **Vyner Street**, not quite as sizzling as it used to be, but still a gallery hot spot. Cross back over Cambridge Heath Road and head west along Andrews Road, paralleling Regent's Canal with its residential houseboats. Here you can either turn right to visit **Broadway Market** or left, going straight until you reach Hackney Road. Turn right and then take your first left at the Ion Square Gardens. Bear right onto **Columbia Road** (helpfully signed for Shoreditch), site of London's best flower market on Sunday.

Shoreditch

A short way past where the shops of Columbia Road end, you'll see another sign for Shoreditch on the left at Virginia Road. Turn left here, bear right, and then turn left again at Hocker Street. This brings you to **Arnold Circus**, an early Arts and Crafts housing development. From the southern end of the Circus, take the first right off Club Row into Old Nichol Street. Here you'll find the **Kate Mac-Garry** gallery, known for its cutting-edge conceptual and video art. Turn left into Boundary Street at the end of the road and stop for a restorative coffee or egg and bacon bap at hipster-vogue **Albion** "caff" at the end of Boundary Street. At this point you can either turn left around the corner to explore more fun boutiques on **Redchurch Street**, or right, which will bring you almost immediately to Shoreditch High Street and the huge Tea Building to the left. Turn left onto Bethnal Green Road, where you'll find the Shoreditch High Street Overground station just above the spunky Boxpark shipping container pop-up mall.

Where to Start:	At Aldgate East Tube station in Whitechapel.
Length:	3½ miles (about 2 hours without stopping).
Where to Stop:	Shoreditch High Street Overground station.
Best Time to Go:	Weekdays for galleries, weekends for markets.
Worst Time to Go:	Busy summer weekends may be too crowded.
Eating and Drinking:	Wine and small plates of charcuterie at Brawn on Columbia Road; excellent modern British food at Upstairs at the Ten Bells on Commercial Street; coffee and light meals at Sir Terence Conran's Albion café on Boundary Street.
Diversions:	Consider crossing to the west side of Shoreditch High Street to explore London's new media hub near the Old Street (aka "Silicon") roundabout. The digerati gather at The Book Club on Leonard Street for coffee by day and drinks by night.
Gallery Highlights:	Maureen Paley Gallery, Whitechapel Gallery, V&A Museum of Childhood, Kate MacGarry Gallery, and Vyner Street Gallery.

AFTERNOON TEA

So, what is Afternoon Tea, exactly? Well, it means real loose-leaf tea—Earl Grey, English Breakfast, Ceylon, Darjeeling, or Assam—brewed in a fine bone china or porcelain pot, and served with fine bone cups and saucers, milk or lemon, and silver spoons, taken between noon and 6 pm.

Tea goers dress smartly (though not ostentatiously), and conversation by tradition should avoid politics and religion. Here are some top places in town to head:

Hands down, the super-glam **Savoy** on the Strand offers one of the most beautiful settings for tea. The Thames Foyer, a symphony of grays and golds centered around a winter garden wrought-iron gazebo, is just the place for the house pianist to accompany you as you enjoy the award-winning house teas along with finger sandwiches, homemade scones, and *yumptious* pastries.

Setting the standard in its English Tea Room for some of London's best-known traditional teas, **Brown's Hotel,** at 33 Albermarle Street—charmingly set in a classic Mayfair town house—offers Afternoon Tea for £41 or, if you wish to splash out, Champagne Tea for £51.

If you seek timeless chic, the sumptuous 1920s dining room at the **Wolseley** Viennese grand café on Piccadilly remains a fashionable hang-out for London's top luvvies. The silver service teas here—light Afternoon Tea is £10.75 and Champagne Tea £33.50—are among the best in town.

Moving west, you can sit looking out onto fab lawns amid mini potted orange trees at **The Orangery** in Prince William and Kate's London pad, Kensington Palace, inside resplendent Kensington Gardens. Afternoon Tea is £22.65 and a suitably Royal Afternoon Tea (with a glass of Laurent-Perrier) is £32.50.

Alternatively, add spice to your Afternoon Tea by trying a popular Moroccan-style Afternoon Tea (£22) at the souk-chic tearoom at **Momo** off Regent Street, where you'll enjoy sweet mint tea in colorful glass cups plus scones with fig jam, Maghrebian pastries, Moroccan chicken wraps, and honey-and-nut-rich Berber-style crêpes.

Bea's of Bloomsbury (motto: "Life is short. Eat More Cake") is one of the best Afternoon Tea and cupcake stops around. With its on-site bakery, Bea's churns out freshly baked delights like blackberry cupcakes or heavenly chocolate fudge cupcake with fudge icing. Cheery Afternoon Tea services (noon–7 pm daily) with loose-leaf Jing tea, cupcakes, scones with jam and clotted cream, mini meringues, marshmallows, and Valrhona brownies is £16 weekdays, and £19 on weekends.

Finally, for frilly trompe l'oeil grandeur, few can compete with Afternoon Tea at **The Ritz** on Piccadilly. It's served in the impressive Palm Court, replete with marble tables, Louis XVI chaises, resplendent bouquets, and musical accompaniment: a true taste of Edwardian London in the 21st century. Afternoon Tea is £47 and Champagne Tea £59. Reserve a few months ahead and remember to wear a jacket and tie.

⇨ *For more information on the above places, see our Where to Stay chapter for the hotels and our Shopping chapter for the shops.*

LONDON WITH KIDS

Education Without Yawns

Kew Gardens. Kew Gardens is great for kids, with activities, the "climbers and creepers" play zone, treetops sky walk, zip wires, scramble slides, and children's trails; it's free for kids.

London Dungeon. Gore galore (did you ever see a medieval disembowelment?) plunges you into the depths of London history, with gruesome Jack the Ripper rides and special effects scary enough to frighten the coolest of kids.

London Zoo. Disappear into the animal kingdom among the enclosures, complete with sessions for kids about all kinds of spiders in this popular animal retreat in Regent's Park.

Natural History Museum. It doesn't get more awe-inspiring than bloodsucking bats, a cabinet of hummingbirds, simulated Kobe earthquakes, and a life-size blue whale. Just make sure you know your dodo from your diplodocus.

Science Museum. Special effects, virtual space voyages, 800 interactive exhibits, puzzles, and mysteries from the world of science can keep kids effortlessly amused all day.

Tower of London. Perfect for playing prince and princess in front of the Crown Jewels, but not so perfect for imagining what becomes of the fairy tale—watch your royal necks.

Performances

Covent Garden street performers. You can't beat the gaggle of jugglers, fire-eaters, unicyclists, mime artists, and the human statues tantalizing crowds at Covent Garden piazza.

Regent's Park Open-Air Theatre. Welcome to the land of fairy dust and magic. Don't miss an evening performance under the stars of *A Midsummer Night's Dream* in summer.

Activities

Ride the London Eye. Europe's biggest observation wheel looks like a giant fairground ride, and you can see across what seems like half of London from the top.

Pose with a Queen's Horse Guard. There's always a soldier in uniform standing watch by the entrance to Horse Guards on the Trafalgar Square end of Whitehall. They don't mind posing for pictures, but they're not allowed to smile (which some kids see as a challenge.)

Ice-skating at the Natural History Museum. Send your kids whizzing, arms whirling, across ice from mid-November to January at this spotlighted ice rink right outside the museum.

Night at the Natural History Museum. Find out what the dinosaurs really do when the lights go out at the monthly Dino Snores sleepover (minimum of one adult and five kids per group).

Pedelo on the Serpentine. Pack a picnic and take a blue pedelo out into the middle of Hyde Park's famed Serpentine lake; settle back and tuck in to lunch.

Lose the kids at Hampton Court Maze. The topiary might be more than 300 years old, but the quest to reach the middle of Hampton Court's world-famous trapezoid-shaped yew hedge maze remains as challenging as ever.

West End musicals. Foot-stompingly good West End musicals and shows like *Les Misérables, Billy Elliot, Matilda, Mamma Mia!, War Horse, Oliver!, Grease,* and *The Phantom of the Opera* will mesmerize the over-seven-years-old crowd.

Millennium Bridge and St. Paul's Cathedral.

THE BUILDING OF LONDON

The past is knit into the very fabric of the lives of Londoners: they live in Regency townhouses, worship in Baroque churches, and chill out in Edwardian-era parks. Unfolding like a gigantic historical pop-up book, London reveals—building by building—the pageant of a nation's history. To make sense of it all, here's a quick architectural tour through time.

Despite invading tribes, an epic fire, and 20th-century bombing, London has always survived, and a surprising amount of yesterday remains visible in its streets today. Starting with remnants of Londinium, the early Roman city contained by a defensive wall some 2,000 years ago, you can trace the city's beginnings. Only pieces of the wall remain, but the name of each entrance to the city has been preserved: Aldgate, Newgate, Bishopsgate, Cripplegate, Aldersgate, and Ludgate.

As commerce grew the city over the centuries, London expanded between two centers of power, Westminster in the west and the Tower in the east. Following both the Great Fire and World War II destruction, the need to rebuild outweighed the desire for sensible street layouts, and often any aesthetic considerations. In fact, London as a whole has rarely been planned, and the financial center is still roughly in the shape of that original Roman wall. London's haphazard streets and alleys are filled with diverse architectural styles side-by-side, each representing a piece of the city's history.

TIMELINE

56, 64 BC Julius Caesar arrives on Britain's shores	43 AD–410 AD Roman rule	61 AD Boudica attacks and destroys Londinium		600s Anglo-Saxon Lundenwic settlemen in Covent Garden are
	0	250	500	750

(top left) Statue of the Roman Emperor Trajan (r. AD 98-117) outside the largest remaining section of the Roman wall at Tower Hill. (right) Tower of London; (left) Carausius coin struck circa 288-290 AD at the Londinium mint.

Pre-410 Roman Londinium

As the Roman Empire expanded, Britain was conquered and the first city where London now stands began to develop along the Thames. Among many building projects, the Romans enclosed Londinium with a wall to protect against invading tribes after the Celtic warrior queen Boudica razed the city. Today chunks of the ancient barrier remain in the City, and at the Guildhall art gallery you can see a partial Roman amphitheatre from this time.

■ Visit: Guildhall (Ch. 6), London Wall at Tower Hill Tube station (Ch. 6), Museum of London (Ch. 5)

410–1485 Saxon and Medieval London

Little is known of the 250 years after the Romans left London. Following these "Dark Ages," most medieval houses and bridges were built of timber or wattle and daub and the perishable materials didn't last in the changing city.

England's royalty began building heavily in the capital as a sign of strength and power, focusing on defensive structures. In 1042, the Saxon King Edward the Confessor moved his court and began a church on the site of the current Westminster Abbey, where almost all the monarchs of England have been crowned since. From

across the English Channel, William the Conqueror brought Norman architectural styles with him. William built the White Tower; later expanded, the solid castle became the heart of the Tower of London complex. His son and heir William II saw the construction of Westminster Hall, the oldest part of the Palace of Westminster (today's Houses of Parliament). St. Bartholomew's Hospital, founded in 1123, and the Guildhall, a center of commerce from the early 15th century, are among the few buildings that survived the later Great Fire.

■ Visit: Guildhall (Ch. 6), St. Bartholomew's Hospital (Ch. 6), Tower of London (Ch. 6)

1000	1250	1500	1750
1066 William the Conqueror becomes King of England	1240 Parliament sits at Westminster for the first time	1348 The Black Death	1605 Guy Fawkes's Gunpowder Plot uncovered	1642–51 Civil War
			1534 Dissolution of the Monasteries	1666 Great Fire

1

IN FOCUS THE BUILDING OF LONDON

(top left) Painted ceiling of Banqueting House by Peter Paul Rubens; (top right) *The Great Fire of London, with Ludgate and old St Paul's;* (bottom right) St. Paul's Cathedral, built 1675–1708, designed by Christopher Wren

Tudor and Stuart London

1485–1700

As London grew, the Tudor royals influenced the architecture of London not only by creating, but also by destroying. Henry VII continued the expansion of Westminster Abbey and his successor, Henry VIII, resided at Hampton Court. The arts flourished under Elizabeth I, and the original Globe Theatre was built in 1599. Yet many fine medieval churches were torn down as England separated from the Roman Catholic Church.

Architects brought continental ideas to London, notably the influential Italian Palladian style introduced by Inigo Jones. You can see this classical style with it's mathematical proportions and balanced lines at the Queen's House in Greenwich and at Banqueting House, where Charles I was executed following the civil war. Eleven years later, Charles II was restored to the throne, returning from exile in France.

The Great Fire of 1666 destroyed five-sixths of London, but it also wiped out the plague that had ravaged the impoverished and overcrowded population the year before. Sir Christopher Wren was given the Herculean charge of rebuilding London. He wanted to map out a more organized grid for the city, but it was rebuilt on the old haphazard lines. It took Wren 35 years to build his baroque masterpiece, St. Paul's Cathedral. Wren also designed 50 other churches (only 23 still stand, including St. Bride's and St. Stephen Walbrook) and Monument to commemorate the fire. Nicholas Hawksmoor assisted Wren and designed his own highly original churches including the splendid Christ Church in Spitalfields.

■ Visit: Banqueting House (Ch. 2), Christ Church, Spitalfields (Ch. 7), Shakespeare's Globe Theatre (Ch. 8), Queen's House, Greenwich (Ch. 12), St. Bride's (Ch. 6), St. Paul's Cathedral (Ch. 6), St. Stephen Walbrook (Ch. 6), Hampton Court (Ch. 13)

(top left) Courtyard of Neo-classical Somerset House, built for George III. (right) The Rotunda of the Victoria and Albert (V&A) Museum with modern Chihuly sculpture; (bottom left) St Martin-in-the-Fields on Trafalgar Square.

Georgian Era

1700–1836

By the beginning of the 18th century, London was the biggest city in Europe and a center of world trade. This growth led to changes in politics, as power moved to a parliamentary system. Increased wealth led to an explosion of art and architecture.

Many different styles flourished—rococo, neo-classical, regency, and Gothic Revival. The predominant neo-classical, based on the styles of ancient Greece, can be seen in many stately homes. You can admire the elegant Regency terraces around John Nash's Regent's Park.

■ Visit: Regent's Park (Ch. 11), Somerset House (Ch. 4), St. Martin-in-the-Fields (Ch. 2)

Victorian Age

1837–1901

Queen Victoria ruled the British Empire for 63 years. London experienced the growth of wealth, industrialization, and philanthropy; this was also a period of desperate poverty, as depicted in Charles Dickens's novels. At the start of the 19th century the population of the city was over a million; by the end of Victoria's reign it was six million.

This rapid growth required many building programs, from worker housing to even bigger projects such as the bridges, government buildings, and the first subway system in the world. Businessmen, artists, and architects helped create many institutions that still exist today from the Tate Britain to the Ragged Schools and Foundling hospitals.

The clean, classical lines of the previous era gave way to more elaborate styles—which were considered more "English"—such as the Gothic Revival Houses of Parliament. Other Victorian projects included covered markets, canal locks, arcades, palaces, memorials, museums, theaters, and parks. So much building took place during this period that it's hard to miss the style: look for elaborate, highly decorated architecture.

■ Visit: Burlington Arcade (Ch. 3), Houses of Parliament (Ch. 2), Leadenhall Market in The City (Ch. 6), V&A and Natural History Museum (Ch. 9)

1851 Great Exhibition held in Hyde Park	1901 Death of Queen Victoria	1939–1945 WWII	1951 Festival of Britain
1863 Underground opens		1914–1918 WWI	
1870	1900	1930	1960

1

IN FOCUS THE BUILDING OF LONDON

(left) Theatergoers at The National Theatre on the South Bank of the Thames River; (right) Tower block at Barbican Centre, a 1980s complex of art venues and apartments.

20th-century building

1901–1979

The turn of the 20th century saw wealthy Westminster widening its streets to accommodate the arrival of motor cars and department stores. Even after the First World War, a "live for today" attitude continued among the upper classes, while the poorest Londoners suffered increasing prices and low wages. While modernism—a cultural movement embracing the future and rejecting anything associated with the past—was gathering pace in 1920s Europe, conservative British architecture continued to hark back to traditional influences of ancient Greece and the middle ages.

The WWII devastation of the Blitz bombings changed this and an enormous amount of post-war building was needed quickly. Émigrés such as Hungarian Ernö Goldfinger and Russian-born Berthold Lubetkin brought the modernist architectural movement to London with their high-rise buildings—a solution to the desperate housing shortage. One of the most exciting post-war projects was the 1951 Festival of Britain, celebrating the great inventions of the century. Out of a host of new architecture at the South Bank for this event, only the Royal Festival Hall remains.

Mass-produced concrete, steel, and glass ushered in the brutalist style in the '60s. This outgrowth of modernism can be seen in the Hayward Gallery and National Theatre. It was not a popular style, partly because the use of raw concrete—pioneered in the sunny south of France—looked gray, ugly, and even sinister against the backdrop of wet and windy London.

London's powers-that-be haven't always embraced modernist architecture, and many examples have been torn down. Today some iconic buildings are protected and the massive concrete Barbican Centre finally brought modernism right into the conservative City.

■ Visit: The Barbican Centre (Ch. 6), Hayward Gallery (Ch. 8), National Theatre (Ch. 8), Royal Festival Hall (Ch. 8) (left) Lloyd's of London by the Richard Rogers Pertnership, completed in 1986. (top right) Current design of the London Aquatics Centre by Zaha Hadid. (bottom right) The 2000 Great Court at the British Museum by Sir Norman Foster.

1980–Present

Modern and Millennium London

While the sun may have set on the British empire, London remains a global city, perhaps more now than ever before. The '80s saw changes in economic policy and ambitious building projects, including the Jubilee Line extension to the Underground system. Great business and banking centers reached higher into the sky as London's importance in financial markets increased. London's disused Docklands area got a revitalizing boost with the Canary Wharf development and the DLR (Docklands Light Railway).

Internationally-known architects began to make

their mark on the city with creative projects. Known as Tower 42, the NatWest Tower opened in 1981 as the tallest skyscraper in the city—for a great view, head to its bar on the 42nd floor. The Richard Rogers Partnership designed the fabulous 1986 Lloyd's of London building. Sir Norman Foster and his associates have designed the Sackler Galleries at the Royal Academy of Arts, the British Museum's Great Court, City Hall, and the Swiss Re Headquarters (known as the "Gherkin").

Building projects to celebrate the Millennium are now so beloved it's hard to imagine London without the pedestrian-only Millennium Bridge and the London Eye.

The stunning structures keep on coming. There's Zaha Hadid's curvaceous Aquatics Center, built for the Olympics but currently undergoing modification for opening to the public in 2014; the Bishopsgate Tower (aka, "Helter Skelter") whose construction is well under way; and the Richard Rogers Partnership's "Cheese Grater", also due for completion in 2014. But dwarfing them all is "The Shard", a 1,016-foot skyscraper designed by Italian Renzo Piano which is now the tallest building in the EU. As London is finding out—the sky's the limit.

■ Visit: Canary Wharf (Ch. 12), Lloyd's of London (Ch. 6), Shard (Ch. 8), Swiss Re (Ch. 6)

WESTMINSTER, ST. JAMES'S, AND ROYAL LONDON

GETTING ORIENTED

Westminster, St. James's,
and Royal London

TOP REASONS TO GO

Glorious Westminster Abbey: This Gothic church was not only the site of William and Kate's marriage but has also seen 38 coronations, starting with William the Conqueror in 1066.

Calling on Buckingham Palace: Even if you miss the palace's summer opening, keep pace with the marching soldiers as they enact the time-honored "Changing the Guard."

Masterpieces Theater: Leonardo, Raphael, Van Eyck, Rembrandt, and many other artistic greats are shown off in the gorgeously renovated rooms at the National Gallery.

Discover the unspoiled Churchill War Rooms: Listen to Churchill's radio addresses to the British people as you explore this cavernous underground wartime hideout.

Hear Big Ben's chimes: As the Eiffel Tower is to Paris, so is Big Ben to London—just follow your ears from Trafalgar Square to catch sight of the 320-foot-high Clock Tower.

FEELING PECKISH?

Gordon's Wine Bar. Gordon's is the oldest dedicated wine bar in the city (1890). The Thames used to lap almost at its doors and Rudyard Kipling was a tenant in the rooms upstairs. Faded art still fills every inch of wall and there's World War II blackout paint on one of the windows by the door. Head to the back room: windowless and lighted entirely by candles, it's been a wine cellar for 800 years. The excellence of the wine list only makes it easier for time to disappear here. ⊠ *47 Villiers St., Trafalgar Sq.* ☎ *020/7930–1408* ⊕ *www.gordonswinebar.com* Ⓜ *Embankment, Charing Cross.*

Inn the Park. With great food, drink, and location, Inn the Park is the perfect place to while away an hour or three, especially on the terrace in the summer. ⊠ *St. James's Park, St. James's* ☎ *020/7451–9999* ⊕ *www.innthepark.com* Ⓜ *St. James's Park.*

GETTING THERE

Trafalgar Square is smack-dab in the center of the action. Take the Tube to Embankment (Northern, Bakerloo, District, and Circle lines) and walk north until you cross the Strand, or alight at the Charing Cross (Bakerloo and Northern lines) Northumberland Avenue exit. Buses are another great option, as almost all roads lead to Trafalgar Square.

Two Tube stations are right in the heart of St. James's: Piccadilly Circus (Piccadilly or Bakerloo lines), and Green Park (Piccadilly, Victoria, or Jubilee lines).

MAKING THE MOST OF YOUR TIME

For royal pageantry begin with Buckingham Palace, Westminster Abbey, and the Guards Museum, followed by the Houses of Parliament and Big Ben. For art, the National Gallery, Tate Britain, and the Queen's Gallery head anyone's list.

NEAREST PUBLIC RESTROOMS

Paid loos (£1.50) are across the street from Westminster Abbey at the bottom of Victoria Street. Banqueting House and the Queen's Gallery have elegant restrooms.

Sightseeing
★★★★★
Nightlife
★★
Dining
★★★
Lodging
★
Shopping
★★

This is postcard London at its best. Crammed with historic churches, grand state buildings, and some of the world's best art collections, Royal London and Westminster unite politics and high culture. (Oh, and the Queen lives here, too.) The places you'll want to explore are grouped into four distinct areas—Trafalgar Square, Whitehall, St. James's, and Buckingham Palace—each nudging a corner of triangular St. James's Park. There is as much history in these few acres as in many whole cities, so pace yourself—this is concentrated sightseeing.

WESTMINSTER

Updated by
James O'Neill

Home to London's most photogenic pigeons (albeit in lesser numbers these days), **Trafalgar Square** is not only the official center of the district known as **Westminster,** it is the official center of London. What will bring you here are the two magnificent museums on the northern edge of the square, the **National Gallery** and the **National Portrait Gallery.** From the square, two boulevards lead to the seats of different eras of governance. The avenue called **Whitehall** drops south to the neo-Gothic **Houses of Parliament,** where members of both Houses (Commons and Lords) hold debates and vote on pending legislation. Just opposite, **Westminster Abbey** is a monument to the nation's history and for centuries the scene of daily worship, coronations, and royal weddings. Poets, political leaders, and 17 monarchs are buried in this world-famous, 13th-century Gothic building. Sandwiched between the two is the **Jewel Tower,** the only surviving part of the medieval Palace of Westminster (a name still given to Parliament and its environs). Halfway down Whitehall, **No. 10 Downing Street** is both the residence and the office of the prime minister. One of the most celebrated occupants, Winston Churchill, is commemorated in the **Churchill War Rooms,** his underground wartime

2

headquarters off Whitehall. Just down the road is the **Cenotaph,** which acts as a focal point for the annual remembrance of those lost in war.

The Mall, a wide, elegant avenue beyond the stone curtain of **Admiralty Arch,** heads southwest from Trafalgar Square toward the **Queen Victoria Memorial** and **Buckingham Palace,** the sovereign's official residence. The building is open to the public only in summer, but you can see much of the royal art collection in the **Queen's Gallery** and spectacular ceremonial coaches in the **Royal Mews,** both open all year. Farther south toward Pimlico, **Tate Britain** focuses on prominent British artists from 1500 to today.

This area can be considered "Royal London" partly because it is neatly bounded by the triangle of streets that make up the route that Queen Elizabeth II usually takes when processing from Buckingham Palace to Westminster Abbey or to the Houses of Parliament on state occasions, and also because it contains so much of British history going back a thousand years. Naturally, in an area that regularly sees the pomp and pageantry of royal occasions, the streets are wide and the vistas long. The main drawback to sightseeing here is that half the world is doing it at the same time as you. So, remember that for a large part of the year a lot of Royal London is floodlit at night (when there's more elbowroom), adding to the theatricality of the experience.

TOP ATTRACTIONS

FAMILY

Fodor'sChoice

★

Churchill War Rooms. It was from this small warren of underground rooms—beneath the vast government buildings of the Treasury—that Winston Churchill and his team directed troops in World War II. Designed to be bombproof, the whole complex has been preserved almost exactly as it was when the last light was turned off at the end of the war. Every clock shows almost 5 pm, and the furniture, fittings, and paraphernalia of a busy, round-the-clock war office are in situ, down to the colored map pins.

During air raids, the leading government ministers met here, and the Cabinet Room is still arranged as if a meeting were about to convene. In the Map Room, the Allied campaign is charted on wall-to-wall maps with a rash of pinholes showing the movements of convoys. In the hub of the room, a bank of different-color phones known as the "Beauty Chorus" linked the War Rooms to control rooms around the nation. The Prime Minister's Room holds the desk from which Churchill made his morale-boosting broadcasts; the Telephone Room (a converted broom cupboard) has his hotline to FDR. You can also see the restored rooms that the PM used for dining and sleeping. Telephonists and clerks who worked 16-hour shifts slept in lesser quarters in unenviable conditions.

A great addition to the War Rooms is the Churchill Museum, a tribute to the great wartime leader himself. Different zones explore his life and achievements—and failures, too—through objects and documents, many of which, such as his personal papers, have never previously been made public. ■ TIP➜ **Although the War Rooms are underground, access is available for wheelchairs.** ✉ *Clive Steps, King Charles St., Westminster* ☎ *020/7930–6961* ⊕ *www.iwm.org.uk* ✇ *£17.50* ☉ *Daily 9:30–6; last admission 5* Ⓜ *Westminster.*

Downing Street. Looking like an unassuming alley but for the iron gates (and armed guards) that block the entrance, this is the location of the famous **No. 10,** London's modest equivalent of the White House. The Georgian entrance to the mid-17th-century mansion is deceptive; it's actually a huge complex of discreetly linked buildings. Since 1732 it has been the official home and office of the Prime Minister—the last private resident was the magnificently named Mr. Chicken—although the current Prime Minister actually lives in the private apartments above No. 11, as those in No. 10 are too small to house a family. (No. 11 is traditionally the residence of the Chancellor of the Exchequer, the head of the treasury). There are no public tours but the famous black front door to No. 10 is clearly visible from Whitehall. Just south of Downing Street, in the middle of Whitehall, is the **Cenotaph,** a stark white mono-lith built to commemorate the 1918 armistice. On Remembrance Day (the Sunday nearest November 11) it's strewn with red poppy wreaths to honor the dead of both world wars and all British and Common-wealth soldiers killed in action since; the first wreath is traditionally laid by the Queen. ⊠ *Whitehall* Ⓜ *Westminster.*

QUICK BITES

Notes Music and Coffee. Next door to the London Coliseum (home of the English National Opera), this hip café serves some of the best sandwiches, salads, and coffee in the neighborhood. Keep an eye out for their popular jazz nights. ⊠ *31 St. Martin's La., Westminster* ☏ *020/7240–0424* ⊕ *notes-uk.co.uk* Ⓜ *Charing Cross.*

FAMILY **Horse Guards Parade.** Once the tiltyard for jousting tournaments, Horse Guards Parade is best known for the annual Trooping the Colour cer-emony, in which the Queen takes the salute on her official birthday tribute, on the second Saturday in June. (Though it's called a birthday it's actually the anniversary of her coronation—the Queen's real birth-day is on April 21.) It's a must-see if you're around, with marching bands and throngs of onlookers. Throughout the rest of the year the changing of two mounted sentries known as the **Queen's Life Guard** at the Whitehall facade of Horse Guards provides what may be London's most popular photo opportunity. The ceremony last about half an hour. ⊠ *Whitehall* ☏ *020/7930–4832* ☉ *Changing of the Queen's Life Guard at 11 am Mon.–Sat. and 10 am Sun.; inspection of the Queen's Life Guard daily at 4 pm* Ⓜ *Westminster.*

Houses of Parliament.

See the highlighted listing in this chapter.

The Jewel Tower. Overshadowed by the far more famous attractions of Parliament to one side and Westminster Abbey to the other, this is the only portion of the Palace of Westminster complex to have survived intact from medieval times. Built in the 1360s to contain treasures belonging to Edward III, it once formed part of the palace's defensive walls—hence the fortress-like appearance. Check out the original ribbed stone ceiling on the ground floor; look up to see the carved stone images of men and beasts. The Jewel Tower was later used as a records office for the House of Lords, but hasn't served in any official function since the rest of the old palace was destroyed by fire in 1834; the ancient

A BRIEF HISTORY OF WESTMINSTER

The Romans may have shaped The City, but England's royals created Westminster. Indeed, technically it's still a separate city—notice it says "City of Westminster" on the street signs, not "City of London"—although any formal divide between the two vanished centuries ago, along with the open countryside that once lay between them. Edward the Confessor started the first Palace of Westminster in the 11th century; he also founded Westminster Abbey in 1050, where every British monarch since then has been crowned. The district became the focus of political power in England after the construction of Whitehall Palace in the 16th century; a vast and opulent building, it was the official residence of the monarch until it burned down in 1698. It survives both as the name of Westminster's most important road, and a term still used in Britain to refer to the seat of government in general. The first Parliament building was part of the same complex; it, too, was nearly destroyed by the Gunpowder Plot of 1605 (still commemorated annually on November 5) and eventually succumbed to fire in 1834. The Westminster we see today took shape during the Georgian and Victorian periods, as Britain reached the zenith of its imperial power. Grand architecture sprang up, and Buckingham Palace became the principal royal residence in 1837, when Victoria acceded to the throne. Trafalgar Square and Nelson's Column were built in 1843, to commemorate Britain's most famous naval victory, and the Houses of Parliament were rebuilt in 1858 in the trendy neo-Gothic style of the time. The illustrious Clarence House, built in 1825 for the Duke of Clarence (later William IV), is now the home of Prince Charles and Camilla, Duchess of Cornwall.

documents were moved to the greater safety of the Tower of London. Today it contains an exhibition on the history of Parliament. ⊠ *Abingdon St., Westminster* ☎ *020/7222–2219* ⊕ *www.english-heritage.org. uk* ⊗ *Mar.–Oct, daily 10–5; Nov.–Feb., daily 10–4; last admission 30 mins before closing* Ⓜ *Westminster.*

FAMILY
Fodor's Choice
★

National Gallery.
See the highlighted listing in this chapter.

FAMILY
Fodor's Choice
★

National Portrait Gallery. Tucked around the corner from the National Gallery, the National Portrait Gallery was founded in 1856 with a single aim: to gather together portraits of famous (and infamous) British men and women. More than 150 years and 160,000 portraits later, it is an essential stop for all history and literature buffs. The spacious galleries make it a pleasant place to visit, and you can choose to take in a little or a lot. Need to rest those legs? Then use the Portrait Explorer in the Digital Space on the ground-floor mezzanine for interactive, computer-aided exploration of the gallery's extensive collection. If you visit with little ones, ask at the desk about the excellent Family Trails, which make exploring the galleries with children much more fun. ■TIP➜ On the top floor, the Portrait Restaurant has one of the best views in London—a panoramic vista of Nelson's Column and the backdrop along Whitehall to the Houses of Parliament.

HOUSES OF PARLIAMENT

✉ St. Stephen's Entrance, St. Margaret St., Westminster ☎ 020/7219–4272 information, 0844/847–1672 public tours, 0161/425–8677 public tours (from overseas) ⊕ www.parliament.uk/visiting ✉ Free; tours £16.50 (booking essential) ⊙ Tour times and hrs for Visitor's Gallery vary week to week; call or check website Ⓜ Westminster.

TIPS

■ Public tours of Parliament cost £16.50 and must be booked in advance throughw-www.ticketmaster.co.uk.

■ Nonresidents can watch debates when Parliament is in session by waiting in line for tickets. Embassies and High Commissions often have a quota of debate tickets available to their citizens, which helps in avoiding long lines.

■ The easiest time to get into the Commons is during an evening session—Parliament is still sitting if the top of the Clock Tower is illuminated.

■ The best view of the Houses is from the opposite (south) bank, across Lambeth Bridge. It is especially dramatic at night when flood-lighted green and gold.

The Palace of Westminster, as the complex is called, was first established by Edward the Confessor in the 11th century. William II started building a new palace in 1087, and this became the seat of English power. Fire destroyed most of the palace in 1834, and the current complex dates largely from the mid-19th century.

Highlights

The **Visitors' Galleries** of the House of Commons afford a view of democracy in action when the benches are filled by opposing MPs (members of Parliament). Debates are formal but raucous—especially during **Prime Minister's Questions** (PMQs), when any MP can put a question to the nation's leader. Tickets to PMQs are free but highly sought after, so the only way for non-U.K. citizens to gain access is by queuing on the day and hoping for no-shows. The action starts at 1 pm Wednesday when Parliament is sitting and broadcast live on television. There are also Visitors Galleries for The House of Lords.

Westminster Hall was the work of William the Conqueror's son William Rufus. It's one of the largest remaining Norman halls in Europe and the scene of the trial of Charles I.

After the 1834 fire, the Clock Tower—renamed **Elizabeth Tower** in 2012, in honor of the Queen's Diamond Jubilee—was completed in 1858, and contains the 13-ton bell known as **Big Ben**. At the southwest end of the main Parliament building is the 323-foot-high Victoria Tower.

Galleries are arranged clearly and chronologically, from Tudor times to contemporary Britain. A Holbein miniature of Henry VIII is perhaps the most famous image in the Tudor Gallery, although the enormous portrait of Elizabeth I—bejeweled and literally astride the world in a powerful display of imperial intent—is by far the most impressive. The huge permanent collections include portraits of Shakespeare, the Brontë sisters, and Jane Austen. Look for the four Andy Warhol *Queen Elizabeth II* silk screens from 1985 and Maggi Hambling's surreal self-portrait. Contemporary portraits range from the iconic (*Julian with T-shirt*—an LCD screen on a continuous loop—by Julian Opie) to the creepy (Marc Quinn's *Self*, a realization of the artist's head in frozen blood) and the eccentric (Tim Noble's ghoulish *Head of Isabella Blow*). Temporary exhibitions can be explored in the ground-floor Wolfson and Porter galleries. ✉ *St. Martin's Pl., Westminster* ☎ *020/7312–2463, 020/730–0555 recorded switchboard information* ⊕ *www.npg.org.uk* ✆ *Free; charge for special exhibitions; audiovisual guide £3* ⊘ *Mon.–Wed. and weekends 10–6, Thurs. and Fri. 10–9; last admission 1 hr before closing* Ⓜ *Charing Cross, Leicester Sq.*

> ## ST. MARTIN'S CONCERTS
>
> Classical concerts (some by candlelight) are held every Thursday to Saturday (and some Tuesdays) at 7:30 pm with evening jazz concerts in the crypt every Wednesday at 8 pm. Tickets are available from the box office in the crypt. Free (£3.50 donation suggested) lunchtime concerts take place Monday, Tuesday, and Friday 1–2 pm.

FAMILY **St. Martin-in-the-Fields.** One of London's best-loved and most welcoming of churches is more than just a place of worship. Named after the saint who helped beggars, St Martin's has long been a welcome sight for the homeless, who have been given soup and shelter at the church since 1914. The church is also a haven for music lovers; the internationally known Academy of St. Martin-in-the-Fields was founded here, and a popular program of concerts continues today. (Although the interior is a wonderful setting for a recital, beware the hard wooden benches!) The crypt is a hive of activity, with a popular café and shop, plus the **London Brass-Rubbing Centre**, where you can make your own life-size souvenir knight, lady, or monarch from replica tomb brasses, with metallic waxes, paper, and instructions from about £5. ✉ *Trafalgar Sq., Westminster* ☎ *020/7766–1100* ⊕ *www.smitf.org* ✆ *Free; concerts £7–£30* ⊘ *Open all day for worship; sightseeing: Mon., Tues., and Fri. 8:30–1 and 2–6; Wed. 8:30–1:15 and 2–5; Thurs. 8:30–1:15 and 2–6; Sat. 9:30–6; Sun. 3:30–5* Ⓜ *Charing Cross, Leicester Sq.*

QUICK BITES

The atmospheric **St. Martin's Café in the Crypt**, with its magnificent high-arched brick vault and gravestone floor, serves full English and continental breakfasts, sandwiches, salads, snacks, afternoon tea, and wine. Lunch and dinner options include vegetarian meals and the setting, at the heart of London, is superb.

NATIONAL GALLERY

✉ *Trafalgar Sq., Westminster* ☏ *020/7747–2885* ⊕ *www. nationalgallery.org.uk* ✉ *Free; charge for special exhibitions; audio guide £3.50* ⊙ *Sun.–Thurs. 10–6, Fri. 10–9* Ⓜ *Charing Cross, Embankment, Leicester Sq.*

TIPS

■ Color coding throughout the galleries helps you keep track of the period in which you're immersed.

■ Begin at an "Art Start" terminal in the Sainsbury Wing or East Wing Espresso Bar. The interactive screens give you access to information on all of the museum's holdings; you can choose your favorites, and print out a free personal tour map.

■ Want some stimulation? Try a free weekday lunchtime lecture, or Ten Minute Talk, which illuminates the story behind a key work of art. One-hour free, guided tours start at the Sainsbury Wing every weekday at 11:30 and 2:30 (also Friday at 7 pm), and on weekends at 4.

■ If you are eager for even more insight into the art, pick up a themed audio guide, which takes in about 20 paintings.

■ If you visit with children, don't miss special programs for young visitors, including free Family Sundays (every Sunday) with special talks for children and their parents. Check the website for other one-off events.

Standing proudly on the north side of Trafalgar Square, this is truly one of the world's supreme art collections, with more than 2,300 masterpieces on show. Michelangelo, Leonardo, Turner, Monet, van Gogh, Picasso, and more—all for free. Watch out for special temporary exhibitions, too.

Highlights

This brief selection is your jumping-off point, but there are hundreds of other paintings to see, enough to fill a full day. In chronological order: (1) **Van Eyck** (c. 1395–1441), *The Arnolfini Portrait*—a solemn couple holds hands, the fish-eye mirror behind them mysteriously illuminating what can't be seen from the front view. (2) **Holbein** (1497–1543), *The Ambassadors*— two wealthy visitors from France stand surrounded by what were considered luxury goods at the time. Note the elongated skull at the bottom of the painting, which takes shape only when viewed from an angle. (3) **Da Vinci** (1452–1519), *The Virgin and Child*—this exquisite black-chalk "Burlington Cartoon" depicts the master's most haunting Mary. (4) **Velázquez** (1599–1660), *Christ in the House of Martha and Mary*—in this enigmatic masterpiece the Spaniard plays with perspective and the role of the viewer. (5) **Turner** (1775–1851), *Rain, Steam and Speed: The Great Western Railway*, the whirl of rain, mist, steam, and locomotion is nothing short of astonishing (spot the hare). (6) **Caravaggio** (1573–1610), *The Supper at Emmaus*—a freshly resurrected Christ blesses bread in an astonishingly domestic vision from the master of chiaroscuro. (7) **Van Gogh** (1853–1890), *Sunflowers*—painted during his sojourn with Gauguin in Arles, this is quintessential Van Gogh. (8) **Seurat** (1859–91), *Bathers at Asnières*—this summer day's idyll is one of the pointillist extraordinaire's best-known works.

The Tate Britain showcases British art from the last 500 years, including contemporary works.

Tate Britain. The stately neoclassical institution may not be as ambitious as its sibling Tate Modern on the South Bank, but Tate Britain's bright galleries lure only a fraction of the Modern's overwhelming crowds and are a great place to explore British art from 1500 to the present. First opened in 1897, funded by the sugar magnate Sir Henry Tate, the museum includes the Linbury Galleries on the lower floors, which stage temporary exhibitions, and a permanent collection on the upper floors. And what a collection it is—classic works by John Constable, Thomas Gainsborough, David Wilkie, Francis Bacon, Duncan Grant, Barbara Hepworth, and Ben Nicholson, and an outstanding display from J.M.W. Turner in the Clore Gallery, including many later vaporous and light-infused works such as *Sunrise with Sea Monsters*. Sumptuous Pre-Raphaelite pieces are a major draw, while the Contemporary British Art galleries bring you face to face with Damien Hirst's *Away from the Flock* and other recent conceptions. The Tate Britain also hosts the annual Turner Prize exhibition, with its accompanying furor over the state of contemporary art, from about October to January each year. Details of activities for families are on the website. There's a good little café, and the excellent Rex Whistler Restaurant has been something of an institution since it first opened in 1927. It's open daily for lunch, but evening hours are mercurial to say the least—you can dine here only on the first Friday of December, February, April, June, August, and October.

■TIP➔ Craving more art? Head down the river on the Tate to Tate boat (£6.50 one way) to Tate Modern, running between the two museums every 40 minutes. A River Roamer ticket (£15) permits a day's travel, with stops including the London Eye and the Tower of London. You get a discount of roughly a third if you have a Travelcard. ⊠ *Millbank, Westminster* ☎ *020/7887–8888* ⊕ *www.tate.org.uk/britain* 🎟 *Free, special exhibitions £9–£15* ⊙ *Sat.–Thurs. 10–6 (last entry at 5:15), Fri. 10–10 (last entry at 9:15)* Ⓜ *Pimlico.*

Fodor'sChoice **Trafalgar Square.** This is literally the center of London: a plaque on the
★ corner of the Strand and Charing Cross Road marks the spot from which distances on U.K. signposts are measured. Medieval kings once kept their aviaries of hawks and falcons here; today the humbler gray pigeons flock en masse to the open spaces around the ornate fountains (although feeding them is banned). The square was designed in 1830 by John Nash, who envisaged a new public space with striking views of the Thames, the Houses of Parliament, and Buckingham Palace. Of those, only Parliament is still clearly visible from the square, but it remains a magnet for open-air concerts, political demonstrations, and national celebrations, such as Victory in Europe Day and New Year's Eve. Dominating the square is the 170-foot **Nelson's Column**, erected as a monument to the great admiral in 1848. Note that the lampposts on the south side, heading down Whitehall, are topped with ships— they all face in the precise direction of Portsmouth, home of the British navy. The column is flanked on either side by enormous bronze lions. ⚠ Climbing them is a very popular photo op—but be extremely careful, as there are no guardrails and it's a long fall onto concrete if you slip. Four plinths border the square; three contain militaristic statues, but one was left empty—it's now used for contemporary art installations, often with a wry and controversial edge. Surprisingly enough, given that this was a square built to honor British military victories, the lawn at the north side, by the National Gallery, contains a statue of George Washington—a gift from the state of Virginia in 1921. At the southern point of the square is the **equestrian statue of Charles I.** After the Civil War and the king's execution, Oliver Cromwell, the anti-Royalist leader, commissioned a brazier, John Rivett, to melt the statue. The story goes that Rivett buried it in his garden and made a fortune peddling knickknacks wrought, he claimed, from its metal, only to produce the statue miraculously unscathed after the restoration of the monarchy—and make a fortune reselling it in the process. In 1667 Charles II had it placed where it stands today, near the spot where his father was executed in 1649. Each year, on January 30, the day of the king's death, the Royal Stuart Society lays a wreath at the foot of the statue. ⊠ *Westminster* Ⓜ *Charing Cross.*

Fodor'sChoice **Westminster Abbey.**
★ *See the highlighted listing in this chapter.*

WORTH NOTING

Admiralty Arch. This stately gateway is an impressive counterpoint to Buckingham Palace, at the opposite end of the Mall (rhymes with "shall"). On the southwest corner of Trafalgar Square, the arch, named after the adjacent Royal Navy headquarters, was designed by Sir Aston Webb and completed in 1912 as a memorial to Queen Victoria. Actually comprised of five arches—two for pedestrians, two for traffic, and the central arch which is only opened for state occasions—it was a

Continued on page 58

WESTMINSTER ABBEY

A monument to the rich—and often bloody and scandalous—history of Great Britain, Westminster Abbey rises on the Thames skyline as one of the most iconic sites in London.

The mysterious gloom of the lofty medieval interior is home to more than 600 monuments and memorial statues. About 3,300 people, from kings to composers to wordsmiths, are buried in the abbey. It has been the scene of 14 royal weddings and no less than 38 coronations—the first in 1066, when William the Conqueror was made king here.

TOURING THE ABBEY

There's only one way around the abbey, and as there will almost certainly be a long stream of shuffling tourists at your heels, you'll need to be alert to catch the highlights. Enter by the north door.

When you enter the church, turn around and look up to see the ❶ painted-glass rose window, the largest of its kind.

The ❷ Coronation Chair, at the foot of the Henry VII Chapel, has been briefly graced by nearly every regal posterior since Edward I ordered it in 1301. Look for the graffiti on the back of the Coronation chair. It's the work of 18th- and 19th-century visitors and Westminster schoolboys who carved their names there.

The ❸ Henry VII's Lady Chapel contains the tombs of Henry VII and his queen, Elizabeth of York. Close by are monuments to the young daughters of James I, and an urn purported to hold the remains of the so-called Princes in the Tower—Edward V and Richard. Interestingly, arch enemies Elizabeth I and her half-sister Mary Tudor share a tomb here. Begun in 1503, the chapel is famed for its ceiling—a dazzling fan-vaulted roof with carved pendants—and the heraldic banners of living knights that hang above its oak stalls.

In front of the ❹ High Altar, which was used for the funerals of Princess Diana and

the Queen Mother, is a black-and-white marble pavement laid in 1268. The intricate Italian Cosmati work contains three Latin inscriptions, one of which states that the world will last for 19,683 years.

The ❺ Shrine of St. Edward the Confessor contains the shrine to the pre-Norman king. Because of its great age, you must join a tour with the verger to be admitted to the chapel. (Details are available at the

admission desk; there is a small extra charge.)

Geoffrey Chaucer was the first poet to be buried in ❻ Poets' Corner in 1400. Other memorials include: William Shakespeare, William Blake, John Milton, Jane Austen, Samuel Taylor Coleridge, William Wordsworth, and Charles Dickens.

A door from the south transept and south choir aisle leads to the calm of the ❼ Great Cloisters.

North Entrance
1 North Transept
2
3
North Ambulatory
Sanctuary **6**
4 **5**
South Ambulatory
South Transept
6
8
9
10

and actual clothing of Charles II and Admiral Lord Nelson (complete with eye patch).

The **10** **Little Cloister** is a quiet haven, and just beyond, the **11** **College Garden** is a delightful diversion. Filled with medicinal herbs, it has been tended by monks for more than 900 years.

The **12** **Dean's Yard** is the best spot for a fine view of the massive flying buttresses above.

The medieval **8** **Chapter House** is adorned with 14th-century frescoes. The King's Council met here between 1257 and 1547. Be sure to look at the floor, one of the finest surviving tiled floors in the country.

The **9** **Abbey Museum** includes a collection of deliciously macabre effigies made from the death masks

In the choir screen, north of the entrance to the choir, is a marble **13** **monument to Sir Isaac Newton.**

14 **A plaque to Franklin D. Roosevelt** is one of the Abbey's very few tributes to a foreigner.

The **15** **Grave of the Unknown Warrior,** in memory of the soldiers who lost their lives in both world wars, is near the exit of the abbey.

QUIRKY LONDON

Near the Henry VII chapel, keep an eye open for St. Wilgefortis, who was so concerned to protect her chastity that she prayed to God for help and woke up one morning with a full growth of beard.

A BRIEF HISTORY

960 AD Benedictine monastery founded on the site by King Edward and King Dunstan.

1045–65 King Edward the Confessor enlarges the original monastery, erecting a stone church in honor of St. Paul the Apostle. Named "west minster" to distinguish from "east minster" (St. Paul's Cathedral).

1065 The church is consecrated on December 28. Edward doesn't live to see the ceremony.

1161 Following Edward's canonization, his body is moved by Henry III to a more elaborate resting place behind the High Altar. Other medieval kings are later buried around his tomb.

1245–54 Henry III pulls down the abbey and starts again with a new Gothic style influenced by his travels in France. Master mason Henry de Reyns ("of Rheims") constructs the transepts, north front, and rose windows, as well as part of the cloisters and Chapter House.

1269 The new abbey is consecrated and the choir is completed.

1350s Richard II resumes Henry III's plan to rebuild the monastery. Henry V and Henry VII continue as benefactors.

1503 The Lady Chapel is demolished and the foundation stone of Henry VII's Chapel is laid on the site.

1540 The abbey ceases to be used as a monastery.

1560 Elizabeth I refounds the abbey as a Collegiate Church. From this point on it is a "Royal Peculiar," exempt from the jurisdiction of bishops.

1745 The western towers, left unfinished from medieval times, are finally completed, based on a design by Sir Christopher Wren.

1995 Following a 25-year restoration program, saints and allegorical figures are added to the niches on the western towers and around the Great West Door.

PLANNING YOUR DAY

GETTING HERE: The closest Tube stop is Westminster. When you exit the station, walk west along Great George Street, away from the river. Turn left on St. Margaret Street.

CONTACT INFO: ✉ Broad Sanctuary, Westminster SW1 P3PA ☎ 020/7222-5152 ⊕ www.westminster-abbey.org.

ADMISSION: Adults: Abbey and museum £18. **Family tickets:** 2 adults and 2 children, £44. **Children under 11:** free.

HOURS: The abbey is a house of worship. Services may cause changes to the visiting hours on any given day, so be sure to call ahead.
Abbey: Weekdays 9:30–6; Sat. Apr.–Sept. 9:30–3:30, Oct.–Mar. 9:30–1:30 (last admission 1 hour before closing); Sun, worship only.
Museum: Mon.–Sat. 10:30–4.
Cloisters: Daily 8–6
College Garden: Apr.–Sept.: Tues.–Thurs. 10–6; Oct.–Mar.: Tues.–Thurs. 10–4.
Chapter House: Mon.–Sat. 10–4

WHAT'S NEARBY: To make the most of your day, arrive at the abbey early (doors open at 9:30), then make an afternoon visit to the Parliament buildings and finish with a sunset ride on the **London Eye.** Post-flight, take a walk along the fairy-lit South Bank and have dinner (or a drink in the bar) with a view, at the **Oxo Tower Restaurant** (☎ 020/7803–3888) or the Royal Festival Hall's **Skylon Restaurant** (☎ 020/7654–7800).

Please note that overseas visitors can no longer visit the **Houses of Parliament** during session. However, tours of the buildings are available in August and September. For more information and booking call ☎ 0844/847–1672. Also, it's advisable to prebook tickets for the London Eye. Do this online at www.londoneye.com, or call 0871/781–3000.

IN A HURRY?

If you're pressed for time, concentrate on the following four highlights: the Coronation Chair; Chapter House; Poets' Corner; and Grave of the Unknown Warrior.

THINGS TO KNOW

■ Photography and filming are not permitted anywhere in the abbey.

■ In winter the interior of the abbey can get quite cold; dress accordingly.

■ For an animated history of the Abbey, join one of the verger-led tours (90 minutes) that depart from the North Door: Apr.–Sept.: Mon.–Fri. 10, 10:30, 11, 2, 2:30, Sat. 10, 10:30, 11; Oct.–Mar.: Mon.–Fri. 10:30, 11, 2, 2:30, Sat. 10:30, 11. Ask at information desk, £3 per person (in addition to entrance charge).

■ Touring the abbey can take half a day, especially in summer, when lines are long.

■ To avoid the crowds, make sure you arrive early. If you're first in line you can enjoy parts of the abbey in relative calm before the mad rush descends.

■ If you want to study up before you go, visit www.westminster-abbey.org, which includes an in-depth history and self-guided tour of the abbey. Otherwise pick up a free leaflet from the information desk.

■ On Sundays the abbey is not open to visitors. Join a service instead. Check the Web site for service times, as well as details of concerts, organ recitals, and special events.

government building until 2012, and even served as an alternative residence for the Prime Minister when Downing Street was under renovation. It is now expected to be turned into a luxury hotel. ⊠ *The Mall, Cockspur St., and Trafalgar Sq., Westminster* Ⓜ *Charing Cross.*

Banqueting House. James I commissioned Inigo Jones, one of England's great architects, to undertake a grand building on the site of the original Tudor Palace of Whitehall, which was (according to one foreign visitor) "ill-built, and nothing but a heap of houses." Jones's Banqueting House, finished in 1622 and the first building in England to be completed in the neoclassical style, bears all the hallmarks of the Palladian sophistication and purity which so influenced Jones during his time in Italy. James's son, Charles I, enhanced the interior by employing the Flemish painter Peter Paul Rubens to glorify his father and himself (naturally) in a series of vibrant painted ceiling panels called "The Apotheosis of James I." As it turned out, these allegorical paintings, depicting a wise monarch being received into heaven, were the last thing Charles saw before stepped through the open first-floor window onto the scaffold which had been erected directly outside for his execution by Cromwell's Parliamentarians in 1649. Yet 20 years later his son, Charles II, would celebrate the restoration of the monarchy in the exact same place. ⊠ *Whitehall, Westminster* ☎ *084/4482–7777* ⊕ *www.hrp.org.uk* 💳 *£5.50* ⊙ *Daily 10–5; last admission 4:15. Can close at short notice for events; call ahead* Ⓜ *Charing Cross, Embankment, Westminster.*

Carlton House Terrace. Architect John Nash designed Carlton House, a glorious example of the Regency style, under the patronage of George IV (the Prince Regent, who ruled in place of George III while the "mad king" was considered too unstable to rule). Carlton House was considered a most extravagant building for its time and it was demolished after the prince's accession to the throne in 1820. In its place Nash built Carlton House Terrace—no less imposing, with white-stucco facades and massive Corinthian columns. Carlton Terrace was a smart address, home to several of the 19th-century's greatest luminaries—including two prime ministers, William Gladstone (1856) and Lord Palmerston (1857–75). Today Carlton House Terrace houses the Royal Society (No. 6–9), Britain's most prestigious society of scientific minds; still active today, its previous members have included Isaac Newton and Charles Darwin. ⊠ *The Mall, St. James's* Ⓜ *Charing Cross.*

FAMILY **Household Cavalry Museum.** Hang around Horse Guards for even a short time and you'll see a member of the Household Cavalry on guard, or trotting past on horseback, resplendent in a bright crimson uniform with polished brass armor. Made up of soldiers from the British Army's most senior regiments, the Life Guards and the Blues and Royals, membership is considered a great honor; they act as the Queen's official bodyguards and play a key role in state occasions. (It is they who perform the Changing the Guard ceremony every day at 11 am.) Located in the cavalry's original 17th-century stables, the museum has displays of uniforms and weapons going back to 1661 as well as interactive exhibits on the regiments' current operational roles. In the tack room you can handle saddles and bridles, and try on a trooper's uniform, including a distinctive brass helmet with horsehair plume. You can also observe the working horses being tended to in their stable block behind a glass wall. ✉ *Horse Guards, Whitehall* ☎ *020/7930–3070* ⊕ *www. householdcavalrymuseum.co.uk* 🎫 *£6* ⊙ *Mar.–Sept., daily 10–6; Oct.– Feb., daily 10–5* Ⓜ *Charing Cross, Westminster.*

St. Margaret's Church. Dwarfed by its neighbor, Westminster Abbey, St. Margaret's was founded in the 11th century and rebuilt between 1488 and 1523. It's the unofficial parish church of the House of Commons— Winston Churchill tied the knot here in 1908. Samuel Pepys, Geoffrey Chaucer, and John Milton worshipped here, and, since 1681, a pew off the south aisle has been set aside for the Speaker of the House (look for the carved portcullis). The stained glass in the north windows is classically Victorian, facing abstract glass from John Piper in the south, replacing the originals, which were ruined in World War II. ✉ *St. Margaret's St., Parliament Sq., Westminster* ☎ *020/7654–4840* ⊕ *www.westminster-abbey.org/st-margarets* ⊙ *Weekdays 9:30–3:30, Sat. 9–1:30, Sun. 2–4:30 (entry via east door). Church may close on short notice for services, so call ahead* Ⓜ *Westminster.*

The Supreme Court. The highest court of appeal in the United Kingdom is housed in the carefully restored Middlesex Guildhall. Visitors are welcome to pop in (for free) and look at the three courtrooms, including the impressive Court Room 1 on the second floor, with its magnificent carved wood ceiling. The Court's art collection, on permanent display, includes portraits by Thomas Gainsborough and Joshua Reynolds. There is a café downstairs. ✉ *Parliament Sq., Westminster* ☎ *020/7960–1500* ⊕ *supremecourt.uk* 🎫 *Free* ⊙ *Weekdays 11–4, Sat. 10:30–4:30* Ⓜ *Westminster (take Exit 6 for Whitehall west).*

FAMILY **Wellington Barracks.** These are the headquarters of the Guards Division, the Queen's five regiments of elite foot guards (Grenadier, Coldstream, Scots, Irish, and Welsh) who protect the sovereign and, dressed in tunics of gold-purled scarlet and tall bearskin caps, patrol her palaces. Guardsmen alternate these ceremonial postings with serving in current conflicts, for which they wear more practical uniforms. If you want to learn more about the guards, visit the **Guards Museum,** which has displays on all aspects of a guardsman's life in conflicts dating back to 1642; the entrance is next to the Guards Chapel. Next door is the **Guards Toy Soldier Centre,** a great place for a souvenir. ✉ *Birdcage Walk, Westminster* ☎ *020/7414–3428* ⊕ *www.theguardsmuseum.com* 🎫 *£5* ⊙ *Daily 10–4; last admission 3:30* Ⓜ *St. James's Park, Green Park.*

Westminster Cathedral. Tucked away on traffic-clogged Victoria Street lies this remarkable neo-Byzantine gem, seat of the Archbishop of Westminster, head of the Roman Catholic Church in England and Wales. Faced with having Westminster Abbey as a neighbor, architect John Francis Bentley looked to the east for inspiration, to the basilicas of St. Mark's in Venice and the Hagia Sofia in Istanbul. The asymmetrical redbrick edifice, dating from 1903, is banded with stripes of Portland stone and abutted by a 273-foot-high bell tower (the bell is nicknamed "Big Edward") at the northwest corner, ascendable by elevator for sterling views. The interior remains incomplete but the unfinished overhead brickwork of the ceiling lends the church a dark, brooding intensity.

Several side chapels, such as the Chapel of the Blessed Sacrament and the Holy Souls Chapel, are beautifully finished in glittering mosaics. The Lady Chapel—dedicated to the Virgin Mary—is also sumptuously decorated. Look out for the Stations of the Cross, a meditative representation of the *Via Dolorosa* found in all Catholic churches (by Eric Gill), and the striking baldachin—the enormous stone canopy standing over the altar with a giant cross suspended in front of it. The nave, the widest in the country, is constructed in green marble, which also has a Byzantine connection—it was cut from the same place as the marble used in the Hagia Sofia, and was almost confiscated by warring Turks as it traveled west. All told, more than 200 different types of marble can be found within the cathedral's interior. Just inside the main entrance is the tomb of Cardinal Basil Hume, head of the Catholic Church in England and Wales for more than 25 years. There's a café in the crypt. ⊠ *Ashley Pl., Westminster* ☎ *020/7798–9055* ⊕ *www.westminstercathedral.org. uk* 🖾 *Bell Tower and viewing gallery £5; Treasures of the Cathedral exhibition £5; joint ticket for Bell Tower and exhibition £8* ☉ *Cathedral weekdays 7–6, weekends 8–7; Bell Tower and Treasures of the Cathedral exhibition weekdays 9:30–5, weekends 9:30–6* Ⓜ *Victoria.*

ST. JAMES'S

As a fitting coda to all of Westminster's pomp and circumstance, St. James's—packed with old-money galleries, restaurants, and gentlemen's clubs that embody the history and privilege of traditional London—is found to the south of Piccadilly and north of the Mall.

When Whitehall Palace burned down in 1698, all of London turned its attention to St. James's Palace, the new royal residence. In the 18th and 19th centuries, the area around the palace became the place to live, and many of the estates surrounding the palace disappeared in a building frenzy, as mansions were built and streets laid out. Most of the homes here are privately owned and so closed to visitors, but there are some treasure houses that you can explore (such as Spencer House), as well as a bevy of fancy shops that have catered to the great and good for centuries.

Today, St. James's remains a rather masculine enclave, containing most of the capital's celebrated gentlemen's clubs (especially the classic Atheneum), long-established men's outfitters and clothiers, and some interesting art galleries and antiques shops. In one corner is St. James's Park, framed on its western side by the biggest monument in the area: Buckingham Palace, official residence of the Queen. The smaller St. James's Palace is where much of the office work for the House of Windsor gets done; nearby is Clarence House, London home of Prince Charles and his wife, Camilla.

TOP ATTRACTIONS

Fodor's Choice **Buckingham Palace.**

★ *See the highlighted listing in this chapter.*

The Mall. This stately, 115-foot-wide processional route sweeping from Admiralty Arch to the Queen Victoria Memorial at Buckingham Palace

ROYALTY WATCHING

You've seen Big Ben, the Tower, and Westminster Abbey. But somehow you feel something is missing: a close encounter with Britain's most famous attraction—Her actual Maj, Elizabeth II. The Queen and the Royal Family attend hundreds of functions a year, and if you want to know what they are doing on any given date, turn to the Court Circular, printed in the major London dailies, or check out the Royal Family website, ⊕ www. royal.gov.uk, for the latest events on the Royal Diary. Trooping the Colour is usually held on the second Saturday in June, to celebrate the Queen's official birthday. This spectacular parade begins when she leaves Buckingham Palace in her carriage and rides down the Mall to arrive at Horse Guards Parade at 11 exactly. To watch, just line up along the Mall with your binoculars.

Another time you can catch the Queen in all her regalia is when she and the Duke of Edinburgh ride in state to open the Houses of Parliament. The famous black and gilt-trimmed Irish State Coach travels from Buckingham Palace—on a clear day, it's to be hoped, for this ceremony takes place in late October or early November. The Gold State Coach, an icon of fairy-tale glamour, is used for coronations and jubilees only.

But perhaps the most relaxed, least formal time to see the Queen is during Royal Ascot, held at the racetrack near Windsor Castle—a short train ride out of London—usually during the third week of June (Tuesday–Friday). The Queen and members of the Royal Family are driven down the track to the Royal Box in an open carriage, giving spectators a chance to see them. After several races, the famously horse-loving Queen invariably walks down to the paddock, greeting race goers as she proceeds. If you meet her, you're supposed to address her as "Your Majesty."

is an updated 1904 version of a promenade laid out around 1660 for the game of *paille-maille* (a type of croquet crossed with golf), which also gave the parallel road Pall Mall its name. The tarmac is colored red, to represent a ceremonial red carpet. The **Duke of York Memorial** up the steps toward Carlton House Terrace is a towering column dedicated to George III's second son, further immortalized in the English nursery rhyme "The Grand old Duke of York." Sadly, the internal spiral steps are inaccessible. ■TIP→ Be sure to stroll along The Mall on Sunday when the road is closed to traffic, or catch the bands and troops of the Household Division on their way from St. James's Palace to Buckingham Palace for the Changing the Guard. ⊠ *St. James's* Ⓜ *Charing Cross, Green Park*.

Piccadilly Circus. The origins of the name "Piccadilly" relate to a humble 17th-century tailor from the Strand named Robert Baker who sold picadils—a stiff ruffled collar all the rage in courtly circles—and built a house with the proceeds. Snobs dubbed his new-money mansion Piccadilly Hall, and the name stuck.

Pride of place in the circus—a circular junction until the construction of Shaftesbury Avenue in 1886— belongs to the statue of **Eros** (although even most Londoners don't know that the 1893 work is a representation

A classic photo op: cavalry from the Queen's Life Guard at Buckingham Palace

of Eros's brother Anteros, the Greek God of requited love). The creation of young sculptor Alfred Gilbert is a memorial to the selflessness of the philanthropic Earl of Shaftesbury (the god's bow and arrow are an allusion to the earl's name). Gilbert cast the statue in the then-novel medium of aluminum. ■ TIP→ The other instantly recognizable feature of Piccadilly Circus is the enormous bank of illuminated advertising hoardings on the north side; if you're passing at night, frame them behind the Tube entrance sign on the corner of Regent Street for an unforgettable photo. ⊠ *St. James's* Ⓜ *Piccadilly Circus.*

The Queen's Gallery. Technically speaking, the sovereign doesn't "own" the rare and exquisite works of art in the Royal Collection, she merely holds them in trust for the nation—and what a collection it is! Only a selection is on view at any one time, presented in themed exhibitions. Let the excellent (free) audio guide take you through the elegant galleries filled with some of the world's greatest art works.

A rough timeline of the major royal collectors starts with Charles I (who also commissioned Rubens to paint the Banqueting House ceiling). An avid art enthusiast, Charles established the basis of the Royal Collection, purchasing works by Raphael, Titian, Caravaggio, and Dürer. During the Civil War and in the aftermath of Charles's execution, many masterpieces were sold abroad and subsequently repatriated by Charles II. George III, who bought Buckingham House, scooped up a notable collection of Venetian (including Canaletto), Renaissance (Bellini and Raphael), and Dutch (Vermeer) art, and a large number of baroque drawings, in addition to patronizing English contemporary artists such as Gainsborough and Beechey. He also took a liking to American artist

Benjamin West. The Prince Regent, later George IV, had a particularly good eye for Rembrandt, equestrian works by Stubbs, and lavish portraits by Lawrence. Queen Victoria had a penchant for Landseer animals and landscapes, and Frith's contemporary scenes. Later, Edward VII indulged Queen Alexandra's love of Fabergé, and many royal tours around the empire produced gifts of gorgeous caliber, such as the Cullinan diamond from South Africa and an emerald-studded belt from India.

More than 3,000 other objects from the Royal Collection reside in museums and galleries in the United

> **BEARSKIN, NOT BUSBY**
>
> While on duty, guardsmen take their job very, very seriously. They don't speak, don't acknowledge anyone (even those tourists trying in vain to make them laugh), don't even swat away troublesome flies from their noses. Worse: they're not even allowed to keel over under the weight of their enormous hats. Called "bearskins," the headdresses were originally worn by the French Imperial Guard defeated in the Battle of Waterloo in 1815.

Kingdom and abroad: check out the National Gallery, the Victoria & Albert Museum, the Museum of London, and the British Museum. ■TIP→ The E-gallery provides an interactive electronic version of the collection, allowing the user to open lockets, remove a sword from its scabbard, or take apart the tulip vases. It's probably the closest you could get to eyeing practically every diamond in the whole glittering diadem. ⊠ *Buckingham Palace, Buckingham Palace Rd., St. James's* ☏ *020/7766–7301* ⊕ *www.royalcollection.org.uk* 🖾 *£9.50; joint ticket with Royal Mews £16.75; joint ticket with Mews and Buckingham Palace £34.50* ☉ *Daily 10–5:30; last admission 4:30* Ⓜ *Victoria, St. James's Park, Green Park.*

FAMILY **Royal Mews.** Fairy-tale gold-and-glass coaches and sleek Rolls-Royce state cars emanate from the Royal Mews, next door to the Queen's Gallery. The John Nash–designed Mews serves as the headquarters for Her Majesty's travel department (so beware of closures for state visits), complete with the Queen's own special breed of horses, ridden by wigged postilions decked in red-and-gold regalia. Between the stables and riding school arena are exhibits of polished saddlery and riding tack. The highlight of the Mews is the splendid Gold State Coach, like a piece of art on wheels, with its sculpted tritons and sea gods. Mews were originally falcons' quarters (the name comes from their "mewing," or feather shedding), but nowadays the horses rule the roost. There are activities for children, and guided tours are available March to October; call for details. ⊠ *Buckingham Palace Rd., St. James's* ☏ *020/7766–7302* ⊕ *www.royalcollection.org.uk* 🖾 *£8.25; joint ticket with Queen's Gallery £16.75; joint ticket with Queen's Gallery and Buckingham Palace £34.50* ☉ *Apr.–Oct., daily 10–5; Nov.–Mar., Mon.–Sat. 10–4; last admission 45 mins before closing* Ⓜ *Victoria, St. James's Park.*

St. James's Palace. Commissioned by Henry VIII, this Tudor brick palace was the residence of kings and queens for more than 300 years; indeed, while all monarchs have actually lived at Buckingham Palace since Queen Victoria's day, it is still the official residence of the Sovereign.

BUCKINGHAM PALACE

✉ *Buckingham Palace Rd., St. James's* ☎ *020/7766–7334* ⊕ *www.royalcollection.org. uk/visit* 🎫 *£19.75; joint ticket with Queen's Gallery and Royal Mews £34.50* ⊙ *Aug., daily 9:30–7 (last admission 4:45); Sept., daily 9:30–6:30 (last admission 3:45). Times subject to change; check website* Ⓜ *Victoria, St. James's Park, Green Park.*

TIPS

■ If bought directly from the palace ticket office, tickets are valid for a repeat visit over the course of 12 months from the first visit.

■ Admission is by timed ticket with entry every 15 minutes throughout the day. Allow up to two hours.

■ A Royal Day Out ticket, available only in August and September, gives you the regal triple whammy of the Royal Mews, the Queen's Gallery, and the State Rooms, and is valid throughout the day. Tickets cost £33.25. Allow four hours.

■ Get there by 10:30 to grab a spot in the best viewing section for the Changing the Guard (www.changing-the-guard.com), daily at 11:30 from May until the end of July (varies according to troop deployment requirements) and on alternate days for the rest of the year, weather permitting.

The doors of the monarch's official residence are only open to the public in August and September, when the Queen heads to Scotland on holiday (you can tell because the famous red, white, and blue Union Flag will be flying above the palace instead of the Royal Standard). The standard tour covers the palace's 19 State Rooms with their gilt moldings and walls adorned with old masters.

Highlights

The **Grand Hall,** followed by the **Grand Staircase** and **Guard Room,** are visions in gold leaf. Don't miss the theatrical **Throne Room,** with the original 1953 coronation throne, or the sword in **the Ballroom,** used by the Queen to bestow knighthoods. Royal portraits line the **State Dining Room,** and the **Blue Drawing Room** is dazzling in its splendor. The bow-shape **Music Room** features lapis columns between floor-to-ceiling windows, and the alabaster-and-gold plasterwork of the **White Drawing Room** is a dramatic statement.

The **Changing the Guard,** also known as **Guard Mounting,** culminates in front of the palace. Marching to military bands, the old guard proceeds up the Mall from St. James's Palace to Buckingham Palace. Shortly afterward, the new guard approaches from Wellington Barracks. The captains of the old and new guards then symbolically transfer the keys to the palace.

BUCKINGHAM PALACE: GROUND FLOOR

BUCKINGHAM PALACE: FIRST FLOOR

(Foreign ambassadors, for instance, are received by the "Court of St. James.") Today it contains various royal apartments and offices, including the working office of Prince Charles. It's not open to the public but the surprisingly low-key Tudor exterior is well worth the short detour from the Mall to see. Friary Court out front is a splendid setting for Trooping the Colour, part of the Queen's official birthday celebrations. Everyone loves to take a snapshot of the scarlet-coated guardsman standing sentry outside the imposing Tudor gateway. Note that the Changing the Guard ceremony at St. James's Palace occurs only on days when the guard at Buckingham Palace is changed. ⇨ *See entry for Buckingham Palace for details.* If you're approaching from St. James Street, take a quick peek at the wonderfully old-looking **Berry Bros. & Rudd** wine store at No. 3, near the back entrance to the palace; it's been trading here continuously since 1698. ⊠ *Friary Ct., St. James's* ⊕ *www. royal.gov.uk* Ⓜ *Green Park.*

FAMILY
Fodor's Choice
★

St. James's Park. In a city of royal parks, this one—bordered by three palaces (the Palace of Westminster, St. James's Palace, and Buckingham Palace)—is the most regal of them all. It's not only London's oldest park, but also its smallest and most ornate. Once marshy meadows, the land was acquired by Henry VIII in 1532 as royal deer-hunting grounds (with dueling and sword fights strictly forbidden). Later, James I drained the land and installed an aviary and zoo (complete with crocodiles, camels, and an elephant). When Charles II returned from exile in France, where he had been hugely impressed by the splendor of the gardens at the Palace of Versailles, he transformed the park into formal gardens, with avenues, fruit orchards, and a canal. Lawns were grazed by goats, sheep, and deer, and in the 18th century the park became a different kind of hunting ground, for wealthy lotharios looking to pick up nighttime escorts. A century later, John Nash redesigned the landscape in a more naturalistic, romantic style, and if you gaze down the lake toward Buckingham Palace, you could easily believe yourself to be on a country estate.

A large population of waterfowl—including pelicans, geese, ducks, and swans (which belong to the Queen)—breed on and around Duck Island at the east end of the lake. From April to September, the deck chairs (charge levied) come out, crammed with office workers at midday, eating lunch while being serenaded by music from the bandstands. One of the best times to stroll the leafy walkways is after dark, with Westminster Abbey and the Houses of Parliament rising above the floodlit lake. The popular Inn the Park restaurant is a wood-and-glass pavilion with a turf roof that blends in beautifully with the surrounding landscape; it's an excellent stopping place for a meal or a snack on a nice day. ⊠ *The Mall or Horse Guards approach or Birdcage Walk, St. James's* ⊕ *www.royalparks.org. uk* ☉ *Daily 5 am–midnight* Ⓜ *St. James's Park, Westminster.*

WORTH NOTING

Clarence House. The London home of the Queen Mother for nearly 50 years until her death in 2002, Clarence House is now the residence of Prince Charles, the Prince of Wales; his wife, Camilla, the Duchess of Cornwall; and Prince Harry. The Regency mansion was built by John Nash for the Duke of Clarence (later to become William IV) who considered next-door St. James's Palace to be too cramped for his liking,

Gentlemen's shops in St. James's specialize in high-quality, handmade goods.

although postwar renovation work means that little remains of Nash's original. Since then it has remained a royal home for princesses, dukes, and duchesses, including the present monarch, Queen Elizabeth, as a newlywed before her coronation. The rooms have been sensitively preserved to reflect the Queen Mother's taste, with the addition of many works of art from the Royal Collection, including works by Winterhalter, Augustus John, and Sickert. You'll find it less palace and more home, with informal family pictures and comfortable sofas. The tour (by timed ticket entry only) is of the ground-floor rooms and includes the Lancaster Room, so called because of the marble chimneypiece presented by Lancaster County to the newly married Princess Elizabeth and the Duke of Edinburgh. Clarence House is usually open only for the month of August and tickets must be booked in advance. ⊠ *St. James's Palace, The Mall, St. James's* ☎ *020/7766–7303* ⊕ *www.royalcollection.org.uk* ☜ *£9.50; exclusive guided tour £35* ☉ *Aug. 1–Sept. 1, weekdays 10–4, weekends 10–5:30; last admission 2 hrs before closing* Ⓜ *Green Park.*

Institute of Contemporary Arts (ICA). You would never suspect that behind the stately white-stucco facade in the heart of Establishment London is to be found that champion of the avant-garde, the ICA. Since 1947, the ICA has been pushing boundaries in visual arts, performance, theater, dance, and music. There are two movie theaters, a performance theater, three galleries, a highbrow bookstore, a reading room, a café, and a bar. ⊠ *The Mall, St. James's* ☎ *020/7930–3647* ⊕ *www.ica.org.uk* ☜ *Free; films £6–10; performances and exhibitions vary (most are free)* ☉ *Galleries Tues.–Sun. 11–11; exhibitions Tues., Wed., and Fri.–Sun. 11–6; Thurs. 11–9* Ⓜ *Charing Cross, Piccadilly Circus.*

ICA Café Bar. Overlooking The Mall, this café and bar offers a tasty, reasonably priced lunch and dinner menu, with coffees and snacks available throughout the day. It's open Tuesday–Sunday 11–11. ⊠ *The Mall, St. James's* ☎ *020/7930–8619* ⊕ *www.ica.org.uk.*

Spencer House. Ancestral abode of the Spencers—Princess Diana's family—this is perhaps the finest example of an elegant 18th-century town house extant in London. Reflecting his passion for the Grand Tour and classical antiquities, the first Earl Spencer commissioned architect John Vardy to adapt designs from ancient Rome for a magnificent private palace. Vardy was responsible for the exteriors, including the gorgeous west-facing Palladian facade, its pediment adorned with classical statues, and the ground-floor interiors, notably the lavish Palm Room, with its spectacular screen of columns covered in gilded carvings that resemble gold palm trees. The lavish style was meant not only to attest to Spencer's power and wealth but also to celebrate his marriage, a love match then rare in aristocratic circles (the palms are a symbol of marital fertility). Midway through construction—the house was built between 1756 and 1766—Spencer changed architects and hired James "Athenian" Stuart, whose designs were based on a classical Greek aesthetic, to decorate the gilded State Rooms on the first floor. These include the Painted Room, the first completely neoclassical room in Europe. Since the 1940s the house has been leased by the Spencers to a succession of wealthy residents. In 2010 the Spencer family scandalously decided to sell off all the house's best furnishings, so today's viewers see a decidedly denuded interior. The garden, which is open on certain Sundays in summer only, has been replanted in the 18th- and 19th-century fashion. Check the website for details. ⊠ *27 St. James's Pl., St. James's* ☎ *020/7499–8620 recorded information, 020/7514–1958 tour reservations* ⊕ *www.spencerhouse.co.uk* ⬚ *£12* ⊙ *Sept.–Dec. and Feb.–July, Sun. 10:30–5:45; last tour 1 hr before closing* Ⓜ *Green Park.*

St. James's Church. Bombed by the German Luftwaffe in 1940 and not restored until 1954, this was one of the last of Sir Christopher Wren's London churches—and his favorite. Completed in 1684, it envelops one of Grinling Gibbon's finest works, an ornate lime-wood reredos (the screen behind the altar). The organ was brought here in 1691 from Whitehall Palace. The church is a lively place, with all manner of lectures and concerts (some are free). A café occupies a fine location right alongside the church, while a small, sedate garden is tucked away at the rear. The market out front is full of surprises; come on Tuesday for antiques, Wednesday to Saturday for arts and crafts. ⊠ *197 Piccadilly, St. James's* ☎ *020/7734–4511, 020/7381–0441 concert program and tickets* ⊕ *www.sjp.org.uk* Ⓜ *Piccadilly Circus, Green Park.*

MAYFAIR AND MARYLEBONE

GETTING ORIENTED

Mayfair and Marylebone

TOP REASONS TO GO

At home with the Duke of Wellington: His Apsley House—known as No. 1, London—is filled with splendid salons lined with grand old-master paintings.

Get a passion for fashion: The shopping on Bond and Mount streets will keep your credit card occupied at McQueen and McCartney, but don't forget stylish, gigantic Selfridges.

London's most charming shopping arcade: Built for Lord Cavendish in 1819, the beautiful Burlington Arcade is right out of a Victorian daguerreotype.

The Wallace Collection: Savor room after room of magnificent furniture, porcelain, silver, and top old-master paintings, in the former residence of the marquesses of Hertford.

Dress to Impress at Claridge's: Afternoon tea at this sumptuous art deco gem is the perfect end to a shopping spree in Mayfair.

FEELING PECKISH?

Crussh. This successful chain serves up delicious juices and smoothies, as well as sandwiches, soups, and wraps. Decamp to nearby Green Park, where—if you're lucky—you can grab one of the deck chairs. It's not open on weekends. ⊠ *1 Curzon St., Mayfair* ☏ *020/7629–2554* ⊕ *www.crussh. com* Ⓜ *Green Park.*

Richoux. Since 1909, Richoux has been an affordable refuge from busy Piccadilly. Simple but well-executed French bistro food is served all day, as well as scrumptious afternoon tea. ⊠ *172 Piccadilly, Mayfair* ☏ *020/7493–2204* ⊕ *www.richoux. co.uk* Ⓜ *Green Park, Piccadilly Circus.*

Truc Vert. Just up from Grosvenor Square, rustic French café Truc Vert has a daily changing menu and is open for breakfast, lunch, and dinner. ⊠ *42 N. Audley St., Mayfair* ☏ *020/7491–9988* ⊕ *www.trucvert.co.uk* Ⓜ *Bond St.*

GETTING THERE

Three Tube stations on the Central line will leave you smack in the center of these neighborhoods: Marble Arch, Bond Street (also on the Jubilee line), and Oxford Circus (also on the Victoria and Bakerloo lines).

You can also take the Piccadilly or Bakerloo line to the Piccadilly Circus Tube station, the Piccadilly line to the Hyde Park Corner station, or the Piccadilly, Victoria, or Jubilee line to the Green Park station.

The best buses are the 8, which takes in Green Park, Berkeley Square, and New Bond Street, and the 9—one of the few routes that still uses the traditional double-decker Routemaster model—which runs along Piccadilly.

MAKING THE MOST OF YOUR TIME

Reserve at least a day to experience Mayfair and Marylebone. Leave enough time for shopping and also to wander casually through the streets and squares.

The only areas to avoid are the Tube stations at rush hour, and Oxford Street if you don't like crowds. At all costs, stay away from Oxford Circus around 5 pm, when the commuter rush can, at times, resemble an East African wildebeest migration—but without the charm.

The area becomes as quiet at night—so plan to party elsewhere.

3

Sightseeing
★★★★
Nightlife
★
Dining
★★★★
Lodging
★★★★
Shopping
★★★★

Mayfair forms the core of London's West End, the city's smartest central area. This neighborhood epitomizes the stately flavor that is peculiarly London's—the sense of being in a great, rich, powerful city is almost palpable as you wander along the posh and polished streets. Scoot across the district's one exception to all this elegance—Oxford Street—and you'll discover the pleasant streets of Marylebone, the most central of London's many "villages."

MAYFAIR

Updated by
James O'Neill

Ultra-ritzy Mayfair, lined with beautiful 18th-century mansions (along with Edwardian apartment buildings faced with deep-red brick), is the address of choice for many of London's wealthiest residents. Once you note the sheer number of Rolls-Royces, Bentleys, and Jaguars, you may become acutely aware of how poor you are. Even the delivery vans hereabouts all seem to bear some royal coat of arms, proclaiming them to be purveyors of fine goodies for as long as anyone can remember.

The district can't claim to be stuffed with must-sees—but that is part of its appeal. There is no shortage of history and gorgeous architecture; the streets here are custom-built for window-shopping, expansive strolling, and getting a peek into the lifestyles of London's rich and famous, past and present. Mayfair is primarily residential, so its homes are off-limits except for one satisfyingly grand house: Apsley House, the Duke of Wellington's home, built by Robert Adam in 1771, and once known as No. 1, London.

Despite being bounded by four of the busiest streets in London—bustling budget-shopping mecca Oxford Street to the north, traffic artery Park Lane with Hyde Park beyond to the west, and elegant boulevards Regent Street and Piccadilly to the east and south, respectively—Mayfair itself is remarkably traffic-free and a delight to explore. Starting at **Selfridges** on Oxford Street, a southward stroll will take you through quiet residential streets lined with Georgian town houses (the area was largely developed in the 17th and 18th centuries) and, with a bit of artful navigating, to four lovely greenswards: **Grosvenor Square, Berkeley Square, Hanover Square,** with its splendid **St. George's Church** where Handel worshipped, and the quiet **St. George's Gardens,** bounded by a maze of atmospheric streets and mews. Mayfair is also London's most exclusive shopping destination, with such enclaves as **Mount Street, Bruton Street, Savile Row,** and the **Burlington Arcade.** At the

<table>
<tr><td>

A BRIEF HISTORY

The name Mayfair derives from the 15-day May fair that was once held in the charming warren of small streets known as Shepherd Market. But in the 18th century, the residents of this now-fashionable neighborhood felt the fair was lowering the tone and so put a stop to it.

</td></tr>
</table>

3

western end of Mayfair at Hyde Park corner are two memorials to England's great hero, the Duke of Wellington: **Wellington Arch** and the duke's restored London residence, **Apsley House.**

The **Royal Academy of Arts** is at the southern fringe of Mayfair on Piccadilly, and just across the road begins more sedate St. James's, with its old-money galleries, restaurants, and gentlemen's clubs that embody the history and privilege of traditional London. You'll get the best sense of the neighborhood just to the south on **St. James's Square** and **Pall Mall,** with its private clubs tucked away in 18th- and 19th-century patrician buildings.

TOP ATTRACTIONS

Fodor's Choice
★

Apsley House (Wellington Museum). Reopened in early 2014 after a major refurbishment, the mansion built by Robert Adam and presented to the Duke of Wellington in thanks for his victory over Napoléon at the Battle of Waterloo in 1815 was long celebrated as the best address in town. Once popularly known as No. 1, London, because it was the first and grandest house at the old tollgate from Knightsbridge village, the mansion was the residence of the Duke of Wellington from 1817 until his death in 1852. The years of war against the French made the "Iron Duke"—born in Ireland as Arthur Wellesley—the greatest soldier and statesman in the land (and on the walls of the nearby subway, beneath the turmoil of traffic, his heroic exploits are extolled in a series of murals). Opposite the house is the 1828 **Wellington Arch** ⇨ *See below*, designed by Decimus Burton, with the four-horse chariot of peace at its pinnacle (open to the public as an exhibition area and viewing platform); the **Achilles** statue (legendarily naked and cast from captured French guns) points the way with thrusting shield to the ducal mansion from the edge of Hyde Park, entered through an elaborate gateway designed and built by Burton at the same time as the arch.

The duke's former residence shows off his uniforms, weapons, a fine collection of paintings (partially looted from his war campaigns), and his porcelain and plate collections acquired as a result of his military success, such as a Sèvres dessert service commissioned by Napoléon for his empress, Josephine. Wellington's extensive art collection includes works by Brueghel, Van Dyck, and Rubens, as well as the famous Velázquez portrait of Pope Innocent X and a portrait of the duke on horseback by Goya. A gigantic Canova statue of a nude (fig-leafed) Napoléon presides over the grand staircase that leads to the many elegant reception rooms.

Old Bond Street is great for window-shopping—it has some of the most exclusive stores in London.

The free audio guide highlights the most significant works and the superb interior, most notably the stunning Waterloo Gallery, where an annual banquet for officers who fought beside Wellington was held beneath the gilded ceiling. Special events take place on the annual Waterloo weekend and occasionally on Waterloo Day (June 18) itself. Check the website for details. Limited disabled access. ⌧ *149 Piccadilly, Hyde Park Corner, Mayfair* ☎ *020/7499–5676* ⊕ *www.english-heritage.org.uk* ⌧ *£6.70 (includes audio tour); joint ticket with Wellington Arch £8.20* ☼ *Mar.–Oct., Wed.–Sun. and bank holiday Mon. 11–5; Nov.–Feb., weekends 10–4. Subject to change, so check website* Ⓜ *Hyde Park Corner.*

Bond Street. This world-class shopping haunt is divided into northern "New" (1710) and southern "Old" (1690) halves. You can spot the juncture by a bronzed bench on which Franklin D. Roosevelt sits companionably next to Winston Churchill. On New Bond Street you'll find **Sotheby's,** the world-famous auction house, at No. 35, as well as upscale retailers like Asprey's, Burberry, Louis Vuitton, Georg Jensen, and Church's. You'll find even more opportunities to flirt with financial ruin on Old Bond Street: flagship boutiques of top-end designers like Chanel, Gucci, and Yves St. Laurent; an array of fine jewelers including Tiffany; and art dealers Colnaghi, Spink Leger, and Agnew's. **Cork Street,** which parallels the top half of Old Bond Street, is where London's foremost dealers in contemporary art have their galleries. ⌧ *Mayfair* Ⓜ *Bond St., Green Park.*

Fodor's Choice
★ **Burlington Arcade.** With ceilings and lights now restored to how they would have looked when it was built in 1819, Burlington Arcade is the finest of Mayfair's enchanting covered shopping alleys. Originally

built for Lord Cavendish, it was meant to stop the hoi polloi from flinging rubbish into his garden at next-door Burlington House. Top-hatted watchmen called Beadles—the world's smallest private police force—still patrol, preserving decorum by preventing you from singing, running, or carrying an open umbrella. ⊠ *Piccadilly, Mayfair* ☏ *020/7493–1764* ⊕ *www.burlingtonarcade.com* ⊗ *Mon.–Sat. 9–8, Sun. 11–8; opening times of shops within the arcade vary* Ⓜ *Green Park, Piccadilly Circus.*

QUICK BITES Several of London's most storied and stylish hotels are in Mayfair. Even if you're not staying at one, sample the high life by popping into their glamorous bars for a cocktail or some afternoon tea. **Claridge's Bar** takes its cue from art deco, as do the Ritz's intimate **Rivoli Bar** and **The Connaught's** eponymous drinking hole; the bar at **Brown's Hotel** is modernist.

Marble Arch. John Nash's 1827 arch, moved here from Buckingham Palace in 1851, stands amid the traffic whirlpool where Bayswater Road segues into Oxford Street, at the top of Park Lane. The arch actually contains three small chambers, which served as a police station until the mid-20th century. Search the sidewalk on the traffic island opposite the movie theater for the stone plaque recalling the Tyburn Tree, an elaborately designed gallows that stood here for 400 years, until 1783. The condemned would be conveyed here in their finest clothes from Newgate Prison in The City, and were expected to affect a casual indifference or face a merciless heckling from the crowds. Towering across the grass from the arch toward Tyburn Way is a vast patina-green statue of a horse's head called *Horse at Water* by sculptor Nic Fiddian. Cross over (or under) to the northeastern corner of Hyde Park for Speakers' Corner, a parcel of land long-dedicated to the principle of free speech, and where every Sunday people of all views—or none at all—come to pontificate, listen, and debate about anything and everything under the sun. ⊠ *Park La., Mayfair* Ⓜ *Marble Arch.*

Fodor's Choice ★ **Royal Academy of Arts.** Burlington House was built in 1664, with later Palladian additions for the 3rd Earl of Burlington in 1720. The piazza in front is a later conception from 1873, when the Renaissance-style buildings around the courtyard were designed by Banks and Barry to house a gaggle of noble scientific societies, including the Royal Society of Chemistry and the Royal Astronomical Society.

Marble Arch was originally a gateway to Buckingham Palace before it was moved to the corner of Hyde Park.

The house itself is home to the draw-card tenant, the Royal Academy of Arts. In a city with heavyweight galleries such as Tate Modern, Tate Britain, and the National Gallery, the Royal Academy more than holds its own. The statue of the academy's first president, Sir Joshua Reynolds, palette in hand, is prominent in the piazza of light stone with fountains by Sir Phillip King. Within the house and up the stairs are statues of creative giants J.W.M. Turner and Thomas Gainsborough. Free tours show off part of the collection and the excellent temporary exhibitions. Every June for the past 240 years, the RA has put on its Summer Exhibition, a huge and always surprising collection. ⊠ *Burlington House, Piccadilly, Mayfair* ☎ *020/7300–8000, 0207/300–5839 lectures, 0207/300–5995 family programs* ⊕ *www.royalacademy.org.uk* ✉ *Prices vary with exhibition £8–£16* ☉ *Sat.–Thurs. 10–6, Fri. 10–10; tours Tues. 1, Wed.–Fri. 1 and 3, Sat. 11:30* Ⓜ *Piccadilly Circus, Green Park.*

QUICK
BITES

Restaurant at the Royal Academy of Arts. With its walls covered in Gilbert Spencer murals, the restaurant at the Royal Academy is almost as beautiful as the art hanging in the galleries. The accent is on flexibility: you can linger over a three-course meal, order a selection of tapas, or just pop in for a quick, delicious bite. It's open daily 10–5:30, except Friday when it closes at 9:30 pm. ⊠ *Burlington House, Piccadilly, Mayfair* ☎ *020/7300–5608* ⊕ *www.royalacademy.org.uk* Ⓜ *Piccadilly Circus, Green Park.*

Wellington Arch. Opposite the Duke of Wellington's mansion, **Apsley House** ⇨ *See above*, this majestic stone arch surveys the traffic rushing around Hyde Park Corner. Designed by Decimus Burton and built in 1828, it was created as a grand entrance to the west side of London and echoes the design of that other landmark gate, **Marble Arch** ⇨ *See above*. Both were triumphal arches commemorating Britain's victory against France in the Napoleonic Wars. The exterior of the arch was intended to be much more ornate but King George IV was going vastly over budget with his refurbishment of Buckingham Palace and cutbacks had to be made else-

WORD OF MOUTH

"I think Mayfair is a great location...you have access to three major tube lines...[and] if you need to hop on a cab, Mayfair is about as central as you can be, so fares won't break the bank."

—hsv

where. Atop the building, the Angel of Peace descends on the quadriga, or four-horse chariot of war. This replaced the Duke of Wellington on his horse, which was considered too large and moved to an army barracks in Aldershot. Inside the arch, three floors of permanent and temporary exhibits reveal the monument's history and explores the world's other great arches. Don't miss the platform at the top of the arch, where you can enjoy a panoramic view over Hyde Park and peer into the private gardens of Buckingham Palace. ⊠ *Hyde Park Corner, Mayfair* ☎ *020/7930–2726* ⊕ *www.english-heritage.org.uk* ⊠ *£4; joint ticket with Apsley House £8.20* ☉ *Sun.–Wed. 10–4, but platform sometimes closed for exhibition installations; check website* Ⓜ *Hyde Park Corner*.

WORTH NOTING

Grosvenor Square. Pronounced *Grove*-na, this leafy square was laid out in 1725–31 and is as desirable an address today as it was then. Americans have certainly always thought so—from John Adams, the second president, who as ambassador lived at No. 38, to Dwight D. Eisenhower, whose wartime headquarters was at No. 20. Now the massive 1960s block of the U.S. Embassy occupies the entire west side (although a new one is being built south of the river), and a British memorial to Franklin D. Roosevelt stands in the center. There is also a classically styled memorial to those who died in New York on September 11, 2001. Grosvenor Chapel, completed in 1730 and used by Eisenhower's men during World War II, stands a couple of blocks south of the square on South Audley Street, with the entrance to pretty **St. George's Gardens** to its left. ⊠ *Mayfair* Ⓜ *Bond St.*

Handel House Museum. The former home of the composer, where he lived for more than 30 years until his death in 1759, is a celebration of his genius. It's the first museum in London solely dedicated to one composer. In rooms decorated in fine Georgian style you can linger over original manuscripts and gaze at portraits—accompanied by live music if the adjoining music rooms are being used by musicians in rehearsal. Some of the composer's most famous pieces were created here, including *Messiah* and *Music for the Royal Fireworks*. To hear a live concert here is to imagine the atmosphere of rehearsals and "salon" music in its day (check the website for details of recitals and events). ⊠ *25 Brook St., entrance in Lancashire Court, Mayfair* ☎ *020/7495–1685* ⊕ *www.handelhouse.org* ⊠ *£6.50* ☉ *Tues., Wed., Fri., and Sat. 10–6, Thurs. 10–8, Sun. noon–6 (last admission ½ hr before closing)* Ⓜ *Bond St.*

Regent Street, home to Liberty department store and Hamleys toy shop, decorated for the holidays

MARYLEBONE

A favorite of newspaper style sections everywhere, Marylebone High Street forms the heart of Marylebone (pronounced "Marr-le-bone") Village, a vibrant, upscale neighborhood that encompasses the squares and streets around High Street and nearby Marylebone Lane. The district took its name from a church dedicated to St. Mary and the bourne (another word for "stream") that ran through the original village. Its development, by various members of the aristocracy, began in the early 18th century. Today, it's hard to believe that you're just a few blocks north of gaudy Oxford Street as you wander in and out of Marylebone's small shops and boutiques, the best of which include La Fromagerie (2–6 Moxon Street), an excellent cheese shop; Daunt Books (Nos. 83–84), a travel bookshop; "Cabbages and Frocks" market on the grounds of the St. Marylebone Parish Church, held Saturday 11–5, which purveys specialty foods and vintage clothing; and on Sunday 10–2, a large farmers' and artisanal-food market in a parking lot on Cramer Street, just behind High Street. But some memorable sights await, too, including that best remnant of ancient régime France in London, the fabled Wallace Collection. The best metro stop for the area is Bond Street.

TOP ATTRACTIONS

Sherlock Holmes Museum. Outside Baker Street station, by the Marylebone Road exit, is a 9-foot-high bronze statue of the celebrated detective. Nearby is number 221B Baker Street—the address of Arthur Conan Doyle's fictional detective. Inside, Mrs. Hudson, "Holmes's housekeeper," conducts you into a series of Victorian rooms full of

Sherlock-abilia. There are more than enough photo ops, and it's all carried off with such genuine enthusiasm that you almost believe that the fictional detective really lived here. ⊠ *221B Baker St., Marylebone* ☎ *020/7224–3688* ⊕ *www.sherlock-holmes.co.uk* ⊡ *£6* ⊙ *Daily 9:30–6* Ⓜ *Baker St.*

FAMILY   **Wallace Collection.** Undergoing refurbishment of its Great Gallery and
Fodor's Choice   due to reopen in autumn 2014, this exquisite labyrinth of an art gal-
★   lery is housed in Hertford House, an 18th-century mansion that was bequeathed to the nation, along with its contents, by the widow of Sir Richard Wallace (1818–90). Wallace was the last in a line of wealthy aristocrats who voraciously scoured Europe in search of beautiful art. His father, the 4th Marquess of Hertford, was a particularly shrewd dealer. After the French Revolution he took a house in Paris and set about snapping up paintings by what were then dangerously unpopular artists, for a song. Frans Hals's *Laughing Cavalier* is probably the most famous painting here, or perhaps Jean-Honoré Fragonard's *The Swing*, which perfectly encapsulates the frilly rococo decadence of pre-revolutionary French art. The full list of painters in the collection reads like a roll call of classical European masters, from Rubens, Rembrandt, and Van Dyck to Canaletto, Titian, and Velázquez. English works include paintings by Gainsborough and Turner, plus a dozen by Joshua Reynolds. Stay for lunch at the restaurant, which is elegantly sited in a glass-roofed courtyard. ⊠ *Hertford House, Manchester Sq., Marylebone* ☎ *020/7563–9500* ⊕ *www.wallacecollection.org* ⊡ *Free* ⊙ *Daily 10–5* Ⓜ *Bond St.*

QUICK   **Wallace Restaurant.** Bringing the outside in, this restaurant enjoys the
BITES   elegant setting of the glass-roofed courtyard of the Wallace Collection. It's open daily for breakfast, lunch, and afternoon tea (10–4:30), and for dinner on Friday and Saturday evenings (last seating is at 9:30 pm). The brasserie menu highlights French food from pâtés and cheeses to scallops, lobster, and succulent steaks. If you don't want to strain your budget too much, you can just linger over coffee in the gorgeous surroundings. ⊠ *Wallace Collection, Hertford House, Manchester Sq., Marylebone* ☎ *020/7563–9505* Ⓜ *Bond St.*

WORTH NOTING

FAMILY   **Madame Tussauds.** One of London's busiest tourist attractions, this is nothing less—but also nothing more—than the world's most famous exhibition of lifelike waxwork models of celebrities. Madame T. learned her craft while making death masks of French Revolution victims, and in 1835 she set up her first show of the famous ones near this spot. Top billing still goes to the murderers in the Chamber of Horrors, who stare glassy-eyed at visitors—one from an electric chair, one sitting next to the tin bath where he dissolved several wives in quicklime. What, aside from ghoulish prurience, makes people stand in line to invest in one of London's most expensive museum tickets? It must be the thrill of all those photo opportunities with royalty, Hollywood stars, and world leaders—all in a single day. ■ TIP→ **Beat the crowds by booking timed entry tickets in advance. You can also buy non-dated, "priority access"**

221B Baker Street and "Holmes" himself

tickets via the website (at a premium). ✉ *Marylebone Rd., Marylebone* ☎ *0870/400–3000 for timed entry tickets* ⊕ *www.madame-tussauds. com* 🎟 *£15–£35 according to time; call or check website. Combination ticket with London Eye, London Dungeons, and London Aquarium £35–£57* ⊙ *Early Apr. and mid-July–Aug., daily 9–7; Sept.–Mar. and mid-Apr.–mid-July, weekdays 9–5:30 (last admission), weekends 9:30–6 (last admission)* Ⓜ *Baker St.*

FAMILY **Ripley's Believe It Or Not!.** Six floors of the weird, the wacky and the downright bizarre (life-size knitted Ferrari, anyone?) to astonish and delight even the most tired and jaded among us. Inspired by the legendary American traveler/cartoonist/curator Robert Ripley, nothing is considered too unusual or outlandish to take its place among the 700-plus authentic artifacts. From dinosaur eggs to an albino alligator, from a maze of mirrors to a sculpture of the Beatles made entirely from chewing gum (yes, chewing gum!), from Ecuadorean shrunken heads to pieces of the Berlin Wall, there is so much to see, with interactive exhibits a-plenty. ✉ *The London Pavilion, 1 Piccadilly Circus, Mayfair* ☎ *020/3238–0022* ⊕ *www.ripleyslondon.com* 🎟 *£26.95* ⊙ *Daily 10 am–midnight (last admission 10:30 pm)* Ⓜ *Piccadilly Circus (use exit 4 to Coventry St.).*

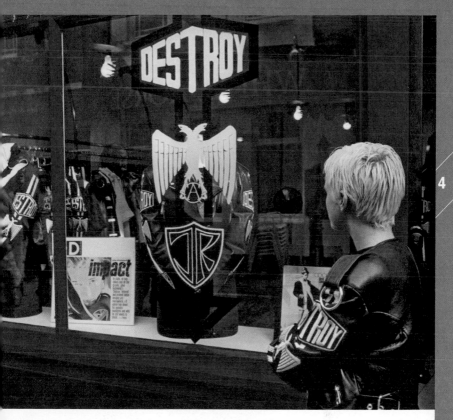

SOHO AND
COVENT GARDEN

Visit Fodors.com for advice, updates, and bookings

GETTING ORIENTED

GETTING THERE	TOP REASONS TO GO
Almost all Tube lines cross the Covent Garden and Soho areas, so it's easy to hop off for a dinner or show in the hippest area of London. For Soho, take any train to Piccadilly Circus, or Leicester Square, Oxford Circus, or Tottenham Court Road. For Covent Garden, get off at the Covent Garden station on the Piccadilly line. It might be easier to exit the Tube at Leicester Square or Holborn and walk. Thirty buses connect to the Covent Garden area from all over London; check out the area's website, ⊕ *www.coventgarden.uk.com.*	**Find tomorrow's look in the Newburgh Quarter:** Head to this adorable warren of cobblestone streets for an ultra-hip array of specialist boutiques, edgy stores, and young indie upstarts.
	Indulge yourself in Gourmet Country: London has fallen in love with its chefs, and Soho is home to many of the most talked-about restaurants in town.
	Covent Garden Piazza: Eliza Doolittle's former backyard has been taken over by fun boutiques and street performers (who play to the crowds at night).
	Royal Opera House: Even if you're not going to the opera or ballet, take in the beautiful architecture and sense of history.
	See a West End hit in Theatreland: Shaftesbury Avenue is the heart of London's theater district, where more than 40 West End theaters pull in the crowds with a mix of extravagant musicals and Shakespeare.

Soho and Covent Garden

Royal Courts of Justice

Royal Opera House
Bow Street Magistrates' Court
COVENT GARDEN
Theatre Royal, Drury Lane
Courtauld Institute Gallery
Covent Garden Piazza
London Transport Museum
Somerset House
Inner Temple Gardens
U TEMPLE
Adam Houses
The Savoy
Victoria Embankment
River Thames
Cleopatra's Needle
Embankment Gardens
U EMBANKMENT
Golden Jubilee Bridges

| 0 | 1/8 mile |
| 0 | 200 meters |

4

MAKING THE MOST OF YOUR TIME

You can comfortably tour all the sights around Soho and Covent Garden in a day. Visit the small but perfect Courtauld Gallery on Monday, when entry costs just £3. That leaves plenty of time to watch street entertainment or shop at the stalls around Covent Garden Piazza or in the fashion boutiques of Soho. Save some energy for a night on the town in Soho.

FEELING PECKISH?

The coffee shops on Covent Garden Piazza can be overpriced and mediocre. Head north for Neal Street or west for Soho when the munchies strike.

Food for Thought. Customers line up here for a tasty range of vegetarian dishes. ⊠ *31 Neal St., Covent Garden* ☎ *020/7836–0239* ⊕ *foodforthought-london.co.uk* Ⓜ *Covent Garden, Leicester Sq.*

Nordic Bakery. On Golden Square, this is an immaculate Scandinavian café that serves dark breads and the city's best cinnamon rolls. ⊠ *14A Golden Sq., Soho* ☎ *020/3230–1077* ⊕ *www.nordicbakery.com* Ⓜ *Piccadilly Circus.*

Princi. This chic Italian café fills up at lunchtime with regulars who come for colorful salads, fresh lasagna, and warm-from-the-oven cakes and pastries. ⊠ *135 Wardour St., Soho* ☎ *020/7478–8888* ⊕ *princi.com* Ⓜ *Tottenham Court Rd., Piccadilly Circus.*

GAY LONDON

Old Compton Street in Soho is the epicenter of London's affluent, stylish gay scene. There are some smart nightclubs in the area, with crowds forming in Soho Square, south of Oxford Street.

Madame Jojo's. This club has been drawing the crowds for nearly 50 years. Its Kitsch Cabaret, performed every Saturday evening, is so popular (with straights as well as gays) that it's usually booked weeks in advance. ⊠ *8–10 Brewer St., Soho* ☎ *020/7734–3040* ⊕ *www.madamejojos.com* Ⓜ *Piccadilly Circus.*

Sightseeing
★★★
Nightlife
★★★★
Dining
★★★★
Lodging
★★
Shopping
★★★

Once a red-light district, today's Soho is more stylish than seedy and offers some of London's best nightclubs, live music venues, restaurants, and theaters. By day, this hotbed of media production reverts to the business side of its late-night scene. If Soho is all about showbiz, neighboring Covent is devoted to culture. Both districts offer an abundance of narrow streets packed with one-of-a-kind shops and lots of antique character.

SOHO

Updated by Jo Caird

Soho, which, along with Covent Garden, is loosely known as "the West End," has long been known as the entertainment and arts quarter of London's center. Bordered to the north by Oxford Street, Regent Street to the west, and Chinatown and Leicester Square to the south, the narrow, winding streets of Soho are unabashedly devoted to pleasure. Wardour Street bisects the neighborhood, with lots of interesting boutiques and some of London's best-value restaurants to the west (especially around Foubert's Place and on Brewer and Lexington streets). Nightlife central lies to the east—including London's gay mecca, Old Compton Street—and beyond that is the city's densest collection of theaters, on Shaftesbury Avenue. London's compact Chinatown is wedged between Soho and **Leicester Square**. A bit of erudition surfaces to the east of the square on Charing Cross Road, famous for its secondhand bookshops, and on tiny **Cecil Court**, a pedestrianized passage lined with small antiquarian booksellers.

TOP ATTRACTIONS

Fodor's Choice
★

Newburgh Quarter. Want to see the hip style of today's London? Find it just one block east of Carnaby Street—where the look of the '60s "Swinging London" was born—in an adorable warren of cobblestone streets now lined with specialty boutiques, edgy stores, and young indie upstarts. Here, not far from roaring Regent Street, the future of

DID YOU KNOW

Covent Garden was a convent garden for 300 years before it was Britain's first planned public square with a fruit and vegetable market. The greengrocers are gone but the 1830 market building and the courtyard still teem with shoppers.

A BRIEF HISTORY

Almost as soon as a 17th-century housing development covered what had been a royal park and hunting ground, Soho earned a reputation for entertainment, bohemianism, and cosmopolitan tolerance. When the authorities introduced zero tolerance of soliciting in 1991 (the most recent of several attempts to end Soho's sex trade), they cracked down on an old neighborhood tradition that still resurfaces from time to time.

Successive waves of refugees—French Huguenots in the 1680s, followed by Germans, Russians, Poles, Greeks, Italians, and Chinese—settled and brought their ethnic cuisines with them. So when dining out became fashionable after World War I, Soho was the natural place for restaurants to flourish (as they continue to do today).

In the 1950s and '60s, Soho was London's artists' quarter and the place to find the top jazz clubs and art galleries. Among the luminaries who have made their home here are landscape painter John Constable; Casanova, the famous lothario; Canaletto, the great painter of Venice; poet William Blake; and the revolutionary Karl Marx.

Present-day Covent Garden took shape in the 1630s, when Inigo Jones turned what had been agricultural land into Britain's first planned public square. After the Great Fire of 1666, it became the site of England's largest fruit-and-vegetable market (the flower market arrived in the 19th century). This, along with the district's many theaters and taverns, gave the area a somewhat dubious reputation, and after the produce market relocated in 1973, the surviving buildings were scheduled for demolition. A local campaign saved them, and the restored market opened in 1980.

England's fashion is being incubated in stores like Lucy in Disguise and Flying Horse Jeans. A check of the ingredients reveals one part '60s London, one part Futuristic Fetishism, one part Dickensian charm, and one part British street swagger. The Nouveau Boho look best flourishes in shops like Peckham Rye, a tiny boutique crowded with rockers and fashion plates who adore its grunge–meets–*Brideshead Revisted* vibe. Quality independent coffee shops abound—take a break at Speakeasy Espresso & Brew Bar, where you can also browse for home coffee-making equipment. ⊠ *Newburgh St., Foubert's Pl., Ganton St., and Carnaby St., Soho* ⊕ *carnaby.co.uk* Ⓜ *Oxford Circus.*

COVENT GARDEN

To the east of Charing Cross Road lies Covent Garden, the famous marketplace turned shopping mall. Although boutiques and haute fashion shops line the surrounding streets, many Londoners come to Covent Garden for its two outposts of culture: the **Royal Opera House** and the **Donmar Warehouse,** one of London's best and most innovative theaters. The area becomes more sedate just to the north, at the end of Wellington Street, where semicircular Aldwych is lined with grand buildings, and from there the Strand leads to the huge, stately piazza of **Somerset**

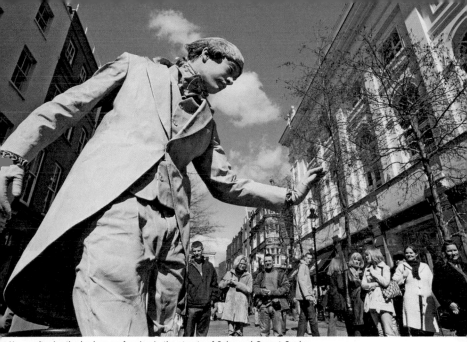
You can't miss the buskers performing in the streets of Soho and Covent Garden.

House, a vibrant center of contemporary arts and home to the many masterpieces on view at the **Courtauld Gallery.** You'll get a sense of old-fashioned London just behind the Strand, where small lanes are little changed since the 18th century. On the way to the verdant **Embankment Gardens** bordering the Thames, you may pass the **Adam Houses,** the remnants of a grand 18th-century riverside housing development, and the **Benjamin Franklin House,** where the noted statesman lived in the years leading up to the American Revolution.

Covent Garden joins Soho as an arts-and-entertainment center in the city, popularly referred to as "the West End." The neighborhood centers on the Piazza, site of the original Covent Garden market. High Holborn to the north, Kingsway to the east, and the Strand to the south form its other boundaries.

TOP ATTRACTIONS

The Courtauld Gallery. One of London's most beloved art collections, the Courtauld is to your right as you pass through the archway into the grounds of the beautifully restored, grand 18th-century neoclassical **Somerset House.** Founded in 1931 by the textile magnate Samuel Courtauld to house his remarkable private collection, this is one of the world's finest Impressionist and post-Impressionist galleries, with artists ranging from Bonnard to van Gogh. A déjà-vu moment with Cézanne, Degas, Seurat, or Monet awaits on every wall (Manet's *Bar at the Folies-Bergère* and *Le Déjeuner sur L'Herbe* are two of the stars). Botticelli, Bruegel, Tiepolo, and Rubens are also represented, thanks to the exquisite bequest of Count Antoine Seilern's Princes Gate collection. German Renaissance paintings, bequeathed in 1947, include the colorful and delightfully wicked *Adam and Eve* by Lucas Cranach the Elder. The second floor has a more provocative, experimental feel, with masterpieces such as Modigliani's iconic *Female Nude*. Don't miss the little café downstairs—a perfect place for a spot of tea. ⊠ *Somerset House, Strand, Covent Garden* ☎ *020/7848–2526* ⊕ *www.courtauld.ac.uk* ⊡ *£6; £3 Mon.* ⊙ *Daily 10–6; last admission 5:30* Ⓜ *Temple, Covent Garden.*

Covent Garden Piazza. Once home to London's main flower market, where *My Fair Lady*'s Eliza Doolittle peddled her blooms, the square around which Covent Garden pivots is known as the Piazza. In the center, the fine old market building now houses stalls and shops selling higher-class clothing, plus several restaurants and cafés and knickknack stores that are good for gifts. One particular gem is Benjamin Pollock's Toyshop at No. 44 in the market. Established in the 1880s, it sells delightful toy theaters. The superior **Apple Market** has good crafts stalls on most days, too. On the south side of the Piazza, the indoor **Jubilee Market,** with its stalls of clothing, army-surplus gear, and more crafts and knickknacks, has a distinct flea-market feel. In summer it may seem that everyone in the huge crowds around you in the Piazza is a fellow tourist, but there's still plenty of office life in the area. Londoners who shop here tend to head for Neal Street and the area to the north of Covent Garden Tube station rather than the market itself. In the Piazza, street performers—from global musicians to jugglers and mimes—play to the crowds, as they have done since the first English Punch and Judy Show, staged here in the 17th century. ⊠ *Covent Garden* ⊕ *www.coventgardenlondonuk.com* Ⓜ *Covent Garden.*

FAMILY **London Transport Museum.** Housed in the old flower market at the southeast corner of Covent Garden, this stimulating museum is filled with impressive vehicle, poster, and photograph collections. As you watch the crowds drive a Tube-train simulation and gawk at the horse-drawn trams (and the piles of detritus that remained behind) and steam locomotives, it's unclear who's enjoying it more, children or adults. Best of all, the kid-friendly museum (under 16 admitted free) has a multilevel approach to education, including information for the youngest visitor to the most advanced transit aficionado. Food and drink are available at the Upper Deck café and the shop has lots of good options for gift-buying. ■TIP→ Tickets are valid for unlimited entry for 12 months. ⊠ *Covent Garden Piazza, Covent Garden* ☎ *020/7379-6344* ⊕ *www. ltmuseum.co.uk* ⊡ *£15* ⊙ *Sat.–Thurs. 10–6 (last admission 5:15), Fri. 11–6 (last admission 5:15)* Ⓜ *Covent Garden, Leicester Sq.*

FAMILY
Fodor's Choice
★
Somerset House. In recent years this huge complex—the work of Sir William Chambers (1723–96), and built during the reign of George III to house offices of the Navy—has completed its transformation from dusty government offices to one of the capital's most buzzing centers of

culture and the arts, hosting several interesting exhibitions at any one time. The cobblestone Italianate courtyard, where Admiral Nelson used to walk, makes a great setting for 55 playful fountains and is transformed into a romantic ice rink in winter; the grand space is the venue for music and outdoor movie screenings in summer. The **Courtauld Gallery** (⇨ *See above*) occupies most of the north building, facing the busy Strand. Across the courtyard are the Embankment Galleries, with a vibrant calendar of design, fashion, architecture, and photography exhibitions. Creative activities for children are a regular feature (the website has details). The East Wing has another fine exhibition space and events are sometimes also held in the atmospherically gloomy cellars below the Fountain Court. Tom's Kitchen offers fine dining and the Deli has mouthwatering cakes and pastries. In summer, eating and drinking spills out onto the large terrace next to the Thames. ✉ *Strand, Covent Garden* ☎ *020/7845–4600* ⊕ *www.somersethouse. org.uk* ✉ *Embankment Galleries price varies, Courtauld Gallery £6 (£3 Mon.), other areas free* ☾ *Daily 10–6; last admission times vary* Ⓜ *Charing Cross, Waterloo, Blackfriars.*

ICE-SKATING

It's hard to beat the skating experience at Somerset House, where from November through January a rink is set up in the grand courtyard of this central London palace. Check the website for current prices; its popularity is enormous, and if you can't get a ticket, other venues such as Hampton Court, the Tower of London, the London Eye, and the Natural History Museum are following Somerset House's lead in having temporary winter rinks. ☎ *0844/847–1520* ⊕ *www. somersethouse.org.uk/ice-rink.*

WORTH NOTING

The Adam Houses. Only a few structures remain of what was once a regal riverfront row of houses on a 3-acre site, but such is their quality that they are worth a detour off the Strand. The work of 18th-century Scottish architects and interior designers (John, Robert, James, and William Adam, known collectively as the Adam brothers), the original development was damaged in the 19th century during the building of the embankment, and mostly demolished in 1936 to be replaced by an art deco tower. The original houses still standing are protected, and give a glimpse of their former grandeur. Nos. 1–4 Robert Street and Nos. 7 and 10 Adam Street are the best. ✉ *Robert St. and Adam St., off The Strand, Covent Garden* Ⓜ *Charing Cross, Embankment.*

Royal Society of Arts. At the Royal Society of Arts, you can sometimes see a suite of Adam rooms; ring ahead to check. ✉ *8 John Adam St.* ☎ *020/7930–5115* ⊕ *www.thersa.org* ✉ *Free* Ⓜ *Charing Cross, Embankment.*

Benjamin Franklin House. This architecturally significant 1730 house is the only surviving residence of American statesman, scientist, writer, and inventor Benjamin Franklin, who lived and worked here for 16 years preceding the American Revolution. The restored Georgian town house has been left unfurnished, the better to show off the original features—18th-century paneling, stoves, beams, bricks, and windows. Visitors are led

Leicester Square is home to many cinemas and a half-price theater ticket booth.

around the house by the costumed character of Polly Hewson, the daughter of Franklin's landlady, who interacts with engaging video projections and recorded voices. On Monday you can take a guided tour focusing on the architectural details of the building. ✉ *36 Craven St., Covent Garden* ☎ *020/7839–2006, 020/7925–1405 booking line* ⊕ *www. benjaminfranklinhouse.org* ✉ *Historical Experience £7; architectural tour £3.50* ⊗ *Historical Experience Wed.–Sun. noon, 1, 2, 3:15, and 4:15; architectural tour Mon. noon, 1, 2, 3:15, and 4:15* Ⓜ *Charing Cross.*

Leicester Square. Looking at the neon of the major movie houses, the fast-food outlets, and the disco entrances, you'd never guess that this square (pronounced *Lester*) was a model of formality and refinement when it was first laid out around 1630. By the 19th century the square was already bustling and disreputable, and although it's not a threatening place, you should still be on your guard, especially at night—any space so full of people is bound to attract pickpockets, and Leicester Square certainly does. Although there's a bit of residual glamour (red-carpet film premieres) Londoners generally tend to avoid the place, though it's worth a visit for its hustle and bustle, its mime artists, and a pleasant green area in its center. In the middle is a statue of a sulking Shakespeare, perhaps remembering the days when the movie houses were live theaters—burlesque houses, but live all the same. On the northeast corner, in Leicester Place, stands the church of **Notre Dame de France,** with a wonderful mural by Jean Cocteau in one of its side chapels. For more in the way of atmosphere, head north and west from here, through Chinatown and the narrow streets of Soho. ✉ *Covent Garden* Ⓜ *Leicester Sq.*

St. Paul's Church. If you want to commune with the spirits of Vivien Leigh, Noël Coward, Edith Evans, or Charlie Chaplin, this might be just the place. Memorials to them and many other theater greats are found in this 1633 work of the renowned Inigo Jones, who, as the King's Surveyor of Works, designed the whole of Covent Garden Piazza. St. Paul's Church has been known as "the actors' church" since the Restoration, thanks to the neighboring theater district and St. Paul's prominent parishioners. (Well-known actors often read the lessons at services, and the church still hosts concerts and small-scale productions.) Fittingly, the opening scene of Shaw's *Pygmalion* takes place under its Tuscan portico (you might know it better from the musical *My Fair Lady,* starring Audrey Hepburn). The western end of the Piazza is a prime pitch for street entertainers, but if they're not to your liking, you can repair to the serenity of the garden entered from King or Bedford streets. ⊠ *Bedford St., Covent Garden* ☎ *020/7836–5221* ⊕ *www.actorschurch.org* Ⓜ *Covent Garden.*

> ### CHEAP TICKETS
>
> One landmark certainly worth a visit by theatergoers is the **Society of London Theatre ticket kiosk (TKTS)**, on the southwest corner of Leicester Square, which sells half-price tickets for many of that evening's performances. It's open Monday to Saturday from 9 to 7, and Sunday from 11 to 4:30. The kiosk also sells advance tickets for many shows. Watch out for illegal ticket touts (scalpers), who target tourists around the square.

Theatre Royal, Drury Lane. This is London's best-known auditorium and almost its largest. Since World War II, Drury Lane's forte has been musicals (from *My Fair Lady* and *South Pacific* to *Miss Saigon* and *Shrek*)—though David Garrick, who managed the theater from 1747 to 1776, made its name by reviving the works of the by-then-obscure William Shakespeare. Drury Lane enjoys all the romantic accessories of a London theater—a history of fires (it burned down three times), riots (in 1737, when a posse of footmen demanded free admission), attempted regicides (George II in 1716 and his grandson George III in 1800), and even sightings of the most famous phantom of Theatreland, the Man in Grey (in the Circle during matinees). Seventy-five-minute dramatized tours, led by actors, are available. ⊠ *Catherine St., Covent Garden* ☎ *0844/412–4660, 0871/297–0777 tour bookings* ⊕ *www.reallyuseful. com* ⊠ *Tours £10.50* ⊙ *Tours Mon., Tues., and Thurs. 2:15 and 4:15; Wed. and Sat. 10:30 and 11:45* Ⓜ *Covent Garden.*

BLOOMSBURY AND HOLBORN

With Islington

GETTING ORIENTED

Bloomsbury and Holborn

TOP REASONS TO GO

Take a tour of "Mankind's Attic": From the Rosetta Stone to the Elgin Marbles, the British Museum is the golden hoard of booty amassed over centuries by the British Empire.

Stroll through the Inns of Court: The quiet courts, leafy gardens, and magnificent halls that comprise the heart of Holborn are the closest thing to the spirit of Oxford in London.

Time travel at Sir John Soane's Museum: Quirky and fascinating, the former home of the celebrated 19th-century architect is a treasure trove of antiquities and oddities.

View rare treasures at the British Library: In keeping with Bloomsbury's literary traditions, this great repository shows off the Magna Carta, a Gutenberg Bible, Shakespeare's First Folio, and other masterpieces of the written word.

Pay your respects to Charles Dickens: The former residence of the *Oliver Twist* author is now a fascinating museum.

FEELING PECKISH?

The Betjeman Arms. Inside St. Pancras International's wonderfully renovated Victorian station, this pub is the perfect place to stop for a pint and some traditional pub fare. Perched above the tracks of the Eurostar Terminal, the view of the trains and travelers will keep you occupied while you put your feet up. ⊠ *Unit 53, St. Pancras International Station, Pancras Rd., King's Cross* ☎ *020/7923–5440* Ⓜ *King's Cross St. Pancras.*

The Hare and Tortoise Dumpling & Noodle Bar. This bright café, serving scrumptious Asian fast food from noon to 11 pm, is a favorite with students, and it's easy to see why: ingredients are all natural, the portions are huge, and the price is always reasonable. ⊠ *15–17 Brunswick Shopping Centre, Brunswick Sq., opposite the Renoir Cinema, Bloomsbury* ☎ *020/7278–9799* ⊕ *www.hareandtortoise.co.uk/bloomsbury* Ⓜ *Russell Sq.*

GETTING THERE

The Russell Square Tube stop on the Piccadilly line leaves you right at the corner of Russell Square.

The best Tube stops for the Inns of Court are Holborn on the Central and Piccadilly lines or Chancery Lane on the Central line.

Tottenham Court Road on the Northern and Central lines is best for the British Museum.

Once you're in Bloomsbury, you can easily get around on foot.

MAKING THE MOST OF YOUR TIME

If you plan to visit the Inns of Court as well as the British Museum, and you'd like to get a feel for the neighborhood, then devote an entire day to this literary and legal enclave.

An alternative scenario is to set aside a separate day for a visit to the British Museum, which can easily consume as many hours as you have to spare.

It's a pleasure to wander through the leafy squares at your leisure, examining historic Blue Plaques or relaxing at a street-side café. The students in the neighborhood add a bit of street life.

5

Sightseeing
★★★
Nightlife
★★
Dining
★★
Lodging
★★★★
Shopping
★★

Guarded by the British Library to the north, the British Museum at its heart, and the Inns of Court of the Holborn district (right by the Thames), Bloomsbury might appear all bookish and cerebral—but fear not, it's much more than that. There's a youthfulness about its buzzing thoroughfares—not surprising, given all the nearby universities and colleges, let alone students heading to the British Library. To the southeast, Holborn was once Dickens territory and now is home to legal London.

BLOOMSBURY

Updated by
James O'Neill

Fundamental to the region's spirit of open expression and scholarly debate is the legacy of the Bloomsbury Group, an elite corps of artists and writers who lived in this neighborhood during the first part of the 20th century. **Gordon Square** was at one point home to Virginia Woolf, John Maynard Keynes (both at No. 46), and Lytton Strachey (at No. 51). But perhaps the best-known square in Bloomsbury is the large, centrally located **Russell Square,** with its handsome gardens. Scattered around the **University of London** campus are Woburn Square, Torrington Square, and Tavistock Square. The **British Library,** with its vast treasures, is a few blocks north, across busy Euston Road.

Bloomsbury is bordered by Tottenham Court Road on the west, Euston Road on the north, Woburn Place (which becomes Southampton Row) on the east, and New Oxford Street on the south.

The area from Somerset House on the Strand, all the way up Kingsway to the Euston Road, is known as London's **Museum Mile** for the myriad historic houses and museums that dot the area. **Charles Dickens Museum,** where the author wrote *Oliver Twist,* pays homage to the master, and artists' studios and design shops share space near the majestic **British Museum.** And guaranteed to raise a smile from the most blasé and footsore tourist is **Sir John Soane's Museum,** where the color-ful collection reflects the eclectic interests of the namesake founder. Bloomsbury's liveliness extends north to the exciting redevelopment of King's Cross—once the ugly sister of *all* ugly sisters—and farther north to quaint, bustling Islington.

TOP ATTRACTIONS

FAMILY **British Library.** Once a part of the British Museum, the 18 million–volume collection of the British Library has had its own state-of-the-art home since 1997. The library's greatest treasures are on view to the general public: the Magna Carta, a Gutenberg Bible, Jane Austen's writings, and Shakespeare's First Folio. Musical manuscripts by G.F. Handel as well as Sir Paul McCartney are on display in the Sir John Ritblat Gallery. Also in the gallery are headphones with which you can listen to pieces in the **National Sound Archive** (the world's largest collection), such as the voice of Florence Nightingale or George V or an extract from the Beatles' last tour interview. Marvel at the six-story glass tower that holds the 65,000-volume collection of George III. On weekends and during school vacations there are hands-on demonstrations of how a book comes together, and the library frequently mounts special exhibi-tions. If all this wordiness gets too much, you can relax in the library's piazza or take in one of the occasional free concerts in the amphitheater outside. ⊠ *96 Euston Rd., Bloomsbury* ☎ *0843/208–1144* ⊕ *www.bl.uk* ✉ *Free, donations appreciated; charge for special exhibitions* ☉ *Mon. and Wed.–Fri. 9:30–6, Tues. 9:30–8, Sat. 9:30–5, Sun. and public holi-days 11–5* Ⓜ *Euston, Euston Sq., King's Cross St. Pancras.*

Fodor'sChoice **British Museum.**
★ *See the highlighted listing in this chapter.*

Charles Dickens Museum. This is one of the few London houses Charles Dickens (1812–70) inhabited that is still standing, and it's the place where the master wrote *Oliver Twist* and *Nicholas Nickleby* and fin-ished *Pickwick Papers.* The house looks exactly as it would have in Dickens's day, complete with first editions, letters, and a tall clerk's desk (Dickens wrote standing up, often while chatting with visiting friends and relatives). Down in the basement is a replica of the Ding-ley Dell kitchen from *Pickwick Papers.* A varied program of special exhibitions explores both Dickens's works and his family life—check out the "costumed tours" (details at the website) where you're guided through the Dickens residence by his housemaid. The museum also houses a shop and café. ⊠ *48 Doughty St., Bloomsbury* ☎ *020/7405–2127* ⊕ *www.dickensmuseum.com* ✉ *£9* ☉ *Daily 10–5 (last admis-sion 4)* Ⓜ *Chancery La., Russell Sq.*

Lamb's Conduit Street. If you think Bloomsbury is about all things cerebral, then think again. Lamb's Conduit Street, a partly pedestrianized street of gorgeous Georgian town houses nestled to the east of Russell Square, is slowly but surely building a reputation as one of the capital's most charm-ing—and fashionable—shopping thoroughfares. Avail yourself of what the many boutique shops have to offer, from fashion to ceramics, fine art to flowers; there's even an excellent run-by-locals food cooperative called The People's Supermarket. Alternatively, you could just window-shop your

Continued on page 106

THE BRITISH MUSEUM

Anybody writing about the British Museum had better have a large stack of superlatives close at hand: most, biggest, earliest, finest. This is the golden hoard of nearly three centuries of the Empire, the booty brought from Britain's far-flung colonies.

The first major pieces, among them the Rosetta Stone and the Parthenon Sculptures (Elgin Marbles), were "acquired" from the French, who "found" them in Egypt and Greece. The museum has since collected countless goodies of worldwide historical significance: the Black Obelisk, some of the Dead Sea Scrolls, the Lindow Man. And that only begins the list.

The British Museum is a vast space split into 94 galleries, generally divided by continent or period of history, with some areas spanning more than one level. There are marvels wherever you go, and—while we don't like to be pessimistic—it is, yes, impossible to fully appreciate everything in a day. So make the most of the tours, activity trails, and visitors guides that are available.

The following is a highly edited overview of the museum's greatest hits, organized by area. Pick one or two that whet your appetite, then branch out from there, or spend two straight hours indulging in the company of a single favorite sculpture. There's no wrong way to experience the British Museum, just make sure you do!

✉ Great Russell St., Bloomsbury WC1

☎ 020/7323–8299

⊕ www.britishmuseum.org

▦ Free; donations encouraged. Tickets for special exhibits vary in price.

🕙 Galleries (and Reading Room exhibition space): Sat.–Thurs. 10–5:30, Fri. 10–8:30. Great Court: Sat.–Thurs. 9–6, Fri. 9–8:30.

Ⓤ Russell Square, Holborn, Tottenham Court Rd.

(left) The Great Court
(top) *Cradle to Grave* by Pharmacopoeia

MUSEUM HIGHLIGHTS

Ancient Civilizations

The Rosetta Stone. Found in 1799 and carved in 196 BC by decree of Ptolemy V in Egyptian hieroglyphics, demotic, and Greek, it was this multilingual inscription that provided French Egyptologist Jean-François Champollion with the key to deciphering hieroglyphics. *Room 4*.

Colossal statue of Ramesses II. A member of the 19th dynasty (ca. 1270 BC), Ramesses II commissioned innumerable statues of himself—more than any other preceding or succeeding king. This one, a 7-ton likeness of his perfectly posed upper half, comes from his mortuary temple, the Ramesseum, in western Thebes. *Room 4*.

(top) Portland vase
(bottom) Colossal statue of Ramesses II

The Parthenon Sculptures. Perhaps these marvelous treasures of Greece shouldn't be here—but while the debate rages on, you can steal your own moment with the Elgin Marbles. Carved in about 440 BC, these graceful decorations are displayed along with an in-depth, high-tech exhibit of the Acropolis; the **handless, footless Dionysus** who used to recline along its east pediment is especially well known. *Room 18*.

Mausoleum of Halikarnassos. All that remains of this, one of the Seven Wonders of the Ancient World, is a fragmented form of the original "mausoleum," the 4th-century tomb of Maussollos, King of Karia. The highlight of this gallery is the marble forepart of the **colossal chariot horse from the** *quadriga*. *Room 21*.

The Egyptian mummies. Another short flight of stairs takes you to the museum's most popular galleries, especially beloved by children: the Roxie Walker Galleries of Egyptian Funerary Archaeology have a fascinating collection of relics from the Egyptian realm of the dead. In addition to real corpses, wrapped mummies, and mummy cases, there's a menagerie of animal companions and curious items that were buried alongside them. *Rooms 62–63*.

Portland Vase. Made in Italy from cameo glass at the turn of the first century, it is named after the Dukes of Portland, who owned it from 1785 to 1945. It is considered a technical masterpiece—opaque white mythological figures cut by a gem-cutter are set on cobalt-blue background. *Room 70*.

The **Enlightenment Gallery** should be visited purely for the fact that its antiquarian cases hold the contents of the British Museum's first collections—Sir Hans Sloane's natural-history loot, as well as that of Sir Joseph Banks, who acquired specimens of everything from giant shells to fossils to rare plants to exotic beasts during his voyage to the Pacific aboard Captain Cook's *Endeavour*. *Room 1*.

Asia Galleries

Egypt Galleries 60–66

Egyptian Mummies

TO GALLERIES 90–94

67

66

North Korean Socialist Realism Art

Asia Galleries 91–94

94   93   92

91   90

TO GALLERIES 36–67

UPPER FLOOR

61   62   63   64   65

59 58 57   56   55 54 53

73   52

72   51

71   50

Greece & Rome Galleries 69–73

70

Portland Vase

Roman Britain Gallery

Mildenhall Treasure

49

Sutton Hoo Treasure

Europe Galleries 41–48

69a 69   36   40   41   42   43

68   37   44

Lindow Man

Prehistory Galleries

47   46   45

48   34

33a   33

Cradle to Grave

World Cultures Galleries

24

Americas Galleries 26–27

Native American Skin Map

33b

26   27

Mausoleum of Halikarnassos

20   21

19   9 Rosetta Stone

Greece Galleries 11–23

22   8 **Egypt Galleries**

18   17   23

16   10

Elgin Marbles

15   7   4

Colossal Statue of Ramesses II

35

Reading Room

1 Enlightenment Gallery

The Great Court

14

13   6   3   2

12   11

GROUND FLOOR

ooooooo

Great Russell St. Entrance

Paul Hamlyn Library

5

IN FOCUS THE BRITISH MUSEUM

Asia

The Korea Foundation Gallery. Delve into striking examples of **North Korean Socialist Realism art** from the 1950s to the present and a reconstruction of a **sarangbang**, a traditional scholar's study, complete with hanji paper walls and tea-making equipment. *Room 67.*

The Percival David Collection. More than 1400 pieces of Chinese ceramics (the most comprehensive collection outside China) are on display. *Room 95.*

World Cultures

The JP Morgan Chase North American Gallery. This is one of the largest collections of native culture outside North America, going back to the earliest hunters 10,000 years ago. Here a 1775 **native American skin map** serves as an example of the importance of such documents in the exploration and cartography of North America. Look for the beautifully displayed **native American costumes.** *Room 26.*

Colossal chariot horse from the *quadriga* of the Mausoleum at Halikarnassos

The Mexican Gallery. The most alluring pieces sit in this collection side by side: a 15th-century **turquoise mask of Xiuhtecuhtli,** the Mexican Fire God and Turquoise Lord, and a **double-headed serpent** from the same period. *Room 27.*

Britain and Europe

The Mildenhall Treasure. This glittering haul of 4th-century Roman silver tableware was found beneath the sod of a Suffolk field in 1942. *Room 49.*

The Sutton Hoo Treasure. Next door to the loot from Mildenhall—and equally splendid, including brooches, swords, and jewel-encrusted helmets—the treasure was buried at sea with (it is thought) Redwald, one of the first English kings, in the 7th century, and excavated from a Suffolk field in 1938–39. *Room 41.*

Lindow Man. "Pete Marsh"—so named by the archaeologists who unearthed the body from a Cheshire peat marsh—was ritually slain, probably as a human sacrifice, in the 1st century and lay perfectly pickled in his bog until 1984. *Room 50.*

Theme Galleries

Living & Dying. The "Cradle to Grave" installation pays homage to the British nation's wellbeing—or ill-being, as it were. More than 14,000 drugs (the number estimated to be prescribed to every person in the U.K. in his lifetime) are displayed in a colorful tapestry of pills and tablets. *Room 24.*

LOWER GALLERY

The three rooms that comprise the **Sainsbury African Galleries** are of the main interest here: together they present a staggering 200,000 objects, featuring intricate pieces of old ivory, gold, and wooden masks and carvings—highlighting such ancient kingdoms as the Benin and Asante. The displays include a collection of **55 throwing knives**; ceremonial garments including a dazzling pink and green **woman's coif** (*qufiya*) from Tunisia made of silk, metal, and cotton; and the *Oxford Man,* a 1992 woodcarving by Owen Ndou, depicting a man of ambiguous race clutching his Book of Knowledge.

DID YOU KNOW?

Galleries help divide this sprawling space into manageable sizes for visitors. The Sainsbury African Galleries are just some of the 94 galleries; the British Museum's collection totals more than 7 million objects.

THE NATION'S ATTIC: A HISTORY OF THE MUSEUM

The collection began when Sir Hans Sloane, physician to Queen Anne and George II, bequeathed his personal collection of curiosities and antiquities to the nation. The collection quickly grew, thanks to enthusiastic kleptomaniacs after the Napoleonic Wars—most notoriously the seventh Earl of Elgin, who obtained the marbles from the Parthenon and Erechtheion on the Acropolis in Athens during his term as British ambassador in Constantinople.

Soon thereafter, it seemed everyone had something to donate—George II gave the old Royal Library, Sir William Hamilton gave antique vases, Charles Townley gave sculptures, the Bank of England gave coins. When the first exhibition galleries opened to visitors in 1759, the trustees agreed to admit only small groups guided by curators. The British Museum quickly became one of the most fashionable places to be seen in the capital, and tickets, which had to be booked in advance, were treated like gold dust.

The museum's holdings quickly outgrew their original space in Montague House. After the addition of such major pieces as the Rosetta Stone and other Egyptian antiquities (spoils of the Napoleonic War) and the Parthenon sculptures, Robert Smirke was commissioned to build an appropriately large and monumental building on the same site. It's still a hot ticket: the British Museum now receives more than 5 million visitors every year.

THE GREAT COURT & THE READING ROOM

The museum's classical Greek-style facade features figures representing the progress of civilization, and the focal point is the awesome Great Court, a massive glass-roofed space. Here is the museum's inner courtyard (now the largest covered square in Europe) that, for more than 150 years, had been used for storage.

The 19th-century Reading Room, an impressive 106-foot-high blue-and-gold-domed library, forms the centerpiece of the Great Court. H.G. Wells, Thomas Hardy, Lord Tennyson, Oscar Wilde, George Orwell, T.S. Elliot, and Beatrix Potter are just a few writers who have used this space as a literary and academic sanctuary over the past 150 years or so. Temporary exhibitions here now include "Vikings: life and legend" and "Ming: 50 years that changed China."

(above) Reading Room

PLANNING YOUR VISIT

Tours

The **30–40 minute eyeOpener tour (free)** by Museum Guides does just what it says; ask for details at the information desk. After this tour, you can then dip back into the collections that most captured your imagination at your leisure.

An excellent **multimedia guide (£5)** is a good way to explore the galleries at your own pace, via a series of differently-themed tours.

Alternatively, the **Visitor's Guide (£3.50)** gives a brief but informative overview of the museum's history and is, again, divided into self-guided themed tours.

Before you go, take a look at the online **COMPASS tour** using the museum's navigation tool (www.thebritishmuseum.org/compass), which allows users to browse past and present exhibits as well as search for specific objects. A children's version can also be found here. Computer stations in the Reading Room offer onsite access to COMPASS.

■ TIP→ The closest underground station to the British Museum is Russell Square on the Piccadilly line. However, since you will be entering via the back entrance on Montague Place, you will not experience the full impact of the museum's grand facade. To do so, alight at Holborn on the Central and Piccadilly lines or Tottenham Court Road on the Central and Northern lines. The walk from these stations is about 10 minutes.

WITH KIDS

■ Take a look at the "Family Visits" page online for the top 12 objects to see with children.

■ The Families Desk in the Great Court has trails for kids ages 3 to 5 and 6 to 11. The Ford Centre for Young Visitors has free activity backpacks.

■ Art materials are available for free from information points, where you can also find out about workshops, performances, storytelling sessions, and other free events.

■ Around the museum, there are Hands On desks open daily 11–4, which let visitors handle objects from the collections.

WHERE TO REFUEL

The British Museum's self-service **Gallery Café** gets very crowded but serves an acceptable menu beneath a plaster cast of a part of the Parthenon frieze that Lord Elgin didn't remove. It's open daily, but isn't particularly family friendly.

The **café in the Great Court** keeps longer hours and is a great place to people-watch and admire the spectacular glass roof while you eat your salad and sandwich.

If the weather is nice, exit the museum via the back entrance on Montague Place and amble over to **Russell Square,** which has grassy lawns, water fountains, and a glass-fronted café for post-sandwich coffee and ice cream.

way down this pretty little street, or re-fuel at **The Lamb**—an atmospheric Victorian-era pub whose previous patrons have included Ted Hughes, Sylvia Plath, and a certain Mr. Dickens. ⊠ *Lamb's Conduit St., Bloomsbury* Ⓜ *Russell Sq.*

Fodor's Choice
★ **Sir John Soane's Museum.** Sir John (1753–1837), architect of the Bank of England, bequeathed his wonderful, eccentric house to the nation on one condition: nothing be changed. It's truly a house full of surprises. In the Picture Room, for instance, two of Hogarth's *Rake's Progress* series are among the paintings on panels that swing away to reveal secret gallery pockets with even more paintings. Everywhere, mirrors and colors play tricks with light and space, and split-level

> ### KING'S CROSS STATION
>
> Sick of living in the shadow of its sumptuously renovated next-door neighbor, St. Pancras station, King's Cross—and the area behind it—is undergoing a major makeover of its own, with bars, restaurants, shops, and even a stunning fountain display. That said, its chief attraction is still the imaginary platform 9¾, the departure point for Harry Potter and his fellow aspiring wizards aboard the *Hogwarts Express.* The station has helpfully put up a sign for platform 9¾ if you want to take a picture there—just don't try to run through the wall.

floors worthy of a fairground funhouse disorient you. In a basement chamber sits the vast 1300 BC sarcophagus of Seti I, lighted by a domed skylight two stories above. (When Sir John acquired this priceless object for £2,000, after it was rejected by the British Museum, he celebrated with a three-day party.) The tranquil courtyard gardens are also open to the public, and a below-street-level passage joins two of the courtyards to the museum. Because of the small size of the museum, limited numbers are allowed entry at any one time, so you may have a short wait outside—but it's worth it. Hour-long tours are offered (check the website for details), and on the first Tuesday of the month there's a very popular candlelight evening opening, from 6 to 9 pm (best to arrive at 5:30). ⊠ *13 Lincoln's Inn Fields, Bloomsbury* ☎ *020/7405–2107* ⊕ *www.soane.org* 🎟 *Free; tours £10* ⊙ *Tues.–Sat. 10–5; also 6–9 on 1st Tues. of month* Ⓜ *Holborn.*

WORTH NOTING

Lincoln's Inn. There's plenty to see at one of the oldest, best preserved, and most attractive of the Inns of Court—from the Chancery Lane Tudor brick gatehouse to the wide-open, tree-lined, atmospheric Lincoln's Inn Fields and the 15th-century chapel remodeled by Inigo Jones in 1620. The chapel and the gardens are open to the public, but to see more you must book a place on one of the official tours in advance. But be warned: they tend to prefer group bookings of 15 or more, so it's best to check the website or call for details and note that there are no tours at weekends or in August. ⊠ *Chancery La., Bloomsbury* ☎ *020/7405–1393* ⊕ *www.lincolnsinn.org.uk* 🎟 *Free* ⊙ *Gardens weekdays 7–7; chapel weekdays 9–5* Ⓜ *Chancery La.*

Royal Courts of Justice. Here is the vast Victorian Gothic pile of 35 million bricks containing the nation's principal law courts, with 1,000-odd rooms running off 3½ miles of corridors. This is where the most important civil law cases—that's everything from divorce to fraud, with libel in between—are heard. You can sit in the viewing gallery to watch any trial you like, for a live version of Court TV. The more dramatic criminal cases are heard at the Old Bailey. Other sights are the 238-foot-long main hall and the compact exhibition of judges' robes. Guided tours must be booked in advance. ⊠ *The Strand, Bloomsbury* ☎ *020/7947–6000, 020/7947–7684 tour reservations* ⊕ *www.hmcourts-service.gov. uk (search for "Royal Courts of Justice" in A–Z option)* 🎫 *Free; tours £12* ☉ *Weekdays 9–4:30* Ⓜ *Temple, Holborn, Chancery La.*

Temple Church. As featured in *The Da Vinci Code*, this church was built by the Knights Templar in the late 12th century. The Red Knights held their secret initiation rites in the crypt here. Having started poor, holy, and dedicated to the protection of pilgrims, they grew rich from showers of royal gifts until, in the 14th century, they were stripped of their wealth, charged with blasphemy and sodomy, and thrown into the Tower. So it goes. Featuring a rare, circular nave, it's not quite as atmospheric as you'd expect—thanks largely to Victorian and postwar restorers. That said, it remains a fine Gothic-Romanesque church and occasionally holds concerts (check website for details). ⊠ *King's Bench Walk, The Temple, Bloomsbury* ☎ *020/7353–3470* ⊕ *www. templechurch.com* 🎫 *£4* ☉ *Mon., Tues., and Thurs–Sat. 11–4; Wed. 2–4; check website for closures* Ⓜ *Temple.*

University College London. Founded in 1826, the college is set in a classical edifice designed by the architect of the National Gallery, William Wilkins. Committed to providing higher education without religious exclusion, in 1878 it also became the first British University to accept women on an equal footing with men. The college has within its portals the **Slade School of Fine Art,** which did for many of Britain's artists what the nearby Royal Academy of Dramatic Art (on Gower Street) did for actors. The South Cloisters contain one of London's weirder treasures: the skeleton of one of the university's founders, Jeremy Bentham, who bequeathed himself to the college. Legend has it that students from a rival college, King's College London, once stole Bentham's head and played football with it. Whether or not the story is true, Bentham's clothed skeleton, stuffed with straw and topped with a wax head, now sits (literally) in the UCL collection. Be sure to detour past the stunning Gotham-esque Senate House on Malet Street. ⊠ *Malet Pl., Bloomsbury.*

Petrie Museum. If you didn't get your fill of Egyptian artifacts at the British Museum, you can see more in the neighboring Petrie Museum, located on the first floor of the DMS Watson library. The museum houses an outstanding collection of Egyptian archaeological objects—jewelry, toys, papyri, and some of the world's oldest garments. ⊠ *Malet Pl.* ☎ *020/7679–2884* ⊕ *www.ucl.ac.uk/museums/petrie* 🎫 *Free, donations appreciated* ☉ *Tues.–Sat. 1–5; closed over Christmas and Easter holidays* Ⓜ *Euston Sq., Goodge St.*

OFF THE BEATEN PATH

London Canal Museum. This quirky little museum, dedicated to the rise and fall of London's once-extensive canal network, is based in the former warehouse of ice-cream maker, Carlo Gatti (hence it also partly features the ice-cream trade as well as London's canals). Children enjoy the activity zone and learning about Henrietta, the museum's horse. Outside, on the Battlebridge Basin, float the painted narrow boats of modern canal dwellers—a stone's throw from the hustle and bustle of St. Pancras International train station. You can walk to the museum along the towpath from Camden Lock—download a free audio tour from the museum's website to accompany the route. ⊠ *12–13 New Wharf Rd., King's Cross* ☎ *020/7713–0836* ⊕ *www.canalmuseum.org. uk* ⊡ *£4* ⊘ *Tues.–Sun. and holiday Mon. 10–4:30; last admission 30 mins before closing. First Thurs. in month open until 7:30* ⊘ *Closed Dec. 23–Jan. 1* Ⓜ *King's Cross.*

HOLBORN

Southeast of Bloomsbury and west of The City, Holborn may appear to be little more than a buffer zone between the two—but while it may lack the panache and of its neighbors, don't underestimate this varied slice of the capital. Home to legal London and the impressive Inns of Court, this is also Charles Dickens territory, with the Old Curiosity Shop snug within its borders and the Dickens museum close by *(⇨ See listing above)*. Add to that its fair share of churches and quirky places of interest, and you'll soon discover that Holborn can be a rewarding place to while away an hour or three. Holborn's massive Gothic-style **Royal Courts of Justice** ramble all the way to the Strand, and the **Inns of Court— Gray's Inn, Lincoln's Inn, Middle Temple,** and **Inner Temple**—are where most British trial lawyers have offices to this day. Geographically, Holborn is probably best defined as: west, Kingsway; north, Theobald's Road; east, Gray's Inn Road; south, where the Strand becomes Fleet Street.

WORTH NOTING

Gray's Inn. Although the least architecturally interesting of the four Inns of Court and the one most damaged by German bombs in the 1940s, Gray's still has romantic associations. In 1594 Shakespeare's *Comedy of Errors* was performed for the first time in the hall—which was restored after World War II. You must make advance arrangements to view the hall, but the secluded and spacious gardens, first planted by Francis Bacon in 1597, are open to the public. ⊠ *Gray's Inn Rd., Holborn* ☎ *020/7458–7800* ⊕ *www.graysinn.org.uk* ⊡ *Free* ⊘ *Weekdays noon–2:30* Ⓜ *Holborn, Chancery La.*

ISLINGTON

Islington is the most central of London's residential village-like neighborhoods. Upper Street, with its high-street stores, independent boutiques, and myriad restaurants and bars, is where most of the action takes place. You'll also find a handful of topflight Off West End theaters and music venues in the area, including the Almeida, Sadler's Wells, and the hugely atmospheric Union Chapel. Wander into the residential streets off the main drag for charming local pubs, many of which serve fantastic food.

6

THE CITY

GETTING ORIENTED

The City

The City

FARRINGDON Ⓤ

BARBICAN Ⓤ

Barbican
Centre ◆

Ropemaker
St.

Silk
St.

Clerkenwell Rd.

Cowcross St.

St. Bartholomew
the Great ◆

MOORGATE Ⓤ

Fore St.

Museum of
London ◆

Basinghall
Ave.

Smithfield ◆
Market

West
Smithfield

Little
Britain

London Wall

**CHANCERY
LANE** Ⓤ

**THE
CITY**

Guildhall ◆

Holborn
Viaduct

Ⓤ **HOLBORN**

Central ◆
Criminal
Court

Holborn
Viaduct
Station ◆

Newgate St.

St. Vedast
Alias Foster ◆

St. Mary-
le-Bow ◆

BANK
Ⓤ

Lincoln's
Inn Fields

Dr. Johnson's
House ◆

Ye Olde
Cheshire
Cheese ✕

Old
Seacoal
La.

Cheapside

Café Below ✕

Lincoln's
Inn
Fields

Gough
Sq.

ST. PAUL'S Ⓤ

Temple ◆
Bar

Ludgate
Circus

Ludgate Hill

St. Paul's ◆
Cathedral

Paul's Ch.

Temple of
Mithras

The Old ✕
Bank of England

Bolt Ln.

Carter La.

Cannon St.

Fleet Street

Fleet St.

Temple ◆
Church

St. Bride's ◆

New Bridge St.

**MANSION
HOUSE** Ⓤ

Temple Bar
Memorial ◆

Queen Victoria St.

Cloak La.

Tudor St.

Upper Thames St.

Sweetings ✕

The Strand

Ⓤ
BLACKFRIARS

Blackfriars
Station ◆

Victoria Embankment

Blackfriars Br.

Millennium ◆
Bridge

Bow Ln.

River Thames

The Queen's Walk

Bankside

Southwark St.

0 _____ 1/4 mile

0 _____ 1/4 km

GETTING THERE

The City area is well served by a concentrated selection of Tube stations—St. Paul's and Bank are on the Central line, and Mansion House, Cannon Street, and Monument are on the District and Circle lines. Liverpool Street and Aldgate border The City's eastern edge, while Chancery Lane and Farringdon lie to the west. Barbican and Moorgate provide easy access to the theaters and galleries of the Barbican, and Blackfriars, to the south, leads to Ludgate Circus and Fleet Street.

TOP REASONS TO GO

St. Paul's Cathedral, the "Symbolic Heart of London": Now increasingly crowded by skyscrapers, St. Paul's still manages to dominate the skyline. Once inside, you'll see the beauty of this 17th-century masterpiece by Sir Christopher Wren's.

Linger on the Millennium Bridge: Hurtle across centuries with this promenade between Tate Modern and St. Paul's—and get a great river view, too.

Treachery and treasures at the Tower: This minicity of melodramatic towers is stuffed to bursting with heraldry, pageantry, and the stunning Crown Jewels (bring sunglasses).

Channel history at the Museum of London: From a Roman leather bikini to Queen Victoria's crinoline gowns; from Selfridges' art deco elevators to a diorama of the Great Fire (sound effects! flickering flames!), this gem of a museum's got it all.

6

MAKING THE MOST OF YOUR TIME

The "Square Mile" is as compact as the nickname suggests, with little distance between points of interest, making an afternoon stroll a rewarding experience. For full immersion in the Tower of London, however, set aside half a day, especially if seeing the Crown Jewels is a priority. Allow an hour minimum each for the Museum of London, St. Paul's Cathedral, and Tower Bridge. On weekends, without the scurrying suits, The City is nearly deserted, making it hard to find lunch—and yet this is when the major attractions are at their busiest.

A GOOD WALK

Crossing the Millennium Bridge from Tate Modern to St. Paul's is one of the finest walks in London—with the river to either side and Christopher Wren's iconic dome towering at one end. Dubbed the "blade of light," the shiny aluminum-and-steel span was the result of a collaboration between architect Norman Foster and sculptor Anthony Caro.

FEELING PECKISH?

The Old Bank of England. It's fun to give directions to this grand old pub next to the Royal Courts of Justice on Fleet Street; just look for the flaming torches next to the statue of a dragon. They serve good, hearty pub food—try one of the tasty pies. ⊠ *194 Fleet St., The City* ☎ *020/7430–2255* ⊕ *www.oldbankofengland.co.uk* Ⓜ *Temple.*

Sweetings. Here since 1889, Sweetings is not cheap, takes no reservations, is only open weekdays, and it closes at 3 pm—but it serves one of the best fish lunches in London. Refuel here on Dover sole or Cornish Brill, and observe the pinstripes at play in their natural habitat. ⊠ *39 Queen Victoria St., The City* ☎ *020/7248–3062* ⊕ *www.sweetingsrestaurant. com* Ⓜ *Mansion House.*

Ye Olde Cheshire Cheese. This wonderfully higgledy-piggledy, multilevel inn on Fleet Street was built in 1667, but the basement bar is centuries older, making this possibly London's oldest pub. It's closed on Sunday. ⊠ *145 Fleet St., The City* ☎ *020/7353–6170* Ⓜ *St. Paul's.*

Sightseeing
★★★★★
Nightlife
★
Dining
★★★
Lodging
★
Shopping
★★★

The City is the capital's fast-beating financial heart, with a powerful architectural triumvirate at its epicenter: the Bank of England, the Royal Exchange, and Mansion House. The "Square Mile" also has currency as the place where London began, its historic heart. St. Paul's Cathedral has been looking after Londoners' souls for hundreds of years, and the Tower of London—that moat-surrounded royal fortress, prison, and jewel house—has occasionally taken care of their heads.

Updated by
Jack Jewers

The City is a dizzying juxtaposition of the old and the new. You'll find yourself immersed in historic London if you begin your explorations on **Fleet Street,** the site of England's first printing press and the undisputed seat of British journalism until the 1980s. Nestled behind Fleet Street is **Dr. Johnson's House,** former home of the author of *Dictionary of the English Language*, who claimed that "when a man is tired of London, he is tired of life." The nearby church of **St. Bride's,** recognizable by its tiered wedding-cake steeple, is a Sir Christopher Wren gem and still the church for journalists, while eastward rises the iconic **St. Paul's Cathedral,** also designed by Wren and largely considered the architect's masterpiece. You'll encounter more of traditional London at the **Central Criminal Court** (nicknamed **The Old Bailey,** and home to London's most sensational criminal trials) and the 800-year-old **Smithfield Market,** whose Victorian halls are the site of a daily early-morning meat market. Nearby are the ancient church of **St. Bartholomew the Great** and St. Bartholomew Hospital, both begun in 1123; the **Guildhall,** the site of the only Roman amphitheater in London; the church of **St. Mary-le-Bow;** and the maze of charmingly old-fashioned, narrow streets around **Bow Lane.**

You can put all this history into context at the **Museum of London,** where archaeological displays include a portion of the original **Roman Wall** that ringed The City.

Just beyond rises the modern **Barbican Centre,** a concrete complex of arts venues and apartments that was controversial at the time it was built, but now has become an indispensible part of the London landscape. The sight of some other new structures rising above The City—especially the **Lloyd's of London Building** and the **Swiss Re Tower,** popularly known as "the Gherkin"—may or may not be more reassuring.

The **Monument,** near the banks of the Thames, was built to commemorate the Great Fire of London of 1666. From here, the river leads to one of London's most absorbing and bloody attractions, the **Tower of London. Tower Bridge** is a suitably giddying finale to an exploration of this fascinating part of London.

There is another reason that makes The City such an intriguing place to visit at the moment: with the constant building of new skyscrapers in the financial district, the ancient skyline is changing at a rapid pace. Cross the Thames anywhere from Waterloo to Tower Bridge and half the people you'll see taking in the view are probably Londoners, paused to wonder in astonishment as yet another glass-and-steel monolith seems to have popped up since last week. You could leave years between your visits, or merely months; either way The City will literally never be the same as when you saw it last.

6

TOP ATTRACTIONS

FAMILY **Monument.** Commemorating the "dreadful visitation" of the Great Fire of London, in 1666, this huge stone column stands both 202 feet tall and exactly 202 feet from Farrier's baking house in Pudding Lane, where the fire started. (Note the gilded urn of fire at the column's pinnacle.) It was designed by Sir Christopher Wren and Dr. Robert Hooke, who were asked to erect it "on or as neere unto the place where the said Fire soe unhappily began as conveniently may be." The view of The City from the top is spectacular, but if climbing the 311 steps seems too arduous, you can watch a live view relayed on a screen at the entrance. ✉ *Monument St., The City* ☎ *020/7626–2717* ⊕ *www.themonument. info* 🖰 *£3; combined ticket with Tower Bridge exhibition £9* ⊗ *Daily 9:30–5:30; last admission 5* Ⓜ *Monument.*

FAMILY **Museum of London.** If there's one place to absorb the history of London,
Fodor's Choice from 450,000 BC to the present day, it's here. There are 7,000 objects
★ to wonder at in all, from Oliver Cromwell's death mask to Queen Victoria's crinoline gowns; Selfridges' art deco elevators to an original Newgate Prison Door. The collection devoted to Roman London contains some extraordinary gems, including an astonishingly well-preserved floor mosaic uncovered just a few streets away. (Appropriately enough, the museum itself shelters a section of the 2nd- to 4th-century London wall, which you can view through a window.) Permanent displays highlight prehistoric, Medieval, and Tudor London. The Galleries of Modern London are equally enthralling: experience the "Expanding City," "People's City," and "World City," each gallery dealing with a section of London's history from 1666 until the 21st century. Innovative interactive displays abound, and you can even wander around a 19th-century London street with impressively detailed shop fronts and interiors, including a pawnbroker, a pub, a barber, and a bank

DID YOU KNOW?

In The City—the oldest part of London—streets still follow a medieval pattern. Here you can see financial institutions and notable buildings, like the Bank of England and Lloyd's of London.

A BRIEF HISTORY

Although there is evidence of Celtic habitation on the north bank of the Thames, in many ways London begins with the Romans, who established the settlement of Londinium in AD 47 as an outpost of the Empire (before those pesky Celts, led by Queen Boudicca, returned and burnt it to the ground 17 years later). The Saxons came and stayed for a while, as did the Vikings, and by the time the Normans turned up in the 11th century, London was already established as the most important city in England. William the Conqueror began building the palace that was to become the Tower of London, which by Tudor times was known as the world's most forbidding prison, and where two of Henry VIII's six wives were executed. During the

Middle Ages, powerful guilds that nurtured commerce took root in the capital, followed by the foundation of great trading companies, such as the Honourable East India Company, which started up in 1600.

London's history has often been one of disaster and renewal. The Great Fire of 1666 spared only a few of the cramped, labyrinthine streets upon which the Great Plague had delivered such devastation the previous year. Yet the gutted wastelands ushered in an era of architectural renaissance, led by Sir Christopher Wren. Further punishment would come during the Blitz of World War II, when German bombers destroyed many buildings—but yet again London rebounded. As always.

manager's office. There's also a fine schedule of temporary exhibitions. ⊠ *London Wall, The City* ☎ *020/7001–9844* ⊕ *www.museumoflondon. org.uk* 🖼 *Free* ⊗ *Daily 10–6; last admission 5:30; galleries start to close 5:40* Ⓜ *Barbican, St. Paul's.*

Fodor's Choice   **St. Paul's Cathedral.**
★   *See the highlighted listing in this chapter.*

FAMILY   **Tower Bridge.** Despite its medieval, fairy-tale appearance, Britain's most
Fodor's Choice   iconic bridge was actually built at the tail end of the Victorian age,
★   first opening to traffic in 1894. Constructed of steel, then clothed in Portland stone, the Horace Jones masterpiece was built in the Gothic style that was highly popular at the time (and nicely complements the Tower of London, next door). The bridge is famous for its enormous bascules—the 1,200-ton "arms" that open to allow large ships to glide beneath. This still happens a few times per month (the website lists upcoming times), but when river traffic was dense, the bascules were raised about five times a day.

The **Tower Bridge Exhibition** is a family-friendly tour where you can discover how the bridge actually works before heading out onto the walkways for wonderful city views. First, take in the romance of the panoramas from the east and west walkways between those grand turrets. On the east are the modern superstructures of the Docklands, and on the west is the Tower of London, St. Paul's, the Monument, and the misshapen steel-and-glass egg that is Greater London Assembly's City Hall (famously described as "a glass testicle" by former mayor Ken Livingstone). Then it's back down to explore the Victorian engine rooms and

Continued on page 122

ST. PAUL'S CATHEDRAL

Sir Christopher Wren's maxim "I build for eternity" proves no empty boast.

Sublime, awesome, majestic, and inspirational are just some of the words to describe Wren's masterpiece, St. Paul's Cathedral—and thanks to a painstaking, recently-completed 15-year restoration project, it's now looking better than ever.

This is the spiritual heart of the nation, where people and events are celebrated, mourned, and honored. As you approach the cathedral your eyes are inevitably drawn skyward to the great dome, one of the largest in the world and an amazing piece of engineering. Visit in the late afternoon for evensong, and let the choir's voices transport you to a world of absolute peace in a place of perfect beauty, as pristine as the day it was completed.

TOURING ST. PAUL'S

Enter the cathedral via the main west entrance, and walk straight down the length of the nave to the central Dome Altar. Nobody can resist making a beeline for the dome, so start your tour beneath it, standing dead center on the beautiful sunburst floor, Wren's focal mirror of the magnificent design above. A simple quotation marks the floor "Lector si momentum requiris, circumspice" (Reader if you seek his monument, look around). The dome crowns the center of the cathedral and rises to 364 feet—but save your strength for the "great climb" to get some fantastic views.

THE CATHEDRAL FLOOR

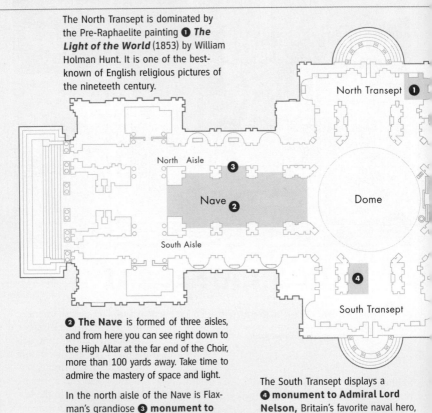

The North Transept is dominated by the Pre-Raphaelite painting **❶ The Light of the World** (1853) by William Holman Hunt. It is one of the best-known of English religious pictures of the nineteeth century.

North Transept ❶

North Aisle ❸

Nave ❷

Dome

South Aisle

❹

South Transept

❷ The Nave is formed of three aisles, and from here you can see right down to the High Altar at the far end of the Choir, more than 100 yards away. Take time to admire the mastery of space and light.

In the north aisle of the Nave is Flaxman's grandiose **❸ monument to the Duke of Wellington,** who sits astride his faithful charger, Copenhagen, the horse that carried him through the Battle of Waterloo.

The South Transept displays a **❹ monument to Admiral Lord Nelson,** Britain's favorite naval hero, with an anchor. Other memorials commemorate the explorer Captain Robert Scott and the darling of British landscape painting J.M.W. Turner.

CELEBRITY STATUS

St. Paul's has witnessed many momentous processions along its checkered nave. The somber state funerals of heroes Admiral Lord Nelson and the Duke of Wellington, and of Sir Winston Churchill, drew huge crowds. It was here, also, that the fairy-tale wedding of Prince Charles and Lady Diana Spencer took place, and the jubilees of Queen Victoria, George V, and the present Queen were celebrated.

The North Choir Aisle features the beautiful **5 gilded gates** by Jean Tijou, perhaps the most accomplished artist in wrought iron of all time, as well as Henry Moore's sculpture **6 *Mother and Child,*** its simple lines complementing the ornate surroundings.

North Choir Aisle

Choir (Quire)

Apse

South Choir Aisle

The South Choir Aisle contains a **7 marble effigy of poet John Donne,** who was Dean of old St. Paul's for his final 10 years (he died in 1631). This is the only statue to have survived the Great Fire of London intact. You can see the scorch marks at the base of the statue.

The Choir contains the **8 Bishop's Throne** or cathedra, hence the name cathedral. Look aloft to the fabulous mosaics. Don't miss the exquisite, delicate carvings by Grinling Gibbons, in particular on the case of the **9 grand organ,** one of the Cathedral's greatest artifacts. It was designed by Wren and played by such illustrious figures as Handel and Mendelssohn.

10 The High Altar, with its glorious canopy, is a profusion of marble and carved and gilded oak.

The Apse is home to the **11 American Memorial Chapel,** which honors the more than 28,000 U.S. soldiers who died while stationed in the U.K. during World War II. The lime-wood paneling incorporates a rocket as a tribute to the United States' achievements in space.

MUSICAL FRICTION

The organ, with its cherubs and angels, was not installed without controversy. The mighty instrument proved a tight fit, and the maker, known as Father Schmidt, and Wren nearly came to blows. Wren was reputed to have said he would not adapt his cathedral for a mere "box of whistles."

6

IN FOCUS ST. PAUL'S CATHEDRAL

THE DOME

The dome is the crowning glory of the cathedral, a must for visitors.

At 99 feet, the **❶ Whispering Gallery** is reached by 259 spiral steps. This is the part of the cathedral with which you bribe children—they will be fascinated by the acoustic phenomenon: whisper something to the wall on one side, and a second later it transmits clearly to the other side, 107 feet away. The only problem is identifying your whisper from the cacophony of everyone else's. Look down onto the nave from here and up to the monochrome frescoes of St. Paul by Sir James Thornhill.

More stamina is required to reach the **❷ Stone Gallery,** at 173 feet and 378 steps from ground level. It is on the exterior of the cathedral and offers a vista of the city and the River Thames.

For the best views of all—at 280 feet and 530 steps from ground level—make the trek to the small **❸ Golden Gallery,** the highest point of the outer dome. A hole in the floor gives a vertiginous view down. You can see the lantern above through a circular opening called the oculus. If you have a head for heights you can walk outside for a spectacular panorama of London.

The top of the dome is crowned with a **❹ ball and cross.** At 23 feet high and weighing approximately 7 tons, it is the pinnacle of St. Paul's.

A BRIEF HISTORY

The cathedral is the masterpiece of Sir Christopher Wren (1632–1723), completed in 1710 after 35 years of building and much argument with the Royal Commission. Wren had originally been commissioned to restore Old St. Paul's, the Norman cathedral that had replaced, in its turn, three earlier versions, but the Great Fire left so little of it standing that a new cathedral was deemed necessary.

Wren's first plan, known as the New Model, did not make it past the drawing board; the second, known as the Great Model, got as far as the 20-foot oak rendering you can see here today before it, too, was rejected, whereupon Wren is said to have burst into tears. The third, however, known as the Warrant Design (because it received the royal warrant), was accepted, with the fortunate coda that the architect be allowed to make changes as he saw fit. Without that, there would be no dome, because the approved design had featured a steeple. Parliament felt that building was proceeding too slowly (in fact, 35 years is lightning speed, as cathedrals go) and withheld half of Wren's pay for the last 13 years of work. He was pushing 80 when Queen Anne finally coughed up the arrears.

■ TIP→ To see Wren's Great Model, you must join a Triforium Tour (Mon. and Tues. at 11:30 and 2, Fri. at 2). These one-hour tours include a visit to the library and a glimpse of the famous Geometric staircase. The visit ends in the Trophy Room, where Wren's Great Model is on display. The tour costs £8 (in addition to admission to the Cathedral). It's best to book in advance by calling ☎ 020/7246-8357 or sending an e-mail to admissions@stpaulscathedral.org.uk.

THE CRYPT

A visit to the vast crypt is a time for reflection and contemplation, with some 200 memorials to see. If it all becomes too somber, take solace in the café or shop near the crypt entrance.

Here lies ❶ **Admiral Nelson,** killed at the Battle of Trafalgar in 1805. His body was preserved in alcohol for the journey home, and his pickled remains were buried here beneath Cardinal Wolsey's unused 16th-century sarcophagus.

The ❷ **tomb of the Duke of Wellington** comprises a simple casket made from Cornish granite. He is remembered as a hero of battle, but his name lives on in the form of boots, cigars, beef Wellington, and the capital of New Zealand.

Surrounded by his family and close to a plethora of iconic artists, musicians, and scientists, the ❸ **tomb of Sir Christopher Wren** is a modest simple slab.

The beautiful ❹ **O.B.E. Chapel** (dedicated 1960) is a symbol of the Order of the British Empire, an order of chivalry established in 1917 by George V. The theme of sovereign and Commonwealth is represented in the glass panels.

The vast ❺ **treasury** houses the cathedral's plate, although a good deal has been lost or stolen over the centuries—in particular in a daring robbery of 1810—and much of the display comes from other London churches.

6

IN FOCUS ST. PAUL'S CATHEDRAL

PLANNING YOUR DAY

WHAT'S NEARBY: Stroll over the Millennium Bridge (look back for a great view of St. Paul's) and have lunch at Tate Modern. The restaurant at the top of the gallery has spectacular views of London. ■ TIP→ To avoid lines visit early in the morning. For a different experience return for Evensong at 5 pm.

CONTACT INFO: ✉ St. Paul's Churchyard, Ludgate Hill EC4 8AD ☎ 020/7236–4128 ⊕ www.stpauls.co.uk Ⓤ St. Paul's.

ADMISSION: Adults: cathedral, crypt, ambulatory, and gallery £17 (includes multimedia guides and guided tours). **Family ticket** (2

adults, 2 children): £39. **Children 6–17:** £7.

TOURS: A guided tour of the cathedral, choir, Geometric staircase, and crypt lasts 1½–2 hours and is included in the price of admission (as are the multimedia guides). Tours start at 10, 11, 1, and 2.

HOURS: The cathedral is a house of worship. Services may cause changes to the visiting hours on any given day, so be sure to call ahead.

Cathedral: Mon.–Sat. 8:30–4.
Shop: Mon., Tues., Thurs.–Sat. 8:30–5, Wed. 9–5, Sun. 10–4:30.
Crypt café: Mon.–Sat. 9–5, Sun. 10–4.

discover the inner workings, which you learn about through hands-on displays and films. ✉ *Tower Bridge Rd., The City* ☎ *020/7403–3761* ⊕ *www.towerbridge.org.uk* ✆ *£8; combined ticket with Monument exhibition £9* ⊙ *Apr.–Sept., daily 10–6; Oct.–Mar., daily 9:30–5:30; last admission 30 mins before closing* Ⓜ *Tower Hill.*

A VIEW TO REMEMBER

At the top of the Monument's 311-step spiral staircase (think of it as the trip to the gym you didn't make that day) is a gallery providing fantastic views from the heart of The City. It is helpfully caged to prevent suicidal jumps, which were a trend for a while in the 19th century.

Fodor'sChoice
★

Tower of London.

See the highlighted listing in this chapter.

WORTH NOTING

Bank of England. The United Kingdom's main bank has been central to the British economy since 1694. Known for the past couple of centuries as "the Old Lady of Threadneedle Street," after the name appeared in a caption to a political cartoon (which can be seen in the museum), the bank manages the national debt and the foreign exchange reserves, issues banknotes, sets interest rates, looks after England's gold, and regulates the country's banking system. Sir John Soane designed the neoclassical hulk in 1788, wrapping it in windowless walls, which are all that survives of his original building. The bank's history is traced in the Bank of England Museum (the entrance is around the corner on Bartholomew Lane), where interactive exhibits chart the bank's more recent history and offer the chance to try your hand at controlling inflation. But most visitors still make a beeline for the solid-gold bar that can be stroked and held in the central trading hall—before you get any ideas, there's security everywhere. ✉ *Threadneedle St., The City* ☎ *020/7601–5545* ⊕ *www.bankofengland.co.uk* ✆ *Free* ⊙ *Weekdays and Lord Mayor's Show day (2nd Sat. in Nov.) 10–5; last admission 4:45* Ⓜ *Bank, Monument.*

Barbican Centre. The Barbican is an enormous 1980s concrete maze that Londoners either love or hate—but the importance of the complex to the cultural life of the capital is beyond dispute. It houses two theaters; the London Symphony Orchestra and its auditorium; the Guildhall School of Music and Drama; a major art gallery for changing exhibitions; two movie theaters; a convention center; an upscale restaurant, cafés, terraces with fountains, and bookshops; and living space in some of the most desirable apartments in The City. Navigation around the complex is via the yellow lines running, Wizard-of-Oz-like, along the floors, with signs on the walls, although it's still easy to get lost. Actors and audiences alike rate the theater for its excellent acoustics and sightlines. The lively and varied program encompasses all kinds of performance, including music, dance, theater, and film. ✉ *Silk St., The City* ☎ *020/7638–8891 box office* ⊕ *www.barbican.org.uk* ✆ *Barbican Centre free; prices for individual performances and exhibitions vary* ⊙ *Barbican Centre Mon.–Sat. 9 am–11 pm, Sun. and holidays noon–11; gallery Sat.–Wed. 10–6, Thurs. and Fri. 10–9* Ⓜ *Barbican, Moorgate.*

Interior of the "Inside-Out" Lloyd's of London building, designed by Richard Rogers Partnership

Dr. Johnson's House. Built in 1700, this elegant Georgian residence, with its paneled rooms and period furniture, is where Samuel Johnson lived between 1748 and 1759. The Great Bear (as he was affectionately known) compiled his *Dictionary of the English Language* in the attic as his health deteriorated. Two early editions are on view, among other mementos of Johnson and his friend, diarist, and later, his biographer, James Boswell. After soaking up the atmosphere, repair around the corner in Wine Office Court to the famed **Ye Olde Cheshire Cheese** pub (⇨ *See Chapter 16*), once Johnson and Boswell's favorite watering hole. ⊠ *17 Gough Sq., The City* ☎ *020/7353–3745* ⊕ *www. drjohnsonshouse.org* ⊒ *£4.50* ⊗ *May–Sept., Mon.–Sat. 11–5:30; Oct.–Apr., Mon.–Sat. 11–5* Ⓜ *Holborn, Chancery La., Temple.*

Guildhall. The Corporation of London, which oversees The City, has ceremonially elected and installed its Lord Mayor here for the last 800 years. The Guildhall was built in 1411, and though it failed to avoid the conflagrations of either 1666 or 1940, its core survived. The Great Hall is a psychedelic patchwork of coats of arms and banners of the City Livery Companies, which inherited the mantle of the medieval trade guilds. Tradesmen couldn't even run a shop without kowtowing to these prototypical unions, and their grand banqueting halls, the plushest private dining venues in The City, are testimony to the wealth they amassed. Inside the hall, Gog and Magog, the pair of mythical giants who founded ancient Albion and the city of New Troy, upon which London was said to be built, glower down from their west-gallery grandstand in 9-foot-high painted lime wood. The hall was also the site of famous trials, including that of Lady Jane

Grey in 1553, before her execution at the Tower of London. To the right of Guildhall Yard is the **Guildhall Art Gallery,** which includes portraits of the great and the good, cityscapes, famous battles, and a slightly cloying pre-Raphaelite section. The construction of the gallery in the 1980s led to the exciting discovery of London's only **Roman amphitheater,** which had lain underneath Guildhall Yard undisturbed for more than 1,800 years. It was excavated and now visitors can walk among the remains, although most of the relics can be seen at the Museum of London. ⊠ *Aldermanbury, The City* ☎ *020/7606–3030, 020/7332–3700 gallery* ⊕ *www.cityoflondon. gov.uk* ✉ *Free (fee for some gallery exhibitions)* ☉ *Hall Mon.–Sat. 9:30–5; gallery Mon.–Sat. 10–5, Sun. noon–4. Last admission ½ hr before closing. Sometimes closed for events; call to check* Ⓜ *St. Paul's, Moorgate, Bank, Mansion House.*

The Old Bailey. England and Wales don't allow cameras in courtrooms, so the only way to see a trial in action is to show up. The most high-profile ones usually happen here, at any of the 16 public courtrooms of the **Central Criminal Court** (universally known as "The Old Bailey"—a reference to the fact that it sits atop a section of the old London wall, or "bailey" in Medieval English). Oscar Wilde stood trial here for "gross indecency" (homosexuality) in 1895, but far darker souls than his have passed through these doors, including the nation's most notorious murderers, fraudsters, gangsters, and traitors. The day's proceedings are posted outside; there are security restrictions and children under 14 are not allowed. The Old Bailey was originally part of Newgate Prison, England's most feared *gaol* (jail) after the Tower, in use from the 12th century all the way to 1902. The present building dates from 1907. Note the 12-foot gilded statue of Justice perched on top; she's not, as is commonly thought, wearing a blindfold—her female form was thought by the Edwardians to imply virtue enough. ⊠ *Newgate St., The City* ☎ *020/7248–3277 information* ⊕ *www.cityoflondon.gov.uk* ✉ *Free* ☉ *Public galleries weekdays 10–1 and 2–5 (approximately). Line forms at Newgate St. entrance or in Warwick St. Passage; closed Mon. holidays and day after* Ⓜ *St. Paul's.*

St. Bartholomew the Great. This is one of London's oldest churches. Construction on the church and the hospital nearby was begun in 1123 by Henry I's favorite courtier, Rahere, who, surviving malaria, dedicated his life to serving the saint who had visited him in his fevered dreams. With the dissolution of the monasteries, Henry VIII had most of the place torn down; the Romanesque choir loft is all that survives from the 12th century. In recent times, this ancient church has become a bit of a movie star, having appeared in *The Other Boleyn Girl, Four Weddings and a Funeral,* and *Shakespeare in Love,* to name but a few. ⊠ *Cloth Fair, West Smithfield, The City* ☎ *020/7606–5171* ⊕ *www.greatstbarts.com* ✉ *Church £4 (free for prayer); photography £1* ☉ *Church weekdays 8:30–5, Sat. 10:30–4, Sun. 8:30–8. Museum Tues.–Fri. 10–4* Ⓜ *Barbican, Farringdon.*

Continued on page 132

THE TOWER OF LONDON

The Tower is a microcosm of the city itself—a sprawling, organic hodgepodge of buildings that inspires reverence and terror in equal measure. See the block on which Anne Boleyn was beheaded, marvel at the Crown Jewels, and pay homage to the ravens who keep the monarchy safe.

An architectural patchwork of time, the oldest building of the complex is the fairytale White Tower, conceived by William the Conqueror in 1078 as both a royal residence and a show of power to the troublesome Anglo-Saxons he had subdued at the Battle of Hastings. Today's Tower has seen everything, as a palace, barracks, a mint for producing coins, an armoury, and the Royal menagerie (home of the country's first elephant). The big draw is the stunning opulence of the Crown Jewels, kept onsite in the heavily fortified Jewel House. Most of all, though, the Tower is known for death: it's been a place of imprisonment, torture, and execution for the realm's most notorious traitors as well as its martyrs. These days, unless you count the killer admission fees, there are far less morbid activities taking place in the Tower, but it still breathes London's history and pageantry from its every brick and offers hours of exploration.

TOURING THE TOWER

Entry to the Tower is via the **Western Entrance** and the **Middle Tower,** which feed into the outermost ring of the Tower's defenses.

Water Lane leads past the dread-inducing **Traitors' Gate,** the final point of entry for many Tower prisoners.

Toward the end of Water Lane, the **Lanthorn Tower** houses by night the ravens rumored to keep the kingdom safe, and by day a timely high-tech recon-struction of the Catholic Guy Fawkes's plot to blow up the Houses of Parliament in 1605.

The **Bloody Tower** earned its name as the apocryphal site

of the murder of two young princes, Edward and Richard, who disappeared from the Tower after being put there in 1483 by their uncle, Rich-ard III. Two little skeletons (now in Westminster Abbey) were found buried close to the White Tower in 1674 and are thought to be theirs.

The **Beauchamp Tower** housed upper-class miscre-ants: Latin graffiti about Lady Jane Grey can be glimpsed today on its walls.

Like a prize gem set at the head of a royal crown, the **White Tower** is the center-piece of the complex. Its four towers dominate the Inner

GOLD DIGGER?

Keep your eyes peeled as you tour the Tower: accord-ing to one story, Sir John Barkstead, goldsmith and Lieutenant of the Tower under Cromwell, hid £20,000 in gold coins here before his arrest and execution at the Restoration of Charles II.

Ward, a fitting and forbidding reminder of Norman strength at the time of the conquest of England.

Once inside the White Tower, head upstairs for the **Armouries,** where the big-gest attraction, quite literally,

Jewel House, Waterloo Barracks

ROYAL BLING

The Crown of Queen Elizabeth, the Queen Mother, from 1937, contains the exotic 105-carat Koh-i-Noor (mountain of light) diamond.

TIME KILLERS

Some prisoners managed to keep themselves plenty amused: Sir Walter Raleigh grew tobacco on Tower Green, and in 1561 suspected sorcerer Hugh Draper carved an intricate astronomical clock on the walls of his Salt Tower cell.

is the suit of armor worn by a well-endowed Henry VIII. There is a matching outfit for his horse.

Other fascinating exhibits include the set of Samurai armor presented to James I in 1613 by the emperor of Japan, and the tiny set of armor worn by Henry VIII's young son Edward.

The **Jewel House** in Waterloo Block is the Tower's biggest draw, perfect for playing pick-your-favorite-crown from the wrong side of bul-

letproof glass. Not only are these crowns, staffs, and orbs encrusted with heavy-duty gems, they are invested with the authority of monarchical power in England, dating back to the 1300s.

Outside, pause at **Tower Green,** permanent departure point for those of noble birth. The hoi polloi were dispatched at nearby Tower Hill. The Tower's most famous female victims—Anne Boleyn, Margaret Countess of Salisbury, Catherine Howard, and Lady Jane Grey—all went this "priviledged" way.

Behind a well-kept square of grass stands the **Chapel Royal of St. Peter ad Vincula,** a delightful Tudor church and final resting place of six beheaded Tudor bodies. ■TIP→ Visitors are welcome for services and can also enter after 4:30 pm daily.

The **Salt Tower,** reputedly the most haunted corner of the complex, marks the start of the **Wall Walk,** a bracing promenade along the stone spiral steps and battlements of the Tower that looks down on the trucks, taxis, and shimmering high-rises of modern London.

The Wall Walk ends at the **Martin Tower,** former home of the Crown Jewels and now host to the crowns and diamonds exhibition that explains the art of fashioning royal headwear and tells the story of some of the most famous stones.

On leaving the Tower, browse the **gift shop,** and wander the wharf that overlooks the Thames, leading to a picture-postcard view of Tower Bridge.

WHO ARE THE BEEFEATERS?

First of all, they're Yeoman Warders, but probably got the nickname "beefeater" from their position as Royal Bodyguards which entitled them to eat as much beef as they liked. Part of the "Yeoman of the Guard," started in the reign of Edmund IV, the warders have formed the Royal Bodyguard as far back as 1509 when Henry VIII left a dozen of the Yeoman of the Guard at the Tower to protect it.

Originally, the Yeoman Warders also served as jailers of the Tower, doubling as torturers when necessary. (So it would have been a Beefeater tightening the thumb screws, or ratchetting the rack another notch on some unfortunate prisoner. Smile nicely.) Today 36 Yeoman Warders (men and women since 2007), along with the Chief Yeoman Warder and the Yeoman Gaoler, live within the walls of the Tower with their families, in accommodations in the Outer Ward. They stand guard over the Tower, conduct tours, and lock up at 9:53 pm every night with the Ceremony of the Keys.

■ TIP➔ Free tickets to the Ceremony of the Keys are available by writing several months in advance; check the Tower Web site for details.

HARK THE RAVENS!

Legend has it that should the hulking black ravens ever leave, the White Tower will crumble and the kingdom fall. Charles II, no doubt jumpy after his father's execution and the monarchy's short-term fall from grace, made a royal decree in 1662 that there should be at least six of the carrion-eating nasties present at all times. There have been some close calls. During World War II, numbers dropped to one, echoing the precarious fate of the war-wracked country. In 2005, two (of eight) died over Christmas when Thor—the most intelligent but also the largest bully of the bunch—killed new recruit Gundolf, named after the Tower's 1070 designer. Pneumonia put an end to Bran, leaving lifelong partner Branwen without her mate.

■ DID YOU KNOW? In 1981 a raven named Grog, perhaps seduced by his alcoholic moniker, escaped after 21 years at the Tower. Others have been banished for "conduct unbecoming."

The six that remain, each one identified by a colored band around a claw, are much loved for their fidelity (they mate for life) and their cheek (capable of 440 noises, they are witty and scolding mimics). It's not only the diet of blood-soaked biscuits, rabbit, and scraps from the mess kitchen that keeps them coming back. Their lifting feathers on one wing are trimmed, meaning they can manage the equivalent of a lop-sided air-bound hobble but not much more. For the first half of 2006 the ravens were moved indoors full-time as a preventive measure against avian flu but have since been allowed out and about again. In situ they are a territorial lot, sticking to Tower Green and the White Tower, and lodging nightly by Wakefield Tower. They've had free front-row seats at all the most grisly moments in Tower history—Anne Boleyn's execution included.

■ TIP➔ Don't get too close to the ravens: they are prone to pecking and not particularly fond of humans, unless you are the Tower's Raven Master.

And *WHAT* are they wearing?

A **pike** (or halberd), also known as a partisan, is the Yeoman Warder's weapon of choice. The Chief Warder carries a staff topped with a miniature silver model of the White Tower.

Anyone who refers to this as a costume will be lucky to leave the Tower with head still attached to body: this is the ceremonial uniform of the Yeoman Warders, and it comes at a cool £13,000 a throw.

This **Tudor-style ruff** helps date the ceremonial uniform, which was first worn in 1552.

The black Tudor **bonnet** is made of velvet; the blue undress consists of a felt top hat, with a single Tudor rose in the middle.

Insignia on a Yeoman Warder's upper right arm denote the rank he carried in the military.

The **medals** on a Yeoman Warder's chest are more than mere show: all of the men and women have served for at least 22 years in the armed forces.

This version of the **royal livery** bears the insignia of the current Queen ("E" for Elizabeth) but originally dates from Tudor times. The first letter changes according to the reigning monarch's Christian name; the second letter is always an "R" for *rex* (king) or *regina* (queen).

Slits in the **tunic** date from the times when Beefeaters were expected to ride a horse.

Red socks and **black patent shoes** are worn on special occasions. Visitors are more likely to see the regular blue undress, introduced in 1858 as the regular working dress of the Yeoman Warders.

The **red lines down the trousers** are a sign of the blood from the swords of the Yeoman Warders in their defense of the realm.

(IN)FAMOUS PRISONERS OF THE TOWER

Anne Boleyn   Lady Jane Grey   Sir Walter Raleigh

Sir Thomas More. A Catholic and Henry VIII's friend and chancellor, Sir Thomas refused to attend the coronation of Anne Boleyn (Henry VIII's second wife) or to recognize the multi-marrying king as head of the Church. Sent to the Tower for treason, in 1535 More was beheaded.

Anne Boleyn. The first of Henry VIII's wives to be beheaded, Anne, who failed to provide the king with a son, was accused of sleeping with five men, including her own brother. All six got the chop in 1536. Her severed head was held up to the crowd, and her lips were said to be mouthing prayer.

Margaret, Countess of Salisbury. Not the best-known prisoner in her lifetime, she has a reputation today for haunting the Tower. And no wonder: the elderly 70-year-old was condemned by Henry VIII in 1541 for a potentially treacherous bloodline (she was the last Plantagenet princess) and hacked to death by the executioner after she refused to put her head on the block like a common traitor and attempted to run away.

Queen Catherine Howard. Henry VIII's fifth wife was locked up for high treason and infidelity and beheaded in 1542 at age 20. Ever eager to please, she spent her final night practicing how to lay her head on the block.

Lady Jane Grey. The nine-days-queen lost her head in 1554 at age 16. Her death was the result of sibling rivalry gone seriously wrong, when Protestant Edward VI slighted his Catholic sister Mary in favor of Lady Jane as heir, and Mary decided to have none of it.

Guy Fawkes. The Roman Catholic soldier who tried to blow up the Houses of Parliament and kill the king in the 1605 Gunpowder plot was first incarcerated in the chambers of the Tower, where King James I requested he be tortured in ever-worsening ways. Perhaps unsurprisingly, he confessed. He met his seriously grisly end in the Old Palace Yard at Westminster, where he was hung, drawn, and quartered in 1607.

Sir Walter Raleigh. Once a favorite of Elizabeth I, he offended her by secretly marrying her Maid of Honor and was chucked in the Tower. Later, as a conspirator against James I, he paid with his life. A frequent visitor to the Tower (he spent 13 years there in three stints), he managed to get the Bloody Tower enlarged on account of his wife and growing family. He was finally executed in 1618 in Old Palace Yard, Westminster.

Josef Jakobs. The last man to be executed in the Tower was caught as a spy when parachuting in from Germany and executed by firing squad in 1941. The chair he sat in when he was shot is preserved in the Royal Armouries' artifacts store.

FOR FURTHER EVIDENCE . . .

A trio of buildings in the Inner Ward, the **Bloody Tower, Beauchamp Tower,** and **Queen's House,** all with excellent views of the execution scaffold in Tower Green, are the heart of the Tower's prison accommodations and home to a permanent exhibition about notable inmates.

TACKLING THE TOWER (without losing your head)

✉ H.M. Tower of London, Tower Hill
☎ 0844/482-7777/7799 ⊕ www.hrp.org.uk
🎫 Adult: £22, children under 16: £11, Family tickets (2 adults, 2 children): £58, children under 5, free. ⏱ Mar.–Oct., Tues.–Sat. 9–5:30, Sun. and Mon. 10–5:30; last admission at 5. Nov.–Feb., Tues.–Sat. 9–4:30, Sun. and Mon. 10–4:30; last admission at 4 Ⓤ Tower Hill

■ TIP➜ You can buy tickets from automatic kiosks on arrival, or up to seven days in advance at any Tube station. Avoid lines completely by booking by telephone (0844 482 7777/7799 weekdays 9–5), or online.

MAKING THE MOST OF YOUR TIME: Without doubt, the Tower is worth two to three hours. A full hour of that would be well spent by joining one of the Yeoman Warders' tours (included in admission). It's hard to better their insight, vitality, and humor—they are knights of the realm living their very own fairytale castle existence.

The Crown Jewels are worth the wait, the White Tower is essential, and the Medieval Palace and Bloody Tower should at least be breezed through.

■ TIP➜ It's best to visit on weekdays, when the crowds are smaller.

WITH KIDS: The Tower's centuries-old cobblestones are not exactly stroller-friendly, but strollers are permitted inside most of the buildings. If you do bring one, be prepared to leave it temporarily unsupervised (the stroller, that is—not your child) outside the White Tower, which has no access. There are baby-changing facilities in the Brick Tower restrooms behind the Jewel House. Look for regular free children's events such as the Knight's school where children can have a go at jousting, sword-fighting, and archery.

■ TIP➜ Tell your child to find one of the Yeoman Warders if he or she should get lost; they will in turn lead him or her to the Byward Tower, which is where you should meet.

IN A HURRY? If you have less than an hour, head down Wall Walk, through a succession of towers, which eventually spit you out at the Martin Tower. The view over modern London is quite a contrast.

TOURS: Tours given by a Yeoman Warder leave from the main entrance near Middle Tower every half-hour from 10–4, and last about an hour. Beefeaters give occasional 30-minute talks in the Lanthorn Tower about their daily lives. Both tours are free. Check website for talks and workshops

6

IN FOCUS THE TOWER OF LONDON

St. Bride's. According to legend, the distinctively tiered steeple of this Christopher Wren–designed church gave rise to the shape of the traditional wedding cake. One early couple inspired to marry here were the parents of Virginia Dare, the first European child born in colonial America in 1587. As St. Paul's (in Covent Garden) is the actors' church, so St. Bride's belongs to journalists, many of whom have been buried or memorialized here. By 1664 the crypts were so crowded that diarist Samuel Pepys, who was baptized here, had to bribe the gravedigger to "justle together" some bodies to make room for his deceased brother. Now the crypts house a museum of the church's rich history, and a bit of Roman sidewalk. Ninety-minute guided tours are held on some Tuesday afternoons (check website for dates). ⊠ *Fleet St., The City* ☎ *020/7427–0133* ⊕ *www.stbrides.com* ✉ *Free; guided tours £6* ⊙ *Weekdays 9–6, Sat. hrs vary (call to confirm), Sun. 10–6:30; tours Tues. at 3* Ⓜ *St. Paul's, Blackfriars.*

> **SUMMER FESTIVAL**
>
> Every year, for four weeks in June and July, the **City of London Festival** (⊕ *www.colf.org*) features numerous walks, dances, and street art, and you can see concerts that are held in buildings not usually open to the public.

St. Mary-le-Bow. Various versions of this church have stood on the site since the 11th century. In 1284 a local goldsmith took refuge here after committing a murder, only to be killed inside by enraged relatives of his victim. The church was abandoned for a time afterward, but was rebuilt as its current form by Sir Christopher Wren after the Great Fire. This 1673 incarnation has a tall steeple (in The City, only St. Bride's is taller) and one of the most famous sets of bells in England—technically, a Londoner must be born within the sound of the "Bow Bells" to be a true Cockney. The origin of that idea may have been the curfew rung on the bells during the 14th century. The Bow takes its name from the bow-shaped arches in the Norman crypt. The church was rebuilt again after severe bomb damage in World War II. The garden contains a statue of local boy Captain John Smith, who founded Virginia in 1606 and was later captured by Native Americans. ⊠ *Cheapside, The City* ☎ *020/7248–5139* ⊕ *www.stmarylebow.co.uk* ⊙ *Mon.–Wed. 7:30–6, Thurs. 7:30–6:30, Fri. 7:30–4* Ⓜ *Mansion House, St. Paul's.*

QUICK BITES

Café Below. In St. Mary-le-Bow's Norman crypt, this café is packed with City workers weekdays from 7:30 am until 2:30 pm for a menu covering breakfasts, scrumptious light lunches, and delicious cakes. ⊠ *Cheapside, The City* ☎ *020/7329–0789* ⊕ *www.cafebelow.co.uk* Ⓜ *Mansion House, St Paul's.*

EAST LONDON

GETTING ORIENTED

East London

TOP REASONS TO GO

Dennis Severs's House by candlelight: The atmospheric set-pieces in this Georgian town house use visuals, sounds, and aromas to evoke the lives of its fictional previous inhabitants.

Eat artisanal at Broadway Market: Check out the more than 100 artisanal food stalls purveying everything from cheeses to oysters at Broadway Market on Saturday.

Check out London's hottest art scene: Edgy galleries mix with large collections.

Trace the footsteps of Jack the Ripper: Track Britain's most infamous serial killer through the former Victorian slum streets of East London.

Peek into the lives of Londoners at the Geffrye Museum of the Home: This former almshouse showcases middle-class domestic interiors over the centuries.

FEELING PECKISH?

Lucky Chip. Once a food truck, Lucky Chip is now in the Seabright Arms pub between Columbia Road and the Broadway Market. Satisfying food is served on paper plates. ✉ *Seabright Arms, 31–35 Coate St., Hackney* ⊕ *www.lucky-chip.co.uk* ⌕ *Reservations not accepted* Ⓜ *Bethnal Green.*

Poppies of Spitalfields. With retro-diner decor and efficient service, this joint serves fish-and-chips (fresh from Billingsgate Market), and free-range grilled chicken. ✉ *6–8 Hanbury St., Spitalfields* ☎ *0207/247–0892* ⊕ *www.poppiesfishandchips.co.uk.*

SAFETY

Around Shoreditch, Spitalfields, and Brick Lane, streets are largely safe during daylight hours. Be cautious on the less gentrified streets of Whitechapel, Bethnal Green, and Hackney at night.

GETTING THERE

The London Overground, with stops at Shoreditch High Street, Hoxton, Whitechapel, Dalston Kingsland, and Hackney Central, is the easiest way to reach East London. Alternatively, the best Tube stations to use are Old Street on the Northern line, Bethnal Green on the Central line, and Liverpool Street on the Metropolitan and Circle lines.

MAKING THE MOST OF YOUR TIME

To experience East London at its most lively, visit on the weekend. Spitalfields Market bustles all weekend, while Brick Lane and Columbia Road are best on a Sunday morning and Broadway Market on Saturday. If you're planning to explore East London's art galleries, pick up a free map at the Whitechapel Art Gallery. As for the area's booming nightlife scene, there's no time limit.

GUIDED TOURS

The 2½-hour **Jack the Ripper Secret London Tour** (⊕ *london-premierwalkingtours.co.uk*), departs from Aldwych Tube station on Tuesday, Wednesday, and Friday at 6:30, Saturday at 6, and Sunday at 1:30. **Street Art London** (⊕ *streetartlondon.co.uk*) offers two- and four-hour walking tours of East London's street art on Tuesday at 10 am and weekends at 11 am.

7

Sightseeing
★★★
Nightlife
★★★★★
Dining
★★★★
Lodging
★
Shopping
★★★★

Made famous by Dickens and infamous by Jack the Ripper, East London is one of London's most enduringly evocative neighborhoods, rich in popular history, architectural gems, and artists' studios. Since the early 1990s, hip gallerists, designers, and new-media entrepreneurs have colonized its handsome Georgian buildings and converted industrial lofts. Today, the collection of neighborhoods that makes up East London lays claim to being the city's most trendsetting neighborhoods.

Updated by
Ellin Stein

The British equivalent of Brooklyn, East London is a patchwork of districts encompassing struggling artists, ethnic enclaves, upscale professionals, and the digerati, occasionally teetering, like its New York equivalent, on the edge of self-parody. The vast area ranges from gentrified districts like Spitalfields—where bankers and successful artists live in desirable renovated Georgian town houses—to parts of Hackney where seemingly derelict, graffiti-covered industrial buildings are hives of exciting creative activity. As with all neighborhoods in transition, it can be a little rough around the edges, so stick to busier streets at night.

At the start of the new millennium, Hoxton, an enclave of Shoreditch, became the glossy hub of London's buzzing contemporary art scene, which accelerated the gentrification process. Some artists, such as Tracey Emin and Gilbert & George, long-term residents of Spitalfields' handsome Georgian terraces (and successful enough to still afford the area), have remained.

One such residence, **Dennis Severs's House,** was transformed two decades ago by American artist Severs into a unique "living house museum" that evokes how past generations of a fictional Huguenot family might have lived there. Not far away, Spitalfields Market offers an ever-changing selection of crafts and funky clothes stalls located under a glass roof in what was once a Victorian produce market. Across from the market, **Christ Church, Spitalfields,** Nicholas Hawkmoor's masterpiece, soars above Fournier Street.

EAST END STREET SMARTS

Brick Lane and the narrow streets running off it offer a paradigm of East London's development. Its population has moved in waves: communities seeking refuge, others moving out in an upwardly mobile direction.

Brick Lane has seen the manufacture of bricks (during the 16th century), beer, and bagels, but nowadays it's primarily known as the heart of Banglatown—Bangladeshis make up one-third of the population in this London borough, and you'll see that the names of the surrounding streets are written in Bengali—where you find many kebab and curry houses along with shops selling videos, colorful saris, and stacks of sticky sweets. On Sunday morning the entire street becomes pedestrianized. Shops and cafés are open, and several stalls are set up, creating a companion market to the one on nearby **Petticoat Lane.**

Fournier Street contains fine examples of the neighborhood's characteristic Georgian terraced houses, many of them built by the richest of the early-18th-century Huguenot silk weavers (note the enlarged windows on the upper floors). Most of those along the north side of Fournier Street have been restored, but some still contain textile sweatshops—only now the workers are Bengali.

Wilkes Street, with more 1720s Huguenot houses, is north of the Christ Church, Spitalfields, and neighboring **Princelet Street** was once important to East London's Jewish community. Where No. 6 stands now, the first of several thriving Yiddish theaters opened in 1886. **Elder Street,** just off Folgate, is another gem of original 18th-century houses. On the south and east side of Spitalfields Market are yet more time-warp streets that are worth a wander, such as **Gun Street,** where artist Mark Gertler (1891–1939) lived at No. 32.

7

In the last decade, the streets around the Old Street roundabout (as well as converted warehouses in Hackney and Dalston) have flourished with start-ups, with attendant stylish boutiques (especially on Redchurch Street), destination restaurants, and hipster bars as part of a government initiative to attract IT oriented businesses to the neighborhood. Old and new Shoreditch meet on **Brick Lane,** the heart of the Bangladeshi community, lined with innumerable curry houses and glittering sari shops, plus vintage clothing emporia. Here you'll also find the **Old Truman Brewery,** an East London landmark converted into a warren of street fashion and pop-up galleries. On Sunday, the Columbia Road Flower Market to the north of Brick Lane becomes a colorful, fragrant oasis of greenery.

As property prices have climbed, up-and-coming artists have sought more affordable studio spaces in former industrial buildings eastward toward Whitechapel and Bethnal Green, where there are also some notable galleries. Here you'll find the **V&A Museum of Childhood,** a delight for children of all ages, and, a design connoisseur's favorite, the **Geffrye Museum,** a collection of domestic interiors that occupies a row of early-18th-century almshouses.

Probably the best start to an East London tour is via the London Over-ground, getting off at the Shoreditch High Street station. Immediately northwest of the station, on the west side of Shoreditch High Street, is the heart of the neighborhood that aspires to be the U.K. equivalent to Silicon Valley. To the northeast is Shoreditch's boutique, gallery, and restaurant zone. The sub-neighborhood of Hoxton is located just above Shoreditch, north of the Old Street roundabout. To the southeast of the station are the handsome Georgian streets of Spitalfields. Bethnal Green is due east, past lively Brick Lane. Whitechapel, formerly Jack the Rip-per's patch, is to the south of Spitalfields. All of these neighborhoods are within what is traditionally referred to as the "East End," although East London extends farther to the North and East.

TOP ATTRACTIONS

Broadway Market. This parade of shops in hipster-centric Hackney (located north of Regent's Canal) is worth visiting for the specialist bookshops, independent boutiques, organic cafés, neighborhood restaurants, and even a traditional (but now rare) pie-and-mash shop. But wait for Satur-day, between 9 and 5, when it really comes into its own with a farmers' market and more than 100 food stalls rivaling those of south London's famed Borough Market. Artisanal breads, cheeses, chocolates, organic meats, produce, oysters, smoked salmon, and ethnic offerings: this is foodie heaven. There are also stalls selling vintage clothes, handmade instruments, and more. ⊠ *Broadway Market, Hackney* ☎ *0787/246–3409* ⊕ *www.broadwaymarket.co.uk* Ⓜ *Bethnal Green.*

Fodor'sChoice
★
Columbia Road Flower Market. On Sunday mornings this largely built-up area is transformed into a riot of color and scent as the Columbia Road Flower Market sells everything from bedding plants to banana trees, including herbs, cut flowers, and bouquets at very reasonable prices. The vendors' patter is part of the fun. Columbia Road itself is lined with some 60 independent shops, so you can pick up some art, antiques, handcrafted jewelry, or, of course, garden accessories to go with your greenery. ⊠ *Columbia Rd., Hackney* ☎ *020/7613–0876* ⊕ *www.columbiaroad.info* ◷ *Sun. 8–3* Ⓜ *Old St., Northern Line.*

Fodor'sChoice
★
Dennis Severs' House. The remarkable interiors of this extraordinary time machine of a house are the creation of Dennis Severs (1948–99), a per-former-designer-scholar from Escondido, California, who dedicated his life to restoring this Georgian terraced house. More than that, he created "still-life dramas" using sight, sound, and smell to evoke the world of a fictitious family of Huguenot silk weavers, the Jervises, who might have inhabited the house between 1728 and 1914. Each of the 10 rooms has a distinctive, compelling atmosphere that encourages visitors to become lost in another time, deploying evocative design details like rose-laden Victorian wallpaper, Jacobean paneling, Georgian wing chairs, Baroque carved ornaments, rich "Catholic" wall colors downstairs, and more sedate "Protestant" shades upstairs. ∎TIP➜ The "Silent Night" can-dlelight tour offered each Monday and Wednesday evening, a silent stroll concluding with champagne by the fire, is the most theatrical and memorable way to experience the house. Private individual Silent Night tours are available one night per month, and private group visits can also be arranged. ⊠ *18 Folgate St., Spitalfields* ☎ *020/7247–4013*

⊕ www.dennissevershouse.co.uk
🖅 £10 Sun., £7 Mon., £14 Mon.
and Wed. evenings ☉ Sun. noon–4
(last admission 3:15); 1st and 3rd
Mon. noon–2 (last admission 1:15);
Mon. and Wed. 6–9 (last admission
8; reservations essential) Ⓜ Overground: Shoreditch High St.

FOR SHOP-TILL-YOU-DROPPERS

One of the delights of exploring East London is coming across
intimate, tucked-away specialty
shops, but for clusters of interesting boutiques it's best to head to
these addresses: Redchurch Street,
Hanbury Street, Cheshire Street,
and Boxpark.

Fodor's Choice
★
Geffrye Museum of the Home. In contrast to the West End's grand aristocratic town houses, this charming
museum is devoted to the life of the
city's middle class over the years.
Originally a row of almshouses built in 1714 by Sir Robert Geffrye,
a former Lord Mayor of London, it contains a series of 11 period
rooms that re-create everyday domestic interiors from the Elizabethan
period through the 1950s to the present day. One of the almshouses
has been restored to its original condition to offer a glimpse into how
the poor and the dependent elderly lived in previous centuries (to visit
the almshouse you must go as part of a tour, which is offered at 11,
noon, 2, and 3 on specific days each month; check website). Outside,
a series of period gardens charts the evolution of the town garden over
the past 400 years, and next to them is a walled herb garden. The
museum's extension wing houses the 20th-century galleries, a lovely
café overlooking the gardens, and a shop. ⊠ 136 Kingsland Rd., Hoxton ☎ 020/7739–9893 ⊕ www.geffrye-museum.org.uk 🖅 Free (charge
for special exhibitions); almshouse £2.50 ☉ Tues.–Sun. 10–5; gardens:
Apr. 1–Oct. 31 ☉ Closed Mon. (except holidays) Ⓜ Old St., then Bus
243; Liverpool St., then Bus 149 or 242. Overground: Hoxton.

Old Spitalfields Market. An impressive piece of architecture in itself, this
large restored Victorian market hall (covered by a glass canopy) is one-
part bazaar and one-part food court. The main market days are Thursday
through Sunday, with a notable antiques markets on Thursday and a
fashion and art market on Friday (plus, on every first and third Friday and
second Saturday, a record fair; and a vintage fair every first Saturday of
the month), as well as markets on other days selling goods ranging from
handmade clothes to toys, hats, and jewelry. While some of the quality is
pedestrian, you can also find interesting clothes, accessories, and leather
goods by new designers. The adjoining brick market building houses
upscale shops. ■ TIP➔ The nearer the weekend, the busier it all gets. ⊠ 16
Horner Sq., Spitalfields ☎ 020/7375–2963 ⊕ www.oldspitalfieldsmarket.
com 🖅 Free ☉ Shops daily 10–7; market stalls Mon.–Wed. 10–5, Thurs.
and Sun. 9–5, Fri. 10–4, Sat. 11–4 Ⓜ Liverpool St.

FAMILY
Fodor's Choice
★
V&A Museum of Childhood. A treat for children of all ages, this East
London outpost of the Victoria & Albert Museum—in an iron, glass,
and brown-brick building transported here from South Kensington in
1868—houses one of the world's biggest toy collections. One highlight
is the Dolls' Houses collection with interiors from 1673 up to the present. The collection is organized into galleries: Moving Toys, which
includes everything from rocking horses to Xboxes; Creativity, which

7

encompasses dolls, puppets, chemistry sets, play kitchens, construction toys, and musical instruments; and Childhood, with areas devoted to babies, an exhibit of children's clothes from the mid-1600s to the present, and toys inspired by adult pursuits, such as toy soldiers, toy guns, and toy hospitals. Don't miss the18th-century *commedia dell'arte* puppet theater, thought to have been made in Venice. There are activities for the under-fives and the shop sells replica toys. ⊠ *Cambridge Heath Rd., Bethnal Green* ☎ *020/8983–5200* ⊕ *www.museumofchildhood. org.uk* ☒ *Free* ☉ *Daily 10–5:45* Ⓜ *Bethnal Green.*

Fodor's Choice   **Whitechapel Art Gallery.** Founded in 1901, this internationally renowned
★   gallery mounts shows that rediscover overlooked masters and exhibits tomorrow's legends today. Painter and leading exponent of abstract expressionism, Jackson Pollock was exhibited here in the 1950s as was pop notable Robert Rauschenberg in the 1960s; the 1970s saw a young David Hockney's first solo show. The exhibitions continue to be on the cutting edge of contemporary art. The gallery also hosts talks, film screenings, workshops, and other events. Pick up a free East London art map to help you plan your visit to the area. ⊠ *77–82 Whitechapel High St., Whitechapel* ☎ *020/7522–7888* ⊕ *www.whitechapelgallery. org* ☒ *Free, charge for some special exhibits* ☉ *Tues., Wed., and Fri.– Sun. 11–6; Thurs. 11–9* Ⓜ *Aldgate East.*

WORTH NOTING

Fodor's Choice   **Christ Church, Spitalfields.** This is the 1729 masterpiece of Sir Chris-
★   topher Wren's associate Nicholas Hawksmoor, one of his six London churches and an example of English baroque at its finest. It was commissioned as part of Parliament's 1711 "Fifty New Churches" Act, passed in response to the influx of immigrants with the idea of providing for the religious needs of the "godless thousands"—actually, to ensure they joined the Church of England as opposed to such nonconformist denominations as the Protestant Huguenots. (It must have worked; you can still see gravestones with epitaphs in French in the crypt.) As the local silk industry declined, the church fell into disrepair, and by 1958 the structure was crumbling, with the looming prospect of demolition. But after 25 years—longer than it took to build the church—and a huge local fund-raising effort, the structure was meticulously restored and is a joy to behold, from the colonnaded Doric portico and tall spire to its soaring, heavily ornamented plaster ceiling. Its excellent acoustics make is a superb concert venue. Tours that take you "backstage" to the many hidden rooms and passages, from the tower to the vaults, are offered by appointment. ■TIP➔ **Don't miss the chance to attend one of the classical concerts held year-round in this atmospheric ecclesiastical venue.** ⊠ *Commercial St., Spitalfields* ☎ *020/7377–6793* ⊕ *www.ccspitalfields.org* ☒ *Free, tours £6* ☉ *Weekdays 10–4 (may be closed for event; call for info), Sun. 1–4* Ⓜ *Overground: Shoreditch High St.*

Kate MacGarry Gallery. Located on what was once one of the worst slum streets in London, this achingly contemporary gallery space (MacGarry's third in the East End—she's been here since 2002) has an excellent reputation for its shows of cutting-edge international artists like Chicks on Speed, Luke Rudolf, and Iain Forsythe & Jane Pollard, with

CLOSE UP

Banksy and The East End Art Scene

Banksy, the Bristol-based artist and provocateur who has maintained his anonymity despite now commanding six-figure prices, is widely credited with making Londoners see street art as more than vandalism. His work can be seen in various locations around the city, from Ladbroke Grove to Fitzrovia to Bemondsey, but he is primarily associated with the East End, where he first came to public attention in the late '80s, and which continues to be an important open-air exhibition space for new talent from around the world. Unfortunately, much of Banksy's early work has been lost, either from being covered over by local councils and building owners, defaced by other graffiti artists, or removed by profiteers. As of this writing, murals remain at Polland Street near Bethnal Green, Rivington Street near Old Street, and Stoke Newington Church Street. Shoreditch Street Art Tours (⊕ www. shoreditchstreetarttours.co.uk/) offers a knowledgeable view, guiding you not only to the remaining Banksy works but also highlighting the best of his successors.

Today, East London is a global hotbed of contemporary art, however, its avant-garde roots go way back. Shoreditch's cheap industrial units and Georgian–Victorian terraced streets have attracted artists since the 1960s, when op-art pioneer Bridget Riley established a service to find affordable studio space for her contemporaries. In the early '90s it gained new notoriety when Young British Artists Sarah Lucas and Tracey Emin began selling their own and their friends' work in The Shop, joining Maureen Paley's influential Bethnal Green gallery, and the long-established Whitechapel Art Gallery, where many leading abstract expressionists and Pop artists had their first U.K. shows. Hoxton truly became a destination for well-heeled collectors when Jay Jopling, the most important modern-art dealer in town, set up his White Cube gallery in 2000 (it's now relocated to Bermondsey), followed by Kate MacGarry's gallery in 2002.

Priced out by the area's fashionability, the emerging artists themselves have relocated farther off the beaten track to edgier neighborhoods such as Hackney and Dalston, with several trendsetting galleries found clustered around Cambridge Heath Road and Vyner Street.

a particular emphasis on conceptual works and video. ⊠ *27 Old Nichol St., Shoreditch* ☎ *020/7613–0515* ⊕ *www.katemacgarry.com* 💷 *Free* ⊙ *Wed.–Sat. 10–6* Ⓜ *Overground: Shoreditch High Street.*

Maureen Paley Gallery. Inspired by the DIY punk aesthetic and the funky galleries of New York's Lower East Side, Maureen Paley started putting on exhibitions in her East End home back in 1984, when it was virtually the only gallery in the area. Since then this American artist and gallerist has shown such respected contemporary artists as Gillian Wearing, Helen Chadwick, Jenny Holzer, Peter Fischli, and Wolfgang Tillmans and, today, is considered the doyenne of East End gallerists. The gallery has been in its current home, a converted warehouse in Bethnal Green, since 1999. ⊠ *21 Herald St., Bethnal Green* ☎ *020/7729–4112* ⊕ *www. maureenpaley.com* ⊙ *Wed.–Sun. 11–6* Ⓜ *Bethnal Green.*

On Sunday, additional clothing and crafts stalls surround Spitalfields covered market.

Old Truman Brewery. The last East End brewery still standing—a handsome example of Georgian and 19th-century industrial architecture, and in late Victorian times the largest brewery in the world—has been transformed into a hipster mall housing galleries, record shops, boutiques, clubs, and restaurants, along with an array of street-food vendors. The retailers are at street level with offices on the upper floors. Events include fashion shows, sample sales, art installations, and, on weekends, a food hall and a vintage clothes fair. The Vibe Bar is a hot spot to chill out behind a traditional Georgian facade—it also has a great outdoor space. ⊠ *91 Brick La., Spitalfields* ☎ *0207/770–6000* ⊕ *www.trumanbrewery.com* Ⓜ *Overground: Shoreditch High St.*

Royal London Hospital Museum. Located in the crypt of a Victorian church, the Royal London Hospital Museum uses exhibits of historic medical equipment, surgical instruments, and archives to document the history of this East London institution from its foundation in 1740 to the present. Highlights include a forensic medicine section with original materials and documentation from the Jack the Ripper murders and the RLH surgeon who investigated them. There are also artifacts and documents relating to Joseph Merrick—better known as "The Elephant Man"—who spent his final years in the hospital. Opening hours are subject to change on short notice, so call before you go. ⊠ *St. Augustine with St. Philip's Church, Newark St., Whitechapel* ☎ *020/7377–7608* ⊕ *www.bartshealth.nhs.uk* 🖾 *Free* ⏱ *Tues.–Fri. 10–4:30* Ⓜ *Whitechapel.*

FAMILY **Spitalfields City Farm.** An oasis of rural calm in an urban landscape, this little community farm raises a variety of animals, including some rare breeds, to help educate city kids about life in the country. A tiny farm

Blimey, Gov'nor, It's Jack the Ripper!

The spirit of Jack the Ripper, one of the world's most infamous serial killers, haunts the "Jack the Ripper Walk" that takes you to the deserted squares and warehouse alleys where he claimed his unfortunate victims.

No. 90 Whitechapel High Street was once the site of the George Yard Buildings, where the body of the Ripper's first victim was discovered in August 1888. His third mutilated victim, Annie Chapman, was left on Hanbury Street, behind what was then a seedy lodging house at No. 29. A double homicide followed, and then, after a month's lull, came the death on the same street of the Ripper's last victim. He had been able to work indoors this time—in a ground-floor apartment today occupied by an Indian restaurant—and left the remains of Mary Kelly, a young widow, strewn around the room. Jack the Ripper's identity has never been proven, although theoretical candidates abound, including, among others, a prominent member of the British aristocracy, the artist Walter Sickert, and Francis Tumblety, an American quack doctor.

Today, many entrepreneurs offer walking tours of the Victorian slums that Jack once stalked. One of the most popular is run by Original London Walks (⊕ www.walks.com); it leaves every night from Tower Hill at 7:30 pm. If you want a walk led by author and Ripper expert Donald Rumbelow, turn up on Sunday nights or alternate Friday nights

shop sells freshly laid eggs, along with organic seasonal produce. ⊠ *Buxton St., Spitalfields* ☎ *020/7247–8762* ⊕ *www.spitalfieldscityfarm.org* 🎫 *Free* ☉ *Tues.–Sun. 10–4* Ⓜ *Overground: Shoreditch High St.*

The Ten Bells. Although the number of bells in its name has varied between 8 and 12 (depending on how many bells were used by neighboring Christ Church Spitalfields), this pub retains its authentic mid-Victorian interior and original tiles, with a tiled frieze depicting the area's weaving tradition on the north wall and particularly fine floral tiling on two others. Legend has it the Ripper's third victim, Annie Chapman, had a drink here before meeting her gory end and the pub is depicted in Alan Moore's acclaimed graphic novel *From Hell.* More recently, the Ten Bells has gained a more positive kind of fame for its outstanding upstairs restaurant. ⊠ *84 Commercial St., Spitalfields* ☎ *020/736–61721* ⊕ *tenbells. com* Ⓜ *Overground: Shoreditch High St.*

SOUTH OF
THE THAMES

GETTING ORIENTED

South of the Thames

GETTING THERE

For the South Bank, use Embankment on the District, Circle, Northern, and Bakerloo lines and walk across the Golden Jubilee Bridges; or Waterloo on the Northern, Jubilee, and Bakerloo lines, from where it's a 10-minute walk.

London Bridge on the Northern and Jubilee lines is five minutes from Borough Market and Southwark Cathedral. The station also serves Bermondsey Street, though, confusingly, the next stop on the Jubilee line is called Bermondsey. Brixton has its own stop on the Victoria Line.

TOP REASONS TO GO

Join the "groundlings" at Shakespeare's Globe: See one of Shakespeare's plays in this historically accurate replica of the Elizabethan theater where they were first performed.

View a new master at Tate Modern: One of the world's great collections of post-1900 modern art, the centerpiece of this Tate branch is the huge renovated electric turbine hall.

Get bloodthirsty at the London Dungeon: Did you ever wonder what a disembowelment looks like? That's just one of the gory tableaux on view in this lively, somewhat jokey history-themed Grand Guignol. You'll be amazed how many children adore this place.

Take in a sunset on Waterloo Bridge: This is one of London's most romantic views, with St. Paul's to the east and the Houses of Parliament to the west.

MAKING THE MOST OF YOUR TIME

Don't attempt to visit the area south of the Thames all in one go. Not only will you exhaust yourself, but you will miss out on the varied delights that it has to offer. Tate Modern alone deserves a whole morning or afternoon, especially if you want to do justice to both the temporary exhibitions and the permanent collection. The Globe requires about two hours for the exhibition theater tour and two to three hours for a performance. Finish with drinks at the Oxo Tower or one of the Shard's restaurants, with their spectacular views, or dinner at one of the many restaurants in the Southbank Centre. You can return across the river to central London via Southwark on the Jubilee line from Tate Modern, although it's a good 15-minute walk to the station. Crossing the elegant Millennium Bridge for St. Paul's on the Central line or the Golden Jubilee Bridge to Embankment station offer longer but more scenic alternatives.

8

FEELING PECKISH?

Konditor & Cook. Known for its handmade cakes and cookies, this chain of bijou patisseries also offers daily specials such as chicken paella or vegetarian moussaka. ✉ *10 Stoney St., Borough* ☎ *020/0844–854–9363* ⊕ *www.konditorandcook.com* ⊗ *Closed Sun.* Ⓜ *London Bridge.*

Pieminister. East of the Southbank Centre in the shopping enclave of Gabriel's Wharf, you'll find Pieminister, which began as a Borough Market stall. Have a locally sourced meat pie. ✉ *56 Upper Ground, Gabriel's Wharf, South Bank* ☎ *020/7928–5755* ⊕ *www.pieminister.co.uk* Ⓜ *Waterloo.*

SAFETY

At night, stick to the Butler's Wharf and Bermondsey Street restaurants, the Southbank Centre, and the Cut near the Old Vic.

Sightseeing
★★★★★
Nightlife
★★★★
Dining
★★★
Lodging
★
Shopping
★★

For decades, south London had a reputation for being down-at-heel, with a considerable criminal element. Tourists rarely ventured across the river to south London except to go to Waterloo station or the Old Vic. But now the area is one of London's leading destinations, with attractions including the IWM London, the Southbank Centre (Europe's largest arts center), and foodie heaven Borough Market. Most are clustered around the Southbank and in Bankside and Southwark, but the surrounding neighborhoods of Bermondsey and Lambeth are rising rapidly, with galleries, shops, and restaurants proliferating.

Updated by
Ellin Stein

A borough of the City of London since 1327, Southwark first became well known for its inns (the pilgrims in Chaucer's *A Canterbury Tale* set off from one), theaters, prisons, tanneries, and brothels, as well as entertainments such as cock-fighting. For four centuries, this was a sort of border town outside the city walls (and jurisdiction) where Londoners went to let their hair down and behave badly. Originally, you were just as likely to see a few bouts of bearbaiting at the Globe as you were Shakespeare's most recent work.

In fact, now that south London encompasses high-caliber art, music, film, and theater venues as well as an aquarium, a historic warship, two popular food markets, and greatly improved transportation links, this region has become one of the leading destinations in England.

Today, the **Thames Path** along the river embankment in South Bank and Bankside is alive with skateboarders, secondhand-book stalls, and street entertainers. At one end the **London Eye**, a 21st-century landmark that became an instant favorite with both Londoners and out-of-towners, rises next to the **London Aquarium** and the **Southbank Centre**, home to the recently renovated **Royal Festival Hall**, the **Hayward Gallery**, the **BFI Southbank**, and the **National Theatre**. Farther east

The restaurant at Tate Modern has some of the best views in London. Here you can see St. Paul's Cathedral in the distance.

you'll come to a reconstruction of Sir Francis Drake's ship the **Golden Hinde; Butler's Wharf,** where some notable restaurants occupy what were once shadowy Dickensian docklands; **The Shard,** at over 1,000 feet the tallest building in the EU, which offers spectacular views over the city; and, next to **Tower Bridge,** the massive headlight-shaped **City Hall.** Nearby Bermondsey Street (the name derives from "Beormund's Eye," as it was known in Saxon times) is home to the bright yellow Fashion Museum, the White Cube Gallery, and lots of trendy shops, restaurants, and cafés. Meanwhile, younger visitors will enjoy the **London Dungeon** and **HMS *Belfast,*** a decommissioned Royal Navy cruiser, while food lovers will head for London's oldest food market, **Borough Market,** now reinvented as a gourmet mecca where independent stall-holders provide farm-fresh produce, artisanal bread and cheese, and specialty fish and meat.

Even from the Shard's lofty viewing platform 1,016 feet up, the area south of the Thames still isn't one of London's most beautiful, but you'll be able to see how this patchwork of neighborhoods fits together. The heart is the South Bank, which extends east from the London Eye to Blackfriars Bridge, with the river to the north and Waterloo station to the south. From Blackfriars Bridge east to London Bridge is Bankside, where you'll find the Globe and Tate Modern. Moving east from London Bridge is Borough, with its cobbled streets and former factories now turned into expensive lofts. Next, southeast of Borough, is buzzy, urban Bermondsey, while leafy Dulwich, with its renowned gallery and charming period streets, is quite a distance to the south. Returning up the river to the west of the South Bank is Lambeth and then Vauxhall, with the imposing IWM London (formerly the Imperial War Museum), a thriving gay scene, and scary through-traffic routes. It's a rapidly changing district, thanks to a regeneration spearheaded by the construction of the new U.S. Embassy in adjacent Nine Elms and a slew of upscale riverside residential developments. South of here is Brixton, long the heartland of London's vibrant Afro-Caribbean community—with a lively club scene—and now attracting young families priced out of nearby Clapham.

TOP ATTRACTIONS

FAMILY

Fodor'sChoice

★

Dulwich Picture Gallery. Famed for its regal old-master painting collection, the Dulwich (pronounced "Dull-ich") Picture Gallery was Britain's first purpose-built art museum when it opened in 1811. The permanent collection includes landmark works by Rembrandt, Van Dyck, Rubens, Poussin, and Gainsborough, and it also hosts three major international exhibitions each year. The gallery has a lovely café serving meals and drinks, and there's a schedule of family activities (see website for details). Development in Dulwich Village is tightly controlled. Consequently, it feels a bit like a time capsule, with old-fashioned street signs and handsome 18th-century houses lining its main street. Take a short wander and you'll find a handful of cute clothing and crafts stores and the well-manicured Dulwich Park, which has lakeside walks and a fine display of rhododendrons in late May. ⊠ *Gallery Rd., Dulwich* ☎ *020/8693–5254* ⊕ *www. dulwichpicturegallery.org.uk* ⊠ *£5–£11; free guided tours weekends at 3* ☉ *Tues.–Sun. and bank holiday Mon. 10–5* ☉ *Closed Mon.* Ⓜ *National Rail: West Dulwich from Victoria or North Dulwich from London Bridge.*

Fashion and Textile Museum. The bright yellow and pink museum (it's hard to miss) designed by Mexican architect Ricardo Legorreta features changing exhibitions devoted to developments in fashion design, textiles, and jewelry from the end of World War II to the present. Founded by designer Zandra Rhodes, and now owned by Newham College, the FTM is a favorite with fashionistas and offers weekday lectures on aspects of fashion history and fashion-based workshops. The excellent gift shop sells books on fashion and one-of-a-kind pieces by local designers. After your visit, check out the many trendy restaurants, cafés, and boutiques that have bloomed on Bermondsey Street. ⊠ *83 Bermondsey St., Bermondsey* ☎ *020/7407–8664* ⊕ *www. ftmlondon.org* ⊠ *£7* ☉ *Tues.–Sat. 11–6; last admission 5:15* Ⓜ *London Bridge.*

FAMILY

Fodor'sChoice

★

The Globe Theatre.

See the highlighted listing in this chapter.

Continued on page 156

"*Within this wooden O...*"
—*William Shakespeare, Henry V*

SHAKESPEARE AND
THE GLOBE THEATRE

At Shakespeare's Globe Theatre, they say the Bard does not belong to the British; he belongs to the world. Not a day has gone by since the Restoration when one of his plays isn't being performed or reinterpreted somewhere. But here, at the site of the original Globe, in a painstaking reconstruction of an open-air theater, is where seeing one of his plays can take on an ethereal quality.

If you are a lover of either British theater or literature, then chances are a pilgrimage to his Globe Theatre is already on your list. But if Shakespeare's works leave you wondering why exactly the play's the thing, then a trip to the Globe—to learn more about his life or to see his words come alive—will reveal all.

The Globe Theatre in Shakespeare's Day

In the 16th and 17th centuries, a handful of theaters—the Rose, the Swan, the Globe, and others whose names are lost—rose above the higgledy-piggledy jumble of rooftops in London's rowdy Southwark neighborhood. They were round or octagonal open-air playhouses, with galleries for the upper classes, and large, open pits for the more lively plebs. People from all social strata, from royalty down, shared the communal experience of drama in these theaters, of which The Globe was one.

A fire in 1613 destroyed the first Globe, which was quickly rebuilt; however, Oliver Cromwell and waves of other puritanical reformers put an end to all the Southwark playhouses in the 1640s. By the time American actor and director Sam Wanamaker visited in 1949, the only indication that the works of the world's greatest dramatist had premiered here was a plaque on a brewery wall. Wanamaker was shocked to find that all evidence of the playwright's legendary playhouse had vanished into air.

And thereby hangs a tale.

Wanamaker's Dream

Over the next several decades, Wanamaker devoted himself to the Bard. He was director of the New Shakespeare Theatre in Liverpool and, in 1959, joined the Shakespeare Memorial Theatre Company (now the Royal Shakespeare Company) at Stratford-upon-Avon. Finally, in the 1970s, he began the project

SHAKESPEARE'S ALL-TIME TOP 10

1. *Romeo and Juliet.* Young love, teenage rebellion, and tragedy are the ingredients of the greatest tearjerker of all time.

2. *Hamlet* (right). The very model of a modern antihero and origin of the most quoted line of any play: "To be or not to be…"

3. *A Midsummer Night's Dream.* Spells and potions abound as the gods use humans for playthings; lovers' tiffs are followed by happy endings for all.

4. *Othello.* Jealousy poisons love and destroys a proud man.

5. *The Taming of the Shrew.* The eternal battle of the sexes.

6. *Macbeth.* Ambition, murder, and revenge. Evil gets its just reward.

7. *The Merry Wives of Windsor.* A two-timing rascal gets his comeuppance from a pack of hysterically funny gossips.

8. *Richard III.* One of literature's juiciest villains. The whole audience wants to hiss.

9. *The Tempest.* On a desert island, the concerns of men amaze and amuse the innocent Miranda: "Oh brave new world, that has such people in't."

10. *King Lear.* A tragedy of old age, filial love, and grasping, ungrateful children.

that would dominate the rest of his life: reconstructing Shakespeare's theater, as close to the original site as possible.

Today's Globe was re-created using authentic Elizabethan materials and craft techniques—green oak timbers joined only with wooden pegs and mortise-and-tenon joints; plaster made of lime, sand, and goat's hair; and the first thatched roof in London since the Great Fire of 1666. The complex, 200 yards from the site of the original Globe, includes an exhibition center, cafés, and restaurants, as well as a 17th-century-style theater, modeled on one built adjacent to the Globe to a design by Inigo Jones.

FUN FACT: Plays are presented in the open air (and sometimes the rain) to an audience of 1,000 on wooden benches in the bays, and 500 "groundlings," who stand on a carpet of hazelnut shells and cinder, just as they did nearly four centuries ago.

The eventual realization of Wanamaker's dream, a full-scale, accurate replica of the Globe, was the keystone that supported the revitalization of the entire district. The new Globe celebrates Shakespeare, his work, and his times, and as an educational trust it is dedicated to making the playwright continually fresh and accessible for new audiences. Sadly, Wanamaker died before construction was completed in 1997. A memorial to him stands beside the statue memorializing Shakespeare himself, in Southwark Cathedral, a few hundred yards west of the Globe.

IN FOCUS 8

SHAKESPEARE AND THE GLOBE THEATRE

The season of plays is limited to the warmer months, from April 23 (Will's birthday) to the first week in October, with the schedule announced in late January on the theater's website. From November through March, the new Sam Wanamaker Playhouse, a re-creation of a Jacobean theater, offers an indoor alternative, with some performances by candlelight. Tickets go on sale in mid-February. The box office takes phone and mail orders as well as in-person sales, but the most convenient way to buy tickets is online. Book as early as possible.

FUN FACT: "Groundlings"—those with £5 standing-only tickets—are not allowed to sit during the performance. Reserve an actual seat, though, on any one of the theater's three levels, and you can join the "Elizabethan" crowd.

If you do have a seat, you can rent cushions for £1 (or bring your own) to soften the backless wooden benches. A limited number of backrests are also available for rent for £4. The show must go on, rain or shine, warm or chilly—so come prepared for whatever the weather throws at you. Umbrellas are banned, but you can bring a raincoat or buy a cheap Globe rain poncho, which doubles as a great souvenir.

MAKING THE MOST OF YOUR TIME

Give yourself plenty of time: there are several cafés and restaurants, as well as fascinating interactive exhibitions, and theater tours with occasional live demonstrations. Performances can last up to three hours.

WITH CHILDREN

Childsplay, a program for 8- to 11-year-olds, is held every Saturday during the theatre season. While Mom and Dad enjoy the play, children—helped by actors, musicians, and teachers—learn the background and story and become accustomed to Shakespearean language. By the time they are admitted to the theater for the last 20 minutes of the play, the children have become Shakespeare enthusiasts for life. There is also a children's playground with games and activities. Workshops start at 1:30 pm and tickets are £15; book in advance.

Year-Round at Shakespeare's Globe

Shakespeare's Globe Exhibition is a comprehensive display built under the theater (the entry is adjacent) that provides background material about the Elizabethan theater and about the surrounding neighborhood, Bankside. The exhibition describes the process of building the modern Globe and the serious research that went into it.

FUN FACT: In Shakespeare's day, this was a rough part of town. The Bear Gardens, around the corner from the Globe, was where bear baiting, a cruel animal sport, took place. Farther along, the local *gaol* (jail) stood on the site of what is now the Clink Prison Museum.

Daily live demonstrations include Elizabethan dressing, stage fighting, and swordplay, performed by drama students and stage-fighting instructors from the Royal Academy of Dramatic Art (RADA) and the London Academy of Music and Dramatic Art (LAMDA).

FUN FACT: Many performances are done in Elizabethan dress. Costumes for "original practices" productions, which aim to recreate the production techniques of Shakespeare's day, are handmade from period materials—wool, silk, cotton, animal skins, and natural dyes.

Admission also includes a tour of the theater. On matinee days, the tour visits the archaeological site of the nearby (and older) Rose Theatre.

FUN FACT: Shakespeare's casts were all male, with young men and boys playing the female roles. The live demonstration of Elizabethan dressing that forms part of the "Elizabethan Experience" shows how this was done—and how convincing it can be.

Visiting the Globe

✉ 21 New Globe Walk, Bankside, Bankside SE1 9DT

☎ 020/7902–1400 box office, 7401–9919 Globe Exhibition & Tour

⊕ www.shakespeares-globe.org

🎟 Exhibition & tour: £13.50, family ticket (2 adults, 3 children) £36; ticket prices for plays vary (Globe £5–£39, Wanamaker £10–£60).

🕐 Exhibition May–early Oct., daily 10–5; mid-Oct.–Apr., daily 9–12:30 and 1–5. Plays: Globe, Apr. 23–Oct.; Wanamaker, Nov.–Apr. 23. Call or check website for performance times.

Ⓤ London Bridge; Mansion House, then cross Southwark Bridge; St. Paul's, then cross the Millennium Bridge.

Borough Market brings hungry shoppers to the London Bridge area every Friday and Saturday.

QUICK
BITES

Gabriel's Wharf. This is a cluster of small shops specializing in jewelry, art, clothing, and ceramics by designer-manufacturers interspersed with informal restaurants. A project of the Coin Street Community Builders, a social enterprise group, it bustles with activity. The same group converted the nearby **Oxo Tower Wharf**, an art deco warehouse with three levels of designer studios that also serve as retail outlets. The Oxo Tower Restaurant, Bar and Brasserie, a pricey restaurant operated by the swish department store Harvey Nichols, occupies the top floor, and you can see the same spectacular views from an adjacent free public viewing area (open daily). ⊠ *56 Upper Ground, South Bank* ☎ *020/7021–1686* ⊕ *www.coinstreet.org* 🎫 *Free* ⊘ *Shops and studios Tues.–Sun. 11–6* Ⓜ *Blackfriars, Waterloo.*

FAMILY **Golden Hinde.** Famed Elizabethan explorer Sir Francis Drake circumnavigated the globe in a little galleon just like this one. Launched in 1973, this exact replica made one full and one partial round-the-world voyage, calling in at ports—many along the Pacific and Atlantic coasts of the United States—to do duty as a maritime museum. Now berthed at the St. Mary Overie Dock, the ship continues its educational purpose, complete with a "crew" in period costumes and three decks of artifacts. Call for information on guided tours. ⊠ *St. Mary Overie Dock, Cathedral St., Bankside* ☎ *020/7403–0123* ⊕ *www.goldenhinde.com* 🎫 *£6* ⊘ *Daily 10–5:30* Ⓜ *London Bridge.*

FAMILY **London Dungeon.** Saved by a keen sense of its own borderline ridiculousness, this Grand Guignol gory attraction is more funny than frightening, with tableaux depicting the bloody demise of famous figures alongside the torture, murder, and ritual slaughter of lesser-known victims, all to a sound track of screaming, wailing, and agonized moaning. There are displays on the Great Plague, Henry VIII, and Jack the Ripper, and, to add to the fear and fun, costumed characters leap out of the gloom to bring the exhibits to life. Perhaps most shocking are the crowds of children baying to get in—kids absolutely adore this place, although those with more a sensitive disposition may find it too frightening (that goes for adults as well). If you've ever wondered what a disembowelment looks like, this is your chance to find out. Be sure to get the souvenir booklet to impress all your friends back home. ■TIP➔ Expect long lines on weekends and during school holidays. Savings are available for online booking. ✉ *County Hall, Westminster Bridge Rd., South Bank* ☎ *0870/423–2240* ⊕ *www.thedungeons.com* 🎫 *From £17.95* ☉ *Mid-July–Aug., Fri.–Wed. 10–7, Thurs. 11–7; Sept.–mid-July, Mon.–Wed. and Fri. 10–5, Thurs. 11–5, weekends 10–6. Phone or check website to confirm times* Ⓜ *Waterloo.*

FAMILY
Fodor's Choice
★

London Eye. To mark the start of the new millennium, architects David Marks and Julia Barfield devised an instant icon that allows Londoners and visitors alike to see the city from a completely new perspective. This giant Ferris wheel is the largest cantilevered observation wheel ever built and among the city's tallest structures. The 25-minute slow-motion ride inside one of the enclosed passenger capsules is so smooth you'd hardly know you were suspended over the Thames. On a clear day you can see for up to 25 miles, with a bird's-eye view of London's most famous landmarks as you circle 360 degrees. If you're looking for a special place to celebrate, champagne and canapés can be arranged ahead of time. ■TIP➔ Buy your ticket online to avoid the long lines and get a 10% discount. For an extra £10, you can save even more time with a Fast Track flight for which you check in 15 minutes before your "departure." You can buy a combination ticket for the Eye and other London attractions—check online for details—and board the London Eye River Cruise here for a 40-minute sightseeing voyage on the Thames. In December, there's a scenic ice rink just below the wheel. ✉ *Westminster Bridge Rd., Riverside Bldg., County Hall, South Bank* ☎ *0871/781–3000* ⊕ *www.londoneye.com* 🎫 *£19.20; cruise £13* ☉ *Visit website for opening times* ☉ *Closed Jan. 7–14* Ⓜ *Waterloo.*

Fodor's Choice
★

Southbank Centre. The public has never really warmed to the Southbank Centre's hulking concrete buildings, products of the Brutalist style popular when the Centre was built in the 1950s and '60s, but they flock to its concerts, recitals, festivals, and exhibitions. The **Royal Festival Hall** is truly a People's Palace, with seats for 2,900 and a schedule that ranges from major symphony orchestras to pop stars (catch the annual summer Meltdown Festival, where "curators" like David Bowie, Patti Smith, or Jarvis Cocker put together a personal selection of concerts by favorite performers). The smaller **Queen Elizabeth Hall** is more strictly classically oriented. It contains the smaller **Purcell Room**, which hosts lectures and chamber performances. For art, head to the **Hayward Gallery**, which hosts shows on top contemporary artists such as Anthony Gormley and Cy Twombly. (The terrace here is home to some exciting restaurants.) Not officially part of the Southbank Centre but moments

8

away on the east side of Waterloo Bridge, the **National Theatre** is home to some of the best productions in London (several, such as *War Horse* and *The History Boys*, have become movies) at prices well below those in the West End. Meanwhile, film buffs will appreciate the **BFI Southbank** (formerly the National Film Theatre), which has a schedule that true connoisseurs of the cinema will relish. The Centre's riverside street level has been overhauled and now offers a terrific assortment of restaurants and bars. The BFI's Benugo bar and the Wahaca restaurant at Queen Elizabeth Hall are particularly attractive. Alterations involving a large boxy glass pavilion over the Hayward Gallery, Purcell Room, and Queen Elizabeth Hall are being mooted for 2015. If they go ahead, the venues will be closed for three years. ■ **TIP→** Hear leading actors, directors, and writers discuss their work at the National Theatre's Platforms, a series of inexpensive early evening and afternoon talks. ⊠ *Belvedere Rd., South Bank* ☎ *020/7960–4200* ⊕ *www.southbankcentre.co.uk* 🎫 *Varies; check website* ☉ *Varies according to venue; check website* Ⓜ *Waterloo, Embankment.*

FAMILY   **Tate Modern.**
Fodor's Choice   *See the highlighted listing in this chapter.*
★

WORTH NOTING

Florence Nightingale Museum. This museum on the grounds of St. Thomas's hospital is dedicated to Florence Nightingale, who founded the first school of nursing and played a major role in establishing modern standards of health care. Exhibits are divided into three areas: one is devoted to Nightingale's Victorian childhood, the others to her work tending soldiers during the Crimean War (1854–56) and her subsequent health-care reforms. The museum incorporates Nightingale's books and lamp as well as interactive displays of instruments and herbs. ⊠ *2 Lambeth Palace Rd., Lambeth* ☎ *020/7620–0374* ⊕ *www.florence-nightingale. co.uk* 🎫 *£5.80* ☉ *Daily 10–5; last admission 4:30* Ⓜ *Waterloo.*

The Garden Museum. This unassuming museum was created in the mid-1970s after two gardening enthusiasts came upon a medieval church which, they were horrified to discover, was about to be bulldozed. The churchyard contained the tombs of two adventurous 17th-century plant collectors, a father and son both called John Tradescant, who introduced many new species to England. The gardeners rescued the church and opened this museum, which has acquired one of the largest collections of historic garden tools and artifacts in Britain with walled gardens that are maintained year-round by volunteers. The church itself contains the tombs of William Bligh, captain of the *Bounty*, members of the Boleyn family, and a few Archbishops of Canterbury. There's a gift shop and **Garden Café**, serving vegetarian lunches and home-baked cakes. ⊠ *5 Lambeth Palace Rd., Lambeth* ☎ *020/7401–8865* ⊕ *www.gardenmuseum.org.uk* 🎫 *£6 (includes garden and all exhibitions)* ☉ *Sun.–Fri. 10:30–5, Sat. 10:30–4; closed 1st Mon. of month* Ⓜ *Lambeth North, Vauxhall.*

FAMILY   **HMS *Belfast*.** At 613½ feet, this is one of the last remaining big-gun armored warships from World War II, in which it played an important role in protecting the Arctic convoys and supporting the

TATE MODERN

✉ *Bankside* ☎ *020/7887–8888* ⊕ *www.tate.org.uk/modern* 🎟 *Free, charge for special exhibitions* ☉ *Sun.–Thurs. 10–6, Fri. and Sat. 10–10 (last admission to exhibitions 45 mins before close)* Ⓜ *Southwark, Mansion House, St. Paul's.*

TIPS

■ Join a free, 45-minute guided tour: Poetry and Dream at 11, Transformed Visions at noon, Structure and Clarity at 2, and Energy and Process at 3. Just show up.

■ Levels 2 and 3 include temporary exhibitions, which cost about £15. Bypass these if you're here to see the main collection, which is free.

■ Make it a two-for-one day by taking the Tate to Tate Boat, which takes visitors back and forth between Tate Britain and Tate Modern every 40 minutes.

■ Private "Tate Tours for Two" can be booked online from £100 to £120, with afternoon tea for an added £25 or a champagne dinner or lunch for £100.

This spectacular renovation of a mid-20th-century power station is one of the most-visited museums of modern art in the world. Its great permanent collection, which starts in 1900 and ranges from modern masters like Matisse to the most cutting-edge contemporary artists, is arranged thematically—Landscape, Still Life, and the Nude. Its blockbuster temporary exhibitions showcase the work of individual artists like Gaugin, Roy Lichtenstein, and Gerhard Richter.

Highlights

The vast **Turbine Hall** is a dramatic entrance point used to showcase big, audacious installations that tend to generate a lot of publicity. Past highlights include Olafur Eliasson's massive glowing sun and Carsten Holler's huge metal slides.

The **Material Gestures** galleries on Level 3 feature an impressive offering of post–World War II painting and sculpture. Room 7 contains a breathtaking collection of Rothkos and Monets; there are also paintings by Matisse, Pollock, and Picasso, and newer works from the likes of the sculptor Anish Kapoor.

Head to the Restaurant on Level 7 or the Espresso Bar on Level 3 for stunning vistas of the Thames. The view of St. Paul's from the Espresso Bar's balcony is one of the best in London.

An extension to the front of the building is not only ambitious but also controversial—you won't be alone if you don't care for it.

8

D-Day landings in Normandy; the ship later saw action during the Korean War. The *Belfast* has been moored in the Thames as a maritime branch of the **IWM London** since 1971. A tour of all nine decks—which include the Admiral's quarters, mess decks, bakery, punishment cells, operations

> ### COMBINATION TICKETS
>
> If you're planning to visit the London Dungeon, Sea Life London Aquarium, and Madame Tussauds, save by booking a combination ticket on any of their websites.

room, engine room, and more—gives a vivid picture of life on board the ship, while the riveting interactive gun turret experience puts you in the middle of a World War II naval battle. ⊠ *The Queen's Walk, Borough* ☎ *020/7940–6300* ⊕ *www.iwm.org.uk* ⊡ *£15.50* ⊙ *Mar.– Oct., daily 10–6; Nov.–Feb., daily 10–5; last admission 1 hr before closing* Ⓜ *London Bridge.*

FAMILY
Fodor's Choice
★

IWM London. Despite its name, the cultural venue formerly known as the Imperial War Museum (one of five IWM branches around the country) does not glorify either Empire or bloodshed but emphasizes understanding through conveying the impact of 20th-and 21st-century warfare. After a major renovation, a dramatic new six-story atrium at the main entrance encloses an impressive amount of hardware—including a Battle of Britain Spitfire, a German V2 rocket, tanks, guns, and submarines—along with interactive material and a new café. The "Trench Experiences" in the new World War I Galleries uses sights, sounds, and smells to re-create the grimness of life in No Man's Land, while an equally effective "Blitz Experience" in the revamped World War II galleries provides a 10-minute glimpse of an air raid. Also in the World War II galleries is an extensive and haunting Holocaust Exhibition, while "Conflict Since 1945" documents the fact that there has been fighting somewhere in the world almost continuously since the end of World War II. Other galleries exhibit war art as well as poetry, photography, and documentary film footage relating to conflicts from World War I to the present day. James Bond fans won't want to miss the Secret War Gallery, which charts the work of secret agents. ⊠ *Lambeth Rd., South Bank* ☎ *020/7416–5000* ⊕ *www.iwm.org.uk* ⊡ *Free (charge for special exhibitions)* ⊙ *Daily 10–6* Ⓜ *Lambeth North.*

FAMILY

Sea Life London Aquarium. The curved, colonnaded, neoclassical former County Hall that once housed London's local government administration is now home to a superb three-level aquarium full of sharks and stingrays, along with many other aquatic species. There are feeding and hands-on displays, including a tank full of shellfish that you can touch. The educational exhibits are particularly well arranged, with areas for different oceans, water environments, and climate zones ranging from a coral reef to a rain forest. Regular feeding times and free talks are offered throughout the day and behind-the-scenes tours are available. ⊠ *County Hall, Westminster Bridge Rd., South Bank* ☎ *0871/663–1678* ⊕ *www.visitsealife.com* ⊡ *£20.70 (10% discount for online booking)* ⊙ *Daily 10–7; last admission 1 hr before closing* Ⓜ *Westminster, Waterloo.*

London City Hall, with the almost finished "Shard" building towering in the background

Southwark Cathedral. Pronounced "Suth-uck," this is the oldest Gothic church in London, with parts dating back to the 12th century. It remains off the beaten track, despite being the site of some remarkable memorials and a concert program that offers regular organ recitals at lunchtime on Monday (except in August and December) and classical music at 3:15 on Tuesday (except in December). Originally the priory church of St. Mary Overie (as in "over the water"—on the South Bank), it became a palace church under Henry VIII and was only promoted to cathedral status in 1905. Look for the gaudily renovated 1408 tomb of the poet John Gower, England's first poet and a friend of Chaucer's, and for the Harvard Chapel, where the founder of the eponymous university, a local butcher's son, was baptized. Another notable buried here is Edmund Shakespeare, brother of William. ■ TIP→ The Refectory serves full English breakfasts, light lunches, and tea 9–6 weekdays, 10–6 weekends. ⊠ *London Bridge, Bankside* ☎ *020/7367–6700* ⊕ *cathedral.southwark.anglican.org* ☐ *Free, suggested donation £4* ⏱ *Daily 10–5* Ⓜ *London Bridge*.

The View from the Shard. At 1,016 feet, this 2013 addition to the London skyline is currently the tallest building in Western Europe. Designed by the noted architect Renzo Piano, it has attracted both admiration and opprobrium. While the building itself is generally highly regarded—many feel it would be better sited in Canary Wharf (or, indeed, Dubai) as it spoils views of St. Paul's Cathedral from traditional vantage points such as Hampstead's Parliament Hill. No matter how you feel about the building, there's no denying that it offers spectacular 360-degree views over London (extending to 40 miles on a clear day) from viewing platforms on floors 68, 69, and 72—almost twice as high as any other vantage point in the city. Digital telescopes provide information about 200 points of interest. ■**TIP→ If you find the price as eye-wateringly high as the viewing platforms, there's a less dramatic but still very impressive—and free—view from the Aquashard restaurant on floor 31, the Oblix restaurant on floor 32, and the Hutong restaurant on floor 33.** ⊠ *Joiner St., Borough* ☎ *0844/499–7111* ⊕ *www.theviewfromtheshard. com* ✉ *From £24.95* ⊙ *Sun.–Wed. 10–5:30, Thurs.–Sat. 10–8:30; admission by timed ticket only* Ⓜ *London Bridge.*

White Cube Gallery. When the United Kingdom's highest-profile commercial gallery moved to this huge converted '70s-era warehouse on Bermondsey Street, it sealed the area's reputation as a rising art-scene hot spot. This is the home gallery of some of today's top contemporary artists, including Jake and Dinos Chapman, Gilbert and George, Gary Hume, Anthony Gormley, Sam Taylor-Wood, Chuck Close, Anselm Kiefer, and several other artists with international reputations. An antiseptic central cuboid gallery, the "white cube"—also called "9 x 9 x 9" (meters, that is)—rests between two other spaces that host smaller exhibitions. There is also a bookshop and auditorium. ⊠ *144–152 Bermondsey St., Bermondsey* ☎ *0207/930–5373* ⊕ *whitecube.com* ⊙ *Tues.–Sat. 10–6, Sun. noon–6* Ⓜ *London Bridge.*

KENSINGTON, CHELSEA, KNIGHTSBRIDGE, AND BELGRAVIA

GETTING ORIENTED

Kensington, Chelsea, Knightsbridge, and Belgravia

GETTING THERE	TOP REASONS TO GO
Several Tube stations are nearby: Sloane Square and High Street Kensington on the District and Circle lines; Knightsbridge and Hyde Park Corner on the Piccadilly line; Earl's Court, South Kensington, and Gloucester Road on the District, Circle, and Piccadilly lines; Holland Park on the Central line; Ladbroke Grove on the Hammersmith and City line; and Victoria on the District, Circle, and Victoria lines.	**Treasure hunt at the V&A Museum:** The Victoria & Albert is the world's best decorative arts museum. Artists have been sketching in the Sculpture Court since Victorian times. **Attract a dinosaur's attention at the Natural History Museum:** Watch children catch on that the museum's animatronic *T. rex* has noticed *them*—and is licking its rather large chops. **Glimpse royal domestic life at Kensington Palace: Visit the public areas and gardens of** this royal family commune that has housed Queen Victoria, Princess Diana, and (currently) the Duke and Duchess of Cambridge (William and Kate). **Enter an Orientalist fantasy at Leighton House:** This small museum and "private palace of art" is right out of the Arabian Nights, with peacock blue tiles and intricate mosaic murals.
SAFETY	
This is one of London's safest districts, but beware of pickpockets in shopping areas.	

MAKING THE MOST OF YOUR TIME

You could fill three or four days in this borough: A shopping stroll along the length of King's Road is easily half a day. Give yourself a half day, at least, for the Victoria & Albert Museum and a half day for either the Science or Natural History Museum.

A GRAZER'S PARADISE

Duke of York Square Food Market. West London's answer to Borough Market, this Saturday open-air market is in a pedestrianized plaza off Duke of York Square, a chic shopping precinct. It hosts 40 stalls purveying artisanal and locally produced meat, game, fish, breads, cakes, cupcakes, honey, pasta, cheese, and chocolate from more than 150 small specialty food producers. Like Borough Market, this is a grazer's paradise, offering the chance to sample fresh oysters and cooked sausages as well as yummy hot snacks from around the world. ⊠ Duke of York Sq., Chelsea ☎ 020/7823–5577 ⊕ www.dukeofyorksquare.com ⏰ Sat. 10–4 Ⓜ Sloane Sq.

9

FEELING PECKISH?

The Café at the V&A. Breakfast, light snacks, tea, and full meals are served throughout the day (10–5:15), all in a grand room at modest prices. You can eat in the courtyard if the weather's good, or have a buffet supper on Friday late nights (until 9:30 pm). Stop by just to see the original Arts and Crafts part of the café, one of William Morris's earliest commissions, with stained-glass panels by Edward Burne-Jones. ⊠ Victoria & Albert Museum, Cromwell Rd., South Kensington ☎ 020/7942–2000 Ⓜ South Kensington.

NEAREST PUBLIC RESTROOMS

Most old-style public restrooms have been replaced by futuristic "autoloos"—podlike booths on street corners that usually cost £1 to use. If you're not brave enough to trust the push-button locks, try the free and clean restrooms at department stores Peter Jones or Harvey Nichols. Or ask for the "loo" in a pub, but be prepared for "sorry" if you're not a paying customer.

Sightseeing
★★★★
Nightlife
★★
Dining
★★★★
Lodging
★★★★
Shopping
★★★★★

The Royal Borough of Kensington & Chelsea (or "K&C" as the locals call it) is where you'll find London at its richest, and not just in the moneyed sense. South Kensington offers a concentration of great museums near Cromwell Road, with historic Kensington Palace located nearby in Kensington Gardens. Once-raffish Chelsea, where the Pre-Raphaelites painted and Mick Jagger partied, is now a thoroughly respectable home for the discreetly wealthy while flashier Knightsbridge has become a bolt-hole for international plutocrats, with shopping to match their tastes.

KENSINGTON

Updated by
Ellin Stein

Kensington incorporates the area along the southern edge of Hyde Park from Exhibition Road (where the big museum complex is) and the area to the west of the park bordered by leafy Holland Park Avenue on the north and traffic-heavy Cromwell Road on the south. This more westerly zone includes the satellite neighborhood of Holland Park, with its serenely grand villas and charming park, as well as local shopping mecca Kensington High Street and the antiques shops on Kensington Church Street.

Kensington's first royal connection was created when King William III, fed up with the dampness arising from the Thames, bought a country place there in 1689 and converted it into **Kensington Palace.** Queen Victoria's consort, Prince Albert, added the jewel in the borough's crown when he turned the profits of the Great Exhibition of 1851 into South Kensington's metropolis of museums: The **Victoria & Albert Museum (V&A),** the **Science Museum,** and the **Natural History Museum.** His namesakes in the area include the **Royal Albert Hall,** with bas-reliefs that make it resemble a giant, redbrick Wedgwood teapot, and the lavish **Albert Memorial.**

Turn into Derry Street or Young Street and enter **Kensington Square,** one of the most complete 17th-century residential squares in London. Holland Park is about ¾ mile farther west; both **Leighton House** and **18 Stafford Terrace,** two of London's most gorgeously decorated Victorian-era houses (the lavish use of Islamic tiles, inlaid mosaics, gilded ceilings, and marble columns make the former into an Arabian Nights fantasy), are nearby as well.

TOP ATTRACTIONS

18 Stafford Terrace. The home of *Punch* cartoonist Edward Linley Sambourne in the 1870s is filled with delightful Victorian and Edwardian antiques, fabrics, and paintings (as well as several samples of Linley Sambourne's work for *Punch*) and is one of the most charming 19th-century London houses extant. The Italianate house was the scene for society parties when Anne Messel was in residence in the 1940s. This being Kensington, there's inevitably a royal connection: Messel's son, Antony Armstrong-Jones, was married to the late Princess Margaret, and their son has preserved the connection by taking the title Viscount Linley. Admission is by guided tour only, and the afternoon tours on weekends are given by costumed actors. ⊠ *18 Stafford Terr., Kensington* ☎ *0207/602–3316* ⊕ *www.rbkc.gov.uk (under Leisure and Libraries)* 🎟 *£8* ☉ *Guided tours Wed. 11:15 and 2:15; weekends 11:15, 1, 2:15, and 3:30. Closed mid-June–mid-Sept.* Ⓜ *High Street Kensington.*

Kensington Palace.
See the highlighted listing in this chapter.

Fodor's Choice ★ **Leighton House Museum.** Leading Victorian artist Frederic (Lord) Leighton lived and worked in this building on the edge of Holland Park *(⇨ see below),* spending 30 years (and quite a bit of money) transforming it into an opulent "private palace of art" infused with an orientalist aesthetic sensibility. The interior is a sumptuous Arabian Nights fantasy, with walls lined in peacock blue tiles designed by Leighton's friend, the ceramic artist William de Morgan, and beautiful mosaic wall panels and floors, marble pillars, and gilded ceilings. The centerpiece is the Arab Hall, its marble walls adorned with even more intricate murals made from 16th- and 17th-century ceramic tiles imported from Syria, Turkey, and Iran, surmounted by a domed ceiling covered in gold leaf with a gold mosaic frieze running underneath. You can also visit Leighton's studio, with its huge north window and dome, and the house is filled with several of his paintings along with works by other Pre-Raphaelites. There are free tours of the house on Wednesday and Sunday at 3. ⊠ *12 Holland Park Rd., Holland Park* ☎ *020/7332–3316* ⊕ *www.rbkc.gov.uk (under Leisure and Libraries)* 🎟 *£5 (includes free return visit within 12 months)* ☉ *Wed.–Mon. 10–5:30* Ⓜ *Holland Park, South Kensington.*

FAMILY **Natural History Museum.**
Fodor's Choice ★ *See the highlighted listing in this chapter.*

FAMILY **Victoria & Albert Museum.**
Fodor's Choice ★ *See the highlighted listing in this chapter.*

KENSINGTON PALACE

⊠ The Broad Walk, Kensington Gardens, Kensington ☎ 0844/482–7799 advance booking, 0844/482–7777 information, 0203/166–6000 from outside U.K. ⊕ www.hrp. org.uk ⊠ £16.50 ☉ Mar.–Sept., daily 10–6; Oct.–Feb., daily 10–5; last admission 1 hr before closing Ⓜ Queensway, High Street Kensington.

TIPS

■ The palace now has a wheelchair-accessible elevator, and Kensington Gardens has electric buggies for mobility-impaired visitors.

■ If you also plan to visit the Tower of London, Hampton Court Palace, Banqueting House, or Kew Palace, become a member of Historic Royal Palaces. It costs £45 per person, or £86 for a family, and gives you free entry to all five sites for a year.

■ Picnicking is allowed on the benches in the palace grounds. (You can also picnic anywhere in the adjoining Kensington Gardens.)

■ There's a delightful café in the Orangery, near the Sunken Garden. Built for Queen Anne, it's a great place for formal afternoon tea, although it gets busy during peak hours.

Neither as imposing as Buckingham Palace nor as charming as Hampton Court, Kensington Palace is something of a Royal Family commune, with various close relatives of the Queen occupying large apartments in the private part of the palace. Bought in 1689 by Queen Mary and King William III, it was converted into a palace by Sir Christopher Wren and Nicholas Hawksmoor, and Royals have been in residence ever since. Its most famous resident, Princess Diana, lived here with her sons after her divorce, and this is where Prince William now lives with his wife, Catherine, Duchess of Cambridge and their young son, George.

The State Apartments, however, are open to the public. One permanent exhibition, called "Victoria Revealed," is devoted to the private life of Queen Victoria (who was born and grew up at KP) based on her diaries, while the Queen's State Apartments are given over to William and Mary and the Glorious Revolution. The lavish King's State Apartments, originally built for George I, has a semipermanent exhibit that explores the world of the Georgian Court through the story of George II and his politically active queen, Caroline. There is also a changing temporary exhibition. Through summer 2015, this will be "Fashion Rules," a collection of gowns worn by Princess Margaret, Princess Diana, and Queen Elizabeth.

Highlights

Look for the King's Staircase, with its panoramic trompe l'oeil painting, and the King's Gallery, with royal artworks in a jewel-box setting of rich red damask walls, intricate gilding, and a beautiful painted ceiling. Outside, the grounds are almost as lovely as the palace itself.

Ice-skaters outside the Natural History Museum in South Kensington

WORTH NOTING

FAMILY **Holland Park.** Formerly the grounds of an aristocrat's house and open to the public only since 1952, Holland Park is an often-overlooked gem and possibly London's most romantic park. The northern "Wilderness" end offers woodland walks among native and exotic trees first planted in the early 18th century. Foxes, rabbits, and hedgehogs are among the residents The central part of the park is given over to the manicured lawns—still stalked by raucous peacocks—one would expect at a stately home, although Holland House itself, originally built by James I's chancellor and later the site of a 19th-century salon frequented by Byron, Dickens, and Disraeli, was largely destroyed by incendiary bombs in 1940. The east wing was reconstructed and has been incorporated into a youth hostel, while the remains of the front terrace provide an atmospheric backdrop for the open-air performances of the April–September **Holland Park Opera Festival** (☎ *0300/999–1000 box office* ⊕ *www.operahollandpark.com*). The glass walled Garden Ballroom (every home should have one) is now the **Orangery,** which hosts art exhibitions and other public events, as does the **Ice House,** while an adjoining former granary has become the upscale Belvedere restaurant. In spring and summer the air is fragrant with aromas from a rose garden, great banks of rhododendrons, and an azalea walk. Garden enthusiasts will also not want to miss the tranquil, traditional **Kyoto Garden,** a legacy of London's 1991 Japan Festival. The southern part of the park is given over to sport and play: cricket and football (soccer) pitches; a golf practice area; tennis courts; a well-supervised children's Adventure Playground; and a giant outdoor chess set. ✉ *Holland Park* ⊕ *www.rbkc.gov.uk (under Leisure and Libraries)* ☉ *Daily 7:30–30 mins before dusk* Ⓜ *Holland Park, High Street Kensington.*

9

NATURAL HISTORY MUSEUM

✉ *Cromwell Rd., South Kensington* ☎ *0207/942–5000* ⊕ *www.nhm.ac.uk* 🖃 *Free (some fees for special exhibitions)* ⊙ *Daily 10–5:50; last admission at 5:30* Ⓜ *South Kensington.*

TIPS

■ "Nature Live" is a program of free, informal talks given by scientists, covering a wildly eclectic range of subjects, usually at 2:30 (and on some days at 12:30) in the David Attenborough Studio in the Darwin Centre.

■ The museum has an outdoor ice-skating rink from November to January, and a popular Christmas fair.

■ Free, daily behind-the-scenes Spirit collection tours of the museum (recommended for children over eight years old) can be booked on the day, but space is limited so come early.

■ Got kids under seven with you? Check out the museum's free "Explorer Backpacks." They contain a range of activity materials to keep the little ones amused, including a pair of binoculars and an explorer's hat.

The ornate terra-cotta facade of this enormous Victorian museum is strewn with relief panels depicting living creatures to the left of the entrance and extinct ones to the right (although some species have subsequently changed categories). Most are represented inside the museum, which contains more than 70 million different specimens. Only a small percentage is on public display, but you could still spend a day here and not come close to seeing everything. The museum is full of exhibits with plenty of interactivity and other cutting-edge technology to appeal to younger visitors.

Highlights

A giant diplodocus skeleton dominates the vaulted, cathedral-like entrance hall, affording the most irresistible photo opportunity in the building. It's just a cast, but the **Dinosaur Gallery** (Gallery 21) contains plenty of real-life dino bones, fossils, and some extremely long teeth.

You'll also come face to face with a giant animatronic Tyrannosaurus rex—who is programmed to sense when human prey is near and "respond" in character. When he does, you can hear the shrieks of fear and delight all the way across the room.

An escalator takes you into a giant globe in the **Earth Galleries,** where there's a choice of levels to explore. Don't miss the earthquake simulation in the **Volcanoes and Earthquake Gallery.**

The **Darwin Centre** houses items the museum itself doesn't have room to display, including "Archie," a 28.3-foot giant squid. The Centre's new **Cocoon Experience** is a 45-minute tour guided by virtual wall-projected scientists where you can see specimens such as huge tarantulas and historic items dating back 400 years.

VICTORIA & ALBERT MUSEUM

✉ *Cromwell Rd., South Kensington* ☎ *020/7942–2000* ⊕ *www.vam.ac.uk* ✆ *Free; charge for some special exhibitions (from £5)* ⊙ *Sat.– Thurs. 10–5:45, Fri. 10–10* Ⓜ *South Kensington.*

TIPS

■ The V&A is a tricky building to navigate, so be sure to use the free map.

■ As a whirlwind introduction, you could take a free one-hour tour (10:30, 11:30, 12:30, 1:30, 2:30, or 3:30). There are also tours devoted just to the British Galleries at 12:30 and 2:30. Occasional public lectures during the week are delivered by visiting bigwigs from the art and fashion worlds (prices vary). There are free lectures throughout the week given by museum staff, who also give an introductory tour of the collection on Friday nights at 7.

■ Whatever time you visit, the spectacular sculpture hall will be filled with artists, both amateur and professional, sketching the myriad artworks on display there. Don't be shy; bring a pad and join in.

■ Although the permanent collection is free—and there's enough there to keep you busy for a week—the V&A also hosts high-profile special exhibitions that run for several months.

Known to all as the V&A, this huge museum is devoted to the applied arts of all disciplines, all periods, and all nationalities. Full of innovation, it's a wonderful, generous place in which to get lost. First opened as the South Kensington Museum in 1857, it was renamed in 1899 in honor of Queen Victoria's late husband and has since grown to become one of the country's best-loved cultural institutions.

Many collections at the V&A are presented not by period but by category—textiles, sculpture, jewelry, and so on. Nowhere is the benefit of this more apparent than in the **Fashion Gallery** (Room 40), where formal 18th-century court dresses are displayed alongside the haute couture styles of contemporary designers, creating an arresting sense of visual continuity.

The **British Galleries** (rooms 52–58 and 118–125), devoted to British art and design from 1500 to 1900, are full of beautiful diversions—among them the Great Bed of Ware (immortalized in Shakespeare's *Twelfth Night*). Here, a series of actual rooms have been painstakingly reconstructed piece by piece after being rescued from historic buildings. These include an ornate music room and the Henrietta St. Room, a breathtakingly serene parlor dating from 1722.

The **Asian Galleries** (rooms 44–47) are full of treasures, but among the most striking items on display is a remarkable collection of ornate samurai armor in the **Japanese Gallery** (Room 44). There are also galleries devoted to China, Korea, and the Islamic Middle East. More recently installed areas include the Buddhist Sculpture gallery, the Ceramics gallery, and the Medieval and Renaissance galleries, which have the largest collection of works from the period outside of Italy.

9

CLOSE UP

Historic Plaque Hunt

As you wander around London, you'll see lots of small blue, circular plaques on the sides and facades of buildings, describing which famous, infamous, or obscure but brilliant person once lived there. The first was placed outside Lord Byron's birthplace (now demolished) by the Royal Society of Arts. There are about 700 blue plaques, erected by different bodies—some green ones originate from Westminster City Council—but English Heritage now maintains the responsibility. If you want to find out the latest, check the website ⊕ *www. english-heritage.org.uk. Below are some of the highlights:*

James Barrie (✉ 100 Bayswater Rd., Bayswater); **Frederic Chopin** (✉ 4 St. James's Pl., St. James's); **Sir Winston Churchill** (✉ 28 Hyde Park Gate, Kensington Gore); **Captain James Cook** (✉ 88 Mile End Rd.,

Tower Hamlets); **T.S. Eliot** (✉ *3 Kensington Court Gardens, Kensington);* **Benjamin Franklin** (✉ *36 Craven St., Westminster);* **Mahatma Gandhi** (✉ *20 Baron's Court Rd., West Kensington);* **George Frederic Handel** and **Jimi Hendrix** (✉ *23 Brook St., Mayfair);* **Alfred Hitchcock** (✉ *153 Cromwell Rd., Earl's Court);* **Karl Marx** (✉ *28 Dean St., Soho);* **Wolfgang Amadeus Mozart** (✉ *180 Ebury St., Pimlico);* **Horatio Nelson** (✉ *103 New Bond St., Mayfair);* **Sir Isaac Newton** (✉ *87 Jermyn St., St. James's);* **Florence Nightingale** (✉ *10 South St., Mayfair);* **George Bernard Shaw** (✉ *29 Fitzroy Sq., Fitzrovia);* **Percy Bysshe Shelley** (✉ *15 Poland St., Soho);* **Mark Twain** (✉ *23 Tedworth Sq., Chelsea);* **H.G. Wells** (✉ *13 Hanover Terr., Regent's Park);* **Oscar Wilde** (✉ *34 Tite St., Chelsea);* **William Butler Yeats** (✉ *23 Fitzroy Rd., Primrose Hill).*

FAMILY
Fodor's Choice
★
Science Museum. This, one of the three great South Kensington museums, stands next to the Natural History Museum in a far plainer building. It has lots of hands-on, painlessly educational exhibits, with entire schools of children apparently decanted inside to interact with them, but don't dismiss the Science Museum as just for kids. Highlights include the Launch Pad gallery, which demonstrates basic laws of physics; *Puffing Billy,* the oldest steam locomotive in the world; and the actual *Apollo 10* capsule. The six floors are devoted to subjects as diverse as the history of flight, space exploration, the Large Hadron Collider, 3D printing, and a sublime exhibition on science in the 18th century. Overshadowed by a three-story blue-glass wall, the Wellcome Wing is an annex to the rear of the museum, devoted to contemporary science and technology. It contains a 450-seat IMAX theater and the Legend of Apollo—an advanced motion simulator that combines seat vibration with other technical gizmos to re-create the experience of a moon landing. ■TIP➔ If you're a family of at least five, you might be able to get a place on one of the popular new Science Night sleepovers by booking well in advance. Aimed at kids 8–11 years old, these nighttime science workshops offer the chance to camp out in one of the galleries, and include a free IMAX show the next morning. Check the website for details. ✉ *Exhibition Rd., South Kensington* ☎ *0870/870–4868*

⊕ *www.sciencemuseum.org.uk*
✉ *Free; charge for special exhibitions, IMAX, and simulator rides*
⊙ *Daily 10–6; last admission 5:15*
Ⓜ *South Kensington.*

Serpentine Gallery. Overlooking the large stream that winds its way through Hyde Park and from which the gallery takes its name, this small brick building set in Kensington Gardens is one of London's foremost showcases for contemporary art, and has featured exhibitions by luminaries such as Louise Bourgeois, John Currin, Gabriel Orozco, and Gerhard Richter. A permanent work on the gallery's grounds, consisting of eight benches and a carved stone circle, commemorates its former patron, Princess Diana. A new second exhibition space, the Serpentine Sackler Gallery, located nearby in a small Georgian gunpowder storeroom with a dramatic extension designed by Zaha Hadid, also contains a stylish restaurant. If you're in town between May and September, check out the annual Serpentine pavilion, which each year is commissioned from a leading architect who is given free rein to interpret the brief—leading to imaginative results. Past designers have included Frank Gehry, Daniel Liebeskind, and Jean Nouvel. ✉ *Kensington Gardens, Kensington* ☎ *0207/402–6075* ⊕ *www.serpentinegallery.org* ✉ *Free* ⊙ *Daily 10–6* Ⓜ *Lancaster Gate, Knightsbridge, South Kensington.*

ARTISTIC CHELSEA

Artists and writers flocked to the area in the 19th century, establishing a creative colony in Cheyne Walk; at one time Turner, Whistler, John Singer Sargent, Dante Gabriel Rossetti, and Oscar Wilde were residents. In the 1960s it was the turn of Mick Jagger and Keith Richards; in the 1970s Bob Marley wrote "I Shot the Sheriff" in a flat off Cheyne Walk. It's now one of London's most expensive streets, completely unaffordable for latter-day Bob Marleys.

9

CHELSEA

Chelsea was settled before the Domesday Book was compiled and already fashionable when two of Henry VIII's wives lived there. On the banks of the Thames are the vast grounds of the **Royal Hospital,** designed by Christopher Wren. A walk along the riverside embankment will take you to **Cheyne Walk,** a lovely street dating back to the 18th century. Several of its more notable residents—who range from J.M.W. Turner and Henry James to Laurence Olivier and Keith Richards—are commemorated by blue plaques on their former houses.

The **Albert Bridge,** a sherbet-color Victorian confection of a suspension bridge, provides one of London's great romantic views, especially at night. Leave time to explore the tiny Georgian lanes of pastel-color houses that veer off King's Road to the north—especially **Jubilee Place** and **Burnsall Street,** leading to the hidden "village square" of **Chelsea Green.** On Saturday there's an excellent farmers' market up from the Saatchi Gallery selling artisanal cheese and chocolates, local oysters, and organic meats, plus stalls serving international food.

Residential Chelsea extends along the river from the Chelsea Bridge west to the Battersea Bridge and north as far as the Old Brompton Road.

TOP ATTRACTIONS

Royal Hospital Chelsea. Charles II founded this hospice for elderly and infirm soldiers in 1682 to reward the troops who had fought for him in the civil wars of 1642–46 and 1648. A creation of three of England's greatest architects—Wren, Vanbrugh, and Hawksmoor—this small village of brick and Portland stone set in manicured gardens (which you can visit) surrounds the Figure Court (the figure being a 1682 gilded bronze statue of Charles II dressed as a Roman general), the Great Hall (dining room), and a chapel. The chapel and the Great Hall, where you can see Antonio Verrio's vast oil painting of Charles on horseback, are open to the public at certain times during the day. There is a small museum devoted to the history of the resident "Chelsea Pensioners," but the real attraction, along with the building, is the pensioners themselves. Recognizable by their traditional scarlet frock coats with gold buttons, medals, and tricorne hats, they are all actual veterans, who wear the uniform, and the history it represents, with a great deal of pride. ⊠ *Royal Hospital Rd., Chelsea* ☎ *020/7881–5298* ⊕ *www.chelsea-pensioners.co.uk* ◻ *Free* ☉ *Grounds, Chapel, Courts, and Great Hall Mon.–Sat. 10–noon and 2–4. Museum weekdays 10–4.* ☉ *Closed Sun., holidays, and for special events* Ⓜ *Sloane Sq.*

Chelsea Flower Show. Also in May (usually the third week), the Chelsea Flower Show, the year's highlight for thousands of garden-obsessed Brits, is held here. Run by the Royal Horticultural Society, this mammoth event takes up vast acreage, and the surrounding streets throng with visitors. ⊠ *Chelsea* ☎ *0844/338–7506 in U.K., 121/767–4063 from outside U.K.* ⊕ *www.rhs.org.uk* Ⓜ *Sloane Sq.*

Saatchi Gallery. Charles Saatchi, who made his fortune in advertising, is one of Britain's most highly regarded collectors of contemporary art, credited with popularizing the Young British Artists movement through his championing of early works by the likes of Damien Hirst and Tracey Emin. The museum's home—its third in ten years—is at the former Duke of York's HQ, just off King's Road. Built in 1803, its grand period exterior belies its imaginatively restored modern interior, which was transformed into 14 gallery exhibition spaces of varying size and shape. Unlike Tate Modern, there is no permanent collection beyond an ongoing site-specific installation; instead, at any one time the galleries are given over to between one and three exhibitions that normally run for up to six months. There's also an excellent café, which is open late. ⊠ *Duke of York's HQ Bldg., King's Rd., Chelsea* ☎ *020/7811–3085* ⊕ *www.saatchigallery.com* ◻ *Free* ☉ *Daily 10–6* Ⓜ *Sloane Sq.*

World-famous Harrods has been attracting shoppers since 1834.

KNIGHTSBRIDGE

There's no getting away from it. With two world-famous department stores—**Harrods** and **Harvey Nichols**, a few hundred yards apart and surrounded by numerous boutiques selling the biggest names in international luxury and expensive jewelry—London's wealthiest enclave (not many other neighborhoods are plagued with street racers in Maseratis) will appeal most to those who enjoy conspicuous consumption.

Nearby Sloane Street is lined with top-end designer boutiques such as Prada, Dior, and Tods. If it all starts to become a bit generic (although expensive generic), **Beauchamp Place** (pronounced "Beecham") is lined with equally luxe boutiques, but they tend to be one-offs and more distinctive and less global.

Posh Knightsbridge is located to the east of Kensington, bordered by Hyde Park on the north and Pont Street just past Harrods on the south.

BELGRAVIA

Steps away from the roaring traffic of Hyde Park Corner is quiet, fashionable Belgravia, one of the most impressive set pieces of 19th-century urban planning, which lies just to the east of Kensington and Chelsea. Street after street is lined with grand cream stucco terraces, once aristocrats' town houses and most still part of the Grosvenor estate owned by the Dukes of Westminster. Many buildings are leased to embassies or organizations, but a remarkable number around **Lowndes Square, Eaton Place,** and **Eaton Square** remain in the hands of private owners, whether old money or the oligarchy who put their security guards in the attached mews houses. Some people consider the area near **Elizabeth Street** to be southern Belgravia, others call it Pimlico–Victoria. Either way, you'll find small, unique stores here specializing in baked goods, wine, gifts, and stationery rather than fashion (except for canine fashion).

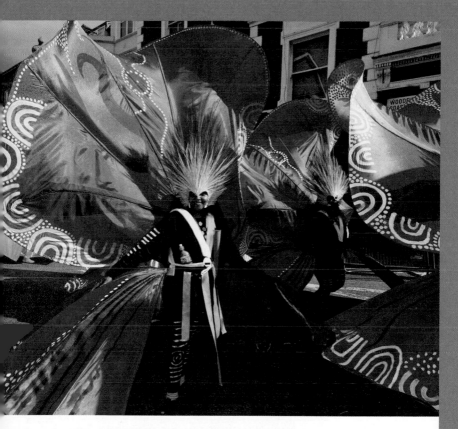

NOTTING HILL
AND BAYSWATER

GETTING ORIENTED

GETTING THERE	TOP REASONS TO GO
For Portobello Market and environs, the best Tube stops are Ladbroke Grove and Westbourne Park (Hammersmith and City lines); ask for directions when you emerge. The Notting Hill Gate stop on the District, Circle, and Central lines enables you to walk the length of Portobello Road on a downhill gradient.	**Unearth a bargain on Portobello Road:** The early bird catches the worm; go before 10 am to find a hidden gem at London's best and most famous antiques market on Saturday, or come during the week for a leisurely browse. **Refresh in Hyde Park:** Explore one of London's largest green spaces by walking, cycling (free "Boris bikes" are available), skating with the Friday Night Skate, or rowing down the Serpentine, the twisty lake that winds through the park.

A GOOD WALK

	Enter an Orientalist fantasy at Leighton House: This small museum and "private palace of art" has a sumptuous Arabian Nights–inspired interior with beautiful peacock blue tiles, gilded ceilings, and intricate mosaic murals.
To find Notting Hill's grandest houses, stroll over to Lansdowne Road, Lansdowne Crescent, and Lansdowne Square—two blocks west of Kensington Park Road.	**Take in contemporary art at the Serpentine Gallery:** Expand your cultural horizons here at one of London's foremost showcases for modern art, or just have a bite at the café in the new Zaha Hadid–designed extension, a piece of artwork in itself.

Notting Hill and Bayswater

MAKING THE MOST OF YOUR TIME

Saturday is the most exciting day for shopping, eating, and drinking here.

The market gets crowded by noon in summer so come early if you are serious about shopping.

Head south from the north end of Portobello Road, using the parks for relaxation.

On Sunday, the Hyde Park and Kensington Gardens railings along Bayswater Road are lined with artists displaying their work, which may slow your progress.

Well-heeled locals are often out on Sunday with friends in the pubs or with kids in the parks.

SAFETY

At night, be wary of straying from the main streets north of Westbourne Park Road towards Ladbroke Grove's high-rise estates and surrounding areas.

FEELING PECKISH?

The Prince Bonaparte. This comfortable yet contemporary gastropub has remained enduringly popular thanks to the high standard of its modern British food and selection of artisanal ales and well-sourced wines. ⊠ *80 Chepstow Rd., Bayswater* ☎ *020/7313–9491* ⊕ *theprincebonapartew2.co.uk* ☾ *Weekdays noon–3:30 and 6–10, Sat. noon–4 and 6–10:30, Sun. noon–9* Ⓜ *Notting Hill Gate, Royal Oak.*

The Tabernacle. This Victorian Gothic bar and café–cum–community arts center serves breakfast, lunch, and dinner daily and also hosts intimate music gigs (some by big names like Jamie Cullum), literary events like an evening with Tales of The City's Armistead Maupin, and 15-minute talks with speakers including Joanna Lumley and Joe Klein. The food is Caribbeaninfluenced and the atmosphere, especially in the large outdoor courtyard, is relaxed (perhaps too relaxed if you're in a hurry). ⊠ *34–35 Powis Sq., Notting Hill* ☎ *020/7221–9700* ☾ *Closed Sun.* Ⓜ *Notting Hill Gate.*

10

Sightseeing
★★

Nightlife
★★★

Dining
★★★

Lodging
★★★

Shopping
★★★★

Notting Hill is a fashionable square mile full of multiethnic finds, music, funky vintage clothing stalls, vibrant street markets, cool bars, and trendy restaurants and shops. It was the heart of London's West Indian community in the 1960s and '70s and a favorite with artists, rock stars, and rich hippies; it's now home to well-off trendy young people who survive without apparent effort (dubbed "trustafarians") and less stuffy investment banker–types. The area is studded with some of London's most handsome period crescents and terraces. Every weekend, hordes descend on Portobello Road to go bargain-hunting at one of the world's great antiques markets. Holland Park to the west has even grander period villas while Bayswater to the east has excellent ethnic restaurants.

NOTTING HILL

Updated by
Ellin Stein

Notting Hill as we know it emerged in the 1840s when the wealthy Ladbroke family developed a small suburb to the west of London. Before then, the area had the far less glamorous name of "the Potteries and the Piggeries," after the two industries it was best known for: ceramics and pig farming.

During the 1980s, Notting Hill transformed from a lively but down-at-heel and somewhat dangerous West Indian enclave to a super-trendy fashionable neighborhood, though a legacy of its previous incarnation remains in the form of the annual Notting Hill Carnival in late August. By the early 2000s the neighborhood's fame had spread—helped massively by the hit movie that bore its name, though the movie itself was criticized by locals for downplaying the area's ethnic diversity. For the Notting Hill of the silver screen, head for fashionable **Westbourne Grove** and **Ledbury Road,** lined with eclectic independent boutiques offering highly desirable designer goods, children's clothing, furniture and home accessories, upscale cookware, shoes, and contemporary art. Prices and taste levels are high.

For less rarified shopping, try **Portobello Road,** with the beautifully restored early-20th-century **Electric Cinema** at No. 191. The famous Saturday antiques market and shops are at the southern end. The central part of the road is home to a weekday produce market interspersed with vintage clothing shops and hot food stalls. On weekends, the more northerly part of the road sells discounted household goods, second-hand goods, and bric-a-brac, while **the Portobello Green Market** under the Westway overpass has clothing stalls selling everything from super-cool baby clothes to jewelry to vintage threads and club wear from youthful new designers. Meanwhile, the boutiques of the **Portobello Green Arcade** carry clothes from more established designers.

To the west of Labroke Grove, before Shepherd's Bush Green, lies the handsome Holland Park neighborhood. On the south side of Holland Park Road (the westerly continuation of Notting Hill Gate) you'll find quiet streets filled with imposing stucco villas, an area even more "stealth wealth" than Notting Hill itself.

TOP ATTRACTIONS

Graffik. Not everyone thinks graffiti adds to the urban landscape, but those who do should head to this leading gallery of contemporary street art. The big name here is Banksy, but there are works for sale by other artists in the same vein such as Tee.WAT and Trust.iCON who are more concerned with social commentary than tagging. This gallery experience especially appeals to young people, especially if the visit includes a two-hour spray-painting class. ✉ *284 Portobello Rd., Notting Hill* ☎ *020/8354–3592* ⊕ *graffikgallery.com* ⊗ *Daily 11–5* Ⓜ *Notting Hill Gate, Ladbroke Grove.*

FAMILY **Hyde Park and Kensington Gardens.**
See the highlighted listing in this chapter.

Portobello Road. Looking for a 19th-century snuff spoon? What about a '60s-era mini-dress? Then head to Portobello Road's famous Saturday market. Arrive at about 9 am to avoid the crowds. Stretching almost 2 miles from Notting Hill, the Portobello Market is actually made up

Continued on page 188

10

HYDE PARK AND KENSINGTON GARDENS

Two verdant oases in the center of London, the royal parks of Hyde Park and Kensington Gardens, which sit side by side and roll out over 590 acres of grassy expanses, provide a welcome respite from London's frenetic pace. The two parks incorporate formal gardens, fountains, sports fields, an art gallery, a palace, great picnic spots, shady clusters of ancient trees, and even outdoor swimming in a small lake.

10

Originally the extended backyard of royals, including King William III, Queen Victoria, and today Prince William, the parks remain the property of the Crown, which is why they weren't devoured by the city's late-18th-century growth spurt.

Londoners flock here when the sun is out to sit in a rented deck chair, walk through the formal gardens, engage in a session of tai chi, or even enjoy a mass in-line skate.

KENSINGTON GARDENS

At the end of the 17th century, William III moved his court to what had been Henry VIII's hunting grounds and began the transformation into **Kensington Gardens.** He was attracted to the location for its clean air and tranquillity and subsequently commissioned Sir Christopher Wren to overhaul the original redbrick building, resulting in the splendid **Kensington Palace.**

To the east of the palace complex is the early-20th-century **Sunken Garden,** complete with a living tunnel of lime trees (i.e., linden trees) and golden laburnum.

On western side of the **Long Water** is George Frampton's 1912 *Peter Pan,* a bronze statue of the boy who lived on Bird's island in the Serpentine and never grew up and whose creator, J.M. Barrie, lived at 100 Bayswater Road, not 500 yards from here.

Back toward Kensington Palace is George Frederick Watts's 1904 bronze horse and rider, a commemoration of diamond king Cecil Rhodes, entitled *Physical Energy.* The **Round Pond** is a magnet for model-boat enthusiasts and duck feeders.

Near the Broad Walk, toward Black Lion Gate, is the

Afternoon tea taken at **the Orangery,** a short walk from the Sunken Garden on the palace grounds, is a quintessentially English experience.

Diana Princess of Wales Memorial Playground, an enclosed space specially designed to evoke Barrie's Neverland. Hook's ship, crocodiles, and "jungles" of foliage provide a fantasy land for kids—more than 70,000 visit every year. Nearby is Ivor Innes's *Elfin Oak,* the remains of a 900-year-old oak with carvings depicting tiny woodland creatures.

One of the park's most striking monuments is the **Albert Memorial.** This high-Victorian Gothic monument to Prince Albert, is adorned with elaborate ornamentation representing his interests and amusements.

The small **Serpentine Gallery,** now joined by the nearby **Serpentine Sackler Gallery,** is known for its exhibitions of challenging contemporary works.

Hyde Park was once a hunting ground of King Henry VIII, who appropriated it from the monks of Westminster Abbey in 1536. The public wasn't granted access to Hyde Park's delights until George II came to the throne.

It was Charles I, in the early 17th century, however, who

HYDE PARK

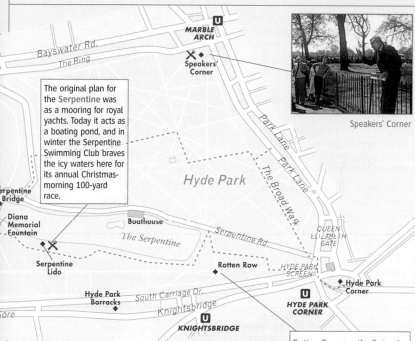

The original plan for the Serpentine was as a mooring for royal yachts. Today it acts as a boating pond, and in winter the Serpentine Swimming Club braves the icy waters here for its annual Christmas-morning 100-yard race.

Speakers' Corner

10

shaped the Hyde Park that visitors see today, creating the Ring (North Carriage Drive), which forms a curve north of the Serpentine and boathouses. Charles opened the park to the general public in 1637. During the Great Plague of 1665, people from crowded neighborhoods east of the city camped in the park, seeking refuge from the deadly disease.

The Serpentine Bridge, built in 1826 by George Rennie, marks the boundary between Hyde Park and Kensington Gardens. Rotten Row, a corruption of the French route de roi ("the king's road"), runs

along the southeastern edge of Hyde Park and is still used by the Household Cavalry, who live at the Hyde Park Barracks—a high-rise and a long, low, red block—to the left. This is where the regiment that mounts the guard at Buckingham Palace resides; you can see them at about 10:30 am, as they leave in full regalia to perform their ceremonial duties.

On the south side of the 1930s Serpentine Lido (open to swimmers from June to September) is the £3.6 million oval Diana Memorial Fountain.

Rotten Row was the first artificially lit highway in Britain. In the late 17th century, William III was concerned that his walk from Kensington Palace to St. James's was too dangerous, so he ordered 300 oil lamps to be placed along the route.

Ever since the 1827 legislation of public assembly, Speakers' Corner near Marble Arch has provided an outlet for political debate. On Sundays, it's a live version of an Internet chat room, with speakers ranging from calm and sensible to vehement and eccentric.

ENJOYING THE PARKS

Ride. **Hyde Park Riding Stables** keeps horses for hacking the sand tracks. Group lessons (usually just a few people) are £64 per person per hour. Private lessons are £89 Tuesday–Friday, £99 on weekends. ⊠ 63 Bathurst Mews, Bayswater W2 ☎ 020/7723–2813 ⊕ www.hydeparkstables.com Ⓤ Lancaster Gate.

Row. **The Serpentine** has paddleboats and rowboats for £10 per person per hour, kids £5, April through October from 10 am to dusk, later in good weather in summer. ☎ 020/7262–1330.

Run. You can run a **4-mi route** around the perimeter of Hyde Park and Kensington Gardens or a **2½-mi route** in Hyde Park alone if you start at Hyde Park Corner or Marble Arch and encircle the Serpentine.

Skate. On Friday, skaters of intermediate ability and upward meet at 8 pm at the Duke of Wellington Arch, Hyde Park Corner, for the **Friday Night Skate**, an enthusiastic two-hour mass skating session, complete with music and whistles. If you're a bit unsure on your wheels, arrive at 6:30 pm for the free lesson on how to break and turn. The **Sunday Rollerstroll**, a more laid-back version of the same thing, runs on Sunday afternoons; meet at 2 pm on the east side of Serpentine Road ⊕ www.thefns.com Ⓤ Hyde Park Corner.

Swim. **Serpentine Lido** is technically a beach on a lake, but a hot day in Hyde Park is surreally reminiscent of the seaside. There are changing facilities, and the swimming section is chlorinated. There is also a paddling pool, sandpit, and kids' entertainer in the afternoons. It's open daily from June through September (and weekends in May), 10–6; admission £4, ☎ 020/7706–3422 ⊕ www.royalparks.org.uk Ⓤ Knightsbridge.

WHERE TO REFUEL

✕ The **Lido Café**, near the Diana Memorial Fountain, has plenty of seating with views across the Serpentine Lake.

✕ **Serpentine Bar and Kitchen** on the eastern side of the lake, is a good pit stop for tasty snacks, salads, and sandwiches.

✕ The **Broadwalk Café & Playcafe** next to the Diana Memorial Playground has a children's menu.

✕ The **Orangery** beside Kensington Palace is a distinctly more grown-up affair for tea and cakes.

SPEAKERS' CORNER

Once the site of public executions and the Tyburn hanging trees, the corner of Hyde Park at Cumberland Gate and Park Lane now harbors one of London's most public spectacles: Speakers' Corner. This has been a place of assembly and vitriolic outpourings and debates since the mid-19th century. The pageant of free speech takes place every Sunday afternoon.

Anyone is welcome to mount a soapbox and declaim upon any topic, which makes for an irresistible showcase of eccentricity—one such being the (now-deceased) Protein Man. Wearing his publicity board, the Protein Man proclaimed that the eating of meat, cheese, and peanuts led to uncontrollable acts of passion that would destroy Western civilization. The pamphlets he sold for four decades are now collector's items. Other more strait-laced campaigns have been launched here by the Chartists, the Reform League, the May Day demonstrators, and the Suffragettes.

PRACTICAL INFO

ADMISSION: Free for both parks

HOURS: Kensington Gardens 6 am–dusk; Hyde Park 5 am–midnight

CONTACT INFO: ☎ 030/0061–2000, ⊕ www.royalparks.gov.uk

GETTING HERE: Ⓤ **Kensington Gardens:** Kensington High Street, Queensway, Lancaster Gate, South Kensington. **Hyde Park:** Hyde Park Corner, Knightsbridge, Lancaster Gate, Marble Arch

EVENTS: Major events, such as rock concerts and festivals, road races, and talks, are regular features of the parks' calendar; check online for what's on during your visit.

Each summer, a different contemporary architect designs an outdoor pavilion for the Serpentine Gallery. Outdoor film screenings, readings, and other cultural events are held there.

Every June or July, Hyde Park hosts Wireless, one of the U.K.'s biggest music festivals. It's held over a weekend, on several stages, and attracts some of the biggest global names in pop, indie, and rock.

(left) Horseback riding, Hyde Park

(top) The Fountains, Kensington Gardens

(bottom) Both parks are lovely year-round, but spring blooms are spectacular.

TOURS: There are **themed guided walks** about once a month, usually on Thursday or Friday afternoons. They are free but must be booked in advance. Check online or call the park offices for dates and details.

A 45-minute tour (£6) of the **Albert Memorial** is available. It's held at 2 and 3 pm on the first Sunday of the month from March to December. For information call ☎ 0207/936–2568.

Kensington Palace is open daily from 10 am to 6 pm, March to September, and 10 am to 5 pm from October to February. Tickets are £16.50; kids with an adult go free. For information call ☎ 0844/482–7779 or visit ⊕ www.hrp.org.uk.

of four sections, each with a different emphasis: antiques, fresh produce, household goods, and a flea market. The antiques stalls are packed in between Chepstow Villas and Westbourne Grove, where you'll also find almost 100 antiques shops plus indoor markets. Around Elgin Crescent, a vibrant neighborhood life kicks in, with a variety of small stores and food stalls interspersed with a fruit-and-vegetable market. On Friday and Saturday the section between Talbot Road and the Westway elevated highway

> **NOTTING HILL CARNIVAL**
>
> Loud, colorful, and very crowded, the annual Carnival (⊕ *www. nottinghillcarnival.biz*) was started by Afro-Caribbean immigrants in the 1960s. Held the last weekend in August, it attracts hundreds of thousands of visitors, mostly young and raucous. Keep your eyes open for pickpockets—even on "family day."

becomes one of London's best flea markets, specializing in discounted household goods, while north of the Westway you'll find secondhand household goods and bric-a-brac. Scattered throughout are vendors selling designer, vintage, and secondhand clothing, together with jewelry, T-shirts, and assorted junk. There's a Trinidad-style Carnival along Portobello Road on the August bank-holiday weekend, a tribute to the area's past as a center of the West Indian community. For more on Portobello Road, see ⇨ *Shopping, Chapter 18.* ⊠ *Portobello Road, Notting Hill* ⊕ *www.portobelloroad.co.uk* Ⓜ *Notting Hill Gate, Ladbroke Grove.*

BAYSWATER

East of Notting Hill Gate Tube station, Notting Hill turns into Bayswater, characterized by wide streets lined with imposing white stucco terraced houses. Traditionally given over to cheap B&Bs, many are being converted back to private homes as the area continues on the up-and-up. The eastern end of Westbourne Grove and the streets around it are known for their excellent ethnic restaurants, particularly Chinese, Lebanese, and Greek. On Queensway, Bayswater's main street, Whiteleys, originally a huge department store built in 1912, has been converted into a shopping center containing a movie theater, restaurants (Le Café Anglais is a good choice for a swanky evening out), a bowling alley, and, of course, shops.

Nearby **Paddington station** is as well known for its association with the world's most famous marmalade fan, Paddington Bear, as for being one of London's most handsome rail terminals.

REGENT'S PARK
AND HAMPSTEAD

GETTING ORIENTED

Regent's Park and
Hampstead

TOP REASONS TO GO

Ramble across Hampstead Heath: Londoners adore the Heath for bringing a bit of countryside to the city.

Go Romantic at Keats House: Visit the rooms where one of England's greatest poets wrote some of his greatest works, inspired by his love for the girl-next-door, Fanny Brawne.

Get sporty in Regent's Park: Cycle past Nash's grand neoclassical stucco terraces and the park's elegant landscaping, or walk up to Primrose Hill for another great view over the city.

Gracious living at Kenwood: See one of Britain's best art collections at this 18th-century gentleman's estate largely designed by Robert Adam.

Meet the penguins at the London Zoo: A VIP ticket will let you get up close and personal with the zoo's personable penguins.

FEELING PECKISH?

Ginger and White. Family-friendly and modern, Ginger and White is a fusion of continental-style café and traditional British coffee shop—all bound up with a sophisticated Hampstead vibe. ⊠ *4A–5A Perrins Ct., Hampstead* ☎ *020/7431–9098* ⊕ *www.gingerandwhite.com* Ⓜ *Hampstead.*

Marine Ices. Near the Camden Lock market, this place has some of London's best ice cream, while the indoor Italian restaurant section lures diners. ⊠ *8 Haverstock Hill, Camden Town* ☎ *020/7482–9003* ⊕ *www.marineices.co.uk* Ⓜ *Chalk Farm.*

SAFETY

It's best to stay out of Hampstead Heath, Primrose Hill, and Regent's Park at night unless there's an event taking place; all are perfectly safe during the day. Also to be avoided after dark: the canal towpath in Primrose Hill and Camden.

GETTING THERE

To get to Hampstead by Tube, take the Northern line (the Edgware branch) to Hampstead station, or take the London Overground to Hampstead Heath station. The south side of Hampstead Heath can also be reached by the London Overground Gospel Oak station. To get to Regent's Park, take the Bakerloo line to Regent's Park Tube station or, for Primrose Hill, the Chalk Farm stop on the Northern line. Little Venice is reachable by the Warwick Avenue stop on the Bakerloo line and St. John's Wood has its own stop on the Jubilee Line.

MAKING THE MOST OF YOUR TIME

Regent's Park, Primrose Hill, and Hampstead can be covered in a day. Spend the morning in Hampstead, with a brief foray onto the Heath, then head south to Regent's Park in the afternoon so that you're closer to central London come nightfall, if that is where your hotel is located. (You'll also be heading downhill instead of up.) You can always return to Hampstead another day for a long walk across the Heath or head west to Little Venice's canals.

A GOOD WALK

A walk from Hampstead Village down through Belsize Park, Primrose Hill, and Regent's Park will take you through some of London's leafiest, prettiest scenery.

Sightseeing
★★★★
Nightlife
★★★
Dining
★★
Lodging
★★
Shopping
★★★

Regent's Park, Primrose Hill, Belsize Park, and Hampstead are four of London's prettiest and most civilized neighborhoods. The city becomes noticeably calmer and greener as you head uphill from Marylebone Road through Regent's Park to the refreshing greenery of Primrose Hill and the handsome Georgian houses and Regency villas of Hampstead. To the west, the less bucolic but equally elegant St. John's Wood and Little Venice also provide a taste of how moneyed London can be.

Leaving the park at the London Zoo, walk up adjoining Primrose Hill for one of the most picturesque views of London. Long a magnet for the creative (though these days within reach of only the most well-heeled creatives), this is the kind of neighborhood where the local library's screening of *The Madness of King George* is introduced by its writer, longtime resident Alan Bennett. Peel off from the Hill to explore Regent's Park Road and its attractive independent shops and cafés, as well as the surrounding streets with their pastel Victorian villas.

Alternatively, continue hugging the Hill heading north along Primrose Hill Road. This will take you to Belsize Park, itself a celebrity hot spot (Helena Bonham Carter, Tim Burton, and Cameron Diaz have houses here) with a mixture of Victorian, Arts and Crafts and art deco buildings. Turn right onto England's Lane, another street full of independent shops and nice cafés, then left onto Haverstock Hill and head farther uphill. At the corner of Pond Street you will see two enormous Victorian Gothic buildings: one, St. Stephen's Church, has been recently restored and is now a community arts center. The other, AIR Studios, founded by Beatles' producer Sir George Martin, is where the scores from movies ranging from *Iron Man 3* to *Les Misérables* and *Brave* have been recorded.

Turn right onto Pond Street and go downhill past the unlovely Royal Free hospital to South End Green and the entrance to Hampstead Heath. Or go straight to stay on Rosslyn Hill and then Hampstead High Street, the neighborhood's main drag. Turn left onto Church Row, with its unspoiled early Georgian terraced houses leading to the St. John's-at-Hampstead, where painter John Constable is buried. To the north of Hampstead Heath is Highgate, another upscale north London "village" with a large concentration of Georgian and early Victorian buildings, particularly around The Grove (home to Kate Moss, George Michael, and Sting).

To reach Little Venice, go to the west entrance of Regent's Park by the gold-domed London Central Mosque and then north past Lord's Cricket Ground to the St. John's Wood Tube stop. Turn left onto Grove End Road, which will bring you to the famous Abbey Road crossroads featured on the Beatles' album of the same name. Head southwest for Little Venice, known as the Belgravia of north London due to its stucco terraces (found on streets such as Randolph Avenue, Clifton Avenue, and Randolph Road) that are very similar to the other neighborhood's. The "Venice" comes from its proximity to a picturesque stretch of the Grand Union Canal along Blomfield Road, where highly decorative houseboats are moored. If you can, visit on the second Sunday in May, when houseboats from all over London's canals gather here in Paddington Basin for the Blessing of the Boats.

REGENT'S PARK

Updated by
Ellin Stein

Commissioned by his patron the Prince Regent (later George IV) to create a master plan for this part of London, formerly a Royal hunting ground, London's great urban planner and architect John Nash laid out the plans for the 410-acre Regent's Park in 1812. Bordered by grand neoclassical terraces, the park is home to many attractions, including the London Zoo and the summer display of more than 400 varieties of roses in Queen Mary's Gardens.

TOP ATTRACTIONS

FAMILY
Fodor'sChoice
★

Primrose Hill. More conventionally park-like than Hampstead Heath, the rolling lawns of Primrose Hill, the northerly extension of Regent's Park which rises to 256 feet, provide outstanding views over the city to the southeast encompassing Canary Wharf and the London Eye. Filled with families and picnickers in nice weather, it has featured in books (it is here that Pongo engaged in "twilight barking" in *The Hundred and One Dalmatians* and the Martians set up an encampment in H.G. Wells' *The War of The Worlds*), been mentioned in songs by Blur, Madness, and Paul McCartney, among others, and served as a location for films including *Bridget Jones: The Edge of Reason* and *Paddington Bear*. ✉ *Regent's Park Rd., Regent's Park* ☎ *0300/061–2300* ⊕ *www. royalparks.gov.uk* ⊠ *Free* Ⓜ *Chalk Farm.*

FAMILY
Regent's Park.
See the highlighted listing in this chapter.

Regent's Park Boating Lake. You can enjoy a pleasant aquatic interlude touring the boating lake in Regent's Park by rowboat or pedalo. Adult rentals cost £7.50 (£5.50 before noon) per hour per person, or £5.50/£4 per half hour. On weekends and school holidays, children under 12 can take to the waters on a smaller lake, where pedalo rentals

A BRIEF HISTORY

Nash's original plan for Regent's Park included a summer palace for his patron the Prince Regent as well as villas for 56 friends, so the concept was to recreate the grounds of a great country estate. The palace was never built (and only eight of the villas were) but Nash's designs for magnificent white-stucco terraces along the park's Outer Circle were, with Cumberland Terrace on the east particularly notable for its neoclassical Ionic columns surmounted by a Wedgewood-blue pediment and statuary personifying Britannia and her empire, an architecturally interesting example of Palladian villa features being incorporated into a residential city terrace. On the opposite side of the park is Winfield House, a neo-Georgian mansion built in the 1930s by heiress Barbara Hutton and now the American Ambassador's (heavily guarded) official residence, with the largest private garden in central London except for Buckingham Palace.

In the early 18th century, the commercial development of the mineral springs in Hampstead led to its success as a spa; people traveled from miles around to drink the pure waters from Hampstead Wells, and small cottages were hastily built to accommodate the influx. Though the spa phenomenon was short-lived, the peace and serenity of Hampstead drew many significant artists and writers (from John Keats to George Orwell and Ian Fleming), along with distinguished refugees from Nazi Germany, whose legacy can be found in notable examples of Modernist architecture scattered among the 18th- and 19th-century period houses.

are £3 per 20 minutes per child going up to £4.50 for an hour (discounted prices before noon). The lake is open April through September, 10–6 ☎ 020/7724–4069 Ⓜ *Baker St.*

FAMILY

Fodor's Choice

★

ZSL London Zoo. Operated by the nonprofit Zoological Society of London, this was the new home of the Royal animals collection when it moved here from the Tower of London in 1828. The zoo itself did not open to the public until 1847. A recent modernization program has seen the introduction of several big attractions, with a focus on education, wildlife conservation, and the breeding of endangered species. The huge **B.U.G.S.** pavilion (Biodiversity Underpinning Global Survival) is a self-sustaining, contained ecosystem for 140 less-cuddly species including invertebrates such as spiders and millipedes, plus some reptiles and fish. At **Gorilla Kingdom,** a walk-through recreation of the habitat of the Western Lowland Gorilla, you can watch the four residents at close range. **Rainforest Life** is an indoor tropical rain forest (complete with humidity) inhabited by the likes of armadillos, monkeys, and sloths. A special nighttime section offers glimpses of nocturnal creatures like slow lorises and bats. The new **Animal Adventures** Children's Zoo allows kids to get up close to animals including mongooses and llamas, as well as feeding and grooming sheep and goats. Two of the most popular attractions are **Penguin Beach,** especially at feeding time before noon, and **Meerkat Manor,** where you can see the sociable animals keeping watch over their own sandy territory. If you're feeling

Regent's Park

0 1/4 mi
0 1/4 km

Haverstock Hill

Maitland Pk. Vs. Rd.

Queens Crescent

Prince of Wales Rd.

Marsden St.

KENTISH TOWN WEST Ⓤ

Prince of Wales Rd.

Eton Ave.

Steele's Rd.

Eton Rd.

Fellows Rd.

CHALK FARM Ⓤ

Chalk Farm Rd.

Wales

Kentish Town Road

Adelaide Rd.

Marden Cl.

Hawley Arms Pub ✕

Henry's Rd.

Gloucester Ave.

Camden Markets ◆   Camden Lock

Elsworthy Rd.

Primrose Hill Rd.

Amber Rd.

Chalcot Rd.

Regent's Canal ◆

Grand

Union Canal

Jamestown Rd.

CAMDEN TOWN

CAMDEN TOWN Ⓤ

Acacia Rd.

Worononzow Rd.

Regent's Rd.

Fitzroy Rd.

Primrose Hill

Prince Albert Rd.

Parkway

Delancey St.

Jewish Museum ◆

St. John's Wood Ter.

Attisten Rd.

Regents Canal

Prince Albert Rd.

Prince Albert Rd.

ZSL London Zoo ◆

Outer Circle

Broad Walk

Park Village East

St. John's Wood High St.

Cumberland Terrace ◆

The Hub ◆

Regent's Park

Cumberland Green ◆

A bany St.

Outer Circle

Lodge Rd.

London Central Mosque ◆

✕ Boathouse Cafe

Long Bridge

Inner

✕ Garden Cafe

Chester Rd.

Chester Terrace ◆

Park Rd.

Boating Lake ◆

Regent's Park Open-Air Theatre ◆

Queen Mary's Gardens ◆

Circle

York Bridge Rd.

Regent's College ◆

Park Square Gardens ◆

Rossmore Rd.

Gloucester Pl.

Sherlock Holmes Museum ◆

Outer Circle

REGENT'S PARK Ⓤ

GREAT PORTLAND STREET Ⓤ

Gibson Grove

Harewood

Balcombe St.

Baker St.

BAKER STREET Ⓤ

Madame Tussauds ◆

Park Cr.

Portland Pl.

Bradley St.

MARYLEBONE Ⓤ

Dorset Square

Marylebone Rd.

◆ RIBA

REGENT'S PARK

✉ Chester Rd., Regent's Park
☎ 0300/061–2300 ⊕ www.
royalparks.gov.uk ⧉ Free
Ⓜ Baker St., Regent's Park,
Great Portland St.

TIPS

■ If watching all this activity works up an appetite, in addition to the Hub's own café there's the Garden Cafe (☎ 020/7935–5729) outside the rose garden that serves breakfast, lunch, and supper on a patio; the Boatyard Cafe by the boating lake; and the Cow and Coffee Bean (☎ 020/7224–3872), which serves coffee and organic Cornish ice cream, and the Honest Sausage, both near the Broad Walk.

■ Regent's Park also hosts two annual events: the Frieze Art Fair, one of the art world's most prestigious, and the Taste of London, a foodie-oriented extravaganza.

The formal, cultivated Regent's Park, more country house grounds than municipal amenity, began life in 1812, when John Nash was commissioned by the Prince Regent (later George IV) to create a master plan for the former royal hunting ground. Nash's original plan included a summer palace for the prince and 56 villas for friends, none of which were realized except for 8 villas (only 2 survive). However, the grand neoclassical terraced houses on the south, east, and west edges of the park were built by Nash and reflect the scope of his ambitions. Queen Mary's Gardens, with some 30,000 roses a favorite spot for weddings, was created in the 1930s. Today the 395-acre park, boasting the largest outdoor sports area in central London, draws the athletically inclined from around the city.

Highlights

At the center of the park is the **Queen Mary's Gardens**, a fragrant 17-acre circle containing more than 400 varieties of roses. Just to the east of the Gardens is the **Regent's Park Open-Air Theatre** and the **Boating Lake**, which you can explore by rental pedalo or rowboat. Heading east from the rose gardens along Chester Road past the Broad Walk will bring you to Nash's iconic white-stucco **Cumberland Terrace**, with its central Ionic columns surmounted by a triangular Wedgwood-blue pediment. At the north end of the Broad Walk you'll find the **London Zoo**, while to the northwest of the central circle is **The Hub** (☎ 0300/061–2323), a state-of-the-art community sports center that has changing rooms, exercise classes, and a café with 360-degree views of the surrounding sports fields that offer soccer, rugby, cricket, field hockey, and softball contests. There are also tennis courts towards the park's southeast (Baker Street) entrance, and the park is a favorite north–south route for cyclists.

flush, try to nab one of the six daily "Meet the Penguins" VIP tickets (2 pm) that offer a 20-minute guided close encounter with the locals (£45 weekdays, £60 weekends.) There's a similar "Meet the Giraffes" VIP encounter as well. Other zoo highlights include **Butterfly Paradise;** the **Blackburn Pavilion,** with its

> **HERE'S WHERE**
>
> London Zoo's reptile house is a special draw for Harry Potter fans—it's where Harry first talks to snakes, to alarming effect on his horrible cousin, Dudley.

hundreds of tropical bird species; the **Big Cats** enclosure, home to a pride of Asian lions; and **Tiger Territory,** a new enclosure for a beautiful pair of endangered Sumatran tigers. For a more grown-up experience, check out Zoo Lates, where comedy, cabaret, and a wine bar are offered to over-18s in addition to all the usual zoo attractions on Friday evenings (6–10 pm) in summer. ■ TIP➜ Check the website or the information board out front for free events, including creature close encounters and "ask the keeper" sessions. ⊠ *Outer Circle, Regent's Park* ☎ *0844/225–1826* ⊕ *www.zsl.org* ⌗ *£21* ⊙ *Mid-Nov.–Feb., daily 10–4; Mar.–early Sept., daily 10–6; early-Sept.–Oct., daily 10–5:30; early–mid-Nov., daily 10–4:30; last admission 1 hr before closing* Ⓜ *Camden Town, then Bus 274.*

WORTH NOTING

Cecil Sharp House. The home of the English Folk Dance and Song Society, this soaring Grade II–listed 1930 building hosts concerts by artists ranging from Mumford & Sons and Laura Marling to the Ukulele Orchestra of Great Britain, as well as family barn dances and céilidhs (Irish barn dances). Meet the locals at drop-in classes offering all forms of folkloric dance, from Morris Dancing to Baroque Dancing, Riverdance-type Irish Dancing, Zydeco Dancing, and Argentinian Tango. There're also British folk arts–related exhibitions, a café and bar, and a small museum devoted to composer Vaughn Williams. ⊠ *2 Regent's Park Rd., Primrose Hill* ☎ *020/7485–2206* ⊕ *www.cecilsharphouse.org* ⊙ *Tues.–Fri. 9:30–5:30, 1st and 3rd Sat. of each month (except Aug.) 10–4; call or check website for evening events* Ⓜ *Chalk Farm, Camden Town.*

QUICK BITES

Regent's Park Road in Primrose Hill has several excellent cafés, notably the organic-minded and child-friendly Greenberry and local favorite Lemonia, which serves Greek food. On Gloucester Avenue at the top of Regent's Park Road, you'll find landmark gastropubs The Lansdowne and The Engineer, plus outstanding artisanal deli Melrose & Morgan.

Jewish Museum. This fascinating museum tells the story of the Jewish people in Britain from 1066 to today (including the period between the 13th and 17th century when Judaism was outlawed in England) through a combination of art, religious artifacts, photographs, manuscripts, and interactive displays. Highlights include a re-creation of a Jewish East End street from the Victorian era and an exhibit about the 10,000 Jewish refugee children who came to Britain just in time, although without their parents, as part of the Kindertransport. There are also temporary themed exhibitions, such as Jews in Football (soccer) or the life of Amy Winehouse. ■TIP→ There's a free over-view of the collection on the ground floor, including a medieval mikveh (ritual bath), excavated a few miles from here in 2001. ⊠ *Raymond Burton House, 129–131 Albert St., Camden Town* ☎ *020/7284–7384* ⊕ *www.jewishmuseum.org.uk* 🖃 *£7.50* ⊗ *Sun.–Wed. 10–5, Thurs. 10–9, Fri. 10–2; last admission 30 mins before closing. Closed on major Jewish holidays* Ⓜ *Camden Town.*

Lord's Cricket Ground & Museum. The spiritual home of this most Eng-lish of games and the headquarters of the MCC (Marylebone Cricket Club), Lord's opens its "behind the scenes" areas to visitors. Highlights of the 100-minute tour include the Long Room, a VIP viewing area where portraits of cricketing greats are on display; the players' dress-ing rooms; and the world's oldest sporting museum, where cricket's 400-year progress from gentlemanly village-green game to worldwide sport is charted via memorabilia, equipment, trophies, and footage of memorable performances. Don't miss the prize exhibit: the urn known as the Ashes—allegedly the remains of a cricket bail (part of the wicket assembly) presented to the English captain in 1883 by a group of Aus-tralian women, a jokey allusion to a newspaper's satirical obituary for the death of English cricket published after a resounding defeat. It's been a symbol of the two nations' long-running rivalry ever since. They still play for possession of the Ashes every two years though it's only been an official (as opposed to joke) trophy since 1998. A Waterford crystal version changes hands these days, though the winners still hold a replica of the original urn aloft. Tours are not available during major matches (they're offered during smaller "county" matches), but the museum remains open to match ticket holders. ⊠ *St. John's Wood Rd., St. John's Wood* ☎ *020/7616–8595* ⊕ *www.lords.org* 🖃 *Tour £18. Museum only £7.50 match days* ⊗ *Museum weekdays 10–5 (hrs vary on match days, call to confirm). Tours Apr., daily 10–2; May–Oct., daily 10–3 on the hr, except during major matches; Jan.–Mar., weekdays 11–2 on the hr, weekends 10–2* Ⓜ *St. John's Wood.*

Regent's Park Open-Air Theatre. There have been works by Shakespeare performed here every summer since 1932, with casts including luminar-ies such as Vivien Leigh, Dame Judi Dench, and Damien Lewis. Today it also mounts productions of classic plays, musicals, and shows for family audiences. However, *A Midsummer Night's Dream* is the one to catch, if it's on—never has that enchanted Greek wood been better evoked, especially if enhanced by genuine birdsong and a rising moon. There's a covered restaurant for pretheater dining, as well as a barbeque, a buffet, prebooked picnic boxes, and, of course, a bar. The park can get chilly, so bring a blanket. Performances are rain or shine (umbrellas aren't allowed) with refunds only in case of very heavy downpours. ⊠ *Inner Circle, Regent's Park* ☎ *0844/826–4242 tickets, 0844/375–3460 enqui-ries* ⊕ *www.openairtheatre.org* 🖃 *£25–£55* ⊗ *May–mid-Sept., evening performances at 8, matinees at 2:30* Ⓜ *Baker St., Regent's Park.*

A match being played at Lord's Cricket Ground

HAMPSTEAD

Even a destitute Romantic poet like John Keats could afford **Hampstead** in 1818 when he moved to what is now **Keats House**, a pretty Regency residence where he spent two years and wrote several of his most famous works. However, Hampstead's bohemian days are long gone, although a few distinguished artists and musicians, plus television stars, still live here. Artisanal food shops and boutiques for the skinny of frame and fat of wallet cluster along Rosslyn Hill, while high-street chains start to proliferate the closer you get to Hampstead Tube station. Be sure to leave the beaten path to explore the numerous narrow charming roads, like Flask Walk, Well Walk, and New End Road. Also hidden among Hampstead's winding streets are **Fenton House,** a Georgian town house with a lovely walled garden, and Burgh House, the oldest (1704) house in the village and a repository of local history. On the way to Highgate you'll find **Kenwood House,** an 18th-century mansion designed by Robert Adam noted for its remarkable art collection and lovely grounds.

Hampstead's crowning glory, however, is **Hampstead Heath** (known locally as "The Heath"), 790 acres of varied habitats including parkland, swimming ponds, and some of Europe's oldest oaks. It's also home to one of London's highest (322 feet) vantage point, Parliament Hill.

TOP ATTRACTIONS

FAMILY
Hampstead Heath

Fodor's Choice
★
See the highlighted listing in this chapter.

Highgate Cemetery. Highgate is not the oldest cemetery in London, but it is probably the best known. After it was consecrated in 1839, Victorians came from miles around to appreciate the ornate headstones, the impressive tombs, and the view. Such was its popularity that 19 acres on the other side of the road were acquired in 1850, and this additional East Cemetery contains what may be the most visited grave—that of Karl Marx (1818–83), only one of several notables interred here. At the summit is the **Circle of Lebanon**, a ring of vaults built around an ancient cypress tree—a legacy of the 17th-century gardens that formerly occupied the site. Leading from the circle is the **Egyptian Avenue**, a subterranean stone tunnel lined with catacombs, itself approached by a dramatic colonnade that screens the main cemetery from the road. Both sides are impressive, with a grand (locked) iron gate leading to a sweeping courtyard built for the approach of horses and carriages. By the 1970s the cemetery had become unkempt and neglected until a group of volunteers, the Friends of Highgate Cemetery, undertook the huge upkeep. Tours are conducted by the Friends, who will show you the most interesting graves among the numerous statues and memorials once hidden by overgrowth. The West side is accessible by tour only, which you must prebook for weekdays but not weekends. Tours of the East side on Saturday are first come, first serve. You're expected to dress respectfully, so forego the shorts and baseball cap. ■TIP➜ Children under eight are not admitted; nor are dogs, tripods, or video cameras. ⊠ *Swains La., Highgate* 🕾 *020/8340–1834* ⊕ *highgatecemetery.org* ✍ *East Cemetery £4, tours £8; West Cemetery tours £12. No credit cards* ⊙ *East: Mar.–Oct., daily 10–5; Nov.–Feb., weekdays 10–4, weekends 11–4. Tours, Sat. at 2. Last admission 30 mins before closing. Hrs may vary according to funeral service schedule—call ahead. West: tours Mar.–Nov., weekdays at 1:45, weekends half-hourly 11–3* Ⓜ *Archway, then Bus 210, 271, or 143 to Highgate Village.*

Keats House. It was while living in this house between 1818 and 1820 that poet John Keats (1795–1821), a leading figure of the Romantic movement, fell in love with girl-next-door Fanny Brawne and wrote some of his best-loved poems before ill health forced him to move to Rome, where he died the following year. After a major refurbishment to make the rooms more consistent with their original Regency decor, the house now displays all sorts of Keats-related material including portraits, letters, many of the poet's original manuscripts and books, the engagement ring he gave to Fanny, and items of Fanny's clothing. A pretty garden contains the plum tree under which Keats supposedly composed *Ode to a Nightingale*. There are frequent guided tours and special events featuring local literary luminaries. The ticket gives you entry for a full year, so you can come back as often as you like. ■TIP➜ Picnics can be taken into the grounds during the summer. ⊠ *10 Keats Grove, Hampstead* 🕾 *020/7332–3868* ⊕ *www. keatshouse.cityoflondon.gov.uk* ✍ *£5* ⊙ *Mar.–Oct., Tues.–Sun. 1–5; Nov.–Feb., Fri.–Sun. 1–5 (last admission 4:30)* Ⓜ *Overground: Hampstead Heath.*

HAMPSTEAD HEATH

11

✉ *Hampstead* ☎ *020/7332–3322 Heath Education Centre* ⊕ *www.cityoflondon.gov.uk/hampstead* 🎫 *Free* Ⓜ *Overground: Hampstead Heath for south of Heath or Gospel Oak for Lido; Hampstead for east of Heath; Golders Green, then Bus 210, 268 to Whitestone Pond for north and west of Heath.*

TIPS

■ At 321 feet above sea level, Parliament Hill is one of the highest points in London. On a clear day, you can see the South Downs, the hills beyond southern London.

■ Perfect for cooling off in summer, the Hampstead "Mens" and "Ladies" ponds are northeast of Parliament Hill with a "Mixed" pond closer to South End Green.

■ Golders Hill Park has a café, tennis courts, a duck pond, a croquet lawn, and a flower garden, plus a Butterfly House (open May–September) and a small zoo.

For generations, Londoners have headed to Hampstead Heath to escape the dirt and noise of the city. A unique expanse of *rus-in-urbe*, its 790 acres encompass a variety of wildlife as well as habitats ranging from grassy meadows to woodland, scrub, wetlands, and, at 500 years old, some of Europe's most venerable oak trees. Be aware that, aside from the southern end, it is more like countryside than a park, with signs and facilities in short supply. Pick up a map at ⇨ *Kenwood House*, or the **Education Centre** near the Lido off Gordon House Road, where you can also get details about the history of the Heath and the flora and fauna growing there. An excellent café near the Athletics Field offers Italian food alfresco.

Today the Heath is popular with walkers, dog walkers, and swimmers. It has inspired artists from John Constable, who painted views several times, to modern author Zadie Smith, to C.S. Lewis, whose *The Lion, The Witch and The Wardrobe* was supposedly inspired by a walk through the Heath's winter landscape.

Highlights

Coming onto the Heath from the South End Green entrance, walk east past a well-equipped children's adventure **Playground** and **Paddling Pool**, turn left, and head to the top of **Parliament Hill**. At 321 feet above sea level, it's one of the highest points in London. You'll find a stunning panorama over the city. On clear days you can see all the way to the South Downs, the hills beyond southern London.

If you keep heading east from the playground instead, you'll come to the **Lido**, an Olympic-size outdoor unheated swimming pool that gets packed on all-too-rare hot summer days.

The fabled cover of the Beatles *Abbey Road* album, with the world's most famous traffic crossing

Fodor's Choice **Kenwood House.** This largely Palladian villa was first built in 1616 and
★ later extended, first by Robert Adam starting in 1767 and later by George
Saunders in 1795. Adam refaced most of the exterior and added the splendid library, which, with its vaulted ceiling and Corinthian columns, is the
highlight of the house for design aficionados. A recent major renovation
has restored four rooms to reflect Adam's intentions as closely as possible,
incorporating the furniture he designed for them and his original color
schemes. Kenwood is also home to the **Iveagh Bequest,** a superb collection of 63 paintings that includes masterworks like Rembrandt's *Portrait
of the Artist* and Vermeer's *The Guitar Player,* along with major works
by Reynolds, Van Dyck, Hals, Gainsborough, and Turner. The grounds,
which are bordered by Hampstead Heath, are equally elegant and serene,
with lawns sloping down to a little lake crossed by a trompe-l'oeil bridge.
All in all, the perfect home for an 18th-century gentleman. ■**TIP→ In
summer the grounds host a series of popular and classical concerts,
culminating in fireworks on the last night.** The Brew House café, occupying part of the old coach house, has outdoor tables in the courtyard
and a terraced garden. ✉ *Hampstead La., Highgate* ☎ *020/8348–1286*
⊕ *www.english-heritage.org.uk* ✉ *Free* ☺ *House daily 10–5; gardens
daily 8–dusk* Ⓜ *Golders Green, then Bus 210.*

WORTH NOTING

Burgh House and Hampstead Museum. One of Hampstead's oldest buildings, Burgh House was built in 1704 to take advantage of the natural
spa waters of the then-fashionable Hampstead Wells. A private house
until World War II, it was saved from near-dereliction in the 1970s by
local residents, who have been restoring and maintaining it ever since.

A TRIP TO ABBEY ROAD

11

The black-and-white crossroads (known as a "zebra crossing") near the Abbey Road Studios at No. 3 is a place of pilgrimage for Beatles' fans from around the world, many of them teenagers born long after the band split up. They converge here to re-create the cover of the Beatles' 1969 *Abbey Road* album, posing on the crossing despite the onrushing traffic. ■TIP➜ Be very careful if you're going to attempt this. Abbey Road is a dangerous intersection. The studio is where the Beatles recorded their entire output, from "Love Me Do" onwards. One of the best—and safer—ways to explore landmarks in the Beatles' story is to take one of the excellent walking tours offered by **Original London Walks** (☎ *020/7624–3978* ⊕ *www.walks.com*). Try **The Beatles In-My-Life Walk** (11:20 am outside Marylebone Underground on Saturday and Tuesday) or **The Beatles Magical Mystery Tour** (Wednesday at 2 pm, February to November, and Thursday and Sunday at 11 am, year-round, at Underground Exit 3, Tottenham Court Road.)

The building is a fine example of the gentle elegance common to the Queen Anne period, with its redbrick box frontage, oak paneled rooms, and terraced garden (originally designed by Gertrude Jekyll). Today the house contains a small but diverting museum on the history of the area, and also hosts regular talks, concerts, and recitals. The secluded garden courtyard of the café is a lovely spot for lunch, tea, or glass of wine on a summer's afternoon. Call ahead if you're visiting on a weekend, however, as the house is often hired out as a wedding venue on Saturday. ✉ *New End Sq., Hampstead* ☎ *020/7431–0144* ⊕ *www.burghhouse.org.uk* ✐ *Free* ☻ *Wed.–Sun. noon–5* Ⓜ *Hampstead.*

Fenton House. This handsome 16th-century merchant's home, Hampstead's oldest surviving house, has fine displays of porcelain, Georgian furniture, and 17th-century needlework. The 2-acre walled garden, with its rose plantings and apple orchard, has been virtually unchanged for 300 years. International musicians give recitals on the important collection of early keyboard instruments throughout the week. Check the website for details. ✉ *Hampstead Grove, Hampstead* ☎ *020/7435–3471* ⊕ *www.nationaltrust.org.uk* ✐ *£6.50, garden only £2* ☻ *Mar.–Oct., Wed.–Sun. 11–5; Dec., weekends 11–4* Ⓜ *Hampstead.*

Freud Museum London. The father of psychoanalysis lived here with his family for a year, between his escape from Nazi persecution in his native Vienna in 1938 and his death in 1939. His daughter Anna (herself a pioneer of child psychoanalysis), remained in the house until her own death in 1982, bequeathing it as a museum to honor her father. The centerpiece is Freud's unchanged study, containing his remarkable collection of antiquities and his library. Also on display is the family's Biedermeier furniture and, of course, *the* couch. As well, there are lectures, study groups, and themed exhibitions, in addition to a psychoanalysis-related archive and research library. ■TIP➜ Looking for a unique souvenir for the person who has everything? The gift shop here sells "Freudian Slippers." ✉ *20 Maresfield Gardens, Swiss Cottage* ☎ *020/7435–2002* ⊕ *www.freud.org.uk* 💷 *£6* ☉ *Wed.–Sun. noon–5* Ⓜ *Swiss Cottage, Finchley Rd.*

St. John's-at-Hampstead. There has been a church here since 1312, but the current building was consecrated in 1747 and later extended in 1877. The nave is classic Georgian, lined with Ionic columns and vaulting arches. The church stands at the end of Church Row, a narrow street lined with flat-fronted brick Georgian houses that gives you a sense of what Hampstead was like when it truly was a rural village as opposed to a traffic-clogged north London neighborhood. Many local notables are buried in the churchyard, including painter John Constable (some of whose most famous works depict the Heath), John Harrison (the inventor of the marine chronometer who inspired *Longitude*), members of the du Maurier family, Jane Austen's aunt, and comedy god Peter Cook. ✉ *Church Row, Hampstead* ☎ *020/7794–5808* ⊕ *www. hampsteadparishchurch.org.uk* 💷 *Free* Ⓜ *Hampstead.*

2 Willow Road. Among the many artists and intellectuals fleeing Nazi persecution who settled in the area was noted architect Erno Goldfinger, who built this outstanding modernist home opposite Hampstead Heath in 1939 as his family residence (his plans drew the ire of several local residents, including novelist Ian Fleming, who supposedly borrowed his neighbor's name for a Bond villain as a result). As well as design touches and pioneering building techniques that were groundbreaking at the time, the unique house, a place of pilgrimage for 20th-century architecture enthusiasts, contains Goldfinger's impressive collection of modern art and self-designed innovative furniture. Before 2 pm admission is by first come, first served hourly tour only, but you can visit independently after 3. ✉ *2 Willow Rd., Hampstead* ☎ *020/7435–6166* ⊕ *www.nationaltrust.org.uk/2-willow-road* 💷 *£6* ☉ *Wed.–Sun. 11–2 (guided tour only), 3–5 (last admission 4:30)* Ⓜ *Overground: Hampstead Heath.*

GREENWICH

GETTING ORIENTED

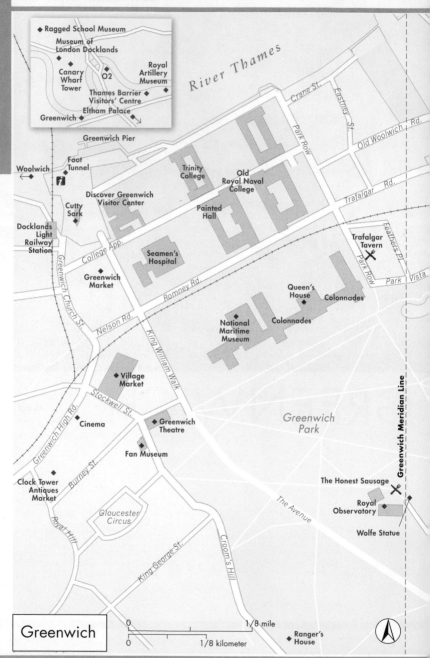

◆ Ragged School Museum

Museum of
London Docklands

Canary
Wharf
Tower

O2

Royal
Artillery
Museum

Thames Barrier
Visitors' Centre

Eltham Palace

Greenwich ◆

River Thames

Greenwich Pier

Woolwich

Foot
Tunnel

Crane St.

Eastney St.

Old Woolwich Rd.

Trinity
College

Old
Royal Naval
College

Park Row

Trafalgar Rd.

Feathers Pl.

Discover Greenwich
Visitor Center

Cutty
Sark

Painted
Hall

Trafalgar
Tavern

Park Row

Park Vista

Docklands
Light
Railway
Station

College App.

Seamen's
Hospital

Greenwich
Market

Queen's
House

Colonnades

Greenwich Church St.

Romney Rd.

Colonnades

Nelson Rd.

National
Maritime
Museum

King William Walk

Village
Market

Stockwell St.

Greenwich
Park

Greenwich Meridian Line

Cinema

Greenwich High Rd.

Greenwich
Theatre

Fan Museum

Burney St.

The Honest Sausage

Clock Tower
Antiques
Market

Royal Hill

Gloucester
Circus

The Avenue

Royal
Observatory

Wolfe Statue

King George St.

Croom's Hill

0   1/8 mile

0   1/8 kilometer

Greenwich

Ranger's
House

TOP REASONS TO GO

Stand astride the Greenwich Meridian Line: At the Royal Observatory—where the world's time is set—you can be in the eastern and western hemispheres simultaneously.

Sir Inigo Jones's Queen's House: This 17th-century building, part of the Old Royal Naval College, was massively influential in its day as the first in England to embrace the styles of the Italian Renaissance. See what all the fuss was about.

Discover Britain's seafaring past at the **National Maritime Museum:** See how Britannia ruled the waves and helped shape the modern world.

Step aboard the *Cutty Sark*: Take a stroll along the deck of the last surviving 19th-century tea clipper, newly shipshape after years of renovation.

FEELING PECKISH?

The Honest Sausage. Inside the park near the Royal Observatory, this delightful little café is a great pit stop for a traditional lunchtime snack. It specializes in straight-down-the-line, traditional sausage or bacon sandwiches, all sourced from an organic, free-range farm in Gloucestershire. And if a porcine snack doesn't curl your tail, you can opt for cake or coffee instead. ⊠ *Pavillion Tea House, Blackheath Ave., Greenwich Park, Greenwich* ☎ *020/8858–9695* ⊕ *www.companyofcooks.com.*

Trafalgar Tavern. With its excellent vista of the Thames, there is no more handsomely situated pub in Greenwich than the Trafalgar Tavern. Featured in Charles Dickens's *Our Mutual Friend*, it's still as grand a place to have a pint and some (upscale) pub grub as it ever was. ⊠ *Park Row, Greenwich* ☎ *020/8858–2909* ⊕ *www.trafalgartavern.co.uk.*

GETTING THERE

Docklands Light Railway (DLR) is a zippy way to get to Cutty Sark station from Canary Wharf and Bank Tube stations in The City. Or take the DLR to Island Gardens and walk the old Victorian Foot Tunnel under the river. (Sitting at the front of a train can be disconcerting, as you watch the controls in the fully automated driver's cab move about, as if a ghost were at the helm.) The best way to arrive, however—time and weather permitting—is like a sea captain of old: by water (though this way takes an hour from central London; ⇨ *for more on cruising the Thames, see Chapter 13).*

MAKING THE MOST OF YOUR TIME

Set apart from the rest of London, Greenwich is worth a day to itself—those who love maritime history will want to spend two—to make the most of walks in the rolling parklands and to immerse yourself in the richness of Greenwich's history, science, and architecture. The boat trip takes about an hour from Westminster Pier (next to Big Ben), or 25 minutes from the Tower of London, so factor in enough time for the round-trip.

NEAREST PUBLIC RESTROOMS

Duck into Discover Greenwich (⇨ *see below*), where loos are free.

About 8 miles downstream—which means seaward, to the east—from central London, Greenwich is a small borough that looms large across the world. Once the seat of British naval power, it is not only home to the Old Royal Observatory, which measures time for our entire planet, but also the Greenwich Meridian, which divides the world into two—you can stand astride it with one foot in either hemisphere.

Updated by
Jack Jewers

Bear in mind that the journey to Greenwich is an event in itself. In a rush, you can take the driverless DLR train—but many opt for arriving by boat along the Thames. This way, you glide past famous sights on the London skyline (there's a guaranteed spine chill on passing the Tower) and ever-changing docklands, and there's usually a chirpy Cock-er-ney navigator enlivening the journey with his fun commentary.

A visit to Greenwich feels like a trip to a rather elegant seaside town—albeit one with more than its fair share of historic sites. The grandiose **Old Royal Naval Hospital,** designed by Christopher Wren, was originally a home for veteran sailors. Today it's a popular visitor attraction, with a more glamorous second life as one of the most widely used movie locations in Britain.

Greenwich was originally home to one of England's finest Tudor palaces, and the birthplace of Henry VIII, Elizabeth I, and Mary I. Inigo Jones built what is considered the first "classical" building in England in 1616—the **Queen's House,** which now houses a collection of fine art. Britain was the world's preeminent naval power for over 500 years, and the excellent **National Maritime Museum** details that history in an engaging way. Its prize exhibits include the coat worn by Admiral Lord Nelson (1758–1805) in his final battle—bullet hole and all. The 19th-century tea clipper *Cutty Sark* was nearly destroyed by fire in 2007, but reopened in 2012 after a painstaking restoration. Now it's more pristine than ever, complete with an impressive new visitor center.

12

Greenwich Park, London's oldest royal park, is still home to fallow red deer, just as it has been since they were first introduced here for hunting by Henry VIII. The **Ranger's House** now houses a private art collection, next door to a beautifully manicured rose garden. Above it all is the **Royal Observatory,** where you can be in two hemispheres at once by standing along the **Greenwich Meridian Line,** before seeing a high-tech planetarium show.

> **FUN FACT**
>
> Hang out beneath the lightning-cracked Elizabeth Oak in Greenwich Park and you'll be following in illustrious footsteps—it's so called because Elizabeth I is supposed to have played in its branches as a girl.

Toward north Greenwich, the hopelessly ambitious Millennium Dome has been successfully reborn as the O2 and now hosts major concerts and stand-up comedy gigs. More adventurous visitors can also go **Up the O2** on a climbing expedition across the massive domed surface. Meanwhile, those who prefer excursions of a gentler kind may prefer to journey a couple of miles south of the borough, farther out into London's southern suburbs, to the shamefully underappreciated **Eltham Palace.** Once a favorite of Henry VIII, parts of the mansion were transformed into an art deco masterpiece during the 1930s.

TOP ATTRACTIONS

Fodor's Choice ★ *Cutty Sark.* This sleek, romantic clipper was built in 1869, one among a vast fleet of tall-masted wooden ships that plied the oceanic highways of the 19th century, trading in exotic commodities—in this case, tea. *Cutty Sark* (named after an old Scottish term for women's undergarments) was the fastest, sailing the London–China route in 1871 in only 107 days. The clipper has been preserved in dry dock as a museum ship since the 1950s, but was severely damaged in a devastating fire in 2007. As luck would have it, however, roughly half the ship had been dismantled and taken away for cleaning at the time. The ship reopened in 2012, with hugely improved visitor facilities; not only can you tour the painstakingly restored ship in its entirety, but the glittering new visitor center (which the ship now rests directly above, in an enormous gold mount) allows you to view the hull from below. A veritable museum of seafaring life, this boat was never too comfortable for the 28-strong crew (as you'll see). And don't forget to take in the very amusing collection of figureheads. ⊠ *King William Walk, Greenwich* ☎ *020/8858–4422* ⊕ *www.rmg.co.uk* ⊠ *£12* ⊙ *Daily 10–5; last admission at 4* Ⓜ *DLR: Cutty Sark.*

Discover Greenwich. Intended as a kind of anchor point for Greenwich's big three attractions—the Old Royal Naval College, *Cutty Sark,* and National Maritime Museum—this excellent, state-of-the-art visitor center includes interactive exhibitions on the history of Greenwich, plus an assortment of local treasures and artifacts. Most intriguing among them is a 17th-century "witch bottle," once used to ward off evil spirits. Modern X-rays have revealed it to contain a mixture of human hair, fingernails, and urine. ⊠ *Pepys Bldg., King William Walk, Greenwich* ☎ *020/8269–4799* ⊕ *www.ornc.org/visit/attractions/discover-greenwich-visitor-centre* ⊠ *Free* ⊙ *Daily 10–5* Ⓜ *DLR: Greenwich.*

ROYAL OBSERVATORY

✉ *Romney Rd., Greenwich*
☎ *020/8858–4422* ⊕ *www.*
rmg.co.uk/royal-observatory
📷 *Astronomy Centre free;*
Flamstead house and Meridian Line courtyard £7; planetarium shows £6.50; combined ticket £11.50 ⊙ *Daily 10–5 (May–Aug., Meridian courtyard until 6); last entry 30 mins before closing; last planetarium show at 4* ⊙ *Closed 1st Tues. of every month except Aug.* Ⓜ *DLR: Greenwich.*

TIPS

■ A brass line laid among the cobblestones marks the meridian. At night, a green laser shoots out, following exactly the path of the meridian line.

■ The Time Ball on Flamsteed House is one of the world's earliest time signals. Daily at 12:58 it rises to the top and at 1, it falls.

■ The hill that is home to the observatory has £1-a-slot telescopes to view the skyline. The Planetarium has three daily shows (purchase tickets online.)

Greenwich is on the prime meridian at 0° longitude, and the ultimate standard for time around the world has been set here since 1884, when Britain was the world's maritime superpower.

Highlights

The observatory is actually split into two sites, a short walk apart—one devoted to astronomy, the other to the study of time. The enchanting **Peter Harrison Planetarium** is London's only planetarium, its bronze-clad turret glinting in the sun. Shows on black holes and how to interpret the night sky are enthralling and enlightening. Even better for kids are the high-technology rooms of the **Astronomy Centre**, where space exploration is brought to life through cutting-edge interactive programs and fascinating exhibits—including the chance to touch a 4.5-billion-year-old meteorite.

Across the way is **Flamsteed House,** designed by Christopher Wren in 1675 for John Flamsteed, the first Royal Astronomer. A climb to the top of the house reveals a **28-inch telescope,** built in 1893 and now housed inside an onion-shaped fiberglass dome. It doesn't compare with the range of modern optical telescopes, but it's still the largest in the United Kingdom. Regular viewing evenings reveal startlingly detailed views of the lunar surface. In the **Time Galleries,** linger over the superb workmanship of John Harrison (1693–1776), whose famous **Maritime Clocks** won him the Longitude Prize for solving the problem of accurate timekeeping at sea, which greatly improved navigation.

DID YOU KNOW?

Once sailors could determine their distance from the Greenwich meridian (longitude), maritime navigation was greatly improved. Look for the brass line marking the two hemispheres throughout the cobblestone streets.

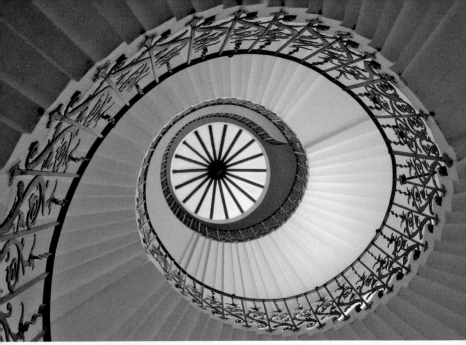

Without a central support, the Tulip Stair spirals up to the Great Hall of Queen's House.

Fodor's Choice **Eltham Palace.** Once a favorite getaway for Henry VIII (who liked to
★ spend Christmas here), Eltham Palace has been drastically remodeled
twice in its lifetime; once each during the 15th and 16th centuries,
and again during the 1930s, when a grand mansion was annexed onto
the Tudor great hall by the super-wealthy Coulthard family. Today
it's an extraordinary combination of late medieval grandeur and art
deco masterpiece, laced with an eccentric whimsy—the Coulthards
even built an entire room for the personal quarters of their beloved
pet lemur. The house and its extensive gardens were fully restored
when the palace finally entered public ownership in the late 1990s.
⊠ *Court Rd., Eltham* ☎ *020/8294–2548* ⊕ *www.english-heritage.org.
uk* ⊠ *£9.90* ☉ *Apr.–Oct. and late Feb., Sun.–Wed. 10–5; Nov.–Mar.,
Sun. 10–4* Ⓜ *Eltham.*

Greenwich Market. Established as a fruit-and-vegetable market in
1700, the covered market now offers mixed stalls of art and crafts
on Wednesday, Saturday, and Sunday; antiques and collectibles on
Tuesday, Thursday, and Friday. You can get food to go on each market day, although the offerings are usually best on weekends. Shopping for handicrafts is a pleasure here, as in most cases you're buying
directly from the artist. ⊠ *College Approach, Greenwich* ☎ *020/8269–
5090* ⊕ *www.greenwichmarketlondon.com* ☉ *Tues.–Sun. 9:30–5:30*
Ⓜ *DLR: Cutty Sark.*

Museum of London Docklands. This wonderful old warehouse building,
on a quaint cobbled quayside beside the tower of Canary Wharf, is
alone worth a visit. With uneven wood floors, beams, and pillars,
the museum used to be a storehouse for coffee, tea, sugar, and rum

THE DOCKLANDS RENAISSANCE

For centuries the Thames was a fevered hub of activity. Great palaces were built along the river, most long gone (such as White-hall, which dwarfed even Versailles in splendor). Dock warehouses sprang up to the east of London in the 18th century to cater to the burgeoning trade in luxury goods, from tea, coffee, and spices to silks and exotic pets. By the 1950s, however, this trade had all but disappeared—partly due to the devastation of World War II, but also because trading vessels had simply gotten too big to fit along the river. The area all but died away until a massive regenera-tion scheme known as Docklands was completed in the 1980s. It brought renewal in the form of cutting-edge architecture, galler-ies, restaurants, and bars. Many of the old warehouses were restored and are now used as museums or shopping malls, such as Hay's and Butler's wharves. The best way to explore is on the **Docklands Light Railway (DLR),** an elevated track that appears to skim over the water past the swanky glass buildings. If you explore on foot, the Thames

Path has helpful plaques along the way, with nuggets of historical information.

Firepower Royal Artillery Museum. Adjacent to the old Royal Dockyard at Woolwich is a brilliant exhibition, the Firepower Royal Artillery Museum. The **Field of Fire** experience is a powerful re-creation of what it was actually like to be in the thick of the London Blitz or the D-Day Landings, complete with giant projections of archive film on all sides, live smoke effects, and a floor that quakes in time to the roar of exploding bombs. The rest of the museum explores the role of the gunner, from the discovery of gunpowder to the present day. Also on show are tanks and guns—some complete with battle scars. Housed in the old Royal Arsenal leading down to the river shore, the museum's setting provides a powerful sense of the Thames and its lingering effect on the capital's history. ✉ *Royal Arsenal, Woolwich* ☎ *020/8855-7755* ⊕ *www. firepower.org.uk* 💷 *£5:30* ⊙ *Tues.– Sat. 10–5; last admission at 4* Ⓜ *DLR: Woolwich Arsenal.*

from the West Indies—hence the name West India Quay. The fasci-nating story of the old port and the river is told using films, together with interactive displays and reconstructions; a permanent exhibition, London, Sugar, and Slavery, outlines the capital's involvement in the slave trade. The museum runs a highlights tour (free) on Wednesday and Sunday at 3 pm. There are also a few special themed tours per season; call or see the website for details. ■ TIP➔ On the second Friday of every month the museum hosts the Docklands Cinema Club, which shows rare and classic films, together with talks, inside the old ware-house. ✉ *No. 1 Warehouse, West India Quay, Canary Wharf, Canary Wharf* ☎ *020/7001–9844* ⊕ *www.museumoflondon.org.uk/docklands* 💷 *Free* ⊙ *Daily 10–6; last admission at 5:40* Ⓜ *Canary Wharf; DLR: West India Quay.*

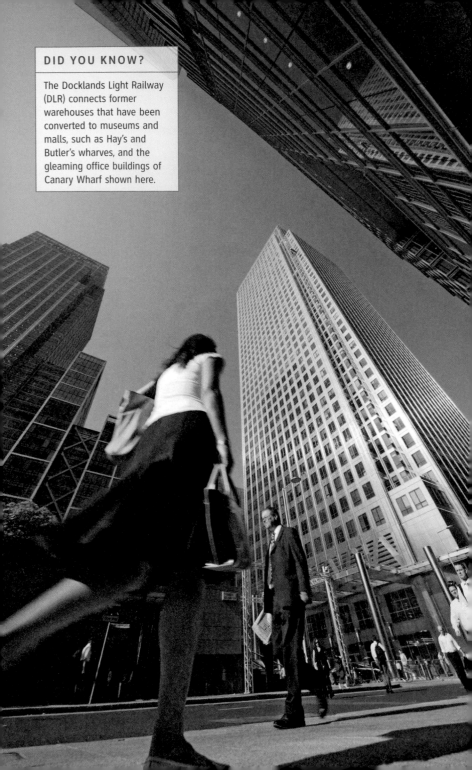

Fodor's Choice ★ **National Maritime Museum.** From the time of Henry VIII until the 1940s Britain was the world's preeminent naval power, and the collections here trace half a millennia of that seafaring history. The story is as much about trade as it is warfare; the "Atlantic Worlds" gallery explores how trade in goods—and people—helped shape the New World, while "Voyagers: Britons and the Sea" focuses on stories of the ordinary people who took to the waves over the centuries. One gallery is devoted to Admiral Lord Nelson, Britain's most famous naval commander, and among the exhibits is the uniform he was wearing, complete with bloodstains, when he died at the Battle of Trafalgar in 1805. Temporary exhibitions here are usually fascinating; those in recent years have included the

> ## GREENWICH FOOT TUNNEL
>
> In a brilliant piece of foresight in 1849, Greenwich Hospital bought Island Gardens, on the other side of the Thames, to guard against industrial sprawl and preserve one of the most beautiful views in London. Take the stone spiral steps down into Greenwich Foot Tunnel and head under the Thames (enjoying the magnificently creepy echo) to Island Gardens, at the southern tip of the Isle of Dogs. Then look back over the river for a magnificent vista: the Old Royal Naval College and Queen's House in all their glory, framed by the verdant green borders of the park.

Arctic convoys of World War II and life in the British navy of the 18th century. ■TIP➔ The museum has a good café with views over Greenwich Park. The adjacent **Queen's House** is home to the museum's art collection, the largest collection of maritime art in the world, including works by William Hogarth, Canaletto, and Joshua Reynolds. Permission for its construction was granted by Queen Anne only on condition that the river vista from the house be preserved, and there are few more majestic views in London than Inigo Jones's awe-inspiring symmetry. Completed around 1638, the Tulip Stair, named for the fleur-de-lis-style pattern on the balustrade, is especially fine, spiraling up without a central support to the Great Hall. The Great Hall itself is a perfect cube, exactly 40 feet in all three dimensions, decorated with paintings of the Muses and the Virtues. ⊠ *Romney Rd., Greenwich* ☎ *020/8858–4422* ⊕ *www.rmg.co.uk/national-maritime-museum* ⊠ *Free* ⊗ *Daily 10–5; last admission at 4:30* Ⓜ *DLR: Greenwich.*

Fodor's Choice ★ **Old Royal Naval College.** Begun by Christopher Wren in 1694 as a rest home for ancient mariners, the college became a school in 1873. It's still used for classes by the University of Greenwich and the Trinity College of Music, although you're more likely to recognize it as a film location—recent blockbusters to have made use of its elegant interiors include *Skyfall*, *Les Misérables*, and *The King's Speech*. Architecturally, you'll notice how the structures part to reveal the **Queen's House** across the central lawns. Behind the college are two more buildings you can visit. The **Painted Hall,** the college's dining hall, which derives its name from the baroque murals of William and Mary (reigned jointly 1689–95; William alone 1695–1702) and assorted allegorical figures. James Thornhill's frescoes, depicting scenes of naval grandeur with a suitably pro-British note of propaganda, were painstakingly completed between 1708–12 and 1718–26, and were good enough to earn him a knighthood. In the opposite building stands the **College Chapel,** which was rebuilt after a fire in 1779 in an altogether more restrained, neo-Grecian style. ■ **TIP→** Check the website for a great program of special events, including talks, tours, and concerts—many of them free. ⊠ *Old Royal Naval College, King William Walk, Greenwich* ☏ *020/8269–4747* ⊕ *www.ornc.org* ⌧ *Free, guided tours £6* ⊙ *Painted Hall and chapel daily 10–5 (Sun. chapel from 12:30); grounds 8–6* Ⓜ *DLR: Greenwich.*

Royal Observatory.

See the highlighted listing in this chapter.

WORTH NOTING

Clock Tower Antiques Market. The weekend Clock Tower Antiques Market on Greenwich High Road has more vintage shopping, and browsing among the "small collectibles" makes for a good half-hour diversion. ⊠ *166 Greenwich High Rd., Greenwich* ☏ *020/7237–2001* ⊕ *www. clocktowermarket.co.uk* ⊙ *Weekends 10–5* Ⓜ *Greenwich Rail.*

Up at the O2. Certainly one of the most unique ways to see London, this thrilling urban expedition takes you on a journey across the giant dome of the O2 arena. After a short briefing, you're dressed in safety gear and taken in small groups across a steep walkway, running all the way to the summit and down the other side. The high point (literally) is a viewing platform, 161 feet above ground, with magnificent views of the city. It's quite an experience, but unsurprisingly there are restrictions: you have to be at least 10 years old, more than 4 feet tall, have a waist measurement that's less than 49 inches, and weigh less than 286 pounds. Wheelchairs can be accommodated on a few tours. ■ **TIP→** Advanced booking is essential. ⊠ *Peninsula Sq.* ☏ *020/463–2000* ⊕ *www.theo2.co.uk/upattheo2* ⌧ *From £25 (varies according to time and date)* ⊙ *Tours daily 10–10 summer, 10–6 winter* Ⓜ *North Greenwich.*

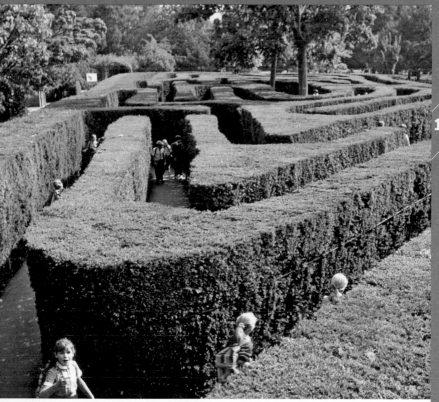

THE THAMES UPSTREAM

GETTING ORIENTED

The Thames Upstream

A GOOD WALK

From Chiswick House, follow Burlington Lane and take a left onto Hogarth Lane—which, in reality, is anything but a lane—to reach Hogarth's House. Chiswick's Church Street (reached by a rather unappealing underpass from Hogarth's House) is the nearest thing to a sleepy country village street you're likely to find in London. Follow it down to the Thames and turn left at the bottom to reach the 18th-century riverfront houses of Chiswick Mall, referred to by locals as "Millionaire's Row." There are several pretty riverside pubs near Hammersmith Bridge.

MAKING THE MOST OF YOUR TIME

Hampton Court Palace requires half a day to experience its magic, though you could make do with a few hours for the other attractions. Because of the distance between sights, it's best to focus on one sight, add in some others within the area, then a riverside walk and pint at a pub.

FEELING PECKISH?

The Original Maids of Honour. This most traditional of Old English tearooms is named for a type of jam tart invented here and still baked by hand on the premises. Legend has it that Henry VIII loved them so much he had the recipe kept under armed guard. Full afternoon tea is served daily 2:30–6, and lunch in two sittings at 12:30 and 1:45. Or opt to take out food for a picnic at Kew Gardens or on Kew Green. ⊠ *288 Kew Rd., Kew* ☎ *020/8940–2752* ⊕ *www.theoriginalmaidsofhonour.co.uk.*

13

GETTING THERE

The District line is the best of the Tube options, stopping at Turnham Green (in the heart of Chiswick but a walk from the houses), Gunnersbury (for Syon Park), Kew Gardens, and Richmond. For Hampton Court, overland train is quickest: South West trains run from Waterloo twice an hour, with roughly half requiring a change at Surbiton. There are also regular, direct trains from Waterloo to Chiswick station (best for Chiswick House), Kew Bridge, Richmond (for Ham House), and St. Margaret's (best for Marble Hill House). London overground trains also stop at Gunnersbury, Kew Gardens, and Richmond.

A pleasant way to go is by river. Boats depart from Westminster Pier, by Big Ben, for Kew (1½ hours), Richmond (2 hours), and Hampton Court (3 hours). The trip is worth taking if you make it an integral part of your day, and know that it gets breezy. Round trip costs between £18 and £23. For more details contact **Transport For London** (☎ 0843/222–1234 ⊕ www.tfl. gov.uk).

TOP REASONS TO GO

Explore Hampton Court Palace: Go ghost hunting or just admire the beautiful Tudor architecture at Henry VIII's beloved home, then lose yourself in the maze as dusk begins to fall.

Go "Goth" at Strawberry Hill: The 19th-century birthplace of connoisseur Horace Walpole's "Gothick" style, this mock-castle is a joyous riot of color and invention.

Escape to magical Kew Gardens: See the earth from above by visiting Kew's treetop walkway at the famous Royal Botanic Gardens.

Pay your respects to Father Thames: Enjoy a pint from the creaking balcony of a centuries-old riverside pub as you watch the boats row by on the loveliest stretch of England's greatest river.

NEAREST PUBLIC RESTROOMS

Richmond Park, Kew Gardens, and all the stately homes have public restrooms.

Sightseeing
★★★★

Nightlife
★★

Dining
★★★

Lodging
★★

Shopping
★★

The upper stretch of the Thames links a string of fashionable districts—Chiswick, Kew, Richmond, and Putney—with winding old streets, horticultural delights, cozy riverside pubs, and Henry VIII's Hampton Court Palace. The neighborhoods along the way are as proud of their villagey feel as of their stately history, witnessed by such handsome estates as Strawberry Hill and Syon House. After the sensory overload of the West End, it's easy to forget you're in a capital city at all.

CHISWICK

Updated by
Jack Jewers

On the banks of the Thames just west of central London, far enough out to escape the crush and crowds you've probably just started to get used to, Chiswick is a low-key, upscale district, content with its run of restaurants, stylish shops, and film-star residents. No doubt its most famous son wouldn't approve of all the conspicuous wealth, though; Chiswick was home to one of Britain's best-loved painters, William Hogarth, who tore the fabric of the 18th-century nation to shreds with his slew of satirical engravings. **Hogarth's House** has been restored to its former glory. Incongruously stranded among Chiswick's row houses are a number of fine 18th-century buildings, which are now some of the most desirable suburban houses in London. By far the grandest of all is **Chiswick House,** a unique Palladian-style mansion born from the third Earl of Burlington's love of classical and Renaissance architecture—a radical style at the time.

TOP ATTRACTIONS

Fodor'sChoice
★

Chiswick House. Completed in 1729 by the 3rd earl of Burlington (also known for Burlington House—home of the Royal Academy—and Burlington Arcade on Piccadilly), this extraordinary Palladian mansion was envisaged as a kind of temple to the arts. Burlington was fascinated by the architecture he saw in Italy while on the Grand Tour as a young man. When his country home was destroyed by fire in 1725, he seized the chance to rebuild it in homage to those classical and Renaissance styles. The building is loosely modeled on the Villa Capra near Vicenza, while the colonnaded frontage is a partial replica of the Pantheon in Rome (which also inspired the domed roof).

The sumptuous interiors were the work of William Kent (1685–1748), his most extraordinary achievement being the Blue Velvet Room, with its gilded decoration and intricate painted ceiling. The design of Chiswick House sparked a great deal of interest—such ideas were radical in England at the time—and turned Kent into a hugely influential figure in British architecture. So great was his fame that wealthy patrons clamored to have him design anything, from gardens to party frocks.

The rambling grounds are one of the hidden gems of west London. Italianate in style (of course), they are filled with classical temples, statues, and obelisks. Also on the grounds are a café and a children's play area. ⊠ *Burlington La., Chiswick* ☎ *020/8995–0508* ⊕ *www.chgt.org. uk* ⊠ *£5.90; grounds free* ☉ *Grounds daily 7 am–dusk; house Apr.– Oct., Sun.–Wed. and holiday Mon. 10–5* Ⓜ *Turnham Green, Chiswick. National Rail: Chiswick.*

Hogarth's House. Besieged by a roaring highway that somewhat spoils the atmosphere, the home of the satirist and painter William Hogarth (1697–1764) is still worth a visit by fans of his amusing, moralistic engravings (such as "The Rake's Progress" and "Marriage à la Mode"). Sadly, the house has had an unlucky few years; closed by a fire in 2008, restoration work was then halted by a second fire the following year. However, now fully reopened, the house contains exhibition spaces devoted to Hogarth and his work. Look out for the 300-year-old mulberry tree in the garden—the remnant of a failed attempt to get silkworms to breed in England. Hogarth's tomb can be found in the cemetery of St. Nicholas's church on nearby Chiswick Mall. ⊠ *Hogarth La., Great West Rd. (A4), Chiswick* ☎ *020/8994–6757* ⊕ *www. hounslow.info/arts/hogarthshouse* ⊠ *Free* ☉ *Tues.–Sun. and holiday Mon. noon–5* Ⓜ *Turnham Green. National Rail: Chiswick.*

HOGARTH HEAVEN

Fosters Bookshop. A great place to buy Hogarth prints is at Fosters Bookshop, based in Chiswick's oldest shop building. The shop has its original Georgian frontage, creaking floorboards, and a glorious number of original Victorian novels and essays. It also offers handwritten gift vouchers from £10 to £50,000. ⊠ *183 Chiswick High Rd., Chiswick* ☎ *020/8995-2768* ⊕ *www.fostersbookshop.co.uk.*

13

QUICK BITES

Some of the loveliest pubs in London sit beside the Thames at Chiswick, dotted along the northern bank of the river as far as Hammersmith Mall— the last remaining fragment of what was once a pretty old village, now all but replaced by urban sprawl.

Blue Anchor. This cozy 18th-century watering hole on the Thames overlooks Hammersmith Bridge—a High Victorian, wrought-iron suspension bridge designed by Sir Joseph Bazalgette in 1887. The rowing memorabilia on the walls hints at the Blue Anchor's importance on the day of the annual Oxford-versus-Cambridge university boat race, when it's an unofficial meeting point for fans and race officials. The pub serves also serves light meals. ⊠ *13 Lower Mall, Hammersmith* ☎ *020/8748–5774* ⊕ *www.blueanchorlondon.com.*

City Barge. One of the few pubs in this upscale quarter of Chiswick that retains a proper, old-school feel, the City Barge overlooks a tiny island in the middle of the Thames. Stop for some excellent pub grub at lunchtime (modern British without too much of a gentrified edge), or just enjoy a pint and watch the river flow by. ⊠ *27 Strand-on-the-Green, Chiswick* ☎ *020/8994–2148* Ⓜ *Gunnersbury. National Rail: Kew Bridge.*

Dove Inn. Retaining the charm of its 300-plus-year heritage, the Dove has a little terrace that's a tranquil place to watch the river flow by. Check out the Lilliputian room immediately on the right as you enter—it's in the Guinness Book of Records for being the smallest bar in the world. ⊠ *19 Upper Mall, Hammersmith* ☎ *020/8748–9474* ⊕ *www.dovehammersmith. co.uk* Ⓜ *Ravenscourt Park, Hammersmith.*

KEW

A mile or so beyond Chiswick is Kew, a leafy suburb with little to see other than its two big attractions: the lovely **Kew Palace** and the **Royal Botanic Gardens**—anchored in the landscape for several miles around by a towering, mock-Chinese pagoda.

TOP ATTRACTIONS

FAMILY **Kew Gardens.**

See the highlighted listing in this chapter.

Fodor'sChoice **Kew Palace and Queen Charlotte's Cottage.** The elegant redbrick exterior of the smallest of Britain's royal palaces seems almost humble ★ when compared with the grandeur of, say, Buckingham or Kensington palaces. Yet inside is a fascinating glimpse into life at the uppermost end of society from the 17th to 19th century. This is actually the third of several palaces that stood here; once known as Dutch House, it was one of the havens to which George III retired when insanity forced him to withdraw from public life. Queen Charlotte had an *orné*—a rustic-style cottage retreat—added in the late 18th century. In a marvelously regal flight of fancy, she kept kangaroos in the paddock outside. The main house and gardens are maintained in the 18th-century style. ⚠ Entry to the palace itself is free, but it lies within the grounds of Kew Gardens, to which you must buy a ticket in order to enter. ⊠ *Kew Gardens, Kew Rd. at Lichfield Rd., Kew* ☎ *0844/482–7777 (only in U.K.), 020/3166–6000* ⊕ *www.hrp.org. uk* 🖼 *Free; separate charge for entering Kew Gardens* ⊙ *Palace late Mar.–Sept., daily 9:30–5:30; Queen Charlotte's Cottage late Mar.– Sept., weekends 10–4* Ⓜ *Kew Gardens.*

KEW GARDENS

✉ *Kew Rd. at Lichfield Rd., for Victoria Gate entrance, Kew* ☎ *020/8332-5655* ⊕ *www.kew.org* 💷 *£16.50* ◷ *Mid-Feb.–Mar., daily 9:30–5:30; Apr.–late Aug., weekdays 9:30–6:30, weekends and holiday Mon. 9:30–7:30; late Aug.–late Oct., daily 9:30–6; late Oct.–mid-Feb., daily 9:30–4:15. Last admission to park, glasshouses, galleries, and treetop walkway 30 mins before closing* Ⓜ *Kew Gardens. National Rail: Kew Gardens, Kew Bridge.*

TIPS

■ Free guided tours, run by volunteers, are held daily at 11 am and 1:30 pm.

■ The Kew Explorer bus runs on a 40-minute, hop-on, hop-off route around the gardens every hour from 11 to 3. Tickets cost £4 in summer, £2 in winter.

■ Discovery Tours are adapted and fully accessible, aimed at disabled visitors.

■ Walking tours are £5 per group, bus tours £30 per group. Book in advance.

■ Enjoy tea at the Victoria Terrace Café or a meal at the Orangery or White Peaks.

Enter the Royal Botanic Gardens, as Kew Gardens are officially known, and you are enveloped by blazes of color, extraordinary blooms, hidden trails, and lovely old follies. Beautiful though it all is, Kew's charms are secondary to its true purpose as a major center for serious research. Academics are hard at work on more than 300 scientific projects across as many acres, analyzing everything from the cacti of eastern Brazil to the yams of Madagascar. First opened to the public in 1840, Kew has been supported by royalty and nurtured by landscapers, botanists, and architects since the 1720s. Today the gardens, now a Unesco World Heritage site, hold more than 30,000 species of plants, from every corner of the globe.

Although the plant houses make Kew worth visiting even in the depths of winter (there's also a seasonal garden), the flower beds are, of course, best enjoyed in the fullness of spring and summer.

Highlights

Two great 19th-century greenhouses—the **Palm House** and the **Temperate House**—are filled with exotic blooms, and many of the plants have been there since the final glass panel was fixed into place. The enormous Temperate House contains the largest greenhouse plant in the world, a Chilean wine palm rooted in 1846. (It's so big that you have to climb the spiral staircase to the roof to get a proper view of it.) Architect Sir William Chambers built a series of temples and follies, of which the crazy 10-story **Pagoda**, visible for miles around, is the star turn. The Princess of Wales conservatory houses 10 climate zones, and the Rhizotron and Xstrata Treetop Walkway takes you 59 feet up into the air.

RICHMOND

Named after the (long-vanished) palace Henry VII started here in 1500, Richmond is still a welcoming suburb with a small-town feel, marred only by choking levels of traffic. Duck away from the main streets to find many handsome Georgian and Victorian houses, antiques shops, a Victorian theater, a grand stately home—and, best of all, the largest of London's royal parks.

TOP ATTRACTIONS

13

Ham House. To the west of Richmond Park, overlooking the Thames and nearly opposite the memorably named Eel Pie Island, Ham House was built in 1610 and remodeled 50 years later. It's one of the most complete examples in Europe of a lavish 17th-century house, together with a restored formal garden that has become an influential source for other European palaces and grand villas. The original decorations in the Great Hall, Round Gallery, and Great Staircase have been replicated, and all the furniture and fittings are on permanent loan from the Victoria & Albert Museum. A tranquil and scenic way to reach the house is on foot, which takes about 30 minutes, along the eastern riverbank south from Richmond Bridge. ⊠ *Ham St., Richmond* ☎ *020/8940–1950* ⊕ *www.nationaltrust.org.uk* ⊠ *House, gardens, and outbuildings £10.90; gardens only £3.65* ☉ *House mid-Feb.–Mar., Sat.–Mon. 11:30–3:30; Apr.–Sept., Sat.–Wed. noon–4; Oct.–Nov., Sat.–Tues. 11:30–3. Gardens Nov.–mid-Feb., daily 11–4; mid-Feb.–Oct., daily 11–5* Ⓜ *Richmond, then Bus 65 or 371.*

Fodor's Choice ★ **Hampton Court Palace.**

See the highlighted listing in this chapter.

Marble Hill House. This handsome Palladian mansion is set in 66 acres of parkland on the northern bank of the Thames, almost opposite Ham House. It was built in the 1720s by George II for his mistress, the "exceedingly respectable and respected" Henrietta Howard. Later the house was occupied by Mrs. Fitzherbert, who was secretly married to the Prince Regent (later George IV) in 1785. The house was restored in 1901 and opened to the public two years later, looking very much like it did in Georgian times, with extravagant gilded rooms in which Ms. Howard entertained the literary superstars of the age, including Pope, Gay, and Swift. A ferry service from Ham House operates during the summer; access on foot is a half-hour walk south along the west bank of the Thames from Richmond Bridge. Note that entry is by guided tour only, run by English Heritage and volunteers from a local history group. ⊠ *Richmond Rd., Twickenham* ☎ *020/8892–5115* ⊕ *www.english-heritage.org.uk* ⊠ *£5.70 (guided tour only)* ☉ *House and park: Apr.–Oct., Sat. 10–2, Sun. and holiday Mon. 10–5; tours 10:30 and noon on weekends, with additional tours 2:15 and 3:30 on Sun. Park only: Nov.–Mar., daily 7–5* Ⓜ *Richmond. National Rail: St Margarets.*

FAMILY **Richmond Park.** This enormous park was enclosed in 1637 for use as a royal hunting ground—like practically all other London parks. Unlike the others, however, Richmond Park still has wild red and fallow deer roaming its 2,360 acres (that's three times the size of New York's Central Park) of grassland and heath. Its ancient oaks are among the last remnants of the vast, wild forests that once encroached on London in medieval times. The Isabella Plantation (near the Ham Gate entrance) is an enchanting and colorful woodland garden, first laid out in 1831. ■TIP➔ There's a splendid, protected view of St. Paul's Cathedral from King Henry VIII's Mound, the highest point in the park. Find it and you have a piece of magic in your sights. The park is also home to White Lodge, a 1727 hunting lodge that now houses the Royal Ballet School. ⊠ *Richmond* ☎ *030/0061–2200* ⊕ *www.royalparks.org.uk* ✉ *Free* ⊙ *Apr.–Oct., 7–dusk; Nov.–Mar., 7:30–dusk* Ⓜ *Richmond, then Bus 371 or 65.*

> **WORD OF MOUTH**
>
> "My mother and I took the train out to Hampton Court and the boat back. It was enjoyable but it does take several [3] hours … it was pleasant to look at the houses, pubs, etc. as we passed by. It was interesting to pass under various bridges coming into London and also we passed the Parliament Buildings."
>
> —raincitygirl

QUICK BITES

White Cross. Overlooking the Thames so closely that the waters almost lap at the door in high tide, the White Cross is a popular spot that serves traditional pub grub. ⊠ *Water La., Richmond* ☎ *020/8940–6844* ⊕ *www.youngs.co.uk.*

Fodor's Choice ★

Strawberry Hill. From the outside, this Rococo mishmash of towers, crenellations, and dazzling white stucco is almost fairy-tale-ish in its faux-medieval splendor. Its architect, Sir Horace Walpole (1717–97), knew a thing or two about imaginative flights of fancy—the flamboyant son of the first British prime minister, Robert Walpole, he all but single-handedly invented the Gothic Revival style with his novel *The Castle of Otranto* (1764). Once inside, the forbidding exterior gives way to a veritable explosion of color and light, for Walpole boldly decided to take elements from the exteriors of Gothic cathedrals and move them inside. The detail is extraordinary, from the cavernous entrance hall with its vast Gothic trompe l'oeil, to the Great Parlour with its Renaissance stained glass, to the Gallery, where extraordinary fan vaulting is a replica of the vaults found in Henry VIII's chapel at Westminster Abbey. Neglected for years, Strawberry Hill reopened in 2011 after a stunningly successful £9-million restoration. The gardens have also been meticulously returned to their original 18th-century design, right down to a white marble love seat sculpted into the shape of a shell. ■TIP➔ You can book a tour of the house at twilight for £20, including a glass of Prosecco. ⊠ *268 Waldegrave Rd., Twickenham* ☎ *020/8744–1241* ⊕ *www.strawberryhillhouse.org.uk* ✉ *£8.40* ⊙ *Timed entry, every 20 mins; Mar.–early Nov., Mon.–Wed. 2–6, weekends noon–6; last admission 1 hr 40 mins before closing. 1 wk. in early Dec., Sat.–Wed. noon–5:30; last admission 50 mins before closing. Garden daily 10–6* Ⓜ *Richmond, then Bus 33; National Rail: Strawberry Hill Station.*

Continued on page 235

Tower Bridge

A TOUR OF THE THAMES

*"I have seen the Mississippi. That is muddy water.
I have seen the St. Lawrence. That is crystal water.
But the Thames is liquid history."*
—John Burns

The twists and turns of the Thames River through the heart of the capital make it London's best thoroughfare and most compelling viewing point. Once famous for sludge, silt, and sewage, the Thames is now the cleanest city river in the world. Whether you take a river cruise or a leisurely stroll along its banks and bridges, traveling on or alongside the river is an unforgettable way to soak up views of the city.

Parliament

MILLENNIUM BRIDGE TO THAMES FLOOD BARRIER

Tower Bridge

The **Millennium Bridge** is the newest span across the river: **St. Paul's Cathedral** and **Tate Modern** eye each other magnificently from either side of the once worryingly wobbly strip of a bridge. Farther east, the reconstructed **Shakespeare's Globe Theatre** is resplendent in whitewash and brown timber on the South Bank.

Between Southwark and London bridges, look for the southside *Golden Hinde*, an exact scale reconstruction of Sir Francis Drake's galleon that sailed around the world.

Moored outside the Victorian shopping mall **Hay's Galleria** is **HMS** *Belfast*, Europe's last existing armored warship that saw action in World War II, now a floating naval museum on nine decks.

London Bridge is admittedly not the river's finest, but it is the birthplace of the city. Some say the river ceases to be picturesque after St. Paul's, but we disagree: look for the flaming crown of the **Monument**, Sir Christopher Wren's tribute to those who died in the 1666 Great Fire of London.

The splendid **Tower of London** sits proudly opposite the shining egg of **City Hall** (also referred to by the former London mayor Ken Livingstone as a giant "glass testicle"—a fine match for its phallic friend across the river, the **Swiss Re Building**, aka the Gherkin, both designed by a mischievous Norman Foster). They frame the 1894 **Tower Bridge**, a magnificent feat of engineering and style, which leads past the elegant confines of **St. Katharine's Docks**, the trendy restaurants of **Butler's Wharf**, and the **Design Museum**.

LONDON BRIDGE

Viking invaders destroyed London Bridge in 1014, hence the nursery rhyme "London Bridge is falling down." By 1962, London Bridge really was falling down again, its 1831 incarnation unable to take the strain of traffic. It was saved by American tycoon Robert McCulloch, who—possibly confusing the bridge with its much more splendid neighbor, Tower Bridge—bought it in 1968 for $2.46 million and had it shipped, stone by stone, to Lake Havasu in Arizona.

Thames Flood Barrier

For the pièce de résistance of London's redevelopment, stay on the river until you reach the bright lights and tall reflective sides of **Canary Wharf**, the city's new business district, robotic in its modernity.

Step back in time at **Greenwich**, with the glorious **Royal Naval College** and the **National Maritime Museum**. Round the bend and you're back to the future, with the alien spaceship **O2** (formerly the Millennium Dome) and the **Thames Flood Barrier** looming.

Walking bridge at Canary Wharf

Limehouse Basin

Canary Wharf
Canary Wharf Pier

Hilton Docklands
Nelson Dock Pier

West India
Millwall Docks

O2

Design Museum

Greenland Docks

Greenland Pier

Millwall
Outer Docks

Thames Flood Barrier

Masthouse Terrace Pier

Royal Naval College

Greenwich Pier

National Maritime Museum

Greenwich

Greenwich Park

0   1/4 mi
0   1/4 km

WANDSWORTH TO BLACKFRIARS

Parliament

Blackfriars Bridge at night.

Battersea Br.

Albert Br.

Chelsea Harbour Pier

Chelsea Br.

Grosvenor Br.

Battersea Park

Battersea Power Station

South Park

0   1/2 mi

0   1/2 km

Wandsworth Br.

WALKING THE THAMES

Even if you lack sea legs, you can still enjoy the river: not much beats a wander beside London's waterway. The Thames Path (www.nationaltrail.co.uk) follows the river 184 miles, from its source to the flood barriers in Greenwich. Some of the best riverside strolls:

- Hammersmith Bridge to Chiswick Mall
- Golden Jubilee Bridges to the South Bank's Queen's Walk
- Cleopatra's Needle to Parliament along Victoria Embankment
- Tate Modern to St. Paul's over Millennium Bridge

Beyond **Wandsworth Bridge**, the early part of this stretch by Battersea Bridge, rebuilt in 1890, was London's real industrial heartland, the southern side chock full of cottage housing for laborers, artisans at work, and factories.

The real treat of this stretch is the view of the **Houses of Parliament** and, beyond that, **Westminster Abbey**. **Victoria Embankment**, stretching all the way from Westminster to Blackfriars, was once all grim mudflats. In 1878 it became the country's first electrically illuminated street, and today its fine architecture, trees, and gardens are perfect strolling territory.

View from London Eye (left); House's of Parliament (right)

You can't miss the **London Eye**, whose parts were brought down the Thames one by one before being assembled on-location. Look out too for the London Aquarium and the Dalí museum, housed in the baroque-style County Hall.

Cleopatra's Needle, overlooking the Thames by Embankment, dates back to Heliopolis in 1450 BC. Look for World War I shrapnel holes and gouges at the base.

Further on is the **Oxo Tower**, whose red-glass letters were designed in 1928 to spell out the brand name while circumventing tight laws on exterior advertising.

By **Blackfriars Bridge**, named after the monks who wore black robes and lived on the north bank during the Middle Ages, the river used to run red by the riverside tanneries and slaughterhouses.

After **Albert Bridge**—glorious at night, with lights like luminescent pearls sweeping down on strings—the Thames is a metropolitan glory of a river, charging through fashionable **Chelsea** and past the now derelict **Battersea Power Station**, under Chelsea, Vauxhall and Lambeth Bridges, with **Lambeth Palace** to the south.

The **Golden Jubilee Bridges** by **Embankment**, two beautifully lit steel-cabled pedestrian walkways, are perfect for reaching the **South Bank**.

Look out for the golden eagle, a monument to World War I RAF fighters, and **Cleopatra's Needle**. For the ultimate double-decker bus-viewing moment, look at **Waterloo Bridge**, once known as Ladies Bridge because it was built by female labor during World War II. The bridge has great views of the South Bank.

Blackfriars Bridge

HAMPTON COURT PALACE TO PUTNEY

The Great Conservatory at Syon Park

Hampton Court Palace is a suitably lavish start or end to any trip on the Thames. The river skirts the grounds, giving magnificent views over the Tudor palace that Henry VIII and his daughter Elizabeth I made home, and continues north to **Kingston Bridge**, starting point for the river voyage of Jerome K. Jerome's *Three Men in a Boat* and home to hectic summer regattas. At **Teddington**, where the poet Alexander Pope and writer Horace Walpole entertained their female admirers in the 18th century, the river turns tidal but remains quiet and unspoiled all the way to **Kew**, passing herons and fine stately homes standing proud on the banks. From **Twickenham Bridge** you round the old deer park (to the south) and **Syon Park** (north), which has belonged to the Duke of

Waterlily House at Kew Gardens

Northumberland's family for centuries. Beyond that is an even greater treat—the UNESCO World Heritage Site of **Kew Botanical Gardens**. All manner of rowboats set up for one, two, four, or eight people pull hard under **Chiswick Bridge** and **Barnes (railway) Bridge**, past the expensive riverside frontage of Chiswick Mall and under **Hammersmith Bridge**, to **Putney** and **Fulham**—smart urban villages facing each other across the banks.

Gunnersbury Park

Kew Br.

Kew Pier

Temperate House

Chiswick Mall

Chiswick Br.

Barnes Br.

Barnes Common

Furnival Gardens

Hammersmith Br.

Barn Elms Water Works

Fulham

Bishops Park

Putney Br.

Hurlingham Park

Wandsworth Park

The stretch between Kew and Hammersmith is real rowing and riverside-pub territory, with a picturesque parade past Strand-on-the-Green by Kew Bridge.

ROWERS' ROW Every spring Britain's oldest universities, Oxford and Cambridge, compete not with their brains but with their brawn, in the **Boat Race**, which began in 1829. The race is 4¼ miles upstream from Putney Bridge to Chiswick Bridge: expect clashing oars, clenched teeth, and the occasional sinking (there have been six). The best views are from Hammersmith at the Surrey bend, which is also where most of the pubs are clustered. ⊕ www.theboatrace.org

A BRIEF HISTORY

An engraving by Claes Van Visscher showing Old London Bridge in 1616, with Southwark Cathedral in the foreground

The Thames has come a long way—and not just from its 344-km (214-mi) journey from a remote Gloucestershire meadow to the sea. In the mid-19th century, the river was dying, poisoned by sewers that flushed into the river. The "Big Stink" was so awful that cholera and typhoid killed more than 10,000 in 1853, and Parliament abandoned sitting in 1858. "The odour is hardly that of frankincense," said one contemporary of the 1884 drought that forced down water levels, leaving elegant Victorian nostrils exposed to slimy ooze on the banks.

Joseph Bazalgette, star civil engineer of his time, was commissioned to design a new sewage system, and by the 1900s nearly all was forgiven. (His efforts did not go unappreciated: Bazalgette was later knighted.) Today 7.2 million people get their drinking water from the Thames River.

PLANNING A THAMES BOAT TOUR

"On the smallest pretext of holiday or fine weather the mighty population takes to the boats," wrote Henry James in 1877. You can follow in the footsteps of James, who took a boat trip from Westminster to Greenwich, or make up your own itinerary.

■ Frequent daily tourist-boat services are at their height between April and October.

■ In most cases you can turn up at a pier, and the next departure won't be far away. However, it never hurts to book ahead if you can.

■ Westminster and Tower piers are the busiest starting points, usually with boats heading east.

■TIP➜ For a rundown of all the options, along with prices and timetables, contact **London River Services** (☎ 020/7222–1234 ⊕ www.tfl.gov.uk/river), which gives details of all the operators sailing various sections of the river.

■ The trip between Westminster Pier and the Tower of London takes about 30 minutes, as does the trip between the Tower and Greenwich.

■ A full round-trip can take several hours. Ask about flexible fares and hop on/off options at the various piers.

THE BEST WAYS TO EXPERIENCE THE THAMES WHILE...

GOING OFF THE BEATEN PATH (LITERALLY)	020/7928–8933 www.londonribvoyages.com	£42
	See the river at high speed! **London RIB Voyages** use rigid inflatable boats (the kind used by coastguards) to shuttle you from Millennium Pier to Canary Wharf and back.	Varies daily according to weather, but generally hourly 10–4. Approximately 1 hr.
SAVING TIME AND MONEY	020/7887–8888 www.tate.org.uk/tatetotate	£5.50 one-way
	The playfully polka-dotted *Tate Boat* sails across the river from the Tate Britain to the Tate Modern with a London Eye stop in between.	Departs from the pier at either museum: Daily every 40 mins. Approximately 13 mins. one-way.
IMPRESSING A DATE OR CLIENT	0870/429–2451 www.bateauxlondon.com	£32–£43 (lunch), £76–£144 (dinner)
	For ultimate glamour (and expense), look into lunch and dinner cruises with **Bateaux London,** often formal affairs with surprisingly good two- to five-course meals. Variations include jazz brunch cruises on Sundays.	Departs from Embankment Pier for lunch at 12: Apr.–Dec., Wed.–Sat. (also Tues. in Jul. and Aug.) and Jan.–Mar., Thur.–Sat.; for dinner at 7:15: Apr.–Dec., daily, and Jan.–Mar., Tue.–Sat.
ENJOYING ON-BOARD ENTERTAINMENT	020/7740–0400 www.citycruises.com	£78
	The *London Showboat* lives up to its name, with four-course meals, snazzy cabaret acts from West End musicals, and after-dinner dancing.	Departs from Westminster Pier at 7:30: Apr.–Sept., Wed.–Sun.; Oct., March, Thurs.–Sun.; Nov., Dec. Thurs.–Sat; Jan.–Feb., Fri.–Sat. (boarding starts 30 mins. prior to departure). Approximately 3½ hours. Book 48 hours in advance.

HAMPTON COURT PALACE

✉ *Hampton Court Rd.,
East Molesley, Surrey*
☎ *0844/482-7799 tickets,
0844/482-7777 informa-
tion (24 hrs)* ⊕ *www.hrp.
org.uk/hamptoncourtpalace*
🎫 *Palace, maze, and gardens
£18.20; maze only £4.40;
gardens only £6* 🕑 *Apr.-
late Oct., daily 10-6; late
Oct.-Mar., daily 10-4:30;
last admission 1 hr before
closing; last entry to maze 45
mins before closing. Formal
Gardens daily 10-6 summer,
10-5:30 winter. Informal
Gardens daily 7-8 summer,
7-6 winter* Ⓜ *Richmond,
then Bus R68; National Rail:
Hampton Court Station, 35
mins from Waterloo (most
trains require change at
Surbiton).*

13

The seat of Henry VIII's court, sprawled beside the Thames, Hampton Court is steeped in more history than any other royal building in England. The Tudor mansion, begun in 1514 by Cardinal Wolsey to curry favor with young Henry, conceals a larger 17th-century baroque building, partly designed by Christopher Wren. The earliest dwellings belonged to a religious order founded in the 11th century and were expanded by subsequent residents, until George II moved the royal household closer to London in the early 18th century.

Highlights

Wander through the **State Apartments** and **Henry's Great Hall**, before taking in the ceiling of the **Chapel Royal**. Reconstructions of Tudor life take place all year, from live appearances by "Henry VIII" to cook-historians preparing Tudor feasts in the 15th-century **Henry's Kitchens**.

Watch for the ghost of Henry VIII's fifth wife, Catherine Howard, who literally lost her head yet is said to scream her way along the **Haunted Gallery**. Joint rulers William and Mary (reigned 1689–1702), were responsible for the **King's and Queen's Apartments** and the elaborate baroque of the **Georgian Rooms**.

Don't miss the famous **maze** (the oldest hedge maze in the world), its half mile of pathways among hedgerows still fiendish to negotiate. There's a trick, but we won't give it away here.

The **Lower Orangery Exotic Garden** displays exotic species that William and Mary collected.

TIPS

■ Family tickets offer huge savings, with £46 covering two adults and up to three children.

■ Choose which parts of the palace to explore based on a number of self-guided audio walking tours. Come Christmas time, there's ice-skating on a rink before the West Front of the palace.

■ Evening ghost tours (£28 per person) are held throughout the year. They're a great way to see the older parts of the palace without the crowds.

FAMILY   **Syon House and Park.** The residence of the duke and duchess of Nor-
Fodor's Choice   thumberland, this is one of England's most lavish stately homes. Set
★   in a 55-acre park landscaped by "Capability" Brown, the core of the
house is Tudor—Henry VIII's fifth wife, Catherine Howard, and the
extremely short-lived monarch, lady Jane Grey ("Queen for thirteen
days"), made pit stops here before they were sent to the Tower. It
was remodeled in the Georgian style in 1761 by famed decorator
Robert Adam. He had just returned from studying the sights of classical antiquity in Italy and created two rooms sumptuous enough to
wow any Grand Tourist: the entryway is an amazing study in black
and white, pairing neoclassical marbles with antique bronzes, and the
Ante-Room contains 12 enormous verd-antique columns surmounted
by statues of gold—and this was just a waiting room for the duke's
servants and retainers. The Red Drawing Room is covered with crimson Spitalfields silk, and the Long Gallery is one of Adam's noblest
creations. ■TIP→ On certain Sundays and bank holidays in the summer you can take a miniature steam-train ride in the grounds. ⊠ *Syon
Park, Brentford* ☎ *020/8560–0882* ⊕ *www.syonpark.co.uk* 🖅 *£11
for house, gardens, conservatory, and rose garden; £5 for gardens and
conservatory* ⊙ *House mid-Mar.–Oct., Wed., Thurs., Sun., and bank
holidays 11–5; gardens mid-Mar.–Oct., daily 10:30–5; Nov.–mid-
Mar., weekends 10:30–4. Last admission 1 hr before closing* Ⓜ *Gunnersbury, then Bus 237 or 267 to Brentlea.*

Tropical Zoo. In the grounds of Syon Park, the Tropical Zoo is a
rescue sanctuary for abused, abandoned, and illegally kept exotic pets,
from snakes and tarantulas to marmosets and crocodiles. Kids get some
major perks here on weekends and holidays: Not only can they handle
(some of) the creatures at 11, 2, and 4, but they can help feed the
tiny squirrel monkeys at 1—or just watch as the other animals get
their lunch. ⊠ *Syon Park* ☎ *020/8847–4730* ⊕ *www.tropicalzoo.org*
🖅 *£7.50* ⊙ *Daily 10–5:30* Ⓜ *Gunnersbury, then Bus 237 or 267 to
Brentlea stop.*

WHERE TO EAT

Updated
by Alex
Wijeratna

Henry James was scathing about London's restaurants, "whose badness is literally fabulous," he declared. But not so now! London has zoomed up the global gastro charts, and can seriously mix it now with the world's top culinary heavyweights. Standards have rocketed at all price points and, dare we ask, might the London restaurant scene be in the most robust health it's ever been in?

A bottom-up local foodie revolution and a top-down cascade of City lucre and hot global monnay has juiced things up fabulously. Feel like the most-tender Wagyu beef steak on planet Earth? Yours for £92 at CUT at 45 Park Lane. You wanna try ultra-modern old English gastronomy from the time of Henry VIII? Ashley Palmer-Watts is your man at Dinner by Heston Blumenthal. You only eat hot dogs and Champagne? No worries, we've got just the thing: try Bubbledogs in Fitzrovia for . . . hot dogs and Champagne, at £8 a pop. Can't stand any more snobby culinary stuff? The low-key British wild game's so good at The Harwood Arms that they've bagged London's first gastropub-based Michelin star.

Everyone's a foodie here now, and it seems everyone's blogging, Facebooking, Tweeting, Snapchatting, Pinteresting, and Instagraming their way through the latest and greatest openings. One week chef Karem Sethi's flavor of the month at ace curry den Gymkhana in Mayfair, the next it's Daniel Doherty ripping it up at Duck & Waffle, 40 floors up the Heron Tower. Thankfully, pride in the best of British food—local, seasonal, foraged, and wild—is witnessing a genuine resurgence. And you, too, will be smitten, because you'll be spending, on average, 25% of your travel budget on eating out. Dig in. Fork up. Enjoy.

To appreciate how far London's risen in the global culinary firmament, just look back to the days of Somerset Maugham, who was once justified in warning, "To eat well in England you should have breakfast three times a day." Change was slow in coming after World War II, for then it was still understood the British ate to live, while the French lived to

REGENT'S PARK

Albany Rd.

HAMPSTEAD
bustling neighborhood eateries

CLERKENWELL
gastro-heaven

NOTTING HILL
trendy cafes and buzzing bars

Albany St.

Gt. Portland St.

Portland Pl.

Euston Rd.

Tottenham Court Rd.

BLOOMSBURY
hip student-filled spots

Gray's Inn Rd.

Clerkenwell Rd.

Marylebone Rd.

MARYLEBONE
slick cafes and ethnic fare

Baker St.

Wigmore St.

FITZROVIA
stylish small-plates restos

THE CITY
expense account dining

Holborn

Kingsway

New Oxford St.

BAYSWATER
best ethnic eats

Oxford St.

OXFORD CIRCUS

Aldwych

Fleet St.

Strand

Bayswater Rd.

New Bond St.

Regent St.

Charing Cross Rd.

Shaftesbury

COVENT GARDEN
avoid the tourist traps

Victoria Embankment

Waterloo Br.

MAYFAIR
chic hotel restaurants

ST JAMES'S
top-notch cuisine for big spenders

Pall Mall

Whitehall

Stamford St.

HYDE PARK

Piccadilly

Green Park

The Mall

St. James's Park

Thames

SOUTH BANK
new foodie destination

Waterloo Rd.

Knightsbridge

Constitution Hill

River

KNIGHTSBRIDGE
up-market food halls

Birdcage Walk

Westminster Br.

Westminster Bridge Rd.

Sloane St.

WESTMINSTER

Lambeth Palace Rd.

KENSINGTON
posh neighborhood eats

BELGRAVIA

Victoria St.

Horseferry Rd.

Lambeth Br.

Lambeth Rd.

Lambeth Rd.

Kennington Rd.

LAMBETH

Buckingham Palace Rd.

Wilton Rd.

Vauxhall Br. Rd.

Millbank

Albert Embankment

Pimlico Rd.

VICTORIA

King's Rd.

CHELSEA
see-and-be-seen scene

Kennington Park Rd.

0   1/2 mile
0   1/2 km

BEST BETS FOR LONDON DINING

With 14,000 restaurants to choose from, how to decide where to eat? Fodor's writers and editors have tramped around and selected their favorite restaurants by price, cuisine, and experience in the Best Bets lists below. In the first column, Fodor's Choice properties represent the "best of the best" in every price category. You can also search by neighborhood for excellent eats—just peruse the following pages. Or find specific details about a restaurant in the full reviews, listed later in the chapter by neighborhood.

Fodor'sChoice★

Berners Tavern, p. 258
Casse-Croûte, p. 266
Dabbous, p. 260
The Delaunay, p. 259
Dinner by Heston Blumenthal, p. 270
Dishoom, p. 256
Duck & Waffle, p. 261
Grain Store, p. 259
Gymkhana, p. 246
The Harwood Arms, p. 269
Hutong, p. 266
The Ledbury, p. 273
Little Social, p. 248
Pétrus, p. 272
Pollen Street Social, p. 249
Restaurant Story, p. 267
The Ritz Restaurant, p. 244
Rules, p. 257

Tommi's Burger Joint, p. 250
Tonkotsu, p. 255
Yashin, p. 268
Zucca, p. 268

Best by Price

$

Berners Tavern, p. 258
Casse-Croûte, p. 266
Dishoom, p. 256, 264
Grain Store p. 259
Pitt Cue Co., p. 254
The Riding House Café, p. 249
Tommi's Burger Joint, p. 250
Tonkotsu, p. 255

$$

Dabbous, p. 260
The Delaunay, p. 259
Duck & Waffle, p. 261

The Harwood Arms, p. 269
Hutong, p. 266
Little Social, p. 248
Yashin, p. 268
Zucca, p. 268

$$$

Gymkhana, p. 246
Pétrus, p. 272
Restaurant Story, p. 267

$$$$

Dinner by Heston Blumenthal, p. 270
The Ledbury, p. 273
The Ritz Restaurant, p. 244

Best by Cuisine

BRITISH

Berners Tavern, p. 258
Duck & Waffle, p. 261

Harwood Arms, p. 269
Rochelle Canteen, p. 265
St. John, p. 262

CHINESE

Hunan, p. 269
Hutong, p. 266

FRENCH

Casse-Croûte, p. 266
The Ledbury, p. 273
Le Gavroche, p. 247
Pétrus, p. 272
The Ritz Restaurant, p. 244

ITALIAN

Bocca di Lupo, p. 252
Cecconi's, p. 245
L'Anima, p. 261
Pizza East, p. 265
Zucca, p. 268

JAPANESE

Koya, p. 253
Tonkotsu, p. 255
Yashin, p. 268
Zuma, p. 272

SEAFOOD

Golden Hind, p. 250
J Sheekey, p. 257
Scott's, p. 249
Sweetings, p. 263

STEAK

Bar Boulud, p. 270
CUT at 45 Park Lane, p. 246
Flat Iron, p. 253
Goodman, p. 246

Best by Experience

BRASSERIE

Balthazar, p. 255
The Delaunay, p. 259
The Riding House Café, p. 249
The Wolseley, p. 245

BRUNCH

The Delaunay, p. 259
Duck & Waffle, p. 261
The Riding House Café, p. 249
The Wolseley, p. 245

BUSINESS DINING

Berners Tavern, p. 258
The Delaunay, p. 259
Le Gavroche, p. 247
Scott's, p. 249
The Square, p. 249

CELEB SPOTTING

Berners Tavern, p. 258
J Sheekey, p. 257
Nobu Berkeley Street, p. 248
Scott's, p. 249
34, p. 250
The Wolseley, p. 245

GASTROPUBS

Anchor & Hope, p. 265
Great Queen Street, p. 256
The Harwood Arms, p. 269

The Mall Tavern, p. 273

GOOD FOR GROUPS

Bistrotheque, p. 263
Dean Street Townhouse, p. 253
Dishoom, p. 256, 264
Duck & Waffle, p. 261
Pizza East, p. 265
The Riding House Café, p. 249

HISTORIC

Maison Bertaux, p. 253
Rules, p. 257
Simpson's Tavern, p. 262
Sweetings, p. 263
Wiltons, p. 244

HOTEL DINING

Bar Boulud at the Mandarin Oriental, p. 270
Berners Tavern at the London Edition, p. 258
CUT at 45 Park Lane, p. 246
Dinner by Heston Blumenthal at the Mandarin Oriental, p. 270
Hélène Darroze at the Connaught, p. 247

HOT SPOTS

Berners Tavern, p. 258
Dabbous, p. 260
Duck & Waffle, p. 261
Gymkhana, p. 246

Hutong, p. 266
Restaurant Story, p. 267

LATE-NIGHT DINING

Coya, p. 245
Duck & Waffle, p. 261
J Sheekey, p. 257
The Wolseley, p. 245

LOCAL FAVORITES

Alounak, p. 273
Chez Bruce, p. 266
Lemonia, p. 275
Pizza East, p. 265

LUNCH PRIX FIXE

Galvin Bistrot de Luxe, p. 250
Hereford Road, p. 275
Le Gavroche, p. 247
The Mall Tavern, p. 273
Zoilo, p. 251

PRETHEATER

Côte, p. 255
Dean Street Townhouse, p. 253
Little Social, p. 248
Opera Tavern, p. 257

QUIET MEAL

Angelus, p. 274
The Greenhouse, p. 246
Hibiscus, p. 247
Koffmann's, p. 271

ROMANTIC

Berners Tavern, p. 258

The Delaunay, p. 259
Duck & Waffle, p. 261
J Sheekey, p. 257
Scott's, p. 249

SPECIAL OCCASION

Berners Tavern, p. 258
Dinner by Heston Blumental, p. 270
Hutong, p. 266
The Ledbury, p. 273
Pétrus, p. 272

WINE LISTS

Bocca di Lupo, p. 252
The Greenhouse, p. 246
Hibiscus, p. 247
The Ledbury, p. 273
The Square, p. 249

EXPERIMENTAL

Dabbous, p. 260
Duck & Waffle, p. 261
Hedone, p. 276
Restaurant Story, p. 267

14

eat. When people thought of British cuisine, fish-and-chips—a greasy grab-and-gulp dish that tasted best wrapped in yesterday's newspaper—first came to mind. Then there was always shepherd's pie, ubiquitously found in smoke-filled pubs—though not made, according to *Sweeney Todd,* "With real shepherd in it."

These days, standards are a million times higher and poor-quality shepherd's pie has been largely replaced by the city's unofficial dish, the ubiquitous Indian curry. London's restaurant revolution is built on its extraordinary ethnic diversity, and you'll find the quality of other international cuisines has also grown immeasurably in recent years, with London becoming known for its Chinese, Japanese, Indian, Thai, Spanish, Italian, French, Peruvian, and North African restaurants. With all of the choices, traditional British food, when you track it down, appears as just one more exotic cuisine in the pantheon.

PLANNING

EATING OUT STRATEGY

Where should you eat? With thousands of London eateries competing for your attention, it may seem like a daunting question. But fret not—our expert writers and editors have done most of the legwork. The selections here represent the best this city has to offer—from haute cuisine to humble dude food. *Search "Best Bets" for top recommendations by price, cuisine, and experience. Or find a review quickly in the neighborhood listings. Whichever way you look at it, you're sure to get a true taste of London.*

RESERVATIONS

Plan ahead if you're determined to snag a sought-after reservation. Some renowned restaurants like Berners Tavern, Dabbous, or Restaurant Story are booked weeks or even months in advance. It's always a good idea to book as far ahead as you can and reconfirm when you arrive in London. Note that some top restaurants also now take credit card details and charge a penalty fee if you're a no-show. *In the reviews, we mention reservations only when they're essential or not accepted.*

WHAT TO WEAR

When in England's style capital, do as the natives do: dress up to eat out. Whatever your style, dial it up a notch. Have some fun while you're at it. Pull out the clothes you've been saving for a special occasion and get a little glamorous. As unfair as it seems, the way you look can influence how you're treated—and where you're seated. Generally speaking, jeans and a button-down shirt will suffice at most table-service restaurants in the budget to moderate range. Moving up from there, many pricier restaurants require jackets, and some like the Ritz insist on ties. Shorts, sweatpants, and sports jerseys are rarely appropriate. *Note that in reviews we mention dress only when men are required to wear a jacket, or a jacket and tie.*

TIPPING AND TAXES

Do not tip bar staff in pubs and bars—though you can always offer to buy them a drink. In restaurants, tip 12.5% of the check for full meals if service is not already included; tip a small token if you're just having coffee or tea. If paying by credit card, double-check that a tip has not already been included in the bill.

CHILDREN

Unless your children behave impeccably, it's best to swerve the haute cuisine establishments, although many top places like The Wolseley are surprisingly child-friendly. London's many burger and rib joints, pizzerias, and Italian restaurants are popular with kids. Other family-friendly establishments include chains like Bill's, Byron, Côte, Carluccio's, Pizza Express, Busaba Eathai, and Wagamama.

HOURS

In London you can find breakfast all day, but it's generally served between 7 am and noon. Lunch is between noon and 3 pm, and brunch between 11 am and 3 pm. Tea, often a meal in itself, is taken between 1 pm and 6 pm, and dinner is typically eaten between 7 pm and 11 pm, though it can be taken earlier. Many ethnic restaurants, especially Indian, serve food until midnight. Sunday is a proper lunch day, and some restaurants are open for lunch only. Over the Christmas period, London has a reputation for shutting down, but a growing number of hotels and other brave bastions are prepared to feed travelers.

PRICES

London is an awfully pricey city by global standards. A modest meal for two can easily cost £50, and the £100-a-head meal is not unknown. Damage-control strategies include making lunch your main meal—the top places have bargain midday menus—going for early- or late-evening deals, or sharing an à la carte entrée and ordering a second appetizer instead. Seek out fixed-price menus, and watch for hidden extras on the check, that is, bread, vegetables, or a cover charged separately.

RESTAURANT REVIEWS

Listed alphabetically within neighborhoods. Use the coordinate (✛ 1:B2) at the end of each listing to locate a property on the Where to Eat and Stay in London atlas at the end of this chapter. Prices in the reviews are the average cost of a main course at dinner or, if dinner is not served, at lunch.

WESTMINSTER, ST. JAMES'S, AND ROYAL LONDON

ST. JAMES'S

St. James's—home to Buckingham Palace and Clarence House, where Prince Charles and Camilla live—has a magnificent olde-world, royal feel. Appropriately, most of the restaurants here are fit for a future king. This is where you'll find London's top-end restaurants—dining experiences that are geared toward a well-heeled, deep-pocketed clientele. Mere mortals should make reservations well in advance to dine at any of these restaurants for dinner (and reserve for the earlier or later shanks of the evening, when demand is less). Keep in mind that no-shows mean last-minute tables often crop up, and lunching here can be a great money-saving strategy.

$$
MODERN
EUROPEAN
FAMILY

✕ **Le Caprice.** Celebville grande dame Le Caprice commands the deepest loyalty of any restaurant in London. Why? Because it gets practically everything right—*every* time. It's the 30-odd-year celebrity history—think Liz Taylor, Joan Collins, and Lady Di—the updated monochrome decor, the haunting David Bailey black-and-white portraits, charming Bolivian-born Jesus Adorno as the veteran maître d', the perfect service, and the long-standing menu that sits somewhere between Euro peasant and trendy fashion plate. Sit at the raised counter or at a coveted corner table and enjoy calves' liver with crispy bacon, pheasant with caramelized quince, John Dory with wild mushrooms, and signature Scandinavian iced berries with a theatrical swirl of hot white-chocolate sauce. $ *Average main: £23* ✉ *Arlington House, Arlington St., St. James's* ☎ *020/7629–2239* ⊕ *www.caprice-holdings.co.uk* ⚱ *Reservations essential* Ⓜ *Green Park* ✛ *5:A1.*

$$$$
BRITISH
Fodor's Choice
★

✕ **The Ritz Restaurant.** Europe's most beautiful dining room at The Ritz would moisten the eye of Louis XVI with its sumptuous Belle Epoque–inspired trompe d'oeil, rococo gilt chandeliers, fairy tale drapery, marble statues, and mirrored wall. A cavalry of liveried waiters glide across the carpeted salon, and gentlemen diners are expected to wear jacket and tie at all times. Sit at the late Baroness Thatcher's favorite seat overlooking Green Park (Table 1) and enjoy British haute cuisine. A Bresse chicken with black Périgord truffle stuffed under its skin arrives in a pig's bladder and is carved table-side and served with sauce suprême. Set and "surprise" menus at ducal prices (£95) might captivate with delicate turbot with cèpe and celeriac or veal with Madeira sauce, and don't miss the crêpes suzette, which are flambéed table-side by the maître d'. $ *Average main: £38* ✉ *The Ritz, 150 Piccadilly, St. James's* ☎ *020/7300–2370* ⊕ *www.theritzlondon.com* ⚱ *Reservations essential* 🎩 *Jacket and tie* Ⓜ *Green Park* ✛ *5:A1.*

$$$$
BRITISH

✕ **Wiltons.** Blue bloods and minor royalty blow the family bank at this old-fashioned bastion of English fine dining on Jermyn Street (the place first opened on the Haymarket as a shellfish stall in 1742). Invariably fresh from a little snooze in their nearby St. James's gentlemen's clubs, gentleman diners are required to wear jackets at all times at this linen-covered clubby time capsule and *frightfully* snooty ode to all things English. Golden signet ring–wearing patrons like to take half a dozen of the finest Colchester oysters, followed by grilled Dover sole on the bone, or fabulous native game in season, such as grouse, woodcock, partridge, or teal. There are antediluvian savories like anchovies or mushrooms on toast, plus desserts like sherry trifle or bread-and-butter pudding. The use of mobile phones is prohibited, the wine's weighed heavily towards Bordeaux and Burgundy, and the service, naturally, would put Jeeves to shame. $ *Average main: £32* ✉ *55 Jermyn St., St. James's* ☎ *020/7629–9955* ⊕ *www.wiltons.co.uk* ⚱ *Reservations essential* 🎩 *Jacket required* ☉ *Closed weekends* Ⓜ *Green Park* ✛ *5:A1.*

$$ ✗ **The Wolseley.** A camel train of stars come for the always-on show spec-
AUSTRIAN tacle and soaring elegance at this bustling Viennese-style grand café on
FAMILY Piccadilly. Framed with 1920s black laquerware, this all-day brasserie,
a few doors down from The Ritz, begins its long decadent days with
breakfast at 7 am and serves highly dependable Dual Monarchy delights
until midnight. Don't be shy to turn up on spec (they hold seats back
for walk-ins) to enjoy such highlights as Hungarian goulash, Austrian
pork belly, chicken soup with a salt-beef sandwich, eggs Benedict, kedg-
eree, or breaded Wiener schnitzel. For dessert, go for luscious *kaiser-
schmarren*—caramelized pancakes with stewed fruit and raisins—and
don't forget to book a return table to savor the Viennoiserie pastries
at one of their classy £10.75 to £23.75 Afternoon Teas. Reservations
are recommended. **$** *Average main: £18* ✉ *160 Piccadilly, St. James's*
☎ *020/7499–6996* ⊕ *www.thewolseley.com* Ⓜ *Green Park* ✛ *5:A1.*

14

MAYFAIR AND MARYLEBONE

If you're looking for something more wallet-friendly, head north to
Marylebone, formerly dowdy but now prized for its chic, village-like
feel. Here are an array of low-key little cafés, boîtes, and tapas bars,
Champagne-and-hot-dog joints, and the odd world-class sizzler, offer-
ing everything from Moroccan and Spanish to Thai and Japanese.

MAYFAIR

$$ ✗ **Cecconi's.** Spot the odd A-lister and wallow in glamorous all-day buzz
MODERN ITALIAN at this upscale Italian brasserie wedged serenely between Old Bond Street,
Cork Street, and Savile Row, and across from the Royal Academy of
Arts. The jet set spill out onto pavement tables for breakfast, brunch, and
cicchetti (Italian tapas), and return later in the day for something more
substantial. À la mode English designer Ilse Crawford's luxe green-and-
brown interior is a stylish backdrop for classics like stuffed baby squid,
Umbrian sausages, lobster spaghetti, *pappardelle* pasta with Chianti ragù,
and a flavorsome pick-me-up tiramisu. It's just the place for a high-end
pit stop during a West End shopping spree or after art buying at the
nearby Mayfair auction houses. **$** *Average main: £23* ✉ *5A Burlington
Gardens, Mayfair* ☎ *020/7434–1500* ⊕ *www.cecconis.co.uk* ⌲ *Reservations essential* Ⓜ *Green Park, Piccadilly Circus* ✛ *3:A6.*

$$ ✗ **Coya.** London's beautiful and the damned binge on Coya's electrifying
PERUVIAN array of top-end Peruvian dishes and sizzily Josper chargrilled offerings,
all boogaloo-ed by star Indian chef Sanjay Dwivedi in a throbbing Inca-
inspired, terra-cotta-floored party zone. London Fashion Week models,
buyers, and bookers devour low-carb diced and marinated yellowfin tuna
or sea bass and white corn *ceviches* and go cuckoo over the sliced raw-
fish *tiraditos*—try salmon and quinoa or scallops and Peruvian chili pep-
pers. Baby squid with rare Peruvian marigold or grilled asparagus spears
are hardly going to pile on the pounds, nor will the *anticuchos* grilled
skewers—look for tiger prawns or monkfish—which join the party when
they're ready. Afterwards, the svelte ones slink off to the Pisco Bar and
its lethal collection of 35 nefarious pisco sours. **$** *Average main: £19*
✉ *118 Piccadilly, Mayfair* ☎ *020/7042–7118* ⊕ *www.coyarestaurant.com*
⌲ *Reservations essential* Ⓜ *Green Park or Hyde Park Corner* ✛ *1:H6.*

$$$$ ✕**CUT at 45 Park Lane.** U.S.–based Austrian star chef Wolfgang Puck
STEAKHOUSE amps up the steak stakes at this ultra-expensive, high-end steak emporium on Park Lane. Against a luxe backdrop of Damien Hirst paintings,
globe lights, and an '80s sound track of T'Pau and Bon Jovi, an army
of hedge fund suits go gangbusters for perfectly seared prime cuts from
the United States, England, and Australia. Grilled over charcoal and
hardwood, and finished under a 650°C broiler, there's awesome Arkan-
sas Creekstone filet mignon for £34 and 8-ounce rib-eye of Wagyu beef
from Darling Downs in Australia for £92. Add bone marrow, French
fries, béarnaise sauce, or creamed spinach with a fried egg on top for
the whole nine yards. $ *Average main: £40* ✉ *45 Park La., Mayfair*
☎ *020/7493–4554* ⊕ *www.dorchestercollection.com* ✍ *Reservations
essential* Ⓜ *Marble Arch, Hyde Park Corner* ✢ *1:G5.*

$$$ ✕**Goodman.** This Manhattan-themed, Mayfair-based upmarket steak-
STEAKHOUSE house, named after Chicago jazz legend Benny Goodman, has every-
one in agreement—these are some of the best steaks in town. There's
token Russian sweet herring, lobster bisque, beef carpaccio, and Caesar
salad, but everyone here's got only one thing on their mind: the sizzling
8–14 ounce charcoal Josper grilled steaks, which come with lobster
tails or fried foie gras, truffles, or chips and creamed spinach, plus pep-
per, béarnaise, or Stilton sauces. $ *Average main: £31* ✉ *24–26 Mad-
dox St., Mayfair* ☎ *020/7499–3776* ⊕ *www.goodmanrestaurants.com*
✍ *Reservations essential* ☾ *Closed Sun.* Ⓜ *Oxford Circus, Piccadilly
Circus* ✢ *3:A5.*

$$$$ ✕**The Greenhouse.** Discreetly tucked away amid imposing redbrick
FRENCH Mayfair mansions and approached through a sumptuous tree-lined,
spotlighted garden, this elegant ground-floor dining salon attracts well-
heeled aficionados of top-class French haute cuisine. Feast on intricately
arranged foie gras with fennel pollen, wild turbot with braised carrot
and ginger, or Galloway beef with garlic and mange tout. A suave
crowd comes for the attentive and achingly smooth service, the soft
lighting, the glassed-off private dining room, and the legendary 110-
page wine list with over 2,000 bottles in all, including a Domaine de la
Romanée-Conti 1929 from Burgundy (a cool £18,000) and a Château
Lafite Rothschild 1870 1er Grand Cru Classé at a piffling £29,500.
$ *Average main: £33* ✉ *27A Hay's Mews, Mayfair* ☎ *020/7499–3331*
⊕ *www.greenhouserestaurant.co.uk* ✍ *Reservations essential* ☾ *Closed
Sun. No lunch Sat.* Ⓜ *Green Park* ✢ *1:H5.*

$$$ ✕**Gymkhana.** Indian curry virtuoso Karam Sethi invokes the last days
MODERN INDIAN of the Raj at London's finest top-end curry emporium in Mayfair.
Fodor's Choice Inspired by the Colonial-era Indian sporting clubs and high-society
★ mustering points of yesteryear, you'll be charmed by the ceiling fans,
rattan chairs, lacquered oak floors, and chocolate leather banquettes.
Try the golden crispy pancake-like *dosa* with fennel-rich Chettinad
duck and coconut chutney, *Kasoori* chicken tikka, or wild Muntjac
rice with pomegranate and mint yogurt sauce. There's also well-spiced
game—like *achari* wild roe deer with keema naan bread. $ *Average
main: £26* ✉ *42 Albemarle St., Mayfair* ⊕ *www.gymkhanalondon.com*
✍ *Reservations essential* ✢ *1:H5.*

$$$$ ✕ **Hélène Darroze at the Connaught.** La crème de la crème flock to French
FRENCH virtuoso Hélène Darroze's restaurant at the Connaught for her dazzling
regional French haute cuisine, served up in an impressive Edwardian
dark wood paneled dining salon. Darroze sallies forth with a procession
of magnificent dishes. Caviar d'Acquitaine might wow with oyster tar-
tare in a sleek martini glass, topped with caviar jelly and white haricot
bean velouté. Spit-roasted and flambéed pigeon is served gloriously
pink, with duck foie gras and mini Brussels sprouts. Darroze is perfect
for important celebrations, but beware the high prices: £35 for lunch,
£55 for brunch, and £85–£120 for set dinner. ⑤ *Average main: £36*
✉ *The Connaught, Carlos Pl., Mayfair* ☎ *020/7107–8880* ⊕ *www.the-
connaught.co.uk* ⤴ *Reservations essential* ⌂ *Jacket required* ⊙ *Closed
Sun. and Mon.* Ⓜ *Green Park* ✛ *1:H5.*

$$$$ ✕ **Hibiscus.** Two-starred French chef Claude Bosi bosses the scene at this
MODERN FRENCH Mayfair gastro mecca with nouvelle Modern French dishes, like carpaccio of hand-dived Isle of Skye scallops with delicate blobs of truffle and
pickled radish, or Cornish John Dory with Morteau sausage and *girolles*
mushrooms. The desserts are as complex as his mains, with an unlikely
sounding but wickedly flavorsome sweet cèpe mushroom tart standing
out. The brilliant bespoke wine list features a 40-odd selection of rare
but top-rank "orange" biodynamic, organic, heirloom, grape variety fine
wines. ⑤ *Average main: £35* ✉ *29 Maddox St., Mayfair* ☎ *020/7629–
2999* ⊕ *www.hibiscusrestaurant.co.uk* ⤴ *Reservations essential* ⊙ *Closed
Sun. and Mon.* Ⓜ *Oxford Circus, Piccadilly Circus* ✛ *3:A5.*

$$$ ✕ **La Petite Maison.** Tucked in an alleyway off New Bond Street, the
FRENCH delightful La Petite Maison boasts an impressively well-sourced French
FAMILY Mediterranean, Côte d'Azur, Liguria, and Provençale menu. Try figure-
friendly broad bean and Pecorino salad, soft burrata cheese with sweet
Datterini-tomato-and-basil spread, or aromatic baked turbot with arti-
chokes, chorizo, five spices, and goopy white wine sauce. Based on
the Southern Med style of the original La Petite Maison in Nice in
the south of France, dishes come to the table as they're ready. More
rosé, anyone? |$| *Average main: £26* ✉ *53–54 Brook's Mews, Mayfair*
☎ *020/7495–4774* ⊕ *www.lpmlondon.co.uk* ⤴ *Reservations essential*
Ⓜ *Bond St., Oxford Circus* ✛ *1:H4.*

$$$$ ✕ **Le Gavroche.** MasterChef judge Michel Roux Jr. works the floor in
FRENCH the old-fashioned proprietorial way at this clubby basement institu-
tion in Mayfair—established by his father and uncle in 1967—and
which many still rate to this day as the best formal dining in London.
With magnificent shiny silver domes and unpriced ladies' menus, Roux's
mastery of classical French haute cuisine hypnotizes all comers with
signatures like foie gras with cinnamon-scented crispy duck pancake,
soufflé Suissesse, roast venison with red wine jus, or saddle of rabbit
with Parmesan cheese. Desserts like Roux's famous chocolate omelet
soufflé or upside-down apple tart are unswervingly accomplished. Nota-
ble three-course set lunches (£54) are the sanest way to experience
Le Gavroche. ⑤ *Average main: £41* ✉ *43 Upper Brook St., Mayfair*
☎ *020/7408–0881* ⊕ *www.le-gavroche.co.uk* ⤴ *Reservations essential*
⌂ *Jacket required* ⊙ *Closed Sun. and bank holiday Mon.* Ⓜ *Marble
Arch, Bond St.* ✛ *1:G5.*

14

CLOSE UP

British Food Decoder

For pure Britishness, roast beef and Yorkshire pudding tops the list. If you want the best, go to a foodie-mad local gastropub. Here the Sunday roasts will be cooked with passion, and crucially with top-quality, organic, or free-range ingredients. The beef is served slightly pink with goose-fat roast potatoes, carrots, parsnips, and peas, and of course Yorkshire puddings, a savory batter baked until crisp. A dark meaty gravy is poured on top, and there's horseradish sauce on the side.

Other top tummy liners include shepherd's pie: made with minced lamb, topped with mashed potato, and baked until lightly brown. Cottage pie is similar, but made with minced beef instead of lamb. Traditional steak-and-kidney pie is made with chunky diced beef and ox kidneys, braised with onions and mushrooms in a thick, brown gravy, and encased with shortcrust pastry.

Fish-and-chips, usually deep-fried battered cod, haddock, or plaice, comes with hand-cut chips that are sprinkled with salt and vinegar. A "ploughman's lunch" is usually served in pubs and consists of "bloomer" crusty white bread, a strong English cheese (Cheddar, Cheshire, or red Leicester), with a side-salad garnish and tangy onion pickle on the side.

For a hot dessert, seek out bread-and-butter pudding if you can, made with overlapping layers of buttered bread scattered with raisins, and baked in egg, cream, and nutmeg until crisp.

$$
MODERN FRENCH
Fodor'sChoice
★

✕ **Little Social.** There's always a hubbub at Jason Atherton's knock-'em-dead French bistro and Mayfair hideaway. Ease into a Burgundy leather banquette booth and admire the hardwood chairs, elm tables, and assorted Michelin road maps before diving into an artfully classic-with-a-twist menu. The crab-salad appetizer comes on a round of tomato with miso dressing and disks of beetroot and radish, while braised Irish ox cheeks with chunky roast bone marrow and horseradish mash is top-end comfort food of the highest order. There's always aged Scottish-beef cheeseburger on the menu (£15), plus a side of unusual Québécois poutine—a bowl of fries piled high with cheese, gravy, chorizo, and jalapeños. Finally, the £7.50 hot chocolate moelleux with a dollop of almond ice cream is near perfection. $ *Average main: £18* ⊠ *5 Pollen St., Mayfair* ☏ *020/7290–7600* ⊕ *www.littlesocial.co.uk* ⌕ *Reservations essential* Ⓜ *Oxford Circus, Piccadilly Circus* ✢ *3:A5.*

$$$
JAPANESE

✕ **Nobu Berkeley Street.** Premier League soccer stars and supermodels converge here for new-style Japanese sashimi with a Peruvian flair at this so-hip-it-hurts Nobu spin-off near Piccadilly. Louder and more fashion-forward than nearby flagship Nobu on Park Lane, this younger sibling cleans up nicely with a combined ground-floor scene bar, a first-floor restaurant, and a West End nightclub vibe. The beautiful people go bananas for miso black cod, California sushi rolls, yellowtail sashimi, Bento boxes, chargrilled peppers, and Wagyu beef. $ *Average main: £30* ⊠ *15 Berkeley St., Mayfair* ☏ *020/7290–9222* ⊕ *www.noburestaurants.com* ⌕ *Reservations essential* Ⓜ *Green Park* ✢ *1:H5.*

$$$
MODERN
EUROPEAN
Fodor'sChoice
★

✕**Pollen Street Social.** Jason Atherton (of el Bulli fame) knocks the London dining scene for a loop at his smash-hit flagship found in a cute alleyway off Regent Street. Fans enjoy refined small and large dishes ranging from a full "English breakfast" appetizer—a cute miniature of poached egg on tomato compote, with parsley-flecked bacon, morels, and croutons—to sublime Scottish ox cheek with 50-day Black Angus rib-eye beef, or wild sea bass with squid and langoustine minestrone. Diners might get up from their tables to sit and perch at the dessert bar to watch staff as they chop, slice, and fiddle away to prepare immaculate Eton Mess with wild strawberries and basil-ash meringue or sashimi-like pressed watermelon with an unlikely basil sorbet. $ *Average main: £28* ⊠ *8–10 Pollen St., Mayfair* ☎ *020/7290–7600* ⊕ *www. pollenstreetsocial.com* ⚶ *Reservations essential* Ⓜ *Oxford Circus, Piccadilly Circus* ✛ *3:A5.*

14

$
BURGER
FAMILY

✕**The Riding House Café.** Hipster-chic London diners flock to this NYC–style small-plates-and-luxe-burgers all-day brasserie behind Oxford Circus in NOHO (North of Soho). Everything's appropriately salvaged, reclaimed, or bespoke here so you'll find stuffed birds and other taxidermy dotted around, reclaimed blue leather theater seats at the long bar, bright orange leather banquettes, or old snooker table legs holding up your dining table. Opt for bargain £5 small plates of sea bass *ceviche* with lime and chili or Waldorf salad starters, and then head for poached egg chorizo hash browns, salt marsh lamb broth, cheeseburger with chips—a steal at £12.50—or their famed lobster lasagna (£25). $ *Average main: £14* ⊠ *43–51 Great Titchfield St., Noho* ☎ *020/7927–0840* ⊕ *www.ridinghousecafe. co.uk* ⚶ *Reservations essential* Ⓜ *Oxford Circus* ✛ *3:A2.*

$$$$
SEAFOOD

✕**Scott's.** Liveried doormen greet the A-list with a nod at this fashionable seafood haven on Mount Street in Mayfair. Originally founded in 1851, and a former haunt of James Bond author Ian Fleming (he liked the potted shrimps, apparently), these days you're more likely to see Bill Clinton in one corner, Kate Winslet in another, and Brit-pack artists Damien Hirst or Tracy Emin joshing around on a banquette nearby. Scott's draws London's movers and shakers who enjoy day-boat-fresh Lindisfarne oysters, baked crab, cod cheeks, and shrimp burgers. Glorious standouts like sautéed razor clams with wild boar sausages or sole Colbert are divine. Prices could make a Saudi sheikh blanch, but fear not: this really is the *hottest* joint in town. $ *Average main: £31* ⊠ *20 Mount St., Mayfair* ☎ *020/7495–7309* ⊕ *www.scotts-restaurant.com* ⚶ *Reservations essential* Ⓜ *Bond St., Green Park* ✛ *1:H5.*

$$$$
MODERN FRENCH

✕**The Square.** Located off beautiful Berkeley Square, this restaurant is a long-standing haven for the titans of business who come for the showy wine list, the well-spaced linen-covered tables, and chef Philip Howard's sophisticated French haute cuisine. In season, you may find marvelously balanced wonders like Dorset crab lasagna with shellfish cappuccino, guinea fowl with truffles and Parmesan, or Lincolnshire hare with beetroot and creamed polenta. Impeccable desserts like fig soufflé with fig leaf ice cream are so good that you're sure to return. $ *Average main: £33* ⊠ *6–10 Bruton St., Mayfair* ☎ *020/7495–7100* ⊕ *www.squarerestaurant.com* ⚶ *Reservations essential* ⊘ *No lunch Sun.* Ⓜ *Green Park, Bond St.* ✛ *1:H5.*

$$$
INTERNATIONAL

✗ **34.** Megawatt celebs from Sandra Bullock to Stella McCartney head straight for 34 in Mayfair because . . . *all* the other stars go there, too! It must be the plush English Edwardian and art deco–inspired dining salon, the swank burnt-orange banquettes, the nightly live jazz, the interesting fish, game, steak, and seafood grill-focused menu, the copious starched white table linens, and the Upper Manhattan–style service. Appetizers like salt-baked beetroot with soft burrata cheese or Dorset crab and gazpacho jelly square off against chunkier delights from the Argentinian *parrilla* charcoal grill—think 28-day Scottish Red Angus sirloin steaks and Creekstone T-bones. Top crowd pleasers include meatball spaghetti, cod and shallots, or Cornish lamb with pumpkin pesto, while game goes down well, too, with roast wood pigeon and damsons standing out. Ⓢ *Average main: £27* ⊠ *34 Grosvenor Sq., Mayfair* ☎ *020/3350–3434* ⊕ *www.34-restaurant.co.uk* ⚞ *Reservations essential* Ⓜ *Marble Arch* ✛ *1:G5.*

MARYLEBONE

$$
BRASSERIE

✗ **Galvin Bistrot de Luxe.** The masterful Galvin brothers, Chris and Jeff, blaze a spectacular trail for the French *bistrot de luxe* formula on a fast-moving stretch of Baker Street in Marylebone. Seasoned fans return time and again for the impeccable food, smart service, Bentwood chairs, and mahogany-paneled Parisian-style salon. There's no finer Dorset crab lasagna in town, and mains consistently punch above their weight: Cornish brill, calves liver with Alsace bacon, classic stuffed pig's trotter, and a sumptuous daube of venison with chestnuts are all devilishly tasty, each one a superbly executed gastro triumph. The £19.50 three-course set lunches or £21.50 early evening dinners (6–7 pm) are top value, and look out for live Sunday-afternoon jazz. Ⓢ *Average main: £20* ⊠ *66 Baker St., Marylebone* ☎ *020/7935–4007* ⊕ *www.galvinrestaurants. com* ⚞ *Reservations essential* Ⓜ *Baker St.* ✛ *1:G3.*

$
SEAFOOD
FAMILY

✗ **The Golden Hind.** You'll land some of the best fish-and-chips in London at this great British "chippy" in a retro 1914 art deco café off Marylebone High Street. Gaggles of tourists and hungry Marylebone village locals and workers alike hunker down for the homemade cod fish cakes, skate wings, feta cheese fritters, and breaded scampi tails at simple dark-wood tables, but it's the neatly prepared and decidedly non-greasy deep-fried or steamed cod, plaice, and haddock from Grimsby (£6–£7.80), the classic hand-cut Maris Piper chips, and the traditional mushy peas that are the big draw. It's BYO (£1 corkage) and take away, but note it's only open for lunch on weekdays and dinner every day but Sunday. Ⓢ *Average main: £7* ⊠ *73 Marylebone La., Marylebone* ☎ *020/7486–3644* ⚞ *Reservations not accepted* ☉ *Closed Sun. No lunch Sat.* Ⓜ *Bond St.* ✛ *1:G3.*

$
BURGER
FAMILY
Fodor'sChoice
★

✗ **Tommi's Burger Joint.** "Be Nice or Leave" and "Sharing is Caring" are a few choice aphorisms found on cardboard signs at this cult Icelandic-run burger boîte in Marylebone. The decor includes overhead fairy lights, chicken wire framing the grill station, and a Chewbacca the Wookiee surfer poster. Everyone here seems to love the cool tunes (from Johnny Cash to Talking Heads), the edgy DIY vibe, and the £9.90 burger, fries, and soda at this hamburger heaven. Aside from beef from top butcher HG Walter, you'll also find grilled cheese sandwiches and veggie burgers, plus a voguish steak burger made with fillet, rump, and rib-eye. All come in awesome fist-size brioche buns with tomato, lettuce, onion, ketchup, and mustard, and help yourself from the estimable condiments bar. ⑤ *Average main: £10* ✉ *30 Thayer St., Marylebone* ☎ *0782/355–7945* ⊕ *www.burgerjoint.co.uk* ⚑ *Reservations not accepted* Ⓜ *Bond St.* ✛ *1:H3.*

$

MODERN
ARGENTINE

✗ **Zoilo.** Sit at the basement kitchen counter at London's top Argentinian tapas joint near Selfridges, where you can watch chef Diego Jacquet work Latin American miracles at the roaring charcoal grill. Swirl a juicy red Finca Perdriel '08 Malbec from Mendoza and watch Jacquet tweak, twerk, and slice away as he conjures dishes of invariable brilliance. Delving into a bubbling oven-hot pan of classic roast Provoleta cheese, almonds, and honey is a gooey must, as is trying the deconstructed chicken *matambre* with quails egg and green peas, or the popular *asado* flank steak, piled high with celeriac and bone marrow. Everyone naturally loves the authentic rib-eye beef with chimichurri. The other char-grilled dishes are sizzling taste bombs, too—try octopus, rump of lamb with quinoa, or garlicky prawns with pork belly and chorizo. Note the £9.95 set lunch with a glass of wine, an excellent value. ⑤ *Average main: £12* ✉ *9 Duke St., Marylebone* ☎ *020/7486–9699* ⊕ *www.zoilo. co.uk* ⚑ *Reservations essential* Ⓜ *Bond St.* ✛ *1:G4.*

14

SOHO AND COVENT GARDEN

Soho and Covent Garden are the city's playground and pleasure zone, an all-day, all-night jostling neon wonderland of glitz, glamour, grit, and greasepaint. This area is London's cultural heart, with old and new media companies, late-night dive bars, cabaret, street performers, West End musicals, and world-class theater, ballet, and opera houses. High rents have recently forced out many of Soho's seedier red-light businesses and ushered in more edgy and top-notch restaurants. Just follow your nose in Covent Garden and Theatreland to find copious options for pretheater dining.

SOHO

$$

MEDITERRANEAN

✗ **Andrew Edmunds.** Candlelit at night and with a haunting Dickensian vibe, Andrew Edmunds is a permanently packed, deeply romantic old-world Soho institution—though it could be larger, less creaky underfoot, and the reclaimed church-pew wooden bench seats more forgiving. Tucked away behind Carnaby Street in a dark and atmospheric 18th-century Soho town house, it's a cozy favorite with the Soho media elite that come for the hand-scribbled, fixed-price lunch menus and the historic vibe. Keenly priced starters and mains draw on the tastes of Ireland, the Med, and Middle East. Harissa-spiced mackerel, woodcock on toast, seafood paella, and Herdwick lamb shanks with mash and broccoli are hale and hearty. Desserts like warm treacle tart or bread-and-butter pudding offer few surprises, but the wine's superb and the markups reasonable. ⑤ *Average main: £17* ✉ *46 Lexington St., Soho* ☎ *020/7437–5708* ⊕ *www.andrewedmunds.com* ⚑ *Reservations essential* Ⓜ *Oxford Circus, Piccadilly Circus* ✛ *3:C5.*

$ ✕ **Bar Italia.** This legendary Italian coffee bar on Frith Street is Soho's
CAFÉ unofficial beating heart and a 22-hour-a-day Soho institution. Established in 1949 during the Italian coffee bar craze and still run by the
founding Polledri family, it's now positively football crazy and a honey-
pot for an assortment of weird and wondrous Soho-ites—from clubbers
and cabbies to stars like Jude Law. Most regulars grab a frothy cappuccino made from the 50-year-old Gaggia coffee machine and wolf down
a slice of pizza, panettone, or chocolate cake at one of the mirrored
bar counters (or pavement seat out front). The walls are plastered with
Italian flags and black-and-white photos of Italian singers, movie legends, and '50s boxing champs, and it's *the* spot in London to watch
Italy play in the soccer World Cup. ⑤ *Average main: £6* ✉ *22 Frith St.,
Soho* ☎ *020/7437–4520* ⊕ *www.baritaliasoho.co.uk* ⌲ *Reservations
not accepted* ⊟ *No credit cards* Ⓜ *Leicester Sq.* ✛ *3:D5.*

$$ ✕ **Barrafina.** London's top Spanish tapas bar is modeled on Cal Pep
TAPAS in old-town Barcelona, and similarly has only a few—23 in total—
raised counter stools. It's no-reservations but the tapas is well worth
the wait. Their motto is "Sourcing Not Saucing," so get ready to
nosh on brilliant small plates prepared in front of you: garlic prawns,
ham *croquetas,* salt cod fritters, rare Galician *percebes* ("goose bar-
nacles") crustaceans, baby squid and octopus with capers, plus obvi-
ous classics like Spanish *torila,* spicy chorizo, and cured Montanera
ham. There's a crack selection of Spanish reds, whites, sherries, and
sparkling Cavas, and leave room for desserts like *crèma Catalana*
or almond-based Santiago tart. ⑤ *Average main: £13* ✉ *54 Frith St.,
Soho* ☎ *020/7813–8016* ⊕ *www.barrafina.co.uk* ⌲ *Reservations not
accepted* Ⓜ *Tottenham Court Rd.* ✛ *3:D4.*

$$ ✕ **Bocca di Lupo.** The place is always packed and the tables jammed
ITALIAN too close together, but everyone still comes for the buzz and chef
Jacob Kenedy's unusual rustic Italian regional fare. Located off Theatreland's Shaftesbury Avenue in Soho, this redbrick, popular family-
run place offers a triumphant procession of small and large plates and
peasant-based dishes from Piedmont to Emilia, Lombardy to Cam-
pania. Try drop-dead offerings like buffalo mozzarella, suckling pig,
and Sicilian lobster spaghetti. Limber up with a Aperol spritz before
plunging into the regional Italian-focused wine list, which weaves
from Super Tuscans to rare Barolos. There's also an intriguing mar-
sala and a range of punchy aged grappas, plus desserts like milk-
free espresso ice cream. ⑤ *Average main: £16* ✉ *12 Archer St., Soho*
☎ *020/7734–2223* ⊕ *www.boccadilupo.com* ⌲ *Reservations essential*
Ⓜ *Piccadilly Circus* ✛ *3:C5.*

$ ✕ **Busaba Eathai.** It's top Thai nosh at this sleek and sultry modern can-
THAI teen in the beating heart of Soho. Fitted with dark-wood bench seats
FAMILY and hardwood tables, this flagship restaurant has communal dining,
rapid service, low-lighting, and fast-moving line ups out front. Pour
yourself a lemongrass tea, then try ginger beef with Thai pepper, classic crunchy green papaya salad, Thai calamari, massaman duck curry,
or myriad other tasty winners. You'll escape well fed for about £17
a head, and, all in all, this makes for a top-value tummy-filler and a
fail-safe pit stop during a West End shopping spree. ⑤ *Average main:*

£10 ✉ 106–110 *Wardour St., Soho* ☎ 020/7255–8686 ⊕ *busaba.com* ✍ *Reservations not accepted* Ⓜ *Tottenham Court Rd.* ✛ 3:C4.

$$ ✕ **Dean Street Townhouse.** Soho media peeps sink into comfy velvet chairs
BRITISH   with frilly cushions for hearty English Afternoon Tea (3–6 pm) at the
FAMILY   cozy Parlour anteroom at this elegant boutique hotel. Besides fine fin-
ger sandwiches and scones and jam, traditional three-tiered Town-
house Teas (£17.50) served on nostalgic Victorian crockery include
extras like buttered crumpets and poppy seed cake. You'll soon find it
makes perfect sense to sink down a little further and segue into High
Tea with sturdy standbys like Welsh rarebit, Scotch eggs, or fish fin-
gers with tartar sauce. Ⓢ *Average main: £17* ✉ *69–71 Dean St., Soho*
☎ 020/7434–1775 ⊕ *www.deanstreettownhouse.com* ✍ *Reservations
essential* Ⓜ *Oxford Circus, Tottenham Court Rd.* ✛ 3:D5.

14

$ ✕ **Flat Iron.** Premium steaks priced at £10 are the only mains on the
STEAKHOUSE   printed menu at this bustling hipster canteen on Beak Street in Soho.
FAMILY   The chargrilled "flat iron" shoulder cuts of beef arrive already sliced on
wooden blocks with watercress and mini meat cleavers. This three-story,
no-reservations steak den and craft-beer basement bar is decked out in
exposed brick walls, enamel lights, and shared wooden tables. Sides
include beef-dripping chips, creamed spinach, and roasted eggplant
with Parmesan, while sauces range from béarnaise to French horserad-
ish cream. Shared seating is first-come, first-served, and at peak times
you'll need to leave a cell number and hang downstairs sipping a vintage
cocktail or rare beer while you wait. Check Twitter for daily specials
like chargrilled Irish belly steak or 48-hour slow-cooked short ribs, and
try the salted chocolate orange mousse for dessert. Ⓢ *Average main: £10*
✉ *17 Beak St., Soho* ⊕ *flatironsteak.co.uk* ✍ *Reservations not accepted*
Ⓜ *Oxford Circus, Piccadilly Circus* ✛ 3:B5.

$ ✕ **Koya.** Is it all the hypnotic kneading that makes the hand-pulled
JAPANESE   Sanuki udon noodles here *so* maddeningly addictive? Ever-present
lines of polite Japanese diners and hip Soho ites are a testament to the
pull of the mega-tasty steaming dishes served at this tiny stripped-back
cult noodle house on Frith Street in Soho. Once inside, start with cold
udon on a bamboo basket with pungent miso and pickled pork, and
then—if you're up for it—slurp hot udon with smoked mackerel and
Japanese green leaves, or fried tofu and green onions. There's pickled
plums, prawn tempura, duck-and-rice-in-a-bowl, slow-cooked *onsen
tamago* poached eggs, and braised pork belly dishes, but it's the mighty
udon noodle that ultimately prevails. Ⓢ *Average main: £12* ✉ *49 Frith
St., Soho* ☎ 020/7434–4463 ⊕ *www.koya.co.uk* ✍ *Reservations not
accepted* Ⓜ *Tottenham Court Rd.* ✛ 3:D5.

$ ✕ **Maison Bertaux.** Die-hard romantics and Francophiles cherish this
CAFÉ   quirky, two-story 1871 French patisserie, vintage tea parlor, and occa-
sional pop-up art space, where happily nothing seems to have changed
since the 1940s. Framed with classic blue-and-white striped awnings,
and decked out in cake stands, antique mirrors, drapes, and fairy lights,
the pastries, tarts, and sweet cakes at this time-warp Soho institution
are renowned, well loved, and baked on-site. The chocolate and fruit
éclairs, Saint-Honoré and Black Forest gâteaux, colorful marzipan figs,
Mont Blancs, strawberry fancies, and flaky almond croissants never

fail to delight. Maison Bertaux also hosts a cheery retro tea service, which comes with tasty savories, like broccoli quiche or Dijon slice, with cheese, peppers, and mustard. $ *Average main: £7* ✉ *28 Greek St., Soho* ☎ *020/7437–6007* ⊕ *www.maisonbertaux.com* ⚖ *Reservations not accepted* ☰ *No credit cards* Ⓜ *Leicester Sq.* ✛ *3:D5.*

$ ✕ **Pitt Cue Co.** Everyone's gone bonkers for the American BBQ beef ribs
BARBECUE   and pulled pork at this Soho trendsetter. A tiny, no reservations joint, Pitt Cue has only 18 basement seats and eight counter stools in the ground-floor bourbon-and-rye crush bar—little wonder line ups snake down the street. Most order the £10–£12.50 finger-lickin' spreads, which come with slaw and house pickles. Charred rib-tips, pig's head sausages, smoked jowl, brisket burgers, and bone-marrow mash sides are other temptations, but the devout devour the sloppy sliders and sticky ribs with their mucky paws. The secret to Pitt Cue's famous BBQ pork and beef ribs? A coal-and-wood-chip smoker, free-range Tamworth, Middle White, and Mangalitsa pork prime cuts from Cornwall. Dry rubs and marinades include smoked paprika, Sriracha chili sauce, blackstrap molasses, and apricot preserve. $ *Average main: £12* ✉ *1 Newburgh St., Soho* ☎ *020/7787–5578* ⊕ *www.pittcue.co.uk* ⚖ *Reservations not accepted* ⊘ *No dinner Sun.* Ⓜ *Oxford Circus* ✛ *3:B5.*

$ ✕ **Spuntino.** Moody tin tile ceilings, dangly filament lights, tattooed
DINER   waitstaff, bluegrass tunes, and only 27 raised counter stools at this pewter-topped rectangular-shaped bar and Lower East Side–inspired diner makes this one of the most unimaginably *cool* gigs in town. Naturally, there's no phone, no reservations, and minimal signage, but that only adds to the hush-hush speakeasy vibe. Once seated after a wait, strike up a conversation with the friendly bar staff and settle in with a whisky-based Brooklyn Manhattan cocktail. Then dive into famed truffled egg toast before moving on to deep-fried grits, soft-shell crab, or three-bites-and-they're-gone Yankee sliders—try beef and bone marrow. Don't overlook the glorious mac 'n' cheese. For dessert, try a PB&J sandwich, and chase it down with a slug or two of Elijah Craig or Knob Creek bourbon. $ *Average main: £12* ✉ *61 Rupert St., Soho* ⊕ *www.spuntino.co.uk* ⚖ *Reservations not accepted* Ⓜ *Piccadilly Circus* ✛ *3:C5.*

$$ ✕ **10 Greek Street.** There may only be 37 seats at this stripped-back
MODERN   Modern European Soho humdinger, but Aussie chef Cameron Emirali
EUROPEAN   and wine guy Luke Wilson have seriously got their schtick together. Great food? *Tick.* Cheap wine? *Tick.* Excellent service? *Tick.* Good prices? *Tick.* Buzz? *Tick.* The only negative is the evenings-only no-reservations policy, but most happily saunter off for a quick shifty in the pub two doors down and wait to be called back on their cell phones. Once seated, expect simple interchangeable starters and mains like butternut ravioli with sage, or pancetta sardines with watercress and fennel. Gutsy meats like Welsh Black short rib, Tamworth pork with apple chutney, or venison with potato galette are big and bold, and swing with the seasons. Top-value £4–£7 desserts, like plum-and-apple crumble, provide a nice finish. $ *Average main: £17* ✉ *10 Greek St., Soho* ☎ *020/7734–4677* ⊕ *www.10greekstreet.com* ⚖ *Reservations not accepted* ⊘ *Closed Sun.* Ⓜ *Tottenham Court Rd.* ✛ *3:D4.*

$ ✗ **Tonkotsu.** Bowls of steaming Japanese ramen with gloopy pork-bone

RAMEN broth and wheat-and-egg-based noodles are the *raison d'être* at this

FAMILY modern restaurant. Ravenous punters line up on the street and peer

Fodor'sChoice into the glass-fronted open-kitchen to ogle steel cauldrons of pork

★ bones bubbling away. Garnish your soup with fatty braised pork belly, *wakame* seaweed, *menma* bamboo shoots, soft-boiled egg, and a slick of black garlic oil. This meal cries out to be lifted up to your mouth and slurped, Japanese-style, with your wooden ladle. There are three ramen soups to chose from and starters like spinach-and-sesame salad, deep-fried *karaage* chicken, or crispy-edged dumplings with house-made chili oil. $ *Average main: £11* ⊠ *63 Dean St., Soho* ☎ *020/7437–0071* ⊕ *www.tonkotsu.co.uk* ⌂ *Reservations not accepted* Ⓜ *Tottenham Court Rd., Oxford Circus, Piccadilly Circus* ✛ *3:D5.*

COVENT GARDEN

$$ ✗ **Balthazar.** Prodigal Brit restaurateur Keith McNally re-creates his

BRASSERIE famed New York all-day brasserie at a winning spot right off the piazza in Covent Garden. The decor of brass-studded red leather banquettes, distressed mirrors, illuminated columns, pewter bar tops, and intricate mosaic floors creates a sparkly, soft patina, and enchanting backdrop in which to enjoy a classic all-day French menu of few surprises. Breakfast, brunch, lunch, afternoon tea, dinner, and pre- and post-theater meals are all well catered for at this buzzy and notably well-serviced 175-seat venue. Pick out flavor-packed dishes like duck shepherd's pie or ox cheek bourguignonne, and kick back and linger over the diverting all-French wine list, which carries everything from a modest Chablis Colombier 2011 (£10 per glass) to a grand Pauillac Château Mouton Rothschild '89 from Bordeaux, at £800 a pop. $ *Average main: £23* ⊠ *4–7 Russell St., Covent Garden* ☎ *020/3301–1155* ⊕ *www.balthazarlondon.com* ⌂ *Reservations essential* Ⓜ *Covent Garden, Charing Cross* ✛ *3:F5.*

$$$ ✗ **Clos Maggiore.** Bag a seat in the low-lighted conservatory at this seri-

FRENCH ously romantic Provençal country inn–style bolt hole in the heart of Covent Garden. A bouquet's throw away from the Royal Opera House, and once a favorite with amorous heir to the throne Prince Harry, service is pretty formal and the warren of candlelit, wood-panel rooms, open fires, old-master oil paintings, and convex mirrors never fails to enchant. Meal deals and theater specials (£15.50–£23.50) are a cute way in, where you'll be wooed by old-fashioned and refined French cuisine, such as Loire Valley rabbit ballotine, Weymouth sea bass, or Charolais beef cheeks with fine French beans. $ *Average main: £24* ⊠ *33 King St., Covent Garden* ☎ *020/7379–9696* ⊕ *www.closmaggiore. com* ⌂ *Reservations essential* Ⓜ *Covent Garden* ✛ *3:F5.*

$ ✗ **Côte.** Where else can you find a cracking two-course French meal in

BISTRO Covent Garden for £9.95? The Côte brasserie chain—softly lighted

FAMILY and decked out with gray-and-white striped awnings, banquettes, and Parisian-style café tables—does the trick, and offers popular meal deals weekdays from noon until 7 pm, weekends from noon until 6 pm. With four choices per course, you'll find all your French brasserie favorites: crêpes with mushrooms and Gruyère cheese, *boeuf bourguignonne*, chargrilled Breton chicken, *moules marinières* (mussels with white

14

wine), steak haché, and iced berries and white-chocolate sauce. Service is brisk and friendly, and if you're lucky enough to be attending the nearby Royal Opera House, this is perfect for pretheater, *or* post-theater come to think of it. $ *Average main: £10* ⊠ *17–21 Tavistock St., Covent Garden* ☎ *020/7379–9991* ⊕ *www.cote-restaurants.co.uk* ⇗ *Reservations essential* Ⓜ *Covent Garden* ✢ *3:G5.*

$

MODERN INDIAN

FAMILY

Fodor's Choice

★

✕ **Dishoom.** Whirring ceiling fans, Indian film posters, checkerboard tiles, oak panels, and old Indian cola bottles create an evocative Bombay backdrop for this inexpensive all-day Indian café off Covent Garden. Try the naan bread with keema minced lamb and peas, or classic handkerchief-thin spicy charred chicken tikka *roomali* roti rolls (£6.90). A succulent lamb *raan* bun comes on a wooden block with slow-cooked pulled lamb in a sourdough bun with pomegranate slaw, *sali* chips, and fried green chilies, while gorgeous creamy black dahl is simmered for 24 hours. Drinks range from a Bollybellini to Limca lemonade or a grenadine-rich lassi. $ *Average main: £8* ⊠ *12 Upper St. Martin's La., Covent Garden* ☎ *020/7420–9320* ⊕ *www.dishoom.com* Ⓜ *Leicester Sq.* ✢ *3:E5.*

$

VEGETARIAN

FAMILY

✕ **Food for Thought.** Covent Garden's throwback 1970s-style subterranean vegetarian café has a cult vegan following, so be prepared to line up down the stairs onto Neal Street. You'll find cramped communal tables and a zingy daily changing menu of wholesome soups, salads, pulses, dhals, stews, quiches, stir fries, bakes, and casseroles—from mushroom Stroganoff to Rajistani red lentil curry. Wheat-free, gluten-free, nut-free, GM–free, free range, Fair Trade, vegan, and organic options are all usually available. Leave room for such desserts as their famous oat-based strawberry and banana "Scrunch." There's take-away and it's BYO, but note it's cash only and only open from noon until 8:30 pm Monday through Saturday, and from noon until 5:30 pm on Sunday. $ *Average main: £9* ⊠ *31 Neal St., Covent Garden* ☎ *020/7836–9072* ⊕ *foodforthought-london.co.uk* ⇗ *Reservations not accepted* ⊟ *No credit cards* Ⓜ *Covent Garden* ✢ *3:F4.*

$$

MODERN BRITISH

✕ **Great Queen Street.** Expect a boisterous best-of-British foodie crowd at one of Covent Garden's leading gastropubs, one that showcases retro-British dishes. Not far from the Royal Opera House, the ground-floor open-kitchen eatery is done up with burgundy walls and bare-oak floors and tables. Unadulterated wine-fueled diners dive into nostalgic offerings like pressed tongue, pickled herrings, chicken pie, or smoked mackerel with rhubarb. You'll find other vintage British dishes from a bygone age, like brown crab on toast, plus great roasts for the table—think seven-hour shoulder of lamb with dauphinoise potatoes (£68 for four). Salads and green veggies are few and far between. $ *Average main: £19* ⊠ *32 Great Queen St., Covent Garden* ☎ *020/7242–0622* ⇗ *Reservations essential* ☉ *No dinner Sun.* Ⓜ *Covent Garden, Holborn* ✢ *3:G4.*

$$

BRITISH

FAMILY

✕ **The Ivy.** The triple A list spurns The Ivy for its upstairs private members' club (and other luxe spots like Scott's, 34, and Berners Tavern) but, nonetheless, this venerable landmark still receives a thousand calls a day! A mesmerizing mix of daytime TV stars, gawkers, day-trippers, and out-of-towners dine on salt-beef hash, squash risotto, Thai-baked sea bass, salmon fish cakes, eggs Benedict, and good ol' English classics like shepherd's pie or kedgeree (curried rice with smoked haddock, egg, and parsley) in a handsome mullioned stained-glass and oak-paneled dining salon. Desserts are standards like Baked Alaska or sticky toffee pudding, service is unfailingly professional, and for low-to-mid wattage West End star-spotting this is still a happy hunting ground. ■ **TIP→ If you can't snag a table by phone or online, try walking in on spec—it's been known to work.** ⑤ *Average main: £22* ✉ *1–5 West St., Covent Garden* ☎ *020/7836–4751* ⊕ *www.the-ivy.co.uk* ⚹ *Reservations essential* Ⓜ *Covent Garden* ✛ *3:E5.*

$$$
SEAFOOD
✕ **J Sheekey.** The A-list sneak into this classy 1896 side-alley seafood haven, a discreet alternative to the more overtly celeb-central Scott's, 34, Berners Tavern, or The Delaunay. Linked with the surrounding Theatreland district, J Sheekey is one of Londoners' all-time favorite West End haunts. Beautifully orchestrated by maître d' John Andrews, Sheekey charms with warm wood paneling, vintage showbiz black-and-white portraits, a warren of alcoves, and twinkly lava-rock bar tops. Opt for snappingly fresh Atlantic prawns, pickled Arctic herrings, scallop, shrimp, and salmon burgers, or the famous Sheekey fish pie. Better still, sip Gaston Chiquet Champagne and sluice down half a dozen Jersey rock oysters at the mirrored bar for the ultimate in true romance. Alternatively, enjoy the £26.50 weekend three-course set lunch deals. ⑤ *Average main: £24* ✉ *28–35 St. Martin's Ct., Covent Garden* ☎ *020/7240–2565* ⊕ *www.j-sheekey.co.uk* ⚹ *Reservations essential* Ⓜ *Leicester Sq.* ✛ *3:F.6.*

$$
TAPAS
✕ **Opera Tavern.** Ibérico pig's head terrine and foie gras and Manchego cheeseburgers are just a few of the outstanding Spanish and Italian tapas dishes found at the Opera Tavern, opposite historic Drury Lane Theatre. Clamber in at the overcrowded ground-floor tapas bar (avoiding the acoustically challenged second-floor dining salon if possible) and, after enjoying a snack of crispy pig's ears or guindilla peppers, opt for rich empanadas of venison, Italian Scotch eggs, braised cuttlefish, wood pigeon with scarmorza cheese, or chargrilled Venetian style sardines. Desserts like *dulche de leche* panna cotta hit the spot, and watch out for the £35 or £40 tapas set meals for groups of seven and up. ⑤ *Average main: £12* ✉ *23 Catherine St., Covent Garden* ☎ *020/7836–3680* ⊕ *www.operatavern. co.uk* ⚹ *Reservations essential* Ⓜ *Covent Garden, Holborn* ✛ *3:G5.*

$$$
BRITISH
Fodor's Choice
★
✕ **Rules.** Come, escape the 21st century. Opened in 1798, London's oldest restaurant is, according to some, still London's most *beautiful.* The main dining salons are, indeed, an old-world wonderland, what Maxim's is to Paris. The decor begins with plush red banquettes, lacquered yellow walls, and spectacular etched-glass skylights. Then, in High Victorian fashion, every cranny is covered with vintage needlepoint, Regency oil paintings, figurines, antlers, antique clocks, stuffed pheasants, and endless framed prints. Little wonder Rules has been a stage across which everyone from Charles Dickens to Laurence Olivier has pranced. For your shining day—be sure to ask for a table in one of the "glass house" skylight rooms, the bar area, or the Margaret Thatcher corner—dig into the menu's historic British dishes like steak-and-kidney pie, jugged hare, partridge, or roast beef and Yorkshire pudding. For a taste of the 18th century, you can choose game specials from the restaurant's Teesdale estate, including grouse, woodcock,

14

snipe, and ptarmigan. ⑤ *Average main: £28* ⊠ *35 Maiden La., Covent Garden* ☎ *020/7836–5314* ⊕ *www.rules.co.uk* ⚖ *Reservations essential* 🏛 *Jacket required* Ⓜ *Covent Garden* ✛ *3:F6.*

$$$$
BRITISH
FAMILY

✕ **The Savoy Grill.** You can *feel* the history in the room at this glamorous 1889 art deco hotel-dining powerhouse, which has hosted everyone from Oscar Wilde and Frank Sinatra to Liz Taylor and Marilyn Monroe. Nowadays—buffed up with Swarovski chandeliers, velvet coverings, gold leaf–backed tortoiseshell walls, and vintage pics and mirrors—it caters to business barons, top-end tourists, and nostalgia freaks who come for the Grill's famed table-side trolley, which might trundle up laden with hulking great roasts like beef Wellington, rack of pork, or saddle of lamb. Savoy legends like omelet Arnold Bennett (with smoked haddock, Parmesan, and cream) or baked egg cocotte with smoked bacon, wild mushrooms, and red wine sauce are to the fore, plus there's timeless standbys like T-bone and chateaubriand steaks, alongside Carlingford oysters and lobster Thermidor. For dessert, you can't top the mandarin Baked Alaska. ⑤ *Average main: £31* ⊠ *The Savoy, 100 The Strand, Covent Garden* ☎ *020/7592–1600* ⊕ *www. gordonramsay.com/thesavoygrill* ⚖ *Reservations essential* Ⓜ *Charing Cross, Covent Garden* ✛ *3:G5.*

$
MEXICAN
FAMILY

✕ **Wahaca.** Brace for line ups for the fab-value Mexican street food at former MasterChef winner Thomasina Miers' brightly colored Covent Garden bolt hole. Concrete walls, shared wooden bench seats, and green ceiling slats make for brisk and breezy basement surrounds, but it's the cheap-as-chips, ethically and sustainably sourced £3.95–£7.95 Mexican market-style tacos, enchiladas, quesadillas, taquitos, and burritos that pull in the budget-conscious studenty and touristy crowds. A generous £19.95 spread for two hungry honchos to share will produce a feast of broad bean quesadillas, pork pibil tacos, slaw, chicken tinga taquitas with green rice, black bean tostadas, and guacamole, but note that the Mexican music can be a bit loud and the restaurant is often heaving by 6:30 pm. ⑤ *Average main: £7* ⊠ *66 Chandos Pl., Covent Garden* ☎ *020/7240–1883* ⊕ *www.wahaca.co.uk* ⚖ *Reservations not accepted* Ⓜ *Covent Garden* ✛ *3:F6.*

BLOOMSBURY, HOLBORN, AND FITZROVIA

BLOOMSBURY

The literary giants of the Bloomsbury set—from Virginia Woolf to E.M. Forster—may be long gone but this bluestocking enclave (centered around the British Library and University of London) still excels at a cultured and a pleasure-loving dining scene. Holborn, bordering Covent Garden, has some of those big, old-establishment hotel dining rooms, and a big, bright elegant shining star in The Delaunay on the Aldwych.

$
MODERN BRITISH
FAMILY
Fodor's Choice
★

✕ **Berners Tavern.** All the cool cats converge at this grand brasserie at Ian Schrager's trendy London Edition hotel. It's hard not to feel like a million dollars as you enter the triple-height all-day dining salon, crammed with 1835 ornate plasterwork, bronze chandeliers, candles, and 150-odd stately home–style paintings. Bag a half-moon banquette and start the day with an impeccable £13 Full English breakfast (with Stornaway black pudding) and return for a light lunch of crispy rock-shrimp roll or pulled Old Spot pork with chips and slaw for £12. Reemerge refreshed for dinner, and swoon over a deep fried duck egg, Cumbrian ham, and pea appetizer, and then it's a toss-up between Creedy caver duck, Cornish sea bass, or Buccleuch Estate bavette. You'll find stunning dishes to share—like *sous vide* Romney Marsh lamb or whole Irish ox, tongue and cheek—and battered cod, chips, and mushy peas on Fish Fridays. $ *Average main: £15* ⊠ *The London Edition, 10 Berners St., Bloomsbury* ☎ *020/7908–7979* ⊕ *www.bernerstavern.com* ⚑ *Reservations essential* Ⓜ *Oxford Circus, Tottenham Court Rd.* ⊕ 3:B3.

$ ✕ **Grain Store.** Vegetables take pride of place at French chef Bruno Lou-
MODERN FRENCH bet's mega-hit 120-seat restaurant. Earthy beetroot, artichoke, corn,
FAMILY quinoa, butternut squash, onions, potatoes, and shiitake mushrooms
Fodor'sChoice take starring roles—and relegate proteins to the margins—on the menu
★ at his quirky 1851 converted former grain warehouse, just behind King's Cross and St. Pancras stations. Watch Loubet in the kitchen-cum-dining room as he concocts veg-centric surprises like spiced mash, pickled cucumber, snowball turnips, broad beans . . . and a *little* confit lamb. You'll smirk at flourishes like a flowerpot of radishes that you roll in "olive soil" (dried black olives), a chilled tomato water lobster "Bloody Mary," and desserts of goat's milk panna cotta with candied tomato. And yet, there's no denying the originality of Loubet's signature butternut squash ravioli or the sheer brilliance of a humble vegetable "Scotch egg" with a wicked tangle of fennel and aioli sauce. $ *Average main: £12* ⊠ *Granary Sq., 1–3 Stable St., King's Cross* ☎ *020/7324–4466* ⊕ *www.grainstore.com* ⚑ *Reservations essential* ⊗ *No dinner Sun.* Ⓜ *King's Cross, St. Pancras* ⊕ 2:C1.

HOLBORN

$$ ✕ **The Delaunay.** It's all *fin de siècle* Vienna at this magnificent art deco–
AUSTRIAN style take on an all-day Viennese coffeehouse on the Aldwych. Dine like
FAMILY Emperor Franz Joseph I on a majestic 60-item menu that would do the
Fodor'sChoice dual-monarchy and Austro-Hungarian Empire proud. Dishes are von
★ Trapp fabulous—think *weiners*, *schnitzels*, goulash, and Viennese hot dogs, served with sauerkraut and onions. There are other goodies like borscht and beef Stroganoff, kedgeree, and *choucroute`a l'Alsacienne* (sauerkraut with sausages). Desserts delight, too, including *apfelstrudel* (apple strudel) and an evocative three-peaked Salzburg soufflé, while the innocuous "Kinder" ice cream coupe bursts with meringue, marsh-mallows, and whipped cream. Classy Viennese breakfast, brunch, Vien-noiserie pastries, and Afternoon Teas are also served. $ *Average main: £21* ⊠ *55 Aldwych, Holborn* ☎ *020/7499–8558* ⊕ *www.thedelaunay. com* Ⓜ *Covent Garden, Charring Cross, Aldwych* ⊕ 3:G5.

FITZROVIA

$ ✕ **Bubbledogs.** Hot dogs and Champagne? Shucks! Why didn't *we* think
AMERICAN of that! Bubbledogs has come up with the most unlikely food combo this side of milk shakes and fries—and has hit the Willy Wonka jack-pot. Husband-and-wife Sandia Chang and James Knappett combine their respective loves of New York hot dogs and independent grower Champagnes, and have gone back to bubbly basics with a bar menu

14

that pays due homage to both. Classic all-British pork, beef, or vegetarian hot dogs cost around £8, while the single-estate and handcrafted Champagnes are some of the most reasonable around—think £7 for a glass of Gaston Chiquet. Sit at raised counters surrounded by brick walls, dog cartoons, and cozy log-cabin paneling, and choose hot dogs ranging from a Fourth of July (bacon wrapped with BBQ sauce), a New Yorker (with NY street-cart onions), or The Reuben (with sauerkraut and Russian dressing). There's slaw and sweet-potato fries, but expect a wait; line ups form after 6 pm. $ *Average main: £8* ⊠ *70 Charlotte St., Fitzrovia* ☎ *020/7637–7770* ⊕ *www.bubbledogs.co.uk* ⌅ *Reservations not accepted* ⊗ *Closed Sun. and Mon.* Ⓜ *Goodge St.* ✛ *3:B2.*

$$
MODERN
EUROPEAN
Fodor's Choice
★

✕**Dabbous.** It's a triumph of taste over technology at wunderkind Ollie Dabbous's extraordinary game changer off Charlotte Street in Bloomsbury. Startlingly minimalist, pure, inventive, and seasonally based new-wave dishes elicit *Oohs! Aahhs!* and *Oh-my-Goshes!* in a flummery-free NYC–industrial chic setting of exposed concrete, overhead ducting, and heavy metal screens and cages. Phenomenal flavors abound. Ingredient-led dishes like a peas-and-mint appetizer ping your taste buds with frozen mint tea, edible violets, and broad bean flowers, and a coddled hen's egg with smoked butter and woodland mushrooms sits handsomely in a slinky bowl of hay. Palette-popping barbecued Ibèrico pork with acorn praline, halibut with coastal herbs (sea aster and oyster leaf), and brittle chocolate ganache with green basil moss are instant classics, and set Dabbous apart as one of London's most dazzling talents. ■TIP➔ **Book far in advance.** $ *Average main: £21* ⊠ *39 Whitfield St., Fitzrovia* ☎ *020/7323–7323* ⊕ *www.dabbous.co.uk* ⌅ *Reservations essential* ⊗ *Closed Sun. and Mon.* Ⓜ *Goodge St.* ✛ *3:C2.*

$$
PERUVIAN

✕**Lima.** Biodiversity-driven cuisine has blasted Lima to the top rank of London's new-wave Peruvian restaurants. Relax in an informal sky-lighted dining room scattered with cushions and Inca-style stitched banquettes, and put yourselves in the hands of the famously smiley staff, who'll guide you first to frisky pisco sours, made with grape brandy, sugar syrup, bitters, and foamy egg white. Next has to be a killer raw-fish sea bream *ceviche*, doused in lime-flavored white tiger's milk (*leche de tigre*), with sweet onion and inka corn. Charred chunks of braised octopus on white quinoa with purple *botija* olive blobs is as vibrant a dish as any, and mains like suckling pig with Amazonian cashews, or crab with purple corn and red *kiwich* (an Andean super grain) will blow your taste buds away. Finish with 75%-cacao Porcelana dessert with mango and mini blue potato chips. $ *Average main: £19* ⊠ *31 Rathbone Pl., Fitzrovia* ⊕ *www.limalondon.com* ⌅ *Reservations essential* Ⓜ *Tottenham Court Rd., Goodge St.* ✛ *3:C3.*

CLERKENWELL AND THE CITY

Historic and just beyond The City limits, chef-centric Clerkenwell is one of the most cutting-edge, radical, and trendy quarters for London gastro-dining, which sets it in marked contrast to the adjacent City, which caters overwhelmingly to business-focused conservative dining. In Clerkenwell, the starchiness of The City fades into relaxed artiness: a fertile ground for avant-garde chefs and restaurants.

$$$ ✗**Bistrot Bruno Loubet.** French chef Bruno Loubet rules the roost at this
FRENCH slick hotel dining room and upscale bistro at the Zetter in historic-yet-cutting-edge Clerkenwell. Loubet tinkers and crafts away and creates so many must-try regional French dishes it's genuinely hard to choose: deliciously pink quail comes with prune, Roquefort, and sautéed wild mushrooms, while guinea fowl *boudin blanc* sausages sit perfectly with delicate leeks and chervil sauce, to name a couple of winners. You'll find fleshy sea bream with Pernod *beurre blanc*, yummy Mauricette snails and meatballs, and soothing *hare royale*, followed by tarragon poached pear, or classic *crêpes Suzette* (served with a touch of cardamom in a copper pan). The bustling ground-floor bistro is kitted with retro lamps, earthenware jars, coat hooks, and artifacts, and overlooks St. John's Square and the crenellated 14th-century St. John's Gate. ⑤ *Average main: £18* ✉ *The Zetter, 86–88 Clerkenwell Rd., Clerkenwell* ☎ *020/7324–4455* ⊕ *www.bistrotbrunoloubet.com* ⌕ *Reservations essential* Ⓜ *Farringdon St., Barbican* ✛ *2:F3.*

$$ ✗**Duck & Waffle.** Zoom up to the 40th floor of the Heron Tower near
MODERN BRITISH Liverpool Street, and head straight for the cult signature dish of crispy
FAMILY confit duck leg, fried duck egg, Belgium waffle, and mustard maple
Fodor's Choice syrup for a taste of awesomeness from rising Brit chef Daniel Doherty.
★ Eclectic flourishes abound amid spectacular views that take in the Tower of London, Tower Bridge, and the Gherkin. A mysterious wax-sealed brown paper bag contains spiced pigs ears, and battered cod tongues have a seafront feel as they come in a faux polystyrene tray with chippy paper and a wooden fork. Handily open 24/7, you might sample an all-day foie gras breakfast, with streaky bacon and homemade Nutella, or share tender octopus with lemon and capers, bacon-wrapped dates, and pollack "meatballs." A stunning vanilla ice cream Baked Alaska with strawberry and mint oil is the ultimate finale. ⑤ *Average main: £19* ✉ *Heron Tower, 110 Bishopsgate, The City* ☎ *020/3640–7310* ⊕ *www. duckandwaffle.com* ⌕ *Reservations essential* Ⓜ *Liverpool St.* ✛ *2:G2.*

$ ✗**E Pellicci.** It's all Cockney banter and all-day full English breakfasts
CAFÉ at this tiny Grade II–listed 1900 family-run greasy spoon near the East
FAMILY End's great Brick Lane and Columbia Road street markets. With atmospheric stained glass, Formica tables, art deco marquetry, and signed pics of *East Enders* TV soap stars, it's a rowdy hole-in-the-wall for the greasy "fry-ups" that the British adore: eggs, bacon, sausages, baked beans, toast, tomatoes, mushrooms, black pudding, tea, and bubble-and-squeak (cabbage and mashed potatoes). Matriarch "Mama" Maria also rustles up Toscana spaghetti and lasagna, plus steamed sponge and bread pudding. Your arteries may clog up, but at least the wallet survives. Everything's less than £8.90, but remember this is the East End, and hence it's *"Cash only, Mate!!"* ⑤ *Average main: £8* ✉ *332 Bethnal Green Rd., Bethnal Green* ☎ *020/7739–4873* ⌕ *Reservations not accepted* ⊟ *No credit cards* ☾ *Closed Sun.* Ⓜ *Bethnal Green* ✛ *2:H1.*

$$$ ✗**L'Anima.** Top-notch southern Italian cuisine in a modern glass-sided
ITALIAN shoe box of a restaurant characterizes the lively business-heavy dining scene here near Bishopsgate. Wavy-haired Italian chef Francesco Mazzei draws inspiration from Sicily, Puglia, Sardinia, and Calabria and prowls the modern high-ceilinged bar, floor, and clear-fronted kitchen

14

like the proud owner he is. With its clean lines, soft music, and distinctive white leather seats, you'll find fresh, simple, and restrained Italian dishes like wild mushroom and black truffle tagliolini and Sardinian fish stew, or incredible crispy fish strips that have been soaked in milk and dipped in double-zero flour. The *baccalà* salt cod with *n'duja* crimson-colored Calabrian sausage is awesome, too. Well-crafted desserts, like ricotta mousse with spicy figs, are *bellissimo,* and the winning wine list is mostly Italian. $ *Average main: £26* ☒ *1 Snowden St., The City* ☎ *020/7422-7000* ⊕ *www.lanima.co.uk* ⚑ *Reservations essential* ⊙ *Closed Sun.* Ⓜ *Liverpool St.* ✛ *2:G1.*

$$

MEDITERRANEAN

FAMILY

✗**Moro.** Up from The City, near Clerkenwell and Sadler's Wells contemporary dance theater, is Exmouth Market, a cluster of cute indie shops, bookstores, vinyl stores, artisan bakeries, an Italian church, and more fine indie-spirited restaurants like Moro. Lovingly nurtured for over a decade by husband-and-wife chefs Sam and Sam Clark, the menu includes an expansive mélange of Spanish, Moroccan, and Moorish North African flavors. Flavor-packed and rustic tapas—like baba ghanoush, Syrian lentils, baby squid with harissa, or ox heart tabouleh—compete with spiced meats, Serrano ham, salt cod, and chargrilled offerings. Wood-fired sea bass with hispi cabbage, grilled lamb with eggplant, or sea bream with chickpea salad are among the standout mains. Sidle up to the long zinc bar, or squeeze into a tiny table and lean in—it's noisy here, but then again that's all part of the buzz. $ *Average main: £18* ☒ *34–36 Exmouth Market, Clerkenwell* ☎ *020/7833–8336* ⊕ *www.moro.co.uk* ⚑ *Reservations essential* ⊙ *No dinner Sun.* Ⓜ *Farringdon, Angel* ✛ *2:E3.*

$

BRITISH

FAMILY

✗**Simpson's Tavern.** The City of London's oldest chophouse and tavern was founded by Thomas Simpson in 1757 (during the reign of George II) and is undoubtedly as raucous now as the day it opened. Approached via a tiny cobbled Dickensian alley off Cornhill, it draws ruddy-faced pin-striped City folk who revel in the old boarding school surrounds and down oodles of claret and rustic old English tavern-style grub: pork belly crackling, potted shrimps, steak-and-kidney pie, grilled chump chops, and "stewed cheese" (the house special of cheese on toast with béchamel sauce). Desserts are public school faves, like spotted dick and custard, and antique six-seater shared oak bench stalls with overhead brass coat racks, House of Commons green cushions, and magnificently merry service only seem to add to the charm. This was once a favorite with Victorian novelists Charles Dickens and William Thackeray. Note it's only open weekdays for breakfast and lunch from 8:30 am until 3:30 pm. $ *Average main: £10* ☒ *Ball Court, 38½ Cornhill, The City* ☎ *020/7626–9985* ⊕ *www.simpsonstavern.co.uk* ⚑ *Reservations essential* ⊙ *Closed weekends. No dinner* Ⓜ *Bank* ✛ *2:G2.*

$$

MODERN BRITISH

✗**St. John.** Gastronauts travel the globe for pioneering Brit-chef Fergus Henderson's nose-to-tail cuisine at this puritan stark-white converted former ham-and-bacon smokehouse near historic Smithfield Market. Henderson famously uses *all* scraps of a carcass, and his waste not, want not chutzpah chimes increasingly with London's age of austerity: one appetizer is pig's skin and others like ox heart, rolled pig's spleen, or calves' brain and chicory are marginally less extreme. Open since 1994, long-standing St. John signatures like bone marrow and parsley salad, chitterlings with dandelion, or pheasant and pig's trotter pie appear stark on the plate, but arrive with aplomb. Look out for a metropolitan art-and-designer crowd, who enjoy feasting meals for the table, like whole roast suckling pig or braised venison with red wine sauce. Finish with Eccles cakes, Lancashire cheese, or half a dozen golden madeleines. ⑤ *Average main: £23* ✉ *26 St. John St., Clerkenwell* ☎ *020/7251–0848* ⊕ *www.stjohnrestaurant.com* ⌛ *Reservations essential* ⊘ *No dinner Sun.* Ⓜ *Farringdon, Barbican* ✚ *2:F4.*

$$
SEAFOOD
✗ **Sweetings.** Sweetings was established in 1889 and little seems to have changed at this time warp since the last days of the British Empire. There are some things Sweetings *doesn't* do: reservations, dinner, coffee, or weekends. It does, mercifully, do seafood—and rather well. Not far from St. Paul's Cathedral, and kitted out with Victoriana, Colonel Blimp, and sporting cartoons, the restaurant is patronized by pin-striped City gents who down pewter tankards of Black Velvet (Guinness and Champagne) and love to eat potted shrimps, roe on toast, Dover sole, and skate wings with black butter sauce, all this perched on high stools at white linen-covered raised wooden counters. West Mersea oysters are fresh and plump, and desserts like spotted dick or baked jam roll are timeless public school favorites. The long-serving waitstaff wear funeral black and white and know all the regulars. ⑤ *Average main: £19* ✉ *39 Queen Victoria St., The City* ☎ *020/7248–3062* ⊕ *www.sweetingsrestaurant.com* ⌛ *Reservations not accepted* ⊘ *Closed weekends. No dinner* Ⓜ *Mansion House* ✚ *2:II6.*

$
INDIAN
✗ **Tayyabs.** Half-hour line ups form at this throbbing neon-fronted east-side Whitechapel mecca and family-owned curry house. Best bets include fiery Pakistani curries, chargrilled lamb chops, and spicy *seekh* and *shami* kebabs. Average price of dinner for two: £36. ⑤ *Average main: £16* ✉ *83–89 Fieldgate St., The City* ☎ *020/7247–9543* ⊕ *www.tayyabs.co.uk* ⌛ *Reservations essential* Ⓜ *Aldgate East* ✚ *2:H2.*

EAST LONDON

$
MODERN
EUROPEAN
✗ **Bistrotheque.** This East End fashionista hangout is located down a side alley in hot Bethnal Green. Once you're inside, see the striking loft dining space and Manchichi bar in its postindustrial chic setting of all-white walls and floors, factory pipes, Crittal windows, and Bentwood chairs. All the men seem to wear caps, spats, 'tashes, trilbys, Acne jeans, or '30s-era three-piece tweed deerstalker suits, while the Alexa Chung look-alike ladies are in capes, *Emmanuelle 2* organza getups, denier 10 tights, and Scooby-Doo specs. Accomplished French and English dishes range from steak tartar, Croque Madame, and towering cheeseburgers, to cod and clams or Longhorn beef with red wine sauce. Fashion-forward desserts like Melba toast or brioche and butter pudding stand out, and be sure to catch Xavior, the resident pianist, at weekend brunch, camping up from Katy Perry to Girls Aloud on the baby grand. ⑤ *Average main: £16* ✉ *23–27 Wadeson St., Bethnal Green* ☎ *020/8983–7900* ⊕ *www.bistrotheque.com* ⌛ *Reservations essential* Ⓜ *Bethnal Green* ✚ *2:H1.*

LOCAL CHAINS WORTH A TASTE

If you're zipping round town or don't have time for a leisurely meal, try a local chain restaurant. *The ones listed below are well priced and are the best in their category.*

Bill's: Linger at this popular chain where you can enjoy porridge, meze, afternoon tea (£9.95), or a steak dinner for two (for £17 each) in a cozy setting. ⊕ *www.bills-website.co.uk.*

Byron: This line of child-friendly hamburger joints mops up the mid-range burger market with its Scotch beef hamburgers, onion rings, and French fries.
⊕ *www.byronhamburgers.com.*

Busaba Eathai: It's always packed at these Thai canteen supremos where you'll find Thai noodles, rice dishes, and spicy meals in a bowl in sultry surrounds.
⊕ *www.busaba.com.*

Café Rouge: A French bistro chain that churns out great £10.25–£14.50 *plats rapides* and prix-fixe deals—so uncool that it's now fashionable.
⊕ *www.caferouge.co.uk.*

Pho: Enjoy serene surrounds at this bargain-priced seven-strong Vietnamese gaggle of pungent pho (pronounced "foh") rice and vermicelli noodle soup stops.
⊕ *www.phocafe.co.uk.*

Côte: High-quality and reliable £9.95–£12.50 classic French brasserie meal deals are the order of the day at this lower–upper-middle-market 22-strong chain.
⊕ *www.cote-restaurants.co.uk.*

Ed's Easy Diner: OD on milk shakes, chili dogs, and made-to-order hamburgers at this chain of shiny, retro-'50s-theme, American-style diners. ⊕ *www.edseasydiner.com.*

Gail's Artisan Bakery: Artisanal sandwiches, breakfasts, and lunches like chorizo, butternut squash, and quinoa salad are found at this chain of gourmet bakeries.
⊕ *www.gailsbread.co.uk.*

Masala Zone: The Covent Garden hub's the most popular of these Indian restaurants, where you can gorge on £12 spreads of curry, vegetables, dhal, and raita.
⊕ *www.masalazone.com.*

Pret a Manger: This take-out sandwich shop has store-made natural sandwiches, chemical-free wraps, sushi, salads, fruit, porridge, and tea cakes, too. ⊕ *www.pret.com.*

Wagamama: Londoners drain billions of bowls of Asian ramen and noodle soups at this high-tech, high-turnover kid-friendly chain of Asian canteens. ⊕ *www.wagamama.com.*

$ ✕ **Dishoom.** The humble curry is England's surrogate national dish and
INDIAN in London you'll find some of the best around. Memorabilia-adorned Dishoom near Leicester Square is modeled on the all-day cafés of Victorian-era Bombay and it expertly churns out mesmerizing street food, from naan breads and handkerchief-thin *roomali* roti wraps, to masala prawns, black dhal, lamb biryani, and yogurt-and-milk-based sweet *lassi* drinks. Average price of dinner for two: £40. ⑤ *Average main: £12* ✉ *7 Boundary St., Shoreditch* ☎ *020/7420–9320* ⊕ *www.dishoom.com* ⚑ *Reservations essential* Ⓜ *Shoreditch High St., Liverpool St.* ✛ *2:G1.*

$ ✕ **Pizza East.** Hoxton locals seem to have taken up residence at this
PIZZA knockabout gourmet pizza parlor, which serves up chewy, 10-inch,
FAMILY wood-fired, thin-crust, crispy pizzas in Hoxton's converted Tea Building—a boisterous and achingly au courant 170-seat setting of exposed
concrete walls, raw brickwork, pipes, pillars, and ducting. Amid a
soundscape of Bow Wow Wow and X-Ray Spex, mix things up at long
refectory-style shared tables with a starter of sea bass carpaccio with
fennel and chili, or broad beans with Italian Pecorino, before tearing
into one of the 11 semolina-crust pizzas, which might be topped with
veal meatballs or San Daniele ham and pesto. There's wine by the tap,
cocktails by the jug, plus karaoke, slam poetry, hip hop, or old-school
vinyl sessions in the Concrete basement bar. ⑤ *Average main: £13* ✉ *56
Shoreditch High St., Shoreditch* ☎ *020/7729–1888* ⊕ *www.pizzaeast.
com* Ⓜ *Overground: Shoreditch High St.* ✛ *2:G1.*

14

$ ✕ **Rochelle Canteen.** You feel quite the foodie insider once you finally
BRITISH find the quirky Rochelle Canteen—it's set in the old former bicycle
FAMILY shed at the restored Victorian-era Rochelle School (off Arnold Circus
in Shoreditch, not far from Liverpool Street and the trendy boutiques
of Redchurch Street). Ring a buzzer next to a pale blue door, go in
through the "Boys" entrance (passing a former playground), and enter
chef Margot Henderson's long white, austere canteen which has an open
kitchen and two long Formica tables, Ercol chairs, and Shaker coat pegs
on the wall. Gloriously understated British fare arrives at a leisurely
pace, from simple deviled kidneys on toast to a retro plate of Yorkshire ham and parsley sauce. Bump along with the Frieze London art,
architecture, and designer crowd, and enjoy seasonal guinea fowl with
bacon, or skate and capers, and finish with lemon posset or quince jelly.
Note it's BYO (£5 corkage), and only open 9 am to 4:30 pm weekdays
for breakfast, elevenses, lunch, and tea. ⑤ *Average main: £16* ✉ *Rochelle School, Arnold Circus, Shoreditch* ☎ *020/7729–5677* ⊕ *www.
arnoldandhenderson.com* ⚃ *Reservations not accepted* ☾ *Closed weekends. No dinner* Ⓜ *Liverpool St.* ✛ *2:G1.*

SOUTH OF THE THAMES

First mentioned in 1276 and believed to have existed in Roman times,
Borough Market in Southwark on the South Bank is a firm favorite with
tourists, chefs, and foodies alike. Open Monday to Thursday (10 am–5
pm), Friday (10 am–6 pm), and Saturday (8 am–5 pm), this Dickensian
location under Victorian wrought-iron railway arches at London Bridge
is packed with food lovers eager to pick up the finest and freshest fruit,
vegetables, and grub in town. There are more than 135 stalls, plus a
bunch of pubs, bars, restaurants, and specialty shops, like Neal's Yard
Diary (✉ *6 Park St.*), where you'll be bowled over by the great moun-
tains of stinky blue Stilton cheese stacked floor to ceiling. There are
other noted eateries in nearby and burgeoning Bermondsey Street, too.

$ ✕ **Anchor & Hope.** Exceptional Brit-focused fish and meaty dishes at wal-
MODERN BRITISH let-friendly prices fly out of the open kitchen at this permanently packed,
no-reservations (apart for Sunday lunchtime) stalwart gastropub on The
Cut in Southwark, and a few doors down from the lively contemporary

Young Vic theater. Pot roast duck, braised pig's cheeks, Swaledale steaks, guinea fowl pie, Arbroath smokies, and Orkney kippers keep the British flag flying high and punch well above their weight in terms of taste and tenderness. Mains are well priced between £9 and £18, but bear in mind it's noisy, cramped, achingly informal, and always frightfully overcrowded. That said, the kitchen has smarts and is highly accomplished, and you'll find great feasting dishes to share—like Sunday lunch seven-hour roast shoulder of lamb or carve-your-own whole roast chicken that will easily feed three to four people. Ⓢ *Average main: £16* ⊠ *36 The Cut, Southwark* ☎ *020/7928–9898* ⚏ *Reservations not accepted* ◌ *No dinner Sun. No lunch Mon.* Ⓜ *Waterloo, Southwark* ✛ *5:F2.*

$ ✕ **Casse-Croûte.** French radio plays in the background and a Michelin
BISTRO Man perches benignly over the bar at this perfectly conceived Parisian-
Fodor's Choice style mini-French bistro on Bermondsey Street near the Shard. Run by
★ three friendly French guys—Hervé, Alex, and Sylvain—and miniscule with 19 tightly packed seats and six counter stools, the daily changing blackboard offers a highly restricted three-course menu of exceptional Gallic bistro riffs and classics. Sip Ricard pastis or an electro-green crème de menthe before lopping off two *ouefs à la coque* (boiled eggs with asparagus soldiers) or untangling your way through a blue cheese salad or perfectly constructed *gratinée à l'oignon* (French onion soup). With mains a steal at £11–£14, it's elbows in as you slice into a generous *bonette* steak with pepper sauce or sublime brill with spinach. The £6 desserts like Paris-Brest choux pastry and cream will instantly transport you back to Montmartre or the Left Bank. Ⓢ *Average main: £12* ⊠ *109 Bermondsey St., Bermondsey* ☎ *020/7407–2140* ⊕ *www.cassecroute.co.uk* ⚏ *Reservations essential* ◌ *No dinner Sun.* Ⓜ *London Bridge* ✛ *5:H2.*

$$$ ✕ **Chez Bruce.** Top-notch French and Mediterranean cuisine, faultless
MODERN FRENCH service, a winning wine list, and a glossy south-of-the-river Wandsworth
FAMILY neighborhood vibe make for one of London's all-star favorite restaurants. Take a taxi or overland train south of the Thames to lauded chef Bruce Poole's cozy, gimmick-free haunt overlooking Wandsworth Common and prepare for gadget-free wonders, ranging from delicious homemade charcuterie or offal to lighter, simply grilled fish dishes. Pot roast pig's cheek with polenta, roast cod with truffle mash, and monkfish with scallops, ham hock, and Jerusalem artichokes are all immaculately conceived and plated. Desserts like poached pear and clementine sorbet are packed with flavor and the sommelier's a hoot. Set three-course lunches are £27.50 weekdays and £35 weekends; three-course dinners are £45 all week. Ⓢ *Average main: £26* ⊠ *2 Bellevue Rd., Wandsworth, South Bank* ☎ *020/8672–0114* ⊕ *www.chezbruce.co.uk* ⚏ *Reservations essential* Ⓜ *Overland: Wandsworth Common* ✛ *4:E6.*

$$ ✕ **Hutong.** Stupendous floor-to-ceiling views of St. Paul's, Tower Bridge,
NORTHERN and The City from the 33rd floor of The Shard intensify the excellence
CHINESE of the high-end northern Chinese cuisine at this swish replica of Hutong
FAMILY restaurant in Hong Kong. A chef carves a Peking duck table-side and
Fodor's Choice places it in neat piles beside cucumber and spring onions, hoisin sauce,
★ and a bamboo steamer of rice paper pancakes. Other staff use chopsticks to delve into a extravagant bowl of fiery "Red Lantern" Sichuan

chilies to help reveal eight hidden tempura soft-shell crabs. Multicolored dim sum dumplings—like crystal crabmeat—are top-class, and best dipped in hot garlic–chili oil, and other standouts like Wuan cod or deboned, marinated, braised, *and* deep-fried spicy lamb ribs are notable for their incredible depth of flavor. The bill arrives in a Chinese jewelry box. $ *Average main: £23* ⊠ *The Shard, 31 St. Thomas St., 33rd Fl., Southwark* ⊕ *www.aquahutong.co.uk* ⌖ *Reservations essential* Ⓜ *London Bridge* ✣ *5:H1.*

$$ ╳ **José.** Rising Spanish chef José Pizarro packs 'em in like so many slices

TAPAS of *jamón jamón* at this tiny tapas-and-sherry treasure trove on hot gastro-trail Bermondsey Street, just south of The Shard. With only 30 seats and no reservations, you'll be hard-pressed to find a spot at the open-kitchen tapas bar or a perch at an upturned sherry barrel after 6 pm, but stick with it *hombre*—the Spanish tapas dishes are superb. Quaff a glass of Amontillado sherry and keep those delicately handcrafted small plates a comin': patatas bravas, croquetas, meatballs, pisto and crispy duck eggs, hake and aïoli, razor clams with chorizo, *pluma* Ibérico pork loin fillets. Everything's impeccably sourced—from the peppery Marques de Valdueza olive oil to the rare Manuel Maldonado chorizo. Service is decidedly *Excelente!*, but you'll either love or hate the crushing crowds. $ *Average main: £16* ⊠ *104 Bermondsey St., South Bank* ☎ *020/7403–4902* ⊕ *www.josepizarro.com/restaurants/jose* ⌖ *Reservations not accepted* Ⓜ *Borough, London Bridge* ✣ *5:H2.*

$$ ╳ **Magdalen.** Not far from The Shard and south of the Thames between

MODERN BRITISH London and Tower bridges, and only a hop from the London Assembly HQ, Magdalen is a self-assured beacon of class in a remarkably rising gastrocentric part of town. Magdalen specializes in bold, inventive, but unpretentious modern British cuisine at fairly keen prices. Punchy surprises like crispy fried calves' brains with gribiche (£8.50), baked Somerset kid with butter beans and fennel (£18.50), and blackberry-and-apple trifle (£6) are hardly going to break the bank. The dark Bentwood chairs, elegant chandeliers, tea candles, and enveloping ox-blood-colored surrounds invite you to sit back with the short but sweet wine list and further ponder whether to indulge in a feast of slow-baked rabbit with roast garlic or whole stuffed suckling pig instead. The £15.50 two-course set lunch is definitely worth a gander. $ *Average main: £17* ⊠ *152 Tooley St., South Bank* ☎ *020/7403–1342* ⊕ *www. magdalenrestaurant.co.uk* ⌖ *Reservations essential* ⊙ *Closed Sun. No lunch Sat.* Ⓜ *London Bridge* ✣ *5:H2.*

$$$ ╳ **Restaurant Story.** Young Brit hotshot Tom Sellers storms the ramparts

MODERN BRITISH at this sell-out gastro-mecca, with his conceptual take on ingredient-

Fodor's Choice led New British and New Nordic cuisine. Housed in a modishly Scan-

★ dinavian-inspired dining space, expect touches like edible nasturtium flowers, cod skin, or eel mousse Oreos to kick things off. The real fun, however, begins with a surprise beef dripping candle that melts into an Ebenezer Scrooge–like silver candleholder, which you mop up with bread throughout the meal. Genius dishes like pureed Désirée heritage potatoes with dandelion *beurre blanc*, coal oil and barley grass, or meadowsweet-pickled scallops with dill ash and horseradish cream pop up throughout the no-choice 6- or 10-course set menu. Stand-out

14

desserts include Earl Grey–soaked prunes with lovage ice cream, edible twig, and a smudge of milk skin. ■ TIP→ Reservations are taken a month in advance. $ *Average main: £26* ✉ *201 Tooley St., Bermondsey* ☎ *020/7183–2117* ⊕ *www.restaurantstory.co.uk* ⌨ *Reservations essential* ⊙ *Closed Sun. and Mon.* Ⓜ *London Bridge* ✛ *2:H6.*

$$
ITALIAN
Fodor'sChoice
★

✕ **Zucca.** River Café alumni Sam Harris nails the elusive winning formula for this *ultimate* modern Italian bistro, doors down from the fab White Cube contemporary art gallery. Any restaurant that notes on its menu that "the use of mobile phones is both unsociable and unnecessary" knows what it's doing, and this sure touch is in evidence throughout from the open kitchen and white melamine tables, to the passionately prepared, all-homemade Italian breads, pasta, and ice cream. Start off sharing a punchy £5.50 antipasto like salt cod with chickpeas, then swoon over the Pietmontese egg-yoke-colored pappardelle pasta with veal ragu, or indulgent Le Marche white truffle and wild mushroom *vincisgrassi* pasta bake. You'll only find three fish or meat mains to choose from at dinner, but anything like the ink-black squid with white polenta or a blush-pink veal chop with spinach and lemon will be *molto bellissimo!* $ *Average main: £17* ✉ *184 Bermondsey St., Bermondsey* ☎ *020/7378–6809* ⊕ *www.zuccalondon.com* ⌨ *Reservations essential* ⊙ *Closed Mon. No dinner Sun.* Ⓜ *London Bridge* ✛ *5:H2.*

KENSINGTON, CHELSEA, KNIGHTSBRIDGE, AND BELGRAVIA

If you're fab, famous, wealthy, or all three, chances are you'll be living—and dining—in one of these neighborhoods among London's world-class museums, Royal parks, shops, hotels, monuments, fashion boutiques, and top restaurants (do the names of super chefs Heston Blumenthal and Tom Aikens ring a bell?). Chelsea, made famous in the swinging '60s, is where today's Stella McCartney–clad yummy mummies bomb around in their Porsche Cayennes and Persol sunglasses. The area's restaurants range from bijou boîtes to exclusive little froufrou places ideal for girly gossip and a bite on the go. Over in upscale Knightsbridge, you'll find Harrods and the high-end fashion boutiques of Sloane Street, plus a heap of platinum-class hotel-based restaurants. Come here for an amazing dining experience, but don't expect bargains (except at lunch). Nearby, Kensington is a Victorian residential neighborhood with a wider range of restaurants, from French bistros to funky Vietnamese hideaways.

KENSINGTON

$$
JAPANESE
Fodor'sChoice
★

✕ **Yashin.** "Without soy sauce . . . but if you want to" proclaims the neon sign on the wall behind the sushi counter at London's top sushi bar off Kensington High Street. Take their advice, bag a ringside seat, and watch head chef and co-founder Yasuhiro Mineno tease, slice, tweak, and blowtorch his way to the most awesome, fresh, funky, spunky, colorful, and exquisite sushi, sashimi, salads, and carpaccios that you're likely to find this side of the East China Sea. Tofu-topped miso cappuccino comes in a Victorian cup and saucer, and soft-shell blue crab salad is a tangle of *mizuna* (Japanese greens). Delectable 8-, 11-, or 15-piece sushi spreads (£30–£60) might mesmerize with ponzu-spiked salmon,

Japanese sea bream with rice cracker dust, salted Wagyu beef, or Japanese prawns. The bargain £12.50 five-piece salmon nigiri set lunch, with hot miso and bracing raw salad, is a smashing way to sample Yashin's below-the-radar brilliance. $ *Average main: £22* ⊠ *1A Argyll Rd., Kensington* ☎ *020/7938–1536* ⊕ *yashinsushi.com* ⌂ *Reservations essential* Ⓜ *High Street Kensington* ✛ *4:B1.*

CHELSEA

$$ ✗ **The Harwood Arms.** British game doesn't get much better than at this
MODERN BRITISH game-lover's paradise and London's only Michelin-starred gastropub
FAMILY off Fulham Broadway. You'll find a catalogue of awesome game-based
Fodor'sChoice dishes like haunch of Berkshire roe deer with pickled mushrooms or
★ Muggleswick grouse with potato and malt to keep you tickled. Tuck into game pie with Somerset cider jelly or Herdwick lamb with rosemary curd in a relaxed comfy-sofas-and-Sunday-newspapers home-away-from-home pub setting. You'll find openers like treacle-cured smoked salmon are served on a gnarled slab of wood, and there are popular carve-your-own whole-roast lamb, pork, or beef joints for the table—and yes, you *can* ask for doggy bags on the way out. $ *Average main: £23* ⊠ *27 Walham Grove, Fulham* ☎ *020/7386–1847* ⊕ *www. harwoodarms.com* ⌂ *Reservations essential* ☉ *No lunch Mon.* Ⓜ *Fulham Broadway* ✛ *4:A5.*

$$ ✗ **Hunan.** There's no printed menu at this quirky, top-rated family-run
HUNAN Chinese stalwart (est. 1982), situated a couple of blocks south of Sloane Square in Pimlico. Instead, baffled diners state their culinary preferences to owner-chef Peng, or his son Michael, and sit back, relax, and chopstick their way through a succession of highly tasty, tapas-size Chinese dishes to share. Using a blizzard of garlic, ginger, fiery Szechuan chilies, and red peppercorns, a loyal, tanned, and gleaming SW1 crowd might enjoy 12 to 14 unfailingly delicious dishes like Hunan water-fried dumplings, sliced duck, signature pork broth with Chinese mushrooms, crispy frogs' legs, pig's ears, or pungent crab noodle soup. There's no particular logic to what you might receive, but portions are generous, the wines intrigue, and the ongoing surprise is all part of the fun. $ *Average main: £22* ⊠ *51 Pimlico Rd., Pimlico, Chelsea* ☎ *020/7730–5712* ⊕ *www.hunanlondon.com* ⌂ *Reservations essential* ☉ *Closed Sun.* Ⓜ *Sloane Sq.* ✛ *4:G3.*

$$ ✗ **Indian Zing.** Indian Zing's chef-patron Manoj Vasaikar woos the west
INDIAN London curry mafia with updated eclectic regional Indian cuisine on King's Street's emergent "Curry Mile." Start with tamarind-spiced Rasam mussels and move onto Khyber Pass shank of lamb or Barbary duck with Chettinad spices. Average price of dinner for two: £75. $ *Average main: £18* ⊠ *236 King St., Hammersmith* ☎ *020/8748–5959* ⊕ *www.indianzing. co.uk* ⌂ *Reservations essential* Ⓜ *Ravenscourt Park* ✛ *1:A2.*

$$ ✗ **Medlar.** What's not to like about Medlar? Sensational Modern Euro-
MODERN pean cuisine, effortless service, elegant oak floors, and mirrored walls
EUROPEAN make for a complete neighborhood package at the quieter strip of King's Road in Chelsea. Weekday set lunches offer good value at £26, where you'll find winners such as crab ravioli with fondant leeks and samphire, roast mallard with pear and star anise, or juicy steak with snails and triple-cooked chips. Deep flavors, balanced ingredients,

14

and technical precision are the watchwords here, where you're sure to find wondrous desserts—like cherry *clafoutis* with vanilla ice cream or blackberry *beignet* with lemon curd—that are gorgeous to the eye and inevitably delicious. $ *Average main: £21* ⊠ *438 King's Rd., Chelsea* ☎ *020/7349–1900* ⊕ *www.medlarrestaurant.co.uk* ⚏ *Reservations essential* Ⓜ *Fulham Broadway, Sloane Sq.* ✛ *4:D4.*

$$$$
INDIAN

✕**Rasoi.** Wizard Indian chef Vineet Bhatia dazzles with some of London's finest contemporary Indian cuisine at this tony Victorian town house. Ring the doorbell on arrival at this romantic celebration venue, which is kitted out with Indian prints, masks, bells, ornaments, and carved wooden deities. Bhatia exhibits god-like qualities of his own with ingenious surprises like popcorn prawns, crab lollies with coconut soup, wild mushroom rice with tomato ice cream, plus Bordeaux-infused lamb rogan josh and Darjeeling tea–soaked chicken. Grilled sea bass comes crusted in South Indian lentil-based "gunpowder" and a beetroot *molee* sauce (with coconut milk, curry leaves, onion, turmeric, and mustard seeds), while Punjabi chicken tikka is revealed from under a plume of smoke. Be sure to try the signature warm chocolate samosas, dubbed "Choca-mosas." $ *Average main: £32* ⊠ *10 Lincoln St., Chelsea* ☎ *020/7225–1881* ⊕ *www.rasoi-uk.com* ⚏ *Reservations essential* ⊘ *No lunch Mon. and Sat.* Ⓜ *Sloane Sq.* ✛ *4:F3.*

KNIGHTSBRIDGE

$$
BRASSERIE
FAMILY

✕**Bar Boulud.** U.S.–based French superchef Daniel Boulud combines the best of French high-end brasserie fare with a winning dash of superior Yankee gourmet burgers and fries, at this popular street-level, all-day hangout at the Mandarin Oriental in Knightsbridge. Lilliputian-size platters of the most delicate Gilles Verot charcuterie, heartier *coq au vin*, or white pork sausages with truffle mash compete with palm-size Yankee, Frenchie, Piggie, or signature "BB" foie gras–beef burgers and fries in black onion or sesame seed buns. The knockout grazing menu has something for everyone, and professional but informal waitstaff make for a convivial vibe in this handy spot opposite Harvey Nichols department store. Note the £24 three-course lunch or 5–7 pm prix fixe deals. $ *Average main: £21* ⊠ *Mandarin Oriental Hyde Park, 66 Knightsbridge, Knightsbridge* ☎ *020/7201–3899* ⊕ *www.barboulud. com/london* ⚏ *Reservations essential* Ⓜ *Knightsbridge* ✛ *4:F1.*

$$$$
BRITISH
Fodor's Choice
★

✕**Dinner by Heston Blumenthal.** Splendid old English dishes executed with modern precision in an open kitchen are the schtick at Ashley Palmer-Watts' award-winner at the Mandarin Oriental (Palmer-Watts is a protégée of TV chef Heston Blumenthal, who's closely involved). As you take in views of Hyde Park, you simply must slice into a chilled Meat Fruit appetizer (c.1500), deceptively shaped like a mandarin, but encasing the smoothest, most creamy foie gras and chicken liver parfait on the planet. A plate of Rice and Flesh (c.1390) is a picture of yellow saffron rice with calf's tails and red wine, and grilled octopus Frumenty (c.1390) is a lively dish of cracked wheat cooked with lovage in a smoked sea broth from the court of Richard II. Marvel at beef royale (c.1720) cooked *sous vide* for 72 hours at 56°C, plus cod in cider (c.1940) or Spiced Pigeon (c.1780) with ale and artichokes. Head off with resplendent spit-roast pineapple Tipsy cake (c.1810)—an homage to English spit-roasting from centuries past. $\boxed{S}$ *Average main: £34* ✉ *Mandarin Oriental Hyde Park, 66 Knightsbridge, Knightsbridge* ☎ *020/7201–3833* ⊕ *www.dinnerbyheston.com* ⇘ *Reservations essential* $\boxed{M}$ *Knightsbridge* ✛ *4:F1.*

$$$
FRENCH
FAMILY

✕ **Koffmann's.** Set in the swish Berkeley in Knightsbridge, this restaurant is run by veteran French superchef Pierre Koffmann. Never paying heed to trends, fads, or fashion, the ducal clientele here enjoy such signatures as stuffed pig's trotters "Tante Claire" with sweetbreads and morels, or delicately seared scallops with a smudge of black squid ink. Culinary godfather to many of London's top chefs—from Gordon Ramsay to Tom Aikens—Gascon-born Koffmann showcases 35-odd-years experience and the best of regional Gascony cuisine in a cute, carpeted, and well-appointed basement setting. Alongside a stream of minor British royalty, be sure to experience other gastro goodies like snails with garlic and parsley, wild duck à l'orange, Gascon apple tart, or signature pistachio soufflé with pistachio ice cream. $\boxed{S}$ *Average main: £26* ✉ *The Berkeley, Wilton Pl., Knightsbridge* ☎ *020/7107–8844* ⊕ *www. the-berkeley.co.uk* ⇘ *Reservations essential* $\boxed{M}$ *Knightsbridge* ✛ *4:G1.*

$$$
RUSSIAN

✕ **Mari Vanna.** This kitsch White Russian fantasy dining salon in Knightsbridge overflows with a maximalist decor of vintage chandeliers, books, pics, knickknacks, Tiffany lamps, *tchotchkes*, mirrors, Cheburashkas, and a Russian *pechka* stove. Note the crochet and linen-covered tables tended by chirpy staff (some in dirndls) and dishes proffered with what feels like great aunt Vanna's old family silver and jumbled crockery. Then snap into character with a horseradish vodka shot or three, and carb-up on pierogi sea bass savories, clear Siberian Pelmeni dumpling soup, or feather-light smoked salmon blinis. There's good borscht and creamy beef Stroganoff with mash and wild mushrooms, and let's not forget the sweet crêpes with condensed milk. But it's the nostalgic dacha-like antebellum home-away-from-home setting that makes you feel like you're participating in some kind of *Anna Karenina*-esque historical reenactment. $\boxed{S}$ *Average main: £27* ✉ *The Wellington Court, 116 Knightsbridge, Knightsbridge* ☎ *020/7225–3122* ⊕ *www.marivanna. co.uk* ⇘ *Reservations essential* $\boxed{M}$ *Knightsbridge* ✛ *4:F1.*

$$
BRASSERIE

✕ **Racine.** There's always an upscale buzz at this star of the Brompton Road dining scene, not far from the V&A and Harrods. This smooth-running chic-and-*fantastique* classic French *brasserie de luxe* excels in doing the simple things well—and not costing the earth. Veteran chef Henry Harris's signature dishes like roast partridge and juniper, foie gras with Calvados, soft roe on toast, skate wing or deep-fried calf's brains, and not-for-the-faint-hearted *tête de veau*—poached calf's head—all hit the high notes and come with a certain Gallic aplomb. While the tables may be a touch too close together and the wine's a little dear, lots of the healthy-looking patrons are stealth wealth loyal local Knightsbridge regulars, and indeed many also seem to cherish the handy £15.50 to £17.75 prix fixe lunch or early evening deals. $\boxed{S}$ *Average main: £19* ✉ *239 Brompton Rd., Knightsbridge* ☎ *020/7584–4477* ⊕ *racine-restaurant.com* ⇘ *Reservations essential* $\boxed{M}$ *South Kensington, Knightsbridge* ✛ *4:E2.*

14

$$ ✕ **Zuma.** Hip, hip, hurray for this ever-fashionable informal Tokyo-style
JAPANESE modern sushi joint and slim-hipsters' hangout near Harrods and Har-
FAMILY vey Nichols in Knightsbridge. Well lighted and designed with polished
granite, blond cedar wood, exposed pipes, and open timberwork, Zuma
takes in a sake bar, robata grill, and sushi counter—and attracts *all* the
J Crew beautiful people from SW7 on a constant rolling news basis.
You can't go wrong with the fresh California maki rolls, tuna sushi, sea
bass sashimi, pork with yuzo, or robata-grilled Wagyu beef that comes
on a hoba leaf. Sip a sake, relax, enjoy the polite service, marvel at the
engrossing petro dollar, Ruski, and spray-tanned "Made In Chelsea"
Mwah! Mwah! set, and be sure to collar the sake sommelier to guide you
through the 40-odd varieties of sake rice wine. ⑤ *Average main: £20* ⊠ *5
Raphael St., Knightsbridge* ☎ *020/7584–1010* ⊕ *www.zumarestaurant.
com* ⌖ *Reservations essential* Ⓜ *Knightsbridge* ✛ *4:F1.*

BELGRAVIA

$$$ ✕ **Pétrus.** Talented chef Sean Burbidge conducts a flawless dining experi-
MODERN FRENCH ence at this Belgravia French haute cuisine hot spot. The soft-carpeted
Fodor's Choice ground-floor dining salon may be a bit beige and dated, and a central
★ circular glass wine cellar a tad passé, but add in the warm welcome,
bonhomie, impeccable nibbles, *bonne bouches*, assured sommelier,
stonking cheese board, *petits fours*, and charming fleet-footed service,
and you've got an unrivaled full-court gastro press. Burbidge's cuisine
is all *Technique! Technique! Technique!* and it's impossible not to gasp
at his starters like exemplary Les Landes duck foie gras with grape jelly,
or lobster ravioli swimming in creamed leaks and Champagne velouté.
Bliss out on 25-day Casterbridge beef fillet with sticky Barolo sauce,
and watch for surprises towards the end, like honeycomb–and–dark
chocolate bomb that theatrically melts before your eyes, or mini white
chocolate ices on sticks that emerge from a bowl of dry ice. ⑤ *Average main: £28* ⊠ *1 Kinnerton St., Belgravia* ☎ *020/7592–1609* ⊕ *www.
gordonramsay.com/petrus* ⌖ *Reservations essential* Ⓜ *Knightsbridge,
Hyde Park Corner* ✛ *4:G1.*

NOTTING HILL AND BAYSWATER

Ever since Hugh Grant and Julia Roberts starred in *Notting Hill* and put
the area on the global map, Notting Hill's had a rep as London's most
glammy neighborhood, with it myriad boutiques, chic cafés, patisseries, restaurants, buzzy bars, and the famous Portobello Road Market's
collection of antiques shops, bric-a-brac, vintage-clothing stands, and
food stalls. Portobello is one of London's most popular street markets,
so get there early on Saturday morning (the market is open 8 am–6
pm) to beat the crowds. Peruse the antiques and vintage clothes stalls,
and when you want to snack, head to the north end where you'll find
fresh fruit-and-veg stalls, artisan bakeries, rare Spanish olive and French
cheese purveyors, plus numerous hot-food stalls peddling savory crêpes,
gourmet hamburgers, spicy German chicken rolls, paella, Moroccan
kebabs, and Malaysian noodles.

NOTTING HILL

$$ — MODERN ASIAN — ✕ **E&O.** Celebs and the perma-tanned Notting Hill brigade give a well-manicured thumbs up to this long-standing Asian tapas supremo off Portobello Road market. E&O's size-8 figure-friendly medley of Japanese, Vietnamese, Chinese, and Thai all-star favorite dishes includes dim sum, sushi, sashimi, and tempura, with a slew of low-carb/no-carb options. Don't skip lychee martinis in the singles-heavy see-and-be-seen bar, before mooching over to the moody monochrome and mirrored dining room for miso black cod, snow-crab maki, papaya salad, Thai rare beef, or lamb rendang; the sea bass sashimi is achingly fresh. There are pavement tables and curbside bench seats to people-watch on Blenheim Crescent. $ *Average main: £17* ⊠ *14 Blenheim Crescent, Notting Hill* ☎ *020/7229–5454* ⊕ *www.rickerrestaurants.com/e-and-o* ⌲ *Reservations essential* Ⓜ *Ladbroke Grove* ✥ *1:B1.*

$$$$ — MODERN FRENCH — **Fodor'sChoice** ★ — ✕ **The Ledbury.** Aussie chef Brett Graham wins hearts, minds—and *serious* global accolades—at this high-ceilinged neighborhood destination modern French (with Pacific and British hints) dining landmark. In a handsome four-square salon full of drapes, mirrored walls, and plush cream leather seats, you won't find a more inventive vegetable dish than Graham's ash-baked celeriac with hazelnut and wood sorrel, and it's impossible to best his complex mains like roast quail with walnut cream, roe deer with bone marrow, or Cornish turbot with Riesling, cockles, and sea lettuce. Besides his obsessive interest in game, Graham's famed for wicked desserts, so why not finish with thinly sliced figs with honey, olives, and sourdough ice cream? The assured service and sommelier round out this winning proposition. $ *Average main: £32* ⊠ *127 Ledbury Rd., Notting Hill* ☎ *0207/7792–9090* ⊕ *www.theledbury.com* ⌲ *Reservations essential* ☾ *No lunch Mon.* Ⓜ *Westbourne Park, Ladbroke Grove* ✥ *1:A4.*

$ — MODERN BRITISH — FAMILY — ✕ **The Mall Tavern.** It's all things British at this charming 1856 Notting Hill gastropub, which overflows with relaxed but discerning Notting Hill locals and Sloanes. Check out the Coronation mugs, Royal wedding trinkets, and Prince Charles and Lady Di memorabilia before sampling some great British bar snacks like pork scratchings, soda bread, or lop eared sausage rolls. Move through to the simple dark-oak-floored dining room to feast on hearty beef pie with bone marrow poking through the crust, or wallow in '70s nostalgia with chicken Kiev, mac 'n' cheese, or high-quality smoked-salmon fish cakes with spinach and a coddled egg. There's salted caramel chocolate Rolos or Victoria plum cheesecake for dessert, plus some stonking British farmhouse cheeses, like Shorrock's Bomb, Isle of Avalon, or Leagram blue. Note the bargain £10 weekday lunches. $ *Average main: £13* ⊠ *71–73 Palace Gardens Terr., Notting Hill* ☎ *020/7229–3374* ⊕ *www.themalltavern.com* ⌲ *Reservations essential* Ⓜ *Notting Hill Gate* ✥ *1:B5.*

BAYSWATER

$ — MIDDLE EASTERN — ✕ **Alounak.** Wondrous Persian dips, unleavened taftoon breads, small tasty plates, steaming lamb bakes, and grilled kebabs are found at this lantern-filled Aladdin's Cave, a warm Iranian canteen beloved by hordes of locals. Lines form onto Westbourne Grove for the hot pita and taftoon breads straight from the clay oven by the door, and you may

14

BEST BREAKFASTS

Bistrot Bruno Loubet. Go east to historic Clerkenwell for a popular vegetarian breakfast (£9.50) at Bistrot Bruno Loubet at The Zetter overlooking St. John's Square, with free-range eggs, smoked bacon, grilled tomatoes, spinach, avocado, and roasted field mushrooms. ⊠ *The Zetter, 86–88 Clerkenwell Rd., Clerkenwell* ☎ *020/7324-4455* ⊕ *www.bistrotbrunoloubet.com* Ⓜ *Farringdon St., Barbican.*

Cecconi's. Cecconi's conjures up a suave Italian scented affair from 7 am weekdays and 8 am weekends for about £16, and offers pink grapefruit, egg-white omelet, bacon sandwiches, wheat-free toast, plus poached eggs, porchetta, and hollandaise—all in a swish green-fringed Ilse Crawford–designed upscale *brasserie super de luxe* setting. ⊠ *5A Burlington Gardens, Mayfair* ☎ *020/7434-1500* ⊕ *www.cecconis. co.uk* Ⓜ *Green Park, Bond St.*

Cinnamon Club. Members of the House of Lords, cabinet ministers, MPs, politicos, and special advisors enjoy Indian Uttapam rice pancakes, green chilies, lentil broth, and coconut chutney for £8 in the converted Old Westminster Library, before ambling over into the nearby Houses of Parliament. ⊠ *The Old Westminster Library, 30–32 Great Smith St., Westminster* ☎ *020/7222-2555* ⊕ *www.cinnamonclub.com* ☉ *No breakfast weekends.*

Dishoom. Curry addicts dart into all-day Bombay-style Indian street food canteen Dishoom off Covent Garden for coriander, onion, and green chili-spiced Bombay omelet, "fire toast," steaming hot spiced *chai* tea, plus egg, bacon, or sausage *naan* bread rolls (about £13). ⊠ *12 Upper St. Martin's La., Covent Garden* ☎ *020/7420-9320* ⊕ *www.dishoom.com.*

The Wolseley. Mayfair's head honchos treat The Wolseley like their staff canteen, and canter through a fine full English breakfast—eggs, bacon, sausage, baked beans, tomatoes, mushrooms, and black pudding (£15.95)—before the global financial markets reopen. ⊠ *160 Piccadilly, Mayfair* ☎ *020/7499-6996* ⊕ *www.thewolseley.com.*

have to wait to get in. Once inside, try grilled eggplant puree with walnuts, feta, mint, and tarragon, the Alounak kebabs, skewered marinated lamb with rice and grilled tomatoes, or the *Zereshk polo*—pungent saffron chicken with sweet-and-sour Iranian forest berries. Enjoy the Persian black cardamom teas and sweets, and lime juice–and-pistachio *faloodeh* Persian sorbet, but know that the sour yogurt drinks are not to everyone's taste. Ⓢ *Average main: £12* ⊠ *44 Westbourne Grove, Bayswater* ☎ *020/7229-4158* ⟁ *Reservations essential* Ⓜ *Queensway, Bayswater* ✛ *1:B4.*

$$$

BRASSERIE

✕**Angelus.** Owner, sommelier, and former pro rugby union player Thierry Tomasin scores at this upmarket French brasserie near Lancaster Gate and Hyde Park. Styled with swirly Art Nouveau mirrors and button-back banquettes in a 200-year-old converted former pub, Angelus has a rep for unrivaled Parisian-style *brasserie de luxe* dishes; the ducks liver crème brûlée, egg cocotte, frog's legs, saddle of lamb or Grand Marnier soufflé are as good as they get. Classy £13 breakfasts, all-day brunch (10 am–10 pm), and light bites like three-egg omelet and truffled brioche steak sandwiches are well conceived, and service is notoriously—*how* should we say this?—*Gallic!* Ex-Le Gavroche sommelier Tomasin is sure to *"Umm"* and *"Ahh!,"*, shrug, sniff, gently smile, and then select an absolutely cracking bottle from the extensive and mainly French-focused wine list and Tomasin's opus and all-round master work. ⑤ *Average main: £26* ✉ *4 Bathurst St., Hyde Park* ☎ *020/402–0083* ⊕ *www.angelusrestaurant.co.uk* ⚓ *Reservations essential* Ⓜ *Lancaster Gate* ✛ *1:D4.*

$$
MODERN BRITISH ✕**Hereford Road.** Bespeckled chef and co-owner Tom Pemberton mans the busy front-of-house grill at this Bayswater favorite, renowned for its pared-down, pomp-free, and ingredient-driven seasonal British fare. With an accent on well-sourced honest-to-goodness regional and seasonal British produce, many dishes are as unfussy as you'll find. Slide into side booths, and work your way though uncluttered combos like steamed mussels with cider and thyme, lemon sole with sea dulse, duck breast with old-fashioned pickled walnuts, or warm and soothing English rice pudding with strawberry jam. Expect to brush past the entire Tory party leadership and the rest of the Notting Hill set on the way out. Note the £9.50, £13 or £15.50 set lunches are arguably the *best* high-quality weekday set lunch deals, bar none. ⑤ *Average main: £15* ✉ *3 Hereford Rd., Bayswater* ☎ *020/7727–1144* ⊕ *www.herefordroad. org* ⚓ *Reservations essential* Ⓜ *Bayswater, Queensway* ✛ *1:B4.*

REGENT'S PARK, HAMPSTEAD, AND ISLINGTON

Stucco-fronted Regent's Park and Primrose Hill attract a boho-chic media and artsy crowd who love the slightly rough and rowdy neighborhood home-away-from-home restaurants like vine-decked Lemonia. Meanwhile, farther north in leafy Hampstead it's all Dick Turpin 17th-century wood-beamed coaching houses and inns with roaring fires, house ales, and trouser-busting Sunday lunches that predominate.

REGENT'S PARK

$
GREEK
FAMILY ✕**Lemonia.** Primrose Hill's favorite Greek Cypriot, vine-decked and '80s-taverna-style Lemonia is large and light, and always packed with hordes of hungry hobo chic locals. Besides an endless supply of Hellenic small-dish meze dips, hot breads, and starters, there are rustic mains like slow-baked *kleftiko* lamb in lemon, classic eggplant, Greek yogurt, and potato moussaka, herb-stuffed tomatoes, grilled prawns, calamari, souvlaki, and pleasing beef on the bone stewed in red wine. Expect friendly Greek service and hospitality, plus bags of noise, an airy glass-domed atrium out the back, and the odd fly-by from the Jude Law Primrose Hill megastar set. Weekday set lunches are a pifling £12.50. ⑤ *Average main: £13* ✉ *89 Regent's Park Rd., Regent's Park* ☎ *020/7586–7454* ⚓ *Reservations essential* ⊘ *No lunch Sat. No dinner Sun.* Ⓜ *Chalk Farm* ✛ *1:F1.*

ISLINGTON

$
CAFÉ
FAMILY ✕**Ottolenghi.** Captivating meringue-filled foodie window displays and a funky modern all-white interior characterize this flagship North African, Middle Eastern, and Mediterranean deli/bakery/café set in Islington's main Upper Street drag. Sit at white tables and dig into

exceptionally inventive, tasty, and healthy dishes like roasted sweet potatoes with burnt eggplant and pomegranate, lamb cutlets with okra, Tunisian harissa-spiced chicken, or golden beetroot, red cabbage, and sour cream, along with cult Ottolenghi fresh salads, savories, soups, flaky pastries, and artisanal cakes. Go home with a take-out chocolate meringue or plum-and-quince tart, and pick up Ottolenghi's outstanding Israeli *and* Palestinian-inspired cookbook, *Jerusalem,* on the way out, too. $ *Average main: £13* ✉ *287 Upper St., Islington* ☎ *020/7288–1454* ⊕ *www.ottolenghi.co.uk* Ⓜ *Angel* ✢ *2:F1.*

THE THAMES UPSTREAM

This wealthy, westerly, leafy suburb may be under the Heathrow flight-path and follow the meandering course of the River Thames, but there's nothing sleepy about the neighborhood dining scene here which is becoming more and more West End in style and substance by the hour. One fanatical locavore maverick stands out: the bearded Mikael Jonsson, a self-taught Swedish genius, who knows his wild scallops from his foraged blueberries, and produces six- and seven-course seasonal tasting menus of staggering class and brilliance.

CHISWICK

$$$

MODERN
EUROPEAN

✕ **Hedone.** Only a loony or genius would serve an appetizer of half a Cévennes onion with a few pear shavings and *beurre blanc*, but luckily maverick Swedish chef Mikael Jonsson falls triumphantly in the latter camp at his wild foodie haven. A former lawyer and prolific food blogger, Jonsson's obsessive approach to the provenance of his largely British-sourced ingredients—very often wild, rare, or foraged—means that his dishes are some of the most vivid and intense around. Sit up on stools and watch Jonsson in an open kitchen prepare ingredient-driven marvels like wild Dorset sea bass with pickled black radishes and hyssop oil, hand-caught Devon scallops with a strikingly stuffed zucchini flower, or gloriously marbled 55-day-aged Darragh O'Shea Black Angus beef on the bone with juniper-smoked potatoes. For afters, a Cox and cobnut tart or English blueberries with rosemary sorbet are as lucid as the mains. ■ TIP➔ Book far in advance. $ *Average main: £27* ✉ *301–303 Chiswick High Rd., Chiswick* ☎ *020/8747–0377* ⊕ *www.hedonerestaurant.com* ⌖ *Reservations essential* ⊘ *Closed Sun. and Mon. No lunch Tues. and Wed.* Ⓜ *Chiswick Park* ✢ *1:A2.*

LONDON
DINING AND
LODGING ATLAS

KEY
☐ Hotels
■ Restaurants
▦ Restaurant in Hotel
U *WESTMINSTER* — Station
London Underground
⇌ *National Rail Connection*

E

N

Barnsbury St

Wynford St

Liverpool Rd

Rodney St

Donegal St

Pentonville Road

Grt Percy St

Amwell St

Myddelton Square

Wharton St

Lloyd Baker St

Margery St

Yardley St

Roseberry Avenue

Exmouth Market

Moro

Phoenix Pl

Gough St

Gray's Inn Rd

Jockey's Fields

Farringdon

Leather Ln

Halton Gdn

Clerkenwell Road

Greville St

High Holborn A40

HOLBORN

Carey St

Fetter Ln

Fleet St

Mitre Ct

THE TEMPLE

Temple Pl

U TEMPLE

Victoria Embankment

0   500 yards
0   500 m

F

One Fine Stay
Ottolenghi

Upper St

Essex Rd A104

Colebrook Row

Noel Rd

ANGEL U

City Road

Goswell Road

St John St

Spencer St

Skinner St

Percival St

Bowling Green Ln

Seward St

Aylesbury St

Bistrot Bruno Loubet
The Zetter

St Johns St

Clerkenwell Road

The Rookery

FARRINGDON U

Cowcross St

St. John

Charterhouse St

Long Ln

W Smithfield

Holborn Viaduct

Giltspur St

Little Britain

Old Bailey

Warwick

New Bridge St

St Bride St

Shoe Ln

Tudor St

Ludgate Hill

ST. PAUL'S ♦

London St. Paul's YHA ▢
Carter Ln

THE CITY

Queen Victoria St

Upper Thames St

BLACKFRIARS U

Crowne Plaza London — The City

RIVER THAMES

Blackfriars Br

G

Shoreditch, Whitechapel and Bethnal Green: see inset above →

Lever St

Central St

Old Street

Whitecross St

Golden Ln

Fann St

Goswell Road

St. Johns St

Aldersgate St

BARBICAN U

BARBICAN CENTRE ♦

BARBICAN

London Wall

Angel St

Gresham St

GUILDHALL ♦

Cheapside

ST. PAUL'S

Watling St

Cannon St

CANNON ST. STATION

Southwark Br

H

OLD STREET U

Featherstone

Bunhill Row

Dufferin St

Shoreditch, Whitechapel and Bethnal Green: see inset above →

Chiswell St

Beech St

Silk St

Moore Ln

Moorfields

Moorgate

MOORGATE

Cable Street Inn ▢ →

BANK OF ENGLAND ♦

BANK U

King William St

Sweetings

CANNON STREET STATION

Restaurant Story

1

2

3

4

5

6

Inset map

N

0   1/4 mi
0   1/4 km

HOXTON

CAMBRIDGE HEATH ⇄
Bistrothequa

Kingsland Rd

Hackney Rd

Columbia Rd

Haggerston Park

Gosset St

Old Bethnal Green Rd

Town Hall Hotel

Viajante

Victoria Park Gardens

Ace Hotel London **Rochelle Canteen**

Old St

Great Eastern St

Bethnal Green Rd

E Pellicci

BETHNAL GREEN

The Hoxton ▢

Dishoom
Pizza East

Weavers Fields

Valiance Rd

SHOREDITCH HIGH ST. ⇄

Buxton St

Sun St Passage

Bishopsgate

Commercial St

WHITECHAPEL

Whitechapel Rd ⇄

L'Anima

London Wall

Threadneedle St

Andaz ▢

Duck & Waffle

ALDGATE

Bevis Marks

Aldgate High St

Leman St

Commercial Rd

Cannon St Rd

Sydney St

Cambridge Heath Rd

Tayyabs ▪

Ramada Docklands

Thread-needles ▪

Simpson's Tavern ▪

Fenchurch St

Mansell St

Minories

MONUMENT

Grange City

Apex City of London ▢

TOWER HILL U

Shoreditch, Whitechapel and Bethnal Green

E   **F**   **G**   **H**

Map 3

- Bloomsbury
- Covent Garden
- Soho

E F G H

1

2

3

4

5

6

ROYAL
NATIONAL
THEATRE

Upper Ground

Stamford St

Hatfields

Cornwall Rd

Roupell St

SOUTHWARK
U

The Cut

Anchor & Hope

WATERLOO
STATION

rk Rd

U

Lwr. Marsh

Baylis Rd

Ln

Westminster Bridge Rd

Hercules Rd

Lambeth Rd

Lambert Walk

Walnut
Tree Walk

Brook Dr

LAMBETH

IMPERIAL WAR
MUSEUM

Hannworth
Park

ncroft St

Cleaver St

Bowling
Green

A23

Kennington Road

Wincott St

St. George's Rd

Hayes St

Dante Rd

Renfrew
Rd

The
val

Prima Rd

A3

Camberwell New Rd

Cranmer Rd

Kennington Park Rd

St. Agnes Pl

Kennington
Park

De Laune St

Braganza St

KENNINGTON
U

A3

Westcott Rd

Kennington
Pk

Otto St

Coals Rd

Larrimore Rd

Hillingdon St

Olney Rd

John Ruskin St

Grosvenor Ter

Bethwin Rd

KENNINGTON

Penton Pl

Manor Pl

Penrose St

Surrey
Gardens

Penrose St

Fielding

Waterloo Rd

Webber St

Blackfriars Road

Pocock St

London Rd

Southwark St

Grt Suffolk St

Hopton St

Holland St

Sumner St

Union St

Southwark Bridge Rd

Borough   Rd

Marshalsea

BOROUGH U

THE
BOROUGH

NEWINGTON

ELEPHANT &
CASTLE
U

ELEPHANT
AND CASTLE

New   Kent   Road

Walworth   Road

Heygate St

Rodney Rd

Browning St

A215

East St

Penrose St

Merrow Rd

Faraday
Gardens

Portland St

WALWORTH

Westmoreland Rd

First St

Chamberwell Rd

New Church Rd

Church St.
Hotel

Premier Travel
Inn Southwark
Park St

SOUTHWARK

Redcross Way

Borough High St

Newcomen St

Tabard

Harper Rd

Trinity St

Farnmouth Rd

Great Dover Street

Manciple St

Tabard St

Long Ln

Southwark
Cathedral

London Br

LONDON
BRIDGE
STATION

London
Bridge
Hotel

Hutong

José →

Magdalen →

Zucca →

Casse-Croûte →

WHERE TO STAY

Updated by
Jack Jewers

Queen Elizabeth hasn't invited you this time? No matter. Staying at one of London's grande-dame hotels is the next-best thing to being a guest at the palace—and some say it's even better. Happily, however, there is no dearth of options where friendliness outdistances luxe—London, thank goodness, has plenty of atmospheric places that won't cost a king's ransom.

That noted, until fairly recently it was extremely difficult to find a decent hotel in the center for less than £150 per night. Things have improved, thanks in part to the global recession, but also to a modest flurry of new midprice hotels that have sprung up in the last few years.

It's all so different if money is no object. London has some of the very best and most luxurious hotels in the world. On the other hand, freshly minted billionaires favor the rash of new hot spots, like the Corinthia or ME London, while fashion plates always book Kit Kemp's super-stylish hotels (such as the Covent Garden and the Charlotte Street). But even these places have sales, and you can sometimes snag a bargain within the reach of ordinary mortals—particularly in the off-season—or just be a spectator to all the glamour by visiting for that most traditional of high-society treats, afternoon tea.

Meanwhile, several midrange hotels have dropped their average prices in response to the choppy waters of the global economy, which has pulled some fantastic places, such as Hazlitt's, the Rookery, and Town Hall, back into the affordable category. And there's a clutch of new, stylish, and super-cheap hotels that are a real step forward for the city. The downside is that these places tend to be a little out of the way, but that's often a price worth paying. Another attractive alternative includes hotels in the Premier and Millennium chains, which offer sleek, modern rooms, lots of up-to-date conveniences, and sales that frequently bring room prices well below £100 a night.

At the budget level, London has also come a long way in the last couple of years, albeit with a catch: to find a good, reasonably priced B&B, you must be prepared to look outside the very center of London. This means that you have to subtract the city's notoriously high transport costs from any savings—but on the plus side, the Tube can shuttle you out to even some far-flung suburbs in under 20 minutes. Prepare to be just a little adventurous with your London base and you will be rewarded by a collection of unique and interesting bed-and-breakfasts, in the kinds of neighborhoods real Londoners live in—places like King Henry's Road, the Cable Street Inn, and the Church Street Hotel. And if you're willing to fend for yourself, the city has some great rental options.

But if you are interested in luxury, London is just the place. Although the image we love to harbor about Olde London Towne may be fast fading in the light of today's glittering city, when it comes time to rest your head, the old-fashioned clichés remain enticing. Choose one of London's heritage-rich hotels—Claridge's supplies perfect parlors; the Savoy has that river view—and these fantasies can, and always will, be fulfilled.

15

PLANNING

LODGING STRATEGY

Where should you stay? With hundreds of London hotels, it may seem like a daunting question. But it doesn't have to be. *The 130-plus selections here represent the best this city has to offer—from the most-for-your-money budget B&Bs to the sleekest designer hotels. Scan "Best Bets" on the following pages for top recommendations by price and experience. Or look through the reviews. To find one quickly, search by neighborhood, then alphabetically. Happy hunting!*

NEED A RESERVATION?

Yes, hotel reservations are an absolute necessity when planning your trip to London, so book your room as far in advance as possible. The further in advance you can book, the better the deal you're likely to get. Just watch out if you change your mind—cancellation fees can be hefty. On the other hand, it is possible to find some amazing last-minute deals at mid- to high-range places, but this is a real gamble, as you could just as easily end up paying full rate. Fierce competition means properties undergo frequent improvements, so when booking inquire about any ongoing renovations that may interrupt your stay.

CHECKING IN

Typical check-in and checkout times are 2 pm and 11 am, respectively. Many flights from North America arrive early in the morning, but having to wait six hours for a room after arriving jet-lagged at 8 am isn't the ideal way to start a vacation. Alert the hotel of your early arrival; large hotels can often make special early check-in arrangements, but almost all will look after your luggage in the meantime. Be prepared to drop your bags and strike out for a few hours. On the plus side, this can effectively give you a whole extra day for sightseeing.

HOTEL QUALITY

Note that rooms can vary considerably in a single hotel. If you don't like the room you're given, ask to see another. Hotels often renovate room by room—you might find yourself allocated a dark, unrenovated room, whereas a bright, newly decorated room awaits just down the hall. Be prepared for the fact that, while smoking is now banned in public areas, this doesn't apply to hotel rooms—so be firm and ask to change if you're given a smoking room and didn't request one.

BREAKFAST

Some hotels include breakfast in the price of the room. It ranges from a gourmet spread to what is known as the "full English" (one fried egg, two "bangers"—that's English-style sausage links—two thick slices of bacon, a grilled tomato, sautéed mushrooms or baked beans, and toast). In many budget hotels and B&Bs, this is the only hot breakfast available. Most expensive hotels (and the most imaginative small ones) may also offer pancakes, French toast, waffles, and omelets. Luckily, virtually all accommodations also offer packaged cereals, muffins, yogurt, and fresh fruit, so when the sausage-and-bacon brigade begins to get you down, go continental.

FACILITIES

Keep in mind that some facilities come with the room rate while others cost extra. So, when pricing accommodations, always ask what's included. Modern hotels usually have air-conditioning, but B&Bs and hotels in older buildings often do not, and it is generally not the norm in London. Wi-Fi is common, but don't assume it's free (large hotels in particular can charge outrageous fees). If you want a double room, specify whether you want a double bed or a twin (two single beds next to each other). *All hotels listed here have private bathrooms unless otherwise noted.*

PRICES

If you're planning to visit in the fall, winter, or early spring, start monitoring bargain online prices a few months before your trip and book whenever you see a good rate. Chains such as Hilton, Premier, and Millennium are known for their low-season sales in which prices can be as little as half the normal rate. And business-oriented hotels frequently have lower rates on weekends.

The exchange rate between the pound and the dollar is also unpredictable, so if it's looking good when you book, an advance-payment deal could end up saving you a decent amount of money. ■TIP→ **The Visit London Accommodation Booking Service (☎ 020/7932–2020 ⊕ www. visitlondon.com) offers a best-price guarantee. Also try the clearing-house websites Late Rooms (⊕ www.laterooms.com), Booking (⊕ www. booking.com), and Last Minute (⊕ www.lastminute.com).**

Prices in the reviews are the lowest cost of a standard double room in high season, including 20% V.A.T.

WHERE SHOULD I STAY?

	Neighborhood Vibe	Pros	Cons
Westminster, St. James's, and Royal London	This historic section is home to major tourist attractions like Buckingham Palace.	Central area near tourist sites; easy Tube access; considered a safe area to stay.	Mostly expensive lodging options; few good restaurants and entertainment venues nearby.
Mayfair and Marylebone	Traditional, old money; a mixture of the business and financial set with fashionable shops.	In the heart of the action; some of London's best hotels are found here.	Pricey part of town; the city-that-never-sleeps buzz makes peace and quiet hard to come by.
Soho and Covent Garden	A tourist hub with endless entertainment—this is party central for young adults.	Buzzing area with plenty to see and do; late-night entertainment abounds; wonderful shopping district.	Perhaps London's busiest (and noisiest) district after dark; few budget hotels.
Bloomsbury and Holborn	Diverse area that is part bustling business center and part tranquil respite with tree-lined streets and parks.	Easy access to Tube, and 15 minutes to city center; major sights, like British Museum in Bloomsbury.	Holborn has busy and noisy streets; the area around King's Cross can be sketchy—particularly at night.
The City	London's financial district, where most of the city's banks and businesses are headquartered.	Extremely central with easy transportation access and great hotel deals.	The City can be as quiet as a tomb at weekends—even the pubs close.
East London	Increasingly trendy area east of the city center, with a great arts scene.	Great for art lovers, shoppers, and business execs with meetings in Canary Wharf.	Still a transitional area; parts of Hoxton can be a bit dodgy at night; 20-minute Tube ride from central London.
South of the Thames	South of the River is a vibrant cultural hub, centered around the South Bank, the Globe, and the Royal National Theatre.	South of the River is London's unofficial cultural quarter, and walking distance from the West End theaters.	You don't have to go very far from the South Bank before you hit some of London's dodgiest neighborhoods.
Kensington, Chelsea, Knightsbridge, and Belgravia	These are some of London's most upscale neighborhoods and a hub of London's tourist universe.	Diverse hotel selection; great area for meandering urban walks; London's capital of high-end shopping.	Depending on where you are, the nearest Tube might be a hike; residential area might be too quiet for some.
Notting Hill and Bayswater	This is an upscale, trendy area favored by locals, with plenty of good hotels.	Hotel deals abound if you know where to look; gorgeous greenery in Hyde Park.	Choose the wrong place and you may end up in a flea pit; residential area may be quiet.
Regent's Park and Hampstead	A mix of arty, fashionable districts with a village-like feel in other places.	Some of London's most fashionable neighborhoods; easy to fall in love with.	Some distance from center; lack of hotel options.

15

HOTEL REVIEWS

Listed alphabetically by neighborhood. Use the coordinate (✢ 1:B2) at the end of each listing to locate a site on the corresponding map. To locate the property on a map, turn to the London Dining and Lodging Atlas at the end of the Where to Eat chapter. The first number after the ✢ symbol indicates the map number. Following that is the property's coordinate on the map grid.

For expanded hotel reviews, visit Fodors.com.

WESTMINSTER, ST. JAMES'S, AND ROYAL LONDON

WESTMINSTER

$$$$
HOTEL
Fodor's Choice
★
The Corinthia. The London outpost of the exclusive Corinthia chain is design heaven-on-earth, with levels of service that make anyone feel like a VIP. **Pros:** so much luxury and elegance you'll feel like royalty. **Cons:** prices jump to the stratosphere once the cheapest rooms sell out. $ *Rooms from: £395* ✉ *Whitehall Pl., Westminster* ☎ *020/7930–8181* ⊕ *www.corinthia.com* ✍ *294 rooms* ⦿ *Breakfast* Ⓜ *Embankment* ✢ *5:C1.*

$$$
HOTEL
FAMILY
DoubleTree by Hilton Hotel London Westminster. Spectacular views of the river, Big Ben, and the London Eye fill the floor-to-ceiling windows in this rather stark, steel-and-glass building steps from the Tate Britain, and a plethora of techy perks await inside. **Pros:** amazing views; flat screens and other high-tech gadgetry. **Cons:** small bedrooms; tiny bathrooms; TV has to be operated through a computer (confusing if you're not used to it). $ *Rooms from: £219* ✉ *30 John Islip St., Westminster* ☎ *020/7630–1000* ⊕ *doubletree3.hilton.com* ✍ *444 rooms, 16 suites* ⦿ *Some meals* Ⓜ *Westminster, Pimlico* ✢ *5:C4.*

$$$$
HOTEL
Fodor's Choice
★
Hotel 41. Designer credentials and high-tech gadgets are everywhere in the impeccably coordinated black-and-white rooms, some split-level and all gorgeously furnished with extraordinary pieces drawn from every corner of the globe. **Pros:** unique place opposite Buckingham Palace; great service; unlimited free Wi-Fi. **Cons:** unusual design is not for everyone. $ *Rooms from: £347* ✉ *41 Buckingham Palace Rd., Victoria* ☎ *020/7300–0041* ⊕ *www.41hotel.com* ✍ *26 rooms, 4 suites, 2 apartments* ⦿ *Breakfast* Ⓜ *Victoria* ✢ *5:A3.*

$$
HOTEL
Lime Tree Hotel. In a central neighborhood where hotels veer from grimy bolt-holes at one extreme to wildly overpriced at the other, the Lime Tree gets the boutique style just about right—and at a reasonable cost for the neighborhood. **Pros:** lovely and helpful hosts; great location; rooms are decent size (though the cheaper rooms are small). **Cons:** some rooms are up several flights of stairs and there's no elevator. $ *Rooms from: £155* ✉ *135–137 Ebury St., Victoria* ☎ *020/7730–8191* ⊕ *www.limetreehotel.co.uk* ✍ *25 rooms* ⦿ *Breakfast* Ⓜ *Victoria, Sloane Sq.* ✢ *4:H2.*

$
B&B/INN
Sanctuary House Hotel. This is a classic example of what the British mean when they refer to an "inn"—a pub with bedrooms, albeit one of exceptionally good quality for London. **Pros:** cozy, authentic London feel; friendly staff; wow-location right in the heart of Westminster. **Cons:** pub can be noisy (light sleepers should ask for a room as far

BEST BETS FOR LONDON LODGING

Fodor's offers a selective listing of high-quality lodging experiences at every price range, from the city's best budget motel to its most sophisticated luxury hotel. Here, we've compiled our top recommendations by price and experience. The very best properties—in other words, those that provide a particularly remarkable experience in their price range—are designated in the listings with the Fodor's Choice logo.

15

from the ground floor as possible). $⑤ Rooms from: £110 ⊠ 33 Tothill St., Westminster ☎ 020/7799–4044 ⊕ www.sanctuaryhousehotel.co.uk ↩ 34 rooms ⟋◯⟍ Breakfast Ⓜ St. James's Park ✛ 5:B2.

ST. JAMES'S

$$$$ ⛨ **The Stafford London by Kempinski.** This is a rare find: a posh hotel
HOTEL   that's equal parts elegance and friendliness, and located in one of the
Fodor'sChoice   few peaceful spots in the area, down a small lane behind Piccadilly.
★   **Pros:** great staff; big, luxurious rooms; quiet location. **Cons:** tra-
ditional style is not to all tastes; perks in the more expensive rooms
could be more generous. $⑤ Rooms from: £348 ⊠ St. James's Pl., St.
James's ☎ 020/7493–0111 ⊕ www.kempinski.com/london ↩ 81 rooms
⟋◯⟍ Breakfast Ⓜ Green Park ✛ 5:A1.

MAYFAIR AND MARYLEBONE

MAYFAIR

$$$$ ⛨ **Athenaeum Hotel and Apartments.** This grand hotel overlooking Green
B&B/INN   Park offers plenty for the money: rooms are both comfortable and
Fodor'sChoice   lavishly decorated, with deeply comfortable Hypnos beds, plasma-
★   screen TVs, luxurious fabrics, and original contemporary artworks.
Pros: peaceful park views; handy for Buckingham Palace and Piccadilly;
great value for elegant setting. **Cons:** bathrooms are almost all small.
$⑤ Rooms from: £342 ⊠ 116 Piccadilly, Mayfair ☎ 020/7640–3557
⊕ www.athenaeumhotel.com ↩ 111 rooms, 46 suites and apartments
⟋◯⟍ Breakfast Ⓜ Green Park ✛ 1:H6.

$$$$ ⛨ **Brown's Hotel.** Founded in 1837 by James Brown, Lord Byron's "gen-
HOTEL   tleman's gentleman," this hotel occupying 11 Georgian town houses
holds a treasured place in London society. **Pros:** elegant spaces; attentive service; good afternoon tea. **Cons:** even the most basic room is very
pricey. $⑤ Rooms from: £348 ⊠ 34 Albemarle St., Mayfair ☎ 020/7493–
6020, 888/667–9477 in U.S. ⊕ www.roccofortehotels.com ↩ 88
rooms, 29 suites ⟋◯⟍ Breakfast Ⓜ Green Park ✛ 1:H5.

$$$$ ⛨ **Claridge's.** The well-heeled have been meeting—and eating—at Clar-
HOTEL   idge's for generations, and the tradition continues in the original art
FAMILY   deco public spaces of this super-glamorous London institution. **Pros:** see-
Fodor'sChoice   and-be-seen dining and drinking; serious luxury everywhere—this is an
★   old-money hotel; comics, books, and DVDs to help keep kids amused.
Cons: better pack your designer wardrobe if you want to fit in with the
locals. $⑤ Rooms from: £420 ⊠ Brook St., Mayfair ☎ 020/7629–8860,
866/599–6991 in U.S. ⊕ www.claridges.co.uk ↩ 136 rooms, 678 suites
⟋◯⟍ Breakfast Ⓜ Bond St. ✛ 1:H4.

$$$$ ⛨ **The Connaught.** A huge favorite of the "we wouldn't dream of staying
HOTEL   anywhere else" moneyed set since its opening in 1917, the Connaught
Fodor'sChoice   has many dazzlingly modern compliments to its famously historic
★   delights. **Pros:** legendary hotel; great for star-spotting. **Cons:** history
comes at a price; bathrooms are small. $⑤ Rooms from: £480 ⊠ Car-
los Pl., Mayfair ☎ 020/7499–7070, 866/599–6991 in U.S. ⊕ www.
the-connaught.co.uk ↩ 87 rooms, 34 suites ⟋◯⟍ Breakfast Ⓜ Bond St.
✛ 1:H5.

$$$$ HOTEL Fodor's Choice ★ **The Dorchester.** Few hotels this opulent manage to be as personable as the Dorchester, which opened in 1939 and boasts a prime Park Lane location with unparalleled glamour—gold leaf and marble adorn the public spaces, and guest quarters are awash in English country house–meets–art deco style. **Pros:** historic luxury in 1930s building; lovely views of Hyde Park; top-notch star-spotting; excellent spa; Michelin-starred dining from Alain Ducasse. **Cons:** traditional look is not to all tastes; prices are high; some rooms are rather small. $ *Rooms from: £414* ⊠ *Park La., Mayfair* ☎ *020/7629–8888* ⊕ *www.thedorchester.com* ⤢ *195 rooms, 55 suites* ⦿| *Breakfast* Ⓜ *Marble Arch, Hyde Park Corner* ✛ *1:H6.*

15

$$ HOTEL **Gloucester Place Hotel.** Just a couple of blocks from Marble Arch and Hyde Park, this small, friendly hotel won't win any style awards—its guest rooms are far from fancy—but, almost better, they are clean and comfortable. **Pros:** great location; huge discounts for stays of four nights or more; free Wi-Fi. **Cons:** shabby decor; stairs to climb and no elevator; some rooms have shared bathrooms; some rooms in separate building. $ *Rooms from: £155* ⊠ *55 Gloucester Pl., Mayfair* ☎ *020/7486–6166* ⊕ *www.gloucesterplacehotel.com* ⤢ *19 rooms* ⦿| *Breakfast* Ⓜ *Marble Arch, Bond St.* ✛ *1:G3.*

$$$ HOTEL **InterContinental London Park Lane.** Overlooking busy Hyde Park Corner and the Queen's back garden (much to her chagrin, allegedly), this hotel's luxurious rooms are aimed at high-end business travelers. **Pros:** central location; business facilities. **Cons:** no park views with standard rooms; prices can shoot up in mid-summer; £15 a day charge for Internet access is a bit rich given the room rates. $ *Rooms from: £323* ⊠ *1 Hamilton Pl., Park La., Mayfair* ☎ *020/7409–3131, 871/422–9200* ⊕ *www.intercontinental.com* ⤢ *447 rooms, 60 suites* ⦿| *Some meals* Ⓜ *Hyde Park Corner* ✛ *1:H6.*

$$$$ HOTEL Fodor's Choice ★ **The Langham.** Hotel pedigrees don't come much greater than this one—built in 1865, the Langham was *the* original luxury hotel in the city, all but inventing the very image of what a great London hotel looked like. **Pros:** beautiful building; impeccably good service; comfortable bedrooms; great restaurant and bar. **Cons:** price rises considerably once cheapest rooms sell out; bathrooms in basic rooms are somewhat utilitarian. $ *Rooms from: £370* ⊠ *1C Portland Pl., Mayfair* ☎ *020/7636–1000* ⊕ *www.langhamhotels.co.uk* ⤢ *331 rooms, 47 suites* ⦿| *Multiple meal plans* Ⓜ *Oxford Circus* ✛ *2:A4.*

$$$ RENTAL FAMILY **No. 5 Maddox Street.** Just five minutes' walk from Oxford Street, this is a great option for those who tire of traditional hotels: 12 luxury suites—some with balconies and working fireplaces—filled with everything you could ever need, including a handy kitchen. **Pros:** cozy and private; room service will deliver meals from local restaurants. **Cons:** no elevator; no communal lobby can make you feel isolated; suites get booked far in advance. $ *Rooms from: £266* ⊠ *5 Maddox St., Mayfair* ☎ *020/7647–0200* ⊕ *www.living-rooms.co.uk* ⤢ *12 suites* ⦿| *No meals* Ⓜ *Oxford Circus* ✛ *3:A5.*

$$$ ⊡ **Radisson Blu Edwardian Berkshire Hotel.** In a dangerously good location
HOTEL for shopaholics, with Oxford Street on the doorstep, the pleasant and
well-run Radisson Berkshire (pronounced 'Bark-sha') offers a similar
level of service to some of the more established hotels in the neighbor-
hood, at a lower rate. **Pros:** great location; good restaurant; free Wi-Fi;
worthwhile deals and promotions. **Cons:** walk-in rate is still quite expen-
sive; small bedrooms. ⑤ *Rooms from: £246* ⊠ *350 Oxford St., Mayfair*
☎ *020/7629–7474, 1800/967–9033 toll-free in U.K., 1800/333–3333
toll-free in U.S.* ⊕ *www.radissonblu-edwardian.com* ⊅ *145 rooms, 2
suites* ⦿⦿ *Multiple meal plans* Ⓜ *Bond St., Oxford Circus* ✛ *1:H4.*

$$ ⊡ **22 York Street.** This Georgian town house has a cozy, family feel, with
B&B/INN polished pine floors and plenty of quilts and French antiques in the homey,
individually furnished guest rooms. **Pros:** good location for shoppers;
friendly hosts; very flexible check-in times; entirely non-smoking. **Cons:**
if you take away the great location, you're paying a lot for a B&B; not
everyone enjoys socializing with strangers over breakfast. ⑤ *Rooms from:
£130* ⊠ *22 York St., Mayfair* ☎ *020/7224–2990* ⊕ *www.22yorkstreet.
co.uk* ⊅ *10 rooms* ⦿⦿ *Breakfast* Ⓜ *Baker St.* ✛ *1:G3.*

MARYLEBONE

$$$ ⊡ **Dorset Square Hotel.** Reopened in June 2012 after extensive updates
HOTEL and refurbishment, this boutique hotel, in one of London's most fash-
Fodor's Choice ionable neighborhoods, occupies a charming town house. **Pros:** ideal
★ location; lovely design; welcoming vibe. **Cons:** some rooms are small;
no bathtub in some rooms; fee for WiFi. ⑤ *Rooms from: £252* ⊠ *39
Dorset Sq., Marylebone* ☎ *020/7723–7874* ⊕ *www.firmdalehotels.com*
⊅ *35 rooms, 3 suites* ⦿⦿ *Breakfast* Ⓜ *Baker St.* ✛ *1:F2.*

$$$ ⊡ **Hyatt Regency London — The Churchill.** Even though it's one of London's
HOTEL largest hotels, the Churchill is always abuzz with guests smiling at the
purring perfection they find here, including warmly personalized service
and calmly alluring guest rooms. **Pros:** comfortable and stylish; efficient
service; up to three can stay in one room. **Cons:** feels more geared to
business than leisure travelers. ⑤ *Rooms from: £269* ⊠ *30 Portman
Sq., Marylebone* ☎ *020/7486–5800* ⊕ *www.london.churchill.hyatt.com*
⊅ *389 rooms, 45 suites* ⦿⦿ *Breakfast* Ⓜ *Marble Arch* ✛ *1:G4.*

$$$ ⊡ **The Landmark London Hotel.** A glass-covered, eight-story atrium sets
HOTEL the scene at this truly grand hotel, where the huge bedrooms are richly
Fodor's Choice furnished and have marble bathrooms (odd-numbered rooms overlook
★ the Winter Garden beneath the glass roof). **Pros:** amazingly luxurious;
one of the few really posh London hotels that doesn't make you dress
up; good discounts are available. **Cons:** two-night minimum stay at cer-
tain times. ⑤ *Rooms from: £234* ⊠ *222 Marylebone Rd., Marylebone*
☎ *020/7631–8000* ⊕ *www.landmarklondon.co.uk* ⊅ *299 rooms, 47
suites* ⦿⦿ *Breakfast* Ⓜ *Marylebone* ✛ *1:F3.*

$$ ⊡ **Park Plaza Sherlock Holmes Hotel.** Named in honor of the fictional
HOTEL detective who had his home on Baker Street, rooms here have a mas-
culine edge with lots of earth tones and pin-striped sheets (along with
hyper-modern bathrooms stocked with fluffy bathrobes). **Pros:** nicely
decorated; near Marylebone High Street; international electrical outlets,
including those that work with American equipment. **Cons:** have to
walk through the bar to get to reception; not well soundproofed from

BED-AND-BREAKFASTS

You can stay in small, homey B&Bs for an up-close-and-personal brush with city life (Parkwood Hotel; Arlington Avenue), or find yourself in what is really a modern guesthouse, where you never meet the owners (B&B Belgravia; The Main House). The main benefit of staying in a B&B is that the price is usually cheaper than a hotel room of comparable quality, and you receive more personal service. However, the limitations may be off-putting for some: although you can sometimes arrange for daily maid service, there's usually no restaurant, bar, or room service. Prices start at around £60 a night, and in that bracket the grimmer places are legion, so make your choice carefully. Prices usually (though not always) go up for more central neighborhoods and larger and more luxurious homes. It's a nice option, both for seasoned travelers who want a more authentic taste of London, and for those trying to travel well without busting their budgets.

AirBnB. This popular global network of private lets and small bed-and-breakfasts has several hundred London-based properties listed on its website. ⊕ *www.airbnb.co.uk.*

Host & Guest Service. Host & Guest Service can find you a room in London as well as in the rest of the United Kingdom. This a great source for bargains, and you know that all properties have been vetted by the agency, but the website functionality is a bit creaky. ⊠ *103 Dawes Rd., Fulham* ☎ *020/7385–9922* ⊕ *www.host-guest.co.uk* ☞ *Full payment in advance.*

15

the noisy street. $ *Rooms from: £168* ⊠ *108 Baker St., Marylebone* ☎ *020/7486–6161* ⊕ *www.sherlockholmeshotel.com* ⮑ *99 rooms, 20 suites* ⦿ *Breakfast* Ⓜ *Baker St.* ✛ *1:G3.*

SOHO AND COVENT GARDEN

SOHO

$$ ⛉ **Dean Street Townhouse.** Discreet and unpretentious, but oh-so-stylish—

HOTEL and right in the heart of Soho—this place has a bohemian vibe and an

Fodor'sChoice excellent modern British restaurant, hung with art by, among others,

★ Peter Blake and Tracy Emin. **Pros:** übercool; resembles an upper-class pied-à-terre. **Cons:** prices can double on certain nights in summer; some rooms are extremely small; rooms at the front can be noisy, especially on weekends. $ *Rooms from: £175* ⊠ *69–71 Dean St., Soho* ☎ *020/7434–1775* ⊕ *www.deanstreettownhouse.com* ⮑ *39 rooms* ⦿ *Breakfast* Ⓜ *Leicester Sq., Tottenham Court Rd.* ✛ *3:D5.*

$$$ ⛉ **Hazlitt's.** This disarmingly friendly place, full of personality, robust

HOTEL antiques, and claw-foot tubs, occupies three connected early-18th-century houses, one of which was the last home of essayist William Hazlitt (1778–1830). **Pros:** great for lovers of art and antiques; historic atmosphere with lots of small sitting rooms and wooden staircases; truly beautiful and relaxed. **Cons:** no in-house restaurant; breakfast is £12 extra; no elevators. $ *Rooms from: £250* ⊠ *6 Frith St., Soho* ☎ *020/7434–1771* ⊕ *www.hazlittshotel.com* ⮑ *20 rooms, 3 suites* ⦿ *No meals* Ⓜ *Tottenham Court Rd.* ✛ *3:D4.*

COVENT GARDEN

$$$$
HOTEL
Fodor'sChoice
★

☷ **Covent Garden Hotel.** It's little wonder this is now the London home-away-from-home for off-duty celebrities, actors, and style mavens, with its Covent Garden location and guest rooms that are *World of Interiors*–stylish. **Pros:** great for star-spotting; super-trendy. **Cons:** you can feel you don't matter if you're not famous; setting in Covent Garden can be a bit boisterous. ⑤ *Rooms from: £342 ⊠ 10 Monmouth St., Covent Garden* ☎ *020/7806–1000, 800/553–6674 in U.S.* ⊕ *www.firmdale. com* ⬌ *55 rooms, 3 suites* ⑩*Some meals* Ⓜ *Covent Garden* ✛ *3:E4.*

$$$$
HOTEL
Fodor'sChoice
★

☷ **ME London.** One can only imagine the endless concept meetings that went into this shiny, new luxury spot that brought a touch of modern cool to the Strand, but the result—a happy mix of high fashion and futuristic hipster—is almost achingly on-trend. **Pros:** sleek and fashionable; full of high-tech comforts; excellent service; stunning views from rooftop bar. **Cons:** design can sometimes verge on form over function; very small closets and in-room storage areas. ⑤ *Rooms from: £450 ⊠ 336 The Strand, Covent Garden* ☎ *0808/234–1953* ⊕ *www.melia.com* ⬌ *141 rooms, 16 suites* ⑩ *Breakfast* Ⓜ *Covent Carden* ✛ *3:G5.*

$$$
HOTEL

☷ **One Aldwych.** An Edwardian building, with an artsy lobby and understated blend of contemporary and classic, provides pure, modern luxury in a great location for theaters and shopping. **Pros:** understated luxury; ultracool atmosphere; good deals and special offers, including big advance booking discounts. **Cons:** all this luxury doesn't come cheap; fashionable ambience is not always relaxing; design sometimes verges on form over function. ⑤ *Rooms from: £298 ⊠ 1 Aldwych, Covent Garden* ☎ *020/7300–1000* ⊕ *www.onealdwych.co.uk* ⬌ *93 rooms, 12 suites* ⑩ *Breakfast* Ⓜ *Charing Cross, Covent Garden* ✛ *3:G5.*

$$$$
HOTEL
Fodor'sChoice
★

☷ **The Savoy.** One of London's most famous hotels has emerged from a £220-million renovation, and the old girl is looking like a superstar again. **Pros:** one of the top hotels in Europe; iconic pedigree; Thames-side location; less snooty than many others of its class. **Cons:** everything comes with a price tag; guest rooms can be surprisingly noisy, particularly on lower floors; right off the super-busy Strand. ⑤ *Rooms from: £390 ⊠ The Strand, Covent Garden* ☎ *020/7836–4343, 800/257–7544 in U.S.* ⊕ *www.fairmont.com/savoy-london* ⬌ *206 rooms, 62 suites* ⑩ *Breakfast* Ⓜ *Covent Garden, Charing Cross* ✛ *3:G5.*

BLOOMSBURY, HOLBORN, AND FITZROVIA

BLOOMSBURY

$
B&B/INN

☷ **Alhambra Hotel.** One of the best bargains in Bloomsbury is a stone's throw from King's Cross and the Eurostar terminal, and though rooms are very small and the neighborhood is still somewhat "edgy," few places are this cheery and clean for the price. **Pros:** low price, with breakfast included; friendly service; central location. **Cons:** zero frills; stairs to climb; some rooms have shared bathrooms. ⑤ *Rooms from: £86 ⊠ 17–19 Argyle St., Bloomsbury* ☎ *020/7837–9575* ⊕ *www.alhambrahotel.com* ⬌ *52 rooms* ⑩ *Breakfast* Ⓜ *King's Cross* ✛ *2:C2.*

$$ 🏨 **Arosfa.** Simple, friendly, and pleasantly quirky, this little B&B, once
B&B/INN the home of pre-Raphaelite painter Sir John Everett Millais, is on an
elegant Georgian street within walking distance of the West End and the
British Museum. **Pros:** friendly staff; check-in from 7 am; good location
for museums and theaters; free Wi-Fi. **Cons:** some rooms are very small;
bathrooms have showers only; few services. Ⓢ *Rooms from: £110* ✉ *83
Gower St., Bloomsbury* ☎ *020/7636–2115* ⊕ *www.arosfalondon.com*
🛏 *16 rooms* ❖*Breakfast* Ⓜ *Goodge St., Euston Sq.* ✛ *3:D1.*

$ 🏨 **Celtic Hotel.** This is a solid, dependable budget choice in a pricey dis-
HOTEL trict (close to the West End and British Museum)—clean and comfort-
able, but with basic amenities. **Pros:** triple and quad rooms available;
free Wi-Fi; good location close to the British Museum and the West End.
Cons: no-frills approach means few extras; no elevator; cheaper rooms
don't have private bathrooms. Ⓢ *Rooms from: £79* ✉ *62 Guilford St.,
Bloomsbury* ☎ *020/7837–6737* ⊕ *www.stmargaretshotel.co.uk* 🛏 *35
rooms* ❖*Breakfast* Ⓜ *Russell Sq.* ✛ *2:C4.*

$$$$ 🏨 **Charlotte Street Hotel.** Tradition and modern flair are fused together in
HOTEL this super-stylish Soho retreat, beautifully decorated with unique printed
Fodor'sChoice fabrics from designer Kit Kemp. **Pros:** elegant, luxurious; great attention
★ to detail. **Cons:** the popular bar can be noisy; reservations are necessary
for the restaurant. Ⓢ *Rooms from: £300* ✉ *15 Charlotte St., Bloomsbury*
☎ *020/7806–2000, 800/553–6674 in U.S.* ⊕ *www.firmdalehotels.com*
🛏 *46 rooms, 6 suites* ❖*Breakfast* Ⓜ *Goodge St.* ✛ *3:C2.*

$ 🏨 **Grange Blooms Hotel.** In this white Georgian town-house hotel, just
HOTEL around the corner from the British Museum, rooms are not too tiny by
London standards, and those in the back look out onto a leafy green
garden. **Pros:** great location; overall good value; good prices if you
book early through the website. **Cons:** bathrooms could use an upgrade;
guests can be bumped to sister hotel if fully booked; no air-condi-
tioning; street noise in some rooms; price rises steeply on weekdays.
Ⓢ *Rooms from: £81* ✉ *7 Montague St., Bloomsbury* ☎ *020/7323–
1717, 800/2247–2643* ⊕ *www.grangehotels.com* 🛏 *26 rooms, 1 suite*
❖*Some meals* Ⓜ *Russell Sq.* ✛ *3:F2.*

$$ 🏨 **Harlingford Hotel.** The most contemporary of the hotels around
HOTEL Bloomsbury's Cartwright Gardens offers sleek, quiet, and comfortable
bedrooms and perfectly appointed public rooms. **Pros:** good location;
friendly staff; use of private garden; wider breakfast choice than many
small London hotels. **Cons:** rooms are quite small; no air-conditioning; no elevator. Ⓢ *Rooms from: £120* ✉ *61–63 Cartwright Gardens,
Bloomsbury* ☎ *020/7387–1551* ⊕ *www.harlingfordhotel.com* 🛏 *43
rooms* ❖*Breakfast* Ⓜ *Russell Sq.* ✛ *2:C3.*

$ 🏨 **Jesmond Hotel.** This friendly little hotel is great value given the loca-
B&B/INN tion: a short walk from the British Museum in one direction, and Soho
and Covent Garden in the other. **Pros:** great location; friendly staff;
free Wi-Fi; 15% discount on stays of one week. **Cons:** some rooms are
very small; nearly half have shared bathrooms. Ⓢ *Rooms from: £85*
✉ *63 Gower St., Bloomsbury* ☎ *020/7636–3199* ⊕ *www.jesmondhotel.
org.uk* 🛏 *15 rooms* ❖*Breakfast* Ⓜ *Goodge St., Euston Sq., Warren
St., Russell Sq.* ✛ *3:C1.*

15

LONDON CHAIN HOTEL PRIMER

Here's a quick rundown of some hotel chains worth considering:

easyHotel: One of the first chains to bring "pod hotels" to London, the easyHotel chain specializes in very cheap (less than £50 a night for a double) rooms that are clean, secure, and offer all the basics, but are teeny-tiny and have no free extras at all. ⊕ www.easyhotel.com.

Grange Hotels: This chain includes a mix of moderately priced hotels with neutral interior design, good service, and gadgets for business travelers. ⊕ www.grangehotels.com.

Malmaison: With lavish, elegant small hotels around the country, this upscale chain offers luxurious designer style, good restaurants, and trendy bars. ⊕ www.malmaison.com.

Millennium: Similar in style to Premier Inns, Millennium (and its other brand, Copthorne) hotels are targeted at both business and leisure travelers. They offer well-designed rooms with plenty of gadgets and have frequent sales. ⊕ www.millenniumhotels.co.uk.

myhotel: A chain of pricey hotels with designer style and trendy bars. myhotels offer reliable comfort and service, if you don't mind the price tag. ⊕ www.myhotels.com.

Premier Inns: This chain features medium-size, moderately priced hotels. They're known for their attractive look, and for frequent sales, which keep prices low. ⊕ www.premierinn.com.

$$
HOTEL
⬚ **Megaro.** Directly across the street from St. Pancras International station (for the Eurostar), the snazzy, well-designed, modern bedrooms here surround guests with startlingly contemporary style and amenities that include powerful showers and espresso machines. **Pros:** comfortable beds; great location for Eurostar; short hop on Tube to city center. **Cons:** neighborhood isn't great; standard rooms are small; interiors may be a bit stark for some. $ *Rooms from: £130* ⊠ *Belgrove St., King's Cross* ☎ *020/7843–2222* ⊕ *www.hotelmegaro.co.uk* ⬎ *49 rooms* ⦿❘ *Breakfast* ✛ *2:C2.*

$
B&B/INN
⬚ **The Ridgemount Hotel.** Mere blocks away from the British Museum and London's West End theaters, this handsomely fronted guesthouse has clean, neat, and plainly decorated rooms at a bargain. **Pros:** good location for theaters and museum; helpful staff; family rooms (accommodating up to five) are excellent value. **Cons:** decoration is basic; no elevator; cheapest rooms have shared bathrooms. $ *Rooms from: £78* ⊠ *65–67 Gower St., Bloomsbury* ☎ *020/7636–1141* ⊕ *www.ridgemounthotel. co.uk* ⬎ *32 rooms, 15 with bath* ⦿❘ *Breakfast* Ⓜ *Goodge St.* ✛ *3:D1.*

$$
B&B/INN
⬚ **Rough Luxe.** Undoubtedly Bloomsbury's most avant-garde hotel, this 19th-century building has been renovated with an appealing mix of shabby chic and modern comfort ("half rough, half luxury" as the owners themselves put it). **Pros:** art and design lovers will be dazzled; free Wi-Fi. **Cons:** no restaurant or bar; cheapest rooms book up fast; in a neighborhood locals would describe as somewhat "dodgy"; some rooms share bathrooms. $ *Rooms from: £159* ⊠ *1 Birkenhead St., Bloomsbury* ☎ *020/7837–5338* ⊕ *www.roughluxe.co.uk* ⬎ *10 rooms* ⦿❘ *Breakfast* Ⓜ *Kings Cross* ✛ *2:C2.*

$$$ **Sanderson Hotel.** At this fashionable and surreal "urban spa" in a
HOTEL converted 1950s textile factory, the lobby looks like a design museum: bedrooms have sleigh beds and a mix of over-the-top Louis XV and postmodern furnishings. **Pros:** popular with design mavens; your every whim gratified. **Cons:** "designer cool" can be self-consciously hip; bar and restaurant are so exclusive it's hard to get in. $ *Rooms from: £275* ⊠ *50 Berners St., Bloomsbury* ☎ *020/7300–1400* ⊕ *www. sandersonlondon.com* ↝ *150 rooms* ⊚ *Breakfast* Ⓜ *Oxford Circus, Tottenham Court Rd.* ✛ *3:B3.*

$$$ **St. Pancras Renaissance.** Reopened in 2011 after nearly a century of
HOTEL dereliction, this stunningly restored Victorian landmark—replete with
Fodor's Choice gingerbread turrets and castle-like ornaments—started as a love letter
★ to the golden age of railways; now it's one of London's most sophisticated places to stay. **Pros:** unique and beautiful; faultless service; just an elevator ride to the Eurostar. **Cons:** very popular bar and restaurant; streets outside are busy 24 hours. $ *Rooms from: £239* ⊠ *Euston Rd., King's Cross* ☎ *020/7841–3540* ⊕ *www.marriott.com* ↝ *207 rooms, 38 suites* ⊚ *Breakfast* Ⓜ *Kings Cross St. Pancras. National Rail: Kings Cross St. Pancras* ✛ *2:C2.*

HOLBORN

$$ **Fleet River Bakery Rooms.** We've heard of a restaurant with rooms
RENTAL before, but never this: four modern, spacious studio suites, upstairs
Fodor's Choice from an artisan bakery. **Pros:** comfortable modern apartments; breakfast
★ from bakery but freedom to prepare your own meals; Sir John Soanes Museum, British Museum, and Covent Garden all within half a mile; free Wi-Fi. **Cons:** few services; no kids aged five and under. $ *Rooms from: £120* ⊠ *71 Lincoln's Inn Fields, Holborn* ☎ *020/7691–1457* ⊕ *www. fleetriverbakery.com* ↝ *4 rooms* ⊚ *Breakfast* Ⓜ *Holborn* ✛ *3:G4.*

$$$ **SACO Holborn.** Down a quiet backstreet, a 10-minute walk from
RENTAL the British Museum, these serviced apartments are spacious, modern, and extremely well equipped, including a kitchen with dishwasher and washing machine. **Pros:** more independence than hotels; pleasant and spacious accommodations; on-site parking. **Cons:** exterior is dated; you must provide own bedding for baby cots. $ *Rooms from: £232* ⊠ *82 Lamb's Conduit St., Holborn* ☎ *0845/122–0405* ⊕ *www. sacoapartments.co.uk* ↝ *30 apartments (mixture of studios, 1-, 2-, and 3-bed)* ⊚ *No meals* Ⓜ *Russell Sq.* ✛ *3:G1.*

FITZROVIA

$$$$ **The London Edition.** A solidly bohemian air permeates this handsome
HOTEL new hotel in the heart of Fitzrovia, which opened to much fanfare in
Fodor's Choice the fall of 2013. **Pros:** very fashionable; great bars; beautifully designed
★ bedrooms. **Cons:** service shows a few teething problems; reservations are essential in the Punch Room. $ *Rooms from: £315* ⊠ *10 Berners St., Fitzrovia* ☎ *020/7781–0000* ⊕ *edition-hotels.marriott.com/london* ↝ *173 rooms* ⊚ *Multiple meal plans* Ⓜ *Oxford Circus* ✛ *3:B3.*

15

THE CITY

$$ HOTEL **Apex City of London.** At this sleek, modern branch of the small Apex chain near the Tower of London, bedrooms are reasonably spacious, with contemporary color schemes, 40-inch flat-screen TVs, and little sofas. **Pros:** great location; helpful staff; good advance booking discounts; free Wi-Fi. **Cons:** geared more to business than leisure travelers; price can rise sharply during busy times. $ *Rooms from: £126* ✉ *1 Seething La., The City* ☎ *020/7702–2020* ⊕ *www.apexhotels.co.uk* ⇌ *130 rooms, 49 suites* |○| *Breakfast* Ⓜ *Tower Hill* ✦ *2:G2.*

$$ HOTEL **Crowne Plaza London—The City.** Don't let the hotel's all-business appearance put you off—it's a polished operation, with stylish minimalist rooms, and just steps from the gleaming new Blackfriars Tube and train station in one direction, and bustling Fleet Street in the other. **Pros:** good prices available with advance booking; great location near the river and transport. **Cons:** neighborhood is super-busy during the day and empty at night. $ *Rooms from: £157* ✉ *19 New Bridge St., The City* ☎ *0871/942–9190* ⊕ *www.cplondoncityhotel.co.uk* ⇌ *203 rooms, 3 suites* |○| *Breakfast* Ⓜ *Blackfriars* ✦ *2:F6.*

$$ HOTEL **Grange City Hotel.** With an eye on business, this sleek City hotel has everything the workaholic needs to feel right at home—chic bedrooms subtly decorated, modern furnishings, plenty of space (by London standards), and more. **Pros:** good-size rooms; prices can drop considerably on weekends; women-only rooms are great for lone female travelers. **Cons:** a bit off the tourist track; some rooms overlook train platform; prices can soar midweek; online discounts tend to not allow changes or cancellation. $ *Rooms from: £152* ✉ *8–14 Cooper's Row, The City* ☎ *020/7863–3700* ⊕ *www.grangehotels.com* ⇌ *307 rooms, 11 suites* |○| *Some meals* Ⓜ *Tower Hill, Aldgate, Monument* ✦ *2:G2.*

$$ HOTEL Fodor's Choice ★ **The Rookery.** An absolutely unique and beautiful 1725 town house, the Rookery is the kind of place where you want to allow quality time to enjoy and soak up the atmosphere. **Pros:** helpful staff; free Wi-Fi; good deals in the off-season. **Cons:** breakfast costs extra; Tube ride to tourist sites. $ *Rooms from: £144* ✉ *12 Peter's La., at Cowcross St., The City* ☎ *020/7336–0931* ⊕ *www.rookeryhotel.com* ⇌ *30 rooms, 3 suites* |○| *No meals* Ⓜ *Farringdon* ✦ *2:F4.*

$$ HOTEL **Threadneedles Hotel.** The elaborate building housing this grand hotel in the financial district is a former bank, and the vast old banking hall—beautifully adapted as the lobby, with luxurious marble and mahogany panels—really sets the scene. **Pros:** lap of luxury; excellent service. **Cons:** a bit stuffy for some tastes; prices rise sharply midweek; neighborhood is quiet at night. $ *Rooms from: £149* ✉ *5 Threadneedle St., The City* ☎ *020/7657–8080* ⊕ *www.hotelthreadneedles.co.uk* ⇌ *63 rooms, 6 suites* |○| *Breakfast* Ⓜ *Bank* ✦ *2:G2.*

$$$ HOTEL Fodor's Choice ★ **The Zetter.** The dizzying five-story atrium, art deco staircase, and slick European restaurant hint at the delights to come in this converted warehouse—a breath of fresh air with its playful color schemes, elegant wallpapers, and wonderful views of The City from the higher floors. **Pros:** huge amounts of character; big rooms; free Wi-Fi; award-winning restaurant. **Cons:** rooms with good views cost

more. $ *Rooms from: £234* ✉ *86–88 Clerkenwell Rd., Clerkenwell* ☎ *020/7324–4444* ⊕ *www.thezetter.com* ⌁ *59 rooms* ❍❘ *Breakfast* Ⓜ *Farringdon* ✛ *2:F3.*

EAST LONDON

$$ ⊡ **Ace Hotel London.** The first European outlet of the super-hip Ace hotel
HOTEL chain fits right into the scenery in achingly cool Shoreditch, surrounded by galleries and on-trend boutiques every bit as style conscious as its own creatively minimalist interiors. **Pros:** extremely fashionable; large and comfortable bedrooms; great bar. **Cons:** not everyone will enjoy being surrounded by hipsters; price rises sharply midweek; street noise can be a problem. $ *Rooms from: £149* ✉ *100 Shoreditch High St., Shoreditch* ☎ *020/7613–9800* ⊕ *www.acehotel.com* ⌁ *258 rooms* ❍❘ *Breakfast* Ⓜ *Shoreditch High St.* ✛ *2:G1*

$$ ⊡ **Andaz.** Swanky and upscale, this hotel sports a modern, masculine
HOTEL design, and novel check-in procedure—instead of standing at a desk, guests sit in a lounge while a staff member with a handheld computer takes their information. **Pros:** nice attention to detail; guests can borrow an iPod from the front desk; no standing in line to check in; "healthy minibars" are stocked with nuts, fruit, and yogurt. **Cons:** sparse interior design is not for all; rates rise significantly for midweek stays. $ *Rooms from: £123* ✉ *40 Liverpool St., East End* ☎ *020/7961–1234, 800/492–8804 in U.S.* ⊕ *www.andaz.hyatt.com* ⌁ *267 rooms* ❍❘ *Breakfast* Ⓜ *Liverpool St.* ✛ *2:G2.*

$ ⊡ **Cable Street Inn.** Wonderful modern art lines the walls of this former
B&B/INN Victorian pub a mile east of the Tower of London, which has been beau-
Fodor'sChoice tifully restored and converted into a modern B&B. **Pros:** true one-of-a-
★ kind place; beautiful art; wonderful host; free Wi-Fi. **Cons:** 20-minute journey by DLR then Tube to the center. $ *Rooms from: £110* ✉ *232 Cable St., East End* ☎ *020/7790–4019* ⊕ *www.cablestreetinn.co.uk* ⌁ *3 rooms* ❍❘ *Breakfast* Ⓜ *DLR: Shadwell* ✛ *2:H5.*

$ ⊡ **The Hoxton Hotel.** The design throughout this trendy East London
HOTEL lodging is contemporary—but not so modern as to be absurd—and
Fodor'sChoice in keeping with a claim to combine a country-lodge lifestyle with true
★ urban living, a fire crackles in the lobby. **Pros:** cool vibe; neighborhood known for funky galleries and boutiques; huge weekend discounts; way-cool restaurant; one hour of free international calls. **Cons:** price rockets during the week; away from tourist sights. $ *Rooms from: £59* ✉ *81 Great Eastern St., East End* ☎ *020/7550–1000* ⊕ *www.hoxtonhotels. com* ⌁ *205 rooms* ❍❘ *Breakfast* ✛ *2:G1.*

$ ⊡ **Ramada Hotel and Suites Docklands.** Many of the sleek and modern
HOTEL rooms at this hotel, dramatically set at the edge of the river in the rejuvenated Docklands area of East London, have water views, while others have views of the city. **Pros:** waterfront views; free Wi-Fi; great value weekend rates. **Cons:** lacks character; area is tumbleweed quiet on weekends; about a 20-minute Tube ride to central London. $ *Rooms from: £89* ✉ *ExCel, 2 Festoon Way, Royal Victoria Dock, East End* ☎ *020/7540–4820* ⊕ *www.ramadadocklands.co.uk* ⌁ *224 rooms* ❍❘ *Breakfast* Ⓜ *Old St.* ✛ *2:H2.*

15

$$ ⊞ **Town Hall Hotel and Apartments.** An art deco town hall, abandoned in
HOTEL   the early 1980s and turned into a chic hotel in 2010, is now a lively
and stylish place, with the best of the building's elegant original features intact. **Pros:** beautifully designed; lovely staff; big discounts on
weekends. **Cons:** though touted as "cool" and "cutting edge," this
is not a good part of town; a 15-minute Tube ride from central London. ⑤ *Rooms from: £148* ✉ *Patriot Sq., Bethnal Green, East End*
☎ *020/7657–8080* ⊕ *www.townhallhotel.com* ⤳ *98 rooms, 86 suites*
|❍| *Breakfast* Ⓜ *Bethnal Green* ✛ *2:H1.*

SOUTH OF THE THAMES

$ ⊞ **Church Street Hotel.** Like rays of sunshine in gritty south London, these
HOTEL   rooms above a popular tapas restaurant are individually decorated in
Fodor's Choice   rich, bold tones and authentic Central American touches—elaborately
★   painted crucifixes; tiles handmade in Guadalajara; homemade iron bed
frames. **Pros:** unique and arty; great breakfasts; lovely staff; closer to
central London than it might appear. **Cons:** a trendy but not great part
of town (stay out of neighboring Elephant and Castle); would suit
adventurous young things more than families; a mile from a Tube station (though bus connections are handier); some rooms have shared
bathrooms. ⑤ *Rooms from: £70* ✉ *29–33 Camberwell Church St.,*
Camberwell, South East ☎ *020/7703–5984* ⊕ *www.churchstreethotel.*
com ⤳ *28 rooms* |❍| *Breakfast* Ⓜ *Oval St.* ✛ *5:H6.*

$$ ⊞ **London Bridge Hotel.** Steps away from the London Bridge rail and
HOTEL   Tube stations, and handy for the South Bank, this thoroughly modern,
stylish hotel is popular with business travelers, but leisure travelers
find it just as handy and appealing. **Pros:** good location for visiting
South Bank attractions; free Wi-Fi; good deals available online in the
off-season. **Cons:** small bedrooms; prices rise by £100 or more midweek. ⑤ *Rooms from: £132* ✉ *8–18 London Bridge St., Southwark*
☎ *020/7855–2200* ⊕ *www.london-bridge-hotel.co.uk* ⤳ *138 rooms,*
3 apartments |❍| *Breakfast* Ⓜ *London Bridge* ✛ *5:H1.*

$$$ ⊞ **London Marriott Hotel County Hall.** This grand hotel on the Thames
HOTEL   enjoys perhaps the most iconic view in the city—right next door is the
London Eye, and directly across the River Thames are the Houses of
Parliament and Big Ben. **Pros:** handy for South Bank arts scene, London Eye, and Westminster; great gym; good weekend discounts. **Cons:**
interior design is overdone; breakfasts are pricey; rooms facing the river
inevitably cost extra. ⑤ *Rooms from: £315* ✉ *County Hall, Westminster Bridge Rd., South Bank* ☎ *020/7928–5200, 888/236–2427 in U.S.*
⊕ *www.marriott.com* ⤳ *186 rooms, 14 suites* |❍| *Breakfast* Ⓜ *Westminster, Waterloo. National Rail: Waterloo* ✛ *5:D2.*

$$ ⊞ **Premier Travel Inn County Hall.** The small but nicely decorated
HOTEL   rooms at this budget choice share the same County Hall complex
FAMILY   as the grander London Marriott Hotel County Hall, and though
they have none of the spectacular river views, their selling point
is the same convenient location at a decidedly lower price. **Pros:**
fantastic location for the South Bank; bargains to be had if you
book in advance; kids stay free. **Cons:** no river views; limited services; cookie-cutter chain hotel atmosphere. ⑤ *Rooms from: £126*

☒ *Belvedere Rd., South Bank* ☎ *0871/527–8648* ⊕ *www.premierinn. com* ⇘ *313 rooms* �🍽 *Breakfast* Ⓜ *Westminster, Waterloo. National Rail: Waterloo* ✣ *5:D2.*

$$
HOTEL

⛱ **Premier Travel Inn Southwark (Borough Market).** This excellent branch of the huge Premier Travel Inn chain is a bit out of the way on the South Bank, but is convenient for visits to Tate Modern, Shakespeare's Globe Theatre, and Borough Market. **Pros:** ideally placed for visiting Tate Modern or the Globe Theatre. **Cons:** small rooms; uninspiring building; limited extras or services; rooms near elevators can be a little noisy (ask for one farther down the hall). Ⓢ *Rooms from: £98* ☒ *34 Park St., Southwark* ☎ *0871/527–8676* ⊕ *www.premiertravelinn.com* ⇘ *56 rooms* �🍽 *Breakfast* Ⓜ *London Bridge* ✣ *5:H1.*

KENSINGTON, CHELSEA, KNIGHTSBRIDGE, AND BELGRAVIA

KENSINGTON

15

$$
HOTEL

⛱ **Ampersand.** A sense of style emanates from every surface of this sumptuous hotel in the heart of Kensington—but the playful, vintage vibe lends the property a refreshingly down-to-earth feel in a neighborhood that often feels cooler-than-thou. **Pros:** flawless design; great service; good restaurant. **Cons:** ground-floor rooms can be noisy. Ⓢ *Rooms from: £174* ☒ *10 Harrington Rd., Kensington* ⊕ *www.ampersandhotel. com* ⇘ *106 rooms, 5 suites* ⛱ *Breakfast* ✣ *4:D2.*

$$
HOTEL

⛱ **Ashburn Hotel.** A short walk from Gloucester Road Tube station and within walking distance of Harrods and the Kensington museums, the Ashburn is one of the better "boutique" hotels in this part of town. **Pros:** friendly atmosphere; free Wi-Fi; turndown gift (different every night). **Cons:** summer prices sometimes hike the cost. Ⓢ *Rooms from: £169* ☒ *111 Cromwell Rd., Kensington* ☎ *020/7938–5970 reservations, 020/7244–1999* ⊕ *www.ashburn-hotel.co.uk* ⇘ *38 rooms, 3 suites* ⛱ *Breakfast* Ⓜ *Gloucester Rd.* ✣ *4:C2.*

$
RENTAL

⛱ **Astons Apartments.** Three redbrick Victorian town houses on a quiet residential street are the setting for Astons's basic but decent studios and apartments. **Pros:** decent alternative to full-service hotel rooms; good location in upscale neighborhood; kitchenettes help save money on long stays. **Cons:** smaller apartments are tiny; furnishings somewhat bland and functional; few customer services; no elevator. Ⓢ *Rooms from: £115* ☒ *31 Rosary Gardens, South Kensington* ☎ *020/7590–6000, 800/525–2810 in U.S.* ⊕ *www.astons-apartments.com* ⇘ *43 rooms, 12 suites* ⛱ *No meals* Ⓜ *Gloucester Rd.* ✣ *4:C3.*

$$$
HOTEL

⛱ **The Bentley London.** Close to but just far enough away to be shielded from the bustle of Kensington, this opulent hotel is an elegant escape within a creamy-white Victorian building. **Pros:** luxurious rooms; gorgeous spa; great location. **Cons:** can be a bit stuffy; old-fashioned style won't please everyone. Ⓢ *Rooms from: £204* ☒ *27–33 Harrington Gardens, South Kensington* ☎ *020/7244–5555* ⊕ *thebentley-hotel.com* ⇘ *39 rooms, 25 suites* ⛱ *Breakfast* Ⓜ *Gloucester Rd.* ✣ *4:C3.*

$$
HOTEL

⛱ **The Cranley Hotel.** Old-fashioned British propriety is the overall feeling at this small, Victorian town-house hotel, where high ceilings, huge windows, and a pale, creamy color scheme flood the bedrooms with light. **Pros:** good-size rooms; attractively decorated; friendly staff; free evening nibbles are a nice touch. **Cons:** steep stairs into lobby; no restaurant; prices rise in mid-summer. *⑤ Rooms from: £184* *✉ 10–12 Bina Gardens, South Kensington ☎ 020/7373–0123 ⊕ www. thecranley.com ✍ 29 rooms, 5 suites, 4 apartments ¶◎¶ Breakfast* *Ⓜ Gloucester Rd. ✛ 4:C3.*

$ **⬚ easyHotel South Kensington.** London's original "pod hotel" has tiny
HOTEL rooms with a double bed, private shower room, and little else, each brightly decorated in the easyGroup's trademark orange and white (to match their budget airline easyJet). **Pros:** amazing price; safe and pleasant space. **Cons:** not for the claustrophobic—rooms are truly tiny and most have no windows; six floors and no elevator. *⑤ Rooms from: £49 ✉ 14 Lexham Gardens, Kensington ☎ 020/7216–1717 ⊕ www. easyhotel.com ✍ 34 rooms ¶◎¶ No meals Ⓜ Gloucester Rd. ✛ 4:B2.*

$$$ **⬚ The Gore Hotel.** Just down the road from the Albert Hall, this gor-
HOTEL geous, friendly hotel has a luxurious mixture of the comfortable and the extraordinary. **Pros:** gorgeously designed spacious rooms; outstanding, attentive service; air-conditioning in all rooms. **Cons:** prices rather high; Wi-Fi is not free; bar can be noisy. *⑤ Rooms from: £204 ✉ 190 Queen's Gate, Kensington ☎ 020/7584–6601, 888/757–5587 in U.S ⊕ www. gorehotel.com ✍ 50 rooms ¶◎¶ Breakfast Ⓜ Gloucester Rd. ✛ 4:D1.*

$$ **⬚ Kensington House Hotel.** A short stroll from High Street Kensington
HOTEL and Kensington Gardens, this refurbished 19th-century town house has streamlined, contemporary rooms with large windows letting in plenty of light, comfortable beds with luxurious fabrics and soft comforters. **Pros:** attractive design; relaxing setting; free Wi-Fi. **Cons:** rooms are small; bathrooms are minuscule; the elevator is Lilliputian. *⑤ Rooms from: £168 ✉ 15–16 Prince of Wales Terr., Kensington ☎ 020/7937– 2345 ⊕ www.kenhouse.com ✍ 39 rooms, 2 suites ¶◎¶ Breakfast Ⓜ High Street Kensington ✛ 4:C1.*

$$ **⬚ London Marriott Kensington.** A big favorite for the business crowd,
HOTEL this pleasant, modern outpost of the Marriott megachain is just one of several big-name hotels in this prime location. **Pros:** friendly, efficient service; good neighborhood; one-minute Tube ride to Kensington museums. **Cons:** "could be anywhere in the world" business vibe feels impersonal; bedrooms are on the small side. *⑤ Rooms from: £169 ✉ 147 Cromwell Rd., Kensington ☎ 020/7973–1000 ⊕ www. marriott.com ✍ 216 rooms ¶◎¶ Some meals Ⓜ Earl's Ct., Gloucester Rd. ✛ 4:B2.*

$ **⬚ Millennium Gloucester.** With a Tube station opposite and Kensington's
HOTEL many attractions nearby, this hotel is both convenient and alluring, its sleek and opulent lobby, with polished wood columns, a warming fireplace, and glittering chandeliers giving way to guest rooms with a traditionally masculine look. **Pros:** good deals available if you book in advance. **Cons:** lighting in some bedrooms is a bit too subtle; bathrooms are relatively small; public areas and restaurant can get crowded. *⑤ Rooms from: £106 ✉ 4–18 Harrington Gardens, Kensington ☎ 020/7373–6030 ⊕ www.millenniumhotels.co.uk ✍ 143 rooms ¶◎¶ Breakfast Ⓜ Gloucester Rd. ✛ 4:C2.*

$$ 🔲 The Nadler. This newly refurbished "aparthotel" in a creamy white
RENTAL Georgian town house offers a useful compromise between full-service
hotel and the freedom of self catering in the form of comfortable rooms
with a stylish, modern look and tiny kitchenettes. **Pros:** great alterna-
tive to hotel; handy mini-kitchens; free Wi-Fi; 24-hour reception. **Cons:**
basic rooms are small; movies in entertainment system are pay-per-
view; 15-minute Tube ride to central London. $ *Rooms from: £148*
✉ *25 Courtfield Gardens, South Kensington* ☎ *020/7244–2255* ⊕ *www.
thenadler.com* 🛏 *65 rooms* ◯ *No meals* Ⓜ *Earls Court* ✛ *4:B3.*

$$$ 🔲 Number Sixteen. Guest rooms at this lovely luxury guesthouse, just
HOTEL around the corner from the Victoria & Albert Museum, look like
they come from the pages of *Architectural Digest,* and the delightful
garden is an added bonus. **Pros:** just the right level of helpful service;
interiors are gorgeous. **Cons:** no restaurant; small elevator. $ *Rooms
from: £276* ✉ *16 Sumner Pl., South Kensington* ☎ *020/7589–5232,
888/559–5508 in U.S.* ⊕ *www.firmdale.com* 🛏 *42 rooms* ◯ *Breakfast*
Ⓜ *South Kensington* ✛ *4:D2.*

$$$ 🔲 The Pelham Hotel. One of the first and most stylish of London's famed
HOTEL "boutique" hotels, this still-chic choice is but a short stroll away from
Fodor's Choice the Natural History, Science, and V&A museums. **Pros:** great loca-
★ tion for museum-hopping; gorgeous marble bathrooms; soigné interior
design; lovely staff; good package deals for online booking. **Cons:** taller
guests will find themselves cursing the top-floor rooms with sloping
ceilings. $ *Rooms from: £220* ✉ *15 Cromwell Pl., South Kensington*
☎ *020/7589–8288, 888/757–5587 in U.S.* ⊕ *www.pelhamhotel.co.uk*
🛏 *47 rooms, 4 suites* ◯ *Breakfast* Ⓜ *South Kensington* ✛ *4:D2.*

$ 🔲 The Rockwell. Despite being on the notoriously traffic-clogged Crom-
HOTEL well Road, this excellent little place is one of the best boutique hotels
in this part of London—and windows have good soundproofing. **Pros:**
large bedrooms; stylish surroundings; helpful staff; advance booking can
drop the price below £100. **Cons:** on a busy, unattractive road; 20-min-
ute Tube ride to central London. $ *Rooms from: £117* ✉ *181 Crom-
well Rd., South Kensington* ☎ *020/7244–2000* ⊕ *www.therockwell.com*
🛏 *38 rooms, 2 suites* ◯ *Breakfast* Ⓜ *Gloucester Rd.* ✛ *4:B2.*

$$ 🔲 Think Earl's Court. These serviced apartments are a stone's throw from
RENTAL Kensington High Street and a short walk from both Earl's Court and
Olympia. **Pros:** brand new building; self-catering offers greater independence. **Cons:** payment is made when you book; bland, officelike
exterior. $ *Rooms from: £118* ✉ *26A Adam and Eve Mews, Kensington*
☎ *020/3465–9100* ⊕ *www.think-apartments.com* 🛏 *206 rooms* ◯ *No
meals* Ⓜ *High Street Kensington* ✛ *4:B1.*

CHELSEA

$ 🔲 At Home Inn Chelsea. King's Road and the rest of super-rich Chelsea
B&B/INN is just a short stroll from this delightfully informal B&B, and you'd be
hard pressed to find a better room in this neighborhood for the price.
Pros: funky, charming, and just a bit eccentric—just like the real Chelsea; short Tube ride to tourist sites; free Wi-Fi; one room can be made a
triple for £25. **Cons:** tiny bathrooms; few extras. $ *Rooms from: £110*
✉ *6 Oakfield St., Chelsea* ☎ *020/7352–2970* ⊕ *www.athomeinnchelsea.
com* 🛏 *2 rooms* ◯ *Breakfast* Ⓜ *Earls Court* ✛ *4:C4.*

15

$$$
HOTEL

⊡ **The Cadogan Hotel.** This elegant and luxurious hotel is one of London's most historically naughty hotels: it was once the home of scandalous actress Lillie Langtry, King Edward's mistress in the 1890s, and where Oscar Wilde was staying (in Room 118) when he was arrested for "indecency" with a young man on April 6, 1895. **Pros:** luxurious but not stuffy; friendly staff; great location for shopping; free Wi-Fi; good special offers online. **Cons:** rooms are quite small. ⑤ *Rooms from: £264* ⊠ *75 Sloane St., Chelsea* ☎ *020/7235–7141* ⊕ *www.cadogan.com* ⇔ *64 rooms* |◯| *Breakfast* Ⓜ *Sloane Sq.* ✛ *4:G2.*

KNIGHTSBRIDGE

$$$
HOTEL

⊡ **The Beaufort.** This gracious boutique hotel is a favorite entry in the little black books of many a visiting high-society *fashionista*—Harrods is the merest toss of a diamond from the front door. **Pros:** gorgeous interiors; friendly and professional staff; air-conditioning; free Wi-Fi. **Cons:** standard doubles are much smaller than the price might indicate. ⑤ *Rooms from: £276* ⊠ *33 Beaufort Gardens, Knightsbridge* ☎ *020/7584–5252* ⊕ *www.thebeaufort.co.uk* ⇔ *20 rooms, 7 suites* |◯| *Breakfast* Ⓜ *Knightsbridge* ✛ *4:F1.*

$$$$
HOTEL

⊡ **The Berkeley.** Convenient for Knightsbridge shopping, the very elegant Berkeley is known for its renowned restaurants and luxuries that culminate—literally—in a splendid penthouse swimming pool. **Pros:** lavish and elegant; attentive service; prices aren't quite as stratospheric as some high-end places. **Cons:** You'll need your best designer clothes to fit in. ⑤ *Rooms from: £420* ⊠ *Wilton Pl., Knightsbridge* ☎ *020/7235–6000, 800/637–2869 in U.S.* ⊕ *www.the-berkeley.co.uk* ⇔ *103 rooms, 55 suites* |◯| *Breakfast* Ⓜ *Knightsbridge* ✛ *4:G1.*

$$$
HOTEL

⊡ **The Capital Hotel.** Nothing is ever too much at this elegant hotel that was formerly a private house—mattresses are handmade, sheets are 450-thread count, bathrooms are marble, and everything is done in impeccable taste. **Pros:** beautiful space; handy for shopping at Harrods. **Cons:** breakfast is expensive. ⑤ *Rooms from: £279* ⊠ *22–24 Basil St., Knightsbridge* ☎ *020/7589–5171, 800/926–3199 in U.S.* ⊕ *www.capitalhotel.co.uk* ⇔ *40 rooms, 10 suites* |◯| *Breakfast* Ⓜ *Knightsbridge* ✛ *4:F1.*

$$$
HOTEL

⊡ **Egerton House.** Sensationally soigné, chicly decorated, and feeling like your own private London home, this hotel has some truly luxuriant design touches, including guest rooms lavishly decorated with rich fabrics and a knockout white-on-gold dining room. **Pros:** lovely staff; great location; magnificent interiors; striking art. **Cons:** some style touches a little too froufrou—even if Toulouse-Lautrec would have approved. ⑤ *Rooms from: £295* ⊠ *17–19 Egerton Terr., Knightsbridge* ☎ *020/7589–2412, 877/955–1515 in U.S.* ⊕ *www.redcarnationhotels.com* ⇔ *23 rooms, 6 suites* |◯| *Breakfast* Ⓜ *Knightsbridge, South Kensington* ✛ *4:F2.*

$$$$
HOTEL
Fodor's Choice
★

⊡ **Mandarin Oriental Hyde Park.** Built in 1880, the Mandarin Oriental welcomes you with one of the most exuberantly Victorian facades in town, then fast-forwards you to high-trend modern London, thanks to striking and luxurious guest rooms filled with high-tech gadgets. **Pros:** great shopping at your doorstep; amazing views of Hyde Park; excellent service. **Cons:** nothing comes cheap; you must dress for dinner (and lunch

APARTMENT RENTALS & HOME EXCHANGES

APARTMENT RENTALS

For a home base that's roomy enough for a family and that comes with cooking facilities, consider renting furnished "flats" (the British word for apartments).

INTERNATIONAL AGENTS

Hideaways International. This company offers boutique hotels, tours, and cruises. ✉ *767 Islington St., Portsmouth, New Hampshire, USA* ☎ *603/430–4433, 800/843–4433* ⊕ *www.hideaways.com.*

LOCAL AGENTS

The Apartment Service. This agency specializes in high-quality executive apartments. ✉ *5 Francis Grove, Wimbledon* ☎ *020/8944–1444* ⊕ *www.apartmentservice.com.*

At Home in London. Rooms in private homes in Knightsbridge, Kensington, Mayfair, Chelsea, and west London are handled by this agency. ✉ *70 Black Lion La., Hammersmith* ☎ *020/8748–1943* ⊕ *www.athomeinlondon.co.uk.*

The Bed and Breakfast Club. Contact this company for delightful apartments in Kensington, Chelsea, and Knightsbridge, from around £50 to £125 per night with full English breakfasts. ✉ *405 Kings Rd., Suite 192, Chelsea* ☎ *01243/370692* ⊕ *www.thebedandbreakfastclub. co.uk* ☞ *There's a 2.5% fee for using a credit card; debit cards incur no fees; the full price of room must be paid in advance. Check cancellation policies carefully.*

Landmark Trust. This agency has flats in historic buildings from £650 for a four-night-minimum stay. ✉ *Shottesbrooke, Maidenhead, Berkshire* ☎ *01628/825925* ⊕ *www.landmarktrust.org.uk.*

One Fine Stay. This agency will provide you with a fine apartment with fresh linen, toiletries, a kitchen full of basics, iPhones loaded with maps, and tips about the area from the owners. ☎ *020/7097–8948.*

HOME EXCHANGES

If you would like to exchange your home for someone else's, join a home-exchange organization, which will send you its updated listings of available exchanges for a year.

Exchange Clubs Intervac U.S. It costs from $99 per year for a listing and online access with this company. ☎ *800/756–4663* ⊕ *us.intervac-homeexchange.com.*

15

and breakfast). ⑤ *Rooms from: £395* ✉ *66 Knightsbridge, Knightsbridge* ☎ *020/7235–2000* ⊕ *www.mandarinoriental.com/london* ⇝ *177 rooms, 23 suites* ⑩ *Breakfast* Ⓜ *Knightsbridge* ✛ *4:F1.*

BELGRAVIA

$$
B&B/INN

Ⓣ **B&B Belgravia.** At this modern guesthouse near Victoria Station, a clean, chic white color scheme, simple modern furniture, and a lounge where a fire crackles away in the winter are all geared to stylish comfort. **Pros:** nice extras like free use of a laptop in the hotel lounge; coffee and tea always available. **Cons:** rooms and bathrooms are small; unimaginative breakfasts; can be noisy, especially on lower floors. ⑤ *Rooms from: £145* ✉ *64–66 Ebury St., Victoria* ☎ *020/7259–8570* ⊕ *www.bb-belgravia.com* ⇝ *17 rooms* ⑩ *Breakfast* Ⓜ *Sloane Sq., Victoria* ✛ *4:H2.*

$$ ⊡ **The Luna Simone Hotel.** This delightful and friendly little family-run
HOTEL   hotel, a short stroll from Buckingham Palace, is a real find for the price
in central London. **Pros:** friendly and well run; family rooms are out-
standing value; superb location. **Cons:** tiny bathrooms; thin walls; no
elevator or air-conditioning. $ *Rooms from: £134* ⊠ *47–49 Belgrave
Rd., Pimlico* ☎ *020/7834–5897* ⊕ *www.lunasimonehotel.com* ⇨ *36
rooms* ❖*Ol Breakfast* Ⓜ *Pimlico, Victoria* ✛ *5:A4.*

$$ ⊡ **Studios@82.** A great little side operation from **B&B Belgravia**, these self-
RENTAL   catering apartments represent fantastic value for money. **Pros:** great price;
lovely location; all the independence of self-catering. **Cons:** lots of stairs
and no elevator; check-in is at B&B Belgravia, six doors down the street.
$ *Rooms from: £125* ⊠ *82 Ebury St., Victoria* ☎ *020/7259–8570* ⊕ *www.
bb-belgravia.com* ⇨ *9 apartments* ❖*Ol Breakfast* Ⓜ *Knightsbridge* ✛ *4:H2.*

NOTTING HILL AND BAYSWATER

NOTTING HILL

$ ⊡ **The Main House.** A stay in this delightfully welcoming B&B feels more
B&B/INN   like sleeping over at a friend's house than in a hotel—albeit a par-
Fodor's Choice   ticularly wealthy and well-connected friend. **Pros:** unique and unusual
★   place; charming and helpful owners. **Cons:** three-night-minimum stay
is restrictive; few in-house services. $ *Rooms from: £110* ⊠ *6 Colvile
Rd., Notting Hill* ☎ *020/7221–9691* ⊕ *www.themainhouse.com* ⇨ *4
rooms* ❖*Ol Breakfast* Ⓜ *Notting Hill Gate* ✛ *1:A4.*

$$$ ⊡ **The Portobello Hotel.** One of London's quirkiest hotels, the little Porto-
HOTEL   bello (formed from two adjoining Victorian houses) has attracted scores
of celebrities to its small but stylish rooms over the years, and the decor
reflects these hip credentials with joyous abandon. **Pros:** stylish and
unique; celebrity vibe; guests have use of nearby gym and pool. **Cons:**
all but the priciest rooms are quite small; may be too eccentric for some.
$ *Rooms from: £234* ⊠ *22 Stanley Gardens, Notting Hill* ☎ *020/7727–
2777* ⊕ *www.portobello-hotel.co.uk* ⇨ *24 rooms* ⊙ *Closed 10 days at
Christmas* ❖*Ol Breakfast* Ⓜ *Notting Hill Gate* ✛ *1:A5.*

BAYSWATER

$ ⊡ **Garden Court Hotel.** In this small hotel, formed from two 19th-century
B&B/INN   town houses in a quiet garden square, each room has a character of
its own—some, such as those with original Victorian fittings, are nicer
than others, but the elevator makes the upper floors more appealing (a
relative rarity in older-style London hotels). **Pros:** lovely garden; lots
of charm; four-person family rooms are exceptional value. **Cons:** very
basic amenities; some rooms much better than others. $ *Rooms from:
£95* ⊠ *30–31 Kensington Gardens Sq., Bayswater* ☎ *020/7229–2553*
⊕ *www.gardencourthotel.co.uk* ⇨ *12 rooms, 10 with bath* ❖*Ol Breakfast*
Ⓜ *Bayswater, Queensway* ✛ *1:B4.*

$ ⊡ **Lancaster Hall Hotel.** This cheap and cheerful choice just north of Hyde
HOTEL   Park offers clean, simple rooms at a decent price, along with a good buffet
breakfast. **Pros:** decent, inexpensive, no-frills accommodations; excellent
central location five-minute walk to Hyde Park; short Tube or bus ride
away from many sights. **Cons:** just the basics; only the Youth Wing has
nonsmoking rooms; street noise; cheap beds; all double rooms have twin

LODGING ALTERNATIVES

London School of Economics Vacations. London School of Economics Vacations costs around £88 for a double with shared bathroom, or £92 for a double with private bathroom. The LSE also rent out self-catering apartments starting from £90 per night, and the earlier you book, the better. ⊠ *Passfield Hall, 1–7 Endsleigh Pl., Bloomsbury* ☎ *020/7955-7676*

⊕ *www.lsevacations.co.uk* ⊙ *No meals.*

University College London. University College London opens up its accommodations from mid-June to mid-September (for two-night minimum stays). ⊠ *Residence Manager, Campbell House, 5–10 Taviton St.* ☎ *020/7837-6704* ⊕ *www.ucl.ac.uk/residences* ⊙ *No meals.*

15

beds. $ *Rooms from: £90* ⊠ *35 Craven Terr., Bayswater* ☎ *020/7723–9276* ⊕ *www.lancaster-hall-hotel.co.uk* ⟿ *180 rooms* ⊙ *Breakfast* Ⓜ *Lancaster Gate, Paddington. National Rail: Paddington* ✛ *1:D4.*

$ ⚎ **London House Hotel.** Set in a row of white Georgian town houses, this
HOTEL excellent budget option in hit-or-miss Bayswater is friendly, well run, and spotlessly clean. **Pros:** friendly and efficient; emphasis on value for money; good location. **Cons:** some public areas feel a bit too clinical; smallest rooms are tiny. $ *Rooms from: £87* ⊠ *81 Kensington Garden Sq., Bayswater* ☎ *020/7243–1810* ⊕ *www.londonhousehotels.com* ⟿ *100 rooms* ⊙ *Breakfast* Ⓜ *Queensway, Bayswater* ✛ *1:B4.*

$ ⚎ **Parkwood Hotel.** Just seconds from Hyde Park in one of London's
B&B/INN swankiest enclaves (the Blairs live a few doors away), this sweet little guesthouse is an oasis of value for money, with warm and helpful hosts and bright guest rooms that are simply furnished with pastel color schemes and reproduction antique beds. **Pros:** lovely hosts; free Wi-Fi; hotel guarantees to match or beat price of any other hotel of its class in the area. **Cons:** often booked up in advance; no elevator; front-facing rooms can be noisy. $ *Rooms from: £79* ⊠ *4 Stanhope Pl., Bayswater* ☎ *020/7402–2241* ⊕ *www.parkwoodhotel.com* ⟿ *18 rooms* ⊙ *Breakfast* Ⓜ *Marble Arch* ✛ *1:F4.*

$$ ⚎ **Space Apart Hotel.** These studio apartments near Hyde Park are done in
RENTAL soothing tones of white and gray, with polished wood floors and attractive modern kitchenettes equipped with all you need to make small meals. **Pros:** especially good value for the money; the larger suites have space for four people; handy location. **Cons:** no in-house restaurant or bar; minimum two-night stay required. $ *Rooms from: £140* ⊠ *32–37 Kensington Gardens Sq., Bayswater* ☎ *020/7908–1340* ⊕ *www.aparthotel-london.co.uk* ⟿ *30 rooms* ⊙ *No meals* Ⓜ *Bayswater* ✛ *1:B4.*

$$ ⚎ **Vancouver Studios.** This pleasant aparthotel, in a converted Victorian
RENTAL town house, is full of quirky design flourishes, from flock wallpaper in the sitting room to a suit of armor at the top of the stairs. **Pros:** more space than most traditional hotel rooms; unique and pleasantly designed little apartments. **Cons:** a bit out of the way. $ *Rooms from: £140* ⊠ *30 Prince's Sq., Bayswater* ☎ *020/7243–1270* ⊕ *vancouverstudios.co.uk* ⟿ *45 studios* ⊙ *No meals* Ⓜ *Bayswater, Queensway* ✛ *1:B4.*

REGENT'S PARK AND HAMPSTEAD

HAMPSTEAD

$
B&B/INN
Glenlyn Guest House. An excellent option for travelers who don't mind being a long Tube ride away from the action, this converted Victorian town house offers a high standard of accommodation a few miles north of Hampstead. **Pros:** comfortable and friendly; you get more for your money than you would in central London; adjoining rooms can be converted to family suites; five-minute walk to Tube station. **Cons:** you have to factor in the cost and inconvenience of a half-hour Tube ride to central London; no restaurant. *⑤ Rooms from: £75 ⊠ 6 Woodside Park Rd., North Finchley ☎ 020/8445–0440 ⊕ www.glenlynhotel.com ➼ 27 rooms, 2 apartments ⍾ Breakfast Ⓜ Woodside Park ✢ 1:D1.*

$
HOTEL
Fodor'sChoice
★
The Hide. This chic hideaway exceeds virtually anything you could hope to find in central London for the price; the downside is the half-hour Tube ride into town. **Pros:** excellent value for money; great service; free Wi-Fi; close to Tube station. **Cons:** far from the center; dull neighborhood. *⑤ Rooms from: £100 ⊠ 230 Hendon Way, Hendon, Hampstead ☎ 020/8203–1670 ⊕ www.thehidelondon.com ➼ 22 rooms ⍾ Breakfast Ⓜ Hendon Central ✢ 1:H1.*

$
B&B/INN
La Gaffe. The name of this simple B&B means "the mistake" in Italian, and is also the punch line to the unlikely tale of how the original husband-and-wife proprietors met—but it neatly chimes with the cockney term "gaff," meaning a simple, cozy residence. **Pros:** unusual place with a cheerful atmosphere; no shared bathrooms. **Cons:** few services; no elevator; outside city center. *⑤ Rooms from: £90 ⊠ 107–111 Heath St., Hampstead ☎ 020/7435–8965 ⊕ www.lagaffe.co.uk ➼ 18 rooms, 3 suites ⍾ Breakfast Ⓜ Hampstead ✢ 1:D1.*

ISLINGTON

$
B&B/INN
Arlington Avenue. A find like this in London is as rare as hen's teeth: a friendly, affordable Georgian town-house B&B, full of character, not too far from the city center. **Pros:** stylish and comfortable; friendly hosts; quiet street; cheap as you'll ever hope to find for a place this nice in London. **Cons:** feels like a private house; shared guest bathroom; neighborhood is trendy but verging on not-so-nice. *⑤ Rooms from: £65 ⊠ Arlington Ave., Islington ☎ 07711/265–183 ⊕ www.arlingtonavenue. co.uk ➼ 2 rooms ⍾ Breakfast Ⓜ Angel, Essex Rd. ✢ 2:D1.*

PRIMROSE HILL

$$
B&B/INN
King Henry's Road. Floor-to-ceiling books and art decorate this lovely B&B in Primrose Hill, the trendy "village" neighborhood north of Regent's Park. **Pros:** unique, homey atmosphere; lovely hosts; great neighborhood. **Cons:** no extras; not very central; smaller rooms share a bathroom. *⑤ Rooms from: £120 ⊠ 30 King Henry's Rd., Primrose Hill ☎ 020/7483–2871 ⊕ www.onefinestay.com/london/king-henrys-road ➼ 5 rooms ⍾ Breakfast Ⓜ Chalk Farm ✢ 1:G1.*

PUBS AND NIGHTLIFE

Updated by Jo Caird

There isn't a London nightlife scene—there are lots of them. As long as there are crowds for obscure teenage rock bands, Dickensian-style pubs, comedy cabarets, and "bodysonic" dance nights, someone will create clubs and venues for them in London. The result? London has become a veritable utopia for excitement junkies, culture fiends, and those who—simply put—like to party.

Nearly everyone who visits London these days will be mesmerized by the city's energy, which reveals itself in layers. Whether you prefer rhythm and blues with fine French food, the gritty guitar-riff music of Camden Town, the boutique beers of East London, a pint and gourmet pizza at a local gastropub, or swanky cocktails and sushi at London's sexiest lair, London is sure to feed your fancy.

PLANNING

GETTING AROUND

If you're out late, the best way to get home is by taxi (the Tube stops running around 12:30 am Monday–Saturday and midnight on Sunday), though the city's night buses are largely safe and reliable. The best place to hail a taxi is at the front door of one of the major hotels; you can also have the staff at your last stop of the evening call one for you. Avoid unlicensed taxis that tout for business around closing time.

LIQUOR AND SMOKING LAWS

Laws now allow London drinking establishments to extend their opening hours beyond the traditional 11 pm closing, and smoking is banned. Most pubs and bars still close by midnight or a few short hours later, and, in general, you'll find yourself drinking in environs that are healthier and more pleasant than was the case in the past.

REGENT'S PARK

Albany Rd.

HAMPSTEAD
villagey pubs for long Sunday lunches

ISLINGTON
off-West-End theaters and fun bar scene

CLERKENWELL
urban cutting edge

Gray's Inn Rd.

Clerkenwell Rd.

NOTTING HILL
arty but smart and rich-hip drinking holes

Euston Rd.

BLOOMSBURY
heritage and learning

Albany St.

Gt. Portland St.

Portland Pl.

Tottenham Court Rd.

Marylebone Rd.

Baker St.

Wigmore St.

Oxford St.

...water Rd.

New Oxford St.

Holborn

HOXTON
arty and on the pulse

Kingsway

Fleet St.

FITZROVIA
secret chic

Charing Cross Rd.

OXFORD CIRCUS

SOHO
lowlife and highlife, music and dance

COVENT GARDEN
a drink before the show

...ych   Strand

Victoria Embankment

Waterloo Br.

MAYFAIR
wine and spirits

New Bond St.

Regent St.

Pall Mall

HYDE PARK

ST JAMES'S
jacket required

SOUTH BANK
real ale, real food

Stamford St.

Waterloo Rd.

Piccadilly

Green Park

The Mall

St. James's Park

Whitehall

River Thames

Knightsbridge

Constitution Hill

Birdcage Walk

Westminster Br.

Westminster Bridge Rd.

KNIGHTSBRIDGE
hotel bar martinis

Sloane St.

WESTMINSTER

Lambeth Palace Rd.

HAMMERSMITH
relaxed and upmarket, evenings by the river

BELGRAVIA
hidden mews gems

Buckingham Palace Rd.

Victoria St.

Horseferry Rd.

Lambeth Rd.

LAMBETH

Kennington Rd.

King's Rd.

Pimlico Rd.

VICTORIA

Wilton Rd.

Vauxhall Br. Rd.

Millbank

Albert Embankment

Lambeth Br.

CHELSEA
sophisticated and moneyed

Kennington Park Rd.

0   1/2 mile
0   1/2 km

CAN I TAKE MY KIDS TO THE PUB?

As pubs increasingly emphasize what's coming out of the kitchen alongside what's flowing from the tap, bringing the kids is more of an option. The law dictates that children 14 to 17 may enter a pub but are not permitted to purchase or drink alcohol, and children under 14 are not permitted in the bar area of a pub unless the pub has a "Children's Certificate" and the kids are accompanied by an adult. Some pubs have a section set aside for families, especially during the day, but many don't allow children in the evening.

WHAT TO WEAR

As a general rule, you won't see too many people in the upscale London nightspots wearing jeans and sneakers. People are more likely to dress down than up for an evening in the pub.

FIND OUT WHAT'S PLAYING WHERE

Because today's cool spot is often tomorrow's forgotten or closed venue, check out the weekly listings in the *Evening Standard* (⊕ *www.standard. co.uk*) and, especially, *Time Out* (⊕ *www.timeout.com/london*). Other websites to consult are ⊕ *www.londontown.com*, ⊕ *www.allinlondon. co.uk*, and ⊕ *www.viewlondon.co.uk*. Although many clubs are for under-thirties, there are plenty of others that are popular with patrons of all ages and types. A particularly useful website for clubs and club nights is ⊕ *www.residentadvisor.net.*

PUBS

Pubs are where Londoners go to hang out, see and be seen, act out the drama of life, and, for some, occasionally drink themselves into varying degrees of oblivion. The pub is still a vital part of London life, though many of the traditions of the pub experience are evolving. There are few better places to meet Londoners in their local habitat. There are somewhere around 4,000 pubs in London—some are dark and woody, others plain and functional, a few still have original Victorian etched glass, Edwardian panels, and art nouveau carvings.

Not long ago, before the smoking ban, pubs tended to be smoky, male-dominated places with a couple of ubiquitous beers on tap and the only available food a packet of salt-and-vinegar-flavor crisps (potato chips). All that has changed. Gastropub fever swept through London around the turn of the 21st century and at many places, char-grills are installed in the kitchen and inventive pub grub is on the menu. A new wave of enthusiasm for craft beers is now having a similar effect on pubs' liquid sustenance.

The big decision is what to drink. The beer of choice among Britons is **"bitter,"** lightly fermented with an amber color that gets its bitterness from hops. It's usually served at cellar temperature (that is, cooler than room temperature but neither chilled, nor, as common misconception would have it, warm). **Real ales,** served from wooden kegs and made without chilling, filtering, or pasteurization, are flatter than other bitters and are enjoying a renaissance. Many small London breweries have sprung up in recent years, and bottled designer and American beers can be found in most bars across London. **Stouts,** like Guinness, are a meal in themselves and something of an acquired taste—they have a dark, caramel-infused flavor and look like thickened flat Coke with a frothy top. Chilled **lagers,** most familiar to American drinkers, are light in color and car-

bonated. ■TIP➔ What Americans call beer, the British call lager, the most commonly served of which are from continental Europe.

Many English pubs are owned by chains such as Mitchells and Butlers, Punch Taverns, or Samuel Smith, and are tenanted. Most are not obviously branded and retain at least some independence. Independently owned pubs, sometimes called "free houses," tend to offer a more extensive selection of beer. Other potations available include apple-based **ciders,** ranging from sweet to dry and from alcoholic to very alcoholic (Irish cider, served over ice, is now also ubiquitous), and **shandies,** a mix of beer and lemonade. Friendly pubs will usually be happy to give you a taste of the brew of your choice before you order.

The list below offers a few pubs selected for interesting beer, historical interest, a pleasant garden, music, or good food, but you might just as happily adopt your own temporary "local."

16

MAYFAIR

The pubs in this central London neighborhood tend to be as smart as the people that frequent them, but you'll find plenty of characterful, informal establishments, too.

Audley. Big, smart, old-school, and a little on the brash side, the Audley makes up in friendly atmosphere what it lacks in charm. There's a good selection of beer on tap, and it's far enough away from the tourist hot spots that, on the right day, it can feel like a village pub. ⊠ *41–43 Mount St., Mayfair* ☎ *020/7499–1843* ⊕ *www.taylor-walker.co.uk* Ⓜ *Bond St., Green Park.*

Fodor's Choice ★ **Punch Bowl.** In a quiet corner of Mayfair, the cozy little Punch Bowl has a worn wood floor and well-spoken staff dressed in pale checked shirts. The pub dates from 1750 and the interior remains steadfastly old-fashioned, with a painting of Churchill, candles, polished dark wood, and engraved windows. Try the place's eponymous ale, made specially in Scotland by Caledonian. A special dining area at the rear buzzes at lunchtime with locals who come for the upscale English pub grub. ⊠ *41 Farm St., Mayfair* ☎ *020/7493–6841* ⊕ *www.punchbowllondon.com* Ⓜ *Green Park, Bond St.*

SOHO AND COVENT GARDEN

Traditional British "boozers" stand side-by-side with informal continental-style drinking dens in this buzzing central neighborhood. Drop by for a late drink and you may find yourself rubbing shoulders with musicians and actors from the West End's many theaters.

SOHO

French House. In the pub where the French Resistance convened during World War II, Soho hipsters and eccentrics rub shoulders now with theater people and the literati—more than shoulders, actually, because this tiny, tricolor-waving, photograph-lined pub is almost always packed. Note that in French style, beer is served in half-pints only. If you're around on July 14, come and join in the rapturous Bastille Day celebrations. ⊠ *49 Dean St., Soho* ☎ *020/7437–2477* ⊕ *www.frenchhousesoho. com* Ⓜ *Tottenham Court Rd.*

COVENT GARDEN

Harp. This is the sort of friendly little local you might find on some out-of-the-way backstreet, except that it's right in the middle of town, between Trafalgar Square and Covent Garden. As a result, the Harp can get crowded, especially since it was named British pub of the year by the Campaign for Real Ale, but the squeeze is worth it for the excellent beer (there are usually eight carefully chosen ales, often including a London micro-brewery) and a no-frills menu of high-quality British sausages, cooked behind the bar. ⊠ *47 Chandos Pl., Covent Garden* ☎ *020/7836–0291* ⊕ *www.harpcoventgarden.com* Ⓜ *Charing Cross.*

Lamb & Flag. This refreshingly un-gentrified 17th-century pub was once known as the Bucket of Blood because the upstairs room was used as a ring for bare-knuckle boxing. Now it's a friendly—and bloodless—place, serving food and real ale. It's on the edge of Covent Garden, up a hidden alley off Garrick Street. ⊠ *33 Rose St., Covent Garden* ☎ *020/7497–9504* ⊕ *www.lambandflagcoventgarden.co.uk* Ⓜ *Covent Garden.*

White Hart. Claiming to be the oldest licensed pub in London, this friendly, family-owned place on Drury Lane had already been here for more than 500 years when it served highwayman Dick Turpin in 1739, just before he was hanged. Nowadays it is one of the best places to mix with cast and crew of the stage, thanks to close relationships with West End theaters. A female-friendly environment, a bright skylight above the lounge area, and house-made pub fare make the White Hart a particularly sociable spot. ⊠ *191 Drury La., Covent Garden* ☎ *020/7242–2317* ⊕ *www.whitehartdrurylane.co.uk* Ⓜ *Holborn, Covent Garden, Tottenham Court Rd.*

BLOOMSBURY, HOLBORN, AND FITZROVIA

The gorgeous historic pubs in this literary neighborhood attract tourists in the daytime and huge crowds of after-work drinkers in the early evening. They tend to quiet down as the night advances, making this area a great spot for a relaxing evening out.

BLOOMSBURY

The Lamb. Charles Dickens and his contemporaries drank here, but today's enthusiastic clientele make sure this intimate and eternally popular pub avoids the pitfalls of feeling too old-fashioned. For private chats at the bar, you can close a delicate etched-glass "snob screen" to the bar staff, opening it only when you fancy another pint. ⊠ *94 Lamb's Conduit St., Bloomsbury* ☎ *020/7405–0713* ⊕ *www.youngs. co.uk* Ⓜ *Russell Sq.*

Museum Tavern. Across the street from the British Museum, this friendly and classy Victorian pub makes an ideal resting place after the rigors of the culture trail. Karl Marx unwound here after a hard day in the Library. He could have spent his *Kapital* on any of 15 well-kept beers available on tap. ⊠ *49 Great Russell St., Bloomsbury* ☎ *020/7242–8987* ⊕ *www.taylor-walker.co.uk* Ⓜ *Tottenham Court Rd., Holborn.*

16

The Queen's Larder. The royal associated with this tiny pub is Queen Charlotte, who is said to have stored food here for her "mad" husband, George III, when he was being treated nearby. The interior preserves its antique feel, with dark wood and old posters, and in the evenings fills up quickly with office workers and students. In good weather, you might prefer to grab one of the seats outdoors. ⊠ *1 Queen's Sq., Bloomsbury* ☎ *020/7837 5627* ⊕ *www.queenslarder.co.uk* Ⓜ *Russell Sq.*

HOLBORN

Holborn Whippet. An impressive number of craft beers are served from unmarked taps set into a brick column behind the bar in this new-breed London pub. Names of the brews are all chalked onto boards, while empty barrels outside testify to the popularity of the best; lunch and supper are served every day. It's popular, especially when nearby offices empty out in early evening, but you can sit outside under umbrellas (with heaters in winter) on small, ornate, pedestrian-only Sicilian Avenue. Inside, it's a deliberately plain affair, with little to detract from the liquid experience. ⊠ *Sicilian Ave., Holborn* ☎ *020/3137–9937* ⊕ *holbornwhippet.com* Ⓜ *Holborn.*

Princess Louise. This fine, popular pub is an exquisite museum piece of a Victorian interior, with glazed tiles and intricately engraved glass screens that divide the bar area into cozy little annexes. It's not all show, either: There's a good selection of excellent-value Yorkshire real ales from the Samuel Smith's brewery. ⊠ *208 High Holborn, Holborn* ☎ *020/7405–8816* Ⓜ *Holborn.*

FITZROVIA

Fodor's Choice ★ **Draft House Charlotte.** The tiniest of a microchain of craft-beer pubs, Draft House Charlotte is well placed for a quick pint of delicious beer (there are dozens of varieties available, both on tap and bottled) en route between the retail juggernaut of Oxford Street and the high culture of Bloomsbury. The food is good, too, with top-notch burgers the specialty, and staff ready to advise on the best beverage to pair with your meal. There's not much space here, though, so you may have to perch on a tiny wooden stool between the young, fashionable people who hang out here. ⊠ *43 Goodge St., Fitzrovia* ☎ *020/7323–9361* ⊕ *www.drafthouse.co.uk* Ⓜ *Goodge St.*

CLERKENWELL AND THE CITY

Workers from The City's many finance firms pour into the neighborhood's pubs at the end of the day, but by 8 pm the party is pretty much over and you'll have no trouble finding a place to sit. It's always worth ducking down a side street as this is where some of the area's most charming establishments can be found.

Fodor'sChoice ★ **The Blackfriar.** A step from Blackfriars Tube station, this spectacular pub has an Arts and Crafts interior that is entertainingly, satirically ecclesiastical, with inlaid mother-of-pearl, wood carvings, stained glass, and marble pillars all over the place. In spite of the finely lettered temperance tracts on view just below the reliefs of monks, fairies, and friars, there is a nice group of ales on tap from independent brewers. The 20th-century poet Sir John Betjeman once led a successful campaign to save the pub from demolition. ⊠ *174 Queen Victoria St., The City* ☎ *020/7236–5474* ⊕ *www. nicholsonspubs.co.uk/theblackfriarblackfriarslondon* Ⓜ *Blackfriars.*

Fodor'sChoice ★ **Craft Beer Company.** With 37 beers on tap and 300 more in bottles (some brewed exclusively for the Craft Beer Company), the main problem here is knowing where to start. Luckily, friendly and knowledgeable staff are happy to advise or give tasters—or why not sign up for a guided tasting session? A huge chandelier and a mirrored ceiling lend antique charm to the interior, and a smattering of tourists and beer pilgrims break up the crowds of Leather Lane workers and locals. ⊠ *82 Leather La., Clerkenwell* ⊕ *thecraftbeerco.com* Ⓜ *Chancery La.*

Fodor'sChoice ★ **Jerusalem Tavern.** Owned by the well-respected St. Peter's Brewery from Suffolk, the Jerusalem Tavern is one-of-a-kind: small, and endearingly eccentric. Ancient Delft-style tiles meld with wood and concrete in a converted watchmaker and jeweler's shop dating back to the 18th century. The beer, both bottled and on tap, is some of the best available anywhere in London. It's loved by Londoners and is often busy, especially after work. ⊠ *55 Britton St., Clerkenwell* ☎ *020/7490–4281* ⊕ *www. stpetersbrewery.co.uk/london-pub* Ⓜ *Farringdon.*

Viaduct Tavern. Queen Victoria opened the nearby Holborn Viaduct in 1869, and this eponymous pub honored the road bridge by serving its first pint the same year. Much of the Victorian decoration is still extant, with gilded mirrors, carved wood, and engraved glass. The tavern's haunted reputation stems from its proximity to the former Newgate Prison, site of London's gallows in the 19th century, which once stood on the site. Ex-prison cells in the basement can be seen with a free tour before or after the lunchtime rush and before 5 pm. There are usually three or four ales on tap; lunch is also served. ⊠ *126 Newgate St., The City* ☎ *020/7600–1863* ⊕ *viaducttavern.co.uk* ☉ *Closed weekends* Ⓜ *St. Paul's.*

PUB NAMES

Pictorial signs traditionally helped illiterate customers identify establishments; these popular names have an interesting historical element behind them.

The many terms related to the coat of arms reflect the fundamental role of heraldry in England's past. Other pub names highlight the importance of specific events (the Trafalgar), and others still reflect myths and legends (Robin Hood). Royal names are ubiquitous, such as the Crown—supposedly the most common pub name in England, with more than 700 establishments—which became popular after the Restoration of the Monarchy in 1660.

Ye Olde Cheshire Cheese. Yes, this extremely historic pub (it dates from 1667, the year after the Great Fire of London) is full of tourists, but it deserves a visit for its sawdust-covered floors, low wood-beam ceilings, and the 14th-century crypt of Whitefriars' monastery under the cellar bar. This was the most regular of Dr. Johnson's and Dickens's many locals. Food is served. ✉ *145 Fleet St., The City* ☎ *020/7353–6170* ☾ *Closed Sun.* Ⓜ *Blackfriars.*

Ye Olde Mitre. Hidden off the side of 8 Hatton Gardens, this cozy pub's roots go back to 1546, though it was rebuilt around 1782. Originally built for the staff of the Bishop of Ely, whose London residence was next door, it remained officially part of Cambridgeshire until the 20th century. It's a friendly little labyrinth-like place, with a fireplace, well-kept ales, wooden beams, and traditional bar snacks. ✉ *1 Ely Ct., The City* ☎ *020/7405–4751* ⊕ *yeoldemitreholburn.co.uk* ☾ *Closed weekends* Ⓜ *Chancery La.*

EAST LONDON

East London is better known these days for its bars and clubs than for its pubs, but in historic neighborhoods such as Spitalfields and Wapping there's a cozy old drinking den around practically every corner.

Prospect of Whitby. Named after a ship, this is London's oldest riverside pub, dating from around 1520. Once upon a time it was called the Devil's Tavern because of the lowlife criminals—thieves and smugglers—who congregated here. Ornamented with pewter ware and nautical objects, this much-loved "boozer" has a terrace with views of the Thames, from where boat trips often point it out. ✉ *57 Wapping Wall, East End* ☎ *020/7481–1095* ⊕ *www.taylor-walker.co.uk* Ⓜ *Wapping; DLR: Shadwell.*

16

SOUTH OF THE THAMES

Head to the area around Borough Market—one of London's oldest neighborhoods—for lively historic pubs where locals and tourists jostle for craft ales and gourmet snacks.

Fodor'sChoice
★

Anchor & Hope. One of London's most popular gastropubs, the Anchor & Hope doesn't take reservations (except for the three-course set Sunday lunch which begins at 2 pm). Would-be diners snake around the red-walled, wooden-floored pub, kept happy by some good real ales and a fine wine list as they wait for at least 45 minutes for a table. The excellent, meaty food is old-fashioned English—think salt cod, tripe, and chips (fries)—with a few modern twists. ⊠ *36 The Cut, South Bank* ☎ *020/7928–9898* ⊕ *www.charleswells.co.uk* Ⓜ *Southwark*.

Market Porter. Opposite the foodie treasures of Borough Market, this atmospheric pub opens at 6 am (weekdays) for the stallholders, and always seems busy. Remarkably, the place manages to remain relaxed, with helpful staff and happy customers spilling out onto the road right through the year. The wide selection of real ales is lovingly tended. The pub was used as a set for one of the Harry Potter movies. ⊠ *9 Stoney St., Borough* ☎ *020/7407–2495* ⊕ *www.markettaverns.co.uk* Ⓜ *London Bridge*.

The Mayflower. An atmospheric 17th-century riverside inn (rebuilt in the following century) with exposed beams and a terrace near the onetime berth of the famous ship on which the Pilgrims sailed to what became the American colonies. The pub has a heated jetty where customers can sit outside; alternatively, opt to enjoy the wood-beamed interiors, although this can get quite packed with sightseers. ⊠ *117 Rotherhithe St., South Bank* ☎ *020/7237–4088* ⊕ *themayflowerrotherhithe.com* Ⓜ *Rotherhithe*.

CHELSEA AND BELGRAVIA

Pubs in this upmarket central west neighborhood range from classy modern affairs with impressive wine lists and sharing platters to tiny local institutions guaranteed to make you feel like you've stepped back in time.

CHELSEA

The Antelope. Just around the corner from chic Sloane Square is the perfect spot to grab an unpretentious pint. Wood paneling and comfy seating create a snug environment, and there's a fancier dining room upstairs. ⊠ *22 Eaton Terr., Chelsea* ☎ *020/7824–8512* ⊕ *www.antelope-eaton-terrace.co.uk* Ⓜ *Sloane Sq.*

BELGRAVIA

The Nag's Head. The landlord of this idiosyncratic little mews pub in Belgravia runs a tight ship, and no cell phones are allowed. If that sounds like misery, the lovingly collected artifacts (including antique penny arcade games) that decorate every inch of the place, high-quality beer, and old-fashioned pub grub should make up for it. ⊠ *53 Kinnerton St., Belgravia* ☎ *020/7235–1135* Ⓜ *Knightsbridge, Hyde Park Corner.*

NOTTING HILL

The line between pub and bar is frequently blurred in this trendy area on the west side of the capital, with the emphasis on good—often haute—food, sleek style, and extensive wine lists.

The Cow. Crowds head to this chic mix of fun, haute food, and friendly, retro style for Guinness and oysters, either enjoying them in the unpretentious downstairs bar or the upstairs more formal restaurant. The food is excellent, if pricey for pub grub, with lots of seafood and steaks (and sometimes a mix, as in the smoked eel with mash and bacon). The atmosphere? Always warm, welcoming, and buzzing. ⊠ *89 Westbourne Rd., Notting Hill* ☏ *020/7221–0021* ⊕ *www.thecowlondon.co.uk* Ⓜ *Royal Oak, Westbourne Park.*

JAZZ AND BLUES

Jazz in London is highly eclectic. You can expect anything from danceable, smooth tunes played at a supper club to groovy New Orleans–style blues to exotic world-beat rhythms, which can be heard at some of the less central venues throughout the capital. London hosts the **London Jazz Festival** (⊕ *www. efglondonjazzfestival.org.uk*) in November, which showcases top and emerging artists in experimental jazz. The **Ealing Jazz Festival** (⊕ *www.ealing.gov.uk*), at the end of July, claims to be the biggest free jazz event in Europe.

16

REGENT'S PARK AND HAMPSTEAD

London's village-like northern neighborhoods—Hampstead, Highgate, and Primrose Hill, to name a few—all boast fantastic local boozers where you can easily while away an afternoon. Camden Town has more of a buzz to it and attracts a younger crowd.

HAMPSTEAD

The Holly Bush. A short walk up the hill from Hampstead Tube station, the friendly Holly Bush was a country pub before London spread this far north. It retains something of a rural feel, with stripped wooden floors and an open fire, and is an intimate place to enjoy great ales and organic and free-range pub food. Try the homemade pork scratchings and pickled eggs. ⊠ *22 Holly Mount, Hampstead* ☏ *020/7435–2892* ⊕ *www.hollybushhampstead.co.uk* Ⓜ *Hampstead.*

Magdala. Now a sedate gastropub located on the edge of Hampstead Heath with chesterfield sofas, fireplace, and small, shady garden, the Magdala has a racier past. In 1955, nightclub hostess Ruth Ellis shot her lover just outside the pub. She turned herself in and was subsequently (and controversially) executed, becoming the last woman in Britain to be hanged. The bullet holes are still there next to pub's entrance, along with an explanatory plaque. ⊠ *2A South Hill Park, Hampstead* ☏ *020/7435–2503* ⊕ *www.the-magdala.com* Ⓜ *Overground: Hampstead Heath.*

Spaniards Inn. Ideal as a refueling point when you're on a hike in Hampstead Heath, this historic, country-style, oak-beam pub has a gorgeous garden—the scene of the tea party in Dickens's *Pickwick Papers*. Dick Turpin, the highwayman, frequented the inn before Dickens's time, and Shelley, Keats, and Byron hung out here as well. The place is extremely popular, especially on Sunday, when Londoners roll in. It's canine friendly, too—there's even a dog wash in the garden. ⊠ *Spaniards Rd., Hampstead* ☎ *020/8731–8406* ⊕ *www.thespaniardshampstead.co.uk* Ⓜ *Hampstead.*

Wells. Although originally built to offer "facilities for the celebration of unpremeditated and clandestine marriages," today this pub is the epitome of Hampstead gentility. It's in a handsome Georgian building, with working fireplace, leather sofas, backgammon (as opposed to darts), and as much emphasis on wine as beer. The upstairs dining room serves good modern British dishes, like grilled scallops with bacon or sea bass with fennel. ⊠ *30 Well Walk, Hampstead* ☎ *020/7794–3785* ⊕ *www.thewellshampstead.co.uk* Ⓜ *Hampstead.*

THE THAMES UPSTREAM

A pint in a riverside pub is a London must, and the capital's western reaches offer some truly picturesque drinking opportunities. Pick a traditional establishment and you'll feel like you've ventured far from the Big Smoke.

RICHMOND

Roebuck. Perched on top of Richmond Hill, the Roebuck has perhaps the best view of any pub in London. The most sought-after seats are the benches found directly across the road, which look out over the Thames as it winds its way into the countryside below. Friendly and surprisingly unpretentious, given its lofty surrounds, it is well worth the long climb up the hill from the center of Richmond. ⊠ *130 Richmond Hill, Richmond* ☎ *020/8948–2329* ⊕ *www.taylor-walker.co.uk* Ⓜ *Richmond. National Rail: Richmond.*

HAMMERSMITH

Fodor'sChoice
★

Blue Anchor. This unaltered Georgian pub has been seen in the movie *Sliding Doors* and was the site where *The Planets* composer Gustav Holst wrote his *Hammersmith Suite*. Sit out by the river, or shelter inside with a good ale. ⊠ *13 Lower Mall, Hammersmith* ☎ *020/8748–5774* ⊕ *www.blueanchorlondon.com* Ⓜ *Hammersmith.*

Dove Inn. Read the list of famous ex-regulars, from Charles II and Nell Gwyn to Ernest Hemingway, as you wait for a beer at this smart, comely, and popular 16th-century riverside pub. An Irish folk band plays on Monday nights, squeezing into the miniature front bar. If (as is often the case) the Dove is too full, stroll upstream along the bank to the Old Ship or the Blue Anchor. ⊠ *19 Upper Mall, Hammersmith* ☎ *020/8748–9474* ⊕ *www.dovehammersmith.co.uk* Ⓜ *Hammersmith.*

NIGHTLIFE

As is true of nearly all cosmopolitan centers, the pace with which bars and clubs go in and out of fashion in London is mind-boggling. New trends, likewise, emerge all time. In one recent development, the dreaded velvet rope has been usurped by the doorbell-ringing mystique of members-only drinking clubs. Some of the city's most talked-about nightlife spots these days are those attached to some of the best restaurants and hotels—no wonder, when you consider the increased popularity of London cuisine in international circles. Moreover, the gay scene in London continues to flourish. One constant on the nightlife scene is variety. The understated glamour of north London's Primrose Hill, which makes movie stars feel so at ease, might be considered dull by the übertrendy club goers of London's East End. Likewise, the price of a pint in Chelsea would be dubbed blasphemous by the musicians and poets of multicultural Peckham.

Whatever your pleasure, however your whim turns come evening, chances are you'll find what you're looking for in London's ever-changing arena of activity and invention.

16

WESTMINSTER, ST. JAMES'S, AND ROYAL LONDON

Elegant drinking holes catering to London's political and social elites abound in these central neighborhoods. Streets that are thronged with tourists and workers by day quiet down by the evening, leaving the area to its few residents and a handful of sophisticated drinker and diners.

WESTMINSTER

BARS

Bedford and Strand. The wine bar enjoyed something of a renaissance in the first decade of the 21st century in London, and this is one of the best of a new generation. It's sunk atmospherically down below the streets of Covent Garden, with dark wood and hanging shades; the wine list is short but well chosen, the service is faultless, and the bistro food is created with plenty of care. ⌗ *1A Bedford St., Charing Cross* ☏ *020/7836–3033* ⊕ *www.bedford-strand.com* ☉ *Weekdays noon–midnight, Sat. 5 pm–midnight* Ⓜ *Charing Cross.*

Cinnamon Club. In the basement of what was once Old Westminster Library, the Club Bar of this contemporary Indian restaurant (treat yourself to a superb curry) has Bollywood scenes projected onto the glass back wall, Asian-theme cocktails (mango mojitos, Delhi mules), delicious bar snacks, and a clientele that includes fashionable young politicos. Upstairs, the Library Bar also serves cocktails through the day. ⌗ *The Old Westminster Library, Great Smith St., Westminster* ☏ *020/7222–2555* ⊕ *www.cinnamonclub.com* ☉ *Mon.–Sat. 4 pm–midnight* Ⓜ *Westminster.*

Fodor'sChoice
★ **Gordon's Wine Bar.** Nab a rickety table in the atmospheric, vaulted interior of what claims to be the oldest wine bar in London, or fight for standing room in the long pedestrianized alleyway that runs alongside it. Either way, the mood is always cheery as a diverse crowd sips on more than 60 different wines, ports, and sherries. Tempting cheese

and meat plates are great for sharing. ✉ *47 Villiers St., Westminster* ☎ *020/7930–1408* ⊕ *www.gordonswinebar.com* ⏱ *Mon.–Sat. 11 am–11 pm; Sun. 12 pm–10 pm* Ⓜ *Charing Cross, Embankment.*

ST. JAMES'S

BARS

Fodor's Choice ★ **American Bar.** Festooned with a chin-dropping array of club ties, signed celebrity photographs, sporting mementos, and baseball caps, this sensational hotel cocktail bar has superb martinis. The name dates from the 1930s, when hotel bars in London started to cater to growing numbers of Americans crossing the Atlantic in ocean liners, but it wasn't until the 1970s, when a customer left a small carved wooden eagle, that the collection of paraphernalia was started. ✉ *Stafford Hotel, 16–18 St. James's Pl., St. James's* ☎ *020/7493–0111* ⊕ *www.thestaffordhotel. co.uk* ⏱ *Daily 11:30 am–11 pm* Ⓜ *Green Park.*

MAYFAIR

Bars in this upmarket central neighborhood—many of which can be found within luxury hotels—attract a polished crowd. Cocktails, fine wines, and rare aged spirits are the tipples of choice.

BARS

Claridge's Bar. This elegant Mayfair meeting place remains unpretentious even when it brims with beautiful people. The bar has an art deco heritage made hip by the sophisticated touch of designer David Collins. A library of rare champagnes and brandies as well as a delicious choice of traditional and exotic cocktails—try the Flapper or the Black Pearl—will occupy your taste buds. Request a glass of vintage Cristal in the darkly moody Fumoir. ✉ *55 Brook St., Mayfair* ☎ *020/7629–8860* ⊕ *www.claridges. co.uk* ⏱ *Mon.–Sat. noon–1 am, Sun. noon–midnight* Ⓜ *Bond St.*

SOHO AND COVENT GARDEN

The center of town is famous for its vibrant gay scene, atmospheric music and cabaret venues, and acclaimed comedy clubs. A spate of recent bar openings is bringing a new buzz to Covent Garden's nightlife scene.

SOHO

BARS

Le Beaujolais. Around 60 lovingly selected French wines are available here, and you can snack on olives, charcuterie, and homemade *croque monsieur* (grilled ham and cheese) sandwiches while snug and warm under the bottle-laden ceiling as a funky blues sound track plays. The romantic, shabby-around-the-edges feel and authentic French insouciance may come as a surprise in the heart of tourist-centric London. ✉ *25 Litchfield St., Soho* ☎ *020/7836–2955* ⏱ *Closed Sun.* Ⓜ *Leicester Sq.*

Opium Cocktail and Dim Sum Parlour. London's passion for speakeasy-style bars shows no sign of flagging and this opium den–themed nightspot in the heart of Chinatown is a particularly fun example of the genre. An innovative cocktail list draws on unusual Eastern ingredients—sweet red bean puree in The Long March, for instance—and tasty dim sum is served until late. Interiors evoke colonial-era China, with plenty of

THE GAY SCENE

The U.K. capital's gay and lesbian culture is as thriving as it is in New York or Los Angeles, with Soho serving as the traditional hub, though "Voho," previously unfashionable Vauxhall, south of the river, is the new upstart area of gay London.

Clubs in London cater to almost every desire, whether that be the suited-up Tommy Hilfiger–look-alike scene, cruisers taking on dingy dives, flamboyant drag shows, lesbian tea dances, or themed fetish nights.

There's also a cornucopia of queer theater and performance art that runs throughout the year. Whatever your tastes, you'll be able to satisfy them with a night on the town in London.

Choices are admittedly much better for males than females here; although many of the gay clubs are female-friendly, those catering strictly to lesbians are in the minority.

The British Film Institute puts on the BFI London Lesbian and Gay Film Festival (⊕ www.bfi.org.uk/flare) in late March and early April every year.

Pride London in June (an annual event that was originally largely political but these days encompasses a parade, sports, art, comedy, theater, music, cabaret, and dance) welcomes anyone and everyone, and claimed a million participants in 2010. This extravagant pageant spirals its way through London's streets, with major events taking place in Trafalgar Square and Leicester Square, then culminates in Victoria Embankment with ticketed parties continuing on afterward. See ⊕ prideinlondon.org for details.

For up-to-date listings, consult *Time Out* (⊕ www.timeout.com/london/lgbt), *Boyz* (⊕ www.boyz.co.uk), *Gay Times* (⊕ www.gaytimes.co.uk), *Attitude* (⊕ www.attitude.co.uk), or the lesbian monthly *Diva* (⊕ www.divamag.co.uk).

BARS, CAFÉS, AND PUBS

Most bars in London are gay-friendly, though there are a number of cafés and pubs that are known as gay hangouts after hours. The latest serve drinks until 3 am (11 pm on Sunday).

CLUBS

Many of London's best gay dance clubs are in mixed clubs like Fabric on theme nights designated for gay clubbers.

Almost all dance clubs in London are gay-friendly, but if you want to cruise or mingle only with other gay people, it's best to call ahead or check website listings.

secret cubbies for moody tête-à-têtes. ⊠ *The Jade Door, 15–16 Gerrard St., Soho* ☏ *020/7734–7276* ⊕ *www.opiumchinatown.com* ☾ *Closed Sun.* Ⓜ *Leicester Sq.*

Fodor'sChoice **Sketch.** One seat never looks like the next at this downright extraordinary
★ collection of esoteric living-room bars. The exclusive Parlour, a patisserie during the day, exudes plenty of rarefied charm; the intimate East Bar at the back is reminiscent of a sci-fi film set; and in the Glade it's permanently sunset in a forest. The restrooms are surely London's quirkiest. ⊠ *9 Conduit St., Soho* ☏ *020/7659–4500* ⊕ *www.sketch.uk.com* ☾ *Parlour weekdays 8 am–2 am, Sat. 10 am–2 am, Sun. 10 am–midnight; The Glade Mon.–Thurs. 1 pm–2 am, Fri. and Sat. noon–2 am, Sun. noon–midnight; East Bar daily 6:30 pm–2 am* Ⓜ *Oxford Circus.*

16

DANCE CLUBS

Disco. At the end of an unlikely looking alley in the Newburgh Quarter is the entrance to Disco, one of central London's most fun new clubs. The dance floor is the focus at this unpretentious basement joint, where staff dressed as airline stewards invite you to "check-in" your coat. Technically it's members only, so email ahead to get your name on the list. You must be over 21 to enter. ⊠ *13 Kingly Court, Soho* ☎ *020/7299–1222* ⊕ *www.disco-london.com* ⊠ *£20* ⊗ *Wed.–Sat. 11 pm–3:30 am* Ⓜ *Piccadilly Circus, Oxford Circus.*

COMEDY AND CABARET

Comedy Store. Known as the birthplace of alternative comedy, this is where the United Kingdom's funniest stand-ups have cut their teeth before being launched onto prime-time TV. Comedy Store Players, a team with six comedians doing improvisation with audience suggestions, entertain on Wednesday and Sunday; the Cutting Edge steps in every Tuesday. Thursday, Friday, and Saturday have the best stand-up acts. There's also a bar with food. Note that children under 18 are not admitted to this venue. ⊠ *1A Oxendon St., Soho* ☎ *0844/871-7699 ticket and booking line* ⊕ *www.thecomedystore.co.uk* ⊠ *£14–£28* ⊗ *Shows daily 7:30 or 8 pm, with extra shows Fri. and Sat. at 11 pm* Ⓜ *Piccadilly Circus, Leicester Sq.*

100 Club. Since this small club opened in 1942, many of the greats have played here, from Glenn Miller and Louis Armstrong to The Who and the Sex Pistols. Saved from closure in 2010 by a campaign led by Sir Paul McCartney, the space now reverberates to jazz, '60s R&B, and northern soul. ⊠ *100 Oxford St., Soho* ☎ *020/7636–0933* ⊕ *www. the100club.co.uk* ⊠ *£7–£15* ⊗ *Fri.–Sun. 7:30 pm–late; weekdays vary, depending on gigs* Ⓜ *Oxford Circus, Tottenham Court Rd.*

ECLECTIC MUSIC

12 Bar Club. This small and rough-and-ready acoustic club hosts notable singer-songwriters. Four different acts of new folk, contemporary country, blues, and even ska and punk perform each night in the intimate venue. There's a good selection of bottled beer and gastropub food here. ⊠ *26 Denmark St., Soho* ☎ *020/7240–2622 tickets, 020/7240–2120* ⊕ *www.12barclub.com* ⊠ *£5–£10* ⊗ *Mon.–Sat. 7 pm–3 am, Sun. 7 pm–12:30 am* Ⓜ *Tottenham Court Rd.*

JAZZ AND BLUES

Ain't Nothin' but . . . The Blues Bar. This sweaty, fun place does exactly what its name suggests. Local musicians, as well as some notable names, squeeze onto the tiny stage and there's good bar food of the chili-and-gumbo variety. Most weekday nights there's no cover. ⊠ *20 Kingly St., Soho* ☎ *020/7287–0514* ⊕ *www.aintnothinbut.co.uk* ⊠ *£5 Fri. and Sat. after 8:30 pm, otherwise free* ⊗ *Mon.–Thurs. 5 pm–1 am, Fri. 5 pm–2:30 am, Sat. 3 pm–2:30 am, Sun. 3 pm–midnight* Ⓜ *Oxford Circus.*

Fodor's Choice
★
 Pizza Express Jazz Club Soho. One of the United Kingdom's most ubiquitous pizza chains also runs a great Soho jazz venue. The dimly lighted restaurant hosts top-quality international jazz acts every night. The Italian-style thin-crust pizzas are good, too, though on the small side. ⊠ *10 Dean St., Soho* ☎ *0845/602–7017 club, 020/7437–9595 restaurant*

⊕ *www.pizzaexpresslive.com* ⊟ *£10–£25* ⊙ *Daily 11:30 am–midnight for food; music after 7:30 pm (times vary)* Ⓜ *Tottenham Court Rd.*

Ronnie Scott's. This legendary jazz club has attracted big names since the 1960s. It's usually crowded and hot, but the food and service are much better than they used to be. The mood can't be beat, even since the sad departure of the eponymous founder and saxophonist. Reservations are recommended. ⊠ *47 Frith St., Soho* ☎ *020/7439–0747* ⊕ *www.ronniescotts.co.uk* ⊟ *£25–£40 nonmembers, 20% off for members (members plus up to 3 guests free after 11 pm weekdays). Annual membership £195* ⊙ *Mon.–Sat. 6 pm–3 am, Sun. noon–4 pm and 6:30 pm–midnight* Ⓜ *Leicester Sq.*

THE GAY SCENE

Fodor's Choice **Friendly Society.** An unremarkable-looking door in a Soho alleyway leads
★ down some dingy steps into one of the most fun joints in the neighborhood. Hopping with activity almost any night of the week, the place is known for being gay yet female-friendly. The decor alone—including garden gnome stools and a ceiling covered in Barbie dolls and disco balls—is enough to lift the spirits. ⊠ *79 Wardour St., Soho* ⊙ *Mon.–Thurs. 4 pm–11:30 pm, Fri. and Sat. 4 pm–midnight, Sun. 4 pm–10:30 pm* Ⓜ *Leicester Sq.*

Ku Bar. A deliciously camp vibe, toned bar staff, and a friendly atmosphere make this one of Soho's most popular gay bars. The crowd is mostly male, but women are very welcome. Head to the quieter upstairs lounge bar for a more laid-back mood, or dance the night away at Ku Klub in the basement. There's a second branch around the corner on Frith Street. ⊠ *30 Lisle St., Soho* ☎ *020/7437–4303* ⊕ *www.ku-bar. co.uk* ⊙ *Mon.–Sat. noon–3 am, Sun. noon–midnight* Ⓜ *Leicester Sq.*

The Shadow Lounge. This fabulous little lounge and dance club glitters with faux jewels and twinkling fiber-optic lights over its sunken dance floor, which comes complete with pole for those inclined to do their thing around it. It has a serious A-list celebrity factor, with the glamorous London glitterati camping out in the VIP booth. Members are given entrance priority when the place gets full, especially on weekends, so show up early, book onto the guest list online, or prepare to wait in line. ⊠ *5–7 Brewer St., Soho* ☎ *020/7317–9270* ⊕ *www.theshadowlounge. co.uk* ⊟ *Mon. free, Tues.–Thurs. £5, Fri. and Sat. £10* ⊙ *Mon.–Sat. 10 pm–3 am* Ⓜ *Leicester Sq.*

The Yard. A corridor of kitsch leads to a surprisingly laid-back bar and spacious terrace at The Yard. This oasis of calm in the middle of Soho attracts a mixed, friendly crowd. ⊠ *57 Rupert St., Soho* ☎ *020/7437–2652* ⊕ *www.yardbar.co.uk* ⊙ *Mon.–Wed. 4 pm–11:30 pm, Thurs. 3 pm–11:30 pm, Fri. and Sat. 2 pm–midnight, Sun. 2 pm–10:30 pm* Ⓜ *Piccadilly Circus.*

COVENT GARDEN

BARS

Earlham Street Clubhouse. Reasonably priced cocktails and super-thin-crust pizzas are the order of the day at this new basement bar in Covent Garden. A fun atmosphere reigns in the main bar area, where the decor is "college kids do speakeasy," according to the manager. There

16

are plenty of cozy nooks and crannies for those more in the mood for a quiet drink. ✉ *35 Earlham St., Covent Garden* ☎ *020/7240–5142* ⊕ *www.esclubhouse.com* ⊘ *Daily noon–midnight* Ⓜ *Covent Garden.*

Terroirs. Specializing in "natural wines" (organic and sustainably produced with minimal added ingredients), Terroirs has an unusually careful selection of 200 wines from artisan French and Italian winemakers. These are served, along with delicious, relatively simple dishes: charcuterie, tapas, and more substantial French-inspired dishes, at a bar and tables in white-washed, wooden-floored environs. ✉ *5 William St., Covent Garden* ☎ *020/7036–0660* ⊕ *www.terroirswinebar.com* ⊘ *Mon.–Sat. noon–11 pm (bar menu only 3 pm–5:30 pm)* Ⓜ *Charing Cross.*

THE GAY SCENE

Fodor's Choice
★

Heaven. With the best light show on any London dance floor, Heaven is unpretentious, loud, and huge, with a labyrinth of rooms, bars, and live-music parlors. Friday and Saturday nights there's a gay comedy night (£13 in advance, 7–10 pm). Tuesday, Wednesday, and Thursday often have live performances. If you go to just one gay club in London, Heaven should be it. ✉ *The Arches, Villiers St., Covent Garden* ☎ *020/7930–2020* ⊕ *www.heavennightclub-london.com* 💳 *£4–£12* ⊘ *Mon. 11 pm–5:30 am, Tues.–Fri. 11 pm–4 am, Sat. 10:30 pm–5 am* Ⓜ *Charing Cross, Embankment.*

BLOOMSBURY, FITZROVIA, AND ISLINGTON

The ongoing redevelopment of the area around King's Cross St. Pancras station has invigorated Bloomsbury's nightlife scene and a host of new bars has recently opened. Fitzrovia, meanwhile, manages to blend sophistication, informality, and a certain edginess that's not found elsewhere in the center of town.

BLOOMSBURY

BARS

Booking Office. Taking full advantage of the soaring Victorian redbrick vaults and arches of the restored St. Pancras Renaissance Hotel, Booking Office is closer in feel to a cathedral than a traditional station bar. Seasonal cocktails using traditional English ingredients are high on flavor and low on mixers and there's also a restaurant and live music Thursday through Saturday evenings. ✉ *St. Pancras Renaissance Hotel, Euston Rd., King's Cross* ☎ *020/7841–3566* ⊕ *www.bookingofficerestaurant.com* ⊘ *Mon.–Wed. 6:30 am–1 am, Thurs. and Fri. 6:30 am–3 am, Sat. 7 am–3 am, Sun. 7 am–midnight* Ⓜ *Kings Cross St. Pancras.*

ROCK

Water Rats. This high-spirited pub hosted Bob Dylan on his 1963 tour, as well as the first Oasis gig. Alt-country, hip-hop, and indie guitar bands thrash it out most nights of the week. ✉ *328 Gray's Inn Rd., Bloomsbury* ☎ *020/7837–7269* ⊕ *www.water-rats.com* 💳 *£6 and up* ⊘ *Mon.–Thurs. 8:30 am–midnight, Fri.–Sat. 8:30 am–1 am, Sun. 4 pm–11 pm* Ⓜ *King's Cross.*

FITZROVIA

BARS

Crazy Bear. This sexy basement bar with cowhide stools and croc-skin tables feels like Casablanca in Fitzrovia. As you enter Crazy Bear, a spiral staircase leads to a mirrored parlor over which presides a 1947 Murano chandelier. But don't let the opulence fool you: Waitstaff here are warm and welcoming to an all-ages international crowd abuzz with chatter. The menu advertises high-quality Thai, Chinese, and Japanese food alongside the drinks. There's another Crazy Bear in nearby Covent Garden. ✉ *26–28 Whitfield St., Fitzrovia* ☎ *020/7631–0088* ⊕ *www. crazybeargroup.co.uk* ⊗ *Mon.–Wed. noon–midnight, Thurs.–Sat. noon–1 am* Ⓜ *Goodge St.*

The London Edition. Visitors to the new London Edition hotel are spoiled for choice when it comes to bars. High ceilings, eclectic artwork, and innovative cocktails can be found at the all-day Berners Tavern and Lobby Bar, which opens in the evening. You'll need a reservation to get into the cozy Punch Room, but the bar's reinventions of traditional (and communal) punches and the exemplary service are worth the extra effort. At the weekend there's dancing until late in the more informal Basement (guest list only; visit ⊕ *www.basementldn.com* for current lineup and contact). ✉ *10 Berners St., Fitzrovia* ☎ *020/7908–7979* ⊕ *www.edition-hotels.marriott.com/london* ⊗ *Berners Tavern daily 7 am–midnight; Lobby Bar daily 9 am–1 am; Punch Room daily 5 pm– 1 am* Ⓜ *Tottenham Court Rd., Oxford Circus.*

ISLINGTON

Exmouth Market and Upper Street are the main nightlife hot spots in this neighborhood just north and east of central London. A fun, informal vibe makes Islington a reliable going-out option.

BARS

Café Kick. This homey continental-style café-bar is open all day for meals, snacks, coffee, and cocktails. It's famous for its foosball tables, which give the place a fun, informal environment. Reductions are available on "cocktails of the month" and house beers during happy hour (4 pm–7 pm). You can reserve foosball tables in advance. There's another branch in Shoreditch. ✉ *43 Exmouth Market, Islington* ☎ *020/7837– 8077* ⊕ *www.cafekick.co.uk* ⊗ *Mon.–Thurs 11–11, Fri. and Sat. 11 am–midnight, Sun. noon–10:30 pm* Ⓜ *Angel.*

ECLECTIC

Union Chapel. The beauty of this sublime old chapel and its impressive multicultural programming make this spot one of London's best musical venues, especially for acoustic shows. Performers have included Björk, Beck, and Goldfrapp, though now you're more likely to hear lower-key alternative country, world music, and jazz, alongside poetry and literary events. ✉ *Compton Terr., Islington* ☎ *020/7226–1686 venue (no box office; ticket sales numbers vary with each event)* ⊕ *www.unionchapel. org.uk* 🎫 *Free–£25* ⊗ *Hrs vary* Ⓜ *Highbury & Islington.*

16

THE CITY

DANCE CLUBS

Fabric. This sprawling subterranean club opposite Smithfield Meat Market is a firm fixture on the London scene and is regularly voted as one of the top clubs in the world. "FabricLive" hosts drum 'n' bass, dubstep, and hip-hop crews and live acts on Friday; international big-name DJs play slow, sexy bass lines and cutting-edge music on Saturday. The devastating sound system and vibrating "bodysonic" dance floor ensure that bass riffs vibrate through your entire body. ■TIP➔ **Get there early to avoid a lengthy line up and don't wear a suit.** ⊠ *77A Charterhouse St., The City* ☎ *020/7336–8898* ⊕ *www.fabriclondon.com* ⊡ *£7–£20; discounts after 3 or 4 am* ⊘ *Fri. 10 pm–6 am, Sat. 11 pm–8 am, Sun. 11 pm–6 am* Ⓜ *Farringdon.*

EAST LONDON

East London's bar scene is ever evolving, with the trendy crowd constantly pushing farther east in search of the next big thing. Shoreditch has bars and clubs to suit nearly all tastes these days, while Dalston, the neighborhood to its north, attracts a younger clientele.

BARS

Birthdays. Dalston is London's hippest neighborhood for nightlife right now and this stark, industrial bar near the top of the main drag is as hot as it gets. Join the youngish crowd for craft beers and gourmet burgers. There's a club in the basement that hosts DJs and live gigs. ⊠ *33–35 Stoke Newington Rd., Dalston* ☎ *020/7923–1680* ⊕ *birthdaysdalston. com* ⊡ *Free–£10* ⊘ *Mon.–Thurs. noon–midnight, Fri. noon–3 am, Sat. 11 am–3 am, Sun. 11 am–midnight* Ⓜ *Dalston Junction.*

Book Club. Light and friendly, the Book Club tops off a dose of Shoreditch's fashionable industrial chic with a dollop of culture. White tiles, bare brick walls, and big black-and-white photos set the tone and there's a separate room for table tennis. Breakfast is served weekday mornings, a full lunch menu is offered through the week, and a modern menu of cocktails accompanies music, book launches, and workshops in the evenings. ⊠ *100 Leonard St., Shoreditch* ☎ *020/7684–8618* ⊕ *www.wearetbc.com* ⊘ *Mon.–Wed. 8 am–midnight, Thurs. and Fri. 8 am–2 am, Sat. 10 am–2 am, Sun. 10 am–midnight* Ⓜ *Shoreditch High St., Old St.*

Comedy Cafe Theatre. This new venue upstairs at the Bedroom Bar hosts at least three mixed-bill comedy nights a week, including the free New Act Night every Wednesday. Up-and-coming comics appear alongside big international names such as Tony Law and Andrew Maxwell on Friday and Saturday, and when the show's over, DJs take the stage, transforming the bare brick space into a dance club. The buzzing downstairs bar hosts five live bands a week, as well as a tasty Korean canteen. ⊠ *68 Rivington St., Shoreditch* ☎ *020/7739 5706* ⊕ *www. comedycafetheatre.co.uk* ⊡ *Free–£12* ⊘ *Tues.–Thurs. noon–1 am, Fri. and Sat. noon–3 am* Ⓜ *Old St., Shoreditch High St.*

DANCE CLUBS

Cargo. Housed under a series of old railroad arches, this spacious brick-wall bar, restaurant, dance floor, and live-music venue pulls a young, international crowd with its hip vibe and diverse selection of music. Long tables bring people together, as does the food, which draws on global influences and is served tapas-style. Drinks, though, are expensive. ⊠ *83 Rivington St., Shoreditch* ☎ *020/7739–3440* ⊕ *www.cargo-london.com* ✉ *Free–£20* ⏱ *Mon.–Thurs. noon–1 am, Fri. and Sat. noon–3 am, Sun. noon–midnight* Ⓜ *Old St.*

XOYO. Big international DJs regularly play this übercool Shoreditch nightspot, which is tucked away in a small side street off the main drag. The decor is industrial chic, with some banquet seating in the relaxed upstairs room and a downstairs with a more hard-core vibe. A youngish crowd dances the night away on the weekend, while weeknight live gigs attract a more diverse bunch. ⊠ *32–37 Cowper St., Shoreditch* ☎ *020/7354–9993* ⊕ *www.xoyo.co.uk* ✉ *Clubnights £12.50–£20; gig ticket prices vary* ⏱ *Fri. and Sat. 9 pm–4 am, Sun.–Thurs. hrs vary* Ⓜ *Old St.*

SOUTH OF THE THAMES

16

Recent years have seen an explosion in south London nightlife, from the gentrification of Brixton, to the artistic colonization of Peckham, and the continuing popularity of Vauxhall as a destination for gay clubbing.

BARS

Fodor's Choice
★

Aqua Shard. This classy bar on level 31 of the Shard, London's new skyscraper and the tallest building in Western Europe, is worth a visit for the phenomenal views alone. The cocktail list is pretty special, too, with ranges inspired by teas and botanicals, as well as all the usual classics. No reservations are taken (except in the restaurant), so be prepared to wait during busy periods. ⊠ *Level 31, The Shard, 31 St. Thomas St., London Bridge* ☎ *020/3011–1256 reservations* ⊕ *www.aquashard. co.uk* ⏱ *Daily noon–1 am* Ⓜ *London Bridge.*

The Dogstar. This popular south London hangout is frequented by local hipsters and counterculture types. It was the first DJ bar in the world and has since enjoyed a fabulous reputation. The vibe at this "surrealist boudoir" is unpretentious, with top-name DJs playing cutting-edge sounds every night in the main bar, comedy and cabaret upstairs, and pizza available until midnight. ⊠ *389 Coldharbour La., Brixton* ☎ *020/7733–7515* ⊕ *dogstarbrixton.com* ✉ *Free; Fri. and Sat. £5 after midnight* ⏱ *Tues. and Wed. 4 pm–11 pm, Thurs. 4 pm–2 am, Fri. 4 pm–4 am, Sat. noon–4 am, Sun. noon–10:30 pm* Ⓜ *Brixton.*

DANCE CLUBS

Ministry of Sound. This is more of an industry than a club, with its own record label, online radio station, and international DJs. Though it's too much a part of the establishment these days to be at the forefront of cool, the stripped-down warehouse-style club has a super sound system and still pulls in the world's most legendary names in dance. Following its latest renovation, there are chill-out rooms, four bars, and four dance floors. ⊠ *103 Gaunt St., Borough* ☎ *0870/060–0010*

⊕ *www.ministryofsound.com* ✆ *£15–£25* ⊙ *Fri. 10:30 pm–6 am, Sat. 11 pm–7 am (last entry 4:30 am)* Ⓜ *Elephant and Castle.*

ECLECTIC MUSIC

Fodor's Choice **O2 Academy Brixton.** This legendary Brixton venue has seen it all—mods
★ and rockers, hippies and punks—and it remains one of the city's top indie and rock venues. Despite a capacity for almost 5,000, this refurbished Victorian hall with original art deco fixtures retains a clublike charm; it has plenty of bars and upstairs seating. ⊠ *211 Stockwell Rd., Brixton* ☎ *0844/477–2000 box office* ⊕ *www.o2academybrixton.co.uk* ✆ *£15–£50* ⊙ *Hrs vary* Ⓜ *Brixton.*

CHELSEA AND KNIGHTSBRIDGE

The pages of society magazines are full of photographs of gorgeous young people dancing the night away at clubs—many of which are members only—in these famously swanky neighborhoods. Dress up and be prepared to splurge.

CHELSEA
JAZZ AND BLUES

606 Club. This civilized Chelsea club showcases mainstream and contemporary jazz by well-known British-based musicians. ■ **TIP→ You must eat a meal in order to consume alcohol, so allow for an extra £30.** Reservations are advisable. Sunday lunchtime jazz takes place on selected Sundays; call ahead. ⊠ *90 Lots Rd., Chelsea* ☎ *020/7352–5953* ⊕ *www.606club.co.uk* ✆ *£8–£12 music charge added to bill* ⊙ *Mon. and Thurs. 7 pm–11:30 pm, Tues. and Wed. 7 pm–12:30 am, Fri. and Sat. 8 pm–1:30 am, Sun. 12:30 pm–4 pm and 7 pm–11:15 pm* Ⓜ *Earl's Ct., Fulham Broadway.*

KNIGHTSBRIDGE
BARS

The Blue Bar at the Berkeley Hotel. With low-slung dusty-blue walls, this hotel bar is ever so slightly sexy. Immaculate service, an excellent seasonal cocktail list, and a trendy David Collins design make this an ideal spot for a romantic tête-à-tête, complete with jazzy music in the background. ⊠ *Wilton Pl., Knightsbridge* ☎ *020/7235–6000* ⊕ *the-berkeley. co.uk* ⊙ *Mon.–Sat. 9 am–1 am, Sun. 9 am–11 pm* Ⓜ *Knightsbridge.*

NOTTING HILL

The focus is more on bars than clubs in this west London neighborhood, though late-night fun is on offer at a few notable exceptions. In general, you can expect a young, moneyed crowd making this their first stop on a wild night out elsewhere.

BARS

Beach Blanket Babylon. In a Georgian house in Notting Hill, close to Portobello Market, this always-packed bar is distinguishable by its eclectic indoor-outdoor spaces with Gaudí-esque curves and snuggly corners—like a fairy-tale grotto or a medieval dungeon. A sister restaurant-bar-gallery offers a slightly more modern take on similar themes in an ex-warehouse in Shoreditch (⊠ *19–23 Bethnal Green Rd.*

☎ 020/7749–3540). ⊠ 45 *Ledbury Rd., Notting Hill* ☎ 020/7229–2907 ⊕ *www.beachblanket.co.uk* ⊗ *Daily noon–midnight* Ⓜ *Notting Hill Gate.*

DANCE CLUBS

Notting Hill Arts Club. Rock stars like Liam Gallagher and Courtney Love have been seen at this small basement club-bar. What the place lacks in looks it makes up for in mood, and an alternative crowd swills beer to eclectic music that spans Asian underground, hip-hop, Latin-inspired funk, deep house, and jazzy grooves. ⊠ *21 Notting Hill Gate, Notting Hill* ☎ 020/7460–4459 ⊕ *www.nottinghillartsclub.com* 🎫 *Free–£8* ⊗ *Tues.–Sat. 7 pm–2 am, alternate Sun. 6 pm–1 am* Ⓜ *Notting Hill Gate.*

REGENT'S PARK AND HAMPSTEAD

Camden Town boasts a handful of dance clubs, but it's this north London neighborhood's music venues that are the big draw for most. Every genre is covered, from folk and pop, to jazz and world music, with interesting gigs taking place every night of the week.

REGENT'S PARK
COMEDY AND CABARET

Canal Café Theatre. Famous comics and cabaret stars perform every night of the week in this intimate, canal-side venue. The long-running News-Revue is a topical song-and-sketch show performed Thursday–Sunday evenings. ⊠ *Bridge House, Delamere Terr., Little Venice* ☎ 020/7289–6054 ⊕ *www.canalcafetheatre.com* 🎫 *Free–£15; NewsRevue £12.50* ⊗ *Pub Mon.–Thurs. noon–11 pm, Fri. and Sat. noon–11:30 pm, Sun. noon–10:30 pm* Ⓜ *Warwick Ave., Royal Oak, Paddington.*

DANCE CLUBS

KOKO. This Victorian theater, formerly known as Camden Palace, has seen acts from Charlie Chaplin to Madonna, and genres from punk to rave. Updated with lush reds not unlike a cockney Moulin Rouge, this is still one of London's most stunning venues. Sounds of live indie rock, cabaret, funky house, and club classics keep the big dance floor moving, even when it's not heaving. ⊠ *1A Camden High St., Camden Town* ☎ 0870/432–5527 ⊕ *www.koko.uk.com* 🎫 *£5–£30* ⊗ *Hrs vary, depending on shows* Ⓜ *Mornington Crescent.*

ECLECTIC

Roundhouse. This former steam-engine repair shed hosts some of the most atmospheric medium-scale rock and pop gigs in the capital, plus a varied program of circus, theater, dance, and the occasional art installation. There's a good restaurant on the first floor, and in the summer the terrace bar is transformed into an "urban beach," complete with sand. ⊠ *Chalk Farm Rd., Chalk Farm* ☎ 0844/482–8008 *box office,* 020/7424–9991 *inquiries* ⊕ *www.roundhouse.org.uk* 🎫 *Free–£40* ⊗ *Daily 9:30–5 (later when performances are taking place; times vary)* Ⓜ *Chalk Farm.*

16

JAZZ AND BLUES

Jazz Café. A palace of cool in bohemian Camden, this remains an essential hangout for fans of both the mainstream end of the jazz repertoire and hip-hop, funk, world music, and Latin fusion. It's also the unlikely venue for Saturday "I Love the 80s" nights. Book ahead if you want a prime table in the balcony restaurant overlooking the stage. ⊠ *5 Parkway, Camden Town* ☎ *020/7485–6834 venue info, 0844/847–2514 tickets (Ticketmaster)* ⊕ *mamacolive.com/thejazzcafe* 🖃 *£6–£35* ⊙ *Sun.–Thurs. 7 pm–10:30 pm, Fri. and Sat. 7 pm–3 am* Ⓜ *Camden Town.*

ROCK

Barfly Club. At one of the finest small clubs in the capital, punk, indie guitar, and new metal rock attract a non-mainstream crowd. Weekend club nights upstairs host DJs (and live bands) who rock the decks. ⊠ *49 Chalk Farm Rd., Camden Town* ☎ *020/7424–0800 venue, 0844/847– 2424 tickets* ⊕ *mamacolive.com/thebarfly* 🖃 *£5–£11* ⊙ *Mon. and Tues. 7 pm–midnight, Wed. and Thurs. 7 pm–2 am, Fri. and Sat. 7 pm–3 am* Ⓜ *Camden Town, Chalk Farm.*

The Forum. The best up-coming and medium-to-big-name rock performers consistently play at this 2,000-capacity club. It's a converted 1920 art deco movie theater, with a balcony overlooking the grungy dance floor. ⊠ *9–17 Highgate Rd., Kentish Town* ☎ *020/7428–4099 venue, 0844/847–2405 tickets* ⊕ *theforumlondon.com* 🖃 *£12–£60* ⊙ *Hrs vary, depending on concert schedule* Ⓜ *Kentish Town.*

ARTS AND
ENTERTAINMENT

Updated by Jo Caird

"All the world's a stage," said Shakespeare, immortal words heard for the first time right here in London. And whether you prefer your theater, music, and art classical or modern, or as contemporary twists on time-honored classics, you'll find that London's vibrant cultural scene more than holds its own on the world stage.

Divas sing original-language librettos at the Royal Opera House, Shakespeare's plays are brought to life at the reconstructed Globe Theatre, and challenging new writing is produced at the Royal Court. Whether you feel like basking in the lighthearted extravagance of a West End musical or taking in the next shark-in-formaldehyde at the White Cube gallery, the choice is yours.

There are international theater festivals, innovative music festivals, and critically acclaimed seasons of postmodern dance. Short trip or long, you'll find the cultural scene in London is ever-changing, ever-expanding, and ever-exciting.

No matter where you head, London's art and performing arts scenes have been setting global trends for decades—and when you include Shakespearean theater and Handel oratorios, for centuries. Fringe theater, classical ballet, participatory chorales, you name it, London probably did it first and often does it best.

PLANNING

TOP THEATER TIPS

Behind the pillars. Many theaters and concert halls sell discounted seats with restricted views.

Matinees. Afternoon performances are almost always better value than evening ones.

Previews. Tickets to shows are usually less expensive in the first few weeks of their run, before the critics have had their say.

Monday. Most cinemas and some theaters, including the Royal Court, have a reduced-price ticketing policy on Monday.

Standing. Globe Theatre and the Proms are the two most prominent places where remaining upright saves you money.

FIND OUT WHAT'S PLAYING WHERE

To find out what's showing now, the weekly magazine *Time Out* (now free, issued every Tuesday outside major stations and around the city; also online at ⊕ *www.timeout.com*) is invaluable.

The free *Evening Standard* carries listings, many of which are also available online at ⊕ *www.standard.co.uk*. *Metro*, London's other widely available free newspaper, is also worth checking out, as are many Sunday papers, and the Saturday *Independent, Guardian,* and *Times*.

The website ⊕ *www.whatsonstage.com* is an invaluable resource for theater listings.

There are hundreds of small private galleries all over London with interesting work by famous and not-yet-famous artists. The bimonthly free pamphlet "new exhibitions of contemporary art" (⊕ *www. newexhibitions.com*), available at most galleries, lists and maps nearly 200 art spaces in London.

ARTS AND ENTERTAINMENT REVIEWS

17

ST. JAMES'S AND WESTMINSTER

Wander the streets of this chic central London neighborhood—home to British aristocracy in the 17th century—and you'll discover a host of small commercial galleries, fine art auction houses, and antiques dealers in among the high-end tailors and gentlemen's clubs.

ART GALLERY

Institute of Contemporary Arts. Housed in an elegant John Nash–designed Regency terrace, the ICA's two galleries have changing exhibitions of contemporary visual art. The ICA also programs performances, underground and vintage movies, talks, and photography, and there's an arts bookstore, cafeteria, and bar. ⊠ *Nash House, The Mall, St. James's* ☎ *020/7930–3647* ⊕ *www.ica.org.uk* ☞ *Free* ☉ *Tues.–Sun. 11–11; galleries Tues., Wed., Fri.–Sun. 11–6; Thurs. 11–9* Ⓜ *Charing Cross, Piccadilly Circus.*

White Cube. The English role in the exploding contemporary art scene has been major, thanks in good portion to Jay Joplin's influential gallery, which has regularly moved around London over the past 15 years. The striking modern concrete structure was the first freestanding building to be built in the area for 30 years when it opened in 2006. It is homebase for an array of British artists who have won the Turner Prize— Hirst, Emin, Hume, et al. A larger space, in an ex-warehouse south of the river in Bermondsey, opened in 2011. ⊠ *25–26 Mason's Yard, St. James's* ☎ *020/7930–5373* ⊕ *whitecube.com* ☞ *Free* ☉ *Tues.–Sat. 10–6* Ⓜ *Green Park, Piccadilly Circus.*

Random Dance Company performs at Sadler's Wells.

CLASSICAL MUSIC

St. James's Church. The organ was brought here in 1691 after fire destroyed its former home, the Palace of Whitehall. St. James's holds regular classical-music concerts and free lunchtime recitals Monday, Wednesday, and Friday at 1:10 pm (free but donation of £3.50 suggested). ✉ *197 Piccadilly, St. James's* ☎ *020/7381–0441 concert program and tickets* ⊕ *www.sjp.org.uk* Ⓜ *Piccadilly Circus, Green Park.*

St. John's Smith Square. This baroque church behind Westminster Abbey offers chamber music and organ recitals as well as orchestral concerts September through July. There are two or three Thursday lunchtime recitals a month for £10. ✉ *Smith Sq., Westminster* ☎ *020/7222–1061* ⊕ *www.sjss.org.uk* Ⓜ *Westminster.*

St. Martin-in-the-Fields. Popular lunchtime concerts (free but £3.50 donation suggested) are held in this lovely 1726 church, as are regular evening concerts. ■ **TIP**➔ **Stop for a snack at the Café in the Crypt.** ✉ *Trafalgar Sq., Westminster* ☎ *020/7766–1100* ⊕ *www.stmartin-in-the-fields.org* Ⓜ *Charing Cross.*

MAYFAIR AND MARYLEBONE

The historic center of the London art world, Mayfair has a thriving gallery scene that has undergone something of a renaissance in recent years. With East End gallerists relocating to central London and a number of top international galleries opening new premises here, there's a real buzz about the place. Directly north of Mayfair, Marylebone has more of a village atmosphere, with a few choice galleries and arts institutions dotted around.

THE ARTS FOR FREE

CLASSICAL MUSIC AND JAZZ

The Barbican, the Royal National Theatre, and the Royal Opera House often have free music in their foyers or in dedicated spaces, usually of high standard. On the South Bank, free festivals and special performances often take place alongside the river.

Many of London's world-class music colleges give free concerts several times a week. The Royal Academy of Music and the Royal College of Music often have free recitals. St. Martin-in-the-Fields has free lunchtime concerts, as does Christchurch Spitalfields. Other churches, including Westminster Abbey, St. James's Piccadilly, and St. Paul's in Covent Garden, also have frequent free music. For the Proms, which run from July to September at the Royal Albert Hall, good seats are expensive, but hundreds of standing tickets are available at £5: not quite free, but good value.

CONTEMPORARY MUSIC

Brixton's Dogstar pub has a great selection of DJs, often playing for free on weekday evenings. Ain't Nothing But Blues Bar in Soho has live music most nights, often without a cover charge, and pubs such as the Monarch and the Hawley Arms near Camden Market offer the chance to see tomorrow's indie stars today. East London establishment Café Oto hosts London's best experimental music performances, while Cecil Sharp House in Camden is the home of traditional and contemporary folk.

DRAMA AND PERFORMANCE ARTS

Look out for occasional festivals where innovative performances take place on the South Bank. Check the newspapers and *Time Out* for upcoming performances.

MUSEUMS AND GALLERIES

Few if any other cities in the world offer the number of free art venues available in London. Most of the city's museums and galleries do not charge entrance fees. The monthly *Galleries* magazine, available from galleries themselves or online at ⊕ *www.galleries.co.uk,* has listings for all private galleries in the capital.

PARK LIFE

London's parks come to life in summer with a wide-ranging program of music, dance, and visual arts (⊕ *www.royalparks.org.uk* for details, or ☎ *020/7298–2000*). There are several summer festivals in London parks, some with lots of big-name pop stars, like the British Summer Time festival in Hyde Park and the somewhat more indie Lovebox in Victoria Park. Notable contemporary art fairs are October's Frieze in Regent's Park (⊕ *www. friezelondon.com*) and the Affordable Art Fair in Battersea Park and Hampstead Heath in spring (⊕ *www.affordableartfair.com*).

RADIO AND TELEVISION

With so much broadcast material made in London, much of it recorded in front of live audiences, there are often opportunities to watch a free quiz show, current-affairs debate, comedy, or even drama. Check the BBC website for forthcoming recordings (⊕ *www.bbc.co.uk/ showsandtours/tickets*).

17

TOP FIVE FOR THE ARTS

Stand with the "plebs" in Shakespeare's Globe Theatre. There are seats, but to really experience theater Shakespearean-style you should stand in the yard, with the stage at eye level (plus, it's a bargain at £5).

Visit the latest grand art installation in the Turbine Hall at Tate Modern. The enormity of the Tate's central space either intimidates or inspires artists challenged to fill it.

Catch a world-class performance at the Proms. There's a surprisingly down-to-earth atmosphere among the elated company at these great concerts.

Enjoy a night at the BFI Southbank. Mingle with the real aficionados at screenings of foreign, classic, and experimental films.

Watch a Hollywood star in a West End production. Film stars often come to London to boost their artistic credibility in small-scale theaters.

MAYFAIR

ART GALLERY

Royal Academy of Arts. Housed in an aristocratic mansion and home to Britain's first art school (founded in 1768), the academy is best known for its blockbuster special exhibitions—like a controversial Sensation show drawn from the Saatchi collection and a record-breaking Monet show—though it also has a permanent collection that includes Michelangelo's marble Taddei Tondo. The annual Summer Exhibition has been a popular London tradition since 1769. ⊠ *Burlington House, Piccadilly, Mayfair* ☎ *020/7300–8000* ⊕ *www.royalacademy.org.uk* ✉ *From £3, prices vary with exhibition* ⊙ *Sat.–Thurs. 10–6, Fri. 10–10* Ⓜ *Piccadilly Circus.*

MARYLEBONE

ART GALLERY

Lisson. Owner Nicholas Logsdail represents about 40 blue-chip artists, including minimalist Sol LeWitt and Dan Graham, at one of the most respected galleries in London. The gallery is most associated with New Object sculptors like Anish Kapoor and Richard Deacon, many of whom have won the Turner Prize. A branch down the road at 27 Bell Street features work by younger, up-and-coming artists, and the gallery has another branch in Milan. ⊠ *52–54 Bell St., Marylebone* ☎ *020/7724–2739* ⊕ *www.lissongallery.com* ✉ *Free* ⊙ *Weekdays 10–6, Sat. 11–5* Ⓜ *Edgware Rd., Marylebone.*

CLASSICAL MUSIC

Fodor's Choice ★ **Wigmore Hall.** Hear chamber music and song recitals in this charming hall with near-perfect acoustics. Don't miss the Sunday morning concerts (11:30 am). ⊠ *36 Wigmore St., Marylebone* ☎ *020/7935–2141* ⊕ *www.wigmore-hall.org.uk* Ⓜ *Bond St.*

Royal Opera House, one of the world's greatest opera houses and home of the Royal Ballet, offers daily tours of the auditorium and backstage.

SOHO AND COVENT GARDEN

London's hip center has it all, from multiplexes playing the biggest blockbuster movies to niche contemporary art galleries tucked away in backstreets, and from world-famous opera houses to sultry cabaret joints. Whatever flavor of culture you're craving, you'll find it here.

SOHO

ART GALLERY

Photographer's Gallery. Reopened in 2012 following a major refurbishment and extension, Britain's first and foremost photography gallery continues to program cutting-edge and provocative photography exhibitions. The prestigious Deutsche Börse Photography Prize is exhibited and awarded here annually. The gallery also has a print sales room, a bookstore, and a café. ✉ *16–18 Ramillies St., off Oxford St., Soho* ☎ *0845/262–1618* ⊕ *www.thephotographersgallery.org.uk* ▨ *Free* ⊙ *Mon.–Wed., Fri., and Sat. 10–6; Thurs. 10–8; Sun. 11:30–6* Ⓜ *Oxford Circus.*

Riflemaker. In the oldest public building in the West End, and taking its name from a former Georgian rifle maker's workshop here, this hip gallery exhibits ambitious works by emerging artists. It hosted debuts by Francesca Lowe, Chosil Kil, Jaime Gili, and Jamie Shovlin. ✉ *79 Beak St., Soho* ☎ *020/7439–0000* ⊕ *www.riflemaker.org* ▨ *Free* ⊙ *Weekdays 10 am–6 pm, Sat. noon–6 pm* Ⓜ *Piccadilly Circus, Oxford Circus.*

Sadie Coles HQ. This light-filled art space overlooking busy Regent Street marked a major expansion for respected British gallerist Sadie Coles when it opened in fall 2013. You'll find the work of important

THEATER: LONDON TODAY

In London the play really *is* the thing, ranging from a long-running popular musical like *Mamma Mia!*, a groundbreaking reworking of Pinter, imaginative physical theater from an experimental company like Complicite, a lavish Disney spectacle, or a small fringe production above a pub. West End glitz and glamour continue to pull in the audiences, and so do the more innovative productions.

In London the words "radical" and "quality," or "classical" and "experimental" are not mutually exclusive. The Royal Shakespeare Company (⊕ www.rsc.org.uk) and the National Theatre (⊕ www.nationaltheatre. org.uk) often stage contemporary versions of the classics. The Almeida, Battersea Arts Centre (BAC), Donmar Warehouse, Royal Court Theatre, Soho Theatre, and Old Vic attract famous actors and have excellent reputations for new writing and innovative theatrical approaches. These are the venues where you'll see an original production before it becomes a hit in the West End or on Broadway (and for a fraction of the cost).

The London theater scene remains vibrant throughout the summer months. Open-air productions of Shakespeare are particularly well served, whether in the faithful reconstruction of the Elizabethan Globe Theatre or under the stars in Regent's Park's Open Air Theatre. Theater festivals such as **LIFT** (the London International Festival of Theatre ⊕ www.liftfestival.com) and **BITE** (Barbican International Theater Events ⊕ www.barbican. org.uk) provide the chance to see international and cutting-edge companies throughout the year.

Theatergoing isn't cheap. Tickets less than £12 are a rarity, although designated productions at the National Theatre have seats at this price. At the commercial theaters you should expect to pay from £20 for a seat in the upper balcony to at least £40 for a good one in the stalls (orchestra) or dress circle (mezzanine). However, last-minute returns available on the night may provide some good deals. Tickets may be booked through ticket agents, at individual theater box offices, or over the phone by credit card. Be sure to inquire about any extra fees—prices can vary enormously, but agents are legally obliged to reveal the face value of the ticket if you ask. All the larger hotels offer theater bookings, but they tack on a hefty service charge.

Ticketmaster (☎ 0844/277–4321 ⊕ www.ticketmaster.co.uk) sells tickets to a number of different theaters, although they charge a booking fee. For discount tickets, **Society of London Theatre** (☎ 020/7557–6700 ⊕ www.tkts. co.uk) operates "tkts," a half-price ticket booth on the southwest corner of Leicester Square, and sells the best available seats to performances at about 30 theaters. It's open Monday–Saturday 9–7, Sunday 11–4:30; there's a £3 service charge (included in the price). Major credit cards are accepted.

■TIP➔ Be very wary of ticket touts (scalpers) and unscrupulous ticket agents outside theaters and working the line at "tkts."

British and international artists such as Sarah Lucas and Wilhelm Sasnal here and at Coles's other gallery, in Mayfair. ⊠ *62 Kingly St., Soho* ☎ *020/7493–8611* ⊕ *www.sadiecoles.com* ⊙ *Tues.–Sat. 11–6.*

FILM

Curzon Soho. This popular, comfortable movie theater runs a vibrant and artsy program of mixed repertoire and mainstream films, with a good calendar of director talks and other events, too. The bar is great for a quiet drink, even when Soho is crawling with people. There are branches in Mayfair, Bloomsbury, Chelsea, and Richmond. ⊠ *99 Shaftesbury Ave., Soho* ☎ *0330/500–1331* ⊕ *www.curzoncinemas.com* Ⓜ *Piccadilly Circus, Leicester Sq.*

FAMILY **Prince Charles Cinema.** This repertory cinema right off Leicester Square offers a chance to catch up with independent features, documentaries, and even blockbusters you may have missed, and tickets start at £8, or £4 if you purchase a £10 annual membership. A second screen upstairs shows newer movies at more usual West End prices. This is where the "sing-along" screening took off—come in character and warble along to *The Sound of Music, Grease,* or *The Rocky Horror Picture Show.* ⊠ *7 Leicester Pl., Soho* ☎ *020/7494–3654* ⊕ *www.princecharlescinema. com* Ⓜ *Leicester Sq., Piccadilly Circus.*

THEATER

Soho Theatre. This sleek theater in the heart of Soho is devoted to fostering new work and is a prolific presenter of plays by emerging writers, comedy performances, cabaret shows, and other entertainment. The bar is always buzzing. ⊠ *21 Dean St., Soho* ☎ *020/7478–0100* ⊕ *www. sohotheatre.com* Ⓜ *Tottenham Court Rd.*

COVENT GARDEN

DANCE

The London Coliseum. Ballet troupes are often booked into the spectacular Coliseum during the summer and the Christmas season, and generally any time when the resident English National Opera is not holding down the fort here. The restored Edwardian baroque theater (1904) is known for its magnificent auditorium and a rooftop glass dome. The top dance company to perform here is the English National Ballet (⊕ *www.ballet.org.uk*). Guided tours (which take place on every other Saturday at 11:30 am, when productions are scheduled) cost £10. ⊠ *St. Martin's La., Covent Garden* ☎ *020/7845–9300* ⊕ *www. eno.org* Ⓜ *Leicester Sq.*

Fodor's Choice **Royal Opera House.** As well as the Royal Opera, the renowned Royal
★ Ballet performs classical and contemporary repertoire in this spectacular theater, where the interior may be Victorian but the stagecraft behind the red velvet curtain is state-of-the-art. Backstage tours are £12. They don't take place when rehearsals or performances are taking place, so check the schedule in advance of your visit. ⊠ *Bow St., Covent Garden* ☎ *020/7304–4000* ⊕ *www.roh.org.uk* ⊙ *Backstage tours (75 mins) weekdays 10:30, 12:30, and 2:30; Sat. 10:30, 11:30, and 12:30* Ⓜ *Covent Garden.*

17

Dominique Gonzalez-Foerster's installation, *TH.2058*, in the Turbine Hall of Tate Modern

OPERA

The London Coliseum. A veritable architectural extravaganza of Edwardian exoticism, the restored baroque-style theater (1904) has a magnificent auditorium and a rooftop glass dome with a bar and great views. As one of the city's largest and most venerable theaters, the Coliseum functions mainly as the home of the English National Opera. Seemingly in better financial shape than it has been for some time, ENO continues to produce innovative opera, sung in English, for lower prices than the Royal Opera House. During opera's off-season, the house hosts a number of dance troupes, including the English National Ballet (⊕ *www. ballet.org.uk*). Guided tours (every other Saturday at 11:30 am, when productions are scheduled) cost £10. ⊠ *St. Martin's La., Covent Garden* ☎ *020/7845–9300 box office, 020/7836–0111 inquiries* ⊕ *www. eno.org* Ⓜ *Leicester Sq.*

Fodor'sChoice
★
Royal Opera House. Along with Milan's La Scala, New York's Metropolitan, and the Palais Garnier in Paris, this is one of the world's greatest opera houses. The resident troupe has mounted famously spectacular productions in the past, though recent productions have tended toward starker, more contemporary operas. Whatever the style of the performance, the extravagant theater itself—also home to the famed Royal Ballet—delivers a full dose of opulence. Tickets range in price from £8 to £230. The box office opens at 10 am, but lines for popular productions can start as early as 7 am; unsold tickets are offered at half price four hours before a performance. If you wish to see the hall but are not able to procure a ticket, you can join a backstage tour (£12) or one of the infrequent tours of the auditorium (£9.50). There are free lunchtime recitals most Mondays in the Crush Room (arrive early to

CONTEMPORARY ART: LONDON TODAY

In the 21st century, the focus of the city's art scene has shifted from the past to the future. Helped by the prominence of Tate Modern, London's contemporary art scene has never been so high profile. In publicly funded exhibition spaces like the Barbican Gallery, the Hayward Gallery, the Institute of Contemporary Arts, and the Serpentine Galleries, London now has a modern-art environment on par with Bilbao and New York. Young British Artists (YBAs, though no longer as young as they once were) Damien Hirst, Tracey Emin, and others are firmly planted in the public imagination. The celebrity status of British artists is in part thanks to the annual Turner Prize, which always stirs up controversy in the media during a monthlong display of the work, usually at Tate Britain.

Depending on whom you talk to, the Saatchi Gallery is considered to be either the savior of contemporary art or the wardrobe of the emperor's new clothes. After a couple of moves it is now ensconced in the former Duke of York's barracks off Chelsea's King's Road.

The South Bank's Tate Modern may house the giants of modern art, but East London is where the innovative action is. There are dozens of galleries in the fashionable spaces around Old Street, and the truly hip have already moved even farther east, to areas such as Bethnal Green. The Whitechapel Art Gallery and Jay Jopling's influential White Cube, with branches in Bermondsey as well as in Soho, remain at the epicenter of the new art establishment and continue to show exciting work by emerging British artists.

On the first Thursday of every month, more than 130 museums and galleries of East London stay open until late (more information at ⊕ www.firstthursdays.co.uk).

17

get a ticket—between 11 am and noon; some tickets are available online from nine days before the event). ROH2, the Opera House's contemporary arm, stages more experimental dance and voice performances in locations including the Linbury Studio Theatre, a 400-seater space below the Opera House. ⊠ *Bow St., Covent Garden* ☎ *020/7304–4000* ⊕ *www.roh.org.uk* ☺ *Public areas generally daily 10–3:30. Backstage tours weekdays 10:30, 12:30, and 2:30; Sat. 10:30, 11:30, 12:30, and 1:30 (please check in advance as tours do not take place when rehearsals or performances are in progress)* Ⓜ *Covent Garden.*

THEATER

Fodor'sChoice ★ **Donmar Warehouse.** Hollywood stars often perform in this not-for-profit theater in diverse and daring new works, bold interpretations of the classics, and small-scale musicals. Nicole Kidman, Gwyneth Paltrow, and Ewan McGregor have all been featured. ⊠ *41 Earlham St., Seven Dials, Covent Garden* ☎ *0844/871–7624* ⊕ *www.donmarwarehouse. com* Ⓜ *Covent Garden.*

BLOOMSBURY AND HOLBORN

Once the heart of fashionable literary London, there's still an air of refinement about this neighborhood. A handful of small theaters with links to the colleges with campuses in the area create a vibrant small-scale performance scene, including theater, dance, and stand-up comedy.

CLASSICAL MUSIC

Kings Place. This airy concert venue opened in 2008: the cultural jewel in the huge new developments near the Eurostar terminal in King's Cross. It is the permanent home of the London Sinfonietta and the Orchestra of the Age of Enlightenment. It offers weeklong programs by musicians in a range of genres, and there are free-to-watch weekly chamber music master classes on Sunday. There's also a hugely varied cultural calendar of jazz, comedy, folk, and political and literary lectures, and two gallery spaces. ⊠ *90 York Way, King's Cross* ☎ *020/7520–1490 box office, 020/7520–1440 inquiries* ⊕ *www.kingsplace.co.uk* Ⓜ *King's Cross.*

DANCE

Peacock Theatre. Sadler's Wells's West End annex, this Modernist theater near the London School of Economics (which uses it as a lecture hall during the day) focuses on younger companies and shows in popular dance genres like flamenco, tango, and hip-hop. ⊠ *Portugal St., Holborn* ☎ *0844/412–4322 box office* ⊕ *www.sadlerswells.com* Ⓜ *Holborn.*

The Place. The Robin Howard Dance Theatre at The Place is London's only theater dedicated to contemporary dance, and with tickets often under £15 (including many free performances by student dancers) it's good value, too. "Resolution!" is the United Kingdom's biggest platform event for new choreographers. ⊠ *17 Duke's Rd., Bloomsbury* ☎ *020/7121–1100* ⊕ *www.theplace.org.uk* Ⓜ *Euston.*

ISLINGTON

Close to central London, yet with its own unique atmosphere, this neighborhood is home to a handful of renowned theaters and music venues that make the short journey northeast well worth the effort.

ART GALLERY

Victoria Miro Gallery. This large, important commercial gallery, in a former furniture factory, has exhibited some of the biggest names on the British contemporary art scene—Grayson Perry, the Chapman brothers, and Peter Doig, to name a few. Some exhibitions spill out into the gallery's own garden. It also brings in exciting talent from abroad. ⊠ *16 Wharf Rd., Islington* ☎ *020/7336–8109* ⊕ *www.victoria-miro.com* ⊠ *Free* ☉ *Tues.–Sat. 10–6* Ⓜ *Old St., Angel.*

DANCE

Fodor's Choice ★ **Sadler's Wells.** This gleaming building opened in 1998, the seventh on the site in its 300-year history, and is devoted to presenting leading classical and contemporary dance companies. The Random Dance Company is in residence, and the little Lilian Baylis Theatre hosts avant-garde work. ⊠ *Rosebery Ave., Islington* ☎ *0844/412–4300 tickets, 020/7863–8198 general inquiries* ⊕ *www.sadlerswells.com* Ⓜ *Angel.*

THEATER

Almeida Theatre. This Off–West End venue, helmed by director Rupert Goold, premiers excellent new plays and exciting twists on the classics, often featuring high-profile actors. There's a good café and a licensed bar that serves "sharing dishes" as well as tasty main courses. ⊠ *Almeida St., Islington* ☎ *020/7359–4404* ⊕ *www.almeida.co.uk* Ⓜ *Angel, Highbury & Islington.*

FAMILY **Little Angel Theatre.** Innovative puppetry performances for children and adults have been taking place in this adorable converted temperance hall since 1961. The theater runs a number of festivals a year, including the biennial Suspense festival of puppetry for adults. ⊠ *14 Dagmar Passage, Islington* ☎ *020/7226–1787 box office* ⊕ *www.littleangeltheatre. com* Ⓜ *Angel, Highbury & Islington.*

THE CITY

It may seem at first glance like the denizens of London's financial center are far too busy to take time out for culture, but if you look a little closer you'll see that arts events are taking place all over, courtesy of a number of acclaimed annual festivals. Art exhibits in empty offices and chamber performances in historic churches are regular occurrences.

PERFORMANCE CENTERS

FAMILY **Barbican Centre.** Opened in 1982, the Brutalist-style Barbican is the largest performing arts center in Europe. The main concrete theater is most famous as the home of the London Symphony Orchestra (LSO). As well as the LSO (⊕ *www.lso.co.uk*), the Barbican is also a frequent host of the English Chamber Orchestra and the BBC Symphony Orchestra, and has an excellent concert season of big-name virtuosos. Performances by British and international theater companies make up part of the year-round **BITE** (Barbican International Theatre Events), which also features groundbreaking performance, dance, drama, and musical theater. Innovative exhibitions of 20th-century and current art and design are shown in the Barbican Gallery and the Curve (usually free). In addition to Hollywood films, obscure classics and film festivals with Screen Talks are programmed in the three movie theaters here. Saturday Framed Film Club has adventure and animation to please all ages. You could listen to Elgar or watch some Russian theater, see some 1960s photography or an exhibition on art and science, and catch some German animation with live musical accompaniment—possibly all in one evening. ⊠ *Silk St., The City* ☎ *020/7638–8891 box office* ⊕ *www.barbican.org.uk* ☯ *Mon.–Sat. 9 am–11 pm, Sun. noon–11 pm* Ⓜ *Barbican.*

17

EAST LONDON

Artists and other creative types, no longer able to afford central London rents, have been making their way eastward for years. It began in Shoreditch, but as rents increased there, too, neighborhoods farther and farther out have been colonized by these creative pioneers. Go gallery hopping in Vyner Street in Bethnal Green or catch a hip band in action at one of Shoreditch's myriad music venues.

ART GALLERY

Whitechapel Art Gallery. Founded in 1901 and recently expanded, this large, independent East End gallery is one of London's most innovative and consistently interesting. Jeff Wall, Bill Viola, Gary Hume, and Mark Rothko have exhibited here and there is an interesting program of events as well as an excellent restaurant. ⊠ *80–82 Whitechapel High St., Shoreditch* ☎ *020/7522–7888* ⊕ *www.whitechapel.org* ✉ *Free* ⊙ *Tues., Wed., and Fri.–Sun. 11–6; Thurs. 11–9* Ⓜ *Aldgate East.*

THEATER

FAMILY **Hackney Empire.** The history of this treasure of a theater is drama in its own right. Charlie Chaplin is said to have appeared here during its days as a thriving variety theater and music hall in the early 1900s. It now hosts traditional family entertainment and variety shows, opera, music, musical theater, dance, and drama, often with a multicultural slant. Its annual Christmas pantomime is legendary. ⊠ *291 Mare St., Hackney* ☎ *020/8985–2424* ⊕ *www.hackneyempire.co.uk* Ⓜ *National Rail: Hackney Central.*

SOUTH OF THE THAMES

The South Bank and its easterly near neighbor Bankside together make up one of the richest areas in London when it comes to arts and entertainment. Whether you want to watch a play, hear a concert, or see an art exhibit, you won't have to wander far to find something top class. Venture a little farther into south London, and you'll be rewarded with a sprinkling of fringe theaters that act as incubators for the capital's mainstream theater scene.

ART GALLERY

Fodor's Choice **Tate Modern.** This converted power station is one of the largest modern-
★ art galleries in the world, so give yourself ample time to take it all in. The permanent collection includes work by all the major 20th-century artists, though only a fraction is shown at any one time. There are also blockbuster touring shows and solo exhibitions of international artists. The huge onetime oil tanks of the old power station were opened up in 2012 for a season of performance art. These new spaces are the first stage in a new extension of the gallery that is scheduled for completion in 2016. ■TIP➔ The bar on the top floor has gorgeous views overlooking the Thames and St. Paul's Cathedral. ⊠ *Bankside, South Bank* ☎ *020/7887–8888* ⊕ *www.tate.org.uk* ✉ *Free–£15* ⊙ *Sun.–Thurs. 10–6, Fri. and Sat. 10–10* Ⓜ *Southwark, St. Paul's, London Bridge.*

FILM: LONDON TODAY

There are many wonderful movie theaters in London and several that are committed to non-mainstream and repertory cinema, in particular the excellent Curzon cinemas and the National Film Theatre. Now nearly 60 years old, the **BFI London Film Festival** (⊕ *www.bfi. org.uk/lff*) brings hundreds of films made by masters of world cinema to London each October, accompanied by often-sold-out talks and other events. The smaller, avant-garde **Raindance Film Festival** (⊕ *www.raindance.co.uk*) highlights Independent filmmaking, September into October.

West End movie theaters continue to do good business. Most of the major houses, such as the Odeon Leicester Square and the Empire, are in the Leicester Square–Piccadilly Circus area, where tickets average £15. Monday and matinees are often cheaper, at around £6–£10, and there are also smaller crowds.

Check out *Time Out*, one of the London papers, or ⊕ *www.viewlondon.co.uk* for listings.

FILM

BFI London IMAX Cinema. The British Film Institute's glazed drum-shaped IMAX theater (now, confusingly, operated by Odeon) has the largest screen in the United Kingdom (approximately 75 feet wide and the height of five double-decker buses), showing state-of-the-art 2-D and 3-D films. ✉ *1 Charlie Chaplin Walk, South Bank* ☎ *0330/333–7878* ⊕ *www.bfi.org.uk/imax* Ⓜ *Waterloo.*

FAMILY **BFI Southbank.** With the best repertory programming in London, the three movie theaters and studio at what was previously known as the National Film Theatre are effectively a national film center run by the British Film Institute. They show more than 1,000 titles each year, favoring art-house, foreign, silent, overlooked, classic, noir, and short films over Hollywood blockbusters. The center also has a gallery, bookshop, and "mediatheque," where visitors can watch film and television from the National Archive for free (closed Mon). This is one of the venues for the BFI London Film Festival; throughout the year there are minifestivals, seminars, and guest speakers. ■TIP➡ **Members (£45) get priority bookings (useful for special events) and £1.50 off each screening.** ✉ *Belvedere Rd., South Bank* ☎ *020/7928–3535 information, 020/7928–3232 box office* ⊕ *www.bfi.org.uk* Ⓜ *Waterloo.*

PERFORMANCE CENTERS

Southbank Centre. The Royal Festival Hall is one of London's best spaces for large-scale choral and orchestral works and is home to the Philharmonia and London Philharmonic orchestras. Other venues in the Southbank Centre host smaller-scale music performances: The Queen Elizabeth Hall is a popular venue for chamber orchestras and top-tier soloists, and the intimate Purcell Room is known for chamber music and solo recitals. Southbank also hosts everything from the London International Mime festival to large-scale dance performances. Also part of the complex is the **Hayward Gallery** (☉ *Mon. noon–6; Tues., Wed., Sat., and Sun. 10–6; Thurs. and Fri. 10–8*), a landmark Brutalist-style

1960s building and one of London's major venues for contemporary art exhibitions. ✉ *Belvedere Rd., South Bank* ☎ *020/7960–4200, 0844/875–0073 box office* ⊕ *www.southbankcentre.co.uk* Ⓜ *Waterloo, Embankment.*

THEATER

BAC. Battersea Arts Centre has a reputation for producing innovative new work. Check out Scratch events, low-tech theater by emerging artists where the audience provides feedback on works-in-progress. Entry for Scratch events is on a pay-what-you-can basis (minimum £1). There's also a fun bar that serves good food. ✉ *176 Lavender Hill, Battersea* ☎ *020/7223–2223* ⊕ *www.bac.org.uk* Ⓜ *National Rail: Clapham Junction.*

National Theatre. When this theater, designed by Sir Denys Lasdun, opened in 1976 Londoners weren't all so keen on the low-slung, multilayered Brutalist block. Prince Charles described the building as "a clever way of building a nuclear power station in the middle of London without anyone objecting." But whatever its merits or demerits as a feature on the landscape, the National Theatre's interior spaces are definitely worth a tour. Interspersed with the three theaters—the 1,150-seat Olivier, the 890-seat Lyttelton, and the revamped 400-seat Dorfman (formerly the Cottesloe)—is a multilayered foyer with exhibitions, bars, restaurants, and free entertainment. Musicals, classics, and new plays are all performed by top-flight professionals. Some shows offer £12 ticket deals. ✉ *Belvedere Rd., South Bank* ☎ *020/7452–3000 box office, 020/7452–3400 information* ⊕ *www.nationaltheatre.org. uk* ✆ *Tour £8.50* ☉ *Foyer Mon.–Sat. 9:30 am–11 pm, selected Sun. noon–6 pm; 75-min tour backstage, times vary* Ⓜ *Waterloo.*

The Old Vic. This grand old theater, former haunting grounds of such stage legends as John Gielgud, Vivien Leigh, Peter O'Toole, Richard Burton, and Judi Dench, is now masterminded by American actor Kevin Spacey. The theater had suffered decades of financial duress before being brought under the ownership of a dedicated trust headed by Spacey. His production record has had a few hiccups but his tenure is these days regarded by most as a success. As well as being artistic director, Spacey often appears on stage. ✉ *The Cut, Southwark* ☎ *0844/871–7628 box office* ⊕ *www.oldvictheatre.com* Ⓜ *Waterloo, Southwark.*

FAMILY

Fodor's Choice

★

Shakespeare's Globe Theatre. This faithful reconstruction of the open-air playhouse where Shakespeare worked and wrote many of his greatest plays marvelously re-creates the 16th-century theatergoing experience. Standing room in the yard or "pit" right in front of the stage costs £5. The season runs April through October, but an exhibition and theater tours run all year round. The Sam Wanamaker Playhouse, a replica Jacobean (early-17th-century) indoor theater named after the Globe's founder, opened in early 2014. ⇨ *For more on the Globe Theatre, see our special photo-feature, "Shakespeare and the Globe Theatre" in Chapter 8.* ✉ *21 New Globe Walk, Bankside, South Bank* ☎ *020/7401–9919 box office, 020/7902–1400 inquiries* ⊕ *www.shakespearesglobe. com* ✆ *Exhibition and Globe Theatre Tour £13.50* ☉ *Exhibition daily 10–5:30; Globe Theatre Tour daily 10:30–5* Ⓜ *London Bridge,*

CLASSICAL MUSIC: LONDON TODAY

Whether it's a concert by pianist Lang Lang or a Mozart requiem by candlelight, it's possible to hear first-rate musicians in world-class venues almost every day of the year. The London Symphony Orchestra is in residence at the Barbican Centre, although other top orchestras—including the Philharmonia and the Royal Philharmonic—also perform here. The Barbican also hosts chamber-music concerts, with celebrated orchestras such as the City of London Sinfonia. Kings Place, the new kid on London's concert block, has a great, and greatly varied calendar of musical events. The Southbank Centre has an impressive international music season, held in the Queen Elizabeth Hall and the small Purcell Room as well as in the Royal Festival Hall, now completely refurbished. Full houses are rare, so even at the biggest concert halls you should be able to get a ticket for £12. If you can't book in advance, arrive at the hall an hour before the performance for a chance at returns.

■ TIP→ Lunchtime concerts take place all over the city in smaller concert halls, the big arts-center foyers, and churches; they usually cost less than £5 or are free, and feature string quartets, singers, jazz ensembles, or gospel choirs. St. John's Smith Square and St. Martin-in-the-Fields are popular locations. Performances usually begin about 1 pm and last one hour.

Classical-music festivals range from the stimulating avant-garde **Meltdown** (⊕ *meltdown.southbankcentre.co.uk*), curated each year by a prominent musician—James Lavelle in 2014—at the Southbank Centre in June, to church hall recitals including the **Spitalfields Festival** (⊕ *www.spitalfieldsfestival.org.uk*), a program of recitals held in beautiful, historic East End churches in June, December, and January, and the month-long **City of London Festival** (⊕ *www.colf.org*) in the Square Mile in summer. A great British tradition since 1895, the **Henry Wood Promenade Concerts** (more commonly known as the "Proms" ⊕ *www.bbc.co.uk/proms*) run eight weeks, from July to September, at the Royal Albert Hall. Despite an extraordinary quantity of high-quality concerts, it's renowned for its (atypical) last night: a madly jingoistic display of singing "Land of Hope and Glory," Union Jack waving, and general madness. For regular Proms, tickets run £5–£95, with hundreds of standing tickets for £5 available at the hall on the night of the concert. ■ TIP→ The last night is broadcast in Hyde Park on a jumbo screen, but even here a seat on the grass requires a paid ticket that can set you back around £35.

Mansion House (then cross Southwark Bridge), Blackfriars (then cross Blackfriars Bridge), St. Paul's (then cross Millennium Bridge).

Young Vic. In a home near Waterloo, big names perform alongside young talent, often in daring, innovative productions of classic plays that appeal to a more diverse audience than is traditionally found in London theaters. Good food is served at the bustling bar. ⊠ *66 The Cut, Waterloo, South Bank* ☎ *020/7922–2922 box office* ⊕ *www.youngvic.org* Ⓜ *Southwark, Waterloo.*

OPERA: LONDON TODAY

The two key players in London's opera scene are the Royal Opera House (which ranks with the Metropolitan Opera House in New York) and the more innovative English National Opera (ENO), which presents English-language productions at the London Coliseum. Only the Theatre Royal, Drury Lane, has a longer theatrical history than the Royal Opera House—the third theater to be built on the site since 1858.

Despite occasional performances by the likes of Björk, the Royal Opera House struggles to shrug off its reputation for elitism and ticket prices that can rise to £800. It is,

however, more accessible than it used to be—the cheapest tickets are less than £10. Conditions of purchase vary; call for information. Prices for the ENO are generally lower, ranging from around £20 to £95.

In summer, the increasingly adventurous Opera Holland Park presents the usual chestnuts alongside some obscure works under a canopy in leafy Holland Park.

International touring companies often perform at Sadler's Wells, the Barbican, the Southbank Centre, and Wigmore Hall, so check the weekly listings for details.

KENSINGTON AND CHELSEA

These refined neighborhoods just west of central London offer a wide variety of art and entertainment options, several of which are located within the area's large public green spaces.

KENSINGTON

ART GALLERY

Serpentine Galleries. Built in 1934 as a tea pavilion in Kensington Gardens, the Serpentine has an international reputation for exhibitions of modern and contemporary art. Henry Moore, Andy Warhol, Bridget Riley, Damien Hirst, and Rachel Whiteread are a few of the artists who have exhibited here. An extension, the **Serpentine Sackler Gallery**, opened in the fall of 2013. It's a seven-minute walk across the park from the main gallery. The annual summer Pavilion, a striking temporary structure designed by a different leading architect every year, is always worth catching. ⊠ *Kensington Gardens, Kensington* ☎ *020/7402–6075* ⊕ *www.serpentinegalleries.org* ⊠ *Free* ⊘ *Tues.–Sun. 10–6* Ⓜ *Lancaster Gate, Knightsbridge, South Kensington.*

CLASSICAL MUSIC

Cadogan Hall. Formerly a church, Cadogan Hall has been turned into a spacious concert venue. It's home to the Royal Philharmonic Orchestra, and the English Chamber Orchestra performs here regularly. ⊠ *5 Sloane Terr., Kensington* ☎ *020/7730–4500* ⊕ *www.cadoganhall.com* Ⓜ *Sloane Sq.*

Royal Albert Hall. Opened in 1871, this splendid iron-and-glass–dome auditorium hosts music programs in a wide range of genres. Its terracotta exterior surmounted by a mosaic frieze depicting figures engaged in artistic, scientific, and cultural pursuits, this domed, circular 5,272-seat

London's Royal Opera House is also home to the Royal Ballet and an in-house orchestra.

auditorium was made possible by the Victorian public, who donated the money to build it. After funds were diverted toward the Albert Memorial (opposite), more money was raised by selling 999-year leases for 1,276 "Members'" seats at £100 apiece—today a box with 5 Members' Seats goes for half a million pounds. The notoriously poor acoustics were fixed after a 2004 renovation and the sight lines are excellent. The RAH hosts everything from pop and classical headliners to Cirque du Soleil, ballet on ice, awards ceremonies, and sumo wrestling championships, but is best known as the venue for the annual July–September BBC Promenade Concerts—the "Proms"—with bargain-price standing (or promenading, or sitting-on-the-floor) tickets sold on the night of the concert. The hall is also open daily for daytime guided tours (£11.50) and occasional afternoon tea (£30–£38). ✉ *Kensington Gore, Kensington* ☎ *0845/401–5034 box office* ⊕ *www.royalalberthall.com* Ⓜ *South Kensington.*

CINEMA

Riverside Studios Cinema. The selection at this converted movie studio showing repertory cinema changes almost daily. Admission fees are reasonable; £9.50 gets you entrance to a double bill. ✉ *Crisp Rd., Hammersmith* ☎ *020/8237–1111* ⊕ *www.riversidestudios.co.uk* Ⓜ *Hammersmith.*

OPERA

Opera Holland Park. In summer, well-loved operas and imaginative productions of relatively unknown works are presented under a spectacular new canopy against the remains of Holland House, one of the first great houses built in Kensington. Ticket prices range from £12 to £67.50, with 1,100 tickets offered free to young people ages 9–18 every season. Tickets go on sale in April. ⊠ *Holland Park, Kensington High St., Kensington* ☎ *0300/999–1000 box office (opens late Apr.), 020/7361–3570 inquiries* ⊕ *www.operahollandpark.com* Ⓜ *High Street Kensington, Holland Park.*

CHELSEA
ART GALLERY
Saatchi Gallery. Charles Saatchi lit the fuse to the contemporary art explosion in Britain and though he and his art investments may not be quite as ubiquitous as they once were, he remains a key figure. After migrating to several museums and being shown around the world, Saatchi's collection now resides in this modern gallery that sprawls through 70,000 square feet of the Duke of York's HQ building in Chelsea, complete with a bookshop and café-bar. ⊠ *Duke of York's HQ, King's Rd., Chelsea* ☎ *020/7811–3070* ⊕ *www.saatchi-gallery.co.uk* ⊠ *Free* ⊙ *Daily 10–6* Ⓜ *Sloane Sq.*

THEATER
Royal Court Theatre. Britain's undisputed epicenter of new theatrical works, the Court is now over 50 years old and continues to produce gritty British and international drama. ■TIP➡ **Don't miss the best deal in town—four 10-pence standing tickets go on sale one hour before each performance, and £10 tickets are available on Monday.** ⊠ *Sloane Sq., Chelsea* ☎ *020/7565–5000* ⊕ *www.royalcourttheatre. com* Ⓜ *Sloane Sq.*

NOTTING HILL

This cosmopolitan west London neighborhood, shown to advantage in the 1999 film that bears its name, is best known for the Notting Hill Carnival, a lively music-focused street festival that takes over the wider area on the final weekend of August each year. There's a year-round culture scene, too, catering mainly to the neighborhood's trendy young professionals.

FILM
FAMILY   **The Electric Cinema.** This refurbished Portobello Road art house screens mainstream and international movies. The emphasis is on comfort, with leather sofas for two, armchairs, footstools, and mini–coffee tables for your tapas-style food and wine. Saturday matinees for kids are popular. Edible Cinema combines experimental food and cocktails with the cinema experience. The Electric also has another sumptuous movie theater in east London—the Aubin, on Redchurch Street, with sofas and wine coolers. ⊠ *191 Portobello Rd., Notting Hill* ☎ *020/7908–9696* ⊕ *www.electriccinema.co.uk* ⊠ *£15.50–£22.50* Ⓜ *Ladbroke Grove, Notting Hill Gate.*

DANCE: LONDON TODAY

Dance fans in London can enjoy the classicism of the world-renowned Royal Ballet, as well as innovative works by several contemporary dance companies—including Rambert Dance Company and Matthew Bourne's New Adventures—and scores of independent choreographers. The English National Ballet and visiting international companies perform at the Coliseum and at Sadler's Wells, which also hosts various other ballet companies and dance troupes. Encompassing the refurbished Royal Festival Hall, the Southbank Centre has a seriously good contemporary dance program that hosts top international companies and important U.K. choreographers, as well as multicultural offerings ranging from Japanese Butoh and Indian Kathak to hip-hop. The Place and the Lilian Baylis Theatre at Sadler's Wells are where you'll find the most daring, cutting-edge performances.

Check ⊕ *londondance.com* for current performances and fringe venues.

Dance Umbrella. The biggest annual event is Dance Umbrella, 10 days in October that host international and British-based artists at various venues across the city.
☎ *020/7407–1200*
⊕ *www.danceumbrella.co.uk.*

REGENT'S PARK AND HAMPSTEAD

17

Leafy north London has long been a stomping ground for the capital's cultural elite—stroll through Primrose Hill and you're practically guaranteed to spot a film star or musician—but there's diversity here, too. Camden Town is justifiably famous for its indie music scene, while respected fringe theaters in Swiss Cottage and Kilburn don't shy away from major topics.

REGENT'S PARK

THEATER

Fodor'sChoice **Open Air Theatre.** On a warm summer evening, open-air classical theater
★ in the pastoral and royal Regent's Park is hard to beat for a magical adventure. Enjoy a supper before the performance, a bite during the intermission on the picnic lawn, or drinks in the spacious bar. The only downside is that warm summer nights in London are not always entirely reliable—a waterproof jacket is advisable. ✉ *Inner Circle, Regent's Park* ☎ *0844/826–4242* ⊕ *openairtheatre.com* Ⓜ *Baker St., Regent's Park.*

HAMPSTEAD

FILM

FAMILY **Everyman Cinema.** Kick off your shoes, curl up on the large comfy sofas, and have tapas and Champagne brought to you in front of classic, foreign, cutting-edge, and Hollywood titles. This venue also screens the Metropolitan Opera live from New York, and is a popular place for Hampstead denizens to bring their kids. Other branches around London also tend to offer a movie experience a cut above the average. ✉ *5 Holly Bush Vale, Hampstead* ☎ *0871/906–9060* ⊕ *www.everymancinema. com* Ⓜ *Hampstead.*

THEATER

FAMILY **Tricycle Theatre.** Committed to representing the cultural diversity of its community, the Tricycle shows the best in black, Irish, Jewish, Asian, and South African drama, and also promotes new work. There is a movie theater, too: Expect the best of new European and international cinema, including films from the United States, occasionally screened at film festivals the theater organizes. A year-round program of film-related activities is geared to children, and discounted movie tickets are available on Monday. ✉ *269 Kilburn High Rd., Kilburn* ☎ *020/7328–1000 box office* ⊕ *www.tricycle.co.uk* Ⓜ *Kilburn.*

SHOPPING

Updated by
Ellin Stein

The keyword of London shopping has always been "individuality," whether expressed in the superb custom tailoring of Savile Row, the nonconformist punk roots of quintessential British designer Vivienne Westwood, or the unique small stores that purvey the owner's private passion, whether paper theaters, toy soldiers, or buttons. This tradition is under threat from the influx of chains—global luxury, domestic mid-market, and international youth—but the distinctively British mix of quality and originality, tradition and character, remains.

You can try on underwear fit for a Queen at Her Majesty's lingerie supplier, track down a leather-bound Brontë classic at an antiquarian bookseller, or find a bargain antique on Portobello Road. Whether you're just browsing—there's nothing like the size, variety, and sheer theater of London's street markets to stimulate the acquisition instinct—or on a fashion-seeking mission, London shopping offers something for all tastes and budgets.

Although it's impossible to pin down one particular look that defines the city, London style tends to fall into two camps: one is the quirky, individualistic, somewhat romantic look exemplified by homegrown designers like Matthew Williamson, Vivienne Westwood, and Lulu Guinness. The other reflects Britain's celebrated tradition of classic knitwear and suiting, with labels like Jaeger, Pringle, and Brora, while Oswald Boateng, Paul Smith, and Richard James take tradition and give it a very modern twist. Traditional bespoke men's tailoring can be found in the menswear stores of Jermyn Street and Savile Row—there's no better place in the city to buy custom-made shirts and suits, while the handbags at Mulberry, Asprey, and Anya Hindmarch are pure classic quality. If your budget can't stretch this far, no problem; the city's chain stores like Topshop, Zara, and H&M, aimed at the younger end of the market, are excellent places to pick up designs copied straight from the

REGENT'S PARK

CAMDEN TOWN
cheap second-hand and club gear

CLERKENWELL
historical hotspot for crafts and design

BLOOMSBURY
antiquarian books and Lamb's Conduit Street

MARYLEBONE
small shops in village-like setting

HOXTON & SHOREDITCH
edgy young designers

NOTTING HILL
antiques, vintage clothing, and boho boutiques

OXFORD CIRCUS
global flagships, department stores, and street style on Carnaby

SOHO
books abound on Charing Cross Road

BAYSWATER

COVENT GARDEN
an urban-wear mecca around Seven Dials

MAYFAIR
catwalk names on Bond St., trad tailors on Savile Row

HYDE PARK

ST JAMES'S
old-fashioned specialists, from hatters to shirtmakers

Green Park

St. James's Park

KNIGHTSBRIDGE
luxe labels and, of course, Harrods

WESTMINSTER

BELGRAVIA

LAMBETH

VICTORIA

CHELSEA
the King's Rd. spans fashion to furniture

1/2 mile

1/2 km

Albany Rd.

Park Rd.

Lisson Grove

Marylebone Rd.

Baker St.

Edgware Rd.

Wigmore St.

Oxford St.

Bayswater Rd.

Kensington Rd.

Brompton Rd.

Sloane St.

King's Rd.

Pimlico Rd.

Knightsbridge

Constitution Hill

Piccadilly

New Bond St.

Regent St.

Albany St.

Gt. Portland St.

Portland Pl.

Euston Rd.

Gray's Inn Rd.

Tottenham Court Rd.

New Oxford St.

Holborn

Kingsway

Charing Cross Rd.

Shaftesbury

Aldwych

Strand

Waterloo Br.

Pall Mall

The Mall

Whitehall

Victoria Embankment

River Thames

Westminster Br.

Victoria St.

Buckingham Palace Rd.

Wilton Rd.

Vauxhall Br. Rd.

Horseferry Rd.

Millbank

Lambeth Palace Rd.

Albert Embankment

Lambeth Br.

Birdcage Walk

catwalk at a fraction of the price, while mid-market chains like Reiss, Jigsaw, and L.K. Bennett offer smart design and better quality for the more sophisticated shopper.

If there's anything that unites London's designers, it's a commitment to creativity and originality, underpinned by a strong sense of heritage. This combination of posh and rock-n-roll sensibilities turns up in everyone from Terence Conran, who revolutionized product and houseware design in the '60s (and is still going strong), to Alexander McQueen, who combined the Punk aesthetic with the rigor of couture. You'll see it in fanciful millinery creations by Philip Treacy and Stephen Jones, and in the work of imaginative shoemakers Nicholas Kirkwood, United Nude, and Terry de Havilland; and it keeps going, right through to current hot designers Erdem, Christopher Kane, and Christopher Bailey, the latter responsible for making traditional label Burberry relevant again.

One reason for London's design supremacy is the strength of local fashion college Central St. Martin's, whose graduates include Conran, Kane, McQueen, his successor at his eponymous label—and designer of the Duchess of Cambridge's wedding dress—Sarah Burton, and Stella McCartney's equally acclaimed successor at Céline, Phoebe Philo.

To find the McQueens, McCartneys, and Baileys of tomorrow, head for the independent boutiques of the East End and Bermondsey. If anything, London is even better known for its vibrant street fashion than for its high-end designers. Stock up from the stalls at Portobello, Camden, and Spitalfields markets.

Aside from bankrupting yourself, the only problem you may encounter is exhaustion. London's shopping districts are spread out all over the city, so do as savvy locals do: plan your excursion with military precision, taking in only one or two areas in a day, and stop for a lunch with a glass of wine or a pint at a pub.

PLANNING

OPENING HOURS

Most shops are open from about 9:30 or 10 am to 6 or 6:30 pm. Some may open at 11 and stay open until 7. Because shop hours, particularly for the smaller shops, are varied, it's a good idea to phone or check websites ahead. Stores that have late shopping—and not all do—are usually open until 7 or 8 pm on Wednesday or Thursday only. Most department stores stay open late one day a week. On Sunday, many shops open between 11 am and noon and close at 5 or 6 pm. Most stores are open on Sunday in December for the Christmas season.

WATCH YOUR LANGUAGE

Locals like to say that Brits and Americans are separated by a common language. Here are a few confusing terms to watch for when out and about in the shops:

Pants means underwear. Every other type of long-legged bottoms (except jeans) are called **trousers.** Also in the underwear category is the **vest** (undershirt in the United States); if you are looking for a vest, ask for a waistcoat.

Knickers are ladies' underwear. If you want pantyhose, ask for **tights**.

Jumper means sweater—unless it's a cardigan, in which case it may be shortened to **cardie**. If you ask for a **sweater**, you may be offered a sweatshirt.

Men use **braces** to hold up their trousers; in England **suspenders** is another word for garters.

If you want some Adidas- or Nike-type athletic shoes, ask for **trainers**, not sneakers.

Don't ask for a **pocketbook** or a **purse** if you mean a handbag—the former will be incomprehensible, and the latter will produce a coin purse. Ask for a **fanny pack** and it will produce a laugh—"fanny" means something altogether different in the United Kingdom, so ask for a "bum-bag."

Nightgowns are usually abbreviated to **nighties** and bathrobes may be **dressing gowns**.

A WORD ABOUT SERVICE

American standards of customer service are rare in London—you may find attentive customer service at old-school, traditional names and some independent stores, but salespeople elsewhere can seem abrupt or indifferent.

SHOPPING REVIEWS

18

ST. JAMES'S

ACCESSORIES: HATS

Fodor'sChoice ★ **James Lock & Co. Hatters.** Need a silk top hat, a flat-weave Panama, or a traditional tweed flat cap? Or, for ladies, an occasion hat? James Lock of St. James's has been providing hats from this cozy shop since 1676 for customers ranging from Admiral Lord Nelson, Oscar Wilde, and Frank Sinatra to, more recently, Robert Downey Jr. and Guy Ritchie, as well as trendsetting musicians and models. ⊠ *6 St. James's St., St. James's* ☎ *020/7930–8884* ⊕ *www.lockhatters.co.uk* ☽ *Closed Sun.* Ⓜ *Green Park.*

Fodor'sChoice ★ **Swaine Adeney Brigg.** Providing practical supplies for country pursuits since 1750, Swaine Adeney Brigg, now in new Mayfair premises, carries beautifully crafted umbrellas, walking sticks, and hip flasks, or ingenious combinations, such as the umbrella with a slim tipple-holding flask secreted inside the stem. The same level of quality and craftsmanship applies to the store's leather goods, which include attaché cases and wallets. You'll find scarves, caps, and the Herbert Johnson "Poet Hat," the iconic headgear (stocked since 1890) worn by Harrison Ford in every Indiana Jones film. ⊠ *7 Piccadilly Arcade, St. James's* ☎ *020/7409–7277* ⊕ *www.swaineadeney.co.uk* ☽ *Closed Sun.* Ⓜ *Green Park.*

Know Your Shopping Personality

"Where is the best place to shop in London?" There are thousands of shops in the city, and dozens of neighborhoods worth shopping in. Start by identifying your shopping personality to narrow your choices for a successful outing.

Easygoing. If you want to pop in and out of a variety of shops, as well as avoid the crowds around Oxford Street, head to King's Road in Chelsea. You'll find department store Peter Jones, plus Marks & Spencer and plenty of chains and trendy boutiques. Another safe bet is High Street Kensington for the usual big chains, in addition to some smaller ones less oriented toward disposable fashion, such as Cos, Karen Millen, and Oliver Bonas.

Eclectic. If you are looking for well-crafted, original items, start at Liberty on Regent Street, then head to Marylebone to the north, or the warren of cobblestone streets lined with independent shops off Carnaby Street, immediately to the south.

Fashionista. When only the top designers will do, start at the designer boutiques along Sloane Street in Knightsbridge before hopping on bus No. 19 to Green Park. From there you can cover Bond Street (both Old and New) finishing at Fenwick, or veer off onto Conduit Street, designer-heavy Bruton Street, or, at the northwest end of Berkeley Square, ultrachic Mount Street. If you still have time and energy, check out South Molton Street opposite Bond Street Tube or St. Christopher's Place across Oxford Street.

Funky and Avant-Garde. For cutting-edge fashion and housewares, head to the East End neighborhoods. Start at Columbia Road in Hoxton, with its charming specialty shops (and the Sunday flower market), then wander through Shoreditch, Spitalfields, and Bethnal Green, where you'll find stores filled with one-of-a-kind designs. There's also lots here to appeal to vintage hunters.

Whirlwind. If you're after a one-stop-shopping experience, head to one of the big department stores. Selfridges and Fenwick are near the Bond Street Tube station, Liberty is near Oxford Circus Tube station, while Harvey Nichols and Harrods share the Knightsbridge Tube station.

BEAUTY

Floris. What do Queen Victoria and Marilyn Monroe have in common? They both used fragrances from Floris, one of the most beautiful shops in London, with gleaming glass-and-Spanish-mahogany showcases salvaged from the Great Exhibition of 1851. In addition to scents for both men and women, Floris makes its own shaving products, reflecting its origins as a barbershop. Other gift possibilities include goose-down powder puffs, a famous rose-scented mouthwash, and beautifully packaged soaps and bath essences. There's another branch in Belgravia. ✉ *89 Jermyn St., St. James's* ☎ *0845/702–3239* ⊕ *www.florislondon. com* ☉ *Closed Sun.* Ⓜ *Piccadilly Circus, Green Park.*

BOOKS

Fodor'sChoice ★ **Hatchards.** This is London's oldest bookshop, open since 1797 and beloved by writers themselves (customers have included Oscar Wilde, Rudyard Kipling, and Lord Byron). Despite its wood-paneled, "gentleman's library" atmosphere, and eclectic selection of books, Hatchards is owned by the large Waterstone's chain. Nevertheless, the shop still retains its period charm, aided by the staff's old-fashioned helpfulness and expertise. Look for the substantial number of books signed by notable contemporary authors on the well-stocked shelves. ✉ *187 Piccadilly, St. James's* ☎ *020/7439–9921* ⊕ *www.hatchards.co.uk* Ⓜ *Piccadilly Circus.*

CLOTHING: MEN

Thomas Pink. This specialist chain is best known for its colorful and stylish formal shirts for both men and women, many in such fine fabrics as Sea Island or Egyptian cotton. More casual shirts are for sale as well, along with ties, boxers, pajamas, belts, and other accessories. For women, there are dresses, skirts, jackets, and knitwear. Bespoke shirts for men can be ordered at the Jermyn Street branch. There are other branches in The City, Chelsea, Canary Wharf, St. Pancras International, Waterloo Station, Heathrow, and the Westfield shopping center. ✉ *85 Jermyn St., St. James's* ☎ *020/7930–6364* ⊕ *www.thomaspink.co.uk* Ⓜ *Green Park, Piccadilly Circus.*

Turnbull & Asser. The Jermyn Street store sells luxurious jackets, cashmere sweaters, suits, ties, pajamas, ready-to-wear shirts, and accessories perfect for the billionaire who has everything. The brand is best known for its superb custom-made shirts—as worn by customers ranging from Prince Charles to Woody Allen and every filmic James Bond—that can be ordered at the nearby Bury Street branch. At least 15 separate measurements are taken, and the cloth, woven to the company's specifications, comes in 1,000 different patterns—the cottons feel as good as silk. The first order must be for a minimum of six shirts, which start from £195 each. There's another branch in The City. ✉ *71–72 Jermyn St., St. James's* ☎ *020/7808–3000* ⊕ *www.turnbullandasser.com* ☙ *Closed Sun.* Ⓜ *Green Park.*

FOOD

Fodor'sChoice ★ **Berry Bros. & Rudd.** Nothing matches Berry Bros. & Rudd for rare offerings and a unique shopping experience. A family-run wine business since 1698, "BBR" stores its vintage bottles and casks in vaulted cellars that are more than 300 years old. The in-house wine school offers educational tasting sessions while the dedicated whisky room also has an excellent selection. The shop has a quirky charm and the staff is extremely knowledgeable—and not snooty if you're on a budget. ✉ *3 St. James's St., St. James's* ☎ *800/280–2440* ⊕ *www.bbr.com* ☙ *Closed Sun.* Ⓜ *Green Park.*

Fodor'sChoice ★ **Fortnum & Mason.** Although F&M is popularly known as the Queen's grocer and the impeccably mannered staff still wear traditional tailcoats, its celebrated food hall stocks gifts for all budgets, such as irresistibly packaged luxury foods stamped with the gold "By Appointment" crest for less than £5. Try the teas, preserves (including the unusual rosepetal jelly), condiments, or Gentleman's Relish (anchovy paste). The store's famous hampers are always a welcome gift. The gleaming food hall spans two floors and incorporates a sleek wine bar, with the rest of the store devoted to upscale housewares, men and women's accessories and toiletries, a dedicated candle room, a jewelry department featuring exclusive designs by breakthrough talent, and clothing and toys for children. If you start to flag, break for afternoon tea at the new juice bar or one of the four other restaurants (one's an indulgent ice-cream parlor)—or a treatment in the Beauty Rooms. There's another branch at St. Pancras International. ⊠ *181 Piccadilly, St. James's* ☎ *020/7734–8040* ⊕ *www.fortnumandmason.com* Ⓜ *Green Park.*

Paxton & Whitfield. In business for more than 200 years, this venerable and aromatic London shop stocks hundreds of the world's greatest artisanal cheeses, particularly British and French varieties (a homesick General de Gaulle shopped here during World War II). The cheeses are laid on straw on refrigerated shelves, with tasting samples set out on a marble-top counter. You can pick up some ham, pâté, condiments, preserves, wine, or port, as well as cheese-related accessories like boards or knives. ⊠ *93 Jermyn St., St. James's* ☎ *020/7930–0259* ⊕ *www.paxtonandwhitfield.co.uk* ⊗ *Closed Sun.* Ⓜ *Piccadilly Circus, Green Park.*

SHOES
Loake Shoemakers. Long established in England's Midlands and a provider of boots to the British armed forces in both world wars, this family-run firm specializes in classic handcrafted men's shoes at reasonable prices. Whether you're after brogues, loafers, or deck shoes, the staff will take the time to ensure you have the right fit. In terms of quality and service, Loakes represents real value for money. There's another branch on Bow Street in The City. ⊠ *8–10 Princes Arcade, off Jermyn St., St. James's* ☎ *020/7734–8643* ⊕ *www.loake.co.uk* ⊗ *Closed Sun.* Ⓜ *Piccadilly.*

SPECIALTY STORES
Geo F. Trumper. If you don't have the time for an old-fashioned hot-towel shave, pick up some accessories to take home for yourself or as a gift. The Extract of West Indian Lime is a popular, zingy aftershave, and the Coconut Oil Hard Shaving Soap, which comes in a hand-turned wooden bowl, is a classic. There is also a store at 9 Curzon Street in Mayfair. ⊠ *1 Duke of York St., St. James's* ☎ *020/7734–6553* ⊕ *www.trumpers.com* ⊗ *Closed Sun.* Ⓜ *Piccadilly Circus.*

TOYS
The Armoury of St. James's. The fine toy soldiers and military models in stock here are collectors' items. Painted and mounted knights only 6 inches high can cost up to £1,200 (though figures start at a mere £7.50 for a toy soldier). Besides lead and tin soldiers, the shop has regimental brooches, historic orders and medals, and military antiques. ⊠ *17 Piccadilly Arcade, St. James's* ☎ *020/7493–5082* ⊕ *www.armoury.co.uk* ⊗ *Closed Sun.* Ⓜ *Piccadilly Circus.*

LONDON SHOPPING STEALS AND DEALS

Even at the best of times London has never been known as a budget-shopping destination, and when the pound is strong prices can seem stratospheric. However, whatever the exchange rate, there are still bargains to be had as long as you know where, and when, to look. To get the maximum mileage out of your cash, visit during the widespread biannual sales, which kick off in late June and just after Christmas, and last about a month.

Fashion insiders attend the many sales held throughout the year, from big warehouse clearances, such as the Designer Warehouse Sales (⊕ www.designerwarehousesales. com) and Designer Sales UK (⊕ designersales.co.uk), to individual designers' sample sales—check out ⊕ www.fashionconfidential.co.uk

or *Time Out* (⊕ www.timeout.com) for information, and to register for updates. London outlets, such as Browns Labels for Less, Paul Smith Sale Shop, and the Joseph Sale Shop on King's Road offer year-round designer bargains. If time permits, travel outside London to Bicester Village (⊕ www.bicestervillage.com), a luxury outlet mall in Oxfordshire. It's completely worth the nearly one-hour train journey, if only for the opportunity to score an item from such highly coveted British brands as Alexander McQueen, Temperley, Mulberry, Burberry, and Aquascutum, as well as top international labels.

If you're not fussy about labels, there are even more choices, including Pokit and Primark (⇨ see Soho listings).

MAYFAIR AND MARYLEBONE

18

MAYFAIR
ACCESSORIES

Mulberry. Staying true to its roots in rural Somerset, this luxury goods company epitomizes *le style Anglais*, a sophisticated take on the earth tones and practicality of English country style. Best known for highly desirable luxury handbags such as the Alexa and the Bayswater, the company also produces gorgeous leather accessories, from wallets to luggage, as well as shoes and clothing for men and women. Aside from the New Bond Street flagship, there are branches in Knightsbridge and Covent Garden, and Mulberry concessions in most of the major department stores. The small store on St. Christopher's Place in Marylebone stocks accessories only. ✉ *50 New Bond St., Mayfair* ☎ *020/7491–3900* ⊕ *www.mulberry.com* Ⓜ *Bond St.*

William & Son. William Asprey, scion of the jewelry dynasty, has opened his own store with a more friendly, less formal approach to selling carefully chosen, British-made luxury goods. Here's where you'll find all sorts of items you didn't know you needed, like silver-tipped retractable pencils, lizard-skin passport holders, crocodile backgammon sets, or a silver piggy bank. The jewelry is tasteful rather than knock-your-eyes-out and the store encourages requests for custom-made pieces. ✉ *10 Mount St., Mayfair* ☎ *020/7493–8385* ⊕ *www.williamandson. com* ☉ *Closed weekends* Ⓜ *Bond St.*

ANTIQUES

Grays Antique Market. Open weekdays from 10 to 6 and from 11 to 5 on Saturday (when not all stalls are open), Grays has approximately 200 dealers specializing in everything from Bakelite home wares to Mughal art. The majority focus on jewelry, ranging from contemporary to antique. Bargains are not out of the question, and proper pedigrees are guaranteed. Also try Grays in the Mews around the corner—stalls there sell less expensive merchandise, including antique dolls at Glenda's and excellent vintage clothing at Vintage Modes. ⊠ *58 Davies St., Mayfair* ☎ *020/7629–7034* ⊕ *www.graysantiques. com* ☉ *Closed Sun.* Ⓜ *Bond St.*

> **BESPOKE LONDON**
>
> Having anything made to order used to be restricted to the upper class. One had one's tailor, one's milliner, one's dressmaker, and so forth. Things are more egalitarian these days, but whether you want a bespoke Savile Row suit or custom-made leather shoes, the prices are still steep.

BOOKS AND STATIONERY

Alfred Dunhill. For over 100 years, Dunhill has been synonymous with the most luxurious and sophisticated men's goods, including accessories, briefcases, and superbly tailored clothes. This Georgian mansion, the mothership (or possibly fathership), also offers a barbershop, men's spa, humidor, cellar bar, courtyard restaurant, and bespoke services, where you can order custom-fitted menswear or unique versions of the brand's celebrated leather goods. There's another branch in St. James's. ⊠ *2 Davies St., Mayfair* ☎ *020/7853-4429* ⊕ *www.dunhill.com* ☉ *Closed Sun.* Ⓜ *Bond St.*

Fodor'sChoice
★
Heywood Hill. Established for more than 70 years on Curzon Street, and considered by some to be the best small bookstore in the English-speaking world (John Le Carré, who set a scene in *Tinker Tailor Soldier Spy* here, is a long-standing customer), Heywood Hill stocks both new and antiquarian books. Here's where you can pick up a leather-bound volume on architecture, gardening, natural history, and topography—in which the antiquarian collection specializes. The contemporary selection emphasizes literature, history, biography, travel, architecture, and children's books. During World War I, author Nancy Mitford helped keep the bookstore going. Today, the descendant of her brother-in-law, the Duke of Devonshire, remains the major stockholder. ⊠ *10 Curzon St., Mayfair* ☎ *020/7629–0647* ⊕ *www.heywoodhill.com* ☉ *Closed Sun.* Ⓜ *Green Park.*

Maggs Bros. Ltd. How could any book lover resist a shop with such a deliciously Dickensian name? Located in a Georgian town house in one of Mayfair's toniest squares, Maggs, established 1853, is one of the world's oldest and largest rare-book dealers. Shop staff is expert enough to advise important collectors, but is nonetheless friendly and helpful to all interested visitors. Far from being fussy, the store includes a "counterculture" section with works on subversion, extremism, punk, the occult, and more. ⊠ *50 Berkeley Sq., Mayfair* ☎ *020/7493–7160* ⊕ *www.maggs.com* ☉ *Closed weekends* Ⓜ *Green Park.*

LOTH SOLD BY THE METRE

Those who want the best and have the budget to afford it head for Mayfair and St. James's.

Smythson of Bond Street. Hands down, this is the most elegant stationer in Britain. No hostess of any standing would consider having a leather-bound guest book made by anyone else, and the shop's distinctive pale-blue–page diaries and social stationery are thoroughly British. Diaries, stationery, and small leather goods can be personalized. Smythson also produces a small range of leather handbags and purses. You'll find other branches in Chelsea, Notting Hill, and the City. ⊠ *40 New Bond St., Mayfair* ☎ *020/7629–8558* ⊕ *www.smythson.com* Ⓜ *Bond St., Oxford Circus.*

Waterstone's. At this mega-bookshop (Europe's largest) located in a former art deco department store near Piccadilly Circus, browse through your latest purchase or admire the view with a glass of wine or a snack at the 5th View Bar and Food, which is open until 9. Waterstone's is the country's leading book chain, and they've pulled out all the stops to make their flagship as comfortable and welcoming as a bookstore can be. There are several smaller branches located throughout the city. ⊠ *203–206 Piccadilly, Mayfair* ☎ *0207/851–2400* ⊕ *www.waterstones. com* Ⓜ *Piccadilly Circus.*

CLOTHING

Belstaff. For years purveyors of Britain's coolest motorcycle leathers, Belstaff has expanded into dresses, skirts, and handbags, as well as knitwear, boots, tops, and trousers for both men and women, all reflecting the brand's functional but unconventional heritage (previous customers include Lawrence of Arabia, Amelia Earhart, and Che Guevara). Outerwear in general and leather jackets in particular remain a strength. ⊠ *135–137 New Bond St., Mayfair* ☎ *020/7495–5897* ⊕ *www.belstaff. co.uk* Ⓜ *Bond St.*

Burberry. Known for its trademark tartan, this company has cultivated an edgy, high-fashion image in recent years, with designs like fetish-y boots and sexy leather jackets perfect for any catwalk. The raincoats are still a classic buy, along with plaid scarves in every color imaginable and handbags. If you're up for a trek, there's a huge factory outlet in Hackney on Chatham Place that has clothes and accessories for men, women, and children at half price or less. There are also branches in Mayfair, Knightsbridge, and Covent Garden, in addition to this spectacular flagship store. ⊠ *121 Regent St., Mayfair* ☎ *020/7806–8904* ⊕ *uk.burberry.com* Ⓜ *Piccadilly Circus.*

Fodor's Choice

★

Dover Street Market. Visiting this six-floor emporium isn't just about buying; with its creative displays and eclectic, well-chosen mix of merchandise, it's as much art installation as store. The creation of Comme des Garçons' Rei Kawakubo, it showcases all of the label's collections for men and women alongside a changing roster of other designers including Peter Piloto, Alexander Wang, and Givenchy—all of whom have their own customized mini-boutiques—plus avant-garde art books, vintage couture, and curiosities such as antique plaster anatomy models. With merchandize and configuration changing every six months, you never know what you will find, which is half the fun. ■ **TIP→ An outpost of the Rose Bakery on the top floor makes for a yummy break.** ⊠ *17–18 Dover St., Mayfair* ☎ *020/7518–0680* ⊕ *www.doverstreetmarket.com* ⊘ *Closed Sun.* Ⓜ *Green Park.*

Fodor's Choice

★

Isabel Marant London. The first London store from of-the-moment designer Marant, a favorite of French fashion editors, this airy sky-lighted space is full of her signature skinny jeans, slouchy knits, wedge sneakers, and rock-chick miniskirts, all exuding Left Bank boho cool. ⊠ *29 Bruton St., Mayfair* ☎ *020/7499–7887* ⊕ *www.isabelmarant.com* ⊘ *Closed Sun.* Ⓜ *Bond St.*

Mackintosh. Think of Victorian and you think of corsets and frock coats— but did you know that in 1823 a Glaswegian chemist named Mackintosh was able to interweave rubber with cloth, thus creating the modern rubberized raincoat (then used for horse-riding). It was so popular that the brand name has become synonymous with the item. This byword for tradition has now been revitalized with designs that infuse the label's classic outerwear with contemporary zing. ⊠ *104 Mount St., Mayfair* ☎ *020/7493–4678* ⊕ *www.mackintosh.com* ⊘ *Closed Sun.* Ⓜ *Bond St.*

CLOTHING: MENSWEAR

Gieves and Hawkes. One of the grand men's tailoring houses of Savile Row, this company made its name outfitting British Royals who served as officers in the armed forces and they still supply custom-made military uniforms, as well as beautifully tailored civilian wear. Prices for a bespoke suit start around £3,800 but there are also off-the-peg designs starting at around £600. There's also a branch in The City. ⊠ *1 Savile Row, Mayfair* ☎ *020/7432–6403* ⊕ *www.gievesandhawkes.com* Ⓜ *Piccadilly Circus.*

Ozwald Boateng. The dapper menswear by Ozwald Boateng (pronounced Bwa-teng) combines contemporary funky style with traditional Savile Row quality. His made-to-measure suits have been worn by trendsetters such as Jamie Foxx, Mick Jagger, and Laurence Fishburne, who appreciate the sharp cuts, luxurious fabrics, and occasionally vibrant colors (even the more conservative choices sport jacket linings in bright silk). ✉ *30 Savile Row, Mayfair* ☎ *020/7437–2030* ⊕ *www. ozwaldboateng.co.uk* ⊘ *Closed Sun.* Ⓜ *Piccadilly Circus.*

CLOTHING: WOMEN'S WEAR

Alexander McQueen. Since McQueen's untimely death in 2010, his right-hand woman Sarah Burton has been at the helm, receiving raves for continuing his tradition of theatrical, darkly romantic, and beautifully cut clothes incorporating corsetry, lace, embroidery, and hourglass silhouettes, all of which were exemplified in Burton's celebrated wedding dress for Kate Middleton. Can't afford a gala gown? Go home with a skull-printed scarf. ✉ *4–5 Old Bond St., Mayfair* ☎ *020/7355–0088* ⊕ *www.alexandermcqueen.com* Ⓜ *Bond St.*

Browns. This shop—actually a collection of small shops—was a pioneer designer boutique in the 1970s and continues to talent-spot the newest and best around. You may find the windows showcasing the work of top graduates from this year's student shows or displaying well-established designers such as Erdem, Dries Van Noten, or Balenciaga. The men's store at No. 23 has a similar designer selection, while Browns Focus at No. 24 showcases youthful, hip designs and denim. There is a smaller boutique on Sloane Street and if you're about to go down the aisle, check out the two bridal boutiques; one at 12 Hinde Street, which stocks various designers, and another at 59 Brook Street devoted to Vera Wang gowns exclusive to Browns in the United Kingdom. ✉ *24–27 S. Molton St., Mayfair* ☎ *020/7514–0016* ⊕ *www.brownsfashion.com* ⊘ *Closed Sun.* Ⓜ *Bond St.*

Fodor's Choice
★

Fenwick. A manageably sized department store, Fenwick is a welcome haven of affordability in a shopping area where stratospheric prices are the norm. The store is particularly strong on accessories (notably lingerie, wraps, and hats), cosmetics, perfumes, and chic, wearable fashion by both established and emerging designers such as Issa, Goat, and Theory. There are also three small spas (Chantecaille, Clarins, and Pure Massage), a nail bar, a brow bar, and a restaurant, plus a men's department in the basement. ✉ *163 New Bond St., Mayfair* ☎ *020/7629–9161* ⊕ *www.fenwick.co.uk* Ⓜ *Bond St.*

Matthew Williamson. Sinuous, feminine, and floaty, Williamson's designs, often incorporating bright prints and embellishment, are the epitome of rich-hippie chic, and are favorites with such well-heeled free spirits as Kate Moss and Sienna Miller. Even if you can't manage to get to a beach party on Ibiza, a Williamson dress will put you in the spirit. ✉ *28 Bruton St., Mayfair* ☎ *020/7629–6200* ⊕ *www.matthewwilliamson. com* ⊘ *Closed Sun.* Ⓜ *Bond St.*

Nicole Farhi. Busy working women who value unfussy quality invest in Farhi's softly tailored yet functional dresses and separates, and her contemporary yet timeless styles are wardrobe staples. This flagship Conduit Street store sells clothes for both men and women as well as shoes and home ware. There are also branches in Covent Garden, Fulham, and Hampstead. ✉ *25 Conduit St., Mayfair* ☎ *020/7499–8368* ⊕ *www.nicolefarhi.com* Ⓜ *Bond St.*

18

Stella McCartney. It's not easy emerging from the shadow of a Beatle father, but Stella McCartney has become a major force in fashion in her own right. Her signature jumpsuits and tuxedo pantsuits embody her design philosophy, combining minimalist tailoring with femininity and sophistication with ease of wear. Her love of functionality and clean lines has led to her branching off into sportswear, designing a line for Adidas and dressing Team GB for the London Olympics. A vegetarian like her parents, she refuses to use fur or leather, making her a favorite with ethical fashionistas. There's another boutique in South Kensington. ⊠ *30 Bruton St., Mayfair* ☎ *020/7518–3100* ⊕ *www.stellamccartney. com* Ⓜ *Bond St.*

Vivienne Westwood. From beginnings as the most shocking and outré designer around, Westwood (now Dame Vivienne) has become a standard bearer for high-style British couture. The Chelsea boutique is where it all started: the lavish corseted ball gowns, the dandified nipped-waist jackets, and the tartan with a punk edge that formed the core of her signature look. Here you can still buy ready-to-wear, mainly the more casual Anglomania diffusion line and the exclusive Worlds End label based on the archives. The small Davies Street boutique sells only the more exclusive, expensive Gold Label and Couture collections (plus bridal), while the flagship Conduit Street store carries all of the above. ⊠ *44 Conduit St., Mayfair* ☎ *020/7439–1109* ⊕ *www. viviennewestwood.co.uk* ⊗ *Closed Sun.* Ⓜ *Oxford Circus.*

DEPARTMENT STORES

Thomas Goode. This spacious luxury housewares shop has been at the same smart Mayfair address since 1845. The china, silver, crystal, and linen, whether from the store's own line or from luxury brands like Christofle and Puiforcat, are simply the best that money can buy, a legacy of its original customer base of international royals and heads of state. The store still holds two royal warrants, but anyone who can afford it can commission their own bespoke set of china. ■ TIP→ If such luxury is beyond you, visit anyway for the shop's small museum of plates, either antique or designed for royalty, including some created for Princess Diana's wedding. ⊠ *19 S. Audley St., Mayfair* ☎ *020/7499– 2823* ⊕ *www.thomasgoode.co.uk* Ⓜ *Green Park.*

FOOD

Charbonnel et Walker. Established in 1875, this master chocolatier's Mayfair shop specializes in traditional handmade chocolates (violet and rose-petal creams, for example) and has been creating these beautifully packaged, high-quality sweets from long before most of today's fashionable brands appeared. ■ TIP→ Their drinking chocolate—coarsely grated fine chocolate in a tin—is worth carrying home in a suitcase. ⊠ *The Royal Arcade, 28 Old Bond St., Mayfair* ☎ *020/7491–0939* ⊕ *www.charbonnel.co.uk* ⊗ *Closed Sun.* Ⓜ *Green Park.*

JEWELRY

Fodor's Choice ★ **Asprey.** Created by architect Norman Foster and interior designer David Mlinaric, this "global flagship" store displays exquisite jewelry—as well as silver and leather goods, watches, china, and crystal—in a discreet, very British setting that oozes quality, expensive good taste, and hushed comfort. If you're in the market for an immaculate 1930s cigarette case, a silver cocktail shaker, a pair of pavé diamond and sapphire earrings, or a ladylike handbag, you won't be disappointed. And, for the really well-heeled, there's a custom-made jewelry service available as well. ☒ *167 New Bond St., Mayfair* ☎ *020/7493–6767* ⊕ *www.asprey.com* ⊘ *Closed Sun.* Ⓜ *Green Park.*

Garrard. Formally known as "Garrard, the Crown Jeweler," this company has been creating royal crowns since Queen Victoria's reign (you can see several on display in the Tower of London). Today the focus is on precious gems in simple, classic settings, along with silver accessories. Although some collections are definitely contemporary with items like minimalist hoop earrings, many of the designs are traditional and impressive, should you be in the market for an old-school diamond tiara. ☒ *24 Albemarle St., Mayfair* ☎ *0870/871–8888* ⊕ *www.garrard. com* ⊘ *Closed Sun.* Ⓜ *Green Park.*

SHOES

Fodor's Choice ★ **Nicholas Kirkwood.** Kirkwood is one of Britain's most fashionable shoe designers and this is his first retail boutique. You won't be able to hike in his imaginative, elegant, sky-high stilettos (be warned: prices are similarly high), but you will be able to make quite an entrance. There are also more wearable shoes that are equally flattering and distinctive. ☒ *5 Mount St., Mayfair* ☎ *020/7290–1404* ⊕ *www.nicholaskirkwood. com* ⊘ *Closed Sun.* Ⓜ *Green Park.*

Fodor's Choice ★ **Rupert Sanderson.** Designed in London and made in Italy, Sanderson's elegant shoes have been a huge hit in fashion circles. Red-carpet-ready high heels as worn by Claire Danes and Sandra Bullock, bright colors, tough motorcycle boots, and a penchant for peep toes are signature elements. Prices reflect the impeccable craftsmanship. ☒ *19 Bruton Pl., Mayfair* ☎ *0207/491–2260* ⊕ *www.rupertsanderson.com* ⊘ *Closed Sun.* Ⓜ *Bond St., Green Park.*

MARYLEBONE

ANTIQUES

Alfie's Antique Market. This four-story, bohemian-chic labyrinth is London's largest indoor antiques market, housing dealers specializing in art, lighting, glassware, textiles, jewelry, furniture, and collectibles, with a particular strength in vintage clothing and 20th-century design. Come here to pick up vintage (1900–70) clothing, accessories, and luggage from Tin Tin Collectables, mid-20th-century furniture at Decoratum that will make you feel like you've stepped into the set of *Mad Men*, or a spectacular mid-20th-century Italian lighting fixture at Vincenzo Caffarrella. There's also a rooftop restaurant if you need a coffee break. In addition to the market, this end of Church Street is lined with excellent antiques shops. ☒ *13–25 Church St., Marylebone* ☎ *020/7723–6066* ⊕ *www.alfiesantiques.com* ⊘ *Closed Sun. and Mon.* Ⓜ *Marylebone.*

BOOKS

Daunt Books. An independent bookstore chain (there are additional branches in Belsize Park, Chelsea, Hampstead, Holland Park, and Cheapside), Daunt favors a thoughtful selection of contemporary and classic fiction and nonfiction over self-help books and ghost-written

18

celebrity "autobiographies." The striking Marylebone branch is an original Edwardian bookstore where a dramatic room lined with oak galleries under lofty skylights houses the noted travel section, which includes not only guidebooks but also related literature and poetry. The Hampstead branch is strong on children's books. ⊠ *83 Marylebone High St., Marylebone* ☎ *020/7224–2295* ⊕ *www.dauntbooks.co.uk* Ⓜ *Baker St.*

CLOTHING

Matches. The rising British designers featured in this carefully curated boutique include Christopher Kane, Charlotte Olympia, Issa, and Richard Nicholl, as well as more-established figures like McCartney and McQueen and international labels such as J Brand, Acne, Bottega Veneta, Lanvin, and Chloe. There's also an equally stylish menswear department, plus jewelry, lingerie, and accessories. Other branches are in Notting Hill and southwest London. ⊠ *87 Marylebone High St., Marylebone* ☎ *020/7487–5400* ⊕ *www.matchesfashion.com* Ⓜ *Regent's Park, Baker St.*

DEPARTMENT STORES

Marks & Spencer. You'd be hard-pressed to find a Brit who doesn't have something in the closet from Marks & Spencer (or "M&S," as it's popularly known). This major chain is famed for its classic, dependable clothing for men, women, and children—affordable cashmere and lambs-wool sweaters are particularly good buys—and occasionally scores a fashion hit. The food department at M&S is consistently good, especially for frozen food, and a great place to pick up a sandwich or premade salad on the go (look for M&S Simply Food stores all over town). The flagship branch at Marble Arch and the Pantheon location at 173 Oxford Street have extensive fashion departments. ⊠ *458 Oxford St., Marylebone* ☎ *020/7935–7954* ⊕ *www.marksandspencer.com* Ⓜ *Marble Arch.*

Fodor's Choice **Selfridges.** This giant, bustling store (the second largest in the United
★ Kingdom after Harrods) gives Harvey Nichols a run for its money as London's most fashionable department store. Packed to the rafters with clothes ranging from mid-price lines to the latest catwalk names, the store continues to break ground with its innovative retail schemes, especially the high-fashion Superbrands section, the ground-floor Wonder Room showcasing extravagant jewelry and luxury gifts, the self-contained Louis Vuitton town house, an array of pop-up shops, and the Concept Store, which features a rotating series of themed displays. There are so many zones that merge into one another—from youth-oriented Miss Selfridge to audio equipment to the large, comprehensive cosmetics department—that you practically need a map. Don't miss the Shoe Galleries, the world's largest shoe department filled with more than 5,000 pairs from 120 brands, displayed like works of art under spotlights. ■TIP➔ Take a break with a glass of wine from the Wonder Bar, or pick up some rare tea in the Food Hall as a gift. ⊠ *400 Oxford St., Marylebone* ☎ *0800/123–400* ⊕ *www.selfridges.com* Ⓜ *Bond St.*

JEWELRY

Fodor's Choice ★ **The Button Queen.** This store is one of the small, comprehensive, niche shops that made London so distinctive but which are now disappearing. It began life as a market stall in the 1950s and now has a vast selection of buttons, from antique to modern, encompassing an array of styles and price points. You can also have a set made using fabric you supply. ⊠ *76 Marylebone La., Marylebone* ☎ *020/7935–1505* ⊕ *www. thebuttonqueen.co.uk* ☉ *Closed Sun.* Ⓜ *Oxford Circus.*

Kabiri. A dazzling array of exciting contemporary jewelry by emerging and established designers from around the world is packed into this small shop. There is something to suit most budgets and tastes, from flamboyant statement pieces to subtle, delicate adornment. Look out for British talent Johanne Mills, among many others. There's another branch in Chelsea. ⊠ *37 Marylebone High St., Marylebone* ☎ *020/7317–2150* ⊕ *www.kabiri.co.uk* Ⓜ *Baker St.*

SOHO AND COVENT GARDEN

SOHO

ACCESSORIES

Fodor's Choice ★ **Peckham Rye.** On the small cobblestone streets leading off Carnaby Street you'll find small specialist boutiques such as Peckham Rye, a tiny shop showcasing heritage-style men's accessories—handmade silk and twill ties, bow ties, and scarves, all using traditional patterns from the archives of this family-run business that go back to 1799. More Ralph Lauren than Ralph Lauren, the socks, striped shirts, and handkerchiefs attract modern-day Beau Brummels such as Mark Ronson and David Beckham. ⊠ *11 Newburgh St., Soho* ☎ *0207/734–5181* ⊕ *www. peckhamrye.com* Ⓜ *Oxford St.*

18

BOOKS

Fodor's Choice ★ **Foyles.** Founded in 1903 by the Foyle brothers after they failed the Civil Service exam, this family-owned store, recently relocated into this historic 1930s art deco building, carries almost every title imaginable. One of London's best sources for textbooks, Foyles also stocks everything from popular fiction to military history, sheet music, medical tomes, graphic novels, and handsome illustrated fine arts books. It also offers the store-within-a-store Ray's Jazz (one of London's better outlets for music) and a cool café. Foyles has branches in the Southbank Centre, St. Pancras International train station (the Eurostar's U.K. terminus), and the Westfield shopping centers in Shepherd's Bush and Stratford. ⊠ *107–109 Charing Cross Rd., Soho* ☎ *020/7437–5660* ⊕ *www.foyles. co.uk* Ⓜ *Tottenham Court Rd.*

CLOTHING

Other. Aimed at men and women in search of stylish cool, this independent boutique stocks its own brand of entirely made-in-England clothing, as well as accessories, housewares, books, and clothing from other carefully selected brands such as b store, Opening Ceremony, Sophie Hulme, and Peter Jensen. The look is understated, slightly geeky, and totally contemporary. ⊠ *21 Kingly St., Soho* ☎ *020/7734–6846* ⊕ *www. other-shop.com* Ⓜ *Oxford Circus.*

Pokit. Sharp but comfortable made-to-measure suits for men and women start from just £800 (jackets £500) at this contemporary tailor shop. It also has a wide range of leather goods. ✉ *132 Wardour St., Soho* ☎ *020/7434–2875* ⊕ *www.pokit.co.uk* Ⓜ *Oxford Circus.*

Primark. Fantastic for low-cost, trendy clothing, this is Primark's huge, two-story flagship (there are other branches in Hammersmith and Kilburn). But keep in mind, you get what you pay for: some of the fabrics and finishes reflect the store's budget prices and its labor practices have attracted criticism. This is the home of fast, youthful, disposable fashion, so don't expect attentive service or classic styling and you won't be disappointed. ✉ *499–517 Oxford St., Soho* ☎ *020/7495–0420* ⊕ *www.primark.co.uk* Ⓜ *Marble Arch.*

CLOTHING: WOMEN'S WEAR
Wolsey. Specializing in men's knitwear since 1755, Wolsey now sells rugged but stylish outerwear, sweaters, shirts, hats, scarves, socks, T-shirts, sweatshirts, and underwear (as worn by both Roald Amundsen and Captain Robert Scott on their race to the South Pole). There's another branch in Covent Garden. ✉ *83 Brewer St., Soho* ☎ *020/7434–4257* ⊕ *www.wolsey.com* Ⓜ *Piccadilly Circus.*

DEPARTMENT STORE
Fodor's Choice
★
Liberty. The wonderful black-and-white mock-Tudor facade, created from the timber of two Royal Navy ships, reflects this store's origins in the late-19th-century Arts and Crafts movement. Leading designers were recruited to create the classic art nouveau Liberty prints that are still a centerpiece of the brand, gracing everything from cushions and silk kimonos to embossed leather bags and photo albums. Inside, Liberty is a labyrinth of nooks and crannies stuffed with thoughtfully chosen merchandise. Clothes for both men and women focus on high quality and high fashion with labels like Helmut Lang and Marc by Marc Jacobs. The store regularly commissions new prints from contemporary designers, and sells both these and its archival patterns by the yard. If you're not so handy with a needle, an interior design service will create soft furnishings for you. ✉ *Regent St., Soho* ☎ *020/7734–1234* ⊕ *www.liberty.co.uk* Ⓜ *Oxford Circus.*

FOOD
Fodor's Choice
★
The Vintage House. If whisky is more to your taste than wine, visit the Vintage House, which has the country's largest selection of single malts (more than 1,400), many notable for their age. The shop is open late—to 11 pm most nights. ✉ *42 Old Compton St., Soho* ☎ *020/7437–2592* ⊕ *freespace.virgin.net/vintagehouse.co* Ⓜ *Leicester Sq.*

MUSIC
BM Soho. House, drum 'n' bass, electro, dubstep—this shop (formerly Black Market Records) is London's longest-established dance music store and stocks the hottest club music around. They carry some CDs, but this is really a shop for vinyl lovers. ✉ *25 D'Arblay St., Soho* ☎ *020/7437–0478* ⊕ *www.bm-soho.com* Ⓜ *Oxford Circus, Tottenham Court Rd.*

SHOES

Irregular Choice. If you want to blend in with the crowd, these shoes are not for you. But if you like footwear that is fun and flattering (not to mention reasonably priced), head for Irregular Choice. Styles tend towards Louis XIV like court shoes ornamented with ribbon ties or silk flowers; pumps in interesting patterns ranging from polka dots to houndstooth; as well as bejeweled flats, leopard-print boots, and red patent-leather stilettos. Best of all, many have round toes and supportive heels, proving that comfortable doesn't have to be dull. There's another branch in Shoreditch. ☒ *35 Carnaby St., Soho* ☎ *020/7494–4811* ⊕ *www.irregularchoice.com* Ⓜ *Oxford Circus.*

TOYS

FAMILY **Hamleys.** Besieged by pester power? Don't worry, help is at hand—this London institution has six floors of the latest dolls, soft toys, video games, and technological devices (plus such old-fashioned pleasures as train sets, drum kits, and magic tricks), with every must-have on the pre-teen shopping list. Some may find the offerings to be overly commercialized (it's heavy on movie and TV tie-ins), and the store only got rid of its separate pink and blue floors for girls and boys in 2011 after a protest campaign. Nevertheless, when British children visit London, Hamleys is at the top of their agenda. It's a madhouse at Christmastime, but Santa's grotto is one of the best in town. There's a smaller branch in St. Pancras International train station. ☒ *188–196 Regent St., Soho* ☎ *0871/704–1977* ⊕ *www.hamleys.com* Ⓜ *Oxford Circus, Piccadilly Circus.*

COVENT GARDEN
BOOKS AND PRINTS

Grosvenor Prints. London's largest collection of 17th- to-early 20th-century prints emphasizes views of the city and architecture as well as sporting and decorative motifs. The selection is eclectic, with prices ranging from £5 into the thousands. ☒ *19 Shelton St., Covent Garden* ☎ *020/7836–1979* ⊕ *www.grosvenorprints.com* ⊘ *Closed Sun.* Ⓜ *Covent Garden, Leicester Sq.*

Fodor's Choice **Stanfords.** When it comes to encyclopedic coverage, there is simply no
★ better travel shop on the planet. Stanfords is packed with a comprehensive selection of maps, travel books, travel gadgets, globes, notebooks, replicas of antique maps, and more. Even the floor is decorated with giant maps. Whether you're planning a day trip to Surrey or an adventure to the South Pole, this should be your first stop. ☒ *12–14 Long Acre, Covent Garden* ☎ *020/7836–1321* ⊕ *www.stanfords.co.uk* Ⓜ *Covent Garden.*

CLOTHING

Paul Smith. British classics with an irreverent twist define Paul Smith's collections for women, men, and children. Beautifully tailored suits for men and women take hallmarks of traditional British style and turn them on their heads with humor and color, combining exceptional fabrics with flamboyant linings or unusual detailing. Gift ideas abound—wallets, scarves, diaries, spectacles, even a soccer ball—all in Smith's signature rainbow stripes. There are several branches throughout London, in Notting Hill, Soho, and Borough Market, plus

18

BRING A BIT OF ENGLAND HOME

To avoid panic-buying a bulk pack of Cadbury chocolate at Heathrow, it's wise to plan your gift purchasing with care.

For a well-chosen, eclectic selection, unique department store Liberty is hard to beat—here you'll find everything from exquisite Miller Harris fragrances by British perfumer Lyn Harris to small leather goods embossed with the famous Liberty prints.

Fortnum & Mason has equally carefully curated, though perhaps more sedate, offerings, such as leather-covered hip flasks and model boats with Union Jack sails.

The big attraction here is the world-famous food hall with its beautifully packaged cookies, teas, and unusual condiments. A. Gold is another source of British-made treats.

Looking for a gift for the hard-to-shop-for man in your life? Consider some traditional shaving cream from Geo. F. Trumper.

The museum shops are also bursting with original gift ideas, from art books and posters at Tate Modern or the Fashion Museum to double-decker bus models and Tube-map mouse pads at the London Transport Museum in Covent Garden.

a Mayfair shop that includes vintage furniture and a shoes-and-accessories shop on Marylebone High Street. ⊠ *40–44 Floral St., Covent Garden* ☎ *020/7379–7133* ⊕ *www.paulsmith.co.uk* Ⓜ *Covent Garden.*

Fodor's Choice
★ **Tabio.** For everything hosiery—knee socks, ankle socks, leggings, leg warmers, pantyhose, tights—this is the place. Patterns range from simple and elegant to lively and attention-getting and come in a wide assortment of weights, but all are functional without being boring. There's another branch on King's Road in Chelsea. ⊠ *66 Neal St., Covent Garden* ☎ *020/7836–3713* ⊕ *www.tabio.com* Ⓜ *Covent Garden.*

Fodor's Choice
★ **United Nude.** Co-created by noted architect Rem D Koolhaas (who also designed this Covent Garden flagship store) and Galahad Clark (of the Clark's shoes dynasty), these distinctive, futuristic designs that use up-to-the-minute techniques such as carbon fiber heels and injection-molded soles are flattering and surprisingly comfortable. There's another Covent Garden branch on Neal Street and one on Regent Street. ⊠ *13 Floral St., Covent Garden* ☎ *0207/240–7106* ⊕ *www.unitednude. com* Ⓜ *Covent Garden.*

HOUSEHOLD

Cath Kidston. If you love chintz and colorful patterns, you'll love Cath Kidston's bright feminine signature look. Textiles bearing ginghams, polka dots, and lots of big, blooming roses are pasted over everything in sight, from ceramics and bed linens to fine china, stationery, and doggie beds. There are clothing and nightwear lines for women and children, along with handbags, totes, and cosmetic bags. Branches can be found throughout the city, including ones in Chelsea, Marylebone, Notting Hill, and a new flagship store on Piccadilly. ⊠ *28–32 Shelton St., Covent Garden* ☎ *020/7240–8324* ⊕ *www.cathkidston.co.uk* Ⓜ *Covent Garden.*

TOYS

FAMILY
Fodor's Choice
★

Benjamin Pollock's Toyshop. This landmark shop still carries on the tradition of its eponymous founder, who sold miniature theater stages made from richly detailed paper from the late-19th century until his death in 1937. Among his admirers was Robert Louis Stevenson, who wrote, "If you love art, folly, or the bright eyes of children, speed to Pollock's." Today the antique model theaters tend to be expensive, but there are plenty of magical reproductions for under 10 pounds. There's also an extensive selection of new but nostalgic puppets, marionettes, teddy bears, spinning tops, jack-in-the-boxes, and similar traditional children's toys from the days before batteries were required. ⊠ *44 The Market, Covent Garden* ☎ *020/7379–7866* ⊕ *www.pollocks-coventgarden. co.uk* Ⓜ *Covent Garden.*

BLOOMSBURY, HOLBORN, ISLINGTON, AND FITZROVIA

BLOOMSBURY

ACCESSORIES

Fodor's Choice
★

James Smith & Sons Ltd. This has to be the world's ultimate umbrella shop, and a must for anyone interested in real Victorian London. The family-owned shop has been in this location on a corner of New Oxford Street since 1857, and sells every kind of umbrella, cane, and walking stick imaginable. The interior is unchanged since the 19th century; you will feel as if you have stepped back in time. If the umbrellas are out of your price range, James Smith also sells smaller accessories and handmade wooden bowls. ⊠ *Hazelwood House, 53 New Oxford St., Bloomsbury* ☎ *020/7836–4731* ⊕ *www.james-smith.co.uk* ☯ *Closed Sun.* Ⓜ *Tottenham Court Rd., Holborn.*

BOOKS

Gay's the Word. Open since 1979, this is London's leading gay and lesbian bookshop. Thousands of titles, from literature and thoughtful nonfiction to erotica and pro-diversity children's books, fill the shelves. The shop is a well-loved fixture on the scene and often hosts discussion groups, readings, and other events. ⊠ *66 Marchmont St., Bloomsbury* ☎ *020/7278–7654* ⊕ *www.gaystheword.co.uk* Ⓜ *Russell Sq.*

Persephone Books. A must for all lovers of women's fiction and nonfiction, Persephone is a gem of a bookshop specializing in reprints of mostly neglected 20th-century works from predominately female writers. Exquisitely decorated endpapers make these books perfect gifts for your bibliophile friends. ⊠ *59 Lamb's Conduit St., Bloomsbury* ☎ *020/7242–9292* ⊕ *www.persephonebooks.co.uk* ☯ *Closed Sun.* Ⓜ *Russell Sq., Holborn.*

SPECIALTY STORES

Blade Rubber. This unique shop near the British Museum specializes in rubber stamps, with everything from businesslike "Paid" stamps to Alice in Wonderland characters, Egyptian gods, VW Beetles, flying saucers, and more. Get a custom-made personal stamp—a great gift for a young person—or bring back an iconic double-decker bus stamp as a souvenir. ⊠ *12 Bury Pl., Bloomsbury* ☎ *020/7831–4123* ⊕ *www. bladerubber.co.uk* Ⓜ *Holborn.*

18

HOLBORN
ANTIQUES

Fodor'sChoice ★ **London Silver Vaults.** Housed in a basement vault, this extraordinary space holds stalls from more than 30 silver dealers. Products range from the spectacularly over-the-top costing thousands to smaller items—like teaspoons, candlesticks, or a set of Victorian cake forks—starting at £25. ■TIP➜ Most of the silver merchants actually trade out of room-size, underground vaults, which were originally rented out to London's upper crust to store their valuables. ✉ *53–64 Chancery La., Holborn* ☎ *020/7242–3844* ⊕ *www.thesilvervaults.com* ⊙ *Closed Sat. after 1 and Sun.* Ⓜ *Chancery La.*

ISLINGTON
HOUSEHOLD

Fodor'sChoice ★ **TwentyTwentyOne.** The best in modern and vintage furniture is showcased here. There are design classics like a chaise longue from Le Corbusier, as well as curvy daybeds from designer Jacob Pringiers. The kids' range is particularly cool, with items like the classic elephant sculpture/toy from husband-and-wife design team Charles and Ray Eames. Small accessories like tote bags and cushions will easily fit into your luggage. There's another branch in The City. ✉ *274–275 Upper St., Islington* ☎ *020/7288–1996* ⊕ *www.twentytwentyone.com* Ⓜ *Highbury & Islington.*

FITZROVIA
CLOTHING

Reiss. With an in-house design team whose experience includes stints at Gucci and Calvin Klein and customers like Beyoncé and the Duchess of Cambridge, who wore a Reiss dress for her official engagement picture, this hot chain brings luxury standards of tailoring and details to mass-market women- and menswear. The sleek and contemporary style is not cheap, but does offer value for money. There are branches in Knightsbridge, The City, Covent Garden, Chelsea, Hampstead, Islington, Soho, Kensington, and basically all over London. ✉ *10 Barrett St., Fitzrovia* ☎ *020/7486–6557* ⊕ *www.reiss.com* Ⓜ *Oxford St.*

Topshop. A hot spot for straight-from-the-runway affordable fashion, Topshop is destination shopping for teenagers and fashion editors alike. Clothes and accessories are geared to the youthful end of the market, although women who are young at heart and girlish of figure can find plenty of wearable items here. However, you will need a high tolerance for loud music and busy dressing rooms. The store also features collections designed by a rotating roster of high-end designers as well as offering its own premium designer line called Topshop Unique. Topman brings the same fast-fashion approach to clothing for men. ■TIP➜ If the crowds become too much, head to one of the smaller Topshops in Kensington High Street, Knightsbridge, Victoria, Marble Arch, or Holborn. ✉ *216 Oxford St., Fitzrovia* ☎ *0844/848–7487* ⊕ *www.topshop.com* Ⓜ *Oxford Circus.*

THE CITY

JEWELRY

Fodor's Choice ★ **Lesley Craze Gallery.** This serene gallery displays unique pieces by some 100 innovative designers from around the world (with a strong British bias). A textiles room showcases colorful handmade scarves. Prices start at £45. ✉ *33–35A Clerkenwell Green, Clerkenwell* ☎ *020/7608–0393* ⊕ *www.lesleycrazegallery.co.uk* ⊗ *Closed Sun.; closed Mon. Jan.–Oct.* Ⓜ *Farringdon.*

EAST LONDON

ACCESSORIES: HATS

Fodor's Choice ★ **Bernstock Speirs.** Here since 1982, Paul Bernstock and Thelma Speirs turn traditional hats for men and women on their head: street-smart trilbies, whimsical baseball caps (with rabbit ears), and knitted hats that feature unusual colors and quirky details. ✉ *234 Brick La., Spitalfields* ☎ *020/7739–7385* ⊕ *www.bernstockspeirs.com* Ⓜ *London Overground: Shoreditch High St.*

CLOTHING

Absolute Vintage. This is a warehouse of handpicked items from the 1930s through the 1980s, but the specialty here is shoes and bags. The shop has the largest collection of vintage shoes in the United Kingdom—more than 1,000 pairs—and, best of all, prices are reasonable. There's another branch on Berwick Street in Soho. ✉ *15 Hanbury St., Spitalfields* ☎ *020/7274–3883* ⊕ *www.absolutevintage.co.uk* Ⓜ *London Overground: Shoreditch High St.*

b Store. Some people regard b Store as the best small clothing boutique in London. Head here for cutting-edge pieces from avant-garde designers such as Sophie Hume, plus the store's quirky own-label shoes, men and women's clothing, and accessories. ✉ *345 Old St., Hoxton* ☎ *020/7734–6846* ⊕ *www.bstorelondon.com* ⊗ *Closed Sun.* Ⓜ *Old St.*

Beyond Retro. More than 10,000 vintage items for men and women, from cowboy boots to bowling shirts to prom dresses—it's got the largest collection of American retro in the United Kingdom. There's another outpost in Hoxton and one in Soho. ✉ *110–112 Cheshire St., Spitalfields* ☎ *020/7613–3636* ⊕ *www.beyondretro.com* Ⓜ *Whitechapel. London Overground: Shoreditch High St.*

Blitz. This vast former furniture factory, the world's first (self-proclaimed) "vintage department store," now has separate floors devoted to antiques and vintage clothing as well as period goods ranging from bikes to luggage. Look for racks filled with denim jackets, '80s Ralph Lauren, chunky ski sweaters, and Liberty shirts. ✉ *55–59 Hanbury St., Spitalfields* ☎ *020/7377–0730* ⊕ *www.blitzlondon.co.uk* Ⓜ *London Overground: Shoreditch High St.*

Fodor's Choice ★ **Hostem.** Drawing style-conscious customers from nearby tech start-ups, Hostem is for the man who wants to be well dressed without looking like he's trying too hard, with a mixture of casual luxury, street wear, and fashion-forward edge. You'll find established names like Phillip Lim and Ann Demeulemeester as well as beautiful cashmere sweaters from

18

newcomers like The Elder Statesmen. A new women's-wear area offers pieces by designers like Commes des Garcons and Rick Owens. It's achingly hip, so expect lots of black. ✉ *41–43 Redchurch St., Shoreditch* ☎ *020/7739–9733* ⊕ *www.hostem.co.uk* Ⓜ *London Overground: Shoreditch High St.*

The Laden Showroom. Sienna Miller and Victoria Beckham are among the celebs who regularly check out emerging talent at this East End showroom for young designers. The store retails the work of more than 50 new designers, some selling one-off items. ✉ *103 Brick La., Spitalfields* ☎ *020/7247–2431* ⊕ *www.laden.co.uk* Ⓜ *Shoreditch High St. London Overground: Shoreditch High St.*

Rokit. Magazine and rock stylists love this place. It consists of two shops along Brick Lane that carry everything from handbags and ball gowns to jeans, military garb, and Western wear. The ever-changing stock spans the 1920s to the 1990s. There are also branches in Camden and Covent Garden. ✉ *101 and 107 Brick La., Spitalfields* ☎ *020/7375– 3864* ⊕ *www.rokit.co.uk* Ⓜ *London Overground: Shoreditch High St.*

Fodor's Choice ★ **Start London.** An ever-changing roster of cutting-edge designers like Richard Nicholl, Helmut Lang, and Alexander Wang is on offer here, and, for men (down the street at No. 59), everything from Comme des Garcons to Nudie Jeans. Although the emphasis is on chic directional fashion, co-owner and American expat Brix Smith-Start is more mother hen than formidable fashionista and is happy to gently guide customers into trying something new. ✉ *42–44 Rivington St., Shoreditch* ☎ *020/7729–3334* ⊕ *www.start-london.com* Ⓜ *Old St. London Overground: Shoreditch High St.*

Fodor's Choice ★ **Sunspel.** This British firm has been making fine men's underwear since the mid-19th century and it's still their specialty, along with luxury basics. Prince Charles is an actual customer and James Bond a filmic one (he wore their shorts in "Thunderball" and polo shirt in "Quantum of Solace"). They also carry elegant, minimalist T-shirts, sweaters, and sweats for women. There are other branches in Marylebone, St. James's, and Soho. ✉ *7 Redchurch St., Shoreditch* ☎ *020/7739–9729* ⊕ *www.sunspel. com* Ⓜ *Shoreditch High St. London Overground: Shoreditch High St.*

FOOD

Fodor's Choice ★ **A. Gold.** All of the traditional or retro foodstuffs—such as jars of London-produced honey and relish, or even locally produced gin—sold in this re-creation of a village shop in an old milliner's premises are British-made and make excellent portable presents. Stylish gift baskets and old-fashioned picnic hampers are available, as are takeout sandwiches and hot daily specials. ✉ *42 Brushfield St., Spitalfields* ☎ *020/7247–2487* ⊕ *www.agoldshop.com* Ⓜ *Shoreditch High St. London Overground: Shoreditch High St.*

HOUSEHOLD

Fodor's Choice ★ **Labour & Wait.** Although mundane items like colanders and clothespins may not sound like ideal souvenirs, this shop will make you reconsider. The owners are on a mission to revive retro, functional British household goods, such as enamel kitchenware, genuine feather dusters, bread bins, and traditional Welsh blankets. ✉ *85 Redchurch St., Shoreditch*

☎ *020/7729–6253* ⊕ *www. labourandwait.co.uk* Ⓜ *Shoreditch High St. London Overground: Shoreditch High St.*

Maison Trois Garcons. If your motto is "too much ain't enough," you'll love this shrine to all things over the top. A mixture of antique, vintage, and contemporary pieces sourced in England, France, Sweden, and elsewhere, this eclectic interiors shop–cum-café does not shy away from the rococo, the opulent, and even kitsch. But there's also plenty of lovely porcelain, glassware, mirrors, furniture, and light fixtures. ✉ *45 Redchurch St., Shoreditch* ☎ *020/3370–7761* ⊕ *www.lestroisgarcons.com/shop* Ⓜ *Shoreditch High St. London Overground: Shoreditch High St.*

MUSIC

Rough Trade East. While many London record stores are struggling, this veteran indie-music specialist in the Old Truman Brewery seems to have gotten the formula right. The spacious surroundings are as much a hangout as a shop, complete with a stage for live gigs, a café, and Internet access. There's another branch on Portobello Road in Notting Hill. ✉ *Dray Walk, Old Truman Brewery, 91 Brick La., Spitalfields* ☎ *020/7392–7788* Ⓜ *Liverpool St. London Overground: Shoreditch High St.*

SPECIALTY STORES

The Village Bicycle. With a style that might best be described as punk *luxe*, this "lifestyle concept store" offers witty, *haute* Goth home wares like a diamanté-covered skull phone (a take on a notorious Damien Hirst artwork). There are also toys, coffee-table books, trinkets, shoes, hi-tops, and art, as well as clothes from ultrahip labels like House of Holland, Opening Ceremony, Sass & Bide, and Mark Fest that are designed for girls with small frames and big credit limits. ✉ *91 Brick La., Shoreditch* ☎ *020/7313–9031* ⊕ *www.imavillagebicycle.com* Ⓜ *Notting Hill Gate, Westbourne Park.*

18

KENSINGTON, CHELSEA, KNIGHTSBRIDGE, AND BELGRAVIA

KENSINGTON

CLOTHING

FAMILY **Marie-Chantal.** If you love beautiful, tasteful clothing for babies and children, head to this boutique created by Princess Marie-Chantal of Greece. As you'd imagine, the look is elegant and the prices are high. Materials used include silk, linen, and Liberty prints. There's another branch in Notting Hill. ✉ *148 Walton St., South Kensington* ☎ *020/7838–1111* ⊕ *www.mariechantal.co.uk* ⊙ *Closed Sun.* Ⓜ *South Kensington.*

Orsini. Designer fashion from the 1930s to 1980s is the trademark at this tiny but desirable boutique, with big names like Pucci, Hermès, Chanel, and Alaïa at bargain prices. Victoria Beckham is a fan. ✉ *76 Earl's Court Rd., Kensington* ☎ *020/7937–2903* ⊕ *www.orsinivintage.co.uk* Ⓜ *Earl's Ct.*

HOUSEHOLD

The Conran Shop. This is the brainchild of Sir Terence Conran, who has been informing British taste since he opened Habitat in the 1960s. Although he is no longer associated with Habitat, his eponymous stores are still bastions of similarly clean, unfussy modernist design. Housewares from furniture to stemware and textiles—both handmade and mass-produced, by famous names and emerging designers—are housed in a building that is a modernist design landmark in its own right. Both the flagship store and the branch on Marylebone High Street are bursting with great gift ideas. ⊠ *Michelin House, 81 Fulham Rd., South Kensington* ☎ *020/7589–7401* ⊕ *www.conranshop.co.uk* Ⓜ *South Kensington.*

Fodor's Choice **Mint.** Owner Lina Kanafani has scoured the globe to curate an eclectic
★ mix of conceptual statement furniture, art, ceramics, and home acces-sories. Mint also showcases works by up-and-coming designers and sells plenty of limited edition and one-off pieces. If you don't want to ship a couch home, consider a miniature flower vase or a handmade ceramic pitcher. ⊠ *2 North Terr., Alexander Sq., South Kensington* ☎ *020/7225–2228* ⊕ *www.mintshop.co.uk* ⊙ *Closed Sun.* Ⓜ *South Kensington.*

Skandium. Largely thanks to its thrillers and chefs, Scandinavia is having a moment in Britain. Skandium brings together many of the region's top designers of furniture, lighting, rugs, and housewares under one roof. Designers include Knoll, Fritz Hansen, Artek, and Georg Jensen. Clean lines and stripped-back, unfussy elegance abounds (although the Moomins make an appearance on ceramics). There's another branch in Marylebone. ⊠ *245–249 Brompton Rd., South Kensington* ☎ *020/7584–2066* ⊕ *www.skandium.com* Ⓜ *South Kensington.*

JEWELRY

Butler & Wilson. Specialists in bold costume jewelry and affordable glam-our, Butler & Wilson have added semiprecious stones to their foundation diamanté, colored rhinestone, and crystal collections. Flamboyant skull brooches or dainty floral earrings make perfect gifts. ⊠ *189 Fulham Rd., South Kensington* ☎ *020/7352–3045* ⊕ *www.butlerandwilson.co.uk* Ⓜ *South Kensington.*

CHELSEA

ACCESSORIES

The Shop at Bluebird. The brainchild of the couple behind popular women's-wear brand Jigsaw, this 10,000-square-foot space in the old Bluebird garage brings together men's and women's fashion from of-the-moment designers like Raf Simons and Christopher Kane. There's also furniture, collectibles, designer tech accessories, and music—all chosen for style and originality. It's worth visiting for the displays alone, which change regularly, although the funky ceiling-light installation of more than 1,000 bulbs seems to be a constant feature. After brows-ing, unwind with a treatment at the on-site spa or join the ladies who lunch at the restaurant in the same complex. ■ TIP→ It's a good 20-min-ute walk from the nearest Tube station at Sloane Square, so catch a No. 11 or No. 22 bus along King's Road. ⊠ *350 King's Rd., Chelsea* ☎ *020/7351–3873* ⊕ *www.theshopatbluebird.com* Ⓜ *Sloane Sq.*

ANTIQUES

Rupert Cavendish. This most elevated of Chelsea dealers had the Biedermeier market cornered, so he has now expanded to Empire and art deco antiques, several of which are museum quality. ⊠ *610 King's Rd., Fulham* ☎ *020/7731–7041* ⊕ *www.rupertcavendish.co.uk* Ⓜ *Fulham Broadway.*

BOOKS

Fodor'sChoice
★

Green & Stone. This fabulous cave of artists' materials, papers, art books, easels, and mannequins is one of the longest-established shops on King's Road. It began life in 1927 as part of the Chenil Gallery, run by a distinguished group that included artist Augustus John and playwright George Bernard Shaw. At the current location since 1934, the shop also has a framing service, antique paint boxes, and craft supplies. ⊠ *259 King's Rd., Chelsea* ☎ *020/7352–0837* ⊕ *www.greenandstone. com* Ⓜ *Sloane Sq.*

John Sandoe [Books] Ltd. This atmospheric warren that crams some 25,000 titles into an 18th-century building off King's Road is the antithesis of a soulless chain bookstore—no surprise it has attracted equally idiosyncratic customers like Tom Stoppard and Keith Richards. Staff members are wonderfully knowledgeable (don't try to figure out how the stock is organized without their help) and there are a lot of them per customer. If a book isn't in stock, they will try to source it for you, even if it is out of print. ⊠ *10 Blacklands Terr., Chelsea* ☎ *020/7589–9473* ⊕ *www.johnsandoe.com* Ⓜ *Sloane Sq.*

CLOTHING

Austique. Fans of such trendy brands as Markus Lupfer or Goat need look no further than Austique. This sophisticated boutique is home to a gorgeous array of dresses, lingerie, jewelry, and accessories for the ultimate fashionista. There's another branch in Marylebone. ⊠ *330 King's Rd., Chelsea* ☎ *020/7376–4555* ⊕ *www.austique.co.uk* Ⓜ *Sloane Sq.*

FAMILY
Fodor'sChoice
★

Brora. The knitwear is cozy, but the style is cool in this contemporary Scottish cashmere emporium for men, women, and kids. There are dressed-up camisoles, sweaters, and cardigans, and adorable baby ensembles, as well as non-cashmere items such as picnic blankets and scarves. Other branches can be found in Notting Hill, Marylebone, Islington, Covent Garden, and Sloane Square. ⊠ *344 King's Rd., Chelsea* ☎ *020/7352–3697* ⊕ *www.brora.co.uk* Ⓜ *Sloane Sq.*

Hackett. If J. Crew isn't preppy enough for you, try Hackett, with branches in Covent Garden, Spitalfields, St. James's, Soho, Mayfair, and The City. Originally a posh thrift shop recycling cricket flannels, hunting pinks, Oxford brogues, and other staples of a British gentleman's wardrobe, Hackett now creates its own line and has become a genuine—and very good—men's outfitter. The look is traditional and classic, with best buys including polo shirts, corduroys, and striped scarves. There's also a boys' line for the junior man-about-town. ⊠ *137–138 Sloane St., Chelsea* ☎ *020/7730–3331* ⊕ *www.hackett. com* Ⓜ *Sloane Sq.*

18

Jack Wills. The British preppie's answer to Abercrombie & Fitch, Jack Wills specializes in heritage and country sports-inspired styles for men and women but gives them a fresh, sexy edge. This means crowds of lithe young things who don't mind the pumping music while browsing for slim-line Fair Isle sweaters, fitted plaid shirts, and short floral sundresses for the girls, plus sweatshirts, blazers, skinny cords, and rugby shirts for the boys. They also have Union Jack carry-on bags, bobble hats galore, knitted jackets for hot-water bottles, and other ironically traditional items. Other branches are in Notting Hill, Covent Garden, Islington, Soho, and Shoreditch. ⊠ *72 Kings Rd., Chelsea* ☎ *020/7581–0347* ⊕ *www.jackwills.com* Ⓜ *Sloane Sq.*

Jigsaw. Jigsaw specializes in clothes that are classic yet trendy, ladylike without being dull. The style is epitomized by the former Kate Middleton, who was a buyer for the company before her marriage. The quality of fabrics and detailing belie the reasonable prices and cuts are kind to the womanly figure. Although there are numerous branches across London, no two stores are the same. The preteen set have their own line, Jigsaw Junior. ⊠ *The Chapel, Duke of York Sq., King's Rd., Chelsea* ☎ *020/730–4404* ⊕ *www.jigsawonline.com* Ⓜ *Sloane Sq.*

FOOD

L'Artisan du Chocolat. Praised by top chefs Gordon Ramsay and Heston Blumenthal, L'Artisan raises chocolate to an art form. "Couture" chocolates are infused with fruits, nuts, and spices (including such exotic flavorings as Szechuan pepper and tobacco). This is one of the few chocolate shops in the world that makes liquid salted caramels. There are also branches in Notting Hill and Borough Market. ⊠ *89 Lower Sloane St., Chelsea* ☎ *0845/270–6996* ⊕ *www.artisanduchocolat.co.uk* Ⓜ *Sloane Sq.*

SHOES

Fodor's Choice ★ **Manolo Blahnik.** Blink and you'll miss the discreet sign that marks fashionista footwear central. Blahnik, the man who single-handedly managed to revive the sexy stiletto and make it classier than ever, has been trading out of this small shop on a Chelsea side street since 1973. It's a must for shoe lovers with a generous budget. If you decide to wear your new Manolos, hop on the No. 11 or No. 22 bus or grab a cab—the nearest Tube station is about a 20-minute totter away. ⊠ *49–51 Old Church St., Chelsea* ☎ *020/7352–8622* ⊕ *www.manoloblahnik.com* ⊙ *Closed Sun.* Ⓜ *Sloane Sq., South Kensington.*

KNIGHTSBRIDGE

ACCESSORIES

Fodor's Choice ★ **Anya Hindmarch.** Exquisite leather bags and personalized, printed canvas totes are what made Hindmarch famous. Here you'll find her complete collection of bags and shoes. You can also order a bespoke piece such as the "Be A Bag," a tote bag imprinted with your chosen photo. There are also branches around the corner on Pont Street, in Mayfair, and in Notting Hill. ⊠ *157–158 Sloane St., Knightsbridge* ☎ *020/7730–0961* ⊕ *www.anyahindmarch.com* Ⓜ *Sloane Sq., Knightsbridge.*

CLOTHING

Egg. Tucked away in a residential mews, this spartan shop in a former Victorian dairy is the brainchild of Maureen Doherty, once Issey Miyake's right-hand person. More than half the minimalist, unstructured styles for men and women in natural fabrics such as silk, cashmere, and antique cotton are handmade. Garments may be casually hung on hooks or folded on wooden tables but the price tags are anything but unassuming and the clientele includes the likes of Donna Karan and photographer Bruce Weber. Unusual ceramics and jewelry are also on display. ⊠ *36 Kinnerton St., Knightsbridge* ☎ *020/7235–9315* ⊙ *Closed Sun.* Ⓜ *Knightsbridge.*

FAMILY **Rachel Riley.** Specializing in traditional English style for boys and girls, Riley's luxurious, vintage-inspired collection includes classics like duffle coats and hand-smocked floral dresses. Mothers who love the Riley look can pick up coordinating outfits for themselves here or at the Marylebone High Street location. ⊠ *14 Pont St., Knightsbridge* ☎ *020/7259–5969* ⊕ *www.rachelriley.co.uk* Ⓜ *Knightsbridge.*

Rigby & Peller. Lovers of luxury lingerie shop here for brands like Prima Donna and Aubade, as well as R&P's own line. If the right fit eludes you, the made-to-measure service starts at around £300. Many of London's most affluent women shop here, not only because this is the Queen's favored underwear supplier but also because the quality is excellent and the service impeccably knowledgeable while being much friendlier than you might expect. There are also branches in Mayfair, Chelsea, and The City. ⊠ *2 Hans Rd., Knightsbridge* ☎ *020/7225–4760* ⊕ *www.rigbyandpeller.com* Ⓜ *Knightsbridge.*

DEPARTMENT STORES

Harrods. With an encyclopedic assortment of luxury brands, this Knightsbridge institution has more than 300 departments and 20 restaurants, all spread over 1 million square feet on a 5-acre site. If you approach Harrods as a blingtastic tourist attraction rather than as a center of elegant sophistication, you won't be disappointed. Focus on the spectacular food halls, the huge ground-floor perfumery, the revamped toy and technology departments, the excellent Urban Retreat spa, and the Vegas-like Egyptian Room. Nevertheless, standards of taste are enforced with a customer dress code (no shorts, ripped jeans, or flip-flops). ■TIP➔ Be prepared to brave the crowds, especially on weekends. ⊠ *87–135 Brompton Rd., Knightsbridge* ☎ *020/7730–1234* ⊕ *www.harrods.com* Ⓜ *Knightsbridge.*

Fodor's Choice **Harvey Nichols.** While visiting tourists flock to Harrods, true London
★ fashionistas shop at Harvey Nichols, aka "Harvey Nicks." The women's-wear and accessories departments are outstanding, featuring of-the-moment designers like Victoria Beckham, Peter Pilotto, and 3.1 Phillip Lim. The furniture and housewares are equally gorgeous (and pricey), though they become somewhat more affordable during the twice-annual sales in January and July. The Fifth Floor restaurant is the place to see and be seen, but if you're just after a quick bite, there's also a more informal café on the same floor or sushi-to-go from Yo! Sushi. ⊠ *109–125 Knightsbridge, Knightsbridge* ☎ *020/7235–5000* ⊕ *www.harveynichols.com* Ⓜ *Knightsbridge.*

18

BELGRAVIA

ACCESSORIES

Fodor's Choice

★ **Lulu Guinness.** Famous for her flamboyantly themed bags (think the satin "bucket" topped with roses or the elaborately beaded red "lips" clutch), Guinness also showcases vintage-inspired luggage and beauty accessories in this frilly little shop, which is just as whimsical as her designs. There are other branches in Mayfair, Covent Garden, and The City. ✉ *3 Ellis St., Belgravia* ☎ *020/7823–4828* ⊕ *www.luluguinness.com* ☉ *Closed Sun.* Ⓜ *Sloane Sq.*

Fodor's Choice

★ **Philip Treacy.** Magnificent hats by Treacy are annual showstoppers on Ladies Day at the Royal Ascot races and regularly grace the glossy magazines' society pages. Part Mad Hatter, part Cecil Beaton, Treacy's creations always guarantee a grand entrance (remember Princess Beatrice's eye-catching headdress at the Royal Wedding?). In addition to the extravagant, haute couture hats handmade in the atelier, ready-to-wear hats, and bags are also for sale. ✉ *69 Elizabeth St., Belgravia* ☎ *020/7730–3992* ⊕ *www.philiptreacy.co.uk* ☉ *Closed Sun.* Ⓜ *Sloane Sq.*

SPECIALTY STORES

Mungo & Maud. If you don't want to leave London without buying something for your best friend, pick up a well-designed coat, collar, leash, blanket, bowl, toy, or comfortable bed that will make your dog the snazziest pooch in town. Cats are also catered for with baskets, suede collars, and catnip toys. Even owners get a nod with luxurious merino throws (soon to be covered in pet hair) and a leather poop pouch. There's also a branch in Notting Hill. ✉ *79 Elizabeth St., Belgravia* ☎ *020/022–1207* ⊕ *www.mungoandmaud.com* Ⓜ *Sloane Sq.*

NOTTING HILL

BOOKS

Fodor's Choice

★ **Books for Cooks.** It may seem odd to describe a bookshop as delicious-smelling, but the aromas wafting out of the tiny test kitchen—which serves daily-changing lunch dishes drawn from recipes in the 8,000 cookbooks on the shelves, as well as cakes and culinary experiments—will whet your appetite even before you've opened one of the books. Just about every world cuisine is represented along with a complete lineup of works by celebrity chefs. ■ TIP➔ Before you come to London, visit the shop's website to sign up for a cooking class. ✉ *4 Blenheim Crescent, Notting Hill* ☎ *020/7221–1992* ⊕ *www.booksforcooks.com* ☉ *Closed Sun. and Mon.* Ⓜ *Notting Hill Gate, Ladbroke Grove.*

CLOTHING

Aimé. French-Cambodian sisters Val and Vanda Heng-Vong launched this shop to showcase the best of French clothing and designer housewares. Expect to find fashion by Isabel Marant, Forte Forte, and A.P.C. along with housewares and a well-edited collection of ceramics. Just next door, Petit Aimé sells children's clothing. There's also a Shoreditch branch. ✉ *32 Ledbury Rd., Notting Hill* ☎ *020/7221–7070* ⊕ *www.aimelondon.com* Ⓜ *Notting Hill Gate.*

FAMILY **Caramel Baby & Child.** Here you'll find adorable clothes for children six months and up: handcrafted Peruvian alpaca cardigans, floral cotton dresses for girls; check shirts and tees for boys; comfortable pants in twill, corduroy, and cotton for both; and merino cashmere sweaters for fashionable babies. Caramel also sells a small selection of decorative-functional items like mobiles and child-friendly chairs. There are also branches in South Kensington and Chelsea. ⊠ *77 Ledbury Rd., Notting Hill* ☎ *020/7727–0906* ⊕ *www.caramel-shop.co.uk* Ⓜ *Westbourne Park, Notting Hill Gate.*

Rellik. Now in the modernist landmark known as the Trellick Tower and favored by the likes of Kate Moss, Rellik began as a stall in the Portobello Market. Vintage hunters looking to splurge can find a selection of YLS, Dior, and Ossie Clark as well as items from lesser-known designers. ⊠ *Trellick Tower, 8 Golborne Rd., Notting Hill* ☎ *020/8962–0089* ⊕ *www.relliklondon.co.uk* ☾ *Closed Sun.* Ⓜ *Westbourne Park.*

Fodor's Choice **Virginia Antiques.** With perhaps the best collection of vintage clothing
★ in London, Virginia Bates's shop offers dresses, hats, and accessories from the late Victorian era (circa 1880) to the early 1930s. These are wearable collector's items in perfect condition and are priced accordingly. ⊠ *98 Portland Rd., Holland Park, Notting Hill* ☎ *020/7727–9908* ☾ *Closed Sun.; open Sat. by appointment only* Ⓜ *Holland Park, Ladbroke Grove.*

MUSIC

Music & Video Exchange. This store is a music collector's treasure trove, with a constantly changing stock refreshed by customers selling and exchanging as well as buying. The main store focuses on rock pop, soul, and dance, mainstream and obscure, in formats ranging from vinyl to CD, cassette, and even mini-disk. Don't miss the discounts in the basement and the rarities upstairs. Classical music is at No. 40 and there are branches in Soho and Greenwich. ⊠ *38 Notting Hill Gate, Notting Hill* ☎ *020/7243–8573* ⊕ *www.mgeshops.com* Ⓜ *Notting Hill Gate.*

SHOES

Emma Hope. The signature look of the footwear here is ladylike, with pointed toes and kitten heels, often ornamented with bows, lace, or exquisite embroidery. Ballet flats and sneakers in velvet or animal prints provide glamour without sacrificing comfort. Small-but-perfectly formed handbags, as well as shoes and accessories for men, are stocked both here and in the Sloane Square branch. ⊠ *207 Westbourne Grove, Notting Hill* ☎ *020/7313–7490* ⊕ *www.emmahope.com* Ⓜ *Notting Hill Gate.*

REGENT'S PARK AND HAMPSTEAD

HOUSEHOLD

Graham & Green. Combining style with practicality and an added whimsical twist, this delightful interiors shop has everything from faux fur and mohair throws to elegant lamps and lampshades, embroidered cushions, felt animal rugs for children, Venetian glass doorknobs, folding deck chairs (as found in the Royal Parks), shabby chic

18

sofas, and even a pedal-powered kiddie car that's a replica of a classic Bugatti. There's another branch in Notting Hill. ✉ *164 Regent's Park Rd., Primrose Hill* ☎ *020/7586–2960* ⊕ *www.grahamandgreen.co.uk* Ⓜ *Chalk Farm.*

SHOES

Spice. Touring London requires a lot of walking, so if your feet are crying out for mercy, stop in at this long-established boutique that specializes in spiffy but comfortable shoes and boots for men and women from brands like Unisa, Aubrey, and their own Spice line. There's another branch in Islington. ✉ *162 Regents' Park Rd., Primrose Hill* ☎ *020/7722–2478* ⊕ *www.spiceshu.co.uk* Ⓜ *Chalk Farm.*

GREATER LONDON

CLOTHING

The Cross. One of the first "lifestyle boutiques" and still one of the best, this west London favorite carries fashion by in-the-know favorites like Vanessa Bruno, Collette Dinnigan, J Brand, Dosa, and more, plus accessories, housewares, and kids clothes. The emphasis is on the feminine and quirky. ✉ *141 Portland Rd., Holland Park* ☎ *202/7727–6760* ⊕ *www.thecrossshop.co.uk* ⊗ *Closed Sun.* Ⓜ *Holland Park.*

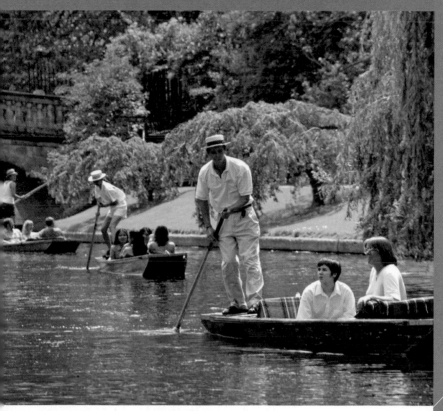

SIDE TRIPS
FROM LONDON

Updated by
Kate Hughes
and Jack
Jewers

Londoners are undeniably lucky. Few urban populations enjoy such glorious—and easily accessible—options for day-tripping. Even if you have only one day to spare, head out of the city. A train ride past hills dotted with sheep, a stroll through a medieval town, or a visit to one of England's great castles could make you feel as though you've added another week to your vacation.

Not only is England extremely compact, the train and bus networks, although somewhat inefficient and expensive compared with their European counterparts, are extensive and easily booked (though pricing structures can be confusing), making "a brilliant day out" an easy thing to accomplish.

Although you can do the Warner Bros. Harry Potter Studio Tour in a day, visiting many of the towns near London will be a frenzied day trip. Heavy summer crowds make it difficult to cover the sights in a relaxed manner, so consider staying for a day or two. You'd then have time to explore a different England—one with quiet country pubs, tree-lined lanes, and neat fields. No matter where you go, lodging reservations are a good idea from June through September, when foreign visitors saturate the English countryside.

PLANNING

GETTING AROUND

Normally the towns near London are best reached by train. Bus travel costs less, but can take twice as long. Wherever you're going, plan ahead: check the latest timetables before you set off, and try to get an early start. ⇨ *Also see Travel Smart London.*

STATION TIPS

You can reach any of London's main-line train stations by Tube. London's bus stations can be confusing for the uninitiated, so here's a quick breakdown:

Green Line Coach Station is on Bulleid Way (in front of the Colonnades Shopping Centre on Buckingham Palace Road) and is the departure point for most Green Line and Megabus services.

Victoria Bus Station is where many of the local London bus services arrive and depart, and is directly outside the main exits of the train and Tube stations.

Victoria Coach Station is on Buckingham Palace Road: it's a five-minute walk from Victoria Tube station. This is where to go for coach departures; arrivals are at a different location, a short walk from here.

TO GET TO . . .		
	TAKE THE TRAIN FROM . . .	TAKE THE BUS FROM . . .
Cambridge	King's Cross (45–90 minutes; every 10 or 20 minutes); Liverpool St. (80 minutes; every 30 minutes)	Victoria Coach (about 3 hours; every hour–90 minutes)
Oxford	Paddington (55–110 minutes; every 3–20 minutes)	Victoria Coach (100 minutes; every half hour; Oxford Tube, Buckingham Palace Rd. (100 minutes; every 12–20 minutes)
Stratford-upon-Avon	Marylebone (2 hours to 2½ hours; every 2 hours); or Euston (1½ hours; every 20 or 40 minutes or hourly)	Victoria Coach (3 hours, 25 minutes; about 3 times daily)
Warner Bros. Harry Potter Studio Tour	Euston Station (20 minutes) to Watford; then shuttle bus to attraction	Watford (15 minutes; every 20 minutes; after taking London train from Euston).
Windsor	Paddington (25–50 minutes; every 5–30 minutes) or Waterloo (1 hour, 5 minutes; every half hour)	Green Line Bus Station, Victoria (1 hour, 5 minutes; hourly)

19

CAMBRIDGE

60 miles northeast of London.

With the spires of its university buildings framed by towering trees and expansive meadows, its medieval streets and passages enhanced by gardens and riverbanks, the city of Cambridge is among the loveliest in England. The city predates the Roman occupation of Britain, but there's confusion over exactly how the university was founded. The most widely accepted story is that it was established in 1209 by a pair of scholars from Oxford, who left their university in protest over the wrongful execution of a colleague for murder.

This university town may be beautiful, but it's no museum. Even when the students are on vacation, there's a cultural and intellectual buzz here. Well-preserved medieval buildings sit cheek-by-jowl next to the latest in modern architecture (for example the William Gates building, which houses Cambridge University's computer laboratory) in this growing city dominated culturally and architecturally by its famous university (whose students make up around one-fifth of the city's 109,000 inhabitants), and beautified by parks, gardens, and the quietly flowing River Cam. A quintessential Cambridge pursuit is punting on the Cam (one occupant propels the narrow, square-end, flat-bottom boat with a long pole), followed by a stroll along the Backs, the left bank of the river fringed by St. John's, Trinity, Clare, King's, and Queens' colleges, and by Trinity Hall.

VISITING THE COLLEGES

College visits are certainly a highlight of a Cambridge tour, but remember that the colleges are private residences and workplaces, even when school isn't in session. Each is an independent entity within the university; some are closed to the public, but at others you can see the chapels, dining rooms (called halls), and sometimes the libraries, too. Some colleges charge a fee for the privilege of nosing around. All are closed during exams, usually from mid-April to late June, and the opening hours often vary. Additionally, all are subject to closures at short notice, especially King's; check the websites in advance. For details about visiting specific colleges not listed here, contact Cambridge University.

TOURS

City Sightseeing. This company operates open-top bus tours of Cambridge—the Backs, the colleges, the Imperial War Museum in Duxford, and the Grafton shopping center. Tours can be joined at marked bus stops in the city. Ask the tourist office about additional tours. ⊠ *Cambridge Train Station, Station Rd.* ☎ *01223/433250* ⊕ *www.city-sightseeing.com* 🎫 *From £14.*

Visit Cambridge. Walking tours, as well as other tours, are led by an official Blue Badge guide. The two-hour tours leave from the tourist information center at Peas Hill. Hours vary according to the tour, with the earliest leaving at 11 am and the latest at 1 pm in winter, 2 in summer. ⊠ *Peas Hill* ☎ *0871/226–8006* ⊕ *www.visitcambridge.org* 🎫 *From £18.50.*

ESSENTIALS

Visitor Information Cambridge University ☎ *01223/337733* ⊕ *www.cam.ac.uk.*

EXPLORING

TOP ATTRACTIONS

Fodor'sChoice
★

Fitzwilliam Museum. In a Classical Revival building renowned for its grand Corinthian portico, the Fitzwilliam, founded by the seventh viscount Fitzwilliam of Merrion in 1816, has one of Britain's most outstanding collections of art and antiquities. Highlights include two large Titians, an extensive collection of French impressionist paintings, and many works by Matisse and Picasso. The opulent interior displays its treasures to marvelous effect, from Egyptian pieces such as inch-high figurines and painted coffins, to sculptures from the Chinese Han dynasty of the 3rd century BC. ⊠ *Trumpington St.* ☎ *01223/332900* ⊕ *www.fitzmuseum.cam.ac.uk* 🎫 *Free* ☉ *Tues.–Sat. 10–5, Sun. noon–5.*

Side Trips
from London

King's College. Founded in 1441 by Henry VI, King's College has a magnificent late-15th-century chapel that is its most famous landmark. Other notable architecture is the neo-Gothic Porters' Lodge, facing King's Parade, which was a comparatively recent addition in the 1830s, and the classical Gibbs building. ■TIP→ **Head down to the river, from where the panorama of college and chapel is one of the university's most photographed views.** Past students of King's College include the novelist E.M. Forster, the economist John Maynard Keynes, and the World War I poet Rupert Brooke. ⊠ *King's Parade* ☎ *01223/331212* ⊕ *www.kings.cam.ac.uk* 🖾 *£7.50, includes chapel* ⊗ *Term time, Mon. 9:45–3:30, Tues.–Fri. 9:30–3:30, Sat. 9:30–3:15, Sun. 1:15–2:30; out of term, Mon. 9:45–4:30, Tues.–Sun. 9:30–4:30.*

Fodors Choice
★

King's College Chapel. Based on Sainte-Chapelle, the 13th-century royal chapel in Paris, this house of worship is perhaps the most glorious flowering of Perpendicular Gothic in Britain. Henry VI, the king after whom the college is named, oversaw the work. From the outside, the most prominent features are the massive flying buttresses and the finger-like spires that line the length of the building. Inside, the most obvious impression is of great space—the chapel was once described as "the noblest barn in Europe"—and of light flooding in from its huge windows. The brilliantly colored bosses (carved panels at the intersections of the roof ribs) are particularly intense, although hard to see without binoculars. An exhibition in the chantries, or side chapels, explains more about the chapel's construction. Behind the altar is *The Adoration of the Magi*, an enormous painting by Peter Paul Rubens. ■TIP→ **The chapel, unlike the rest of King's College, stays open during exam periods.** Every Christmas Eve, a festival of carols is sung by the chapel's famous choir. To compete for the small number of tickets available, join the line at the college's main entrance early—doors open at 7 am. ⊠ *King's Parade* ☎ *01223/331212* ⊕ *www.kings.cam.ac.uk* ☞ *£7.50, includes college and grounds* ⊙ *Term time, weekdays 9:30–4, Sat. 9:30–3:45, Sun. 1:15–3; out of term, daily 9:30–5; last admission 30 mins before closing. Chapel occasionally closed for services and private events; call or check online.*

Fodor's Choice **Polar Museum.** Beautifully designed, this museum at the university's Scott
★ Polar Research Institute chronicles the history of polar exploration. There's a particular emphasis on the British expeditions of the 20th century, including the ill-fated attempt by Robert Falcon Scott to be the first to reach the South Pole in 1912. Norwegian explorer Roald Amundsen reached the pole first; Scott and his men perished on the return journey, but his story became legendary. There are also collections devoted to the science of modern polar exploration and the indigenous people of northern Canada, Greenland, and Alaska. ⊠ *Scott Polar Research Institute, Lensfield Rd.* ☎ *01223/336540* ⊕ *www.spri. cam.ac.uk/museum* ☞ *Free* ⊙ *Tues.–Sat. and bank holiday Mon. 10–4. Closed Sat. of bank holiday weekends.*

WORTH NOTING

Emmanuel College. The master hand of architect Christopher Wren (1632–1723) is evident throughout much of Cambridge, particularly at Emmanuel, built on the site of a Dominican friary, where he designed the chapel and colonnade. A stained-glass window in the chapel has a likeness of John Harvard, founder of Harvard University, who studied here. The college, founded in 1584, was an early center of Puritan learning; a number of the Pilgrims were Emmanuel alumni, and they remembered their alma mater in naming Cambridge, Massachusetts. ⊠ *St. Andrew's St.* ☎ *01223/334200* ⊕ *www.emma.cam.ac.uk* ☞ *Free* ⊙ *Daily 9–6, except exam period.*

Queens' College. One of the most eye-catching colleges, Queens' is named after Margaret, wife of Henry VI, and Elizabeth, wife of Edward IV. Founded in 1448, the college is tucked away on Queens' Lane, next to the wide lawns that lead down from King's College to the Backs. The secluded "cloister court" looks untouched since its completion in the 1540s. Queens' masterpiece is the **Mathematical Bridge,** the original version of which is said to have been built without any fastenings. The current bridge (1902) is said to have been built without any fastenings. The current bridge (1902) is actually bolted. The college is closed to visitors late May to late June. ⊠ *Queens' La.* ☎ *01223/335511* ⊕ *www. quns.cam.ac.uk* ☞ *Mid Mar.–Sept. £2.50; Oct. weekends and Nov.– mid Mar. free for parties of 5 or fewer.* ⊙ *Mid-Mar.–mid-May and late June–Sept., daily 10–4:30; Oct., weekdays 2–4, weekends 10–4:30; Nov.–mid-Mar., daily 2–4.*

Trinity College. Founded in 1546 by Henry VIII, Trinity replaced a 14th-century educational foundation and is the largest college in either Cambridge or Oxford, with nearly 700 undergraduates. In the 17th-century great court, with its massive gatehouse, is **Great Tom**, a giant clock that strikes each hour with high and low notes. The college's greatest masterpiece is Christopher Wren's **library,** colonnaded and seemingly constructed with as much light as stone. Among the things you can see here is A. A. Milne's handwritten manuscript of *The House at Pooh Corner.* Trinity alumni include Isaac Newton, William Thackeray, Lord Byron, Alfred Tennyson, and 31 Nobel Prize winners. ✉ *St. John's St.* ☎ *01223/338400* ⊕ *www.trin.cam.ac.uk* 🎫 *£1* ⊙ *College and chapel daily 10–4, except exam period and event days; Wren Library weekdays noon–2, Sat. in term time 10:30–12:30; Great Court daily 10–4:30.*

WHERE TO EAT

$$ ✕ **Loch Fyne.** Part of a Scottish chain that harvests its own oysters, this
SEAFOOD airy, casual place across from the Fitzwilliam Museum is deservedly popular. The seafood is fresh and well prepared, served in a traditional setting with a modern ambience. Try the Bradan Rost smoked salmon if it's on the menu; it's flavored with Scotch whisky. The restaurant is also open for breakfast. ⑤ *Average main: £16* ✉ *37 Trumpington St.* ☎ *01223/362433* ⊕ *www.lochfyne-restaurants.com.*

$$ ✕ **River Bar & Kitchen.** Across the river from Magdalene College, this
MODERN BRITISH popular waterfront bar and grill serves delicious steak and burgers, plus specialties such as lobster macaroni and cheese and roast chicken with a bourbon barbecue glaze. Light lunches are served in the afternoon, and the evening cocktail list is small but elegant. Try the French 75, which is gin with lemon juice, sugar, and sparkling wine. ⑤ *Average main: £20* ✉ *Quayside, Thompsons La., off Bridge St.* ☎ *01223/307030* ⊕ *www.riverbarsteakhouse.com* 🔑 *Reservations essential.*

19

OXFORD

55 miles northwest of London.

With arguably the most famous university in the world, Oxford has been a center of learning since 1167, with only the Sorbonne preceding it. It doesn't take more than a day or two to explore its winding medieval streets, photograph its ivy-covered stone buildings and ancient churches and libraries, and even take a punt down one of its placid waterways. The town center is compact and walkable, and at its heart is Oxford University. Alumni of this prestigious institution include 48 Nobel Prize winners, 26 British prime ministers (including David Cameron), and 28 foreign presidents (including Bill Clinton), along with poets, authors, and artists such as Percy Bysshe Shelley, Oscar Wilde, and W. H. Auden.

Oxford is northwest of London, at the junction of the rivers Thames and Cherwell. The city is more interesting and more cosmopolitan than Cambridge, and although it's also bigger, its suburbs aren't remotely interesting to visitors. The interest is all at the center, where the old town curls around the grand stone buildings, great restaurants, and historic pubs. Victorian writer Matthew Arnold described Oxford's "dreaming spires," a phrase that has become famous. Students rush past on the way to exams, clad with antiquarian style in their requisite mortar caps, flowing dark gowns, stiff collars, and crisp white bow ties. ■TIP→ Watch your back when crossing roads, as bikes are everywhere.

> ### WORD OF MOUTH
>
> "It's perfectly possible to get a HUGE amount out of a 6-hour Oxford stay—especially by following the self-guided tours on the Oxfordshire official tourist site or booking a Blue Badge walking tour at the city's Tourist Information Centre. Or opt to spend a month there. Neither strategy (or anything in between) is self-evidently wrong."
>
> —flanneruk

VISITING THE COLLEGES

You can explore major sights in town in a day, but it takes more than a day to spend an hour in each of the key museums and absorb the college scene. Some colleges are open only in the afternoons during university terms. When undergraduates are in residence, access is often restricted to the chapels, dining rooms, and libraries, and you're requested to refrain from picnicking in the quadrangles. All are closed certain days during exams, usually from mid-April to late June.

TOURS

City Sightseeing. This company offers hop-on, hop-off bus tours with 19 stops around Oxford; your ticket, purchased from the driver, is good for 24 hours. ☎01865/790522 ⊕ www.citysightseeingoxford. com ✉ From £14.

Oxford Tourist Information Centre. You can find information here on the many guided walks of the city. The best way of gaining access to the collegiate buildings is to take the two-hour university and city tour, which leaves the Tourist Information Centre at 10:45 and 1 daily, 1 and 2 on Saturday. You can book in advance. ✉ 15/16 Broad St. ☎01865/252200 ⊕ www.visitoxfordandoxfordshire.com.

EXPLORING

TOP ATTRACTIONS

Fodor's Choice
★

Ashmolean Museum. Britain's oldest public museum displays its rich and varied collections from the Neolithic to the present day over five floors. Innovative and spacious galleries on the theme of "Crossing Cultures, Crossing Time" explore connections between the priceless Greek, Roman, and Indian artifacts, as well as the Egyptian and Chinese objects. In regards to the superb art collection, not to be missed are drawings by Raphael, the shell-encrusted mantle of Powhatan (father of Pocahontas), the lantern belonging to Guy Fawkes, and the Alfred Jewel, set in gold, which dates from the reign of King Alfred the Great (ruled 871–899). ■TIP→ There's too much to see in one visit, but the free admission makes return trips easy. The Ashmolean Dining Room, Oxford's first rooftop restaurant, is a good spot for

Radcliffe Camera, an unmissable circular library at Oxford University

refreshments. ⊠ *Beaumont St.* ☎ *01865/278002* ⊕ *www.ashmolean. org* ⊠ *Free* ⊙ *Tues.–Sun. and national holidays 10–5.*

Fodor's Choice
★
Magdalen College. Founded in 1458, with a handsome main quadrangle and a supremely monastic air, Magdalen (pronounced *maud*-lin) is one of the most impressive of Oxford's colleges and attracts its most artistic students. Alumni include such diverse people as P.G. Wodehouse, Oscar Wilde, and John Betjeman. The school's large, square tower is a famous local landmark. ■**TIP→** To enhance your visit, take a stroll around the Deer Park and along Addison's Walk; then have tea in the Old Kitchen, which overlooks the river. ⊠ *High St.* ☎ *01865/276000* ⊕ *www.magd.ox.ac.uk* ⊠ *£5* ⊙ *July–Sept., daily noon–7 or dusk; Oct.–June, daily 1–6 or dusk.*

FAMILY
Fodor's Choice
★
Pitt Rivers Museum. More than half a million intriguing archaeological and anthropological items from around the globe, based on the collection bequeathed by Lieutenant-General Augustus Henry Lane Fox Pitt Rivers in 1884, are crammed into glass cases and drawers. Items are organized thematically, an eccentric approach that's surprisingly thought-provoking. Labels are handwritten, and children are given flashlights to explore the farthest corners and spot the world's smallest dolly. Give yourself plenty of time to wander here. Children will have a field day. ⊠ *S. Parks Rd.* ☎ *01865/270927* ⊕ *www.prm.ox.ac. uk* ⊠ *Free, suggested donation £3* ⊙ *Mon. noon–4:30, Tues.–Sun. and national holidays 10–4:30.*

WORTH NOTING

Christ Church. Built in 1546, the college of Christ Church is referred to by its members as "The House." This is the site of Oxford's largest quadrangle, Tom Quad, named after the huge bell (6¼ tons) that hangs in the Christopher Wren–designed gate tower and rings 101 times at five past nine every evening in honor of the original number of Christ Church scholars. The vaulted, 800-year-old chapel in one corner has been Oxford's cathedral since the time of Henry VIII. The college's medieval dining hall, re-created for the Harry Potter films, contains portraits of many famous alumni, including 13 of Britain's prime ministers. ■TIP➔ Plan carefully, as the dining hall is only open weekdays 10:30–11:40 and 2:30–4:30 and weekends 2:30–4:30. Lewis Carroll, author of *Alice in Wonderland*, was a teacher of mathematics here for many years; a shop opposite the meadows on St. Aldate's sells Alice paraphernalia. ⊠ *St. Aldate's* ☎ *01865/276492* ⊕ *www.chch.ox.ac.uk* 🖃 *£8; £9 in July and Aug.* ⊙ *Mon.–Sat. 10–5, Sun. 2–5; last admission 30 mins before closing.*

Radcliffe Camera and Bodleian Library. A vast library, the domed Radcliffe Camera is Oxford's most spectacular building, built in 1737–49 by James Gibbs in Italian baroque style. It's usually surrounded by tourists with cameras trained at its golden-stone walls. The Camera contains part of the Bodleian Library's enormous collection, begun in 1602. Much like the Library of Congress in the United States, the Bodleian contains a copy of every book printed in Great Britain and grows by 5,000 items a week. Tours reveal the Duke Humfrey's Library, which was the original chained library and completed in 1488. Guides will show you spots used for Hogwarts School in the *Harry Potter* films. ■TIP➔ Arrive early to secure tickets for the three to six daily tours. These are sold on a first-come, first-served basis (except for the extended tour on Wednesday and Saturday, which can be prebooked). Audio tours, the only tours open to kids under 11, don't require reservations. Call ahead to confirm tour times. ⊠ *Broad St.* ☎ *01865/287400* ⊕ *www.bodleian.ox.ac.uk* 🖃 *Audio tour £2.50, minitour £5, standard tour £7, extended tours £13* ⊙ *Bodleian and Divinity School weekdays 9–5, Sat. 9–4:30, Sun. 11–5.*

St. John's College. One of Oxford's most attractive campuses, St. John's has seven quadrangles surrounded by elaborately carved buildings. You enter the first through a low wooden door. This college dates to 1555, when Sir Thomas White, a merchant, founded it. His heart is buried in the chapel (by tradition, students curse as they walk over it). The Canterbury Quad represented the first example of Italian Renaissance architecture in Oxford, and the Front Quad includes the buildings of the old St. Bernard's Monastery. ⊠ *St. Giles* ☎ *01865/277300* ⊕ *www. sjc.ox.ac.uk* 🖃 *Free* ⊙ *Daily 1–5 or dusk.*

University Church of St. Mary the Virgin. Seven hundred years' worth of funeral monuments crowd this spacious church, including the tombstone, on the altar steps, of Amy Robsart, the wife of Robert Dudley, Elizabeth I's favorite. One pillar marks the site where Thomas Cranmer, author of the *Anglican Book of Common Prayer*, was brought to trial under Queen Mary for his marital machinations on behalf of Henry

VIII. ■ TIP➜ The top of the 14th-century tower has a panoramic view of the city's skyline. It's worth the 127 steps. The Vaults and Garden Café, a part of the church accessible from Radcliffe Square, serves breakfasts and cream teas as well as good lunches. ✉ *High St.* ☎ *01865/279111* ⊕ *www.university-church ox ac uk* ✉ *Church free, tower £1* ⊗ *Mon.– Sat. 9–5, Sun. noon–5; last admission 30 mins before closing.*

WHERE TO EAT

$$

FRENCH

✕ **Brasserie Blanc.** Raymond Blanc's sophisticated brasserie in the Jericho neighborhood, a hipper cousin of Le Manoir aux Quat' Saisons in Great Milton, is one of the best places to eat in Oxford. Wood floors and large windows keep the restaurant open and airy. The changing menu lists stunning adaptations of bourgeois French fare, sometimes with Mediterranean or Asian influences. Try the chicken confit and Armagnac prune paté or Jervaulx blue cheese to start and a boeuf bourguignonne to follow. The £11.50 fixed-price lunch is a good value, and kids have their own menu. ⑤ *Average main: £15* ✉ *71–72 Walton St.* ☎ *01865/510999* ⊕ *www.brasserieblanc.com.*

$

CAFÉ

✕ **Grand Café.** The grand, gold-topped columns of the café's facade draw you here, to the country's oldest coffeehouse (est. 1650) and now an excellent spot for sandwiches and salads. It's packed with tourists and the service can be slow, but this is still a pretty spot for afternoon tea. From Thursday through Saturday night, it transforms into a popular cocktail bar. ⑤ *Average main: £8* ✉ *84 High St.* ☎ *01865/204463* ⊕ *www.thegrandcafe.co.uk.*

$

ITALIAN

✕ **Jamie's Italian.** One of chef Jamie Oliver's missions is to re-create the best rustic Italian fare all over the country, and it's no different at this buzzing eatery. There's a diverting range of starters, pastas, and mains such as truffle tagliatelle with Parmesan and nutmeg or British lamb lollipops with toasted nuts and lemon yogurt. The various dishes served on a wood plank are a steal, desserts are light—granola crumble, for example—and the crowd is lively. ⑤ *Average main: £12* ✉ *24–26 George St.* ☎ *01865/838383* ⊕ *www.jamieoliver.com.*

19

STRATFORD-UPON-AVON

104 miles north of London.

Stratford-upon-Avon has become adept at accommodating the hordes of people who stream in for a glimpse of William Shakespeare's world. Filled with distinctive, Tudor half-timber buildings, this is certainly a handsome town, and the Royal Shakespeare Theatre is a don't-miss for those who want to see Shakespeare performed in England. But the town can feel, at times, like a literary amusement park, so if you're not a fan of the Bard, you may want to explore elsewhere.

TOURS AND TICKETS

City Sightseeing. Hop-on, hop-off guided tours of Stratford are run by City Sightseeing, and you can combine the tour (about an hour with no stops) with entry to either three or five Shakespeare houses. In summer, the same company's Heart of Warwickshire tour includes Compton

Stratford-upon-Avon honors Shakespeare's birthday with an annual procession.

Verney, Charlecote Park, and Warwick (four trips on weekends from April through July, daily in August). ☎ *01789/412680* ⊕ *www.city-sightseeing.com* ✉ *From £12.50.*

Shakespeare Birthplace Trust. The main places of Shakespearean interest (Anne Hathaway's Cottage, Hall's Croft, Mary Arden's Farm, Nash's House and New Place, Shakespeare's Birthplace, and Shakespeare's Grave) are run by the Shakespeare Birthplace Trust. Buy a money-saving combination ticket to all five properties for £22.50, or pay separate entry fees if you're visiting only one or two. Family tickets are an option, too. Advance booking online gives you a 10% saving, and tickets are valid for a year. Tickets for Hall's Croft and Nash's House and New Place are available only as a rather pricey (£14.95) joint ticket that includes the birthplace and grave. ☎ *01789/204016* ⊕ *www. shakespeare.org.uk.*

Stratford Town Walk. This walking tour runs year-round and also offers ghost-themed walks and cruises. ☎ *01789/292478, 0785/576–0377* ⊕ *www.stratfordtownwalk.co.uk* ✉ *From £5* ☉ *Mon–Thurs. at 11, Fri.–Sun. at 11 and 2.*

ESSENTIALS
Visitor Information Stratford-upon-Avon Tourist Information Centre ✉ *Bridgefoot* ☎ *01789/264293* ⊕ *www.discover-stratford.com.*

EXPLORING

Hall's Croft. One of the finest surviving Jacobean (early 17th-century) town houses, this impressive residence has a delightful walled garden. Hall's Croft was the home of Shakespeare's elder daughter, Susanna, and her husband, Dr. John Hall, a physician who, by prescribing an herbal cure for scurvy, was well ahead of his time. His consulting room and medical dispensary are on view along with the other rooms, all containing Jacobean furniture of heavy oak, including a fine child's high chair, and some 17th-century portraits. The café serves light lunches and afternoon teas. ⊠ *Old Town* ☏ *01789/292107* ⊕ *www.shakespeare.org. uk* 🎫 *£15.90, includes admission to Shakespeare's Birthplace, Nash's House and New Place, and Shakespeare's Grave* ⊗ *Apr.–Oct., daily 10–5; Nov.–Mar., daily 11–4.*

Holy Trinity Church. The burial place of William Shakespeare, this 13th-century church sits on the banks of the Avon, with a graceful avenue of lime trees framing its entrance. Shakespeare's final resting place is in the chancel, rebuilt in 1465–91 in the late Perpendicular style. He was buried here not because he was a famed poet but because he was a lay rector of Stratford, owning a portion of the township tithes. On the north wall of the sanctuary, over the altar steps, is the famous marble bust created by Gerard Jansen in 1623 and thought to be a true likeness of Shakespeare. The bust offers a more human, even humorous, perspective when viewed from the side. Also in the chancel are the graves of Shakespeare's wife, Anne; his daughter Susanna; his son-in-law John Hall; and his granddaughter's husband, Thomas Nash. Nearby, the Parish Register is displayed, containing Shakespeare's baptismal entry (1564) and his burial notice (1616). ⊠ *Trinity St.* ☏ *01789/266316* ⊕ *www.stratford-upon-avon.org* 🎫 *£2 for chancel* ⊗ *Mar. and Oct., Mon.–Sat. 9–5, Sun. 12:30–5; Apr.–Sept., Mon.–Sat. 8:30–6, Sun. 12:30–5; Nov.–Feb., Mon.–Sat. 9–4, Sun. 12:30–5; last admission 20 mins before closing.*

Nash's House and New Place. The house where Shakespeare died in 1616, called **New Place**, was built in 1483 "of brike and tymber" for a lord mayor of London, and was Stratford's grandest piece of real estate when Shakespeare bought it in 1597 for £60. It was torn down in 1759 by the Reverend Francis Gastrell, who was angry at the hordes of Shakespeare-related sightseers. You can see finds from the excavations carried out here from 2010 to 2012 in the heavily restored **Nash's house** next door, the residence of Thomas Nash, who married Shakespeare's last direct descendant, his granddaughter Elizabeth Hall. It's now furnished in 17th-century style, and the gardens contain an extensive Elizabethan knot garden and a fine display of cloud topiary. ⊠ *Chapel St.* ☏ *01789/292325* ⊕ *www.shakespeare.org.uk* 🎫 *£15.90, includes admission to Shakespeare's Birthplace, Hall's Croft, and Shakespeare's Grave* ⊗ *Apr.–Oct., daily 10–5; Nov.–Mar., daily 11–4.*

Fodor's Choice **Royal Shakespeare Company.** One of the finest repertory troupes in the
★ world and long the backbone of the country's theatrical life, the company performs plays year-round in Stratford and at venues around Britain. The Royal Shakespeare Theatre, home of the RSC, has a thrust

19

stage based on the original Globe Theater in London. The Swan Theatre, part of the theater complex and also built in the style of Shakespeare's Globe, stages plays by Shakespeare and contemporaries such as Christopher Marlowe, as well as works by contemporary playwrights. Prices range from £5 to £50. ■TIP➜ Seats book up fast, but day-of-performance and returned tickets are sometimes available. ⊠ *Waterside* ☎ *0844/800–1110 ticket hotline* ⊕ *www.rsc.org.uk.*

Fodor's Choice
★
Shakespeare's Birthplace. A half-timber house typical of its time, the playwright's birthplace is a much-visited shrine that has been altered and restored since he lived here. Passing through the modern visitor center, you are immersed in the world of Shakespeare through a "Famous Beyond Words—Shakespeare All Around Us" visual and audio exhibition created for his 450th birthday celebrations in 2014. The house itself is across the garden from the visitor center. Colorful wall decorations and furnishings reflect middle-class Elizabethan domestic life. Shakespeare's father, John, a glove maker and wool dealer, purchased the house; a reconstructed workshop shows the tools of the glover's trade. Mark Twain and Charles Dickens were both pilgrims here, and you can see the signatures of Thomas Carlyle and Walter Scott scratched into Shakespeare's windowpanes. In the garden, actors present excerpts from the plays. There's also a café and bookshop on the grounds. ⊠ *Henley St.* ☎ *01789/201822* ⊕ *www.shakespeare.org.uk* ⊠ *£15.90, includes entry to Hall's Croft, Nash's House and New Place, and Shakespeare's Grave* ۞ *Apr.–June, Sept., and Oct., daily 9–5; July and Aug. daily 9–6; Nov.–Mar., daily 10–4.*

STRATFORD ENVIRONS

Two additional stops on the Shakespeare trail are just outside Stratford; also nearby is spectacular Warwick Castle.

Fodor's Choice
★
Anne Hathaway's Cottage. The most picturesque of the Shakespeare Trust properties, on the western outskirts of Stratford, was the family home of the woman Shakespeare married in 1582. The "cottage," actually a substantial Tudor farmhouse, has latticed windows and a grand thatch roof. Inside is period furniture, including the settle where Shakespeare reputedly conducted his courtship, and a rare carved Elizabethan bed; outside is a garden planted in lush Edwardian style with herbs and flowers. A stroll through the adjacent orchard takes you to willow cabins where you can listen to sonnets and view sculptures with Shakespearean themes, while the nearby arboretum has trees, shrubs, and roses mentioned in Shakespeare's works. ■TIP➜ The best way to get here is on foot, especially in late spring when the apple trees are in blossom. The signed path runs from Evesham Place (an extension of Grove Road) opposite Chestnut Walk. Pick up a leaflet with a map from the tourist office; the walk takes a good half hour. ⊠ *Cottage La., Shottery* ☎ *01789/295517* ⊕ *www.shakespeare.org.uk* ⊠ *£9.50; £23.90 with the Five House Pass which includes Hall's Croft, Mary Arden's Farm, Nash's House and New Place, Shakespeare's Birthplace, and Shakespeare's Grave* ۞ *Apr.–Oct., daily 9–5; Nov.–Mar., daily 10–4; last admission 30 mins before closing.*

FAMILY **Mary Arden's Farm.** A working farm, where food is grown using methods common in the 16th century, is the main attraction at Mary Arden's House (the childhood home of Shakespeare's mother) and Palmer's Farm. This bucolic stop is great for kids, who can try their hand at basket weaving and gardening, listen as the farmers explain their work in the fields, and watch the cooks prepare food in the Tudor farmhouse kitchen. It all brings the past to life. There are crafts exhibits, a café, and a garden. The site is 3 miles northwest of Stratford; you need to walk or drive here, or else go with a tour. ⊠ *Off A3400, Wilmcote* ☎ *01789/293455* ⊕ *www.shakespeare. org.uk* ⊒ *£12.50; £23.90 with the Five House Pass which includes Anne Hathaway's Cottage and Gardens, Hall's Croft, Nash's House and New Place, Shakespeare's Birthplace, and Shakespeare's Grave* ☉ *Apr.–Oct., daily 10–5.*

> **DID YOU KNOW?**
>
> The Queen uses Windsor often— it's said she likes it much more than Buckingham Palace—spending most weekends here, often joined by family and friends. You know she's in when the Royal Standard is flown above the Round Tower but not in when you see the Union Jack.

FAMILY
Fodor's Choice
★
Warwick Castle. The vast bulk of this medieval castle rests on a cliff overlooking the Avon—"the fairest monument of ancient and chivalrous splendor which yet remains uninjured by time," to use the words of Sir Walter Scott. Today the company that runs the Madame Tussauds wax museums owns the castle, and the exhibits and diversions can occupy a full day. Warwick is a great castle experience for kids, though it's pricey (there are family rates). Warwick's two soaring towers, bristling with battlements, can be seen for miles: the 147-foot-high Caesar's Tower, built in 1356, and the 128-foot-high Guy's Tower, built in 1380. Warwick Castle's monumental walls enclose an impressive armory of medieval weapons, as well as state rooms with historic furnishings and paintings by Rubens, Van Dyck, and other masters. Exhibits display the sights and sounds of a great medieval household as it prepares for an important battle, and of a princess's fairy-tale wedding; in the Dragon Tower, Merlin and a talking dragon breathe life into the Arthurian legend. Below the castle strutting peacocks patrol the 60 acres of grounds elegantly landscaped by Capability Brown in the 18th century. ■ TIP→ Arrive early to beat the crowds. If you book online, you save on ticket prices. Lavish medieval banquets (extra charge) and special events, including festivals, jousting tournaments, and a Christmas market, take place throughout the year, and plenty of food stalls serve lunches. ⊠ *Castle La. off Mill St., Warwick* ☎ *01926/495421, 0871/265–2000 24-hr information line* ⊕ *www. warwick-castle.com* ⊒ *Castle, Dragon Tower, and Dungeon £30.60; Castle and Dungeon £28.20; Castle £22.80; parking £6* ☉ *Late July and Aug., daily 10–6; mid-Sept.–mid-July, daily 10–5; last admission 30 mins before closing.*

19

WHERE TO EAT

$ ✕ **The Black Swan/The Dirty Duck.** The only pub in Britain to be licensed
BRITISH   under two names (the more informal one came courtesy of American
Fodor's Choice   GIs who were stationed here during World War II), this is one of Strat-
★   ford's most celebrated pubs—it's attracted actors since the 18th-century
thespian David Garrick's days. A little veranda overlooks the theaters
and the river here. Along with your pint of bitter, you can choose from
the extensive menu of daily specials, wraps, ciabattas, steaks, burgers,
and grills. Few people come here for the food, though you will need
to book ahead for dinner: the real attraction is the ambience and your
fellow customers. ⑤ *Average main: £10* ✉ *Waterside* ☎ *01789/297312*
⊕ *www.dirtyduck-pub-stratford-upon-avon.co.uk.*

$ ✕ **Opposition.** Hearty, warming meals are offered at this informal,
MODERN BRITISH   family-style restaurant in a 16th-century building on the main dining
street near the theaters. The English and international dishes—chicken
roasted with banana and served with curry sauce and basmati rice, for
instance—win praise from the locals. There's a good range of lighter
and vegetarian options and fixed-price menus as well. Make reservations a month ahead in summer. ⑤ *Average main: £14* ✉ *13 Sheep St.*
☎ *01789/269980* ⊕ *www.theoppo.co.uk* ◔ *Closed Sun.*

WARNER BROS. HARRY POTTER STUDIO TOUR

20 miles northwest of London.

Popular and family friendly, the Warner Bros. Harry Potter Studio Tour
has sets and props from the successful films, and plenty of engaging
interactive diversions for all ages. The train and a special shuttle bus
from Watford get you here.

EXPLORING

FAMILY   **Warner Bros. Harry Potter Studio Tour.** Muggles, take note: this spectacular
Fodor's Choice   attraction just outside Watford will give you at least three hours of expe-
★   riencing the magical world of the wizards and witches of *Harry Potter*.
From the Great Hall of Hogwarts to magical props, each section of this
attraction showcases the real sets, props, and special effects used in the
eight movies. Visitors enter the Great Hall, a fitting stage for costumes
from each Hogwarts house. Admire the intricacies of the Hogwarts
Castle model (50 feet in diameter), ride a broomstick, try butterbeer,
or just take refuge in the comforting confines of Dumbledore's office.
Tickets, pegged to a 30-minute arrival time slot, must be prebooked
online. The studio tour is a 20-minute drive from St. Albans. You can
also get here by taking a 20-minute train ride from London's Euston
Station to Watford Junction (then a 15-minute shuttle bus ride). Via car
from London, use M1 and M25 and enjoy the free parking. ✉ *Studio
Tour Dr., Leavesden* ☎ *0845/084–0900* ⊕ *www.wbstudiotour.co.uk*
✉ *£30* ◔ *Daily 10–4 (until 6:30 at some times of year).*

WINDSOR CASTLE

21 miles west of London.

The tall turrets of Windsor Castle, one of the homes of the Royal Family, can be seen for miles around. The grand stone building is the star attraction in this quiet town with some remaining medieval elements—though Eton College, England's most famous public school, is also just a lovely walk away across the Thames.

ESSENTIALS

Visitor Information Royal Windsor Information Centre ⊠ *Old Booking Hall, Windsor Royal Station, Thames St.* ☎ *01753/743900, 01753/743907 for accommodations* ⊕ *www.windsor.gov.uk.*

EXPLORING

Fodor'sChoice
★
Windsor Castle. From William the Conqueror to Queen Victoria, the kings and queens of England added towers and wings to this brooding, imposing castle, visible for miles and now the largest inhabited castle in the world. Despite the multiplicity of hands involved in its design, the palace manages to have a unity of style and character. The most impressive view of Windsor Castle is from the A332 road, coming into town from the south. Admission includes an audio guide and, if you wish, a guided tour of the castle precincts. Entrance lines can be long in season and you're likely to spend at least half a day here, so come early.

William the Conqueror began work on the castle in the 11th century, and Edward III modified and extended it in the mid-1300s. One of Edward's largest contributions was the enormous and distinctive **Round Tower.** Later, between 1824 and 1837, George IV transformed the castle into the fortified royal palace you see today, the only royal residence in continuous use by the Royal Family since the Middle Ages.

As you enter the castle, **Henry VIII's gateway** leads uphill into the wide castle precincts, where you're free to wander. Across from the entrance is the exquisite St. George's Chapel (closed Sunday). Here lie 10 of the kings of England, including Henry VI, Charles I, and Henry VIII (Jane Seymour is the only one of his six wives buried here). One of the noblest buildings in England, the chapel was built in the Perpendicular style popular in the 15th and 16th centuries. The elaborate **Albert Memorial Chapel** was created by Queen Victoria in memory of her husband.

The **North Terrace** provides good views across the Thames to Eton College, perhaps the most famous of Britain's exclusive "public" boys' schools. From the terrace, you enter the **State Apartments,** which are open to the public most days. On display to the left of the entrance to the State Apartments in Windsor Castle, **Queen Mary's Dolls' House** is a perfect miniature Georgian palace-within-a-palace, created in 1923. Electric lights glow, the doors all have tiny keys, and a miniature library holds Lilliputian-size books written especially for the young queen by famous authors of the 1920s.

19

Although a fire in 1992 gutted some of the State Apartments, hardly any works of art were lost. Phenomenal repair work brought to new life the **Grand Reception Room,** the **Green and Crimson Drawing Rooms,** and the **State and Octagonal Dining Rooms.** A green oak hammer-beam roof looms magnificently over the 600-year-old **St. George's Hall,** where the Queen gives state banquets. The State Apartments contain paintings by Rubens, Van Dyck, and Dürer, among others. The tour's high points are the **Throne Room** and the **Waterloo Chamber,** where Sir Thomas Lawrence's portraits of Napóleon's victorious foes line the walls. ■ TIP➔ To see the castle come magnificently alive, check out the Changing the Guard, which takes place daily at 11 am from April through July and on alternate days at 11 am from August through March. Confirm the exact schedule before traveling to Windsor. ⊠ *Castle Hill* ☎ *020/7766–7304 tickets, 01753/831118 recorded information* ⊕ *www.royalcollection. org.uk* ⊡ *£18.50 for Precincts, State Apartments, Gallery, St. George's Chapel, and Queen Mary's Dolls' House; £10 when State Apartments are closed* ⊙ *Mar.–Oct., daily 9:45–5:15, last admission at 4; Nov.– Feb., daily 9:45–4:15, last admission at 3*

Fodor'sChoice
★
Eton College. Signs warn drivers of "Boys Crossing" as you approach the Tudor-style buildings of Eton College, the distinguished boarding school for boys ages 13 through 18 that was founded in 1440 by King Henry VI. It's all terrifically photogenic, because during the college semester students still dress in pin-striped trousers, swallow-tailed coats, and stiff collars. Rivaling St. George's at Windsor in terms of size, the Gothic **Chapel** contains 15th-century grisaille wall paintings juxtaposed against modern stained glass by John Piper. Beyond the cloisters are the school's playing fields where, according to the duke of Wellington, the Battle of Waterloo was really won, since so many of his officers had learned discipline and strategy during their school days. Among the country's prime ministers to be educated here is David Cameron. The **Museum of Eton Life** has displays on the school's history. The school offers public tours, although as of this writing they were suspended due to construction. They are set to resume again in 2015, but call ahead for more information. ⊠ *Brewhouse Yard, Eton, Berkshire* ☎ *01753/671177* ⊕ *www.etoncollege.com.*

WHERE TO EAT

$$
BRITISH
✕ **Two Brewers.** Locals congregate in a pair of low-ceiling rooms at this tiny 17th-century establishment by the gates of Windsor Great Park. Those under 18 aren't allowed inside the pub (though they can be served at a few outdoor tables), but adults will find a suitable collection of wine, espresso, and local beer, plus an excellent menu with such dishes as fish cakes and hot and cold sandwiches. On Sunday the pub serves a traditional, hearty lunchtime roast. ⑤ *Average main: £15* ⊠ *34 Park St.* ☎ *01753/855426* ⊕ *www.twobrewerswindsor.co.uk* ⌛ *Reservations essential* ⊙ *No dinner Fri.–Sun.*

UNDERSTANDING LONDON

LONDON AT-A-GLANCE

ENGLISH VOCABULARY

BOOKS AND MOVIES

LONDON AT-A-GLANCE

FAST FACTS

Type of government: Representative democracy. In 1999 the Greater London Authority Act reestablished a single local governing body for the Greater London area, consisting of an elected mayor and the 25-member London Assembly. Elections, first held in 2000, take place every four years.

Population: Inner city 3 million, Greater London 7.7 million

Population density: 12,331 people per square mile

Median age: 38.4

Infant mortality rate: 5 per 1,000 births

Language: English. More than 300 languages are spoken in London. All city government documents are translated into Arabic, Bengali, Chinese, Greek, Gujurati, Hindi, Punjabi, Turkish, Urdu, and Vietnamese.

Ethnic and racial groups: White British 70%, White Irish 3%, Other White 9%, Indian 6%, Bangladeshi 2%, Pakistani 2%, other Asian 2%, Black African 6%, Black Caribbean 5%, Chinese 1%, Other 3%.

Religion: Christian 58%, nonaffiliated 15%, Muslim 8%, Hindu 4%, Jewish 2%, Sikh 1%, other religion 1%, Buddhist 0.8%.

When a man is tired of London, he is tired of life; for there is in London all that life can afford.

—Samuel Johnson

GEOGRAPHY AND ENVIRONMENT

Latitude: 51° N (same as Calgary, Canada; Kiev, Ukraine; Prague, Czech Republic)

Longitude: 0° (same as Accra, Ghana). A brass line in the ground in Greenwich marks the prime meridian (0° longitude).

Elevation: 49 feet

Land area: City, 67 square miles; metro area, 625 square miles

Terrain: River plain, rolling hills, and parkland

Natural hazards: Drought in warmer summers, minor localized flooding of the Thames caused by surge tides from the North Atlantic

Environmental issues: The city has been improving its air quality, but up to 1,600 people die each year from health problems related to London's polluted air. Only half of London's rivers and canals received passing grades for water quality from 1999 through 2001. More than £12 million ($22 million) is spent annually to ensure the city's food safety.

I'm leaving because the weather is too good. I hate London when it's not raining.

—Groucho Marx

ECONOMY

Workforce: 3.8 million; financial/real estate 28%, health care 10%, manufacturing 4%, education 7%, construction 5%, public administration 5%

Unemployment: 7.2%

Major industries: The arts, banking, government, insurance, tourism

London: a nation, not a city.

—Benjamin Disraeli, Lothair

ENGLISH VOCABULARY

You and a Londoner may speak the same language, but some phrases definitely get lost in translation once they cross the Atlantic.

British English	American English
BASIC TERMS AND EVERYDAY ITEMS	
bill	check
flat	apartment
holiday	vacation
lift	elevator
nappy	diaper
note	bill (currency)
plaster	Band-Aid
queue	line
row	argument
rubbish	trash
tin	can
toilet/loo/WC	bathroom
CLOTHING	
braces	suspenders
bum bag	fanny pack
dressing gown	robe
jumper	sweater
pants/knickers	underpants/briefs
rucksack	backpack
suspender	garter
tights	pantyhose
trainers	sneakers
trousers	pants
vest	undershirt
waistcoat	vest
TRANSPORTATION	
bonnet	hood
boot	trunk

coach	long-distance bus
pavement	sidewalk
petrol	gas
pram	baby carriage
puncture	flat
windscreen	windshield

FOOD

aubergine	eggplant
banger	sausage
biscuit	cookie
chips	fries
courgette	zucchini
Crisps	potato chips
Jam	jelly
main course (or main)	entrée
Pudding	dessert
Rocket	arugula
Starter	appetizer
Sweet	candy
Tea	early dinner

SLANG

all right	hi there
Cheers	thank you
Chuffed	pleased
Fit	attractive
Geezer	dude
guv'nor, gaffer	boss
Hard	tough
Mate	buddy
Sound	good
Ta	thank you

BOOKS AND MOVIES

London in Books

London has been the focus of countless books and essays. For sonorous eloquence, you still must reach back more than half a century to Henry James's *English Hours* and Virginia Woolf's *The London Scene*. Today most suggested reading lists begin with V. S. Pritchett's *London Perceived* and H. V. Morton's *In Search of London*, both decades old. Four more-up-to-date books with a general compass are Peter Ackroyd's *Thames* and anecdotal *London: The Biography,* which traces the city's growth from the Druids to the 21st century; John Russell's *London*, a sumptuously illustrated art book; and Christopher Hibbert's *In London: The Biography of a City*. Stephen Inwood's *A History of London* explores the city from its Roman roots to its swinging '60s heyday. Piet Schreuders's *The Beatles' London* follows the footsteps of the Fab Four.

That noted, there are books galore on the various facets of the city. *The Art and Architecture of London,* by Ann Saunders, is fairly comprehensive. *Inside London: Discovering the Classic Interiors of London,* by Joe Friedman and Peter Aprahamian, has magnificent color photographs of hidden and overlooked shops, clubs, and town houses. For a wonderful take on the golden age of the city's regal mansions, see Christopher Simon Sykes's *Private Palaces: Life in the Great London Houses*. For various other aspects of the city, consult Mervyn Blatch's helpful *A Guide to London's Churches*, Andrew Crowe's *The Parks and Woodlands of London*, Sheila Fairfield's *The Streets of London*, Ann Saunders's *Regent's Park*, Ian Norrie's *Hampstead, Highgate Village, and Kenwood*, and Suzanne Ebel's *A Guide to London's Riverside: Hampton Court to Greenwich*. For keen walkers, there are two books by Andrew Duncan: *Secret London* and *Walking Village London*. *City Secrets: London*, edited by Robert Kahn, is a handsome book of anecdotes

from London writers, artists, and historians about their favorite places in the city. For the last word on just about every subject, see *The London Encyclopaedia,* edited by Ben Weinreb and Christopher Hibbert. HarperCollins's *London Photographic Atlas* has a plethora of bird's-eye images of the capital. For an alternative view of the city, it would be hard to better Iain Sinclair's witty and intelligent *London Orbital: A Walk Around the M25* in which he scrutinizes the history, mythology, and politics of London from the viewpoint of its ugly ring road. Sinclair is also the editor of *London: City of Disappearances*, an anthology exploring what has vanished.

Of course, the history and spirit of the city are also to be found in celebrations of great authors, British heroes, and architects. Peter Ackroyd's massive *Dickens* elucidates how the great author shaped today's view of the city; Martin Gilbert's magisterial, multivolume *Churchill* traces the city through some of its greatest trials; J. Mansbridge's *John Nash* details the London buildings of this great architect. Liza Picard evokes mid-18th-century London in *Dr. Johnson's London*. For musical theater buffs, Mike Leigh's *Gilbert and Sullivan's London* takes a romantic look at the two artists' lives and times in the capital's grand theaters and wild nightspots. *Rodinsky's Room*, by Rachel Lichtenstein and Iain Sinclair, is a fascinating exploration of East End Jewish London and the mysterious disappearance of one of its occupants.

Maureen Waller's *1700: Scenes from London Life* is a fascinating look at the daily life of Londoners in the 18th century. Nineteenth-century London—the city of Queen Victoria, Tennyson, and Dickens—comes alive through *Mayhew's London*, a massive study of the London poor by Henry Mayhew, and Gustave Doré's *London*, an unforgettable series of engravings of the city (often reprinted in modern editions) that detail its horrifying slums and grand avenues. When it comes to fiction, of course, Dickens's immortal works top the list. Stay-at-home detectives have long walked the streets of London, thanks to great mysteries by Dorothy L. Sayers, Agatha Christie, Ngaio Marsh, and Antonia Fraser. Cops and bad guys wind their way around 1960s London in Jake Arnott's pulp fiction books, *The Long Firm* and *He Kills Coppers.* Martin Amis's *London Fields* tracks a murder mystery through west London. For so-called "tart noir," pick up any Stella Duffy book. Marie Belloc-Lowndes's *The Lodger* is a fictional account of London's most deadly villain, Jack the Ripper. Victorian London was never so salacious as in Sarah Waters's story of a young girl who travels the theaters as a singer, the Soho squares as a male prostitute, and the East End as a communist in *Tipping the Velvet.* Late-20th-century London, with its diverse ethnic makeup, is the star of Zadie Smith's famed novel *White Teeth.* The vibrancy and cultural diversity of London's East End come to life in Monica Ali's *Brick Lane.*

London in Film

Many films—from *Waterloo Bridge* and *Georgy Girl* to *Secrets and Lies* and *Notting Hill*—have used London as their setting. The great musicals Walt Disney's *Mary Poppins,* George Cukor's *My Fair Lady,* and Sir Carol Reed's *Oliver!* evoke the Hollywood soundstage version of London.

Children of all ages enjoy Stephen Herek's *101 Dalmatians,* with Glenn Close as fashion-savvy Cruella de Vil. King's Cross Station in London was shot to cinematic fame by the movie version of J.K. Rowling's *Harry Potter and the Philosopher's Stone.* Look for cameos by the city in all other *Harry Potter* films.

The swinging '60s are loosely portrayed in M. Jay Roach's *Austin Powers: International Man of Mystery,* full of references to British slang and some great opening scenes in London. For a truer picture of the '60s in London, Michelangelo Antonioni weaves a mystery plot around the world of a London fashion photographer in *Blow-Up.* British gangster films came into their own with Guy Ritchie's amusing tales of London thieves in *Lock, Stock, and Two Smoking Barrels,* filmed almost entirely in London, and the follow-up *Snatch.* More sobering portraits of London criminal life include Neil Jordan's *Mona Lisa,* Paul McGuigan's *Gangster No. 1,* and John Mackenzie's *The Long Good Friday.* Of course, the original tough guy is 007, and his best exploits in London are featured in the introductory chase scene in *The World Is Not Enough.*

Sir Arthur Conan Doyle knew the potential of London as a chilling setting, and John Landis's *An American Werewolf in London* and Hitchcock's *39 Steps* and *The Man Who Knew Too Much* exploit the Gothic and sinister qualities of the city. For a fascinating look at Renaissance London, watch John Madden's *Shakespeare in Love.* Dickens's London is indelibly depicted in David Lean's *Oliver Twist.*

Some modern-day romantic comedies that use London as a backdrop are Peter Howitt's *Sliding Doors* with Gwyneth Paltrow and the screen adaptations of Helen Fielding's *Bridget Jones's Diary* (and its sequel), starring Renée Zellweger, Hugh Grant, and Colin Firth. Glossy London is depicted in Woody Allen's *Match Point,* bohemian London in David Kane's *This Year's Love,* gritty London in Shane Meadow's *Somers Town,* and post-zombie London in Danny Boyle's *28 Days Later,* while Patrick Kellior's *London* offers a uniquely informed, idiosyncratic view of the city.

TRAVEL SMART
LONDON

GETTING HERE AND AROUND

Central London and its surrounding districts are divided into 32 boroughs—33, counting the City of London. More useful for finding your way around, however, are the subdivisions of London into postal districts. Throughout the guide we've given the full postal code for most listings. The first one or two letters give the location: N means north, NW means northwest, and so on. Don't expect the numbering to be logical, however. You won't, for example, find W2 next to W3. The general rule is that the lower numbers, such as W1 or SW1, are closest to Buckingham Palace, but it is not consistent—SE17 is closer to the city center than E4, for example.

■ AIR TRAVEL

Flying time to London is about 6½ hours from New York, 7½ hours from Chicago, 11 hours from San Francisco, and 21½ hours from Sydney.

For flights out of London, the general rule is that you arrive at least one hour before your scheduled departure time for domestic flights and two hours before international flights for off-peak travel.

Airline Security Issues Transportation Security Administration ☎ 866/289–9673 ⊕ www.tsa.gov.

AIRPORTS

International flights to London arrive at either Heathrow Airport (LHR), 15 miles west of London, or at Gatwick Airport (LGW), 27 miles south of the capital. Most flights from the United States go to Heathrow, which is the busiest and is divided into five terminals, with Terminals 3, 4, and 5 handling transatlantic flights. Gatwick is London's second gateway. It has grown from a European airport into an airport that also serves dozens of U.S. destinations. A smaller third airport, Stansted (STN), is 35 miles northeast of the city. It handles mainly European and domestic traffic, although there's also scheduled service from New York. Two smaller airports, Luton (LTN), 30 miles north of town, and business-oriented London City (in East London E16) mainly handle flights to Europe.

Airport Information Gatwick Airport ☎ 0844/892–0322 ⊕ www.gatwickairport.com. **Heathrow Airport** ☎ 0844/335–1801 ⊕ www.heathrowairport.com. **London City Airport** ☎ 020/7646–0088 ⊕ www.londoncityairport.com. **Luton Airport** ☎ 01582/405–100 ⊕ www.london-luton.co.uk. **Stansted Airport** ☎ 0844/355–1803 ⊕ www.stanstedairport.com.

GROUND TRANSPORTATION

London has excellent if pricey bus and train connections between its airports and central London. If you're arriving at Heathrow, you can pick up a map and fare schedule at the Transport for London (TfL) Information Centre located in the Underground station serving Terminals 1, 2, and 3. Train service can be quick, but the downside (for trains from all airports) is that you must get yourself and your luggage to the train via a series of escalators and connecting trams. Airport link buses (generally National Express Airport buses) may ease the luggage factor and drop you closer to central hotels, but they're subject to London traffic, which can be horrendous and make the trip drag on for hours. Taxis can be more convenient than buses, but beware that prices can go through the roof. Airport Travel Line has additional transfer information and takes advance booking for transfers between airports and into London. The BAA (British Airport Authority) website is a useful resource, giving all transportation options from Gatwick, Heathrow, and Stansted.

FROM HEATHROW TO CENTRAL LONDON		
TRAVEL MODE	TIME	COST
Taxi	1 hour+	£55+
Heathrow Express Train	15 minutes	£20 (£34 round-trip) and £28 for first class
Underground	50 minutes	£5.70 one way (less with Oyster card)
National Express Bus	1 hour	From £5 one way
Hotel by Bus	1 hour+	£22.50 one way

Heathrow by Bus: National Express buses take one hour to reach the city center (Victoria) and cost from £5 one way and £9 round-trip (book online for best prices). A rival service, easyBus, offers buses from as little as £2 (book online for best prices). The National Express Hotel Hoppa service runs from all airports to around 20 hotels near the airport (from £4). Alternatively, nearly every hotel in London itself is served by the Hotel By Bus service. Fares to central London average around £22.50. Sky-Shuttle also offers a shared minibus service between Heathrow and any London hotel. The N9 night bus runs to Aldwych every half hour from midnight to 5 am; it takes an hour and costs £2.40.

Heathrow by Train: The cheap, direct route into London is via the Piccadilly line of the Underground (London's extensive subway system, or "Tube"). Trains normally run every four to eight minutes from all terminals from early morning until just before midnight. The 50-minute trip into central London costs £5.70 one way and connects with other central Tube lines. The Heathrow Express train is comfortable and convenient, if costly, speeding into London's Paddington station in 15 minutes. Standard one-way tickets cost £20 (£34 round-trip) and £28 for first class. Book ahead (online is the cheapest option; at a

NAVIGATING LONDON

London is a confusing city to navigate, even for people who've visited it a few times. Its streets are arranged in medieval patterns that no longer make much sense, meaning that you can't always use logic to find your way around. A good map is essential, and public transportation can be a lifesaver: buses will take you magically from point A to point B, and the Tube is often the quickest way to reach your destination. Here are some basic tips to help you find your way around.

■ Although free tourist maps can be handy, they're usually quite basic and include only major streets. If you're going to be doing lots of wandering around, buy the pocket-size map book London A–Z sold in bookstores and Tube and train stations throughout the city. Its detailed maps are invaluable.

■ To find your way, look for tall landmarks near where you are headed: the London Eye, for example, or the cross atop St. Paul's Cathedral—or the most obvious of all, Big Ben.

■ If you get properly lost, the best people to ask are the Londoners hustling by you, who know the area like nobody else. The worst people to ask are the people working in souvenir kiosks, and street vendors handing out the local Evening Standard newspaper; they're famously rude and unhelpful to lost tourists.

■ The tourist hubs of Soho, Covent Garden, Leicester Square, and Trafalgar Square are separated from one another by only a few blocks. Taking the Tube from one to another actually takes longer than walking.

■ On the other hand, when you're lost, the Tube is often the shortest distance between two points. Don't hesitate to use it.

counter/kiosk less so), as tickets are more expensive to buy on board. There's daily service from 5:10 am (5:50 am on Sunday) to 11:25 pm (10:50 pm on Sunday), with departures every 15 minutes. The Heathrow Connect service leaves from Paddington station and makes five local stops before arriving at Terminals 1, 3, and 5. At 25 minutes, journey time is only slightly slower than the Express and one-way tickets are £9.50.

Gatwick by Bus: An hourly bus service runs from Gatwick's north and south terminals to London's Victoria station, with stops at Hooley, Coulsdon, Mitcham, Streatham, Stockwell, and Pimlico. The journey takes up to 90 minutes and costs from £7.50 one way. The easyBus service runs to west London (Fulham) from as little as £2; the later the ticket is booked online, the higher the price (up to £10 on board).

Gatwick by Train: The fast, nonstop Gatwick Express leaves for Victoria station every 15 minutes 4:35 am–1:35 am. The 30-minute trip costs £19.90 one way, £34.90 round-trip. Book in advance, as tickets cost more on board. The First Capital Connect rail company's non-express services are cheaper; Capital Connect train runs regularly throughout the day to St. Pancras International, London Bridge, and Blackfriars stations; departures are every 15 minutes (hourly during the night), and the journey takes 45–55 minutes. Tickets are from £10 one way from St.Pancras International. FlyBy service to Victoria (£14.40 single) is not express, takes almost an hour, and the fare applies only on trains operated by Southern Trains.

Stansted by Bus: Hourly service on National Express Airport bus A6 (24 hours a day) to Victoria Coach station costs from £10 one way, £17 round-trip, and takes about 1 hour and 40 minutes. Stops include Golders Green, Finchley Road, St. John's Wood, Baker Street, Marble Arch, and Hyde Park Corner. The easyBus service to Victoria via Baker Street costs from £2 one-way but book early and online for best prices.

Stansted by Train: The Stansted Express to Liverpool Street station (with a stop at Tottenham Hale) runs every 15 minutes 6 am–12:30 am, Monday to Thursday; until 1:30 am, Friday to Sunday. The 45-minute trip costs £23.40 one way, £32.80 round-trip if booked online. Tickets cost more when purchased on board.

Luton by Bus and Train: A free airport shuttle runs from Luton Airport to the nearby Luton Airport Parkway station, from which you can take a train or bus into London. From there, the First Capital Connect train service runs to St. Pancras, Farringdon, Blackfriars, and London Bridge. The journey takes about 35 minutes. Trains leave every 10 minutes or so during the day, and hourly during the night. Single tickets cost from £14 one-way. The Green Line 757 bus service from Luton to Victoria station runs three times an hour, takes about 90 minutes, and costs from £10 one way.

Heathrow, Gatwick, Stansted, and Luton by Taxi: This is an expensive and time-consuming option. The city's congestion charge (£10) may be added to the bill if your hotel is in the charging zone, you run the risk of getting stuck in traffic, and if you take a taxi from the stand, the price will be even more expensive (whereas a minicab booked ahead is a set price). The trip from Heathrow, for example, can take more than an hour and cost more than £55.

TRANSFERS BETWEEN AIRPORTS

Allow at least two to three hours for an inter-airport transfer. The cheapest option—but most complicated—is public transportation: from Gatwick to Stansted, for instance, you can catch the non-express commuter train from Gatwick to Victoria station, take the Tube to Liverpool Street station, then catch the train to Stansted from there. To get from Heathrow to Gatwick by public transport, take the Tube to King's Cross, then change to the Victoria line, get to Victoria station, and then take the commuter train to Gatwick.

The National Express Airport bus is the most direct option between Gatwick and Heathrow. Buses pick up passengers every 15 to 20 minutes from 5:20 am to midnight from both airports. The trip takes around 70 minutes, and the fare is from £20 one way, but it's advisable to book tickets in advance. National Express buses between Stansted and Gatwick depart every 30 to 45 minutes and can take around 3 hours and 45 minutes. The adult one-way fare is from £22. Some airlines may offer shuttle services as well—check with your travel agent in advance of your journey.

Contacts easyBus ⊕ *www.easybus.co.uk.* **First Capital Connect** ☎ *0845/026-4700* ⊕ *www.firstcapitalconnect.co.uk.* **Gatwick Express** ☎ *0845/850-1530* ⊕ *www. gatwickexpress.com.* **Heathrow Express** ☎ *0845/600-1515* ⊕ *www.heathrowexpress. com.* **National Express** ☎ *08717/818178* ⊕ *www.nationalexpress.com.* **SkyShuttle** ☎ *0845/481-0960* ⊕ *www.skyshuttle.co.uk.* **Stansted Express** ☎ *0845/600-7245* ⊕ *www.stanstedexpress.com.*

Transfer Information Airport Travel Line ☎ *0871/200-2233* ⊕ *www.travelline.co.uk.*

FLIGHTS

British Airways is the national flagship carrier and offers mostly nonstop flights from 16 U.S. cities to Heathrow and Gatwick airports, along with flights to Manchester, Birmingham, and Glasgow. It also offers flights to New York from London City Airport near Docklands.

Airline Contacts American Airlines ☎ *800/433-7300, 0844/499-7300 in London* ⊕ *www.aa.com.* **British Airways** ☎ *800/247-9297, 0844/493-0787 in London* ⊕ *www. ba.com.* **Delta Airlines** ☎ *800/241-4141 for international reservations, 0871/221-1222 in London* ⊕ *www.delta.com.* **United Airlines** ☎ *800/864-8331 for international reservations, 0845/607-6760 in London* ⊕ *www. united.com.* **US Airways** ☎ *800/428-4322 for international reservations, 0845/600-3300 in London* ⊕ *www.usairways.com.* **Virgin Atlantic** ☎ *800/862-8621, 0844/209-7777 in London* ⊕ *www.virgin-atlantic.com.*

▌ BIKE TRAVEL

London's mayor, Boris Johnson, is a real cycling enthusiast and keen to make the capital more bike-friendly. A 24-hour cycle-for-hire scheme, the Barclays Cycle Hire, introduced in 2010 to enable Londoners to pick up a bicycle at one of more than 720 docking stations and return it at another, has proved very popular. The first 30 minutes are free. After that, charges rise incrementally from £1 for one hour up to £50 for the entire 24 hours. There is also a £1-per-day access charge. Fees are payable online, by phone, or at docking stations, by credit or debit cards only—cash is not accepted. To sign up, a user goes to the TfL (Transport for London) website and then receives a bike key in the mail, so this scheme is really meant for locals, not tourists.

▌ BUS TRAVEL

ARRIVING AND DEPARTING

National Express is the biggest British long-distance bus operator and the nearest equivalent to Greyhound. It's not as fast as traveling by train, but it's comfortable (with washroom facilities on board). Services depart mainly from Victoria Coach station, a well-signposted short walk behind the Victoria mainline train station. The departures point is on the corner of Buckingham Palace Road; this is also the main information point. The arrivals point is opposite, at Elizabeth Bridge. National Express buses travel to all large and mid-size cities in southern England and the midlands. Scotland and the north are not as well served. The station is extremely busy around holidays and weekends. Arrive at least 30 minutes before departure so you can find the correct exit gate. Smoking is not permitted on board.

Another bus company, Megabus, has been packing in the budget travelers in recent years, since it offers cross-country fares for as little as £1 per person. The company's single- and double-decker buses serve an extensive array of cities across Great

Britain with a cheerful budget attitude. In London, buses for all destinations depart from the Green Line bus stand at Victoria station. Megabus does not accommodate wheelchairs, and the company strictly limits luggage to one piece per person checked, and one piece of hand luggage.

Green Line serves the counties surrounding London, as well as airports. Bus stops (there's no central bus station) are on Buckingham Palace Road, between the Victoria train station and Victoria Coach station.

Tickets on some long-distance routes are cheaper if purchased in advance, and traveling midweek costs less than over weekends and at holiday periods.

GETTING AROUND LONDON

Private, as opposed to municipal, buses are known as coaches. Although London is famous for its double-decker buses, the old beloved rattletrap Routemasters, with the jump-on/off back platforms, now only serve two "heritage" routes: the No. 9 travels through Piccadilly, Trafalgar Square, and Knightsbridge, and the No. 15 travels from Trafalgar Square down Fleet Street and on to St. Paul's Cathedral. That said, a modernized Routemaster has taken to the streets in recent times, replacing the failed experiment that was the so-called "bendy buses" (long, articulated vehicles that struggled to navigate London's narrow roads).

Bus stops are clearly indicated; signs at bus stops feature a red TfL symbol on a plain white background. You must flag the bus down at some stops. Each numbered route is listed on the main stop, and buses have a large number on the front with their end destination. Not all buses run the full route at all times; check with the driver to be sure. You can pick up a free bus guide at a TfL Travel Information Centre (at Euston, Liverpool Street, Piccadilly Circus, King's Cross, and Victoria Tube stations; and at Heathrow Airport).

Buses are a good way of seeing the town, particularly if you plan to hop on and off to cover many sights, but don't take a bus if you're in a hurry, as traffic can really slow them down. To get off, press the red "Stop" buttons mounted on poles near the doors. You will usually see a "Bus Stopping" sign light up. Expect to get sardined during rush hour, from 8 am to 9:30 am and 4:30 pm to 6:30 pm.

Night buses, denoted by an "N" before their route numbers, run from midnight to 5 am on a more restricted route than day buses. However, some night-bus routes should be approached with caution and the top deck avoided. All night buses run by request stop, so flag them down if you're waiting or push the button if you want to alight.

All journeys cost £2.40, and there are no transfers. If you plan to make a number of journeys in one day, consider buying a Travelcard (⇨ *Underground Travel: The Tube*), good for both Tube and bus travel. Also consider getting a prepaid Oyster card, as single journeys are just over a pound using a prepaid card. Travelcards are also available in one-, three-, or seven-day combinations. Visitor Oyster cards cost £5 and can be topped up. They are available from ticket desks at Gatwick and Stansted airports or at any Tube station and are transferable if you have money left over. Traveling without a valid ticket makes you liable for a fine (£40). Buses are supposed to swing by most stops every five or six minutes, but in reality, you can often expect to wait a bit longer, although those in the city center are quite reliable.

In central London, if you don't have a prepaid Oyster or Travelcard, you must pay before you board the bus. Automated ticket machines are set up at these bus stops, which are clearly marked with a yellow sign "Buy Tickets Before Boarding." Otherwise, you can buy tickets at most central London Tube stations as well as at newsagents and shops that display the sign "Buy Your Travel Cards & Bus Passes Here." Outside the central zone, payment may be made to the driver as you board (exact change is best so as to avoid incurring the driver's wrath).

Bus Information **easyBus** ⊕ *www.easybus. co.uk.* **Green Line** ☎ *0844/801-7261* ⊕ *www.greenline.co.uk.* **Megabus** ☎ *0900/160-0900* ⊕ *www.megabus.com.* **National Express** ☎ *08717/818-178* ⊕ *www.nationalexpress.com.* **Transport for London** ☎ *0343/222-1234* ⊕ *www.tfl.gov.uk.* **Victoria Coach Station** ☎ *0843/222-1234.*

▌ CAR TRAVEL

The best advice on driving in London is this: don't. London's streets are a winding mass of chaos, made worse by one-way roads. Parking is also restrictive and expensive, and traffic is tediously slow at most times of the day; during rush hours—from 8 am to 9:30 am and 4:30 pm to 6:30 pm—it often grinds to a standstill, particularly on Friday, when everyone wants to leave town. Avoid city-center shopping areas, including the roads feeding Oxford Street, Kensington, and Knightsbridge. Other main roads into the city center are also busy, such as King's Cross and Euston in the north. Watch out also for cyclists and motorcycle couriers, who weave between cars and pedestrians that seem to come out of nowhere, and you may be fined heavily for straying into a bus lane during its operating hours—check the signs.

If you are staying in London for the duration of your trip, there's virtually no reason to rent a car since the city and its suburbs are widely covered by public transportation. However, you might want a car for day trips to castles or stately homes out in the countryside. Consider renting your car in a medium-size town in the area where you'll be traveling, and then journeying there by train and picking up the car once you arrive. Rental rates are generally reasonable, and insurance costs are lower than in comparable U.S. cities. Rates generally begin at £40 a day for a small economy car (such as a subcompact General Motors Vauxhall Corsa, or Renault Clio), usually with manual transmission. Air-conditioning and unlimited mileage generally come with the larger-size automatic cars.

In London your U.S. driver's license is acceptable (as long as you are over 23 years old, with no driving convictions). If you have a driver's license from a country other than the United States, it may not be recognized in the United Kingdom. An International Driver's Permit is a good idea no matter what; it's available from the American (AAA) or Canadian (CAA) Automobile Association and, in the United Kingdom, from the Automobile Association (AA) or Royal Automobile Club (RAC). International permits are universally recognized, and having one may save you a problem with the local authorities.

Remember that Britain drives on the left, and the rest of Europe on the right. Therefore, you may want to leave your rented car in Britain and pick up a left-side drive if you cross the Channel.

CONGESTION CHARGE

Designed to reduce traffic through central London, a congestion charge has been instituted. Vehicles (with some exemptions) entering central London on weekdays from 7 am to 6 pm (excluding public holidays) have to pay a £10 daily fee; it can be paid up to 90 days in advance, on the day of travel, or on the following charging day, when the fee goes up to £12. Day-, month-, and yearlong passes are available on the Congestion Charging page of the Transport for London website, at gas stations, parking lots (car parks), by mail, by phone, and by SMS text message. One day's payment is good for all access into the charging zone on that day. Traffic signs designate the entrance to congestion areas, and cameras read car license plates and send the information to a database. Drivers who don't pay the congestion charge by midnight of the next charging day following the day of driving are penalized £130, which is reduced to £65 if paid within 14 days.

Information Congestion Charge Customer Service ☎ *0343/222-2222 in U.K., 0044/207/649-9122 outside U.K.* ⊕ *www.cclondon.com.* **Transport for London** ☎ *0343/222-1234* ⊕ *www.tfl.gov.uk.*

GASOLINE

Gasoline (petrol) is sold in liters and is expensive (at this writing about £1.35 per liter—around $8 per gallon). Unleaded petrol, denoted by green pump lines, is predominant. Premium and Super Premium are the two varieties, and most cars run on regular Premium. Supermarket pumps usually offer the best value. You won't find many service stations in the center of town; these are generally on main, multilane trunk roads out of the center. Service is self-serve, except in small villages, where gas stations are likely to be closed on Sunday and late evening. Most stations accept major credit cards.

PARKING

During the day—and probably at all times—it's safest to believe that you can park nowhere except at a meter, in a pay-and-display bay, or in a garage; otherwise, you run the risk of an expensive ticket, plus possibly even more expensive clamping and towing fees (some boroughs are clamp-free). Restrictions are indicated by the "No Waiting" parking signpost on the sidewalk (these restrictions vary from street to street), and restricted areas include single yellow lines or double yellow lines, and Residents' Parking bays. Parking at a bus stop is prohibited; parking in bus lanes, restricted. On Red Routes, indicated by red lines, you are not allowed to park or even stop. It's illegal to park on the sidewalk, across entrances, or on white zigzag lines approaching a pedestrian crossing.

Meters have an insatiable hunger in the inner city—a 20p coin may buy just three minutes—and some will permit only a maximum two-hour stay. Meters take 20p and £1 coins, pay-and-display machines 10p, 20p, 50p, £1, and £2 coins. Some take payment by credit card. In some parts of central London, meters have been almost entirely replaced by pay-and-display machines that require payment by cell phone. You will need to set up an account to do this (⊕ *www.westminster. gov.uk*). Meter parking is free after 6:30

or 8:30 in the evening, on Sunday, and on holidays. Always check the sign. In the evening, after restrictions end, meter bays are free. After meters are free, you can also park on single yellow lines—but not double yellow lines. In the daytime, take advantage of the many NCP parking lots in the center of town (from about £7 per hour, up to six hours).

Information NCP ☎ *0845/050–7080*
⊕ *www.ncp.co.uk.*

ROADSIDE EMERGENCIES

If your car is stolen, you're in a car accident, or your car breaks down and there's nobody around to help you, contact the police by dialing ☎ 999.

The general procedure for a breakdown is the following: position the red hazard triangle (which should be in the trunk of the car) a few paces away from the rear of the car. Leave the hazard warning lights on. Along highways (motorways), emergency roadside telephone booths are positioned at intervals within walking distance. Contact the car-rental company or an auto club. The main auto clubs in the United Kingdom are the Automobile Association (AA) and the RAC. If you're a member of the American Automobile Association (AAA), check your membership details before you depart for Britain, as, under a reciprocal agreement, roadside assistance in the United Kingdom should cost you nothing. You can join and receive roadside assistance from the AA on the spot, but the charge is higher—around £95—than a simple membership fee.

Emergency Services American Automobile Association ☎ *800/564–6222*
⊕ *www.aaa.com.* **Automobile Association** ☎ *0800/085–2721, 161/333–0004 from outside the U.K., 0800/887–766 for emergency roadside assistance from cell phones* ⊕ *www. theaa.com.* **RAC** ☎ *01922/437000 inquiries, 0800/828–282 for emergency roadside assistance, 0333/200–0999 for emergency roadside assistance* ⊕ *www.rac.co.uk.*

RULES OF THE ROAD

London is a mass of narrow, one-way roads, and narrow, two-way streets that are no bigger than the one-way roads. If you must risk life and limb and drive in London, note that the speed limit is either 20 or 30 mph—unless you see the large 40 mph signs found only in the suburbs. Speed bumps are sprinkled about with abandon in case you forget. Speed is strictly controlled and cameras, mounted on occasional lampposts, photograph speeders for ticketing.

Medium-size circular intersections are often designed as "roundabouts" (marked by signs in which three curved arrows form a circle). On these, cars travel left in a circle and incoming cars must yield to those already on their way around from the right. Signal when about to leave the roundabout.

Jaywalking is not illegal in London and everybody does it, despite the fact that striped crossings with blinking yellow lights mounted on poles at either end—called "zebra crossings"—give pedestrians the right-of-way to cross. Cars should treat zebra crossings like stop signs if a pedestrian is waiting to cross or already starting to cross. It's illegal to pass another vehicle at a zebra crossing. At other crossings (including intersections) pedestrians must yield to traffic, but they do have the right-of-way over traffic turning left at controlled crossings—if they have the nerve.

Traffic lights sometimes have arrows directing left or right turns; try to catch a glimpse of the road markings in time, and don't get into the turn lane if you mean to go straight ahead. Turning on a red light is not permitted. Signs at the beginning and end of designated bus lanes give the time restrictions for use (usually during peak hours); if you're caught driving on bus lanes during restricted hours, you will be fined. By law, seat belts must be worn in the front and back seats. Drunk-driving laws are strictly enforced, and it's safest to avoid alcohol altogether if you'll be driving. The legal limit is 80 milligrams of alcohol per 100 milliliters of blood, which roughly translated means two units of alcohol—two small glasses of wine, one pint of beer, or one glass of whiskey.

▌DLR: DOCKLANDS LIGHT RAILWAY

For destinations in East London, the quiet, driverless Docklands Light Railway (DLR) is a good alternative, offering interesting views of the area.

The DLR connects with the Tube network at Bank and Tower Hill stations as well as at Canary Wharf. It goes to London City Airport, the Docklands financial district, and Greenwich, running 5:30 am–12:30 am Monday–Saturday, 7 am–11:30 pm Sunday. The DLR takes Oyster cards and Travelcards, and fares are the same as those on the Tube. A £17 River Rover ticket (£15.30 if booked online) combines one day DLR travel with hop on, hop-off travel on City Cruises riverboats between Westminster, Waterloo, Tower, and Greenwich piers.

Information Transport for London ☎ 0343/222–1234 ⊕ www.tfl.gov.uk.

▌RIVER BUS

One legacy of the 2012 Olympics has been a new push to develop river travel as part of London's overall public transportation system. The service now stops at 10 piers between London Eye/Waterloo and Greenwich, with peak-time extensions to Putney in the west and Woolwich Arsenal in the east. The Waterloo-Woolwich commuter service runs 6 am–midnight on weekdays, 8:30 am–midnight on weekends (peak time frequency: every 20 minutes). Tickets are £6.50, with a one-third discount for Travelcard holders and a 10% discount for Oyster card holders. When there are events at the O2 (North Greenwich Arena), a half-hourly express service runs to and from Waterloo starting three hours before the event. There is also the special Tate to Tate express, a

20-minute trip between Tate Modern and Tate Britain that costs £6.50. Boats run every 40 minutes from 10 am to 5 pm. A £13.10 per day River Roamer ticket offers unlimited river travel after 9 am.

Contacts Thames Clippers ☎ 020/7001–2222 ⊕ www.thamesclippers.com.

▌TAXI

Universally known as "black cabs" (even though many of them now come in other colors), the traditional big black London taxicabs are as much a part of the city's streetscape as red double-decker buses, and for good reason: the unique, spacious taxis easily hold five people, plus luggage. To earn a taxi license, drivers must undergo intensive training on the history and geography of London. The course, and all that the drivers have learned in it, is known simply as "the Knowledge." There's almost nothing your taxi driver won't know about the city.

Hotels and main tourist areas have cabstands (just take the first in line), but you can also flag one down from the roadside. If the yellow "For Hire" sign on the top is lighted, the taxi is available. Cabdrivers often cruise at night with their signs unlighted so that they can choose their passengers and avoid those they think might cause trouble. If you see an unlighted, passengerless cab, hail it: you might be lucky.

Fares start at £2.40 and charge by the minute—a journey of a mile (which might take between 6 and 13 minutes) will cost anything from £5.60 to £8.80 (the fare goes up between 10 pm and 6 am—a system designed to persuade more taxi drivers to work at night). A surcharge of £2 is applied to a telephone booking. At Christmas and New Year, there is an additional surcharge of £4. You can, but do not have to, tip taxi drivers 10% of the tab. Usually passengers round up to the nearest pound.

Minicabs, which operate out of small, curbside offices throughout the city, are generally cheaper than black cabs, but are less reliable and trustworthy. These are usually unmarked passenger cars, and their drivers are often not native Londoners, and do not have to take or pass "the Knowledge" test. Still, Londoners use them in droves because they are plentiful and cheap. If you choose to use them, do not ever take an unlicensed cab: anyone who curb-crawls looking for customers is likely to be unlicensed. Unlicensed cabs have been associated with many crimes and can be dangerous. All cab companies with proper dispatch offices are likely to be licensed. Look for a small purple version of the Underground logo on the front or rear windscreen with "private hire" written across it.

There are plenty of trustworthy and licensed minicab firms. For London-wide service try Lady Mini Cabs, which employs only women drivers, or Addison Lee, which uses comfortable minivans but requires that you know the full postal code for both your pickup location and your destination. When using a minicab, always ask the price in advance when you phone for the car, then verify with the driver before the journey begins.

Black Cabs Dial-a-Cab ☎ 020/7253–5000 cash bookings, 020/7426–3420 credit/debit card bookings ⊕ www.dialacab.co.uk. **Radio Taxis** ☎ 020/7272–0272 ⊕ www.radiotaxis. co.uk.

Minicabs Addison Lee ☎ 020/7387–8888 ⊕ www.addisonlee.com. **Lady MiniCabs** ☎ 020/7272–3300 ⊕ www.ladyminicabs.co.uk.

▌TRAIN TRAVEL

The National Rail Enquiries website is the clearinghouse for information on train times and fares as well as to book rail journeys around Britain—and the earlier the better. Tickets bought two to three weeks in advance can cost a quarter of the price of tickets bought on the day of travel. However, journeys within commuting distance of city centers are sold at unvarying set prices, and those can be purchased on the day you expect to make your journey without any financial penalty. You may also be able to purchase a PlusBus ticket, which adds unlimited bus travel at your destination. Note that, in busy city centers such as London, all travel costs more during morning rush hour. You can purchase tickets online, by phone, or at any train station in the United Kingdom. Check the website or call the National Rail Enquiries line to get details of the train company responsible for your journey and have them give you a breakdown of available ticket prices. Regardless of which train company is involved, many discount passes are available, such as the 16–25 Railcard (for which you must be under 26 and provide a passport-size photo), the Senior Railcard, and the Family & Friends Travelcard, which can be bought from most mainline stations. But if you intend to make several long-distance rail journeys, it can be a good idea to invest in a BritRail Pass (which you must buy in the United States).

You can get a BritRail Pass valid for London and the surrounding counties, for England, for Scotland, or for all of Britain. Discounts (usually 20%–25%) are offered if you're between 16 and 25, over 60, traveling as a family or a group, or accompanied by a British citizen. The pass includes discounts on the Heathrow Express and Eurostar. BritRail Passes come in two basic varieties. The Classic pass allows travel on consecutive days and the FlexiPass allows a number of travel days within a set period of time. The cost (in U.S. dollars) of a BritRail Consecutive Pass adult ticket for eight days is $249 standard and $369 first class; for 15 days, $369 and $549; and for a month, $549 and $825. The cost of a BritRail FlexiPass adult ticket for four days' travel in two months is $270 standard and $338 first class; for eight days' travel in two months, $438 and $650; and for 16 days' travel in two months, $630 and $938. Prices drop by about 25% for off-peak travel passes between November and February.

Most long-distance trains have refreshment carriages, called buffet cars. Most trains these days also have "quiet cars" where use of cell phones and music devices is banned. Smoking is forbidden in all railcars.

Generally speaking, rail travel in the United Kingdom is expensive and the ticketing system unnecessarily convoluted: for instance, a round-trip ticket to Bath from London can cost more than £150 per person at peak times but for an off-peak ticket purchased far enough in advance, that fee can drop to £20 or even less. It's best to avoid the frantic business commuter rush (before 9:30 am and after 4:30 pm). Credit cards are accepted for train fares paid both in person, by phone and online.

Delays are not uncommon, but they're rarely long. You almost always have to go to the station to find out if there's going to be one (because delays tend to happen at the last minute). Luckily, most stations have coffee shops, restaurants, and pubs where you can cool your heels while you wait for the train to get rolling. National Rail Enquiries provides an up-to-date state-of-the-railroads schedule.

Most of the time, first-class train travel in England isn't particularly first-class. Some train companies don't offer at-seat service, so you still have to get up and go to the buffet car for food or drinks. First class is generally booked by business travelers on expense accounts because crying babies and noisy families are quite rare in first class and quite common in standard class.

Short of flying, taking the Eurostar train through the Channel Tunnel is the fastest way to reach the continent: 2 hours and 15 minutes from London's St. Pancras International station to Paris's Gare du Nord. The high-speed Eurostar trains use the same tunnels to connect St. Pancras International directly with Midi station in Brussels in around two hours. If purchased in advance, round-trip tickets from

London to Belgium or France cost from as little as £69, especially if you travel in the very early or very late hours of the day. If you want to bring your car over to France (if it's a rental, ask the rental company if this is permitted), you can use the Eurotunnel Shuttle, which takes 35 minutes from Folkestone to Calais, plus at least 30 minutes to check in. The Belgian border is just a short drive northeast of Calais.

Information BritRail Travel ☎ *866/938–7245 in U.S. and Canada* ⊕ *www.britrail.com.* **Eurostar** ☎ *08432/186186, 1233/617575 outside U.K.* ⊕ *www.eurostar.com.* **National Rail Enquiries** ☎ *0845/748–4950, 020/7278–5240 outside U.K.* ⊕ *www.nationalrail.co.uk.*

Channel Tunnel Car Transport Eurotunnel ☎ *0844/335–3535 in U.K., +33/3–21–00–20–61 from outside Europe* ⊕ *www.eurotunnel.com.*

▌UNDERGROUND TRAVEL: THE TUBE

London's extensive Underground train (Tube) system has color-coded routes, clear signage, and many connections. Trains run out into the suburbs, and all stations are marked with the London Underground circular symbol. (Do not be confused by similar-looking signs reading "subway"—in Britain, the word subway means "pedestrian underpass.") Trains are all one class; smoking is *not* allowed on board or in the stations. There is also an Overground network serving the farther reaches of Inner London. These now accept Oyster cards.

Some lines have multiple branches (Central, District, Northern, Metropolitan, and Piccadilly), so be sure to note which branch is needed for your particular destination. Do this by noting the end destination on the lighted sign on the platform, which also tells you how long you'll have to wait until the train arrives. Compare that with the end destination of the branch you want. When the two match, that's your train.

London is divided into six concentric zones (ask at Underground ticket booths for a map and booklet, which give details of the ticket options), so be sure to buy a ticket for the correct zone or you may be liable for an on-the-spot fine of £40. Don't panic if you do forget to buy a ticket for the right zone: just tell a station attendant that you need to buy an "extension" to your ticket. Although you're meant to do that in advance, generally if you're an out-of-towner, they don't give you a hard time.

For one-way fares paid in cash, a flat £4.70 price per journey now applies across all central zones (1–3), whether you're traveling 1 stop or 12 stops. If you're planning several trips in one day, it's much cheaper to buy a tourist Oyster card or even a Travelcard, which is good for unrestricted travel on the Tube, buses, and some Overground railroads for the day. The off-peak Oyster-card fare for Zones 1–2, for example, is £2.20. Bear in mind there is no longer an Off-Peak one-day Travelcard. A one-day Travelcard for Zones 1–2 now costs £9.20 and you can travel at anytime. The more zones included in your travel, the more the Travelcard will cost. For example, Kew is Zone 4, and Heathrow is Zone 6. If you're going to be in town for several days, buy a seven-day Travelcard (£31.60 for Zones 1–2, £58 for Zones 1–6). Children 11–15 can travel at discounted rates on the Tube and free on buses and trams with an Oyster photocard (order at least four weeks before date of travel), while children under 11 travel free on the Tube if accompanied by an adult or with an Oyster photocard and on buses at all times. Young people 16–18 and students over 18 get discounted Tube fares with an Oyster photocard.

Oyster cards are "smart cards" that can be charged with a cash value and then used for discounted travel throughout the city. Each time you take the Tube or bus, you place the blue card on the yellow readers at the entrance and the amount of your fare is deducted. Passengers using Oyster cards pay lower rates. Oyster-card Tube fares start at £1.60 and go up depending on the number of zones you're covering, time of day, and whether you're traveling into Zone 1. You can open an Oyster account online or pick up an Oyster card at any London Underground station, and then prepay any amount you wish for your expected travel while in the city. Using an Oyster card, bus fares are £1.45 instead of £2.40. If you make numerous journeys in a single day, your Oyster-card deductions will always be capped at the standard price of a one-day Travelcard.

However, although Oyster cards sound like the way of the future, they will soon be a thing of the past. From late 2014, Oyster cards will begin to be gradually phased out and passengers encouraged to move to a system of direct payments using their bank debit cards. In practice, this will mean swiping your "contactless" debit card instead of your Oyster card at ticket barriers.

From fall 2015, Tube trains will run for 24 hours a day on weekends on five major lines: Piccadilly, Victoria, Northern, Central, and Jubilee. If successful, this pilot scheme will be expanded to other lines. Until then, the usual timetable will apply on all lines, with trains running from just after 5 am Monday–Saturday, and with the last services leaving central London between midnight and 12:30 am. On Sunday, trains start two hours later and finish about an hour earlier. The frequency of trains depends on the route and the time of day, but normally you should not have to wait more than 10 minutes in central areas.

There are TfL Travel Information Centres at the following Tube stations: Euston, Liverpool Street, Piccadilly Circus, King's Cross, and Victoria, open 7:15 am–9:15 pm; and at Heathrow Airport (in Terminals 1, 2, and 3), open 6:30 am–10 pm.

Important note: as with the Metro system in Paris—and unlike the subway system in New York City—you need to have your ticket (Oyster-card pass or regular ticket) handy in order to exit the turnstiles of the Tube system, not just to enter them.

Information Transport for London
☎ *0343/222–1234* ⊕ *www.tfl.gov.uk.*

ESSENTIALS

▌ BUSINESS SERVICES AND FACILITIES

There are several The Color Company outlets (formerly known as FedEx Kinko's) and Mail Boxes Etc. locations in London to handle your photocopying, next-day mail, and packaging needs. Check their websites for more locations.

Contacts The Color Company (*FedEx Kinko's*). ⊠ *1 Curzon St., Mayfair* ☎ *0800/939–493* ⊕ *www.color.co.uk.* **Mail Boxes Etc.** ⊠ *19–21 Crawford St., Marylebone* ☎ *020/7224–2666* ⊕ *www.mailboxes-etc.co.uk.*

▌ COMMUNICATIONS

INTERNET

If you're traveling with a laptop, carry a spare battery and adapter: new batteries and replacement adapters are expensive. If you do need to replace them, head to Tottenham Court Road (W1), which is lined with computer specialists. For Macintosh computers, Micro Anvika is a good chain for parts and batteries, and the Apple Stores on Regent Street off Oxford Street and in the Covent Garden Piazza do repairs. John Lewis department store and Selfridges, on Oxford Street (W1), also carry a limited range of computer supplies.

The United Kingdom is finally catching up to the United States in terms of the spread of high-speed and Wi-Fi. In London, free Wi-Fi is increasingly available in hotels, pubs, coffee shops—even certain branches of McDonald's—and broadband coverage is widespread; generally speaking, the pricier the hotel, the more likely you are to find Wi-Fi there.

Contacts Cybercafes. More than 4,000 Internet cafés worldwide are listed. ⊕ *www.cybercafes.com.* **My Hot Spots** ⊕ *www.myhotspots.co.uk.*

PHONES

The good news is that you can now make a direct-dial telephone call from virtually any point on Earth. The bad news? You can't always do so cheaply. Calling from a hotel is almost always the most expensive option; hotels usually add huge surcharges to all calls, particularly international ones. Calling cards usually keep costs to a minimum, but only if you purchase them locally. And then there are cell phones, which are sometimes more prevalent—particularly in the developing world—than landlines; as expensive as cell phone calls can be, they are still usually a much cheaper option than calling from your hotel.

The minimum charge from a public phone is 60p for a 120-second call. To make cheap calls it's a good idea to pick up an international phone card, available from newsstands, which can be used from residential, hotel, and public pay phones. With these, you can call the United States for as little as 5p per minute.

To dial from the United States or Canada, first dial 011, then Great Britain's country code, 44. Continue with the local area code, dropping the initial "0." The code for London is 020 (so from abroad you'd dial 20), followed by a 7 for numbers in central London, or an 8 for numbers in the Greater London area. Freephone (toll-free) numbers start with 0800, 0500, or 0808; low-cost national information numbers start with 0845 or 0844.

A word of warning: 0870 numbers are *not* toll-free numbers; in fact, numbers beginning with this, 0871, or the 0900 prefix are "premium rate" numbers, and it costs extra to call them. The amount varies and is usually relatively small when dialed from within the country but can be excessive when dialed from outside the United Kingdom.

CALLING WITHIN BRITAIN

There are three types of phones: those that accept (1) only coins, (2) only British Telecom (BT) phone cards, or (3) BT phone cards and credit cards, although with the advent of cells, it's increasingly difficult to find any type of public phone, especially in London.

The coin-operated phones are of the push-button variety; the workings of coin-operated telephones vary, but there are usually instructions on each unit. Most take 10p, 20p, 50p, and £1 coins. Insert the coins *before* dialing (the minimum charge is 10p). If you hear a repeated single tone after dialing, the line is busy; a continual tone means the number is unobtainable (or that you have dialed the wrong—or no—prefix). The indicator panel shows you how much money is left; add more whenever you like. If there is no answer, replace the receiver and your money will be returned.

There are several different directory-assistance providers. For information anywhere in Britain, try dialing 118–888 (49p per call, then 9p per minute) or 118–118 (49p per call, then 14p per minute); you'll need to know the town and the street (or at least the neighborhood) of the person or organization for which you're requesting information. For the operator, dial 100.

You don't have to dial London's central area code (020) if you are calling inside London itself—just the eight-digit telephone number. However, you do need to use it if you're dialing a 0207 (Inner London) number from a 0208 (Outer London) number, and vice versa.

For long-distance calls within Britain, dial the area code (which begins with 01), followed by the number. The area-code prefix is used only when you are dialing from outside the destination. In provincial areas, the dialing codes for nearby towns are often posted in the booth.

CALLING OUTSIDE BRITAIN

For assistance with international calls, dial 155.

To make an international call from London, dial 00, followed by the country code and the local number.

When calling from overseas to access a London telephone number, drop the first 0 from the prefix and dial only 20 (or any other British area code) and then the eight-digit phone number.

The United States country code is 1.

Access Codes AT&T Direct ☎ *0800/890–011 in U.K., 0500/890–011 in U.K.* **MCI** ☎ *0800/279–5088 in U.K., 800/888–8000 for U.S. and other areas.* **Sprint International Access** ☎ *0808/234–6616 in U.K.*

CALLING CARDS

Public card phones operate either with cash or with special cards that you can buy from post offices or newsstands. Ideal for longer calls, they are composed of units of 10p, and come in values of £5, £10, and more. To use a card phone, lift the receiver, insert your card, and dial the number. An indicator panel shows the number of units used. At the end of your call, the card will be returned. Where credit cards are taken, slide the card through, as indicated.

CELL PHONES

If you have a multiband phone (Britain uses different frequencies from those used in the United States) and your service provider uses the world-standard GSM network (as do T-Mobile, AT&T, and Verizon), you can probably use your phone abroad. Roaming fees can be steep, however: 99¢ a minute is considered reasonable. And overseas you normally pay the toll charges for incoming calls. It's almost always cheaper to send a text message than to make a call, since text messages have a very low set fee (often less than 5¢).

If you just want to make local calls, consider buying a new SIM card (note that your provider may have to unlock your phone for you to use a different SIM card) and a prepaid service plan in London. You'll then have a local number and can make local calls at local rates. If your trip is extensive, you could also simply buy a new cell phone in your destination, as the initial cost will be offset over time.

■ **TIP→ If you travel internationally frequently, save one of your old cell phones or buy a cheap one online; ask your cell phone company to unlock it for you, and take it with you as a travel phone, buying a new SIM card with pay-as-you-go service in each destination.**

Any cell phone can be used in Britain if it's tri-band/GSM. Travelers should ask their cell phone company if their phone is tri-band and what network it uses, and make sure it is activated for international calling before leaving their home country.

You can rent a cell phone from most car-rental agencies in London. Some upscale hotels now provide loaner cell phones to their guests. Beware, however, of the per-minute rates charged, as these can be shockingly high.

Contacts Cellular Abroad. This company rents and sells GMS phones and sells SIM cards that work in many countries. ☎ *800/287–5072 in U.S., 310/862–7100 international, 800/3623–3333 in U.K.* ⊕ *www.cellularabroad.com.* **Mobal.** Cell phone rentals and GSM phone purchases (starting at $49) that will operate in 150 countries are available here. Per-call rates vary throughout the world. ☎ *888/888–9162 in U.S., 01543/426999 in U.K.* ⊕ *www.mobal. com.* **Planet Fone.** Here, you can rent cell phones, but the per-minute rates are expensive. ☎ *888/988–4777* ⊕ *www.planetfone. com.* **Rent a Mobile Phone.** Phones with short contracts can be rented. ☎ *020/7353–7705* ⊕ *www.rent-mobile-phone.com.*

■ CUSTOMS AND DUTIES

You're always allowed to bring goods of a certain value back home without having to pay any duty or import tax. But there's a limit on the amount of tobacco and liquor you can bring back duty-free, and some countries have separate limits for perfumes; for exact figures, check with your customs department. The values of so-called "duty-free" goods are included in these amounts. When you shop abroad, save all your receipts, as customs inspectors may ask to see them as well as the items you purchased. If the total value of your goods is more than the duty-free limit, you'll have to pay a tax (most often a flat percentage) on the value of everything beyond that limit.

There are two levels of duty-free allowance for entering Britain: one for goods bought outside the European Union (EU) and the other for goods bought within the EU.

Of goods bought outside the EU you may import the following duty-free: 200 cigarettes or 100 cigarillos or 50 cigars or 250 grams of tobacco; 4 liters of still wine and 16 liters of beer and, in addition, either 1 liter of alcohol over 22% by volume (most spirits), or 2 liters of alcohol under 22% by volume (fortified or sparkling wine or liqueurs).

Of goods bought within the EU, you should not exceed the following (unless you can prove they are for personal use): 800 cigarettes, 400 cigarillos, 200 cigars, or 1 kilo of tobacco, plus 10 liters of spirits, 20 liters of fortified wine such as port or sherry, 90 liters of wine, or 110 liters of beer.

Pets (dogs and cats) can be brought into the United Kingdom from the United States without six months' quarantine, provided that the animal meets all the PETS (Pet Travel Scheme) requirements, including microchipping and vaccination. Other pets have to undergo a lengthy quarantine, and penalties for breaking this law are severe and strictly enforced.

Fresh meats, vegetables, plants, and dairy products may be imported from within the EU. Controlled drugs, flick knives, obscene material, counterfeit or pirated goods, and self-defense sprays may not be brought into the United Kingdom; firearms (both real and imitation) and ammunition, as well as souvenirs made from endangered plants or animals, are barred except with relevant permits.

Information HM Revenue and Customs
✉ *Crownhill Court, Tailyour Rd., Plymouth*
☎ *0300/200–3700* ⊕ *www.hmrc.gov.uk.*
U.S. Customs and Border Protection
⊕ *www.cbp.gov.*

■ ELECTRICITY

The electrical current in London is 220–240 volts (coming into line with the rest of Europe at 230 volts), 50 cycles alternating current (AC); wall outlets take three-pin plugs, and shaver sockets take two round, oversize prongs. For converters, adapters, and advice, stop in one of the many STA Travel shops around London or at Nomad Travel.

Consider making a small investment in a universal adapter, which has several types of plugs in one lightweight, compact unit. Most laptops and cell phone chargers are dual voltage (i.e., they operate equally well on 110 and 220 volts), and thus require only an adapter. These days the same is true of small appliances such as hair dryers. Always check labels and manufacturer instructions to be sure. Don't use 110-volt outlets marked "For Shavers Only" for high-wattage appliances such as hair dryers.

Contacts Nomad Travel ✉ *43 Bernard St., Bloomsbury* ☎ *020/7833–4114* ⊕ *www.nomadtravel.co.uk.* **STA Travel** ☎ *0333/321–0099* ⊕ *www.statravel.co.uk.* **Steve Kropla's Help for World Travelers.** Information is available here on electrical and telephone plugs around the world. ⊕ *www.kropla.com.* **Walkabout Travel Gear.** Offers some helpful advice on electricity; search for "Adapters." ⊕ *www.walkabouttravelgear.com.*

■ EMERGENCIES

London is a relatively safe city, though crime does happen (even more so than in New York City), especially in areas of built-up public project housing or tourist meccas. If you need to report a theft or an attack, head to the nearest police station (listed in the Yellow Pages or the local directory) or dial 999 for police, fire, or ambulance (be prepared to give the telephone number you're calling from). National Health Service hospitals give free round-the-clock treatment in Accident and Emergency sections, where waits can be up to four hours, depending on the severity of your ailment or injury. As a non-EU foreign visitor, you will be expected to pay for any treatment you receive before you leave the country. Prescriptions are valid only if made out by doctors registered in the United Kingdom. All branches of Boots are dispensing pharmacies.

Doctors and Dentists Dental Emergency Care Service ☎ *020/8748–9365* ⊕ *www.24hour-emergencydentist.co.uk.* **Medical Express Clinic** ✉ *117A Harley St., Marylebone* ☎ *020/7499–1991, 0800/980–0700* ⊕ *www.medicalexpressclinic.com.* **UCL Eastman Dental Hospital** ✉ *256 Gray's Inn Rd., King's Cross* ☎ *020/3456–7899* ⊕ *www.uclh.nhs.uk.*

Foreign Embassies U.S. Embassy ✉ *24 Grosvenor Sq., Mayfair* ☎ *020/7499–9000* ✉ *londonpassport@state.gov* ⊕ *www.usembassy.org.uk.*

General Emergency Contacts Ambulance, fire, police ☎ *999 U.K. only, 112 pan-European.*

Hospitals and Clinics Charing Cross Hospital ✉ *Fulham Palace Rd., Fulham* ☎ *020/3311–1234* ⊕ *www.imperial.nhs.uk/charingcross.* **Royal Free Hospital** ✉ *Pond St., Hampstead* ☎ *020/7794–0500* ⊕ *www.royalfree.nhs.uk.* **St. Thomas's Hospital** ✉ *Westminster Bridge Rd., Lambeth* ☎ *020/7188–7188* ⊕ *www.guysandstthomas.nhs.uk.* **University College Hospital** ✉ *235 Euston Rd., Bloomsbury* ☎ *0845/155–5000, 020/3456–7890* ⊕ *www.uclh.nhs.uk.*

Hotlines Samaritans. Counseling service. ☎ *020/7734–2800* ⊕ *www.cls.org.uk.*

Pharmacies Boots ✉ *44–46 Regent St., Piccadilly Circus* ☎ *0845/070–8090* ⊕ *www.boots.com.*

■ HOLIDAYS

Standard holidays are New Year's Day, Good Friday, Easter Monday, May Day (first Monday in May), spring and summer bank holidays (last Monday in May and August, respectively), Christmas, and Boxing Day (December 26). On Christmas Eve and New Year's Eve, some shops, restaurants, and businesses close early. Some museums and tourist attractions may close for at least a week around Christmas, or operate on restricted hours—call to verify.

■ MAIL

Stamps can be bought from post offices (generally open weekdays 9–5:30, Saturday 9–noon), from stamp machines outside post offices, and from some newsagents and newsstands. Mailboxes are known as post or letter boxes and are painted bright red; large tubular ones are set on the edge of sidewalks, whereas smaller boxes are set into post-office walls. Allow seven days for a letter to reach the United States. Check the Yellow Pages for a complete list of branches, though you cannot reach individual offices by phone.

Airmail letters up to 10 grams (0.35 ounce) to North America, Australia, and New Zealand cost 88p. Letters under 9.4 inches by 6.4 inches within Britain are from 60p for first class, 50p for second class. Large letters (over 9.4 inches by 6.4 inches, under 13.8 inches by 9.8 inches) cost from 90p first class, 69p second class within the United Kingdom, depending on weight. Airmail is assessed by weight alone.

If you're uncertain where you'll be staying, you can have mail sent to you at the London Main Post Office, c/o poste restante. The post office will hold international mail for one month.

Contact Post Office ☎ 0845/611–2970 ⊕ www.postoffice.co.uk.

Main Branches London Main Post Office ✉ 24–28 William IV St., Charing Cross ⊕ www.postoffice.co.uk ✉ 43–44 Albemarle St., Mayfair ✉ 111 Baker St., Marylebone ✉ 54–56 Great Portland St., Fitzrovia ✉ 181 High Holborn, Holborn.

SHIPPING PACKAGES

Most department stores and retail outlets can ship your goods home. You should check your insurance for coverage of possible damage. Private delivery companies such as DHL, FedEx, and Parcelforce offer two-day delivery service to the United States, but you'll pay a considerable amount for the privilege.

Express Services DHL ☎ 0844/248–0844 ⊕ www.dhl.com. **FedEx** ☎ 0845/607–0809 ⊕ www.fedex.com. **Parcelforce** ☎ 0844/800–4466 ⊕ www.parcelforce.com.

■ MONEY

No doubt about it, London is one of the most expensive cities in the world: getting around is expensive, eating can be pricey, travel costs are steep, and hotels aren't cheap. However, for every yin there's a yang, and travelers do get a break in other places: most museums are free, for example, and Oyster cards help cut the price of travel.

ATMS AND BANKS

Your own bank will probably charge a fee for using ATMs abroad; the foreign bank you use may also charge a fee. Nevertheless, you'll usually get a better rate of exchange at an ATM than you will at a currency-exchange office or even when changing money in a bank. And extracting funds as you need them is a safer option than carrying around a large amount of cash.

■**TIP➔ PIN numbers with more than four digits are not recognized at ATMs in many countries. If yours has five or more, remember to change it before you leave.**

Credit cards or debit cards (also known as check cards) will get you cash advances at ATMs, which are widely available in London. To make sure that your Cirrus or

Plus card (to cite just two of the leading names) works in European ATMs, have your bank reset it to use a four-digit PIN number before your departure.

CREDIT CARDS

■TIP➔ Remember to inform your credit-card company before you travel, especially if you're going abroad and don't travel internationally very often. Otherwise, the credit-card company might put a hold on your card owing to unusual activity—not a good thing halfway through your trip. Record all your credit-card numbers—as well as the phone numbers to call if your cards are lost or stolen—in a safe place, so you're prepared should something go wrong. Both MasterCard and Visa have general numbers you can call (collect if you're abroad) if your card is lost, but you're better off calling the number of your issuing bank, since MasterCard and Visa usually just transfer you to your bank; your bank's number is usually printed on your card.

If you plan to use your credit card for cash advances, you'll need to apply for a PIN at least two weeks before your trip. Although it's usually cheaper (and safer) to use a credit card abroad for large purchases (so you can cancel payments or be reimbursed if there's a problem), note that some credit-card companies *and* the banks that issue them add substantial percentages to all foreign transactions, whether they're in a foreign currency or not. Check on these fees before leaving home, so there won't be any surprises when you get the bill.

■TIP➔ Before you charge something, ask the merchant whether he or she plans to do a dynamic currency conversion (DCC). In such a transaction the credit-card processor (shop, restaurant, or hotel, not Visa or MasterCard) converts the currency and charges you in dollars. In most cases you'll pay the merchant a 3% fee for this service in addition to any credit-card company and issuing-bank foreign-transaction surcharges.

Dynamic currency conversion programs are becoming increasingly widespread. Merchants who participate in them are supposed to ask whether you want to be charged in dollars or the local currency, but they don't always do so. And even if they do offer you a choice, they may well avoid mentioning the additional surcharges. The good news is that you *do* have a choice. And if this practice really gets your goat, you can avoid it entirely thanks to American Express; with its cards, DCC simply isn't an option.

Credit cards are accepted virtually everywhere in London.

Reporting Lost Cards American Express ☎ 800/528–4800 in U.S., 01273/696933 in U.K. ⊕ www.americanexpress.com. **Diners Club** ☎ 800/234–6377 in U.S., 514/877–1577 collect from abroad ⊕ www.dinersclub. com. **MasterCard** ☎ 800/627–8372 in U.S., 0800/964-767 in U.K. ⊕ www.mastercard.com. **Visa** ☎ 800/847–2911 in U.S., 020/7795–5777 in U.K. ⊕ www.visa.com.

CURRENCY AND EXCHANGE

The units of currency in Great Britain are the pound sterling (£) and pence (p): £50, £20, £10, and £5 bills (called notes); £2, £1 (100p), 50p, 20p, 10p, 5p, 2p, and 1p coins. At this writing, the exchange rate was about Australian $1.55, Canadian $1.61, New Zealand $1.94, U.S. $1.63, and €1.23 to the pound (also known as quid).

Even if a currency-exchange booth has a sign promising no commission, rest assured that there's some kind of huge, hidden fee. (Oh . . . that's right. The sign didn't say no *fee*.) And as for rates, you're almost always better off getting foreign currency at an ATM or exchanging money at a bank or post office.

■TIP➔ Banks never have every foreign currency on hand, and it may take as long as a week to order. If you're planning to exchange funds before leaving home, don't wait until the last minute.

▌ PACKING

London's weather is unpredictable. It can be cool, damp, and overcast, even in summer, but the odd summer day can be uncomfortably hot, as not many public venues, theaters, or the Tube are air-conditioned. In general, you'll need a heavy coat for winter and light clothes for summer, along with a lightweight coat or jacket. Always pack a small umbrella that you can easily carry around with you. Pack as you would for any American city: jackets and ties for expensive restaurants and nightspots, casual clothes elsewhere. Jeans are popular in London and are perfectly acceptable for sightseeing and informal dining. Sports jackets are popular with men. In five-star hotels men can expect to be asked to wear a jacket and tie in the restaurant and bar, and women might feel out of place unless they're in smart clothes. Otherwise, for women, ordinary dress is acceptable just about everywhere.

▌ PASSPORTS AND VISAS

U.S. citizens need only a valid passport to enter Great Britain for stays of up to six months. If you're within six months of your passport's expiration date, renew it before you leave—nearly extinct passports are not strictly banned, but they make immigration officials anxious, and may cause you problems.

PASSPORTS

It's always surprising how few Americans have passports—only 35% at this writing. This number is expected to grow now that it is impossible to reenter the United States from trips to neighboring Canada or Mexico without one. Remember this: a passport verifies both your identity and nationality—a great reason to have one.

U.S. passports are valid for 10 years. You must apply in person if you're getting a passport for the first time; if your previous passport was lost, stolen, or damaged; or if your previous passport has expired and was issued more than 15 years ago

or when you were under 16. All children under 18 must appear in person to apply for or renew a passport. Both parents must accompany any child under 14 (or send a notarized statement with their permission) and provide proof of their relationship to the child.

There are 24 regional passport offices, as well as 7,000 passport acceptance facilities in post offices, public libraries, and other governmental offices. If you're renewing a passport, you can do so by mail. Forms are available at passport acceptance facilities and online.

The cost to apply for a new passport is $140 for adults, $95 for children under 16; renewals are $140. There is an additional "execution fee" of $25. Allow six weeks for processing, both for first-time passports and renewals. For an expediting fee of $60 you can reduce this time to about two weeks. If your trip is less than two weeks away, you can get a passport even more rapidly by going to a passport office with the necessary documentation. Private expediters can get things done in as little as 48 hours, but charge hefty fees for their services.

■TIP➜ Before your trip, make two copies of your passport's data page (one for someone at home and another for you to carry separately). Or scan the page and email it to someone at home and/or yourself.

VISAS

A visa is essentially formal permission to enter a country. Visas allow countries to keep track of you and other visitors—and generate revenue (from application fees). You *always* need a visa to enter a foreign country; however, many countries routinely issue tourist visas on arrival, particularly to U.S. citizens. When your passport is stamped or scanned in the immigration line, you're actually being issued a visa. Sometimes you have to stand in a separate line and pay a small fee to get your stamp before going through immigration, but you can still do this at the airport on arrival. Getting a visa isn't always that easy. Some countries require that you arrange for one in advance of your trip. There's usually—but not always—a fee involved, and said fee may be nominal ($10 or less) or substantial ($100 or more).

If you must apply for a visa in advance, you can usually do it in person or by mail. When you apply by mail, you send your passport to a designated consulate, where your passport will be examined and the visa issued. Expediters—usually the same ones who handle expedited passport applications—can do all the work of obtaining your visa for you; however, there's always an additional cost (often more than $50 per visa).

Most visas limit you to a single trip—basically during the actual dates of your planned vacation. Other visas allow you to visit as many times as you wish for a specific period of time. Remember that requirements change, sometimes at the drop of a hat, and the burden is on you to make sure that you have the appropriate visas. Otherwise, you'll be turned away at the airport or, worse, deported after you arrive in the country. No company or travel insurer gives refunds if your travel plans are disrupted because you didn't have the correct visa.

U.S. Passport Information
U.S. Department of State ☎ *877/487-2778* ⊕ *travel.state.gov/passport.*

U.S. Passport and Visa Expediters
A. Briggs Passport & Visa Expeditors ☎ *800/806-0581, 202/388-0111* ⊕ *www.abriggs.com.* **American Passport Express** ☎ *800/455-5166* ⊕ *www. americanpassport.com.* **Passport Express** ☎ *800/362-8196* ⊕ *www.passportexpress.com.* **Travel Document Systems** ☎ *800/874-5100, 202/638-3800* ⊕ *www.traveldocs.com.* **Travel the World Visas** ☎ *866/886-8472* ⊕ *www.world-visa.com.*

▌ SAFETY

The rules for safety in London are the same as in New York City or any big metropolis. If you're carrying a considerable amount of cash and do not have a safe in your hotel room, it's a good idea to keep it in something like a money belt, but don't get cash out of it in public. Keep a small amount of cash for immediate purchases in your pocket or handbag.

Beyond that, use common sense. In central London, nobody will raise an eyebrow at tourists studying maps on street corners, and don't hesitate to ask for directions. However, outside of the center, exercise general caution about the neighborhoods you walk in: if they don't look safe, take a cab. After midnight, outside of the center, take cabs rather than wait for a night bus. Although London has plenty of so-called "minicabs"—normal cars driven by self-employed drivers in a cab service—don't ever get into an unmarked car that pulls up offering you "cab service." Take a licensed minicab only from a cab office, or, preferably, a normal London "black cab," which you flag down on the street. Unlicensed minicab drivers have been associated with a slate of violent crimes in recent years.

If you carry a purse, keep a firm grip on it (or even disguise it in a local shopping bag). Store only enough money in the purse to cover casual spending. Distribute the rest of your cash and any valuables among deep front pockets, inside jacket or vest pockets, and a concealed money pouch. Some pubs and bars have "Chelsea clips" under the tables where you can hang your handbag at your knee. Never leave your bag beside your chair or hanging from the back of your chair. Be careful with backpacks, as pickpockets can unzip them on the Tube, or even as you're traveling up an escalator.

Advisories U.S. Department of State ⊕ *travel.state.gov.*

▋ TAXES

Departure taxes are divided into four bands, depending on destination. The Band A tax on a per-person Economy fare is £13, Band B is £69, Band C is £85, and Band D is £97. The fee is subject to government tax increases.

The British sales tax (V.A.T., value-added tax) is 20%. The tax is almost always included in quoted prices in shops, hotels, and restaurants.

Most travelers can get a V.A.T. refund by either the Retail Export or the more cumbersome Direct Export method. Many, but not all, large stores provide these services, but only if you request them; they will handle the paperwork. For the Retail Export method, you must ask the store for Form VAT 407 when making a purchase (you must have identification—passports are best). Some retailers will refund the amount on the spot, but others will use a refund company or the refund booth at the point when you leave the country. For the latter, have the form stamped like any customs form by U.K. customs officials when you leave the country, or, if you're visiting several European Union countries, when you leave the EU. After you're through passport control, take the form to a refund-service counter for an on-the-spot refund (which is usually the quickest and easiest option), or mail it to the address on the form (or the envelope with it) after you arrive home. You receive the total refund stated on the form (the retailer or refund company may deduct a handling fee), but the processing time can be long, especially if you request a credit-card adjustment. This may be preferable to a check, however, as U.S. banks will charge a fee for depositing a check in a foreign currency.

With the Direct Export method, the goods are shipped directly to your home. You must have a Form VAT 407 certified by customs, the police, or a notary public when you get home and then send it back to the store, which will refund your money. For inquiries, contact Her Majesty's Customs & Excise office.

Global Refund is a worldwide service with 240,000 affiliated stores and more than 200 Refund Offices. Its refund form, called a Tax Free Check, is the most common across the European continent. The service issues refunds in the form of cash, check, or credit-card adjustment. Again, the cost of cashing a foreign currency check may exceed the amount of the refund.

V.A.T. Refunds Global Refund ☎ 866/706–6090 in U.S., 800/32–111–111 in U.K., 800/32–222–555 in U.K. ⊕ www.globalrefund.com. **Her Majesty's Revenue & Customs** ☎ 0300/200–3700 within U.K., 292/050–1261 from outside U.K. ⊕ www.hmrc.gov.uk/vat.

▋ TIME

London is five hours ahead of New York City. In other words, when it's 3 pm in New York (or noon in Los Angeles), it's 8 pm in London. Note that Great Britain and most European countries also move their clocks ahead for the one-hour differential when daylight saving time goes into effect (although they make the changeover several weeks after the United States).

Time Zones Timeanddate.com. This site can help you figure out the correct time anywhere in the world. ⊕ www.timeanddate.com/worldclock.

▋ TIPPING

Tipping is done in Britain just as in the United States, but at a lower level. So, although it might make you uncomfortable, tipping less than you would back home in restaurants—and not tipping at all in pubs—is not only accepted, but standard. Tipping more can look like you're showing off. Do not tip movie or theater ushers, elevator operators, or bar staff in pubs—although you can always offer to buy the latter a drink.

TIPPING GUIDELINES FOR LONDON	
Bartender	In cocktail bars, if you see a tip plate, it's fine to leave £1 or £2. For table service, tip 10% of the cost of the bill. However, the gratuity is often included in the check at more expensive bars.
Bellhop	£1 per bag, depending on the level of the hotel.
Hotel Concierge	£5 or more, if a service is performed for you.
Hotel Doorman	£1 for hailing taxis or for carrying bags to check-in desk.
Hotel Maid	It's extremely rare for hotel maids to be tipped; £1 or £2 would be generous.
Porter at Airport or Train Station	£1 per bag
Skycap at Airport	£1–£3 per bag
Taxi Driver	Optional 10%–12%, perhaps a little more for a short ride.
Tour Guide	Tipping optional; £1 or £2 would be generous.
Waiter	10%–15%, with 15% being the norm at high-end restaurants; nothing additional if a service charge is added to the bill.
Other	Restroom attendants in expensive restaurants expect some small change (50p or so). Tip coat-check personnel £1 unless there is a fee (then nothing). Hairdresser and barbers get 10%–15%.

▌ TOURS

BIKE TOURS

Whether you join the Barclays Cycle Hire scheme or just, per usual, get one from a rental shop, remember that London is still a busy metropolis: unless you're familiar with riding in London traffic, the best way to see it on two wheels is probably to contact one of the excellent cycle-tour companies.

Tour Operators Barclays Cycle Hire ☎ *0343/222–6666 within U.K., 208/216–6666 from outside U.K.* ⊕ *www.tfl.gov.uk/roadusers.* **Cycle Tours of London** ☎ *07788/994430* ⊕ *www.biketoursoflondon.com.* **Fat Tire Bike Tours** ☎ *07882/338779* ⊕ *www.fattirebiketours.com.* **London Bicycle Tour Company** ☎ *020/3318–3088* ⊕ *www.londonbicycle.com.*

BOAT TOURS

Year-round, but more frequently from April to October, boats cruise the Thames, offering a different view of the London skyline. Most leave from Westminster Pier, Charing Cross Pier, and Tower Pier. Downstream routes go to the Tower of London, Greenwich, and the Thames Barrier via Canary Wharf. Upstream destinations include Kew, Richmond, and Hampton Court (mainly in summer). Most of the launches seat between 100 and 250 passengers, have a public-address system, and provide a running commentary on passing points of interest. Some include musical entertainment. Depending upon the destination, river trips may last from one to four hours.

Details on all other operators are available as a PDF from Transport for London's River Services page ⊕ *www.tfl.gov.uk.*

River Cruise Operators Bateaux London ☎ *020/7695-1800* ⊕ *www.bateauxlondon. com.* **London Duck Tours** ☎ *020/7928–3132* ⊕ *www.londonducktours.co.uk.* **Thames Cruises** ☎ *020/7928–9009* ⊕ *www. thamescruises.com.* **Thames River Boats** ☎ *020/7930–2062* ⊕ *www.wpsa.co.uk.* **Thames River Services** ☎ *020/7930–4097* ⊕ *www.thamesriverservices.co.uk.*

BUS, COACH, AND TAXI TOURS

Guided sightseeing tours from the top of double-decker buses, which are open-top in summer, are a good introduction to the city, as they cover all the main central sights. A number of companies run daily bus tours that depart (usually between 8:30 and 9 am) from central points. In hop-on, hop-off fashion, you may board or alight at any of the numerous stops to view the sights, and reboard on the next bus. Most companies offer this hop-on, hop-off feature but others, such as Best Value, remain guided tours in traditional coach buses. Tickets can be bought from the driver and are good all day. Prices vary according to the type of tour, although £25 is the benchmark. For that more personal touch, try out a tour in a guided taxi. Other guided bus tours, like those offered by Golden, are not open-top or hop-on, hop-off, but enclosed (and more expensive) coach bus versions.

Bus Tour Operators Best Value Tours ☎ *0870/803–1316* ⊕ *www.bestvaluetours. co.uk.* **Big Bus Tours** ☎ *020/7808–6753* ⊕ *www.bigbustours.com.* **Black Taxi Tour of London** ☎ *020/7935–9363* ⊕ *www. blacktaxitours.co.uk.* **Golden Tours** ☎ *020/7630–2028 in U.K., 800/509–2507 in U.S.* ⊕ *www.goldentours.co.uk.* **Original London Sightseeing Tour** ☎ *020/8877–1722* ⊕ *www.theoriginaltour.com.* **Premium Tours** ☎ *020/7713–1311, 800/815–4003 from the U.S.* ⊕ *www.premiumtours.co.uk.*

CANAL TOURS

The tranquil side of London can be found on narrow boats that cruise the city's two canals, the Grand Union and Regent's Canal; most vessels operate on the latter, which runs between Little Venice in the west (nearest Tube: Warwick Avenue on the Bakerloo line) and Camden Lock (about 200 yards north of Camden Town Tube station). Fares start at about £9 for 1½-hour round-trip cruises.

Canal Tour Operators Canal Cruises ☎ *020/8440–8962* ⊕ *www.londoncanalcruises. com.* **Jason's Trip** ⊕ *www.jasons.co.uk.* **London Waterbus Company** ☎ *020/7482– 2550* ⊕ *www.londonwaterbus.co.uk.*

EXCURSIONS

Evan Evans, Green Line, and National Express all offer day excursions by bus to places within easy reach of London, such as Hampton Court, Oxford, Stratford-upon-Avon, and Bath.

Tour Operators Evan Evans ☎ *020/7950– 1777, 800/422–9022 in U.S.* ⊕ *www. evanevanstours.co.uk.* **Green Line** ☎ *0844/801–7261* ⊕ *www.greenline.co.uk.* **National Express** ☎ *0871/781–8178* ⊕ *www.nationalexpress.com.*

WALKING TOURS

One of the best ways to get to know London is on foot, and there are many guided and themed walking tours from which to choose. Richard Jones's London Walking Tours includes the Jack the Ripper Walk, following in the footsteps of the titular killer, as does the Blood and Tears Walk. Other tours include Secret London, the West End with Dickens, and Hampstead—A Country Village. Context London's expert docents lead small groups on walks with art, architecture, and similar themes. The London Walks Company hosts more than 100 walks every week on a variety of themes, including a Thames pub walk, Literary Bloomsbury, and Spies and Spycatchers. For more options, pick up a copy of *Time Out* magazine and check the weekly listings for upcoming one-off tours.

Walking Tour Operators Blood and Tears Walk ☎ *07905/746733* ⊕ *www.shockinglondon.com.* **Blue Badge** ☎ *020/7403–1115* ⊕ *www.blue-badge-guides. com.* **Context London** ☎ *020/3514–1780, 800/691–6036 in U.S.* ⊕ *www.contexttravel. com/london.* **London Walks** ☎ *020/7624– 3978* ⊕ *www.walks.com.* **Richard Jones's London Walking Tours** ☎ *020/8530–8443* ⊕ *www.londondiscoverytours.co.uk.* **Shakespeare City Walk** ☎ *07905/746733* ⊕ *www.shakespeareguide.com.*

❚ VISITOR INFORMATION

When you arrive in London, you can get good information at the Travel Information Centre near the Eurostar arrivals area at St. Pancras International train station and at Victoria and Liverpool Street stations. These are helpful if you're looking for brochures for London sights, or if something's gone horribly wrong with your hotel reservation—if, for example, you don't have one—as they have a useful reservations service. The Victoria station center, opposite Platform 8, is open Monday–Saturday 7:15 am–9:15 pm, Sunday 8:15 am–7 pm; the St. Pancras center Monday–Saturday 7:15 am–9:15 pm, Sunday 8:15 am–8:15 pm; while Liverpool Street and Euston station centers open Saturday–Thursday 8:15 am–7:15 pm, Friday 8:15 am–8:15 pm. The one at Piccadilly Circus Tube station is open daily 9:15 am–7 pm. The Travel Information Centre at Heathrow is open Monday–Saturday 7:15 am–8 pm and Sunday 8:15 am–8 pm. There are also London Tourist Information Centres in Greenwich and some other Outer London locations.

Official websites ⊕ *www.visitbritain.com,* ⊕ *www.visitlondon.com.*

Other websites ⊕ *www.londontown.com,* the *Evening Standard* online ⊕ *www.standard. co.uk,* and the BBC ⊕ *www.bbc.co.uk.*

Entertainment Information ⊕ *www.timeout. com/london* ⊕ *www.officiallondontheatre.co.uk.*

INDEX

PHOTO CREDITS

Front cover: Steve Vidler/eStockphoto [Description: Beefeater, Costume detail]. 1, Sylvain Grandadam / age fotostock. 2-3, Herb Christian. 5, Rich B-S/Flickr. Chapter 1: Experience: 8-9, William Helsel/age fotostock. 10, Angelina Dimitrova/Shutterstock. 11 (left), British Tourist Authority. 11 (right), PCL/ Alamy. 12, gary718/Shutterstock. 13 (left), Pres Panayotov/Shutterstock. 13 (right), Kathy deWitt/ Alamy. 14, Jan Kranendonk/Shutterstock. 15 (left), Dominic Burke/Alamy. 15 (right), Doug Scott/ age fotostock. 17, Marc Pinter/Shutterstock. 18 (left), Sean Nel/Shutterstock. 18 (top center), Vinicius Tupinamba/Shutterstock. 18 (bottom center), WH Chow/Shutterstock. 18 (top right), Jan Kranendonk/ iStockphoto. 18 (bottom right), Thomas Sztanek/Shutterstock. 19 (top left), Bob Masters/Alamy. 19 (bottom left), Andrew Ward/Life File/Photodisc. 19 (top center), Jack Sullivan/Alamy. 19 (bottom center), Dominic Burke/Alamy. 19 (right), Walter Bibikow/viestiphoto.com. 20 (left), wikipedia.org. 20 (top center), The Print Collector/Alamy. 20 (bottom center and top right), wikipedia.org. 20 (bottom right), www.wga.hu. 21 (top left, bottom left, and right), wikipedia.org. 21(top center), newsphoto / Alamy. 22, British Tourist Authority. 25 (left), Lebrecht Music and Arts Photo Library/ Alamy. 25 (right), Visit London. 30, Sean Neil/Shutterstock. 31, Sylvain Grandadam/age fotostock. 32, British Tourist Authority. 33, David Peta/Shutterstock. 34 (top left), UK21/Alamy. 34 (bottom left), wikipedia. org. 34 (right), Kobby Dagan/Shutterstock. 35 (left), Mike Booth/Alamy. 35 (top right), wikipedia.org. 35 (bottom right), INTERFOTO Pressebildagentur/Alamy. 36 (top left), Robert Stainforth/ Alamy. 36 (bottom left), Jeffrey Blackler/Alamy. 36 (right), Andrew Dunn/wikipedia.org. 37 (left), Eric Nathan/ Alamy. 37 (right), Chris Batson/Alamy. 38 (left), Directphoto.org/Alamy. 38 (top right), Zaha Hadid/ wikipedia.org. 38 (bottom right), Nigel Young/British Museum. Chapter 2: Westminster, St. James's & Royal London: 39, British Tourist Authority. 41, Eric Nathan/ britainonview.com. 42, Peter Adams/ age fotostock. 46, Pres Panayotov/Shutterstock.48-49, Doug Pearson/age fotostock. 50, British Tourist Authority. 51, John Sturrock/Alamy. 53 (left), F. Monheim/R. von G.t/Bildarchiv Monheim/age fotostock. 53 (top right), Dean and Chapter of Westminster. 53 (center right), Mark Thomas/Alamy. 53 (bottom right) and 55, Dean and Chapter of Westminster. 57, British Tourist Authority. 62, ktylerconk/ Flickr. 64, Mark William Richardson/Shutterstock. 67, Matthew Mawson/Alamy. Chapter 3: Mayfair & Marylebone: 69, Derek Croucher/Alamy. 71, British Tourist Authority. 72, David Noton Photography/Alamy. 74, Tibor Bognar / age fotostock. 76, Pawel Libera/Alamy. 78, Jess Moss. 80, PCL/Alamy. Chapter 4: Soho & Covent Garden: 81, 83 and 84, British Tourist Authority. 85, Julian Love/John Warburton-Lee Photography/photolibrary.com. 87, Jon Arnold/age fotostock. 89, Ann Steer/iStockphoto. 91, British Tourist Authority. Chapter 5: Bloomsbury & Holborn: 93, Michael Jenner/Alamy. 95 and 96, British Tourist Authority. 98, Jarno Gonzalez Zarraonandia/Shutterstock. 99 and 100 (top), British Museum. 100 (bottom), Grant Rooney/Alamy. 102, British Museum. 103, James McCormick/britainonview.com. 104, Eric Nathan/Alamy. Chapter 6: The City:109, PSL Images/Alamy. 110, Ryan Fox/age fotostock. 112, Jerry Millevoi/age fotostock. 114-15, Jason Hawkes. 117 (left), F. Monheim/R. von G.t/ Bildarchiv Monheim/age fotostock. 117(top right), Jeff Gynane/Shutterstock. 117 (center right), Ken Ross/viestiphoto.com. 117 (bottom right), Marcin Stalmach/iStockphoto. 119, Rene Ramos/Shutter stock. 121, Russ Merne/Alamy. 123, Imagestate/age fotostock.com. 125, iStockphoto. 127 (left), Wal ter Bibikow/ viestiphoto.com. 127 (right), Tom Hanley/Alamy. 128 (top), Natasha Marie Brown/HRP/ newsteam.co.uk. 129, Peter Phipp/Peter Phipp/age fotostock.130 (left), Mary Evans Picture Library/ Alamy. 130 (center), Reflex Picture Library/Alamy. 130 (right), Classic Image/Alamy. 131, Jan Kranendonk/iStockphoto. Chapter 7: East London: 133, MAISANT Ludovic hem / age footstock.135, Neil Setchfi eld/Alamy. 136, foybles/Alamy. 141, Jon Arnold/age fotostock. 143, Elly Godfroy/Alamy. Chapter 8: South of the Thames: 145, Mike Peel/wikipedia/org. 147,Eric Nathan/britainonview.com. 148, PCL/Alamy. 149, Melba / age footstock.151 (top), Shutterstock. 151 (bottom), Duncan Soar/Alamy. 152, Vehbi Koca/Alamy. 153 (top), Lebrecht Music and Arts Photo Library/Alamy. 153 (bottom), Eric Nathan/ britainonview.com. 155, AA World Travel Library/Alamy. 156, Jess Moss. 159, Terry Walsh/ Shutterstock. 161, i4lcocl2 / Shutterstock.com. Chapter 9: Kensington, Chelsea, Knightsbridge & Belgravia: 163, Cahir Davitt/age fotostock. 165, British Tourist Authority. 166, Robert Harding Picture Library Ltd/Alamy. 168, John Warburton-Lee Photography/Alamy. 169, Londonstills.com/Alamy. 170, British Tourist Authority. 171, Ant Clausen/Shutterstock. 175, PCL/Alamy. Chapter 10: Notting Hill & Bayswater: 177, Roger Cracknell 01/classic / Alamy. 179, Doug Scott/age fotostock. 180, David H. Wells/age fotostock. 182, Peter Cook/age fotostock. 183, Corbis. 185, Joe Viesti/viestiphoto.com. 186, TNT MAGAZINE/Alamy. 187 (left), Andrew Holt/Alamy. 187 (top right), Dominic Burke/Alamy. 187 (bottom right), David Berry/Shutterstock. Chapter 11: Regent's Park & Hampstead: 189, ARCO/R. Kiedrowski/age fotostock. 191, British Tourist Authority. 192, Bildarchiv Monheim GmbH/Alamy. 196, PCL/Alamy. 199, Earl Patrick Lichfi eld/britainonview.com. 201, (c) Davidmartyn | Dreamstime. com. 202, Pictorial Press Ltd/Alamy. Chapter 12: Greenwich: 205, Michael Booth/Alamy. 207, Visit

NOTES

NOTES

NOTES

NOTES

ABOUT OUR WRITERS

Jack Jewers updated the Where to Stay chapter, along with the neighborhood chapters on Greenwich, Thames Upstream, Westminster, St. James and Royal London, and The City. A resident of London and its penumbra since public transport was cheap, Jack knows slightly more than is healthy about the city's secret underground world of abandoned train lines, mysterious tunnels, and other things hidden below the streets. When he isn't writing guidebooks, he makes independent films.

James O'Neill loves London and—as his work updating our chapters on Mayfair and Marylebone, Bloomsbury and Holborn, and Travel Smart for this edition proves—loves rediscovering it, too. Although originally from Ireland, he's lived in London for almost 20 years—and still loves it just as much now as he did back then. He has written extensively for TV (BBC and Channel 4), the stage, and the page. He is currently finishing his debut novel, which is set in—where else?—London.

Ellin Stein has written for publications on both sides of the Atlantic, including the *New York Times*, the *Times [London]*, the *Guardian*, the *Telegraph*, and *InStyle*, for whom she was European correspondent. Her book *That's Not Funny, That's Sick: The* National Lampoon *and the Comedy Insurgents Who Captured the Mainstream*, was published by W. W. Norton & Co. in 2013. Originally from Manhattan, she has lived in London for two decades. For this edition, she updated our chapters on Kensington, Chelsea, Knightsbridge, and Belgravia; East London; South of the Thames; Notting Hill and Bayswater; Regent's Park and Hampstead; and Shopping.

London restaurant maven **Alex Wijeratna** is permanently blown away by the capital's rocket-fueled restaurant scene. From locavore heroes and street food gourmet-democrats, to global gastropanjandrums, Alex tickles out the best joints that restaurant-mad London has to offer. With his first full Fodor's guidebook out last year (*Around London with Kids*), Alex has written for *The Times, Guardian, Independent, Daily Mail, Daily Express,* and *The Face.* For this edition, he updated the Where to Eat and Experience London chapters.

Jo Caird is a travel and arts journalist who writes on theater, visual arts, film, literature, and food and drink, as well as cycling and scuba diving. Her travel stories, city guides, and arts features appear regularly in *The Guardian, The Independent, The Sunday Telegraph, The Economist, Condé Nast Traveller,* and *World of Interiors.* Born and raised in London, Caird has an endless fascination for the city, and is delighted to write about it whenever the opportunity arises. For this edition, she updated the Nightlife, Arts and Entertainment, and Soho and Covent Garden chapters. Follow her on Twitter at www.twitter.com/jocaird or visit her website at www.jocaird.com.

Writer and editor **Kate Hughes** studied classical literature in Liverpool and also has a master's degree in garden history, so she feels qualified to pass judgment on matters both urban and rural. She is responsible for Stratford-upon-Avon and various Thames Valley side trips in *Fodor's London,* and also updates parts of *Fodor's England.*